Michael Trzdale

Foundations of the Portuguese Empire, 1415–1580

Europe and the World
in the Age of Expansion

edited by Boyd C. Shafer

FOUNDATIONS
of the
PORTUGUESE EMPIRE,
1415–1580

by
BAILEY W. DIFFIE
and
GEORGE D. WINIUS

(Chapters 1–13 and Appendixes 1–16 are by Bailey W. Diffie.
Chapters 14–22 are by George D. Winius.)

UNIVERSITY OF MINNESOTA PRESS
OXFORD UNIVERSITY PRESS
1977

Library of Congress Catalog Card Number 76-7880

ISBN 019 690419 6

Europe and the World in the Age of Expansion

SPONSORS

Department of History of the
University of Minnesota

James Ford Bell Library of the
University of Minnesota Library

SUPPORTING FOUNDATIONS

Northwest Area Foundation
(formerly Louis W. and Maud Hill
Family Foundation), St. Paul

James Ford Bell Foundation,
Minneapolis

ADVISORY COUNCIL

EDITORS

To Our Wives
Edilla Xavier Diffie
and
Margriet Hoffman Winius

Editor's Foreword

The expansion of Europe since the thirteenth century has had profound influences on peoples throughout the world. Encircling the globe, the expansion changed men's lives and goals and became one of the decisive movements in the history of mankind.

This series of ten volumes explores the nature and impact of the expansion. It attempts not so much to go over once more the familiar themes of "Gold, Glory, and the Gospel," as to describe, on the basis of new questions and interpretations, what appears to have happened insofar as modern historical scholarship can determine.

No work or works on so large a topic can include everything that happened or be definitive. This series, as it proceeds, emphasizes the discoveries, the explorations, and the territorial expansion of Europeans, the relationships between the colonized and the colonizers, the effects of the expansion on Asians, Africans, Americans, Indians, and the various "islanders," the emergence into nationhood and world history of many peoples that Europeans had known little or nothing about, and, to a lesser extent, the effects of the expansion on Europe.

The use of the word *discoveries*, of course, reveals European (and American) provincialism. The "new" lands were undiscovered only in the sense that they were unknown to Europeans. Peoples with developed cultures and civilizations already had long inhabited most of the huge areas to which Europeans sailed and over which they came to exercise their power and influence. Nevertheless, the political, economic, and social expansion that came with and after the discoveries affected the daily lives, the modes of producing and sharing, the ways of governing, the customs, and the values of peoples everywhere. Whatever their state of development, the expansion also brought, as is well known, tensions, conflicts, and much injustice. Perhaps most important in our own times, it led throughout the developing world to the rise of nationalism, to reform and revolt, and to demands (now largely realized) for national self-determination.

The early volumes in the series, naturally, stress the discoveries and explorations. The later emphasize the growing commercial and political involvements, the founding of new or different societies in the "new" worlds, the emergence of different varieties of nations and states in the often old and established societies of Asia, Africa, and the Americas, and the changes in the governmental structures and responsibilities of the European imperial nations.

The practices, ideas, and values the Europeans introduced continue, in differing ways and differing environments, not only to exist but to have consequences. But in the territorial sense the age of European expansion is over. Therefore the sponsors of this undertaking believe this is a pro-pitious time to prepare and publish this multivolumed study. The era now appears in new perspective and new and more objective statements can be made about it. At the same time, its realitie are still with us and we may now be able to understand intangibles that in the future could be overlooked.

The works in process, even though they number ten, cover only what the authors (and editors) consider to be important aspects of the expansion. Each of the authors had to confront vast masses of material and make choices in what he should include. Inevitably, subjects and details are omitted that some readers will think should have been covered. Inevitably, too, readers will note some duplication. This arises in large part because each author has been free, within the general themes of the series, to write his own book on the geographical area and chronological period allotted to him. Each author, as might be expected, has believed it necessary to give attention to the background of his topic and has also looked a bit ahead; hence he has touched upon the time periods of the immediately preceding and following volumes. This means that each of the studies can be read independently, without constant reference to the others. The books are being published as they are completed and will not appear in their originally planned order.

The authors have generally followed a pattern for spelling, capitalization, and other details of style set by the University of Minnesota Press in the interests of consistency and clarity. In accordance with the wishes of the Press and current usage, and after prolonged discussion, we have used the word *black* instead of *Negro* (except in quotations). For the most part American usages in spelling have been observed. The last is sometimes difficult for historians who must be concerned with the different spellings, especially of place names and proper nouns, at different times and in different languages. To help readers the authors have, in consequence, at times added the original (or the present) spelling of a name when identification might otherwise be difficult.

The discussions that led to this series began in 1964 during meetings of the Advisory Committee of the James Ford Bell Library at the University of Minnesota, a library particularly interested in exploration and discovery. Members of the university's Department of History and the University of Minnesota Press, and others, including the present editor, joined in the discussions. Then, after the promise of generous subsidies from the Bell Foundation of Minneapolis and the Northwest Area Foundation (formerly the Hill Family Foundation) of St. Paul, the project began to take form under the editorship of the distinguished historian Herbert Heaton. An Advisory Council of six scholars was appointed as the work began. Professor Heaton, who had agreed to serve as editor for three years, did most of the early planning and selected three authors. Professor Boyd C. Shafer of Macalester College (now at the University of Arizona) succeeded him in 1967. He selected eight authors and did further planning. He has been in constant touch with all the authors, doing preliminary editing in consultation with them, reading their drafts, and making suggestions. The Press editors, as is usual at the University of Minnesota Press, have made valuable contributions at all stages. Between Professor Shafer and the authors — from England, Canada, New Zealand, and the United States — there have been voluminous and amicable as well as critical exchanges. But it must be repeated, each author has been free to write his own work within the general scope of the series.

Bailey W. Diffie and George D. Winius are joint authors of *Foundations of the Portuguese Empire, 1415–1580*, volume I in the series. They wrote their respective parts of the book separately, though in frequent consultation with each other. Professor Diffie, with his Doctor en Filosofia y Letras (Madrid), taught chiefly at the City College of New York and also at several other universities. He has studied and traveled widely

xii   FOUNDATIONS OF THE PORTUGUESE EMPIRE

in Latin America and Europe. His principal and well-known publications are *Latin American Civilization: Colonial Period* and *Prelude to Empire: Portugal Overseas before Henry the Navigator*. Professor Winius, who has a Ph.D. from Columbia University, was a working journalist at Time, Inc., taught briefly at Hood College, from 1965 to 1976 at the University of Florida, and is now at the University of Leyden. Harvard University Press published his *Fatal History of Portuguese Ceylon: Transition to Dutch Rule* in 1971. He has lived and studied in Holland and Portugal. In Professor Diffie's words, "the principal theses of the authors" are: "Portuguese expansion was the result of long-trend economic and maritime developments, rather than the work of one man; Portugal led all other nations in revealing the world to Europe, but there is no basis for 'secret' discoveries before the known voyages of Dias, da Gama, Cabral, and others, and . . . Portugal's overseas administration set the model that other nations copied and modified." Professor Winius adds that his part of the volume principally addresses "itself to the need for a modern, continuous narrative of the political, military, and economic aspects of Portuguese exploration and empire building, 1498–1580."

University of Arizona   Boyd C. Shafer

PREFACE TO PERIOD 1415–1500

Bailey W. Diffie

No other people in history made such extensive geographical explorations as the Portuguese. During the course of the fifteenth century they were the first to reveal to Europe the unknown coast of West Africa, reaching and passing the Cape of Good Hope. They made the first all-water voyage from the West to the East in 1497–99, for the first time circumventing the land barrier that long separated the East from the West. Cabral touched on Brazil en route to India in 1500. Afonso de Albuquerque established the Portuguese as far east as Malacca in 1511. Many of the islands of the East Indies had been visited by Portuguese ships before Magellan, a Portuguese sailing in the service of Spain, began the first voyage around the world in 1519. Christopher Columbus, who discovered America in 1492, was an Italian who largely learned his trade as navigator in Portugal. By the end of the sixteenth century the Portuguese banner was flying around the world.

The question inevitably arises of why Portugal, a small country with only approximately a million people, led the way in exploration in the fifteenth century. Some of the answer is evident and some requires more subtle deductions. The geographical position of Portugal at the southwest extreme of Europe gave it lead over northern countries — though not over Spain. The existence of a seagoing merchant class that had long carried on overseas trade and of a shipbuilding industry provided the kind of manpower needed for an extension of activities further afield, if motivation came. The motivation, as will be seen later, included a number of elements. For the merchants and seamen there was opportunity for profits in a new area of trade. The mysteries of the Atlantic Ocean and the

African coast challenged those of adventurous spirit. The young fighting class found a place to win honors and new lands. The religious saw an opportunity to convert infidels to Christianity. The presence in Africa of men rather easily enslaved brought increased enthusiasm to shipowners, merchants, adventurers, nobles, and the crown. The strong throne ruling a unified nation supported the overseas expansion; and one member of the royal family, Prince Henry the Navigator, became the chief promotor of exploration.

If other peoples of Europe shared some of these things, no other — not even Spain — had them all to the same degree that Portugal did. At the beginning of the fifteenth century when other nations were fighting old battles of international and dynastic rivalry, Portugal had been provided by destiny with the opportunity and was ready to assume the leadership in bringing in a great new epoch of history.

The contribution of Portugal to world history has been forgotten by many modern historians who write their works as if Europe consisted of only the northern countries. Edward P. Cheyney, in his justly praised *The Dawn of a New Era, 1250–1453* (published in 1936), did not mention either Portugal or Henry the Navigator. He wrote on "The Idea of Nationality" and made not a single reference to Portugal, the first nation-state in Europe; and of "The Unity of History" without putting in even the name of the nation that did most to make European history into world history. The same sad fact is true of many others who either do not include Portugal in their narratives or, worse still, copy from out-of-date, ill-informed texts which perpetuate misinformation easily discredited. This neglect of Portuguese history needs to be redressed. The history of Portugal overseas deserves careful study, not merely a repetition of past romantic accounts.

The history of Portuguese expansion can be — must be — told on two separate levels of historical writing: on the first level is the simple narrative of the great achievements of Henry the Navigator, Diogo Cão, Bartolomeu Dias, Vasco da Gama, Pedro Álvares Cabral, and many other Portuguese; on the second is the necessary critical examination of the sources of information about the great explorations. Early in the nineteenth century Alexander von Humboldt, followed by other writers from northern Europe, put forth claims to priority for their nationals for geographical discoveries and advances in navigational science that evidently belonged to the Portuguese. The rightfully indignant replies of the

Visconde de Santarém and later Portuguese historians, as well as some scholars of other nations, set in motion a sequence of claims and counterclaims that has become more polemic and less scientific in the present century.

The problem of knowing the truth comes from both the scantiness of documentation and the difficulty of understanding the meaning of what is left to us. To fill the gap where no documentation exists, some historians, of Portugal and other countries as well, have interpreted a minimum of evidence very broadly. To account for lack of evidence for what "must have happened" they have sometimes gone further and postulated "lost" documents and a "Policy of Secrecy" by Portuguese kings to keep hidden from other nations the areas of the world known, they say, only to Portugal. Such historians, as for example Jaime and Armando Cortesão, and Gago Coutinho, Portuguese, with some non-Portuguese in agreement, have asserted that before Henry there must have been explorations; before Vasco da Gama, secret voyages in the Atlantic and Indian oceans; before Columbus, discovery of America; before Cabral, secret Portuguese voyages to Brazil. The effect of their reasoning is to reduce all the great explorers to pygmies following in the already known wake of the "first" anonymous discoverers.

The expansion of Portugal overseas does not mean the same thing to the person not acquainted with the literature on discovery as it does to the historians of the period. The former are more apt to see the true story — the phenomenal things that were accomplished by a small nation. The latter get involved in the details, most of them disputed, and fail to stress the profound influence of Portugal on civilization. Their arguments are so destructive of the grandeur of Portugal's greatest explorers that if offered by foreigners they could be considered a conspiracy to rob Portugal of credit for its accomplishments.

The reader will soon see that I have little patience with what I regard as elaborate guesswork. The unquestionable greatness of a Vasco da Gama is preferable to an unknown pre-da Gama. For the positive and matchless achievements of the Portuguese I am filled with endless admiration; but I do not accept the claims of those writers who have tried to make a physically small nation greater because they were sensitive about its size and have only succeeded in belittling it and making it seem petty.

Whoever writes of exploration must come to grips with the "evidence" set forth by such writers. A general reader may have little interest in this material. It destroys the continuity of the narrative and even obscures the real Portuguese accomplishments. It has, therefore, been placed in footnotes and appendixes. The text that follows can be read with minimal reference to the appendixes without losing any of the essential story of Portugal's expansion. I hope to achieve the double purpose of satisfying both general reader and specialist.

The known published primary accounts have been studied in the preparation of this book as well as the principal secondary books and articles. In recent times there have not been any highly significant discoveries of documents that changed the existing body of knowledge, though some relatively minor disclosures from the archives have been hailed because such new material is so rare. The appropriate citation appears in the footnotes and in the general bibliography. Because much of the evidence of discoveries, as well as the fancies of medieval cartographers, appears in maps and marine charts, the most essential examples of these are reproduced.

The rule used for spelling the names is in general to take the English form for popes, kings, and other principal persons. However, the names of the kings of Portugal appear in their Portuguese forms, i.e., João (John), and Spanish kings in their Spanish forms, i.e., Juan (John), to avoid frequent repetition such as John of Castile, John of Portugal, etc. Henry the Navigator appears as Henry, not Henrique. Geographical names where verifiable follow modern spellings. Many places are not easily and accurately equated with their medieval names.

During the forty plus years of my interest in Portuguese history, I have accumulated many debts of gratitude to people, libraries, and archives. In Portugal and Brazil, as well as in various western European countries, courtesies too many in number to be mentioned have facilitated my work. Various foundations have also helped finance me, among them the Rotary Club of Fort Worth, Texas; The American Philosophical Society; the Social Science Research Council; the Fulbright Commission; and the Rockefeller Foundation. And let us not forget the Internal Revenue Service, which has been taught to look at times with lenient eyes on expenses for educational travel.

As a college professor, I acknowledge with pleasure and gratitude the help of many students who have contributed to my knowledge in the City

College of New York, New York University, Columbia, Yale and Cornell Universities, and the Universities of Washington, Texas, and Southern California. Without the acute questions of students many dubious bits of "knowledge" would have passed as accurate. Concerning Portuguese exploration we can quote a famous saying of the nineteenth-century humorist Artemus Ward: "It ain't that the people are ignorant; it is just that what they know ain't so." This has certainly been the case with Portuguese exploration. Myths have accumulated and are still accumulating and being defended. I have no doubt retained some of my preferred myths — but many others are dispelled. I wish to thank those who have read this manuscript and suggested corrections of errors and viewpoints, and to apologize for rejecting their wisdom. In the last analysis every student of history must make his own decisions.

To two of my students at the University of Southern California, Mr. Oliver Rink and Mr. Francis R. Provencher, I am indebted for help in preparing the maps showing Portugal's principal discoveries. Professor Barbara Worcester of Texas Christian University gave expert advice on matters concerning astronomy.

To my wife Edilla, who has helped me at all stages of the writing of this work, I give thanks with only the regret that no words can adequately express my debt.

PREFACE TO PERIOD 1500–80

George D. Winius

The writing of a preface is the time to reveal one's own views about the work one has completed, and in the instance of assessing my own contribution to *Europe and the World in the Age of Expansion* series, I must confess I was more conditioned by what others had written, or not written, than I was by trying to present a balanced survey of Portuguese Asia in all the dimensions known to modern historiography. To do the General Editor credit, he has never insisted that I do so, but has given me my own gait.

There is a sharp break in the historiography of Portuguese overseas expansion that begins at the discovery of India. Historians have argued for generations about the motives and priorities of the era of Henrician and Columbian discoveries, but it would almost seem that they lost interest in what happened to the Portuguese after they had rounded the Cape of Good Hope. They have largely been content thereafter to weave the chronicle accounts of Barros, Castanheda, Corrêa, Couto, and Damião de Góis into a single narrative and let matters go at that. It is difficult to find a controversy or even a major difference in interpretation — in fact, there is hardly any interpretation. The accounts merely seem to fall into two categories: short and long.

For over seventy years, the standard histories of Portuguese Asia in English that cover the period 1500–80 have been those of Frederick C. Danvers (*The Portuguese in India*, 1894) and Richard S. Whiteway (*The Rise of the Portuguese Power in India*, 1899). These are also both political and military narrative accounts based largely on the chronicles, and their main defect for modern readers is that they are too detailed in their battle accounts, contain too little information about who the Portuguese were fighting, and why, and do not reflect any of the work done subsequently on economic or institutional history. To make much sense of them today requires too much reading in companion volumes for any but the most intrepid student to undertake. My aim has been to save others the trouble by pruning the battle accounts and incorporating other types of institutional and economic information not available to Messrs. Danvers and Whiteway in their day. I still feel, however, that their books are useful, and I have referred to them extensively to establish a continuity between events because the chronicles meander at such a digressive and leisurely pace that one often loses one's way in them — though always enjoyably.

Two other writers in English, Charles R. Boxer and Donald F. Lach, have influenced this book, and I must confess that I stand in awe of their achievements. Boxer's works are too voluminous and too well known to describe in detail here, but their unfailing characteristics are a revelation of the author's vast command of sources, a graceful narrative style, and judicious generalization, especially in regard to social history. Fortunately for myself, Professor Boxer has so far chosen to write little about Portuguese India itself, especially in the sixteenth century, and it is as if for that reason alone that I have undertaken to write this work. However, I was conscious as I wrote that to attempt a chapter on social history would be to repeat his citations endlessly and to rehash, less ably, what he has already written. I would urge readers to undertake his *Portuguese Seaborne Empire* (1969), among his many other books, if they have not already done so. I dislike the idea of trying to say everything in one book, even if it were possible.

Donald Lach has dealt extensively with Portugal in his first volumes of *Asia in the Making of Europe*. He has summed up virtually all there is to be said about Portuguese missionary efforts and cultural contacts, at least insofar as they have been written about in secondary sources or reflected in printed accounts or documents. His influence has been such that I did not feel compelled to write a specific chapter on the general missionary activities of the Portuguese empire in Asia to 1580, but only dealt with them when they moved to the fore in imperial affairs, namely in Ethiopia and Japan. To readers who are sufficiently interested in missionary and in cultural contacts, I commend his Volume I.

My own concern as a historian of European expansion has been to examine the Portuguese empire as a unit and to explain what factors made it possible and motivated it, and what ones inhibited its ultimate success. The Portuguese were (and are) a remarkable race, with a tenacity and a zest for survival matched only by a few other nations, notably the Dutch and the Finns. In early modern Europe, they were the true geniuses for adventure, the iron men to whom seemingly insuperable odds were no more than a challenge. All the seafaring people of the Renaissance shared this daring to some larger or lesser degree, but the Portuguese were clearly the first among them. I hope I have given them their due, and I would caution those preoccupied with the humanitarian and egalitarian concerns of the midtwentieth century that one must not judge Albuquerque and his contemporaries by standards of conduct more applicable to today's statesmen and generals. They marched very well, but to another drum.

Finally, I wish to caution readers that I have written a history of Portuguese power in Asia, not a history of Asia at the time of Portuguese expansion, or even a full-scale history of Portuguese Asia. No doubt Asian readers have long ago tired of exclusively Europocentric accounts written about the expansion of Europe in their own lands, but I feel this does not preclude any history of Europe in Asia. I have tried to include as much background material as I could, but I felt the book would have suffered from diffuseness, not to speak of more ignorance than I display already, if I had strayed much farther afield than I did.

I wish to thank my collaborator and my editor, Beverly Kaemmer, for their willingness and understanding of my foibles (mostly sloth and always having a better rewording to spring upon them). Similarly, Mrs. Frankie Hammond and Mrs. Beth Ramey, of Gainesville, Florida, my typists, who were cheerful and unstinting of their efforts. My friends, António de Oliveira Marques, Charles Boxer, and Padre António da Silva Rego all helped to clarify my ideas and, I might add, to inspire me. Three others lent me more practical aid: Sr. Alexandre Marques Pereira of the Sociedade de Geografia de Lisboa, who spared no trouble in locating books for me, and my two new colleagues, Drs. Gerard Telkamp and Leonard Blussé, both of Leyden University, who read proof expertly, made last-minute suggestions, and straightened out my orthography of Chinese and Japanese names. And finally, I must thank my beloved spouse, Margriet, for her lovely patience: hence the dedication.

Contents

            Illustrations 1–19 and Maps I–VI follow p. 192

A powerful Portuguese squadron shown while visiting the Mediterranean in 1521. The lead
ship is the *Santa Maria do Monte Sinai*, built in India about 1512. Courtesy of the National
Maritime Museum, Greenwich.

Foundations of the Portuguese Empire, 1415–1580

It is astonishing how it is possible to extract from the same documentation, in good faith, conclusions that are diametrically opposed.

DUARTE LEITE

CHAPTER 1

West-East Relations from Ancient Times to the Fourteenth Century A.D.

West-East Contacts to Roman Times

The Portuguese accomplished in their expansion the fulfillment of a centuries-old dream. The desire to know other lands and people, to travel, conquer, trade, and spread one's religion is perhaps as old as mankind itself. Earliest recorded history reveals the peoples of the Mediterranean and India reaching toward one another at least as early as 2000 B.C.[1] The stories of Jason and the Argonauts and the siege of Troy in the twelfth century B.C. show Greek expansion. The Phoenicians sailed westward to Carthage in the ninth century B.C., while at the same time their fleets were in the Red Sea. Herodotus recounts a story of a Phoenician fleet sent by the Pharaoh Necho from east to west around Africa and back to Egypt in a three-year voyage about 600 B.C. Herodotus also established the traditional view that the land masses of the world were divided into three continents: Asia, Africa, and Europe. The world he knew reached to the Caspian Sea, the Indus River, and the Arabian Sea, and from the Niger River in Africa to the Danube River in Europe. The Carthaginians expanded to the west coast of Africa where, it was reported, Hanno of Carthage settled 30,000 people in various towns during the sixth century B.C. The Phoenicians pushed into Spain and Portugal and perhaps to the British Isles in their search for tin and other trade products.

[1] Concerning the period to ca. A.D. 300 see the following works: Lloyd A. Brown, *The Story of Maps*, pp. 3–80; Max Cary and E. H. Warmington, *The Ancient Explorers*; Lionel Casson, *The Ancient Mariners*; Donald Harden, *The Phoenicians*; Charles E. Nowell, *The Great Discoveries*; Boies Penrose, *Travel and Discovery*, pp. 3–27; Percy Sykes, *A history of Exploration*, pp. 1–44.

The Greeks, from about 800 to 500 B.C., spread westward to the end of the Mediterranean and eastward along the shores of the Black Sea. They mingled with their practical desire for commerce and colonization great scientific curiosity. They sought explanations of the earth on which they stood and all that seemed to surround them. Anaximenes, in the sixth century B.C., proposed that the world was a rectangle floating on air, not entirely an incorrect concept. Pythagoras thought of the world as a sphere; Hecataeus wrote the first geography.

People of the great ancient empires contributed to geographical knowledge. Darius extended his power from India in the east to the shores of the Mediterranean. The Persian emperor Xerxes, in the fifth century B.C., dispatched Sataspes to sail through the Mediterranean and around Africa as atonement for raping a lady of the court. Sataspes failed, returned to Persia, and was executed. Alexander the Great came nearer than anyone to joining Eastern and Western worlds. In the brief period from 334 to 323 B.C., he conquered to the Indus River and to Bactria east of the Caspian Sea. At Khojan he was 3500 miles east of his homeland. So little did he understand geography that he confused the Jaxartes, which flows into the Aral Sea, with the Don, which flows into the Black Sea. Nor did Alexander realize the size of India whose western edges only he had touched, nor did he know, apparently, that China and the Indies lay beyond. A contemporary, Pytheas of Marseilles (Massilia), was reported to have sailed to England, Scotland, and the Baltic, and to have heard of "Thule," the outermost part of the world. He is said to have learned to fix his latitude by observing the varying lengths of the days. If true, this would give him a high rank as a scientific observer; but some later writers have doubted the story.

Closer ties were soon to be formed between East and West with the simultaneous rise of three great empires. In China, Emperor Shih Huang Ti (221–210 B.C.) began building the Great Wall to ward off the nomads who, having thrown themselves in vain against it, turned westward to begin a series of attacks which culminated in assaults on the Roman Empire. The Han Empire in China, founded in 206 B.C., endured for four centuries and established a *Pax Sinica*, which extended from China across Siberia to the Caspian Sea. Here it came into contact with the Parthian Empire (220 B.C.–A.D. 226). Contemporaneously the Romans, whose maximum empire extended from Scotland to the Persian Gulf, completed the trio of great empires with contiguous boundaries from the Atlantic to the Pacific. One result was a mutual exchange of commerce and culture. Emperor Wu Ti (140–87 B.C.) sent an ambassador, Chang Kien, westward in 138 B.C. to seek trade and allies. He was able, it is said, to open up the great Silk Route across Siberia into the Roman Empire. It was during this period that Hinduism triumphed over Buddhism in India and Buddhism spread across Siberia into China and the Island of Ceylon. In the Roman Empire, Christianity, a future expansive force, began to grow at the expense of other religions.

Rome, though blocked from direct trade with the Chinese across the hostile Parthian Empire, was able to establish commerce through the Black Sea northward across the Caspian Sea and along the land route to China. Roman commerce from the Levant down the Tigris and Euphrates rivers or by way of the Nile or the Red Sea and across to India was much increased when, about 120 B.C., Eudoxus returned from India with news of the monsoons. Credit for bringing this news to the Greeks, which meant to the Romans, was given to Hippalus. The southwest monsoon, blowing spring and summer, carried ships to India; the northeast monsoon in fall and winter enabled them to return to the Red Sea or to the African coast.

Roman Expansion and World Concepts

The Romans continued to conceive of the world as three continents and a few islands. The Roman Strabo, a geographer, mathematician, historian, and political observer, who lived in the reign of Emperor Augustus (30 B.C.–A.D. 14), described the Roman world. He regarded the story of Pytheas's exploration of the north as fanciful and rejected — unfortunately for later scientific geography — much of the work of Eratosthenes, who had correctly postulated a world 25,000 miles in circumference. Strabo reported a flourishing trade with India, some 120 ships plying this route. The coast of East Africa as far as Zanzibar was known, and wearing Chinese silk became a status symbol for Roman women.

Pomponius Mela (fl. ca. A.D. 43), in *De situ orbis*, divided the world into five zones, only two of which were habitable. He suggested an antipodes, beyond the tropics, not accessible to the northern zones. He was to have a great influence centuries later on the Portuguese geographer Duarte Pacheco Pereira. Ptolemy, a Greco-Roman of Alexandria (fl. A.D. 150), was the most scientific geographer of Roman times. He recorded

with fair accuracy the world from Thule, which he placed at about 63°
north latitude, to India. He knew of Africa south of the Sahara and recognized the possibility of sailing to China by sea, believing, however, that
there was a great "terra incognita" which enclosed the Indian Ocean,
making impossible a voyage around Africa to India. He accepted the idea
of a great tropical barrier separating the northern from a southern hemisphere. His most important contribution was to draw lines of latitude and
longitude on his maps. Largely lost sight of during the Middle Ages, his
treatise on geography was resuscitated in the early fifteenth century. The
maximum extent of the Romans' knowledge may be judged from the
report that a Roman merchant, described as an ambassador, was in Indochina in approximately A.D. 166.

The great empires collapsed almost simultaneously, as they had risen
four centuries before, and the trade between East and West declined with
them. Rome lapsed into civil war during the third century; the Han
Empire of China fell in A.D. 220; and the Parthian Empire fell to the
Sassanids in A.D. 226. Not for many centuries was there again close inter-
communication between the East and the West.

Roman geographers in the third and later centuries were less interested
in the scientific than they were in the spectacular. Solinus (fl. ca. A.D.
250), known as Polyhistor, collected tales from earlier writers, particularly
from the largely unnatural *Natural History* of Pliny, and often accepted
the unbelievable. Since people nevertheless believed and repeated the
tales for centuries, his influence extended throughout the Middle Ages
and to modern times. He described the strange forms and miraculous
qualities of many kinds of imaginary, marvelous birds, fishes, reptiles,
minerals, and beasts, including men with dogs' heads, or with eyes in their
chests, or with one eye in the center of their foreheads. Others were
pictured with one foot large enough to use as an umbrella or with ears that
reached to the waist. So profoundly did he persuade his readers that
centuries later the explorers of Africa, America, and Asia sought and
"saw" such creatures.

The Small World of Medieval Europe

With the steady decline of the Roman Empire and the triumph of Christianity as the official religion, Christians became more interested in a
future world than in this. Though there seems to be nothing essentially

"Christian" about the inaccurate geographical concepts of the Middle Ages, they were deemed more compatible with what were then considered to be Christian ideas of the world.[2] Thus the Roman geographer Microbius (fl. ca. A.D. 395–423) was acceptable to later Christians because he proposed a stationary sphere as the center of the universe, surrounded by a sea variously called Atlantic, Great Sea, or Ocean. Land, he said, not water, covered most of the world. He believed in the almost accurate 25,000-mile circumference of the earth posited by Eratosthenes rather than the inaccurate 22,500-mile figure of Ptolemy, and he also proposed a torrid zone to the south, dividing the northern from a southern world inhabited by an unknown people and inaccessible to Europeans. Martianas Capella (fifth century) also believed in a global world with a 25,000-mile circumference, a world divided into five zones, one of which was too hot for habitation and one too cold, and surrounded by a great circumnavigable ocean. From his writings it is evident that Pliny, Solinus, and Pomponius Mela had supplanted Eratosthenes, Hipparchus, Strabo, and Ptolemy as sources of information about the world.

In the fifth century, by which time western Europe was losing its knowledge of the East, Chinese ships were sailing westward to India and even into the Euphrates River. China and Persia exchanged ambassadors. After the fall of the Roman Empire almost the only Western contact with the East was through the Byzantine Empire at Constantinople. An example of the traders who still existed was Cosmas, known as the "Indian Traveler." A merchant-contemporary of Emperor Justinian (A.D. 527–565), he retired in A.D. 548 to write a "Christian" geography. His *Christian Topography* denounced the "evil and false" belief in the sphericity of the earth; he held that it was oblong. He scorned the antipodes as an old wives' tale for, he said, those on the opposite side would be standing with their heads downward contrary to nature. Furthermore there could be no antipodes since the apostles who were commanded to go into all the world and preach the gospel were not reported to have gone there.

Christian writers struggled throughout the Middle Ages to conceive of the size and shape of the earth, but they could not get too far from their chief authority, the Bible. All men had to be of one origin, descendants of

[2] Charles Raymond Beazley, *The Dawn of Modern Geography*, vol. I (covering the period from ca. A.D. 300 to ca. 900); Francis S. Betten, "The Knowledge of the Sphericity of the Earth"; Brown, *The Story of Maps*, pp. 81–112; George H. T. Kimble, *Geography in the Middle Ages*; A. P. Newton, ed., *Travel and Travellers of the Middle Ages*, pp. 1–69; Vincent H. Cassidy, *The Sea around Them*.

Adam; the shape of the earth had to be such that all men could have heard the preaching of Jesus. Not until such mental images were destroyed was it possible to recover the more accurate concepts of the geographers.

The Muslim World and Eastern Contacts

While the Christians were struggling with these ideas, there sprang up a new religion, Islam, which was to influence Christian geography profoundly. It spread within a century of the time of the Hegira (622) from Arabia to Egypt, throughout North Africa to central France, briefly, and to the Tigris-Euphrates valley and the gates of Constantinople.

During this period the Chinese were still trading with India and Persia, and soon the Arab leaders of Islam were to meet the people from the farthest East. In the seventh century China again dominated a region that reached to the Caspian Sea. Olopun, a Nestorian Christian missionary, traversed this empire and visited China about 635. Hsüan Tsang, a Chinese Buddhist monk, traveled extensively from about 629 to 645. The Chinese knew so much of the West in fact that the *Annals* of 670 record an Arab attack that failed to capture Constantinople. Chinese junks sailed from Canton to Ceylon, to the Malabar coast, to Cambay, and to Ormuz, before reaching the Euphrates in the seventh and eight centuries. In 671 the Chinese monk I-Ching embarked in China on a Persian ship that visited Sumatra and other areas en route to India.

The Muslims, under Arabic leadership, occupied the Near Eastern world, reaching to Bokhara, Samarkand, Farghana, and Kashgar from 705 to 714. An Arab embassy was dispatched to China in 713, and the Arabs were in India by 750. That there were Christians in China is indicated by an imperial order in 745 requiring that the Christian temples hitherto known as Persian were to be called Roman, "Ta-tsin." There were visits of "priests of great virtue" to China. Shortly after this time a Muslim curtain closed over the East, and Christian visits were less feasible. The Arabs had their trading post at Canton. In 758 war broke out between the Chinese of Canton and the Persian and Arab traders, who sacked the city and fled to their ships. In spite of such incidents, it is clear that from this time on a trade area existed in which products of China, Indonesia, and India were exchanged via the Mediterranean for those of Iberia and Africa on the Atlantic. Sulayman, an Arab merchant, made several voyages to China in the mid-ninth century. Another merchant, Khurdadbih, made an overland trip to Samarkand along the Khorasan road and the "Golden Road" and thence to China by way of the "great Silk Road."

Islamic civilization was reaching its height during the eighth through the tenth centuries. The Omayyad Dynasty which had succeeded the original line of Mohammed in 661 was overthrown in 749 by the Abbasids who ruled from Baghdad. A member of the Omayyads escaped to Spain where he established himself in Córdoba as Abd-er-Rahman I, emir. Later his successors declared themselves caliphs. Their court was the principal cultural center of the Muslim West, as was Baghdad of the East. Harun al-Rashid, caliph of Baghdad, was famous even in the European West and exchanged embassies with Charlemagne. Under Mamun, a ninth-century caliph, science became highly developed. A school of geography, the first known since Roman times, was created in Baghdad where there was an astronomical observatory as well. Many studies were made in mathematics, physics, optics, and medicine, which only later were to be known in the West. Much of this learning had come down from Hellenistic Greeks, and much could be attributed to Islamic toleration of Nestorian Christians, who had created a University at Nisibis (or Nisibin, modern Nusaybin in southwest Turkey on the Syrian border near Iraq) where many translations from Greek to Arabic were made of works not known at that time in the West. Nestorianism spread during the ninth century into India, Syria, Persia, Arabia, Samarkand, and China. Cartographic art in tenth-century Islam may be judged from the world map of Masudi, who had traveled from Spain to Turkistan, and who also mentioned Sofala, Zanzibar, and China. *The Arabian Nights'*, although only a storybook, shows that the area from Africa and India to the East was known and traveled.

The Gradual Awakening of Western Europe

The Christian world to the west of the Byzantine Empire, except Iberia and Sicily, had slight knowledge before the tenth century of the culture and trade that existed under Islam. The awakening in the West that eventually was to make it triumphant over the East came with the rise of Feudalism, the voyages of the Vikings, and the growth of the Italian cities.

When Charlemagne's empire began disintegrating after the Treaty of Verdun in 843 divided his domains among his three grandsons, it seemed for a while as if the West would find no means to pull itself back to a semblance of Roman organization. But feudalism restored to Europe some elements 'of organized government. By the end of the tenth century a few large states such as Normandy, Flanders, Brittany, Burgundy, and Aquitania had arisen, where before there were hundreds of petty states. In the tenth and eleventh centuries five Christian kingdoms rose across northern Spain, including the region that was to become Portugal. The existence of these larger states made more travel and commerce possible.

A few Italian cities, namely Venice, Brindisi, Amalfi, Pisa, and Genoa, began in the tenth century to be known in a small way in the commerce of the Mediterranean. Though often victims of Arab raids and sometimes of temporary Arab occupation, they were finding ways to resist and to expand their trade.

From the north had come the Vikings, whose extensive conquests, travels, and trade were to have a profound influence on Europe.[3] At first their incursions were mainly destructive — their raids had helped destroy Charlemagne's empire. They struck as far south as the Iberian Peninsula in the ninth and tenth centuries. Presently they settled in areas where they had previously only raided. Normandy in France became their territory. They pushed into England, Scotland, Ireland, and the Shetland and Orkney islands. Their westward expansion led them in about 874 to Iceland, which they colonized. They found there Irish monks who had settled as early as 790. In 877 the Viking Gunnbjorn sighted Greenland. Erik the Red "discovered" Greenland in 982 and made a settlement on the southwest coast, where Viking communities probably existed continuously to the fifteenth century. Most interesting was the discovery made by Bjarni Heriulfson, who sighted the coast where Leif Ericsson landed about the year 1000. Returning from Norway to Greenland, Leif sailed to or was driven onto a coast that he called Wineland or Vinland, now believed to have been the North American continent, probably New-

[3] Beazley, *Dawn of Geography*, II, 1–111 (the Vikings), 392–464 (commercial travel ca. A.D. 900–1260); Theodore C. Blegen, *The Kensington Rune Stone*; Johannes Brøndsted, *The Vikings*; Charles Home Haskins, *The Normans in European History*; Gwyn Jones, *The Norse Atlantic Saga* and *A History of the Vikings*; Magnus Magnusson and Herman Palsson, eds., *The Vinland Sagas*; Newton, *Travel and Travellers*, pp. 70–87; Tryggvi J. Oleson, *Early Voyages and Northern Approaches, 1000–1632*; M. Postan and E. E. Rich, eds., *The Cambridge Economic History of Europe*, II, Chap. IV and bibliography, pp. 531–536; Sykes, *Exploration*, pp. 52–57; Samuel Eliot Morison, *The European Discovery of America: The Northern Voyages*, p. 32, uses the term *Viking* to distinguish "the Norse freebooters and pirates who raided the coast of Europe" from the *Norsemen*, "comparatively peaceful traders and farmers" who settled in Iceland and Greenland. But see what he says of Frydis on p. 62.

foundland. Thorfinn Karlsefni left Greenland about 1003 with three ships to settle in Vinland. He and his party spent three years somewhere in North America before being driven out by the Eskimos. No known permanent settlements resulted from these expeditions, except those in Greenland and Iceland.

The Vikings had also pushed eastward in the tenth century, penetrating Russia and establishing trade routes along the rivers leading into the Black Sea, where they made contacts with the Byzantine Empire. One of their principal centers of trade in Russia was Kiev. The conversion of the Russians in this region to Christianity would facilitate trade at a later period. The Vikings were converted to Roman Christianity in the eleventh century.

The Christian Counteroffensive against the Muslims

In the eleventh century there was even greater activity in western Europe: the Christian states of Spain made great progress in driving back the Muslims; Portugal was established as a separate political entity;[4] England began a new period of history when it was conquered by William; and the Italian cities that had been hard pressed to defend themselves against the Muslims in the tenth century now went on the offensive. In 1016 Pisa took Sardinia from the Muslims. In the same year the Normans, coming through Gibralter into the Mediterranean, arrived in Italy, where they began a series of conquests of both Muslim and Christian lands.

In Spain the decisive event was the fall of the Muslim caliphate in 1031. This removed for the time being collective Muslim opposition to the Christians and enabled Castile and Aragon to drive against them. From this time on, the history of the Iberian Peninsula was in great part a confrontation between the Muslim and Christian forces.

Events that would later influence the Iberian Peninsula decisively were taking place in the Mediterranean and the Near East. From 1060 to 1091 the Normans proceeded with their conquest of Sicily. The rise of the

---

[4] Pedro Aguado Bleye, *Manual de historia de España*, I, 593–622; Fortunato de Almeida, *História de Portugal*, I, 125–170; Rafael Altamira, *Historia de España*, I, 362–386; Charles E. Nowell, *History of Portugal*, pp. 1–20; Damião Peres, ed., *História de Portugal*, I, 433–504. For more extensive reading see: Reinhart P. A. Dozy, *Histoire des Musulmans d'Espagne* and *Spanish Islam*; Alexandre Herculano, *História de Portugal*; H. V. Livermore, *A History of Portugal*.

Seljuk Turks, converts to Islam, was signalized by the conquest of Baghdad in 1055 and the defeat of the Byzantine Empire in 1071 at the decisive Battle of Manzikert in Central Anatolia. The Muslims were losing slowly in Spain and the Mediterranean, but they were gaining in the East with the conversion of the Seljuks to Islam. The Normans and the Seljuks were destined to come into conflict.

In Spain, Alfonso VI (1065–1109) raided deep into Muslim territory, allegedly as far as the Atlantic at Cádiz and to the walls of Lisbon. In 1085 he captured the city of Toledo, which was never recovered by the Muslims and which became the Castilian capital. The Muslim answer to the conquest of Toledo was the invasion of Spain from Africa by the Almoravids in 1086. A Berber people recently converted to Islam, they would stay in Spain until 1147. The Christian Italians were at the same time advancing against the Muslims in Africa where in 1087 Genoa and Pisa conquered the city of El Mehdia. When the Normans completed their conquest of Sicily in 1091, the Christians were well on their way to controlling the western Mediterranean. With the First Crusade in 1095 the Christians launched a long series of attacks in an effort, eventually unsuccessful, to wrest control of the eastern Mediterranean from the Muslims.

In the course of the half century before the Crusades, many Christian knights from the north had been called into Spain to aid their fellow Christians.[5] The two who gained most were the cousins Counts Raymond and Henry of Burgundy. Raymond married Urraca, daughter of King Alfonso VI of Castile, and was named heir to the throne (he died before his father-in-law). Henry married Teresa, another daughter of Alfonso VI, and with his wife was given the area around Oporto in Portugal to rule in 1095. Henry and Teresa drove hard against the Muslims and also achieved relative autonomy within the Castilian system. By the time of Count Henry's death (1112?), Portugal, which even in the earliest times had distinctive characteristics, was becoming such a clear entity that it could never again be successfully absorbed into Castile. The growth of Portugal in the twelfth century and the further increase in power and trade of Italian cities in the Mediterranean were to bring these two areas into closer economic and political relationships.

The trade rivalries in the Mediterranean embattled not only Christian against Muslim but Christian against Christian. Byzantium, which had

[5] Damião Peres, *Como nasceu Portugal*; Petit de Vausse, "Croisades bourguignonnes."

been the leading Christian power down to the eleventh century, was now challenged. Both Venetians and Normans became powerful enough to exact trade privileges in Byzantium, and in 1111 Byzantium granted privileges to Pisa as a counterweight to Norman-Venetian influence. The Byzantine Empire badly needed the assistance of Western Christians in their struggle against the Muslims, but they also resented the privileges the Christians demanded. In a war, 1122–26, Byzantium attempted in vain to force the Venetians to give up some of the previously granted trade privileges. War against, and trade with, the Italian cities was to become the pattern of Byzantine life. In the war with Roger of Sicily, 1147–58, Emperor Manuel Comnenus (1143–80) was forced to buy the aid of the Venetians by making further trade concessions. In 1155 he also granted trade privileges to the city of Genoa.

The Birth of Portugal: 1095–1211

Events in Portugal were fashioning that state's autonomy. Afonso Henriques (1128–85), son of Count Henry and Countess Teresa, was a vigorous and aggressive ruler who warred against Castile to assure his boundaries in the north and east and against the Muslims in the south to push them out of Portugal.[6] In 1139 somewhere deep in Muslim territory, no one can say where, he defeated a Muslim army, no one can say how large, in the Battle of Ourique. This battle at the time was held to be a great Christian victory, though in later centuries its significance was much debated by historians. Afonso Henriques then declared himself king. In 1143 his cousin King Alfonso VII of Castile recognized his autonomy, if not his independence. Afonso Henriques enhanced his prestige in 1146 with his marriage to Matilde, the daughter of Amador III, Count of Savoy. Not dismayed by the Almohads, Berbers from North Africa, newly converted to Islam, who invaded Spain in 1146 and ruled southern Spain until 1269, Afonso in 1147 captured Lisbon with the assistance of the Crusaders in perhaps 200 ships from northern European countries en

---

[6] Almeida, *História de Portugal*, I, 140–170; H. V. Livermore, *A New History of Portugal*, pp. 50–80; Nowell, *History of Portugal*, pp. 8–41; Peres, *História de Portugal*, II, 7–154. Note: The Christian Portuguese came in the course of time to call themselves Lusitanians, a name derived from a pre-Roman people supposedly descended from Lusus, hence Lusitanians, sons of Lusus. They occupied a region around Mérida (Spain) and gave the Romans a difficult task of conquest. They were pushed west and formed a nucleus for Lusitania (later Portugal). The modern name of Portugal is derived from the region around Oporto, ruled by Henry of Burgundy and Teresa.

route to the Holy Land for the Second Crusade. This placed in Christian hands one of the finest cities and ports in Europe.

The future commercial importance of Portugal was foreshadowed by the trade and fishing carried on in Afonso Henriques's time. The Muslim geographer Edrisi, who in 1154 prepared for Roger II of Sicily a map and a description of the world known to Europe, described Portugal in considerable detail. Oporto and Lisbon were of course the most important Christian ports; Alcácer do Sal on the Sado River, Sines and Odemira farther south on the west coast, as well as Lagos, Silves, Albufeira, and Tavira on the south coast were still important Muslim cities. Such products as fish, salt, olive oil, wine, cork, esparto grass, and pine resin were traded with northern Europe. Many foreigners from the Mediterranean were in Portugal. Lusitanians, i.e. Portuguese, are mentioned by the Greek writer Timarion as trading in the fair of San Demetrius in Thessalonica in the first half of the twelfth century.

Genoa and other Italian cities were making progress against the Muslims in the Mediterranean.[7] Genoa won trade privileges from Boujia and cities on the Moroccan coast in 1137. Italian cities cooperated with Spanish monarchs in attacks on the Balearic Islands, Corsica, and Sardinia. By 1160 Ceuta and Genoa actively traded. In 1161 the Genoese gained important commercial advantages from the Moroccans, twice renewed later in the century. In 1162 they sailed through Gibraltar to the city of Salé on the west coast of present-day Morocco.

It is quite possible that the Christian Portuguese traded in the Muslim ports of North Africa as they did in Portugal itself with Muslims and Jews, an example being in 1166 when Afonso Henriques granted a charter to Évora, recently captured from the Muslims, in which rights were given to Muslims and Jews as well as to Christians. In 1180 Muslims in Lisbon, Palmela, and Alcácer do Sal received the right to travel freely throughout his kingdom. There are numerous other examples of Christian-Muslim trade, one being the municipal price lists which indicate that Christian Portugal was receiving pepper by way of Muslim lands.

Marriage alliances show that Portugal was in touch with both Mediterranean and northern European areas. In 1160 Afonso Henrique's daughter was betrothed to Count Ramón Berenguer of Provence, son of Ramón

---

[7] Bailey W. Diffie, *Prelude to Empire*, pp. 20–27; Luigi Federzoni, ed., *Relazione fra Italia–Portogallo*; Hilmar C. Krueger, "Genoese Trade with Northwest Africa"; M. L. de Mas Latrie, *Traités de paix et de commerce avec les Arabes de l'Afrique*; Roberto S. Lopez, *Storia delle colonie genovese* and *Genova marinara*.

Berenguer III of Barcelona, but the count died before the marriage. Another daughter of Afonso Henriques, Uracca, married Fernando II of Leon in 1165; and Sancho, later king of Portugal, married Dulce, daughter of Ramón Berenguer IV, in 1174. Their daughter Berengaria subsequently married the king of Denmark. Still another daughter Teresa married Phillip, the Count of Flanders, in 1184. The international aspect of these marriages is indicated by the support that Henry II of England gave the marriage of Teresa and Phillip as part of his war against Philip II of France. Afonso sought in these marriages to ally himself with those who could help him in his struggle against Castile. He also constantly appealed to Rome for recognition as king of Portugal and was finally successful in 1179. Portuguese relationships with northern Europe increased. Numbers of Flemings settled in Portugal and Portuguese in Flanders, thus increasing commerce between the areas.

King Sancho I of Portugal (1185–1211) found other opportunities to increase external contacts. When Jerusalem fell to the Muslims in 1187, a new Crusade was called. Two fleets with Flemings, Germans, English, French, and Danes helped Sancho in the conquest of some southern areas of Portugal, including Silves, captured in 1189 but lost shortly afterward to invaders from North Africa and not to be recovered until 1249. Many of the Crusaders remained in Portugal.

The Mongols East of the Muslims: Genghis Khan, 1155–1227

Mediterranean events led to greater East-West relationships. Venice became the dominant Christian power in the eastern Mediterranean, occupying Constantinople from 1204 to 1261 as a result of the misdirected Fourth Crusade. Commerce in the Black Sea and in the Mediterranean increased the flow of Eastern products into western Europe, always through the Muslim middlemen.

In the thirteenth century there was a tremendous increase in East and West exchange. Muslim influence had penetrated India to such a degree that the country was largely divided between two religions, Islam and Hinduism. The formation of the Muslim Delhi sultanate in 1206 soon gave the Muslims a state that extended from Kashmir in the northwest to the Brahmaputra River. In the northwest the sultanate came into contact and conflict with Mongols who had risen in Asia and who were to exert a tremendous economic influence by virtue of the great territory under their control.[8]

The leader of the Mongols was Genghis Khan (ca. 1155–1227). By the time Genghis died in 1227, his forces had reached almost to the Caspian Sea and the Indus River. By 1237 the Mongols had conquered much of what is today Russia. In 1243 they defeated the Seljuks who then dominated Anatolia, and in 1258 they captured Baghdad and crushed the Abbasids. They had also moved eastward in Asia, and in 1258 they were in Hanoi. Their power now reached from the Pacific across Siberia into Russia, to the Baltic, the Caspian, and Black seas, the shore of the eastern Mediterranean, and the Indian Ocean.

The Political and Economic Growth of Portugal: 1211–49

During the half century in which the Mongols were extending their power over such wide areas, Portugal and Spain were pushing back the Muslims. They won a decisive victory at Las Navas de Tolosa in 1212. Other Christian victories followed. Fernando III of Castile captured Córdoba in 1236 and Seville in 1248. He gained the right to establish a fortress and a Christian church in Morocco. Jaime I of Aragon, the Conqueror, took Valencia and Murcia, the latter in the name of the king of Castile. His attacks in North Africa failed. However, he was able to take the Balearic Islands in a campaign, 1229–35, marking the beginning of the Aragonese Mediterranean power. In 1225–36 (or 1238–39) the Genoese besieged Ceuta, which they failed to capture but from which they gained commercial trade privileges. Portuguese kings were simultaneously making their own drive against the remaining Muslim forces in their country. Again taking advantage of the presence of Crusaders on their way to the Fifth Crusade, Afonso II in 1217 recaptured Alcácer do Sal on the Sado River, the key to advance farther south. The final conquest was completed in 1249 under Afonso III.

Portugal and Spain were far distant from sources of Eastern merchandise and greatly affected by the cost of the numerous transfers of goods from one merchant to another. Portugal's trade in the thirteenth century was principally with northern Europe and to some extent with North

[8] Walther Heissig, *A Lost Civilization: The Mongols Rediscovered*; Eustace D. Phillips, *The Mongols*.

Africa. The king of Portugal encouraged trade and participated in it, as shown in the charters to Lisbon and Santarém in 1179, which had a number of provisions for trade promotion. Royal letters patent in 1204–10 provided for an *alcaide dos navios* (commander of the ships), later known as the *alcaide do mar*. Markets were regulated by city governments, the king having his own *tendas* or stores. England sought to encourage Portuguese merchants, granting in 1203, 1205, 1208, and 1220 "safe conducts" (*salvo condutos*) for them to reside and trade in England.[9] A Portuguese merchant was in Dublin, Ireland, before the end of the twelfth century. Henry III of England issued more than 100 safe conducts to Portuguese merchants in 1226. Portuguese merchants were residing in France about 1240. The king of Portugal had his own shipyard at least as early as 1237. Afonso III (1248–79), who had lived many years in France and who married Beatrice, daughter of Afonso X of Castile, was greatly interested in foreign affairs and was a good businessman. He bought or constructed houses, stores, workshops, and inns for rental purposes. Portuguese kings acted as businessmen and economic promoters, and this was characteristic of Portugal for centuries to come.

Business was flourishing and prices were rising so fast that a law of December 1253 was enacted by Afonso III fixing prices on 400 foreign and domestic items from England, Flanders, and France, as well as from Castile and Andalusia, in an attempt to stop inflation.

Portuguese merchants carried on so much business in Spain after the Christians conquered Seville in 1248 that there was a street called "Calle de los Portugueses." The port of Viana in northern Portugal traded with the Muslims of Africa and Granada between 1258 and 1262. In fact, after the final conquest of Portugal from the Muslims in 1249, the products from Algarve continued to flow to their usual market in Muslim territories.

The West Seeks Mongol Aid against the Muslims

The fight against the Muslims did not deflect the Christians from their rivalries with one another for the trade of Africa and the East. Nor did

[9] Armando Marques Guedes, *A aliança inglêsa*; Herculano, *História de Portugal*, III, 212ff.; L. Saavedra Machado, "Os ingleses em Portugal"; V. M. Shillington and A. B. Wallis, *The Commercial Relations of England and Portugal*.

their rivalries make them forget entirely their goal of eventual victory over the Muslims. Thus it was that the appearance of the Mongols in Russia and in the Near East seemed to offer help to the Christians against the hated world of Islam. Pope Innocent IV hoped that he could convert the Mongols to Christianity and win them to an alliance against the Muslims. He sent Giovanni da Pian del Carpine (Plano Carpine) as an envoy to the Great Khan at Karakorum, capital of the Mongols in 1245–47.[10] Carpine was received with courtesy and listened to with respect, but he did not succeed in his mission, either for conversion or for an alliance. Louis IX (1226–70) of France, known as St. Louis, was stung by the failures of the previous Crusades, and attacked the Muslims in 1248 in Egypt and the Holy Land; but his attempt failed utterly. He now felt the necessity of having a powerful ally if the Muslim world was to be defeated. He dispatched William of Rubruck to the Great Khan (1253–55). William made much the same journey as Carpine and wrote one of the most enlightening travel accounts of any traveler to the East; but he achieved little else. The khan listened, allowed William to engage in public discussions with advocates of other religions, and made clear his preference for Buddhism. William returned in 1255; like Carpine he had not converted the Mongols to Christianity or gained them as an ally against the Muslims.

The way to the Far East was, nevertheless, opening; there were fewer barriers to travel than there had been for centuries. Genoa and Venice, feuding constantly for the chance to carry on this trade, fought from 1253 to 1258 over control of the Black Sea, Venice winning a temporary victory. In 1261 the Venetians who had had control of Constantinople since 1204 lost it to the Greeks who, to gain an ally against Venice, turned over Galata on the Golden Horn to the Genoese. The Genoese fleet was destroyed in another Venetian-Genoese war at the Battle of Trepani in 1264. The Venetians regained their privileges in Constantinople and in the few, small territories left to the Byzantine Empire, including Trebizond on the southeast shores of the Black Sea. Trebizond, having successfully resisted the Seljuk Turks as well as the Mongols, had become a great trading post for merchandise coming from the East by way of Persia and Armenia.

---

[10] C. Dawson, ed. and trans., *The Mongol Mission*; Newton, *Travel and Travellers*, pp. 124–158; Giovanni Soranzo, *Il Papato, l'Europa Cristiana e i Tartare*; R. A. Skelton, *The Vinland Map and the Tartar Relation*.

The Polos and Christian Missionaries
in the East: 1260–1328

From Trebizond in 1260 began one of the epic travels of all history and
one that was to have a profound influence on all of western Europe for
centuries. Two Venetian merchants, Nicolo and Maffeo Polo, journeyed
across Central Asia, remained several years in Bokhara, and continued on
to China. Returning, they brought great wealth in goods and colorful
stories of the East.[11]

They reached Acre, then in Christian hands, in 1269, with letters from
Kublai Khan to the pope, requesting 100 Christian missionaries. New
allies were important to the West at this time because a new threat to the
Christians was emerging in the Near East where the Ottomans, a branch
of the Turks, had invaded and had been converted to Islam. St. Louis IX
of France, still determined to strike a blow at the Muslims, made a new
Crusade to Tunis in 1270, but failed again and died. His failure, as well as
that of others, emphasized the value of anti-Muslim allies. The Polos,
unable to recruit the missionaries requested by the khan because of an
interregnum in the church, started again toward the East in 1271 with
only two preaching friars, who soon dropped out. The brothers, however,
had with them seventeen-year-old Marco, son of Nicolo. His personal
qualities and gifts as a linguist attracted the khan who took him into his
service.

The Polos were by no means the only Christians in the Far East.
Nestorians had been there for centuries, and some of the khans had
married Nestorian women. The mother of Kublai was a Nestorian. The
khans, nevertheless, found Buddhism more suitable for their people. The
Nestorian patriarch of Baghdad (Christians were tolerated within Muslim
bounds) appointed an archbishop for Peking in 1275, and several churches
were built in China. One indication of the relative ease of travel through
the Near and Far East was the presence in China from 1268 to 1273 of
engineers and war machines from Mesopotamia to help the Mongols in
their conquests in China. Mar Yabalaha, a Nestorian pilgrim who traveled
from Peking to Jerusalem, was elected patriarch in 1281; his companion
Rabban Bar Sauma went in 1287 as an ambassador for Arghun Khan of
Persia to arouse the West against the Muslims. He was able to make an

---

[11] Marco Polo: see Marco Polo, *The Book of Ser Marco Polo*, ed. by H. Cordier; Newton,
Travel and Travellers, pp. 132–141; Leonardo Olschki, *L'Asia di Marco Polo*.

agreement with Pope Nicholas IV regarding the Nestorian and Roman churches. There were many other pilgrims and emissaries.

Marco Polo traveled extensively in the service of the khan between 1275 and 1292. His travels included north and south China, Burma, and India. Marco reported on the commerce of China. He found the Chinese busily shipping silks and procelains to Java, Malaya, Ceylon, India, and Persia, from which they brought many varieties of spices as well as gems and pearls. Muslims were numerous in China, where Yunnan became a stronghold of Islam in the latter part of the thirteenth century.

John of Monte Corvino, a Roman missionary to China, was en route to China while the Polos were making their return journey and possibly was in India at the same time. John reached China in 1294, remaining there to 1328, where he was said to have converted 5000 to Christianity. In 1307 he was named archbishop of Peking by the pope. He was visited in Peking by Odoric of Pordenone during the period 1324–28.

The Polos started on their return journey from the East in 1292 sailing down the China coast past Indochina, touching in Sumatra, sailing through the Strait of Malacca, and the Bay of Bengal, past India, and along the coast of Persia. Their route home from there is not specifically known. They reached Venice in 1295 and found a Christian world troubled by the aggressive advance of the Ottoman Turks. Tripoli had fallen in 1289, and Acre, the last stronghold in Western Christian hands, fell in 1291. Venice quickly made a new treaty with the conquerors. Genoa attempted in reprisal to close the Dardanelles to Venetian trade and won a victory in 1294. Venice forcibly opened the Dardanelles and sacked the city of Galata, which was in Genoese hands. During the war that followed Marco, in Venetian service, was captured and placed in a Genoese jail. This proved to be fortunate for Marco's future reputation. He dictated his stories to a fellow prisoner, Rusticello (Rusticiano) of Pisa; otherwise his tales might never have become a part of history. Much of what he wrote has stood the test of time for accuracy; but it seemed fabulous and unreal to his contemporaries, as it does to us today. We are no longer certain what Marco Polo dictated and what was later added by others to the numerous copies of his manuscript done before printing made possible a fairly standardized version. His true story had to compete with fanciful accounts of travels, and thus there is a good probability that the many copyists enhanced his account with stories not in the original.

The Polos were the most famous but not the only European travelers

from the West to the East. The *Pax Tatarica* had made possible relatively
easy travel along the land routes from China across Asia to the Caspian
and the Black seas and into the Baltic or the Mediterranean. Chinese and
other merchants of the East, as well as Arab merchants, shipped their
merchandise through the Strait of Malacca, into India, Persia, Arabia, and
Egypt, as well as to the eastern end of the Mediterranean, where the
Venetians, Genoese, Catalans, French, and others from the western
Mediterranean transshipped it for distribution throughout northern
Europe and to Spain, Portugal, and northwest Africa. The rise of the
Ottomans and the conquest of Acre in 1291 did not disturb this trade as
much as it alarmed the Christians of the West about a Muslim menace.

The Continued Economic Growth of Portugal: the Reign of King Dinis, 1279–1325

Contemporary events prepared Portugal for what was at first to be a small
part in revealing knowledge of the African coast and was eventually to be
the decisive contribution to this development. As noted before, Portugal
was in contact with both northern Europe and Africa, and had been a way
station for northern Europeans en route to the Mediterranean. It had not
yet as a nation shown any signs of expansion along the African coast. Its
maritime interests were primarily those of a commercial-minded class
whose trade with northern Europe continued and was extended in several
ways.

King Dinis (1279–1325) of Portugal vigorously promoted the interest of
the merchant class.[12] Its continued participation in the trade of Europe is
indicated by the agreement the merchants drew up among themselves to
establish a *bolsa*, or fund, for mutual protection and insurance, the first of
its kind for which there is documentary evidence in Europe. The king
approved this agreement in 1293. It provided that all vessels of 100 tons
or more loading in Portugal for Flanders, England, Normandy, Brittany,
and La Rochelle pay a tax of twenty *soldos* sterling and that those with less
tonnage pay ten *soldos*. The same tax was to be paid by Portuguese

[12] Álvaro da Veiga Coimbra, "Ordens militares de cavalaria de Portugal"; Anselmo
Braamcamp Freire, "Maria Brandoa, a do Crisfal" (concerns the Portuguese *feitoria* in
Flanders); Henrique da Gama Barros, *História da administração pública em Portugal*, IX,
35ff.; Rui de Pina, *Crónica d' El-Rey D. Diniz;* João Martins da Silva Marques, *Descob-rimentos portugueses*, I, 21–22, document 29.

merchants going *além-mar* (overseas) to Seville or elsewhere. From these taxes a fund of 100 marks in silver or its equivalent was to be kept in Flanders for the mutual protection of the merchants. This association was instrumental in the formation of the institution known as the *feitoria*, trading post, later to be Portugal's chief overseas commercial institution. The archives of Venice registered in 1293 the first of the annual *galere de Fiandra* which helped to furnish Portugal a link with the Mediterranean. In Bruges where the Portuguese were established there were also German, Spanish, Viscayan, Aragonese, Catalan, Italian, and Sicilian merchants, as well as moneylenders from Lombardy, Florence, and Siena.[13]

Portuguese merchants benefited from the English King Edward I's *Carta Mercatoria* issued in 1303, regulating the trade of foreign merchants in England. They were also trading in products that came across the Sahara, as indicated by the inclusion in 1304 of malagueta (grains of paradise, a spice of West African origin), in the goods going into Bruges from Portugal. The war of Philip IV with Flanders, which interrupted much of the trade of the Champagne Fairs at the beginning of the fourteenth century, facilitated new trade agreements between Portugal and England in 1308 and with France in 1310. Portugal's economic progress was a subconscious preparation for the time when it would play the chief role in the linking of East-West trade.

Growing Western Efforts to Get Behind the Muslims

The years of Portuguese progress were those during which the Polos were on their long journey. The East and West were continually reaching toward each other, frustrated by the land barriers that separated them and the conflicts of the forces that sought to control their routes.[14] The Ilkan of Persia sent his representatives, seeking an alliance with the West, as far as France in 1287, 1289, 1290, and 1307. The Mediterranean Christians, though mainly concerned with rivalries among themselves for trade with the Muslims, were also alarmed at the advancing Muslim power. Efforts

[13] Ernest van Bruyssel, *Histoire du commerce et de la marine en Belgique*; Jules Finot, *Étude historique sur les relations commerciales entre la Flandre e l'Espagne*, and two other works by the same author cited in the bibliography; Gama Barros, *História da administração pública*, IX, 357ff.; Émile Vandenbussche, *Flandre et Portugal*, pp. 193–201.

[14] Joaquim Bensaúde, *As origens do plano das Índias*; Attílio Gandi, "Os caminhos do Sahara."

to stimulate new Crusades were made but only by those who were not in a position to organize the military forces required. For example Raymond Lully (1232–1315), the Catalan philospher, was one such advocate. Another was Marino Sanuto, a Venetian who wrote *Secrets for True Crusaders to Help Them to Recover the Holy Land*. He presented this to the pope in 1307 to stimulate an attack on the Muslims in Egypt and Syria, which would break their hold because Christians would then refuse to trade with them. His ideas are mainly interesting to us because they show a growing knowledge of the geography of Africa and Asia.

The preaching of Lully, Sanuto, and others did not gain even lip service for new Crusades. Turkish advances intensified Genoese-Venetian rivalries rather than uniting them in a concerted Christian effort to repel the Infidel. Other Christians, for example Alfonso III of Aragon and his brother Jaime II of Sicily, made a pact with the sultan of Egypt on April 25, 1290, which gave them trade privileges. The Genoese also signed a treaty with Egypt the same year. However, treaties could not ensure easy trade through Egypt and the Red Sea to India. The efforts of the Christians to cooperate with the Persians, who were both anti-Turk and anti-Mameluke, led to confiscation of Christian goods in Egypt in 1295.

While Genoa maintained its position in the eastern Mediterranean and the Black Sea with difficulty against Venetian and Muslim opposition, it also carried on trade with Muslim cities of northern Africa. The caravan routes, which in several places traversed the Sahara and reached into the fertile areas of western Africa, brought a large amount of trade goods exchanged in North African ports where Christian cities had long maintained contact. In fact, the knowledge of the interior of Africa that reached western Europe, though imprecise, was considerably greater than European knowledge of the African coast. Some began to believe that beyond the Muslims there was a road to Eastern trade and that it could be found.

CHAPTER 2

Prelude to Empire:
Portuguese and European
Expansion to 1415

The Search for a Way around
Africa to the East

The birth of the idea that Europeans could get around Africa to reach the East cannot be traced to any precise date. The first to make the attempt were the Genoese. The difficulties of such a voyage did not necessarily seem insurmountable to the sailors of that time, given their misconception of the shape of Africa and the East as may be seen by looking at the maps available to them. It is not necessary to try to determine whether the men of the thirteenth century knew of the voyages allegedly made around Africa in ancient times. The difficulties the Genoese experienced in their rivalry with the Venetians and Muslims were sufficient to explain why they might look for an alternative trade route. Their efforts to organize a fleet in the Gulf of Persia and the Red Sea to cut off the Mamelukes from the rear were related to their efforts to sail around Africa, though no specific documents prove this to be true. Those who sought to sail around Africa to India had to be ignorant of the Ptolemaic belief that land enclosed the Indian Ocean or willing to challenge such an idea.

In May 1291 the Vivaldi brothers, Ugolino and Vadino, left Genoa "volentes ire in Levante ad partes indiarum" (desiring to go to the East, to the regions of the Indies). That they judged their task to be difficult can be seen in their preparation for a ten-year trip and their agreement to pay their backers half the profits.[1]

The Genoese had traded in the Atlantic as early as the twelfth century and had made a settlement on the west coast of Morocco in 1253. It is not improbable that the Vivaldis could have reached Gozora (approximately Cape Nun) as alleged; but after this nothing is known of them for certain. Did they reach the Canaries? Some historians have wishfully thought so. Whatever happened to them, they opened other eyes to Atlantic expansion. In 1325 Sor Leone went into the Atlantic in search of his father, Ugolino, and found traces of him. As one result of the search for Vivaldi, Lanzarote Marocello discovered, perhaps as early as 1312, the island in the Canaries that bears his name and that he claimed for his city, Genoa. In 1335 twelve Genoese ships from Ceuta, under the command of Marocello, demanded reparations from the sultan of Morocco for damages done to them.

Portuguese and Spanish Interest in Northwest Africa

Early in the fourteenth century Genoese and Venetians en route to England and Flanders put in at Portuguese ports. Merchants of both cities soon began to settle in Portugal.

[1] Luis de Albuquerque, *Introdução à história dos descobrimentos*, pp. 98–102; Beazley, *Dawn of Geography*, III, 410–422 (Beazley accepts mid-fourteenth-century discoveries of Madeira and the Azores on the evidence of the maps, which are not exact enough to merit such faith); Diffie, *Prelude*, pp. 49–60; Vitorino Magalhães Godinho, *A economia dos descobrimentos*, pp. 19–35; B. Bonnet Reverón, "Las expendiciones a las Canarias"; Damião Peres, *História dos descombrimentos portuguêses*, pp. 13–14; Florentino Pérez Embid, *Los descubrimientos en el Atlántico*, pp. 51–60; Guido Pó, in *Congresso do Mundo Português* (*CMP*), III, 579–644; Francis M. Rogers, *The Vivaldi Expedition*; Charles Verlinden, "Les découvertes portugaises et la collaboration italienne," and "Lanzarotto Malocello et la découverte portugaise des Canaries." Efforts have been made by J. Cortesão, Verlinden, and others to link the Portuguese family of Admiral Pessanha with alleged later discoveries in the Canaries, using documents published by Fortunato de Almeida, *História de Portugal*, III, 759–789. The authenticity of the documents has been seriously challenged, and the probability of forgery sometime later than 1385 and perhaps in the nineteenth century is strong. See Albuquerque, *História dos descobrimentos*, pp. 117–126, who concludes: ". . . it is evident that the thesis of Charles Verlinden will have to be considered exaggerated and unfounded unless by chance there should be found more solid proof to justify it." Elías Serra Rafols, "Lançarotto Malocello en Canarias," in proceedings of the *Congresso International de História dos Descobrimentos* (*CIHD*) III, 767–778 (1960), holds that the documents are forgeries, probably dating from the nineteenth century and, consequently, that studies based on them are invalid. He points out that in the fourteenth century, the term used for Canarians, "Guanches," was properly applied only to the inhabitants of Tenerife and was not generalized to all Canarians until the nineteenth century.

King Dinis (1279–1325) continued the deliberate policy of encouraging foreign merchants.[2] One of his acts had lasting importance; in 1317 he summoned the Genoese Manuel Pessanha (Pessagno) to Portugal to be his admiral. The assimilation of the Genoese knowledge of ships and the sea, plus the long experience of the Portuguese in the Atlantic, was important in the process by which the Portuguese became masters of ocean navigation. Pessanha, many of his men, and other Italian merchants, became permanent citizens of Portugal, and their descendants are in Portugal to this day.

Another act, unrelated at the time but later to be a significant part of Portugal's overseas policies, was the creation of the Order of Christ in 1319. Dinis seized an opportunity presented to him by the dissolution of the Knights Templar to persuade the pope to create a special order endowed with the extensive holdings of the Knights. The Order of Christ, unique to Portugal, was charged with defending Christians from Muslims and carrying the war to them in their own territory. Since there was no Muslim territory in Portugal, this could only mean overseas, i.e., in North Africa or possibly Granada. Henry the Navigator was later head of this order. The Christians looked on the "reconquest" of Muslim Africa as their right — at one time under Christian rule, it should be recovered. As early as November 1291 Sancho IV of Castile and Jaime II of Aragon made a treaty that fixed the Muluya River as the boundary of their projected conquests in Morocco.[3] The Christian attack in North Africa was to continue from this date for hundreds of years.

[2] Almeida, *História de Portugal*, I, 246–248 (Order of Christ); Diffie, *Prelude*, pp. 38–56; Vitorino Magalhães Godinho, "Les grandes découvertes," pp. 25ff.; José Benedito de Almeida Pessanha, *Os Almirantes Pessanhas*; Guido Pó, in Federzoni, ed., *Italia–Portogallo*, pp. 261–267.

[3] Pérez Embid, *Descubrimientos*, pp. 39–46. A tempest in a teapot has arisen over the title Henry held as head of the Order of Christ. He signed himself as governador and regidor (governor and administrator). Pope Martin V on the request of King João I, named him administrator on May 25, 1420. See D. Charles-Martial de Witte, "Les bulles pontificales," LIII, 470; António Brásio *A acção missionária no período henriquino*, pp. 60–70; *Monumenta Henricina*, III; Francis M. Rogers, *Travels of Infante Dom Pedro*, pp. 333 n. 5. He was referred to as *mestre* by contemporaries, and until a few years ago it was not challenged when he was called grão-mestre (grandmaster) by historians. The argument now runs that Henry could not have been grandmaster because he was not a priest. Yet his father was grandmaster of the Order of Aviz in 1363 at the age of five or seven, though he was not a priest and he later fathered two illegitimate children before he became king. D. Álvaro de Luna, a contemporary who was a favorite of Juan I of Castile, was maestre of the Order of Santiago in Spain. By the bull *Sincerae Devotionis* of September 9, 1434, Pope Eugenius IV named Fernando, son of João I, mestre of the Order of Aviz.

The bull *Dum Tua*, January 25, 1461, named King Afonso V grandmaster of the Order of

Genoese Activities in West Africa
and the Canary Islands

Meanwhile the Genoese continued their trade on the Atlantic Moroccan coast and, at least for a time, the occupation of Lanzarote in the Canary Islands. The first definitely dated voyage to the Canaries in which there was Portuguese participation was 1341.[4] Giovanni Boccaccio, the Italian humanist scholar, records that a letter dated November 15, 1341, arrived in Florence from two Florentine merchants of Seville. They stated that on July 1 three vessels outfitted by the king of Portugal with crews of Florentines, Genoese, "Castilians and other Spaniards" (*et hispanorum Castrensium et aliorum hispanorum*) sailed from Lisbon with horses, arms, and various war machines to conquer cities and castles.[5] The commanders were apparently Niccoloso da Recco, Genoese, and Angiolino del Teggia dei Corbizzi, Florentine. They reached their destination in five days and after some months on the islands returned to Lisbon in November. They brought back with them "four men of the inhabitants of that island, skins of sheep and goats, tallow, fish oil, seal skins, wood which dyed red almost like brazil (*verzinium*), but which the experts say is not brazil, bark of other trees which also dyes red, red earth, and other similar things."

Christ. He renounced it in favor of his brother Fernando who was named grandmaster by the bull *Repetentes Animo*, July 11, 1461. Neither was a priest.

Antônio Caetano de Sousa, in *Provas de história genealógica da Casa Real Portuguêsa*, I, 61, says Afonso V in 1454 "made a large donation to the Order of Christ because the Infante was *Mestre* of it." Also Sousa (I, 442) says that Eugenius IV in 1445 confirmed grants made to Kings Duarte and Afonso V as well as naming Henry to the grandmastership of the Order of Christ. See Fortunato de Almeida, *História da Igreja*, vol. I, *passim*.

Henry acted in all matters as the sole head of the Order and in his will of October 1460 disposed of all its property and power as he did his other properties, saying: "I order by my Letter that I leave to the Mestres, Regidores, e Governadores da Ordem de Cristo who may come after me, etc." No one else in any known document during the life of Henry after 1420 was called *Mestre*. It may be concluded that anyone who wishes to call Henry grandmaster will not be rebuffed by Henry when he passes by St. Peter at the Pearly Gates and offers congratulations to the "Grandmaster" and "Navigator."

[4] Albuquerque, *História dos descobrimentos*, pp. 98–117; Bonnet Reverón, "Canarias" in *Revista de Indias (RIM)*; Jaime Cortesão, "Primordias da expansão marítima, as expedições às Canárias" in *Descobrimentos portuguêses*, I, 179–191; Federzoni, ed., *Italia–Portogallo*; Vitorino Magalhães Godinho, *Documentos sôbre a expansão portuguêsa*, I, 21–33; Peres, *Descobrimentos portuguêses*, pp. 16–34; Pérez Embid, *Descubrimientos*, pp. 54–58; Sérgio da Silva Pinto, "O problema da época do achamento das Canárias"; Pó, in *CMP*, 759ff., stresses the importance of the Italians; Elías Serra Rafols, "Portugal en las Islas Canarias" in *CMP*, III, 211–238; Charles de la Roncière, *La découverte de l'Afrique au Moyen Age*, II, 4ff.

[5] The quotations that follow are from the so-called Boccaccio account in Italian and Portuguese, *CMP*, III, 632ff. and 638ff.

The islands discovered were about 900 Italian miles from Seville and less from Cape St. Vincent. The letter described "men and women who go nude and are savage in their customs and rites." Some who seemed to be more important were dressed in the skins of goats tinted yellow or red. The people were said to speak different languages in each of the inhabited islands, and none spoke the language of any of the expeditionaries. This seems to indicate that the island had not been recently peopled from adjacent Africa, where the languages spoken should have been known to many who lived in Genoa, Spain, and Portugal. Five of the thirteen islands were inhabited. The mariners were impressed with the fields of wheat and other grains, the fig trees, palms, and the gardens of cabbages and other vegetables.

On one of the islands they found beautiful well-constructed houses of square stones. They were entirely white as if "painted with whitewash." In one house they found a stone statue, which they took to Lisbon. The young male inhabitants who were brought back to Portugal were described as light-complexioned, with waist-length hair. They were captured on the most densely populated island and the only one that was given a definite name, Canaria, where "the natives . . . counted by the decimal system" which was reproduced by Boccaccio up to number sixteen. Boccaccio adds the intriguing statement: "In fact they found other things that the said Niccoloso did not wish to recount." But, he says, "It seems that these islands are not rich for the mariners could scarcely recover the expenses of the voyage." Although members of the expedition were armed, "they did not have the courage to penetrate into the interior."

Boccaccio's narrative establishes definitely that the Canaries were visited in 1341, but it leaves many mysteries. Although it is stated in one place that there were thirteen islands, of which five were inhabited, other descriptions give the impression that there were many more, relatively close together and within view of one another. Some historians have wished to see indications that the Madeira Islands were definitely sighted and that even the Azores were seen. The former is a possibility, but the sighting of the Azores seems highly improbable. Nor is it clear whether this can be considered a voyage of Portuguese initiative. There is no specific reference to indicate that any of the expeditionaries were Portuguese, although the word Hispania, or Spain, did include Portugal at this time and in the following centuries. Why did the report come from

Seville rather than from Lisbon? Did the king of Portugal initiate as well as provision the voyage, or did he merely facilitate its provisioning? It seems entirely logical that this could have been a voyage succeeding known earlier Genoese contacts with the Canaries. But nothing in this, nor in any other narrative, says so. That a voyage was made two years after the island of Lanzarote appeared on the 1339 map of Angelino Dulcert, with the arms of Genoa, indicates prior discovery, which is in accord with other accounts. There is no evidence of subsequent Genoese voyages to the Canaries, which could be explained by the relative economic poverty of the islands, although they were occupied during at least part of the fourteenth century.

Portuguese-Spanish Rivalry in Africa and the Canary Islands

The 1341 expedition is difficult to interpret, but Portuguese references to a specific Portuguese expedition sent by the king in 1341 or before are more bewildering. Three years later, on November 15, 1344, Pope Clement VI, in Avignon, gave to Luis de España (Luis de la Cerda), great-grandson of both Alfonso the Wise of Castile and St. Louis of France, the temporal jurisdiction and the right of patronage over the Fortunate Isles, provided no other Christian prince had a previous title.[6] Luis, who had been made admiral of France, took the oath of vassalage to the papacy and agreed to pay an annual rent of 400 French florins. He was invested at a ceremonious public occasion during which he received the crown and the royal seal of the islands he had been granted. Pope Clement VI immediately sent direct messages to the kings of Aragon, Castile, Portugal, France, and Naples, the prince of Dauphiné, and the commune of Genoa, informing them of the concession and requesting that they give all possible aid. Luis and those who were to accompany him received special privileges similar to the benefits granted those on Crusade and also the right of absolution. Eleven islands were given to Luis of which one, Goleta, was said to be in the Mediterranean and the other ten in the Atlantic. The bull of concession assumed that all were ruled by non-Christians. The islands, named Canaria, Ningaria, Pluviana, Capraria, Iunonia, Embronea, Athlantia, Esperidum, Cernent, Gorgones, and Goleta, are those that appear in the work of Pliny. No mention is made of Lanzarote, the map of Angelino

[6] Pérez Embid, *Descubrimientos*, pp. 73–81, for quotations unless otherwise noted.

Dulcert, or the expedition of 1341, nor is it stated that these islands were "newly discovered," which is noted in other grants of the time, particularly those of the Mallorcans to which we shall shortly refer. Thus it is not absolutely clear that the islands granted were the Canaries, although the one known island named was Canary.

One effect of the bull was to give juridical basis to the Castilian-Portuguese rivalry in the Atlantic, which was not to be settled for more than a century. Both nations gave nominal obedience to the papal grant, but neither gave aid to Luis and both used the occasion to set forth their own claims. The Castilian king made a vigorous defense of his rights based on the Convention of Soria with Aragon in 1291, which divided the zone of influence each was to conquer from the Muslims in Africa. It is highly doubtful that Luis occupied any part of the Canaries, but his claims afforded Portugal the opportunity to assert prior discoveries of the Canaries, as detailed above.

The immediate response by Afonso IV of Portugal on February 12, 1345, to Avignon indicated his strong objection to the grant. He made the following points to Clement VI: "Natives of Portugal" (*nossos naturais*) were the first to find the islands; the islands are closer to Portugal than to the territory of any other prince and could be conquered more easily by Portugal than by any other country; he had sent his own people (*nossas gentes*) and ships to explore the nature of the land in the islands, had seized by force men, animals, and other things, and had brought them to Portugal; at the moment when an armada was prepared to sail to the Canaries[7] with a great number of cavalry and infantry (*cavaleiros e peões*), his intention was frustrated by the wars that broke out, first between Portugal and the king of Castile and later with the "Sarracen king." All of this "being very well known," inasmuch as his ambassadors had recently brought it to the pope's attention, Afonso said he could not give the requested supplies because he lacked the means to do so and because "we cannot spare them because of the war which we are carrying on and propose to carry on against the infidel princes (*agarenos*), our perfidious and dangerous neighbors." Nevertheless as "our people have happily begun this project we should be invited by Your Holiness with preference to any other to bring it to a happy conclusion."

This letter brings still more confusion to the question of the settlement

---

[7] Albuquerque, *História dos descobrimentos*, pp. 109–117; Godinho, *Documentos*, I, 29ff.; Peres, *Descobrimentos portuguêses*, pp. 16–27.

of the Canaries. It is interesting that the name of only one of the islands mentioned, Canaria, appears on authentic maps of the Canaries — the other names are from mythology. However, all who study this papal grant regard the Canaries as the islands donated. Afonso IV made a flat statement that his subjects (*os nossos naturais*) were the first to find the islands. To make such a statement, he must have known where the Canaries (if it is the Canaries that were referred to) lay. Afonso also claimed that he sent an expedition: "We sent there our people and some ships to explore the nature of the land." Thus he seems to claim that his subjects made two voyages to the Canaries, a voyage of discovery, followed by one of reconnaissance. He, however, gave no dates for these voyages nor for the wars fought with Castile and the "Sarracens." (He may have been referring to the war of 1336 against Castile and the war of 1340 against the Muslims, particularly the Battle of Salado in which the Christian princes of Iberia were allied and won a decisive victory.) Although his enumeration of the things that were brought back to Portugal from the Canaries was much less complete than the 1341 account, it was not contradictory. If he was referring to the 1341 expedition, why did he not say so, since this would have given him a definite claim? There is no reason to doubt that the Portuguese of that time had the capability to send such expeditions to the Canaries.

Given the evidence which obviously places the Genoese and the Portuguese in the Canaries in 1341 and before, there remains the mystery of why neither followed up the early explorations. Genoa and Portugal play no known role in Atlantic exploration from this time to the coming of Henry the Navigator.[8]

The Catalans and Mallorcans in Africa and the Canary Islands

The Catalans and the Mallorcans now took up the explorations.[9] The expeditions that slight though sufficient documentation justifies mentioning are those of 1342, 1346, 1352, 1369, and 1386. In 1342 Francesco Desvalers received a commission from the representative of the king of Mallorca to sail two light vessels, *cocas*, to the Canaries. There is no certainty that this voyage was made. Also in 1342 Domingo Gual was

[8] See note 1 above.
[9] Pérez Embid, *Descumbrimientos*, pp. 81–107.

named captain of a single *coca* for a proposed voyage of a semiofficial nature. It is not known whether Gual actually sailed.

Information concerning a voyage that supposedly was made by Jacme Ferrer along the coast of Africa in 1346 is equally vague. The legend on the Catalan map drawn by Abraham Cresque about 1375 states that Ferrer sailed in an *uxer* (or *uixer*) for the Rio de l'Or, August 10, 1346. The map has a picture of a vessel, with one mast and oars, which is being rowed toward the coast of Africa. The Villadestes map of 1413 repeats the same information. Documents of the Mallorca archives that might shed some light on this alleged voyage are missing precisely from 1345 to 1348. It would be significant if a vessel had gone south of the Canaries and returned at such an early date, but the legend and drawing on the maps constitute insufficient proof.

In 1352 Arnau Roger of Mallorca was commissioned to lead an expedition under the auspices of Pedro III of Aragon and Catalonia. Whereas the expeditions of 1342 were private, this expedition had a pronounced missionary flavor. Instructions given the expeditionaries provided for building churches and cities and discovering new islands which were to be under the sovereignty of Aragon. On May 13, 1351 two bulls issued by Pope Clement VI, who had made the grant to Luis de la Cerda, gave spiritual concessions to Juan Doria, Jaime Segarra, and other Mallorcans who were to evangelize the Canaries. The pope named Fray Bernardo, a Carmelite, as bishop. The expeditionaries were to have the collaboration of slaves brought from the Canaries on previous voyages, who had learned to speak Catalan in Mallorca and had been converted to Christianity. A third authorization was issued by Guillén de Llagostera, the lieutenant-governor of Mallorca. Whether this expedition ever sailed is unknown.

The attention of Portugal and Europe in general for the rest of the fourteenth century was concentrated on problems considered more urgent than expeditions into the as yet little-known Atlantic. There had been sufficient travel by the middle of the fourteenth century, however, to stimulate the interest of Europeans in a wider world than they had known before.

Travel Accounts, Real and Imaginary, Stimulate Interest

Several travelers or pseudotravelers in imitation of Marco Polo wrote interesting if not always authentic accounts. First, we may notice one from the Arabic world who is considered by some to have been the greatest traveler of the Middle Ages and by others to have been least in part a charlatan. Ibn Battuta,[10] a prosperous resident of Ceuta, spent from 1325 to 1349 traveling across North Africa, Egypt, the Near East, Arabia, East Africa, and into India. In many of these places he lived for some years. He spent eight years in what is now Delhi, India, going later to Ceylon and then on to China. Returning to his home in 1349 he rested for a time, after which he traveled across the Sahara (1352–54) and visited Timbuktu, Mali, and other regions near the Niger River. He records that there were certain areas of Africa into which neither he nor any other white men were allowed to go. He gives an excellent description of the people and customs and of the caravan routes by which Central Africa was known to traders who touched the Mediterranean and Moroccan Atlantic ports.

A "traveler" of a different kind was an anonymous Franciscan who wrote about 1350, shortly before Ibn Battuta started his African trip. His work, known as *Libro del conoscimiento* (*Book of the Knowledge of All the Kingdoms, Lands and Lordships There Are in the World*), purports to be the account of a trip taken by the author to most of the lands from the Atlantic to the Pacific, including the Arctic, the mythical islands of the Atlantic, deep into Africa, and along both the Atlantic and the east coast of Africa.[11] A large part of the work stems from the works of Solinus, Isidore of Seville, and others who peopled the world with bizarre and imaginary animals and humans. The geography is in the main so inaccurate as to be amusing; but to the fanciful parts copied from previous medieval or ancient authors, the anonymous Spanish Franciscan adds information that had to be from recent journeys into Africa and voyages along the African coast. Together with fruit trees of "Ibernia" which bore "very fat and tasty birds," he describes a voyage along the west coast of Africa down to the land of Negroes which, though probably not taken by himself, shows knowledge of those areas.

The most fanciful and the most popular of these travel accounts was by Sir John Mandeville, possibly a pseudonym for Jean d'Outremer of Liège,

---

[10] Albuquerque, *História dos descobrimentos*, pp. 181–194; Beazley, *Dawn of Geography*, III, 535, 538 and *passim*; Ibn Battuta, *The Travels of Ibn Battuta in Asia and Africa*, ed. and trans. H. A. R. Gibb, pp. 320–357; Newton, *Travel and Travellers*, pp. 88–103, 124–173; Sykes, *Exploration*, pp. 84–96 (Ibn Battuta).

[11] Albuquerque, *História dos descobrimentos*, pp. 166–181; B. Bonnet Reverón, "Las Canarias y el primer libro de geografia medieval," says the work is accurate for West Africa as far as the Canaries.

also dated in the middle of the fourteenth century.[12] In a convincing manner which gave the semblance of authenticity — he often wrote "It is said" when relating some of his improbable stories, and he confessed that he had not seen the Terrestrial Paradise because he was not worthy but said that he had talked to those who had been there — he whetted the appetites of his readers for more knowledge of a world they could not otherwise know. He was sufficiently informed to know the world was a sphere. Frequently copied and translated into many languages (though not into Portuguese until modern times), his work became more popular still with the increased use of the printing press in the late fifteenth century. Whether it influenced Portuguese readers or whether it was even known in Portugal is not certain.

The cartographers of the fourteenth century, influenced by some of the stories, decorated their maps with imaginary islands and legends.[13] The map by Dulcert dated 1339 shows Africa with some accuracy and depicts the "road to the land of the Negroes" and a "Saracen King" beyond the mountains who owned a mine "abounding in gold." The creator of the Catalan map of ca. 1375 knew that the kingdom of Mali and the city of Timbuktu were commercial crossroads for ivory and gold in a region known as the Rio d'Ouro to the south of Cape Bojador. The map also reveals that the author knew of different types of life led by the Arabs and the blacks of Africa. This information could have been drawn from merchants who traded with northern African cities.

Land Barriers between East and West: Mamelukes and Ottomans

The pressures in the Mediterranean and in the Near and Far East that had brought about the original Genoese explorations in the Atlantic must have been increasing and demand attention if we are to understand why in the fifteenth century such extensive efforts were made to find a way around Africa and to the East.

The most influential factors were the power of the Mamelukes of Egypt, the rise of the Ottoman Turks, the decline of the Mongol Empire,

[12] See *Mandeville's Travels*; Josephine Waters Bennet, *Rediscovery of Sir John Mandeville*.
[13] See the maps in R. A. Skelton, *Explorers' Maps*; Peres, *Descobrimentos portugueses*; Albuquerque, *História dos descobrimentos*; and La Roncière, *Découverte de l'Afrique*, 3 vols.

and the fractionalization of power in the area of Mesopotamia and Persia. Most important for Portugal and Spain was the power of Venice, Genoa, Catalonia, and other Christian areas of the Mediterranean.

Beginning as slave soldiers, the Mamelukes had revolted in 1250 and assumed rule in Egypt.[14] In the latter part of the fourteenth century they had extended their rule over the Levant, including Syria, and thus stood astride two of the important trade routes from the Mediterranean to the Indian Ocean. When they occupied Armenia Minor (Cilicia) in 1375, they had even more effective control of the commerce in the Tigris-Euphrates valley. The Ottomans, unable to advance against the then stronger Mamelukes, had taken an easier route across Asia Minor, attacking the Byzantine Empire. Byzantium was still a great trade center, but in treaty after treaty the Genoese and Venetians had been able to extract exemptions from duties, obtain special ports for their own control, or gain monopolies of some given line of imports and exports. Among other Christian cities with privileges were Ragusa, Pisa, Florence, Ancona, Barcelona, Marseilles, Montpellier, and Narbonne. The Genoese collected six times as much revenue at Galata on the Golden Horn as was paid to the Byzantine government.

Greatly weakened by the concessions that it had made to its fellow Christians, the empire was unable to defend itself against the advancing Serbians, Bulgarians, Germans, and Turks. The government at Constantinople often became the victim of the mercenary forces that were employed to protect it. It was with comparative ease that the Ottoman rulers advanced across Asia Minor to the Dardanelles. Not yet strong enough to capture Constantinople, they served as mercenaries in its army. Thus were the Ottomans first introduced into Europe. They soon came on their own, crossing the Hellespont in 1354. In 1365 they captured Adrianople, which became their European capital and military center. The Byzantine Empire now became tributary to the Ottomans. Though they did not capture Constantinople for another century, they were in a position to block or control in large part Christian trade into the Black Sea and hence farther to the East. The Serbians, Bulgarians, and Greeks all fell before them. Ragusa, a Christian city on the Adriatic Sea, made a commercial treaty by which it agreed to pay tribute. Genoa and Venice, though alarmed at the success of the Ottomans, were not sufficiently so to make common cause against them or even to join with

[14] Edward P. Cheyney, *The Dawn of a New Era: 1250–1453*, pp. 298–327.

other Christian forces. They in fact flirted with and sold to both sides. Byzantine appeals to Western Christians brought some efforts to unite against the Ottomans, but an allied army was decisively defeated at Nicopolis in 1396.

Fall of the Mongols, 1368: New Trade Difficulties

In Siberia and in China the Mongol Empire was crumbling.[15] A "Chinese" movement beginning in about 1360 succeeded in driving the Mongol emperors from the throne, the last ending his rule in 1368. Soon after, foreigners were expelled from China, and the native Ming dynasty closed its borders to the outside world. The result for the West was a lessening of trade along the overland trans-Asian routes. The closing of China was a blow to East-West travel, but otherwise the conquests that gave the Mamelukes and the Ottomans control over trade routes from the Mediterranean to the East were not in themselves prejudicial to commerce. Frequent wars interrupted commerce, but it was in the interest of the Mamelukes and the Ottomans to encourage trade; and they did so. However, they also charged tariffs on all goods that passed through their kingdoms, and in times of war they seized such goods, making the Christians subject to the conditions that they set.

As noted before, Western Christians, including the popes, were constantly trying to make contact with the Christians behind the Muslim front who supposedly could serve as allies against the Muslims.[16] This hope was to provide considerable inspiration for expansion around Africa. The appearance of an Ethiopian embassy in Venice in 1402, and again in 1408, shows the efforts of Western Christians to arrive at some understanding that would enable them to attack their mutual enemy from both sides. The mission also helped to foster the myth of Prester John and perhaps to create the false impression in Western Christendom that behind the Muslims lay a great Christian empire whose strength combined with that of the West could crush the Muslims utterly. One observation that can be made here is that the Ethiopians could not have traveled

[15] Heissig, *The Mongols Rediscovered*; Phillips, *The Mongols*.
[16] Roberto S. Lopez, "Medieval European Trade with the Far East"; Francis M. Rogers, *The Quest for Eastern Christians*, pp. 28–49 and *passim*, and "Union between Latin and Eastern Christians"; Vsevolod Slessarev, *Prester John*.

through the Mediterranean without crossing Muslim-held territory. The Muslim world was thus not an impenetrable barrier to the Christians but rather a sieve through which Christians and Christian traders could pass, albeit always under Muslim control.

The Economic and Political Progress of Portugal to 1383

Portugal, the nation that would successfully conclude the long efforts of East and West to circumvent the land barrier separating them, was undergoing national growth that would shortly enable it to do what no other Western or any Eastern people had accomplished except fleetingly in ancient times. Portugal's maritime inclinations during the last half of the fourteenth century were mainly to the north, although constant contact was also maintained with the Mediterranean through the annual fleets of Italian galleys which stopped en route northward.[17] In 1350 and 1353 King John II of France confirmed and extended Portuguese privileges. In the latter year the English and Portuguese signed a treaty, brought about by the initiative of the merchants of Lisbon and Oporto, guaranteeing mutual safety and privileges for a period of fifty years. Those who signed for the Portuguese were merchants and mariners, their signature being recognized by Afonso IV as binding on him.

Before any other nation in Europe, Portugal was acquiring the characteristics necessary for organized overseas efforts. During the reigns of Pedro I (1357–67) and Fernando (1367–83), Portugal showed much evidence of continued economic growth.[18] Pedro confirmed the privileges of the Pessanha family, who maintained their ties with Genoa. Additional Italian merchants came to Portugal where they received privileges modeled on those given to the Bardis of Florence in 1338. Pedro named among those so favored Genoese, Milanese, and Piacenzans, as well as the Cahorsins of France. Trade with the Muslims of Granada and Africa

---

[17] Michel Mollat, *Le commerce maritime normand*; A. H. de Oliveira Marques, *Hansa e Portugal*; Gama Barros, *História da administração pública*, IX, 343–346, 357–383, and X, 171–196, 211.; Diffie, *Prelude*, pp. 59–72; Fernão Lopes, *Crónica de Pedro I*, and *Crónica de D. Fernando*; Renée Doehaerd, *L'expansion économique belge*; R. Francisque-Michel, *Les portugais en France*, and *Histoire du commerce à Bordeaux*; Eduardo Freire de Oliveira, *Elementos história de Lisboa*, vol. I; H. G. Rawlinson, "The Flanders Galleys"; Yves Renouard, "Pour les recherches sur . . . la Mediterranée"; Alwyn A. Ruddock, "Italian Trading Fleets in Medieval England," and *Italian Merchants in Southampton*; Charles Verlinden, "Deux aspects de l'expansion commerciale du Portugal-Harfleur."

[18] Fernão Lopes, *Crónica de D. Fernando* and *Crónica de D. Pedro*.

continued. Privileges were granted to Catalans and Mallorcans in 1362 for "their long residence" and their support of the king. In the same year John II of France again confirmed Portuguese privileges, as did Charles V of France in 1364.

Two significant facts emerge from the first of three wars in which Fernando became embroiled with Spain: Admiral Lanzarote Pessanha was able to secure aid from Genoa, and Portugal could assemble thirty-two galleys and thirty other ships (naus) for an attack on Seville in 1369. Fernando at this time carried on commerce in his own ships, not accepting cargo from others until he had loaded his own produce. The Cortes at Lisbon in 1371 complained that he had requisitioned wheat at five *soles* and sold at five *libras*, thus gaining a ratio of twenty to one. Some 400 to 500 ships loaded in Lisbon annually, which in the famous words of the historian Fernão Lopes was a city of "numerous and various foreigners," among them Lombards, Genoese, Milanese, Catalans, Biscayans, Mallorcans, Aragonese, and "others," who would have included Venetians, Florentines, Piacenzans, Flemings, French, English, and Cahorsins. The Portuguese obviously were a commerce-minded and sea-minded people. The same Cortes of Lisbon complained to the king in 1371 that the clergy and the nobility took advantage of their privileges in commerce to avoid the taxes paid by the merchants. In 1372, in Leiria, the Cortes extended this complaint to include the king and queen, grand masters of the religious orders, bishops, clergymen, knights, and government officials including accountants, scriveners, custom collectors, and magistrates, calling them all "merchants and hucksters" (*mercadores e regatões*).

If the king was the rival of his own merchants in some ways, he was their protector and promoter in many others. An act of 1377 regulated matters of dispute between native and foreign merchants and listed in 100 pages the taxes on foreign and domestic goods. A law of June 6, 1377, provided a subsidy to shipbuilders, allowing residents of Lisbon who built ships of 100 tons upward to cut wood free of tax in the royal forests. They were exempt from taxes on wood, iron, sailcloth, and other imported articles pertinent to shipbuilding. The law contained many other provisions to stimulate shipbuilding and shipping. In December 1380 these privileges were granted to all those who built ships of fifty tons or brought such ships from abroad. Oporto received the same privileges in March 1381. In 1380 the *Companhia das Naus* provided maritime insurance on all the decked ships of fifty tons upward, including the king's ships which then numbered twelve. Each ship paid 2 percent of the value of its cargo into the treasury on each trip and received insurance against losses in war and peace or against unexpected foreign taxes. The prototype of this law was the act approved by King Dinis in 1293. As the Belgian historian Goris remarked: "From the fourteenth century the Portuguese developed the rudiments of modern maritime insurance. Under the auspices of the kings of Portugal, entrepeneurs without a par in economic history, they had solved step by step all phases of this complicated problem. . . . The detailed and well-rounded regulations established by Fernando exercised a capital influence on the formation of maritime law in the Mediterranean."[19] That Fernando prospered in spite of his wars may be judged from the remarks about his revenues by Fernão Lopes, the chronicler: "They were so great that it is now difficult to believe."

A New Dynasty in Portugal: The Aviz, João I

Fernando, a model king in the promotion of his merchants and seamen, handled his foreign affairs much less felicitously. He three times involved himself in wars with Spain. As one result of the third war he had married off his daughter Beatriz to Juan I of Castile.[20] The marriage arrangement provided that if Fernando left no sons Beatriz would become queen; if she should die before her husband, he would inherit the Portuguese throne. Fernando's widow, Leonor Teles, assumed the regency. As a pro-Spanish regent she would have been unpopular in any case. However, she suffered the additional stigma of a scandalous reputation. The prospect of a Castilian monarch inheriting the throne not only offended the moral and nationalistic feelings of the Portuguese, but also, and perhaps most important, it aroused the fears of the merchants that their interest might eventually be subordinate at that of their Spanish rivals. A strong anti-Leonor Teles and anti-Spanish party soon arose. They found a leader in João, the illegitimate son of Pedro I, Grand Master of the Order of Aviz. They were joined by the archbishop of Braga, who claimed ecclesiastical primacy over the archbishop of Toledo, and by some members of the nobility. Most of the nobles chose the arrangement considered "legal," upholding

[19] A. Goris [Jan Albert], *Études sur les colonies à Anvers*, pp. 178–179; Francisque-Michel, *Portugais–français*, pp. 274–277.

[20] Almeida, *História de Portugal*, I, 297–316; António Borges Coelho, *A revolução de 1383*.

the claims of Juan I and Queen Beatriz. João of Aviz murdered the queen's alleged lover João Fernando Andeiro with his own hand and was proclaimed regent and "Defender of the Realm."

War followed with Juan I of Castile who invaded Portugal. João of Aviz, supported by the merchants, by a large number of people, and by an alliance with the English Duke John of Gaunt, who was trying to get the Castilian throne for his Spanish wife, was elected king April 6, 1385. His forces, commanded by the remarkable Nuno Álvares Pereira, constable of Portugal, defeated the Spaniards at Aljubarrota on August 14 in one of the really decisive battles of Portuguese and Spanish history.[21]

A treaty was concluded with England on May 9, 1386, which has become known as the most enduring and continuous treaty ever made. Its economic provisions bound the two nations more closely together than ever before. One clause of the alliance called for the marriage of João to Philippa, daughter of John of Gaunt by his first wife. The wedding was in February 1387. Of Philippa's sons, one succeeded his father as king, one died tragically in civil war after being regent, one became a saint, and one was Henry the Navigator. Another of John of Gaunt's daughters, Catherine, by his second (Spanish) wife, married Enrique III of Castile and was the grandmother of Isabella of Castile whose great-grandson, Philip II of Spain, became king of Portugal in 1580, thus in a sense making John of Gaunt's ambitions come true.

The Portuguese Kings as Trade Promotors

In 1389 the privileges of the English merchants in Portugal were reaffirmed. Portugal's trade with other northern regions continued. The merchandise which the Portuguese were carrying to the northern ports in this period included jewels, pearls, spices (of Eastern and African origin?), wines, olive oil, dates, grapes, oranges, figs, almonds, and perhaps wool.[22]

Portuguese merchants were now growing in riches and power from their trade abroad. War with Castile continued on a de facto basis, although an armistice for three years had been signed in 1387 and was

---

[21] J. P. de Oliveira Martins, *A vida de Nun' Álvares*; Joaquim Mendes dos Remédios, ed., *Crónica do condestabre Nuno Álvarez Pereira*; Fernão Lopes, *Crónica de El-Rei D. João I*.

[22] Jacques Heers, "L'expansion maritime portugaise . . . Mediterranée" and "Portugais et génois au XV° siécle"; Luis Suárez Fernández, "El Atlántico y el Mediterráneo"; Diffiie *Prelude*, pp. 73–82.

subsequently renewed for fifteen years. Frequent raids across the border were the rule, each side blaming the other, as Spanish and Portuguese historians still do.

João, to promote commerce, designated Caminha in northern Portugal as a free port, permitting "all ships whatsoever" to anchor in allocated areas, being taxed only on goods actually sold. The *Companhia das Naus* was renewed in 1397. The overwhelming impression gained from reading the detailed history of the period is that Portugal, though frequently beset with conflict and troubles for its merchants, was a vigorous trading nation.

During this period wheat and other cereals, which had usually been exported by Portugal, were increasingly imported. Among the explanations for this are that cultivation of wine grapes took the place of wheat or that the frequent raids from Spain destroyed the wheat crops. In 1399 and at other times João forced his merchants to include cereals in their return cargoes from England, Flanders, and Brittany in preference to lighter products of great unit value.

The king himself was still a participant, as former Portuguese kings had been, in foreign trade. João's own ships sailed to such regions as Norway, Flanders, and Genoa in the year 1405. A price list issued in 1410 for both Lisbon and Oporto shows a great variety of merchandise from all parts of Europe. Portuguese ships were known in the Balearic Islands and in other Mediterranean ports during the early fifteenth century, sometimes their cargoes were wheat brought from northern countries. These ships as well as those of the Genoese and Venetians were a connecting link between the northern seas and the Mediterranean. The *feitoria* in Bruges remained there to protect trade. So large was the number of Portuguese in Flanders and Flemings in Portugal that the Portuguese had their own cemetery in Bruges in 1410, as did the Flemings in Lisbon before 1414.

There is no unquestionable evidence to indicate, however, that during the last half of the fourteenth century Portugal was venturing to unknown seas.[23] Her growing wealth and the increasing importance of the activities of her merchant class, both native and foreign, were confined almost exclusively to trade in the products for which Portugal had a market in northern Europe, Christian Spain, Granada, and North Africa. But this experience, it may be repeated, was preparing Portugal for an expansion overseas that was to come in the fifteenth century.

[23] See note 1 above and Diffie, *Prelude*, p. 106, n. 4.

Rivalry in the Canary Islands:
Catalans and Castilians

Atlantic exploration in the latter part of the fourteenth century was not pursued with system or vigor by any group or nation. The most active voyagers in this area were the Mallorcans and the Catalans and to some extent the popes, who were trying to promote missionary efforts.[24] There was also some enslavement of the Canary Islanders, by whom and exactly on what occasions is not known. To the expeditions mentioned before should be added one authorized by the papal bull *Ad Hoc Semper* of Pope Urban V, in Viterbo, September 30, 1369. Urban V directed the bishops of Barcelona and Tortosa to send ten secular and twenty regular clergy, who could preach in native languages to the Canarians. There is no further notice of this project, but the presumption that thirty missionaries could be found who spoke the language of the islanders surely indicates a long-established relationship.

In 1386 still another expedition, the fifth known of the Catalan-Mallorcan expeditions, was carried out by the "Pauperes Heremite," recommended to Pope Urban VI by Pedro IV of Aragon. This indicates that the papacy was still interested in the evangelization of the Canaries. The fate of the missionaries is not known unless we connect them, not implausibly, with the thirteen "fraires Chrestiens" who were killed in 1391 after having preached the Catholic fath to the Canary Islanders for some seven years.[25]

The Castilians entered the contest in this area in 1393 with a voyage to the Canaries recorded in the chronicle of Enrique III of Castile. This expedition landed in Lanzarote and captured the king and queen and some 160 people, of whom an unspecified number were shipped to Spain

[24] Bonnet Reverón, "Las expediciones a las Canarias" in *RIM*, numbers 18–21 (1944–1945), and in book form, Madrid, 1946. See also a series of articles in *Revista de Historia*, La Laguna, beginning 1941; Pérez Embid, *Descubrimientos*, pp. 81–104.

[25] It should be noted that the historiography of these islands includes accounts of many expeditions which either were confused with those described above or are now considered apocryphal. Those considered apocryphal by Bonnet Reverón, the most recent authoritative writer on the subject, are: 1360, by Mallorcans; about 1377, by Martín Ruiz de Avendaño, Biscayan; about 1380–1382, by a ship allegedly wrecked in Niguiniguada — there were thirteen survivors; 1386, expedition by Fernando de Ormel, confused with the expedition planned by Ferdinand d'Ulm (Olmo), 1486; 1372, by Fernando de Castro, said to be confused with the expedition of the Portuguese Fernando de Castro, 1424–1425; 1385 by Hernán Peraza, a Sevillian who had obtained a permit from Enrique III, King of Castile; 1399, Gonzalo Peraza Martel, confused with his actual voyages of 1393. See Pérez Embid, *Descubrimientos*, pp. 95–96.

along with products which brought "a great deal of profit to those who went there." On returning they informed the king of Castile that these islands would be very "easy to conquer . . . and at small cost." The leader of the expedition was Gonzalo Pérez Martel who three years before, in 1390, had obtained from Castile permission to carry out an occupation of the islands. The result of this was somewhat more than temporary as indicated by the fact that Hernán Peraza, second son of Pérez Martel by his marriage to Doña Ines de las Casas, came to be considered lord of the Canaries.

There is no evidence to confirm other Andalusian or Castilian expeditions before 1402. Nevertheless, it seems clear that some were made. When Bettencourt was made "king of the Canaries" in 1402, it was provided that "nobody shall dare to sail to those islands without express orders or license of Bettencourt." An indication that the island of Fuerteventura was occupied from 1393 to 1402 is found in a statement in the *Canarien* that a crew of fifteen in a *chalupa* (sloop) had captured slaves around Cape Bojador and then returned to Grand Canary to rejoin their ship.[26]

Further evidence for the early presence of Europeans in the Canary Islands is the fact that when Bettencourt later conquered part of the islands he had with him Canarian natives with Castilian names. We need not be confused by the double purpose revealed in these stories, that is, Christianization on the one hand and enslavement on the other, when we reflect on the experience that was to follow European relations with the peoples of Africa and America. In the eyes of the Castilian king, he had now established a claim to the Canary Islands.

A Spanish Foothold in the Canary Islands: Bettencourt, 1402–18

It is amply clear that to 1402 no nation or city had placed sufficient emphasis on the Canary Islands or the Atlantic to make permanent settlement there. Earlier exploratory efforts by the Genoese, Mallorcans, Catalans, and Portuguese had resulted in a considerable knowledge of

---

[26] On the Bettencourt expedition see Pierre Margry, *La conquête et les conquérants des îles Canaries*. Margry should be used rather than *The Canarian or Book of the Conquest and Conversion of the Canarians, 1402*, published by the Hakluyt Society in 1872, which was based on an incomplete version.

North Africa, the Canaries, and possibly the Madeira Islands. Definitive settlement was to wait until the fifteenth century when the Spaniards began serious settlement in the Canaries and the Portuguese began their career as the world's most persistent explorers.

In 1393 when news of the expedition of that year to the Canaries reached the Castilian king, Enrique III, the French ambassador, Roberto de Braquement, representing Charles VI, solicited and received from Enrique a concession to conquer the Canaries. His primary interest was to find an opportunity for his nephew Jean de Bettencourt to better his situation in life. Bettencourt was then chamberlain to the Duke of Turenne, brother of Charles VI. He associated with himself in the enterprise Gadifer de la Salle, who became the true organizer of the expedition, furnishing the ship and most of the soldiers.

Leaving La Rochelle May 1, 1402, they sailed to the island of Lanzarote. Here a number of the expeditionaries revolted and abandoned the expedition, some going to Spain, others into Africa. Bettencourt left the island in October to solicit aid, and during the next year and a half appealed to the pope and to others, finally obtaining help from Enrique III, who granted him the title of king of the Canaries as feudatory of the Castilian crown. Bettencourt was again in the Canaries in 1404, quarreled with Gadifer, and returned to France. In 1405 Bettencourt brought more immigrants from France, among them his nephew Maciot de Bettencourt. His attempt to conquer Grand Canary and Palma failed. In December 1405, having conquered two of the islands, he returned to France, leaving Maciot as his lieutenant. He was never to see the Canaries again. Bettencourt held his claim to the Canaries until 1418 when, with the license of the king of Castile, he sold them to the Count of Niebla.

Renewed Portuguese Interest in Northwest Africa: Ceuta

Meantime the Portuguese had begun their overseas career with the capture of Ceuta, preliminary to Atlantic explorations which were to make them the most effective explorers in the fifteenth century.[27] While the Castilian monarchs were still embroiled in internal quarrels with their

[27] Diffie, *Prelude*, pp. 83–90.

own nobles, the English and French in the Hundred Years War, and the Italian cities in trade rivalries along the old routes, the Portuguese monarchy, now firmly established, was able to give its attention to the Atlantic coastline of Africa as well as to customary trade.

Portuguese interest in Africa was not new. From 1248 when Fernando III of Castile captured Seville, and in 1249 when the last Muslim power was driven from Portuguese territories, Christians and Muslims faced each other across the short distance separating Africa from Iberia. Granada was to remain Muslim for two and a half centuries more. Christians, including Spaniards and Portuguese, traded in Granada and African ports. The Christians looked forward to the time when there would no longer be Muslim power in the Iberian Peninsula and to the future extension of their territories into Africa. Castile and Aragon, as noted above, had defined their respective spheres of African conquests in 1291. The Aragonese were alloted the territory east and the Castilians the territory west of the Muluya River to the Atlantic. The Portuguese at this time set forth no African claims, although their sailors traded with and fought against their opposite Muslim numbers. Nor did Castile attempt so far as is known to enforce the treaty of 1291. Aside from the trade with the Muslims of Morocco and the frequent conflicts at sea, Portugal showed no inclination to enter the territory staked out by Castile and Aragon.

When peace with Castile finally came in 1411, the released energy, though still directed mainly in the traditional trade channels, was free to seek other outlets. It was at this time that João's eyes turned southward, where he began planning the most significant event of his reign, if not the most significant in Portuguese history, an attack on some point in Muslim Northwest Africa.

CHAPTER 3

Ceuta – the Beginning of Empire

Preparation for the Attack on Ceuta

Preparation for the attack on Ceuta was in progress by 1412.[1] When did João I decide on the African invasion, and what were his motives? The first question, though of relatively minor importance, has been hotly debated. Certainly João might have thought of African invasion as early as 1409 or even long before that. His predecessors might have had such thoughts; they would have been natural to kings whose merchants were constantly involved in the Moroccan trade and in unending conflict with the Muslims.

[1] Some historians object to the use of the word *empire* to describe Portuguese overseas territories. One school of thought does so on the grounds that Portugal never had "colonies" but only "overseas provinces." Another objection is based on the statement that in the East, Portugal held port cities and trade but only minor areas of territory. The author shares neither of these views. Portugal fought for and held territory in Northwest Africa, forts and trading posts along the coast of Africa, islands offshore, a large segment of Angola after 1574, and the "empire" of Brazil, later to be an independent empire in the nineteenth century. These facts would seem to justify the title of *empire* for Portugal.

Almeida, *História de Portugal*, II, 23–26; Pedro Augusto de Azevedo, ed., *Documentos relativos à Marrocos*; Charles R. Boxer, *Four Centuries of Portuguese Expansion*; J. Cortesão, *Descombrimentos portuguêses*, I, 249–256; Godinho, *Documentos*, III, 7–11; *HEP*, I, 131–142; Visconde de Lagôa, "Estímulo econômico da conquista de Ceuta," in *CMP*, III, 57–76; Fernão Lopes, *Crónica de D. João I*; António Sérgio, "A conquista de Ceuta". The examination of the reasons for the triumph of João I, his accession to the throne, and later his capture of Ceuta has produced the usual attempts to explain events in terms of "rise of the bourgeoisie," the conflict of "merchants versus nobles," etc. There are also those who see Ceuta as a "crusade," an extension of Christianity to Muslim Africa. Still others stress Portugal's strategy of cutting across the path of Castile in Africa. All these and other motives as well might have moved João I. And if we could look into the minds of the expeditionaries, no doubt we could multiply many times over the reasons for the conquest of Ceuta.

46

There is evidence that the king's own ships, acting as corsairs, had participated in the piracy that customarily took place between Muslim and Christian sailors or even between Christians. As early as 1338, when the king granted privileges to the Bardi of Florence, he referred to his "corsairs" as casually as he did to his "marinheiros" (mariners). The collection of ransom for captives was a good business which gave ample reason for the operations of corsairs at sea. An ordinance of 1388 regulated the division of prisoners captured on land or at sea among the king, the admiral, and the mariners of the royal fleet. The captives belonged to the captor "except a prisoner of great worth of 20 *dobras* up; and if the king takes him himself, he must pay a thousand pounds."[2] The ransom of prisoners between Muslims and Christians was sufficiently well organized even in the twelfth and thirteenth centuries to require definite officials for negotiations. A special type of "broker of prisoners" (*alfaqueque*) arranged such exchanges. Designated Portuguese, particularly Franciscans, were allowed into North Africa to negotiate with their Muslim counterparts; and a special Franciscan convent was established in Portugal for this work.

Legitimate commerce between Africa and Europe had long been established, as already mentioned. West Africa normally supplied cereals, certain kinds of textiles, leather, sugar, and gold to European merchants in exchange for copper, arms, wood, lacquer, and other products. The Italians, Aragonese, and Catalans active in this trade were present not only in Ceuta and Tangier but also in Salé, Safi, and other African cities on the northwest African coast. It may be pointed out that the Portuguese as well as the Spaniards issued strict laws limiting trade with Muslims and prohibiting the sale of arms and food; the church constantly manifested its hostility toward trade with the Infidel, although without marked success.

When João was preparing his armada for the Ceuta expedition, the news spread throughout Europe, causing much uneasiness.[3] The reason for gathering such a large fleet was unknown. The king of Granada, particularly alarmed, sent an embassy to inquire about its purpose. The ambassador, according to Azurara, complained to João that the Granadian merchants were afraid to carry on their usual commerce with Portugal. "Never was there such discord between your people and mine," he said,

---

[2] Quoted in Albuquerque, *História dos descobrimentos*, p. 47.
[3] A considerable number of foreigners came to Portugal to serve, among them some Belgians. See Ernest van Bruyssel, *Histoire du commerce*, II, 64.

"that they ceased to trade . . . your merchandise for ours and ours for yours."[4] Trade with Granada, aside from its economic value, was a part of Portuguese rivalry with Castile. But what the king approved of and promoted for one Muslim territory was equally applicable to another, i.e., North Africa. Muslims resided in Portugal and carried on trade, as indicated in a license granted in 1383 for Muslim residents to go "overseas to the Muslim lands" without putting up a bond. Azurara notes in his *Crónica de Dom Pedro de Menezes* that fruits from Algarve were frequently bought by Moroccans. "Almost in all times of the previous kings" he says, "the Muslims beyond the seas (*além-mar*) traded their merchandise in these kingdoms, buying usually every year the fruits of Algarve, which they paid for only in gold; and most of the *dobras* were made in Tunis."[5] Moroccan coins circulated widely in Portugal. Fernão Lopes, the fifteenth-century Portuguese chronicler, also mentioned this trade in describing the *Companhia das Naus* in 1380.

In 1414 João I, as a war measure preparatory to attack on Ceuta, prohibited his subjects from carrying to the lands of the Moors in either Portuguese or foreign vessels, bread, hazelnuts, fruits, or other foods, as well as steel, iron, or arms on penalty of death and confiscation of their vessels. At that moment North Africa, normally an exporter of breadstuff, was short of cereals. That the Portuguese were informed about this temporary shortage indicates the extent of knowledge gained through trade.[6]

Perennial Trade and War Between Portugal and the Muslims

If it is not difficult to verify a long-established relationship of trade and

[4] Azurara (Gomes Eanes de Zurara), *Crónica da tomada de Ceuta*, p. 106; Mateu de Pisano, *Livro da guerra de Ceuta* (based on Azurara). Gomes Eanes de Zurara (1404[?]–1474), called Zurara or Azurara, wrote four chronicles that are the most extensive and sometimes the only source of information on Portuguese expansion in the first half of the fifteenth century. He was a *comendador* of the Order of Christ and is considered to be biased toward Henry the Navigator and against Pedro, thus making his accounts somewhat suspect. His accounts concern Ceuta and North Africa (the conquest of Ceuta and the governorships of Pedro and Duarte de Meneses) and explorations (*Crónica da Guiné*, which deals with the voyages along the coast of Africa to about 1448). Some references in this chronicle were retouched at a later date. It was discovered in Paris by the Visconde de Santarém and published in 1841. The 1937 edition of José de Braganza is used here. Azurara was made chronicler by Afonso V, July 6, 1454, and served until April 2, 1474, shortly before his death. See Joaquim Veríssimo Serrão, *Historiografia portuguêsa*, pp. 49–59.

[5] Azurara, *Crónica do Conde D. Pedro de Menezes*, quoted in Albuquerque, *História dos descobrimentos*, p. 92.

[6] Godinho, *Documentos*, III, 10–11.

hostilities between Portugal and Northwest Africa, it is much less easy to judge why the Portuguese decided precisely in 1415 to occupy firmly an African port.[7] The possession of a good port located on the Strait of Gibraltar would, of course, greatly increase the defensive strength of the Portuguese against the Muslims and, it was thought, give better access to the trade coming across the Sahara from the interior of Africa. On the other hand, there is no evidence that Portuguese trade with Africa was about to be cut short by Muslim action.[8] Many of the reasons given for João I's decision to move at that time may have been contributing, though not necessarily decisive, factors. We can readily believe, as Azurara says, that João's three energetic sons, Duarte, Pedro, and Henry, wanted to win their spurs of knighthood on the battlefield. João might have, as Azurara also states, invited French knights and planned to hold tournaments where his sons could show their valor. But he was too serious and too able a man to organize a large overseas expedition for this reason alone. If one thinks in modern terms, much more weight might be given to the need to employ a soldiery just released from the Spanish war by the treaty of 1411. João did, in fact, propose to Castile a joint war on Granada, which would have interposed Portugal in what Castile considered its own affairs. Castile rejected the proposal. Granada had long been marked out by Castile as an area for its own future conquest.

João turned his eyes to Africa. Political and strategic reasons offered firm ground for João's decision. In the accord of 1291 made between Castile and Aragon for the division of Africa, there was no provision to leave any part for the Portuguese. It is possible that the 1393 Andalusian voyage to the Canaries, as well as the attack by Castile in 1400 in which Tetuán was captured and sacked, aroused João's fears that Portugal could be cut off from its existing African connections and possible future conquests there. If Portugal could get a firm foothold in North Africa before Castile had attached itself firmly in the Canaries, future conquests in Muslim territories would be Portuguese rather than Castilian or Aragonese.

[7] On the motives for Portuguese expansion and the varied interpretations by modern scholars see: "The Western Rim of Christendom" in Boxer, *Four Centuries*, pp. 1–5; "Factors in the Outburst of Fifteenth Century Expansion," in Godinho, *Economia dos descobrimentos*, pp. 69–81; "Portuguese Feeling and Thought, and Economic Policy," *ibid.*, pp. 83–107; "The Direction of Expansion," *ibid.*, pp. 129–150; "Religion and Discoveries," *HEP*, II, 23–38: "The Imperatives of Expansion," *HEP*, I, 338–352; "Causes of Expansion," in Peres, *Descobrimentos portugueses*, pp. 39–41.
[8] A. de Veiga Simões, *Flandre-Portugal*, pp. 30–31.

Divided Counsel: Renew War with
Spain or Attack in Africa?

The Portuguese leaders were not of a mind on policy. One party wanted an African adventure, and the other favored renewed war on Spain. Azurara, the best source of information on this period, presents picturesquely the two opinions concerning policies, that of the older men versus the younger.

All the elders and those who had good judgement . . . said Portugal is the most excellent and happy kingdom in the whole world, for we have all the good things that a prosperous kingdom should have. We have a great abundance of breadstuff . . . many varieties of wines . . . not only for our own nation but in abundance to export and our fish are so abundant that in no other part of the world are they found in such great sufficiency. . . . A great part of Spain is supplied. Oil and honey are so ample and so good that our neighbors have need of us and we not of them. We have meats of all kinds and of excellent flavor. There are fruits and vegetables and an abundance of other things. What else can we really desire more than peace? . . . Now that we have peace with Castile we need not fear any other power in the world, for on one side the sea surrounds us, and on the other side we have Castile for shield. . . . Now our merchants can go securely throughout Spain to sell their merchandise, from which they can bring us many beautiful things. . . . The farmers who had abandoned the border regions because of the war could return to their homes. People could sleep peacefully in their beds . . . and go on pilgrimages (romarias) to visit the relics of the saints in Spain.[9]

The older men, many of them merchants, saw the economic advantages of peace. But opposition to peace with Spain was offered by the young nobles (fidalgos mancebos) and others of their age, among whom were those who had nothing except the hope of gain from feats of arms. Since the king of Castile was young and weak, they argued, "we have great opportunity to invade that kingdom by the robbery of which we can enrich our land." The young men must learn the arts of war or they would lose the best years of their lives. They might also go outside their kingdom to fight where their gallantry would benefit others in foreign wars. Only through fighting could their ambitions be fulfilled. The desire for peace, the young said, could be laid at the door of the king and all those who fought in the earlier wars who were now "tired and bored."[10] If Azurara

[9] Azurara, Crónica de Ceuta, chap. 6, cited in Godinho, Documentos, I, 35–41.
[10] Ibid.

accurately quotes the opinions of the young men, it is they who were to win the attention of the king. He faced the problem of seeing his young men go abroad to fight for other countries or perhaps using their arms within their own country if he did not provide them an outlet for their ambitions.

This picture of a merchant class which preferred the profits to be gained from peace does not accord with the interpretation that the expansion overseas was for the benefit and at the urging of the merchants and shipowners. Azurara ascribes to João Afonso, royal treasurer, who may be considered representative of the merchant class, the role of chief protagonist for overseas venture. He quotes João Afonso as saying to the princes:

I can show you something that will permit you to carry out your intentions . . . to capture Ceuta . . . a very notable city ready to be taken; and this I know principally from one of my employees that I sent there. . . . He related to me what a large city it is, rich and beautiful. . . . And taking into account the great desire of your father, and yours, I do not know at present anything in which you could more honorably prove your valor than in the capture of that city.

But because the king "had laughed at his proposal to take Ceuta," João Afonso incited the princes to plead with their father. They did, "all four of them," but the king also "began to laugh at them showing that he held their words in jest." [11]

The king's laughter was intended perhaps to disguise for the moment his intentions. Or maybe he was feigning reluctance as a device to sharpen the desires of those who expressed his own ideas. The preparations to attack were then, or soon thereafter, under way. From this version of the reason for the Ceuta attack, there emerges distinctly the view that João Afonso of the merchant class was in agreement with the princes and the fighting nobility. Azurara refers to the "very great honor owed to João Afonso . . . because it was he who promoted such a holy and honorable thing." [12]

The Capture of Ceuta, 1415

No clear picture emerges of who the chief promoters of the conquest of Ceuta were, nor is it obvious when a first decision was made for the

[11] Azurara, *Crónica de Ceuta*, chap. 9, cited in Godinho, *Documentos*, I, 41–43.
[12] Azurara, *Crónica de Ceuta*, chap. 74, cited in Godinho, *Documentos*, I, 44.

venture. At the time of the battle the king referred to "the almost six years that I have worked at this task making all the preparations of which you know."[13] Some have concluded from this statement that the preparation for the expedition had begun as early as 1409 and that the king himself was largely responsible for it. If the date 1409 is taken literally, it would seem unlikely that any of the princes had much to do with such early planning, since his oldest son, Duarte, was only eighteen and Henry was only fifteen.

The tremendous decision that an attack on Ceuta involved was obviously long debated by the king and his advisors. Azurara in his picturesque and redundant speech portrays the king as outlining the difficulties involved. After long soul-searching about whether it would be in the "service of God" and deciding that it was, he took up the question of whether it was within his power to carry out such an attack. "For there are many things that are good and desirable in the will of men who yet lack the power to carry them to a successful conclusion. . . . I was filled with very great doubts" he said; basic among the reasons for them was "money which I do not have, and which at the present moment do not know where or how I could get." The people, he argued further, would resist taxes, the secret of the mission would become known, and soldiers and arms would be needed "from abroad." Ceuta was so distant that a great fleet would be necessary "which I do not have in my realm. . . . The Castilian frontier would have to be garrisoned. . . . Ceuta is very large and strong." Even if God gave the Portuguese victory, it might do more harm than good for it would leave Granada easier for Castile to conquer and would strengthen Castile more than Portugal. "For me and my people" he said, "the Castilians have a very great hate [particularly when the memory of their defeat was so recent] and they would take the opportunity to get their revenge for former injuries."[14]

The loss might outweight the gain. It had to be considered whether once captured the city could be held. The Muslims would be inspired to greater defense and desire for revenge, "and they would come upon those of our kingdom of Algarve who would be unguarded . . . and rob them of their goods and their lives . . . and we would lose all hope that from now on our merchandise could without great fear be transported to any port of the Mediterranean." The Muslims would have their ports full of

[13] Azurara, *Crónica de Ceuta*, chap. 12, cited in Godinho, *Documentos*, I, 44–53.
[14] *Ibid.*

ships designed especially to attack. The great glory of the conquest would be in holding the city; but the king said, "I do not see any way whatever in which we could for long maintain or govern it. . . . It would be better to forget the whole thing if [Portugal] did not intend to carry through."[15]

Ceuta was described as inhabited by "for the most part . . . merchants, officials, and mariners." The palaces were in fact fortified walls and towers outside the city. Between the palaces and the city there were "large gardens and orchards with many trees."[16] Ceuta was the "flower of all other cities of Africa" with people who came from "Ethiopia, Alexandria, Syria, Barbary, Assyria (which is the kingdom of the Turks), as well as those from the Orient who lived on the other side of the Euphrates River, and from the Indies . . . and from many other lands that are beyond the axis and that lie before our eyes."[17] Certainly said Azurara, "it cannot be denied that the city of Ceuta is the key of the whole Mediterranean Sea."[18]

The reasons for conquering and holding Ceuta as seen by Azurara in his four chronicles were: securing the Iberian Peninsula from invasion from Africa; protecting the Algarve coast from raids; providing security for the Italian galleys en route to Flanders and England and for Portuguese commerce to the Mediterranean; establishing a Portuguese base in the Mediterranean which Christian corsairs could use in attacks on Muslim commerce and which would serve for the eventual conquest of Morocco; preventing Castilian penetration into Morocco; and providing a center for the domination of the commercial routes of the Sahara.[19] The well-thought-out geopolitical concepts held by João I and his advisors are clearly demonstrated in Azurara's explanation of the reasons for capturing Ceuta.

The preparations for the attack on Ceuta were almost complete when Queen Philippa died July 18, 1415. The court paused momentarily for grief and mourning, and then continued with the enterprise. The fleet, which has been estimated at more than 200 vessels and with as many as

[15] *Ibid.*, pp. 45–51.

[16] Azurara, *Conde d. Pedro Menezes*, bk. 1, chap. 15, cited in Godinho, *Documentos*, I, 53.

[17] Azurara, *Crónica de Ceuta*, chap. 94, cited in Godinho, *Documentos*, I, 54–56; see also, Godinho, *História econômica e social da expansão, passim*.

[18] Azurara, *Crónica de Guiné*, chap. 5 in Godinho, *Documentos*, I, 56–57.

[19] Those are the points picked by Godinho, *Documentos*, I, 56–57, from Azurara's chronicles. Godinho emphasizes the economic, political and strategic aspects rather than chivalry and crusading.

50,000 men, sailed from Restelo on the Tagus on July 25 and reached Lagos on July 27. After more preparations and after a difficult voyage in which some of the ships were driven past Ceuta into the Mediterranean, the fleet anchored before Ceuta on August 20. The attack was made August 21. At the end of one day of fighting the Muslims abandoned the city. Sacked, it rendered the victors a great quantity of merchandise of many types, as well as gold, silver, and rare jewels. The principal mosque was converted into a Christian church, and there the three sons of João I, Duarte, Pedro, and Henry, were knighted on August 25.[20]

To Hold or Evacuate Ceuta?

After the capture the question arose whether Ceuta should be held or abandoned — at least so Azurara presents the story. The king "held a general council to choose what could be best done for the service of God and for his honor with that city." After "much reasoning," the council was divided. One side advocated abandoning the city because it would cost more to retain than it was worth. The other side advised that to leave the city and return to Portugal after sacking it and "killing the few old Muslims that you killed here" would be viewed as "merely robbery," the actions not of a king but rather of "some powerful corsair." It would be reckoned of little service to God, especially since the Muslims would return and restore Ceuta in a short time and could then easily return every year to visit Algarve and do there what they had done many times before, motivated now by the desire to obtain revenge. The arguments for keeping the city were much the same as those for taking it, and there was the added inducement that the common people "you now send to Castile as exiles (degredados)" could be employed in Ceuta in honor of the king and in the service of God.[21] These arguments, it would seem, did no more than strengthen the reasons for what the king must have already decided to do.

[20] Almeida, História de Portugal, II, 23–25; Edgar Prestage, The Portuguese Pioneers, p. 24, erroneously gives the date of August 15 for the capture. Some like to stress, following Azurara, the chivalric motive for the Ceuta attack — the sons of João I wanted to "win their spurs" on the field of battle, not merely in a tourney held for the purpose. The above description of the doubts, the debate, and the long and extensive preparation of the Armada indicates that João I did not undertake such a dangerous enterprise merely to cater to the vanity — natural in young men, but vanity nevertheless — of his sons.

[21] Azurara, Crónica d. Pedro Menezes, bk. I, chap. IV, in Godinho, Documentos, I, 57–67.

The decision was made to hold Ceuta, and João Pedro de Menezes, Count of Viana, was named governor. He was left with some 2700 men as a garrison, a few ships, food, and ammunition.[22] The fleet sailed for Portugal September 2. On royal request, Ceuta was created a diocese September 6, 1420, in accordance with a bull of Pope Martin V, *Romanus Pontifex*, April 4, 1418.[23]

The retention of Ceuta was as difficult as had been foreseen by the opponents of occupation. The garrison was subjected to constant harassment and was forced to make frequent forays into the surrounding countryside to obtain food and supplies. The Christians were spared an immediate counterattack in force because of divisiveness among the Muslims. But by 1418 they had gathered their armies, and that year and the next they seriously besieged the city, forcing João I to send Prince Henry back to Ceuta with a relief expedition. Though unable to retake the city, the Muslims effectively deprived the Christians of the advantages that holding it was supposed to bring.

The principal center of Muslim trade moved from Ceuta to other cities, and consequently the trade routes across the Sahara were not brought under Portuguese control. To profit from the occupation of Ceuta, the Christians would have had to find a way to expand their power in North Africa or to seek still other means of getting behind the Muslims. The retention of the city was a continual drain on a royal treasure already overburdened. The costs of taking and holding Ceuta would appear in the budget for many years to come, giving force to the reasoning of those who still thought that abandonment was the wisest policy. No effective effort could be made to expand Portuguese power inland. The first reason for seeking an alternative policy to African conquest may be found precisely in the Portuguese disappointment at failing to reap the great benefits anticipated in the occupation of Ceuta.

A Dual Policy: Hold Ceuta and Advance along the African Coast

Portugal adopted the dual policy of holding Ceuta while advancing and trading along the Atlantic African coast. Many elements of the Portuguese

[22] Almeida, *História de Portugal*, II, 23–25.
[23] *Ibid.*, III, 78–79, and Charles M. de Witte, "Les bulles pontificales et l'expansion portugaise au XVe siècle."

population favored this policy: the merchants who wanted to carry on trade; the corsairs, including many of high social status, who wanted to prey on Muslim commerce; the venturesome who wanted to find out what was along the African coast; the young fighting men who wanted activity; the zealous who demanded that the Infidel be attacked in his own land; and royal policy which sought the expansion of the kingdom. Even so there was always opposition to expansionist policy and to further attacks on the Muslims inland. Frequently it is difficult for the historian to determine who was promoting expansion and who was opposing it.

Whether or not Henry alone should be given credit for motivating Portuguese expansion, a view that has become traditional, he was the one who most consistently favored the dual policy of attacking the Muslims by land as well as of advancing along the coast to get behind them.

CHAPTER 4

Portuguese Expansion in Africa and the Atlantic, 1415–37

The Madeiras and Canaries, 1418–25: Portuguese-Spanish Rivalry

The first decisive step in the occupation of the newly discovered lands was the colonization of the Madeira Islands sometime between 1418 and 1425.[1] None of the islands had previously been inhabited, though some do appear on fourteenth-century maps in the approximately correct position and relative size.[2] The Castilians allegedly used them as temporary

[1] The principal documents on the expansion of Portugal along the coast and in the islands are found in Godinho, *Documentos*; João Martins da Silva Marques, *Descobrimentos portuguêses*, 1 vol. and supplement; Alberto Iria, *Descobrimentos*, 2 vols; and Dinis, *Monumenta henricina*, 12 vols. to date. See also Albuquerque, *História dos descobrimentos*, pp. 201–206; Almeida, *História de Portugal*, II, 26–32, III, 451–455; Marquês de Jacome Corrêa, *História da descoberta das ilhas*, pp. 44–71 and *passim*; António J. Dias Dinis, *Estudos henriquinos*, vol. I; António Álvaro Dória, "O problema do descobrimento da Madeira." Diogo Gomes, who was an old man when he told his account of discoveries to Martin Behaim sometime after 1484, places the colonization in the 1420s. See *Boletim da Sociedade de Geografia*, Lisboa, series 17, no. 5, 1900; "The Problem of the Origin of Expansion in Portuguese Historiography," in Godinho, *Economia dos descobrimentos*, pp. 37–50, 165–176; and Godinho, *Documentos*, I, 69–115, 171–192. Valentim Fernándes says Zarco was guided to the Madeira Islands by a Castilian who had been there with Castilian ships en route to the Canaries. For the grant of Madeira to João Gonçalves Zarco by João I, see Godinho, *Documentos*, I, 177–179; and by Duarte to Henry on September 26, 1433, see *ibid.*, 180–181. J. Cortesão, *Descobrimentos portuguêses*, I, 197–400, maintains that Henry envisioned the plan for the discovery of the East from the outset. Peres, *Descobrimentos portuguêses*, pp. 27–32, 57–71, and Charles Verlinden, "Formes féodales et domaniales de la colonisation portugaise," have good discussions.

[2] For the legends of earlier discoveries, of Madeira, see Peres, *Descobrimentos portuguêses*, pp. 57–62; Azurara, *Crónica da Guiné*, chap. 83; Jean Fontvieille, "A lenda de Machim."

stopovers after the occupation of the Canaries in 1402. According to Azurara's account, João Gonçalves Zarco and Tristão Vaz Teixeira, two young men in Henry's service authorized to sail as corsairs, were blown by storms to Porto Santo, one of the Madeira Islands. After remaining there for some days they returned to Portugal and reported to Henry. Later they returned with Bartolomeu Perestrelo, who became captain of Porto Santo. Perestrelo's daughter would much later marry Christopher Columbus. Madeira was divided between Zarco and Teixeira. Two things concerning the settlement need to be noted. The original initiative of settlement came not from Henry but from two of his young retainers, and there is no evidence that Henry had any rights over the islands before a grant was made to him by his brother King Duarte in 1433.

At the time the Portuguese were settling in the Madeira Islands, they began showing an interest in the Canaries. Jean de Bettencourt, through his nephew Maciot as his lieutenant, had remained in possession of his rights until November 1418 when, with the permission of Juan II of Castile, he sold Lanzarote and Fuerteventura, and perhaps Hierro as well, to the Count of Niebla. Juan II granted to Alfonso de las Casas, commonly referred to as Alfonso de las Casas de Canarias, on August 29, 1420, rights of conquest of the Canary Islands not held by other Christians. Las Casas willed the Canaries to his male heirs on November 15, 1421. The concession to Las Casas created a double lordship, the Castilian Count of Niebla showing his authority on June 8, 1422, as lord of the Canaries (señor de las Canarias) by granting freedom from taxes (franqueza de pecho) to the Spaniards on the islands that belonged to him. The Portuguese, taking the view that any island not occupied by Christians was open to conquest, sent a strong expedition under the command of Fernando de Castro against Grand Canary in 1424 or 1425. Azurara says Grand Canary had about 5000 fighting men and that some of the inhabitants "called themselves Christians." The Portuguese expedition consisted of about 2500 men and 120 horses. The resistance being too great, Castro abandoned the island and returned to Portugal. The Castilians protested to Portugal immediately and repeated their protest in 1435.[3] The Fer-

[3] Almeida, *História de Portugal*, II, 50–53, 90–92; Azurara *Crónica da Guiné*, chap. 79; Peres, *Descobrimentos portuguêses*, pp. 55–57; Pérez Embid, *Descumbrimientos*, pp. 111–136. Diogo Gomes gives an account of two Portuguese expeditions to the Canaries in 1415, an expedition to the island of Lanzarote, which he erroneously says was uninhabited, and the expedition of Fernando de Castro, which he says was commanded by João de Castro, Fernando's brother.

nando de Castro armada was the first of many efforts by the Portuguese to get possession of the islands.

The Castilians and the Portuguese were now clearly launched on conflicting courses. Castilian claims to the part of Morocco lying toward the Atlantic from the Muluya River westward were based on the assertion that as successors of the Visigoths they held rights to all of Roman Mauritania-Tingitana. Castile and Aragon, as indicated previously, had divided rights or projected conquests by the Convention of Soria in 1291. During the fourteenth century, Portugal put forth no claims to this part of Africa. In a treaty of 1373 between Castile and Portugal, nothing was said of rights to future African conquest. The next year, when an alliance was signed between Castile and Portugal against Pedro II of Aragon, no territorial provisions were included. The treaty in 1411 which ended the long Portuguese-Castilian war also lacked clauses affecting North African territories. Thus Portugal neither accepted nor challenged the Convention of Soria, nor did Castile abandon its claims. When Portugal captured Ceuta in 1415, Castile made no protest. But Castile did, as noted, protest the effort made by Portugal to capture Grand Canary, inasmuch as it had assumed rights of ownership over all the islands, though some had not yet been conquered or occupied.

At about the time of the attack on the Canaries, the Portuguese were beginning to probe the northwest African coast.[4] Fray Gonçalo Velho, a member of the household of Henry the Navigator and a *commendador* of the Order of Christ who had won his knighthood at the capture of Ceuta, had allegedly sailed to a Terra Alta, somewhere short of Cape Bojador, in 1426. Many other Portuguese ships, according to Azurara, were exploring the same area. In fact, it is plausible that the coast as far as Cape Nun and farther south to Cape Juby, about opposite Grand Canary, was known both to the Portuguese and to the Spaniards who sailed it en route to the

---

[4] Diogo Gomes gives the date as 1416. Godinho, *Documentos*, I, 69ff., and n. 2 on p. 106, shows the date had to be 1426 and the Terra Alta had to lie short of Bojador. On the Portuguese explorations along the coast and the situation they found see Eric Axelson "Prince Henry the Navigator and the Discovery of the Sea Route to India," for an excellent summary of explorations; J. Cortesão, *Descobrimentos portuguêses*, I, 282–288; Abel Fontoura da Costa, "Descobrimentos portuguêses no Atlântico e na costa ocidental africana do Bojador ao Cabo de Catarina," *CMP*, III, 245–283; *HEP*, I, 305–310; and Alberto Iria, *Porque foi o Algarve*. On Moorish and other navigation before the Portuguese see Raymond Mauny, "Navigations sur les côtes sahariennes," and "Le débloquage d'un continent par les voies maritimes," and J. C. Anene "Concurrence du désert et de l'océan: l'exemple du Soudan central et du nord de l'Afrique," in Jacques Heers et al., "Resumé du Rapport," XII, *ICHS*, III:159–167 (Vienna, 1965); Peres, *Descobrimentos* portuguêses, pp. 93–152.

Canaries.[5] The scant information available does not reveal what expeditions sailed from Portugal in the years between the capture of Ceuta in 1415 and the passage of Cape Bojador in 1434. The dispute with Spain over the Canaries and the Moroccan policy occupied the attention of Portugal before the exploration of the African coast got seriously under way. This will be discussed later when another of the mysteries, who discovered the Azores Islands and when, has been probed.

Exploring the Atlantic:
the Azores Islands, 1427–32

Determining the date of the first discovery of the Azores involves not merely the authenticity of information but also the question of the ability of mariners in the fifteenth century to sail the high seas hundreds of miles from land.[6] The customary routes of sailing, at least up to this period, were along the coast, and ships cast anchor at night where the waters were not well known. Whereas the Canary Islands lie close to the continent and could have been discovered easily, — in fact they could hardly have been missed by navigators sailing that far south — the Madeiras are almost 400 statute miles from the mainland. To reach them required not merely sailing far from sight of land but involved the more difficult task of determining a return course. The Castilians did this, according to Valentim Fernandes (the German printer who settled in Lisbon in about 1493 and who gathered much information about exploration and commerce in his time and before), making stops in Madeira or Porto Santo en route

[5] Raymond Mauny et al., "Le probléme des sources de l'histoire de l'Afrique noire jusqu'a la colonisation européene," in XII, *ICHS*, III:177–232 (Vienna, 1965); Roland Oliver and J. D. Fage, *A Short History of Africa*; John J. Saunders, ed., *The Muslin World on the Eve of Europe's Expansion*.

[6] Albuquerque, *História dos descobrimentos*, pp. 206–220; Almeida, *História de Portugal*, II, 70–74; Mario Cardozo, "A tradição náutica"; Corrêa, *Descobertas das ilhas*; Cortesão, *Descobrimentos*, I, 256–269 (including a discussion of "secrecy"); Abel Fontoura da Costa, *A marinharia dos descobrimentos*; Carlos Viegas Gago Coutinho, "A técnica náutica e a história dos descobrimentos," in *A náutica dos descobrimentos*, I, 99–116; "Cabo Bojador, a volta do mar de Baga ou de Sargaço," *ibid.*, I, 234–270; "Descobrimento e achamento," *ibid.*, II, 355–356; Henrique Querino da Fonseca, *A caravela portuguêsa*; Gaspar Frutuoso, *Livro primeiro das saudades da terra*. See new edition in progress of full manuscript, Ponta Delgada, 1963–; Godinho, *Documentos*, I, 104–106, 207–221; Duarte Leite, *Descobrimentos portuguêses*, I, 277–281; J. Custódio de Morais, *O conhecimento dos ventos*; Samuel Eliot Morison, *Portuguese Voyages*, pp. 11–15; *HEP* I, 291–304; António Ferreira de Serpa, *O descobrimento dos Açores*; Luciano Pereira da Silva, "A arte de navegar dos portuguêses," *HCPB*, I, chap. II; Aires de Sá, *Frei Gonçalo Velho*.

home from the Canaries. Winds in the area from Portugal to Madeira are generally from the north and northwest; from Madeira to the Canaries they are generally from the north and northeast, facilitating sailing to those islands. They are seasonally variable, however, the rain-bearing winds coming usually from the southwest in the winter and thus at this season facilitating return from the islands.

To explain the early discovery of the Azores requires that we accept the idea that mariners of the time could navigate a minimum of 745 miles from the Portuguese coast and return. The first Portuguese discovery of the Azores occurred in 1427, according to cartographic evidence. The strong westerlies and northwesterlies rendered difficult a direct westward voyage from Portugal, but of course the return to Portugal was easier. At times the winds shifted and blew from the east, making it possible to sail to the Azores.

A map drawn by Valsequa, dated 1439, shows the right number of Azores islands discovered to that date (Corvo and Flores were not discovered until 1452), aligned for the first time in the right direction, from southeast to northwest. A much-disputed legend on this map has been read: "These islands were found by Diego de Silves pilot of the king of Portugal in the year MCCCCXXVII."[7] The Valsequa map is perhaps not a definitive answer to the puzzle of Azorean discovery. Maps are altered or amended with relative ease, and legends may be place on them after their original date. Detection of alterations made at a date relatively early in the life of the map may be difficult or impossible. The style of handwriting would not have changed substantially, and a difference in the ink or the age of the ink would scarcely be detectable after several centuries. Thus though the Valsequa map and its legend seem authentic, other dates have been suggested for the discovery of the Azores.

Martin Behaim, who lived for some years in Portuguese lands following 1484 and who married a daughter of Jos de Hurtere, donatary in the islands of Fayal and Pico, placed on the globe he issued in 1492 a legend that describes a discovery voyage in 1431 made by two ships and a coloniz-

---

[7]*Aquestes illes foran trobades P. Diogo de Sunis* (Silves) *pelot del rey de Portogall an lay MCCCCXXVII.* Although the rendition of Silves for the much disputed word is arbitrary, it is a logical name for an Algarvian pilot. The date 1427 as it appears on this map is now generally accepted, though for a time it was disputed. The reader may wish to make his own interpretation. (See illustration.) "Sines" can easily be read "Silves." The top letters in this legend have never been satisfactorily explained, and Peres makes no attempt to do so, *Descobrimentos portugueses*, pp. 78–92.

ing expedition in 1432 of sixteen ships. The legend does not indicate who the commanders were.

In the "Memorias" of Diogo Gomes which were dictated to Martin Behaim, two voyages are attributed to Henry's initiative, but no dates are given. The commander of the first expedition is not named, though it is said he sailed 300 leagues to the west of Cape Finisterre and discovered five islands, namely Santa Maria, São Miguel, Terceira, Fayal, and Pico. The commander of the second voyage was said to be Fray Gonçalo Velho, whose objective was to transfer domestic animals to the islands. The grant by which Duarte gave the Madeiras to Henry, September 26, 1433, does not mention the Azores. No official document gives the dates or the circumstances of discovery. We are left to choose between 1427 or 1431 for discovery and to accept 1432 as the possible beginning of settlement. On July 2, 1439, Pedro, Henry's brother, as regent for the infant King Afonso V, granted to Henry the right to colonize seven islands of the Azores to which Henry had already sent ships.[8]

The Policy Debate Continues:
Attack in Africa or Granada?

In 1433 a burning question for João I was what policy should be adopted vis-à-vis the Muslims in Granada and Morocco. The occupation of Ceuta to this date had brought limited results — principally raids on the area around Ceuta to obtain food and other supplies, and corsair activities against Muslim shipping (and Castilian and other shipping as well). Prince Pedro had written to his brother Prince Duarte from Bruges sometime between 1425 and 1428 concerning Ceuta, expressing his opinion that it had been a "sinkhole" of men, arms, and money.[9] Both Pedro and Duarte may have at this point favored the abandonment of Ceuta. By 1433 the issue became pressing.

João I called a council which met in Santarém. In April 1433 the Count of Arraiolos expressed himself to Crown Prince Duarte on the question whether Portugal should attack Morocco or "whether Henry . . . should accept a friendly alliance" with the king of Castile to

[8] Godinho, *Documentos*, I, 180–181, 208–209; Peres, *Descobrimentos portugueses*, pp. 73–92; the discovery of the two westernmost Azores, Flores and Corvo, is attributed to Diogo de Teive and his son João de Teive in about 1452. The Bianco map of 1448 does not show these islands, and no reliable documents indicate an earlier discovery.

[9] Godinho, *Documentos*, II, 55–57.

conquer Granada. The conquest of Granada would, he said, "save many souls" and, furthermore, since "Prince Henry . . . had first proposed the enterprise," it should be carried out. The results could be nothing but good for Portugal in view of the civil war in progress in Spain — the marriage of Duarte's daughter to a Castilian prince would be advantageous. Also, "Henry would have the kingdom of [Castile] in hand, as well as the Canaries which you want." This is a clear example of how the expansion of Portugal was often linked with the political rivalries in the Iberian Peninsula. The count was opposed to the alternative policy of an attack on Morocco from which there could only result "great evils and no good."[10]

The Count of Barcelos expressed himself concerning "the Armada which Prince Henry had asked the king to prepare," advising the king that to take ships, merchants, farmers from the field, and workmen from their jobs might be "to lose the goodwill of the people." He concluded it was "not in the service of God nor the world" to attack Morocco; but, as for Granada, he said, "I feel quite the contrary," for "it could be enduring and God's service."[11]

The Count of Ourém favored help to Castile and the conquest of Granada without seeking any gains of Portugal. He wanted the king of Spain and "all the world to know that you make this war . . . only for the service of God." But he opposed any war whatever because "for this kingdom there is no profit in any war on the Muslims." Ourém admired Henry as being of "great heart" (grande coração) but nevertheless said plainly he was willing to go only if Duarte himself, not Henry, led the expedition.[12]

The situation was thus: for the conquest of Granada, Duarte and the Counts of Barcelos, Arraiolos, and Ourém; for the conquest of Morocco, João I; for the conquest of both Granada and Morocco, Prince Henry. The deathbed desire of João was to continue the war against the Muslims, as we know on the evidence of Azurara, King Duarte, the Venetian merchant-explorer Cadamosto, and Rui de Pina, the chronicler.[13] Pedro saw neither service to God nor profit to the realm in a foreign venture at this time.

[10]Ibid., 58–68.
[11]Ibid., 68–74.
[12]Ibid., 74–78.
[13]Ibid., 56–68, 126–137; E. Simões de Paula, "O Infante D. Henrique e Tanger."

One point stands out very clearly — Henry was the strongest proponent of an expansionist policy for Portugal.

Portuguese Efforts to Capture
the Canaries

The death of João I on August 14, 1433, precisely forty-eight years after the overwhelming victory against the Spanish armies in the Battle of Aljubarrota, brought important changes. Nothing came of the proposals to aid Castile in the conquest of Granada, albeit there was considerable self interest involved, and the proposed attack on some point in Africa was postponed for another four years. The attention of Duarte, the new king, and of his brother Henry, the chief supporters of an expansionist policy at this time, was now turned toward further explorations along the coast and Portugal's claims to the Canaries.

Circumstances offered Portugal another opportunity to put forward a claim to the Canaries.[14] On March 25, 1430, the Count of Niebla sold his rights to Guillén de las Casas, son of Alfonso de las Casas, thus ending the double title that had existed since 1418. Guillén invaded the islands and carried Maciot to Hierro as prisoner. Henry the Navigator now entered the picture, though with what right it is not clear. He ordered Maciot liberated and sent to Portugal, where he gained from him what Maciot seemingly did not own, the cession of the island of Lanzarote. Once again there was double lordship — Henry (Maciot) in Lanzarote and Guillén de las Casas in the other islands. The double ownership would be eliminated later. Juan II confirmed to Guillén in 1433 the rights previously given to Alfonso in 1420, as well as the charge to continue the conquest.

Castile continued nevertheless to assume sovereign power over all the Canary Islands. At about this time, after the death of João I though a specific date cannot be cited, Prince Henry directed a request to Juan II of Castile for rights to conquer the Canaries. From a diplomatic viewpoint this was a mistake, inasmuch as Castile was later to use this petition as a justification for its own claims against Portugal. When Castile refused to grant him the islands, Henry appealed to the pope who, seemingly unaware of the claims made by Castile, granted Henry's request.[15]

[14] Pérez Embid, *Descubrimientos*, pp. 104, 127–150.

[15] António Brásio, "As relações da Cúria Romana com Etiópia." See also on papal policy: Louis Jadin, "L'Afrique et Rome"; Levy Maria Jordão, *Bullarium patronatus portugaliae*;

Castile protested this bull vigorously. On royal instructions, Alfonso of Cartagena, bishop of Burgos, thoroughly reviewed the Castilian claim and obtained from the pope a brief, *Dudum Cum Ad Nos*, dated in Bologna July 31, 1436 and addressed to King Duarte of Portugal, requesting him to obey a communication of 1434 in which it was specified that at the time the concession of the islands had been made, Duarte had said that no Christian prince held sovereignty over them. This was reinforced by the bull *Romani Pontificis*, November 6, 1436. These documents of 1434 and 1436 are the first in which the papacy intervened in the Spanish-Portuguese rivalry, although the pope had previously supported the Portuguese struggle against the Muslims. Six weeks after the death of his father, Henry obtained from Duarte extensive rights. How much initiative Henry took and how much authority he exerted before the death of his father, João I, is brought into question by a charter (*carta de mercê*) issued by João which states; "I give in perpetuity to the new settlers of Madeira the lands which João Gonçalves Zarco by my command went to distribute."[16] Thus it was João, not Henry, who granted the Madeira Islands to João Gonçalves Zarco; and Zarco was, it may be noted, the grandson of João Afonso, who played such an important part in organizing the attack on Ceuta. There is no official document (only accounts by Azurara and other chroniclers) indicating that Henry had sole authority in the Madeira Islands and exclusive rights for other explorations along the coast before the grant he received from his brother Duarte in 1433.

Essentially in this grant Duarte gave Henry "the islands of Madeira, Porto Santo, and Deserta with all of the rights and income from them which we by right have, and should have, with the civil and criminal jurisdiction except in cases of death sentence or dismemberment."[17] Henry received a donation of title by this letter, not a confirmation, without any indication that he had held a previous title to the land. The grant was seignorial in nature and was the forerunner of similar grants that would be made in lands yet to be discovered and conquered. On the same day, September 26, 1433, the Order of Christ of which Henry was ad-

Francisco Mateos, "Bulas portuguesas e españolas"; Pérez Embid, *Descubrimientos*, pp. 127–143; R. F. Wright, "The High Seas and the Church in the Middle Ages"; Charles M. de Witte, "Les bulles pontificales"; Pérez Embid speaks of the *bula* of *Dudum Cum Ad Nos* and dates it July 31, 1436. De Witte says it was a *breve* and that it could not have been dated before November 6, 1436.

[16] Godinho, *Documentos*, I, 177–181.

[17] *Ibid.* and Amaro D. Guerreiro, *Panorama econômico dos descobrimentos henriquinos*.

ministrator and governor (*regedor e governador*) was granted "all the spiritual functions of our islands of Madeira, Porto Santo, and of the islands of Deserta which the prince newly (*novamente*) settles (*povoa*) by our authority in the same manner as in Tomar" (seat of the Order of Christ), reserving for the crown a number of specific rights and "asking the Holy Father" to "confirm to the Order of Christ" the said islands.[18]

Chinese Expansion: Westward Expeditions, 1405–33

On the eve of Portuguese expansion the centuries-long attempt to connect West and East became momentarily a race, though neither of the chief participants, Portugal and China, knew of the other's efforts. Earlier it was stated that the Ming dynasty ruling in China after 1368 had withdrawn largely into its own boundaries in a long period of self-imposed self-sufficiency. Briefly from 1405 to 1433 the Chinese appear as great navigators. Seven expeditions or embassies were sent out.[19] They cannot be called exploring expeditions inasmuch as the seas from the East African shore to China were known to the numerous traders of those days, including the Muslim merchants, who were the most important traders in the Indian Ocean and whose commerce reached to the East Indies. There has been no adequate explanation for the sudden onset of Ming activity or for its abrupt cessation. The chief objectives appear to have been to impose Chinese prestige and to exact obedience and tribute. The commander of the fleets was Cheng Ho, a eunuch castrated at the age of ten for imperial service. The emperor during the time of the first expeditions was Ch'eng-Tsu (1403–24).

The first expedition, 1405–6, described as being composed of sixty-two vessels with 28,000 men, sailed as far as Calicut. This fleet and those that sailed later were commanded to clean the sea of pirates to make legitimate trade possible. At a later time the Ming navy was said to consist of 250 "treasure ships" of great sailing range and fire power, each capable of carrying a crew of 500 and a large quantity of merchandise. The envoys who went with the fleets negotiated trade under Chinese conditions,

[18] Godinho, *Documentos*, I, 182, observes that *novamente* here refers to *settlement* not to discovery "for the first time."
[19] Kuei-Sheng Chang, "A Re-examination of the Earliest Chinese Map of Africa"; "Africa and the Indian Ocean in Chinese Maps of the Fourteenth and Fifteenth Centuries"; and "The Ming Maritime Enterprise." Also for text see Donald F. Lach and Carol Flaumenhaft, *Asia on the Eve*, pp. 115–120.

required foreign kings to accept vassalage, and invited ambassadors to return with them to China. Some rulers were taken to China as prisoners. In 1407 the Chinese established an institute of the languages of "western barbarians," which may have been Arabic and Persian. Of the six expeditions that followed, the second sailed to Siam, Cochin, and Calicut in 1407–9; the third reached the same areas plus Ceylon, where the king was taken captive to China in 1409–11; the fourth went as far as Ormuz and areas in the Indian Ocean in 1413–15; the fifth, in 1417, visited the "western regions" including Ormuz, taking back "lions, leopards with golden spots, and large western horses." In Aden they embarked a giraffe, and in Mogadishu on the coast of Africa they found camels and ostriches. This fleet also visited Calicut. The sixth, in 1421, went again to Ormuz to which they returned "the ambassadors from Ormuz and other countries, who had been in attendance at the capital for a long time back, to their own countries." All these countries were required to pay tribute to China. The seventh and last fleet, in 1431, went once more to the "barbarian countries" to read to them "an imperial edict." Cheng Ho died in Calicut.

Thus were the Chinese at a threshold which might have led them around Africa to the Atlantic, if their primary motive had been discovery of new lands. Whether their failure to persist was owing to lack of interest or interal problems (the eunuch advisers of the Ming emperors were superseded by the Mandarins who were hostile to overseas maritime adventures that were not profitable), there were no Chinese efforts after 1433. The Portuguese during these years took on the responsibilities of exploration.

Portuguese Exploration of the African Coast: the Passage of Cape Bojador, 1434

The Portuguese were actively seeking to push beyond Cape Bojador, long regarded as the utmost limit of sailing along the West African coast. Azurara, in his characteristically picturesque and prolix style, explains "why ships dared not go beyond Cape Bojador."

[Henry] sent many times, not only ordinary men but those whose . . . great deeds of war made them first in the profession of arms, yet . . . not one dared to pass Cape Bojador to learn about the land beyond it. . . . Not from cowardice or lack of good will, but from the newness . . . the old sayings about this . . . fostered by the sailors . . . from generation to generation. . . . There was great doubt about who would be the first to risk his life. . . . Among so many of . . . great and lofty deeds . . . there was not one to date . . . [for], said the mariners, clearly beyond this cape there is no race of men or inhabited lands nor . . . [is] the land less sandy than . . . Lybia. . . . [There are] no water, no trees, no green vegetation. . . . [There are] shallow seas . . . currents [of water] so terrible that no ship, once having passed the cape, will ever be able to return. . . . For during twelve years the Prince sent . . . out his ships . . . finding nobody who dared. . . . Yet . . . as a reward for their failure, some made attacks on . . . Granada and other [places] where they took great booty from the Infidels.[20]

The first to overcome the fears and real difficulties was Gil Eanes of Lagos, a squire of Henry's household.

And finally after twelve years, the Prince [sent] Gil Eanes. . . . But affected by the self-same terror, he went only as far as the Canary Islands . . . took some captives and returned in 1433. . . . The next year the Prince . . . earnestly ordered him to strain every nerve. . . . "You cannot find" said the Prince, "a danger so great that the hope of reward will not be greater. . . . Go on your voyage . . . with the grace of God. . . . you cannot fail to gain . . . honor and profit." [Eanes] doubled the cape scorning all danger. And although the deed was in itself small . . . because of its daring it was considered great. . . . So the accomplishment brought greater honor to Eanes."[21]

On his return, Eanes was sent out again in his *barca* accompanied by Afonso Gonçalves Baldaia in a *barinel*; both ships had sails but were small enough for rowing also.

The final passage of Cape Bojador removed a psychological barrier that had become greater with each failure. The effort had taken twelve years and fifteen voyages.[22] Once the barrier was down, going beyond Cape Bojador became easier, but only for psychological, not physical, reasons. The physical obstacle to sailing past Bojador was real for the ships of that day — as noted by Duarte Pacheco Pereira, the navigator pilot and cos-

---

[20] Azurara, *Crónica da Guiné*, chap. 8. The types of vessels used in these early voyages were the *barca* and the *barinel*. The *barca* was a small boat of perhaps twenty-five tons, only partly decked if decked at all. Its crew numbered about fifteen men, and it was propelled by oars and one or two sails. The *barinel* was slightly bigger and heavier to row, and had a larger crew. The caravel, which became the vessel of exploration, was still larger and had a triangular (lateen) sail. It had the capability of sailing within five points of the wind and not merely with the wind astern.

[21] *Ibid.*, chap. 9.

[22] Peres, *Descobrimentos portuguêses*, p. 95; W. G. L. Randles, "La signification cosmographique du passage du Cap Bojador."

mographer of the fifteenth-sixteenth centuries, three-quarters of a century after hundreds of sailing vessels had made the passage. "The Prince began this discovery for the service of God from Cape Nun and beyond" says Duarte Pacheco, adding that Cape Bojador was about 200 miles beyond Cape Nun. "A wise pilot will . . . pass Bojador eight leagues out at sea. . . . Because Cape Bojador is most dangerous, as a reef of rock juts out in the sea more than four or five leagues, several ships have already been lost. This cape is very low and covered with sand; . . . in ten fathoms you cannot see the land because it is so low."[23]

Eanes and Baldaia had reported that they had found "lands without houses but with signs of men and camels," now identified as Garnet Bay (*Angra dos Ruivos*), 24°51′ N. Henry was encouraged. "It seems," he said, "that the town is not far from there." On a third voyage, in 1436, Henry instructed Baldaia to "make the farthest advance you can . . . capturing some of these people . . . to give me some knowledge of the land."[24] Baldaia sailed, according to Azurara's estimates, usually exaggerated, 120 leagues beyond Cape Bojador to what is today Piedra de Galea, 22°3′ N. Baldaia landed the next day and attempted without success to capture some of the natives. He had already killed a large number of sea lions (*lobos marinhos*) for their skins, and with these he returned to Portugal in 1436. On this voyage Baldaia discovered what the Portuguese called Rio d'Ouro, a bay rather than a river, lying much to the north of the real "goldbearing river" identified later with the upper Senegal and Niger regions.[25]

[23] Duarte Pacheco Pereira, *Esmeraldo de situ orbis*, bk. I, chap. 22. The early records speak of Cape Nun as the starting point of Henry's explorations, as does Henry himself. Cape Bojador is always referred to as the barrier to be passed. Present-day Bojador is some 200 miles southwest of Nun. Some modern historians and navigators have adopted the belief that Cape Juby, as shown on modern maps, has more of the characteristics ascribed to fifteenth-century Bojador than does the Cape now called Bojador, and that therefore Juby must have been the Cape causing the difficulties until 1434. On maps of today Juby is 200 miles north of Bojador, lying slightly north of the Canary Islands, whereas Bojador is a bit to the south of the Canaries. This modern identification of Juby as Bojador brings up a problem. By 1434 sailing as far as the Canaries, i.e., beyond present-day Cape Juby, was common. Both Portuguese and Spaniards frequently went to the Canaries and were already contesting possession of these. If Juby of this century was Bojador of the fifteenth, it had been passed often. But if modern Bojador was fifteenth-century Bojador, the difficulties of passing it were chiefly physchological. See Peres, *Descobrimentos portuguêses*, appendix p. 581; Antônio Joaquim Dias Dinis, "Qual o cabo dobrado em 1434 por Gil Eanes?" Damião Peres holds that "O cabo dobrado por Gil Eanes em 1434 foi o Bojador."

[24] Azurara, *Crónica da Guiné*, chaps. 9–10; Peres, *Descobrimentos portuguêses*, pp. 95–96.

[25] Duarte Leite, in *Descobrimentos*, I, 285–322, estimates an exaggeration of distances in Azurara of some 20 to 50 percent.

If we accept Azurara's statement that the passage of Bojador had been a preoccupation of Henry's since 1422, and that he had made fifteen efforts before he was successful, we have to puzzle over the lack of information about those efforts. The only voyage before 1433 about which there is specific information is Fray Gonçalo Velho's, mentioned above in the discussion of the Azores, which Diogo Gomes, the only and very uncertain source of information, placed in 1416 but which modern historians agree must have been no earlier than 1426 and perhaps as late as 1429.[26]

Sailing along the Moroccan coast as far south as Cape Nun should have been profitable for the voyages made before 1433, judging from the possibilities of commerce and trade with Granada, Castile, Portugal, and the Mediterranean. An analysis of the trading opportunities as drawn from contemporary fifteenth- and sixteenth-century accounts by, for example, Azurara, Duarte Pacheco Pereira, Valentim Fernandes, Damião de Góis, and Leo Africanus, as well as many documents of the time, shows a wide variety of resources. Among the many products of the coast of Morocco and the inland valleys around such towns as Ceuta, Tangier, Larache, Salé, Messa, and Cape Nun were wheat, barley, cattle, horses, honey, wax, indigo, dates, gum arabic, lacquer, grapes, and many other products and vegetables, as well as textiles and other manufactured articles. Gold came across the Sahara from the Niger region. The Christians living in Ceuta had special rights to trade with the Muslims, as indicated by reference to a papal bull in King Duarte's letters of January 29 and August 27, 1437.[27] In the *Esmeraldo de situ orbis* (ca. 1505–08), Duarte Pacheco Pereira, after describing the coast town by town, remarks on the trade "of great value" brought from there as well as things sold there by European traders.[28] There was obviously no lack of merchandise from which to profit while seeking regions farther along the coast.

Attempted Expansion into Northwest Africa: Disastrous Failure at Tangier

While these voyages were in progress, Portugal was occupied with many other problems, which help to explain the four-year pause in explorations.

[26] Godinho, *Documentos*, I, 234–244; Azurara, *Crónica da Guiné*, chap. 9.
[27] Godinho, *Documentos*, II, 36–54, 103.
[28] Pereira, *Esmeraldo*, chaps. 20–23; Godinho, *Documentos*, I, 227, and II, 54–69.

Among the reasons were the preparations for the unsuccessful attack on Tangier in 1437, the death of King Duarte in 1438, and the contest over the regency between the queen and Prince Pedro.[29]

As noted above, the suggested combined attack by Portugal and Castile on Granada was dropped. The claims laid to the Canaries had met the opposition of Castile and were also for the moment in abeyance. All the pressures that had determined Portugal's policies for many years were, however, still strong. The unsatisfactory situation with respect to Ceuta, for example, continued. The young nobles who wanted to find outlets for their energies and increase their estates were restless, and the merchants sought additional trade opportunities and better protection. The ever-present spirit of "Crusade" still stirred in Portugal; and the rivalry with Castile was seldom if ever absent from Portuguese foreign policy. All these problems and more precluded a passive attitude on Duarte's part.

The exploring activities along the African coast, in full development after 1433, were not the sole manifestation of Portugal's expansionist forces. Henry himself was the most active advocate of a determined attack on the Muslims of Morocco and Granada, as well as the chief advocate of exploration. It seems natural that at this moment when Portugal was frustrated in its efforts to gain title to the Canaries, the concept of an attack in Morocco, as advocated in 1433, should be renewed — and so it was in 1436.

Preparations began for what was to become the attack on Tangier the next year. The Portuguese reasoned that the occupation of Tangier would give support to Ceuta and facilitate progress inland against the Muslims. Many of the young nobles, notably Fernando, João I's fifth living legitimate son, who was without great estates, would have an opportunity to establish themselves. Fernando and others had already requested, without success, that Duarte permit them to go abroad to engage in tourneys. The young nobles argued it was as true then as it had been at the time of Ceuta that it would be better to employ them in attacking Muslims in Africa rather than other Christians elsewhere in Europe; at the same time Portuguese power and Christianity would be enhanced.[30]

[29] Peres, *Descobrimentos portuguêses*, p. 100.
[30] Godinho, *Documentos*, II, 81–85; Robert Ricard, *Études sur l'histoire des portugais au Maroc*. João I had six legitimate sons and one acknowledged illegitimate son. See Fortunato de Almeida, *História de Portugal*, II, 45.

Prince Pedro, second son of João I, and just a year younger than his brother King Duarte, had already manifested his doubts concerning the continued occupation of Ceuta in a letter sent home during his travels in western Europe between 1425 and 1428. Pedro now analyzed the proposal for a new attack in Africa in detail and opposed it, saying that "the loss of Portugal is certain without winning Africa. . . . Your Highness should not get entangled in Africa."[31] Duarte nevertheless had obtained a *bula de crusada* from Pope Eugenius IV in 1436, whether for the specific purpose of attacking Tangier or for some future occasion which might arise is a matter of doubt.[32]

Henry was ardently for the African venture "as something which in his belief God inspired."[33] To the king he made his position clear. "That war on the Muslims," Henry said "is in God's service is beyond doubt, for the church has willed it," and the moment was right because the Muslims were divided among themselves, "as never heard of before."[34] Henry's advice to Duarte does not reveal any general plan of expansion, though it does advocate consistent attacks on the Muslims.

The king in a justification after the events cited thirteen reasons for the attack on Tangier, the last of which was that "a great part of the council favored," it. In fact the campaign proved to be but weakly supported by the country, and the attack on Tangier, led by Henry, resulted in a bad defeat.[35] Prince Fernando was captured and held hostage for the return of the city of Ceuta to the Muslims.[36] For eleven years thereafter, while Fernando was prisoner and before he died in 1448, the Portuguese debated whether or not Ceuta should be surrendered for his release.

King Duarte died September 19, 1438, leaving his six-year-old son Afonso V as successor. In a struggle for power in which Henry and Pedro, as well as the other nobles and the queen, were involved, Pedro emerged as regent. Neither he nor Henry made decisive moves to surrender Ceuta for the release of Fernando. Ceuta was held, and at a later date other and more successful attacks were made in Morocco. The expansion of Portugal along the African coast to hitherto unknown areas continued, now un-

[31] Godinho, *Documentos*, II, 128–131.
[32] Rui de Pina, *Crónica de Duarte*, chap. 13, in Godinho, *Documentos*, II, 90–93.
[33] Rui de Pina, *Crónica de Duarte*, chap. 13, in Godinho, *Documentos*, II, 86.
[34] Quoted in Godinho, *Documentos*, II, 104–112, 164–165. Frei João Álvares, *Crónica de Fernando*, chap. 20, discusses this division.
[35] Godinho, *Documentos*, II, 93–102.
[36] Joaquim Mendes dos Remédios, *Crónica do Infante Santo D. Fernando*.

doubtedly promoted largely by Henry but supported by Pedro the regent.[37]

After the disaster of Tangier, Henry returned to Portugal but not immediately to the court. It is only after 1437, more likely after 1443, that he established himself at Sagres on the southwest point of Portugal.[38]

[37] Godinho, *Documentos*, II, 93–165.
[38] Alberto Iria, *Itinerário do Infante Henrique.*

CHAPTER 5

New Discoveries along the African Coast and the Old Spanish Rival

Prince Henry: Reasons for Coastal Exploration

The exploration beyond Bojador so successfully begun between 1434 and 1436 had been interrupted by the disastrous attack on Tangier in 1437. The next year King Duarte died, and "very serious discord" over succession problems occupied Henry's time. Pedro, the second son of King João I, became regent. Azurara attributes the temporary discontinuance of discoveries to Henry's involvements in Portugal's domestic difficulties.[1]

The tendency of some modern historians is to credit Prince Pedro,[2] or even the collective expansionist forces of Portugal at that time, with the outburst of exploration; but Azurara makes a good case for Henry as the strongest force in Portuguese expansion. He entitles chapter VII of his *Crónica da Guiné* "The Five Reasons Why Prince Henry Was Motivated to Send His Ships to Guinea."

[1] To gain knowledge of the land that extended beyond the Canary Islands and of a cape called Bojador. . . . And because he wished to know the truth [of the many rumors about the region] . . . he sent his ships to those parts in order to get reliable information (*manifesta certidão*), being impelled in this by his desire to serve God and King Duarte, his Lord and brother, who reigned at that time. And this may even be

---

[1] Godinho, *Documentos*, II, 167–168.
[2] Godinho, throughout the extensive notes in the three volumes of his *Documentos*, stresses Pedro's role in promoting exploration along the African coast and settlement in the islands. See also for further information and comparison, Júlio Gonçalves, *O Infante D. Pedro*, and Francis M. Rogers, *The Travels of the Infante Dom Pedro*.

considered the first reason that motivated him. (2) [To find] merchandise which might be brought to [Portugal whose products] might be carried there . . . with great profit to our fellow citizens. . . . (3) To gain knowledge of the strength of the enemy . . . and discover . . . how far the power of the [Moors] reached. (4) . . . to find Christians to help against the enemies of the Catholic faith and (5) . . . to expand the Holy Faith . . . the salvation of souls.

But, adds Azurara, more important than these five reasons, there was a sixth, the "root from which all the others came . . . the heavenly circles . . . the stars," which led Henry to be curious about the mysteries of the world, "for his ascendant was Aries, which is the House of Mars. . . . And because Mars was in Aquarius, which is the House of Sagittarius . . . it signified that this Lord [Henry] would work at noble and courageous conquests, especially to search out the things hidden from other men, and secrets, according to the characteristics of Saturn which . . . signified that all his efforts and accomplishments (*tratados e conquistas*) would be done in loyalty for the satisfaction of his king and lord."[3]

These five reasons, even perhaps the sixth, Henry's stars, are logical and reasonable. Azurara was speaking of the year 1433 and later, as he makes perfectly clear when he refers to King Duarte. Trade with the African Coast as far as Cape Nun had shown the Portuguese sailors that much of what they found in the coastal ports had come from inland and from farther south. What was more natural than to want to know what was beyond Bojador, until then an "impossible" barrier, and beyond the Canary Islands, some of which the Spaniards had colonized, but farther than which nobody was known to have sailed.

The second reason, commerce with new lands and peoples which might be discovered, follows logically. The third is equally logical inasmuch as the Portuguese were continuously engaged in war with the Muslims. The search for a Christian king to help them stems from the obvious desire for an ally. As for the fifth motive, the conversion of souls and conquest of territory from Infidels was the frequently expressed overall purpose of Spaniards and Portuguese, somewhat as in our century the spread of democracy has been a justification for our wars. Nor is there any reason to doubt that not merely Henry but many other people of his time, as well as many today, might have believed in and consulted astrologers. Henry's

[3] Azurara, *Crónica da Guiné*, chap. 7.

life need not be interpreted in a literal astrological sense; there is ample evidence that he believed in his own destiny and that he moved with force toward his goals.

Duarte Pacheco Pereira ascribes Henry's motives to a "revelation that he would be doing a service to Our Lord to discover the said Ethiopias where he would find a great multitude of new people." He says nothing of Henry's desire to know of the regions beyond Bojador, but he adds "thus God revealed and pointed the way . . . to the conquests and commerce of these regions all the way to India."[4] João de Barros, the sixteenth-century historian of Portuguese expansion, ascribes to Henry the "desire to make war on the Infidels" and the obligations binding him as "governor of the Order of Knighthood of Our Lord Jesus Christ." He was always inquiring of the Moors about the interior, "not only of the lands of the nomads (Alarves) . . . but of the Azenegues whose lands are adjacent to . . . Guinea. . . . Having this information . . . he began . . . sending . . . vessels beyond Cape Nun . . . [the] limit of discoveries of the navigators of Spain [i.e., Portugal and Spain]."[5]

Coastal Trade: The First Slaves, 1441

After the crisis of the death of Duarte had passed, "the affairs of the kingdom being now somewhat quieter, though not entirely so," as Azurara remarked,[6] development and further exploration could be renewed. On June 1, 1439, the regent Pedro in the name of Afonso V granted Henry a five-year tariff exemption on products from Madeira.

[4] Pereira, *Esmeraldo*, I, chap. 22; Godinho, *Documentos*, I, 112ff.; Albuquerque, *Descobrimentos*, pp. 220–232; Elaine Sanceau, *Portugal in Quest of Prester John*; C. D. Ley, ed., *Portuguese Voyages*, pp. 63–75, "The Land of Prester John."
[5] João de Barros and Diogo Couto, *Da Ásia*, Dec. I, bk. 1, chap. 2. Damião de Góis, *Crónica D. João*, chap. 7, writing a century after the events, places the time of Henry's residence in Sagres to about 1419, which is known to be incorrect. See Godinho, *Descobrimentos*, I, 136–140. Góis is also the author who most explicitly attributes to Henry the ambition to reach India. On the meaning of "India" as used, see Duarte Leite, "O plano henriquino da Índia e os nossos escritores," in *Seára Nova*, nos. 754, 755, 756. Barros, *Ásia*, Dec. I, bk. I, chap. 16, gives his estimate of Henry's characteristics. See also Godinho, *Documentos*, I, 132–135. For contrasting views of Henry, including his motives and achievements, see J. Cortesão, *Descobrimentos portuguêses*, I, 390–400, who exalts Henry, and Leite, *Descobrimentos*, I, 67–267, who assesses him on the basis of stricter adherence to documentation. The reader will note that the early Portuguese historians used "Spain" to refer to the Iberian Peninsula, and that they often spoke of the Castilian language as "our" language.
[6] Azurara, *Crónica da Guiné*, chap. 12.

The next year on May 8, 1440, Henry granted to Tristão Vaz Teixeira a portion of the island of Madeira with extensive economic privileges and political powers, reserving for himself, however, the authority to impose the death penalty or dismemberment.[7]

Exploration was renewed in 1440. Two caravels[8] — this is the first time this type of ship is mentioned in exploration — were sent out but obtained few results. In 1441 the Prince outfitted a small ship (navio), in which he sent as captain Antão Gonçalves "a very young man." Gonçalves was instructed to obtain only a cargo of oil and seal skins; but he was more ambitious. "What a beautiful thing it would be" he said to his crew, "if we could capture some of the natives; the Prince would be not a little happy." He captured two men in Rio d'Ouro, the first brought to Portugal from beyond Bojador.[9]

While in Rio d'Ouro, Gonçalves was joined by Nuno Tristão, also a gentleman of Prince Henry's household, who had orders "to go as far as possible" beyond Porto da Galé. Together they found a group of natives and charged them, crying, "Portugal and Santiago"; they killed four and captured ten, of whom one was Adahu, a nobleman. Gonçalves returned home and Tristão pushed southward in obedience to the command "to capture people in any way and the best way you can," reaching Cape Blanco, also in 1441, the farthest point south yet attained in the explorations (20°46' N).[10]

[7] Godinho, Documentos, I, 186. Henry was in Santarém, north of Lisbon, not in Sagres when this document was prepared. The king confirmed this grant on March 11, 1449. On January 18, 1452, the king granted hereditary rights to Tristão and his sons, and to descendants in the male line.

[8] Henrique Lopes de Mendonça, Estudos sôbre navios; Gago Coutinho, "As caravelas" in A náutica dos descobrimentos, I, 159–194.

[9] Azurara, Crónica da Guiné, chap. 11. For Africa and slavery in general, see Fred Burke, Africa; Manuel Heleno, Os escravos em Portugal; Phillip D. Curtin, The Atlantic Slave Trade, and Africa Remembered; Basil Davidson, The African Slave Trade; Oliver Davies, "Native Culture in the Gold Coast"; Oliver Davies, West Africa before the Europeans; D. B. Davis, The Problem of Slavery in Western Culture; James Duffy, Portugal in Africa; P. J. M. McEwan, ed., Africa from Early Times; Roland Oliver, ed., The Dawn of African History; Roland and Caroline Oliver, Africa in the Days of Exploration; P. E. N. Tindall, A History of Central Africa.

[10] Azurara, Crónica da Guiné, chap. 12. Azurara, the principal contemporary record of the discoveries, is not always easy to follow, either for places or dates. The various accounts and attempts at solutions to problems are discussed in Peres, Descobrimentos portugueses, pp. 93–166, and in Godinho, Documentos, II, 167–266. In Dinis, Monumenta Henricina, vols. 9 and 10, the chronology of Henry's activities is reconstructed from Azurara's chronicle and other sources of information. See also Barros, Ásia, Dec. I, bk. 1, chap. 6.

What kinds of weapons were used by the Portuguese in their fifteenth-century expansion? There is evidence that traditional medieval hand weapons were used exclusively until

The psychological effect of capturing the first African slaves was greater than that caused by the passage of Bojador. Here was visible reason for the hazardous voyage. A great change occurred in the Portuguese attitude toward what had been for some years principally an activity of Prince Henry and the sailors of Algarve. Henry, seeing the great interest on the part of others, obtained from his brother Pedro exclusive rights of navigation toward Guinea. In October 1443 he obtained from the pope a bull confirming his rights. The scant knowledge the Portuguese had had of West Africa was mainly of the interior, not the coast. The maps of Africa drawn to this date, i.e., the atlas of Abraham and Jafuda Cresques of Mayorca, showed an interior with some principal places like Timbuktu, Mali, and Gao; but they were vague and inaccurate about the coast south of the Canary Islands. Whether the Portuguese made use of the atlas or other maps is uncertain. There is no direct evidence that they did. Their knowledge came from their advance along the coast. The way Azurara describes the voyages and the tone of the grants made by the king show how startlingly new everything was to them.

For historical purposes, it may be noted that the Portuguese used the term Guinea to apply to the region extending from Cape Blanco and Arguim Bay southward along the coast to Cape Catarina and beyond the islands of São Tomé and Annobom.[11]

These first captives, perhaps from some branch of the Berbers, were from the desert regions and not from sub-Saharan Africa. Azurara left a glowing picture of the arrival of the captives and their appearance before Henry. "I cannot reflect on the arrival of these ships, with the novelty of these slaves before our Prince, that I do not find pleasure. For it seems to

---

the middle of the century. Azurara speaks of the Portuguese "furbishing their weapons . . . hasten[ing] to rivet their armor . . . battle-axes, . . . swords" in preparation for the attack on Ceuta. Pedro and Henry shed their armor during the battle, because it was too hot. The Muslims used lances and even stones, and Azurara lists among the captured weapons darts, arrows, arbalests, bucklers, and bombard, and powder.

In recounting the conquests in Guinea, Azurara mentions the horses, which were so useful, and swords and lances. The natives who fought against Nuno Tristão and Antão Gonçalves "defended themselves with javelins . . . for they knew nothing of the use of other weapons." Some of the blacks of Guinea fought with bows and iron-tipped, poisoned arrows, which took a considerable toll. They protected themselves with a "buckler, round and rather larger" than that used by the Portuguese, which was "made of an elephant's ear." Though hard put at times, the Portuguese, according to Azurara's account, fought almost entirely with hand weapons and made little use of the bombard and harquebus known in Portugal at least as early as the fourteenth century. When forts were later built at Arguim (1456?) and São Jorge da Mina (1482) they were fortified with firearms.

[11]A. P. Kup, A History of Sierra Leone.

me I see before my eyes how great his joy must have been . . . [to see the first profit from the heavy expenditures], not for the number of those captives, but for the hope, oh Sainted Prince! you had for others you could have in the future. . . . Though their bodies were captive, this was small matter in comparison with their souls which would have eternal true freedom."[12]

The invitation to venture and profit was not rejected. Gonçalves returned again to Africa with his noble captive Adahu, who was released on promise of ransom but ran away and returned to his own people. Two other prisoners were exchanged for "ten Negroes, men and women of various tribes." With Gonçalves was Henry's slave broker (*alfaqueque*).[13] They also obtained gold, "and though it was only a little," it was enough to raise great hopes. The estuary where they were anchored was named 'Rio d'Ouro.' The appetite of Prince Henry was also whetted by "three 'delicacies' [ostrich eggs] as fresh and as good as if from some other domestic fowl."[14] "Thus these things began to develop little by little. The people began to dare to take up that career, some to serve, others to gain honor, and others with the hope of profit."[15]

Slave Raids, 1443–46

From 1443 to 1446 there was an outburst of activity. In 1443 Nuno Tristão sailed beyond Cape Blanco to the islands of Arguim Bay, from one of which came some twenty-five dugouts in which naked rowers were seated astride, using their legs as oars. To the startled mariners they looked like birds; but when the Portuguese saw that they were men, "their hearts were naked with a new kind of joy, principally to see them so easy to capture." Fourteen prisoners were taken.[16]

Henry's exclusive rights prevented anyone except those he sent or licensed from sailing to that area.[17] As more ships went to the newly discovered coast, Henry ordered maps made of the region (there were no detailed coastal maps before) and noted that no Christians had previously

[12] Azurara, *Crónica da Guiné*, chap. 14; Peres, *Descobrimentos portugueses*, p. 105.
[13] On the functions of the *alfaqueque* in the exchange of prisoners, see Godinho, *Documentos*, III, 90–91.
[14] Azurara, *Crónica da Guiné*, chaps. 14–16; Barros, *Ásia*, Dec. I, bk. I. chap. 7.
[15] Azurara, *Crónica da Guiné*, chap. 17.
[16] *Ibid*.
[17] Godinho, *Documentos*, I, 142, quoting the *carta régia* of October 23, 1443.

been to that area. The interior, as I indicated earlier, was better known than the coast, as judged by travel accounts and maps. Evidence is lacking, however, about how the Portuguese knew the interior, and it can only be surmised what maps they were acquainted with at that time. None of the maps made by Henry's orders has survived.[18]

It seems significant that a few days after Henry was granted the monopoly rights over West African trade and discoveries Pedro gave him a league of territory around Cape Trasfalmenar where Sagres and São Vicente now are. Only after this did Henry live in Algarve in a semipermanent way and spend periods of time in other ports of Portugal where he attended to his many other duties. In Algarve Henry was to have the right to construct a town, and it was here that construction was begun on his Villa do Infante in 1443 or later.[19] The exact location of the villa has been a matter of lively discussion among historians, but no satisfactory solution to the problem has been suggested so far. In any case, it is a matter of minor importance in the history of discoveries.

Azurara paints a great skepticism and criticism of the African ventures until the mariners saw the results. "But when they saw the first Moors . . . and the second group . . . and the third . . . [the scoffers] confessed their error . . . feeling foolish . . . [hailing Henry] as another Alexander the Great . . . [seeing] the homes of others bursting at the seams with slaves, male and female."[20] Because after 1443 Henry was frequently in Algarve once construction of his villa had begun there, and because the slaves were brought to Lagos, the citizens of this port were the first who sought licenses from Henry to go to the lands where the prisoners had been captured. After the royal grant to Henry, the first to ask for such a license, according to Azurara, was Lanzarote, tax collector (*almoxarife*) of Lagos, who in 1444 assembled with his friends six caravels.[21] They sailed to the area just beyond Cape Blanco, Heron Island (*Ilha das Garças*), where they rested and feasted on the young birds. Their serious hunt was for slaves. Lanzarote here harangued his crew, saying, according to Azurara: "My friends . . . we left Portugal to do

[18] Armando Cortesão, *Cartografia e cartógrafos portuguêses dos séculos XV e XVI*.
[19] Godinho, *Documentos*, I, 154–156, quoting the *carta régia* from Pedro to Henry of October 27, 1443.
[20] Azurara, *Crónica da Guiné*, chap. 18.
[21] Azurara, *Crónica da Guiné*, chap. 18, does not state clearly the year. See Peres *descobrimentos portuguêses*, pp. 106–107. In Dinis, *Monumenta Henricina*, the known writings and documents concerning Henry are published in chronological order. For these years, see vols. 9 and 10.

service to God and to the Prince Our Lord, [so let us hunt better than] any others who have come here." And so they did, for slaves. To the usual battle cry of "Santiago, São Jorge, and Portugal" they charged, killing many and capturing 165. "The fight over, they all praised God for their many blessings." In the region of Cape Blanco they captured others — Azurara says 235 altogether.[22]

Having loaded his vessels to capacity with captives, Lanzarote and his friends returned to Lagos. The news of their return was sent to Henry "who only a few hours earlier had happened to arrive." The crews "as you can imagine," says Azurara, "were happy to be with their wives and children." The next day Lanzarote made a formal presentation to Henry. "Your Highness well knows," said Lanzarote, "that the *Fifth* of these Moors are yours."[23]

Azurara's description of the captives is more compassionate than his account of their capture. He seems to have been a witness to the scene. Addressing himself to the "Heavenly Father" he prayed that his "tears might not prejudice his conscience" which "cried out piously for their suffering . . . on seeing the miserable group [who] are also . . . the sons of Adam." When the captives landed on August 8, 1444, Azurara found them "a marvellous sight." Some were white, some were mulattoes, "others were as black as Ethiopians, and so ugly in face and body," as if they came from "the lower hemisphere." Their condition was piteous. They were groaning and crying out. "We could not understand their words but the sound . . . was in keeping with their grief." The greatest suffering came when they were separated from one another, "fathers from sons, husbands from wives, brothers from brothers." Azurara describes the misery as "mothers clung to their children and were whipped with little pity." Crowds of people had gathered "only to see this novelty." Prince Henry was there "astride a powerful horse." He received "forty-six souls" as his portion, which he distributed among his subjects. Some of the captives were sold as slaves. Families were divided and sent to different places, "the father in Lagos . . . the mother in Lisbon . . . the children to some other place."

Azurara did not find the results all bad. Those captives who were not

[22] Azurara, *Crónica da Guiné*, chaps. 19–22.
[23] *Ibid.*, chaps. 23–24. Among the taxes imposed by the kings of Portugal and Spain was the Fifth, i.e. 20 percent of the gross product of certain types of economic activities, notably mining, but in this case of the commerce along the African coast. Henry had been given a grant of this royal privilege and thus the Fifth of the slaves belonged to him.

"set in the faith of other Moors" came to Christ willingly. Some were set free and married to Portuguese. Some were adopted by "widows of good family" and treated with kindness. Their condition, he thought, was much better than when they lived in "damnation of souls." Formerly they had "lived like animals . . . without knowing bread and wine." Now they were "dressed . . . fed . . . loved [and had] turned with good will to the path of the Faith. Now you see what glory should be the Prince's before the Lord Our God for bringing thus to the true salvation not only these, but many others who will be mentioned, as you will see, in this history later."[24]

Azurara's justification for slavery was hardly improved on by the apologists of the following centuries, when so many millions of others were "saved."

The Slaving Voyages of 1444–45

Later in the same year, in which Lanzarote returned, Henry sent Gonçalo de Sintra in a caravel with orders to sail directly to Guinea; but he went instead to Cape Blanco and then to the island of Naar just beyond, where he and seven of his companions were killed by the natives in a futile attempt to take more captives.[25] Also in 1444, according to Azurara, Henry sent out Antão Gonçalves, Gomes Pires, and Diogo Afonso, though Regent Pedro obviously participated since Valentim Fernandes reports that Gomes Pires was master of a ship belonging to the king (*patrão de El-Rey*) on a mission to open commerce and seek more souls to be saved; it did not succeed on either count.[26]

Nuno Tristão likewise sailed in 1444, going again at first to the areas just south of Cape Blanco, Heron Island and Arguim, from which the natives had temporarily fled to other parts, causing Tristão to report "we could make no captives in these islands. . . . My desire was to sail on as far as I could until I reached the Negro lands, for you know the wish of the Prince." The point Tristão reached is assumed to be somewhere in the region of the Senegal River. Bad weather forced him to return. This

[24]*Ibid.*, chaps. 25–26. The statement made by Azurara in chap. 25 that he had seen the grandchildren of the captives shows that at least some part of his work was finished many years after 1448, when his chronicle ends, or after 1453, the date given in the Paris manuscript.

[25]Azurara, Crónica da Guiné, chaps. 26–27.

[26]*Ibid.*, chaps. 27–29.

voyage is of principal interest because it pushed further south than anyone had to that date and actually reached "the land of the Negroes."[27] Afterward Dinis Dias "reached a high cape to which they gave the name Cape Verde, disembarking on a small island they called *Ilha da Palma* (in Angra of Bezeguiche), today Gorée Island.[28]

In 1445 Gonçalo Pacheco of Lisbon "a squire of noble lineage . . . who always maintained ships to sail against the Infidels,"[29] was attracted by the "great numbers of captives" and sought license from Henry "who was in Vizeu" (i.e., in the north of Portugal) to send out three caravels. All three carried the banner of Christ. They sailed to Arguim and Tider where they captured some sixty or seventy natives.[30] After debating their next move, they resolved "to go to the Negro lands" where Dinis Dias had made captives the year before — going on, according to Azurara, eighty leagues farther where they found green fields, cattle, and a numerous hostile people who prevented them from going ashore.[31] On their way home they made other captives in the islands of Arguim and Tider but lost a large number of their companions in a battle with the natives "who ate the dead Christians left on the beach."[32]

In 1445 João Gonçalves Zarco, one of the captains of Madeira, sent Álvaro Fernandes, his nephew, in "a very fine caravel" to explore "without any profit motive but only to see and learn whatever news he could," and ordered him to go directly to the "Negro lands" and as far on as possible. They sailed "that great ocean sea until they reached the Nile" (Senegal) which they identified as a western branch of the Egyptian Nile. Beyond Cape Verde they found hostile people, "six boats with 35 to 40 men . . . who acted like men who wished to fight," but who stood off some distance from the caravel. Álvaro Fernandes lowered a boat and attacked but found them very difficult to capture because they could swim and dive like "cormorants." Only two were captured. The prospects not being good there, they sailed on to a place they called Cape of the Masts, because of the gaunt palm trees, where they surprised but failed to capture some of the natives. This was the farthest point reached in 1445.[33]

[27] *Ibid.*, chap. 30.

[28] *Ibid.*, chap. 31.

[29] That is to say, according to Godinho, "corsair or a pirate"; see *Documentos*, II, 203–204.

[30] Valentim Fernandes, chap. 29, quoted in Godinho, *Documentos*, II, 203–204.

[31] Azurara, *Crónica da Guiné*, chaps. 42–44.

[32] Valentim Fernandes, chap. 23, from Godinho, *Documentos*, II, 211–214.

[33] Azurara, *Crónica da Guiné*, chap. 75; Godinho, *Documentos*, II, 214–221. The Ilha da Palma, also called Bezeguiche, is present-day Gorée.

They returned home via Madeira to Lisbon where they found the "Prince." Azurara leaves in doubt whether this Prince was Pedro or Henry.

The Slaving Voyages of 1445–46

In August 1445 some twenty-six vessels sailed from Lagos, Lisbon, and Madeira, possibly with ships from other ports as well. One leader of this expedition, which did not act as one fleet, was again Lanzarote, who had made a voyage the year before. "The news of this fleet spread throughout the kingdom, stirring up others to attach themselves to the company."[34] Henry himself was called away to Coimbra to knight his nephew Pedro, son of the regent, who was off to Spain to assist Juan II in the wars against his cousins of Navarre and Aragon — an example of how the affairs of Portugal and Spain were enmeshed and of the relative importance of discovery at that time in comparison with dynastic quarrels. Fourteen vessels were fitted out in Lagos, and others came from Lisbon and Madeira. Henry's own scrivener accompanied one of the caravels to keep the records, "for such was the custom of the Prince."[35]

Among those who accompanied this fleet was Tristão Vaz Teixeira, one of the captains of Madeira. João Gonçalves Zarco of Madeira sent two caravels of his own. The fourteen vessels of Lagos sailed August 10, with a rendezvous set for Cape Blanco. Later they assembled at Heron Island. In the subsequent attack on the islands and the nearby mainland, twenty or more natives were killed and fewer than 100 captured. Lanzarote announced that he considered his mission as a leader accomplished. "As you all know" he said to his crew, "we left our city with the principal objective the conquest of this island which God has granted," and thus with the task ended "each one may do whatever he wishes, going wherever he feels to his advantage and profit." As for himself, Lanzarote said, "I do not intend to return with such a small prize" to report to Henry.[36]

Gomes Pires of Lisbon, who commanded a caravel which belonged to the king, decided to go further "because you well know how great is the will of the Prince to know more about the Negro lands, especially the Nile." Three other captains decided to sail with Pires: Rodrigo de Travas-

[34] Azurara, *Crónica da Guiné*, chaps. 49–50.
[35] *Ibid.*, chaps. 51–57.
[36] *Ibid.*, chaps. 52–56.

sos, and Lourenço and Vicente Dias. They passed the landmark of two palms already described by Dinis Dias, "which they recognized as where the Negro lands began, the sight of which made them very happy," and began to prepare "to hunt for Negroes." But rough water prevented it. They were amazed to learn that the "Nile" (Senegal) sweetened the ocean water miles out. Also amazing were the elephants "large enough to feed 2500 people," whose "bones" (tusks) were thrown away, though in the Mediterranean they were worth a thousand *dobras*.[37]

Carried by a north wind they made Cape Verde which was already known to Dinis Dias. Further south they learned that the caravel sent by João Gonçalves Zarco had preceded them. The natives, who used poisoned darts, were too numerous and too hostile to permit them to land. They returned and made an unsuccessful effort to enter the Senegal. Lourenço Dias returned to Lagos. Gomes Pires returned via the Rio d'Ouro, where he bought only one Negro but got on such friendly footing with the merchants that they promised the next year "he would find for sale an abundance of Negroes and gold."[38]

The ships of Lanzarote's fleet had devoted most of their time to the search for slaves. They found that in the islands of Arguim Bay, "the caravels sail around here daily," and captives were scarce. Lanzarote, swearing that "we will not leave here without captives," was rewarded, "for God be praised" they captured fifty-seven and killed others, while still others fled. Azurara felt compassion for those who escaped. "Ah, if only . . . those who fled . . . had some comprehension of higher things . . . they would have . . . come to . . . save their souls."[39] Rodrigo Eanes and Dinis Dias sailed to Cape Verde where they found the natives "not so easily captured as we would like, for they are very strong men, cautious and skillful in their fighting; and worse, their arrows are poisoned with a very dangerous herb."[40] They killed a few, captured none, and returned home by way of the islands of Arguim where they made one prisoner. "From there they sailed directly to Lisbon where, paying the tariff to the Prince, they were received with honor and thanks."[41]

[37]*Ibid.*, chaps. 57–60.
[38]*Ibid.*, chap. 63
[39]*Ibid.*, chap. 65.
[40]*Ibid.*, chap. 72.
[41]*Ibid.*, chap. 74. It is more likely that the prince who received them in Lisbon was Pedro rather than Henry, according to José de Bragança, editor of the 1937 edition of Azurara. See

Two vessels returning home encountered a third and were persuaded to join it in raiding the Canaries for slaves. With the aid of two Canarian chieftains of Gomera who had been to Portugal and received excellent treatment at the hands of Prince Henry, they raided Palma, chasing the natives around the mountain peaks until they captured seventeen. Several of the Portuguese were killed in falls from the craggy mountains. Disappointed with the number of their prizes, they treacherously took to Portugal as prisoners twenty-one of their helpers from Gomera. Henry, indignant at this, returned the Canarians to their homes "very nobly dressed."[42]

Two other raids on the Canaries were made by Álvaro Dornelas in 1445 or 1446. The first netted only two captives who were sold in Madeira to buy supplies. Bad weather drove him to Lisbon where his cousin João, half owner of the caravel, refitted the ship. Together, with the aid of natives of Gomera, they captured twenty and killed ten natives on Palma. Álvaro remained in Gomera, and João made a difficult passage home, "supplies being so short that there seemed nothing could be done except eat some of those captives." He finally made Tavira in Algarve.[43]

Some of the slaving parties ended in disaster. In 1445 or 1446 Nuno Tristão landed twenty-two men "60 leagues beyond Cape Verde," of whom twenty were killed by poison arrows, including Tristão. Five of this crew, described as boys, none a navigator, managed to sail home to Lagos in two months.[44]

In 1446 Álvaro Fernandes was again sent out by João Gonçalves Zarco "to go as far as possible and try to take the kind of new prize whose importance would testify to the good will that he had to serve the *Senhor* (Henry) who had raised him." Fernandes again reached the Cape of

---

his footnote 1, vol. II, pp. 61–63. Godinho deduces from the description given by Azurara of the 1445 expedition of Lanzarote that "the men of Lagos seemed to have formed some type of company, though of short term" (Godinho, *Documentos*, III, 49–50, note 6). It is difficult to see anything that approaches our modern concept of company. At most there was a temporary agreement among the various shipowners, in keeping with the custom among the mariners of the times. Such agreements were called *companhias* or *companharias* and were made and dissolved with each voyage. The twenty-six vessels did not act as a single fleet; they sailed either in small groups or singly, making their individual raids along the coast. There is no indication that all profits were divided among the owners and sailors of the twenty-six vessels. See Valentim Fernandes who gives a resumé (chap. 30) based on *Crónica da Guiné*. See also Azurara, *Crónica da Guiné*, chap. 63. Particularly see Virginia Rau and Bailey W. Diffie, "Alleged Fifteenth-Century Portuguese Joint Stock Companies."

[42] Azurara, *Crónica da Guiné*, chaps. 68–69.
[43] *Ibid.*, chaps. 70, 78–79, 85.
[44] *Ibid.*, chaps. 85–86.

Masts, sailing beyond and having several engagements with the Negroes. He was wounded by a poisoned arrow and almost died. Azurara estimates that this voyage reached some 120 leagues beyond Cape Verde, which, allowing for Azurara's usual 30 percent exaggeration would place Fernandes at some point beyond the Senegal but short of the Geba. He had extended the discoveries more than had any other explorer. Prince Pedro the regent rewarded him with 100 *dobras*, and Henry did the same.[45]

In 1446 a fleet of nine caravels, including one belonging to the bishop of Algarve, stopped over in Madeira "by order of the Prince" to provision. They restored to their homes in Gomera nineteen of the Canarians previously kidnapped but made an unsuccessful attempt to capture others on Palma. Three of the caravels returned to Portugal. Others reached sixty leagues (Azurara's estimate) beyond Cape Verde, where they found fields of tree cotton, rice, and many other crops. They had the usual fight with the natives who shot poisoned arrows, killing five of the crew, of whom three were foreigners. On the way home, however, "with little work" they captured "forty-eight Moors."[46]

Gomes Pires "remembered that he had promised the Moors" of Rio d'Oura that he would return. He set out with two caravels in 1446, one fitted out by Henry and the other perhaps by himself.[47] In one of the caravels Henry sent his scrivener João Gorizo, "who was to list all the receipts and expenses."[48] The caravels went first to Madeira "as was now the custom of all the ships sent out by the Prince . . . to be provisioned." After twenty-one days of vain effort to trade with and to buy slaves from merchants who were inland from Rio d'Ouro, they captured eight Moors on one raid and twenty-one men, women, and children on another, returning to their caravel "content with their victory." Some six leagues away they captured another thirty-one, mainly "old men, women,

[45]*Ibid.*, chap. 87; António J. Dias Dinis, *O V [quinto] centenário do descobrimento da Guiné, 1446–1946*.

[46]Azurara, *Crónica da Guiné*, chap. 88. The presence of foreigners in the early and later explorations did not excite any questions by the chroniclers. José de Bragança, editor of the 1937 edition of Azurara, remarks: "The frequent inclusion of foreigners in the expeditions of discovery is without a doubt a serious impediment to belief in the thesis of secrecy about the discoveries" (II, 223, note 1).

[47]Azurara makes it appear that Henry outfitted both caravels, but according to Valentim Fernandes, Gomes Pires outfitted one and Henry outfitted the other. See Godinho, *Descombrimentos*, III, 227, note 2.

[48]Azurara, *Crónica da Guiné*, chap. 89. Godinho deduces from this that Henry was determined not to be "defrauded of his share of the profits granted him by the concession from the regent."

and children." Altogether they had a total of seventy-nine "souls" (*almas*), as Azurara called the slaves. Now overloaded, they threw overboard the salt they had brought along to trade with the natives or to salt seal skins. On returning to Lagos they found that Henry was at the moment nearby in Mexilhoeira.[49]

Not all the activities of Algarve were directed toward discoveries, slave trading along the African coast, or legitimate routine commerce. Tavira, near the Spanish border, complained to the Cortes of Lisbon in 1446 that vessels which outfitted in Portugal "with the pretense of going against the Moors" instead sailed along the coast of Algarve and Castile, going from river to river and port to port, capturing cargoes from Brittany and Galicia which were intended for Spain. Because of this, other foreign vessels were afraid to enter Algarve ports.[50]

Henry the Navigator Granted a Monopoly beyond Bojador

On February 3, 1446, Henry received from the king a further grant of his powers addressed in the usual form "To whomever may see this letter," forbidding anyone to go to the areas beyond Bojador to make war, to carry merchandise without Henry's license, or to bring from that region any captives or any other objects without paying Henry the Fifth customarily paid to the king. The purpose of the monopoly was to compensate Henry for the "great expenses" he had incurred, as detailed in the previous grant of October 22, 1443. Furthermore, the same privileges applied to the Canary Islands, "inasmuch as we know that no ships ever went to those islands from our kingdom before [Henry] sent them, nor do generally go except those of his fleet. . . . Nobody is to go to the said islands, except at his command, and those who go are to pay the Fifth."[51] Any who went without consent would lose both ship and cargo to Henry. The nature of the economic and political powers that Henry had received and that he could grant to others is manifested in the grant he made on November 1, 1446, to Bartolomeu Perestrelo, captain of Porto Santo. This grant was a model for future colonization in other islands and in Brazil in the sixteenth century.[52]

[49] Azurara, *Crónica da Guiné*, chaps. 89–92; Valentim Fernandes, chaps. 55–58.
[50] Godinho, *Documentos*, III, 76–78; and Silva Marques, *Descobrimentos*, I, 451–452.
[51] Godinho, *Documentos*, I, 201–204.
[52] *Ibid.*, 189–192.

Because Gomes Pires failed to establish a trade relationship with the natives of Rio d'Ouro, in 1447 Henry decided to make an effort at the city of Messa, province of Sous, in Morocco, which Valentim Fernandes describes as a "very large town of Moors" on a large river (Sous) with a "great trade of Berbers and nomads where the Genoese trade. . . . From up river comes gold, wax, cattle hides, goat skins, lacquer, and indigo."[53] Duarte Pacheco Pereira describes the region of Sous as fertile and well watered by irrigation, with crops of barley, wheat, sugar, and cattle, as well as trade in gold, silver, copper, lead, rock salt, manufacturing of textiles, and trade with Sudan. It was a point of interchange between Morocco and the "Negro lands" from which came both gold and slaves.[54] Genoese trade with the region dates back to the thirteenth and fourteenth centuries, with an increasing amount in the fifteenth. This expedition of 1447 was commercial, not exploratory, and under the command of Diogo Gil, who had "served well in war with the Moors, at sea as well as on land." Two other expeditions in 1447 went to the Rio d'Ouro, bringing cargoes of oil and seal skins.[55]

Yet another expedition went out to Guinea in 1447. Azurara says that as "the news of these acts [the discoveries] spread around the world," there came from the then united court of Denmark, Sweden, and Norway a nobleman called Vallarte, who lived for a time in the court of Prince Pedro from whom he asked a caravel in which to travel the Negro lands. Pedro entrusted him with the diplomatic mission of attempting to make a treaty with the king of that region "inasmuch as he [Pedro] had been told he was a very great lord . . . they say Christian, who could help in the wars against the Moors of Africa."[56]

The belief that there were Christians in this region was still maintained as late as the sixteenth century when Leo Africanus wrote.[57] With Vallarte went Fernão d'Afonso of the Order of Christ and two interpreters. They sailed beyond Cape Verde to some point (Cacheu?) not easily located with

[53] Valentim Fernandes, fol. 154.

[54] Pereira, *Esmeraldo*, bk. I, chaps. 13–21; Godinho, *Documentos*, II, 25–29 and note 32, pp. 47–48.

[55] Azurara, *Crónica da Guiné*, chap. 93; Godinho. *Documentos*, III, 72, note 2 on p. 75, remarks, "That is to say, one of the rentainers of Henry with long experience in piracy."

[56] Azurara, *Crónica da Guiné*, chap. 94. José Bragança, ed. of Azurara's chronicle, states: "Clearly the prince (Infante) referred to here was the Regent Pedro and not Dom Henrique," an important point in any discussion of to whom credits are due for the expansion of Portugal. Azurara, *Crónica da Guiné*, II, 252, note 1.

[57] Azurara, *Crónica da Guiné*, chaps. 94–96; Godinho, *Documentos*, II, 255–266; Leo Africanus, *The History and Description of Africa*.

precision in the region of the Gambia or São Domingos rivers. Making an effort to get in touch with the Bor-Mali, the Mandinga emperor whose realm extended from the Gambia River on the north to the upper regions of the Senegal and the Niger, the Portuguese read to the local chieftains a letter from their own King Afonso V. They were attacked, Vallarte was either killed or captured, and the caravels returned to Portugal.[58]

By 1448 some fifty-one vessels had gone beyond Bojador; and discovery had been extended as far south as Portuguese Guinea.[59] An estimated 927 slaves, "souls . . . of whom the majority were converted to the true road of salvation," were taken by 1448 when Azurara ends his chronicle.[60]

Prince Pedro and King Afonso V
Take a Share in Expansion

The eyes of both Henry and Pedro, more Pedro's than Henry's, it seems, were now on the Azores. In 1447 Pedro decided to stimulate the economy of the Azores; on April 20, as regent, he obtained from his nephew King Afonso V, "in order that São Miguel be well peopled," an exemption from the tithe on the principal imports from Portugal. Settlers were also "induced" to go, as may be seen in a later pardon permitting one Pedro do Porto to return home after six years of exile. It would appear that between 1431 and 1439 little or no effort had been made to people the islands, though in 1439 Pedro had authorized Henry to do so. Pedro had also granted exemptions from customs in 1443. The exemption from the tithe was a renewed attempt to stimulate colonization.[61]

In 1448 Pedro was dismissed from the regency and Afonso V assumed the throne. Henry moved to reaffirm his rights. On February 25, 1449, the king renewed Henry's privileges.[62] On March 10 the king also repeated the terms of the grant made to Henry in 1439. The extent of

[58] Later Portugal learned of three Christian prisoners inland. Godinho suggests that one of these might have been the white man or some white men reported by Usodimare about ten years later. Azurara, *Crónica da Guiné*, chap. 94; Godinho, *Documentos*, II, 255–266.

[59] Godinho lists the voyages from 1441 to 1444 that he considers to have been initiated by Henry and those from 1444 to 1447 initiated by others. See Appendix XVI.

[60] This is the same number given by Valentim Fernandes. Diogo Gomes's estimate is much higher; he gives 650 as the number captured on the Lanzarote expedition alone in 1445. The 1448 letter of Afonso V mentions more than a thousand "bodies" of the infidels. Azurara, *Crónica da Guiné*, chap. 96.

[61] Godinho, *Documentos*, I, 210–212.

[62] *Ibid.*, 144.

settlement in the Azores to this date is not certain, though indications are that colonization of most of the islands was yet to come.[63]

The rivalry of Portugal and Castile for the trade of the African coast continued. The Duke of Medina Sidonia received a trade monopoly from the king of Castile for the region between Cape Guir (Agadir) and Cape Bojador in 1449. In the same year Afonso V granted to Henry the monopoly from Cape Cantin to Cape Bojador, an overlapping area.[64]

Afonso V, in July 1450, had ordered that the captaincy of Ceuta be given to Henry who had held the title of governor since 1416; but in 1451, before this order could take effect, Afonso himself assumed the government of the city. The king thus began playing an active role shortly after his accession to the throne. He also sent his own caravels along the African coast, though Henry nominally held a monopoly of that area. In 1452 Henry sent Luis Fernandes and his brother João in an *urca* to Morocco and Guinea to trade. In 1453 the king himself sent Cid de Souza, "nobleman of our household and captain of the ships we are sending to Guinea," to take Nuno Antonio de Gois, a nobleman of Henry's household, as "merchant" for "all the merchandise we are sending in the said vessels . . . to exchange for Moors" beyond Cape Blanco. In 1454 the king had a "controller of finance of all matters pertaining to the Ocean Sea," as well as a "receiver of all Muslims and anything else whatsoever concerning our Guinea trade (*resgates*)."[65]

The maintenance of Ceuta, the constant naval engagements with the Muslims, the pursuit of trade along the African coast, and the extension of the known areas farther and farther south, were all important to Portugal; but so were the political and economic relations of Portugal with France, England, and Flanders, as well as with other northern regions which were probably far more profitable up to this time. In any case, as mentioned before, the pursuit of trade with the Muslims of Africa had a direct relation to the trade which the Portuguese had developed along the Guinea coast. The numbers and privileges of foreign merchants continued to be

[63] *Ibid.*, 212–213.

[64] Azurara, *Crónica da Guiné*, chap. 93; Godinho, *Documentos*, III, 72–76, note 1. See also Godinho, *História ecônomica e social*; and Pérez Embid, *Descubrimientos*, pp. 155–157, 204–207, 302–303; John W. Blake, *European Beginnings in West Africa, 1454–1578*, pp. 1–25.

[65] Godinho, *Documentos*, III, 79–84. *Resgatar* means to ransom, free from captivity, or rescue. Here it means to exchange or trade as well as to ransom.

significant for Portugal's commercial policies, of which the new African trade and slavery from beyond Bojador was the added element.

In both 1450 and 1451 English merchants received guarantees against seizure in Portuguese waters. The English maintained a factory (trading post) in Faro.[66] The Genoese Luca Cassano was established in Terceira in the Azores from which he financed several exploring expeditions into the Atlantic.[67] Afonso V granted the French the right to have a consul in Lisbon in 1452.[68] Among others frequently mentioned as receiving trade privileges were Germans and Venetians.

Portugal's Success against Spain on the Coast: Failure in the Canaries

Henry's interest in the Canaries was constant.[69] The double ownership continued after 1435, Maciot still holding Lanzarote while Guillén de las Casas and his successors held Fuerteventura and Hierro. The same division existed for the rights of future conquests. Las Casas sold his rights to Peraza, as previously mentioned, who in turn passed them on to his daughter Inez, who was married to Diego García de Herrera. Herrera conquered the island of Gomera in 1447 and built there the Torre de San Sebastián. The Portuguese claim during these years was only to seignorial rights, not to sovereignty over Lanzarote. In 1446, as already stated, Henry obtained from Afonso V exclusive rights of Portuguese navigation to the Canaries plus the agreement that he was to be paid the Fifth by any vessels that went there. Two years later, in 1448, Henry bought Maciot's rights to Lanzarote and immediately took charge of the government. Two caravels with Álvaro Dornelas and Antão Gonçalves, both Henry's retainers, were sent to the islands. Gonçalves was appointed captain, and all the officials were Portuguese. Henry assumed the title of Lord (*senhor*) of the island. This did not necessarily constitute sovereignty because Maciot, who was French, had held the island under Spanish sovereignty. Maciot was given a pension and went to live in Madeira.[70]

[66] Pedro Augusto de Azevedo, "Comércio anglo português" in *Boletim da Segunda Classe*, 8:53–66 (1913–14).

[67] Próspero Peragallo, *Cenni intorno alla colonia italiana*, pp. 10, 48–49; Ferdinand Columbus, *Columbus*, chap. 9; Bartolomé de las Casas, *Historia*, chap. 13.

[68] Francisque-Michel, *Portugais–Français*, pp. 12–13, 172.

[69] Pérez Embid "La política del Infante según los Pleitos Colombianos."

[70] Pérez Embid, *Descubrimientos*, pp. 143–149.

Inasmuch, however, as Henry was actively pushing claims to the area, his position of "senhor of Lanzarote" was more dangerous to Spanish sovereignty than Maciot's governorship had been. Juan II of Castile protested Henry's occupation through his agent Juan Iñigues de Atabe. Atabe was in the Portuguese court on two occasions before 1451 and there vigorously combatted the claims of the king of Portugal who wanted to force Hernán Peraza to appear before him and prove his rights to the islands that he held.

In 1451 two Spanish caravels under the command of Juan Iñigues de Atabe and accompanied by the bishop of the Canaries, Don Juan Cid, with twenty-five men of arms, was captured by an armada belonging to Prince Henry. In the same year other vessels sailing from Seville were captured by a Portuguese fleet of five caravels which Henry had sent against the island of Lanzarote. "The said five caravels cruised around all the other islands and robbed any vessels of this city [Seville] which they found, and on their return robbed this witness . . . of things his wife had sent in another caravel when she learned that her husband recently had stolen from him the things he carried."[71]

Atabe was again in Lisbon in 1452 accompanied by Diego Gonçalves de Ciudad Real, making another protest without receiving any specific satisfaction. Juan II in his letters to Afonso V referred to the many other letters "we have sent you." Juan II complained to Afonso V that armed men from eight Portuguese caravels and a pinnace (fusta) had stolen cattle and other animals, and had robbed the merchants of the Canaries who were Castilian subjects.[72] Spanish protests continued, the most vigorous coming in 1454 when Juan II made strong threats of taking action. In fact, Antão Gonçalves was expelled from Lanzarote by the Castilians in 1454.

Portugal was anxious to clinch its claims to lands discovered and to get to the Canaries as well. Juan II sent an embassy to Portugal in April or May 1454 to discuss a request by Henry to buy the claims of Diego García de Herrera to the Canaries. He referred to Guinea "which is of our conquests,"[73] and protested Henry's claims to the Canaries. However, Afonso V and Henry wanted a clear admission by Juan II that the islands were Portuguese.

On June 7, 1454, Afonso V conceded to the Order of Christ the

[71]Ibid.
[72]Ibid.
[73]Pérez Embid, Descubrimientos, pp. 158–165.

"spiritual administration and jurisdiction of Guinea, Nubia, and Ethiopia, or by whatever other names they may be called."[74] He stated that it would be referred to the pope for confirmation, as was later done. In the bull *Romanus Pontifex*, January 8, 1455, Nicolas V conceded to Portugal the coast of Africa from Bojador southward.[75] This was based on the previous mission given to the Order of Christ and the discoveries then in progress by Portugal. Later, in 1456, the privileges of the Order of Christ were again confirmed by the pope. All Christians, however, were prohibited from trading with the "Sarracens" in this region, or from navigating, trading, or fishing without the permission of the king of Portugal.

The death of Juan II and the accession of Enrique IV of Castile in 1454 was to give Portugal an advantage in the rivalry for Africa.[76] Enrique IV manifested indifference even to his claims to the Canaries. In 1455 he granted to two Portuguese counts, Atoujia and Villa Real, who accompanied Princess Juana to Spain to marry Enrique IV, lordship over Grand Canary and Tenerife, and over Palma, which was still occupied only by the natives. They sold their rights to Fernando, nephew of Henry the Navigator. This was a clear violation of the rights of the Herrera family who held Lanzarote, Fuerteventura, Gomera, and Hierro, as well as the concession to the unconquered islands. The Count of Villa Real requested

[74] Pérez Embid, *Descubrimientos*, p. 162, from Silva Marques, *Descobrimentos*, I, 518.

[75] Silva Marques, *Descobrimentos*, I, 503–513; Pérez Embid, *Descubrimientos*, pp. 161ff., note pp. 179–180, discusses this bull and two others previously promulgated with the same name. He considers the possibility that it was antedated at the request of Portugal. This bull would be dated January 8, 1455, by the calendar now in use. Beginning in 1098 and to the pontificate of Innocent XII (1691–1700) the papacy dated according to the "Year of the Incarnation" which began on March 25. Thus the dates between January 1 and March 24 must be advanced to the next year to coincide with our calendar — 1454 in the bull is 1455. The same is true of other papal dates, e.g., the bull *Inter Caetera* of March 13, 1455, papal dating, is 1456 our style. The usage among historians is not uniform in this regard. Pérez Embid gives 1454 (not 1455, the modern date) and dates *Inter Caetera* 1456. He makes no comment on the differences in dates. Damião Peres (*Descobrimentos portuguêses*, 2nd. edition, p. 46) gives 1454 and 1456 without mentioning the need to adjust the dates to the modern calendar. Luis Albuquerque says 1454 and 1456 (*História dos descobrimentos*, p. 231). Prestage (*Portuguese Pioneer*, p. 165) says 1454 and 1456. Boxer (*Portuguese Seaborne Empire*, pp. 20–21) gives 1455 and 1456. Lach (*Asia in the Making of Europe*, I, 152, note 8) cites *Romanus Pontifex* as 1455 and does not mention the 1456 bull. Davenport (*European Treaties*, I, pp. 13–26), explains proper dating. De Witte, "Les bulles pontificales," in *Revue d'Histoire Ecclesiastique*, lists and properly dates all the known bulls relating to Portuguese expansion.

[76] Pérez Embid describes this period as "years in which the sterility of policy was a consequence of the bitter rivalry of the stubborn factions, and this in turn was derived from the corruption that permeated all strata of Castilian life. The simeon-seeming Henry IV, sunk in the most unconfessable vices" was incompetent to defend Castilian interest. Pérez Embid, *Descubrimientos*, p. 165.

and obtained from Pope Pius II, on the urging of Afonso V, confirmation of the grant.

Enrique IV thus by neglect left Guinea open to the Portuguese. Not even Castilian fishing along the Moroccan coast was safe, "the Portuguese interfering even with the fishing to which the Andalusians applied themselves." Enrique IV was forced, according to the Spanish chronicler Alfonso de Palencia, to the humiliation of asking the king of Portugal not to molest his Castilian subjects when they went to Guinea to trade if they paid the Fifth of their cargoes to Afonso.[77]

The exclusive rights of Portugal to the African possessions was strengthened further by a bull *Inter Caetera* of Calixtus III, March 13, 1456, by which he gave the Order of Christ "all power, dominion and spiritual jurisdiction" over the regions reserved to Portugal.[78]

[77] Pérez Embid, *Descubrimientos*, pp. 166–172.
[78] *Ibid.*, p. 164; Silva Marquest, *Descobrimentos*, I, 535.

CHAPTER 6

Explorations to Guinea and the Cape Verde Islands

The Venetian Merchant Alvise da Cadamosto

While Portugal and Spain were contending for control of the coast of Africa, Portugal was pushing its claims by making new discoveries. The best record of this comes from Alvise da Cadamosto (1432–88), a young Venetian nobleman and merchant who arrived in Portugal in 1454 and became a participant in the discoveries. Cadamosto had trading experience in the Mediterranean and had made one trip to Flanders before arriving in Portugal.[1]

He embarked from Venice for England in the Flanders galleys August 8. Contrary winds forced them to stop over at Cape St. Vincent where, he says, "by chance I found myself not far from where Prince Henry was . . . at Raposeria." Henry sent a messenger to the galleys with "samples of sugar and dragon's blood" (a dye) from Madeira. The prince "had for sometime past" sent his sailors to seas "never before sailed" and had "discovered . . . strange races and many marvels." Cadamosto became intrigued with the idea of joining Henry's ventures and asked the conditions for going to Guinea. He was informed that "any who wished to sail" could do so under either of two conditions: he could fit out a caravel

---

[1] Alvise Cá da Mosto (Cadamosto), *Voyages of Cadamosto*, covering the period 1454 to 1463; Júlio Gonçalves, "Alvise de Cada Mosto"; João Franco Machado and D. Peres, eds. *Viagens de Cadamosto*; A. Fontoura da Costa, *Cartas de achamento das ilhas do Cabo Verde de Valentim Fernandes, 1506–1508*; Ernesto do Canto, "Diogo Gomes de Cintra"; John W. Blake, *European Beginnings in West Africa*, pp. 1–25; António da Silva Rêgo, "Reflexões sôbre a história Cabo Verdiana."

and load it with his own merchandise, paying one-fourth of the proceeds to Henry; or he could go in one of Henry's caravels and pay one-half of the proceeds. "If any of our nation wished to go there, the said lord would welcome him gladly." Cadamosto resolved to accept Henry's terms, disembarked, and the Venetian galleys rowed on to Flanders. Cadamosto was delighted to sail "toward the south to the land of the Blacks of lower Ethiopia," [2] where Henry's men were the first "to navigate in this portion of the ocean sea towards . . . lower Ethiopia." He called the caravels of Portugal "the best ships that sail the seas." [3]

Cadamosto embarked in a caravel of ninety batti (seventy tons?) belonging to Vicente Dias, on March 22, 1455, and reached Madeira on March 28. [4] In Madeira he found there were "800 men, among whom 100 horsemen." This should probably be understood as the total population or the total number of Europeans, not men only. His description of Madeira's products and exports indicates a very considerable prosperity with "many rich men . . . because it is all a garden and everything gathered there is gold." [5]

He went on to the Canaries and visited Gomera and Hierro, giving a good description of their people and products, and sighted Palma, Grand Canary, and Tenerife, which were still not conquered. "We set sail . . . always south toward Ethiopia . . . to Cape Blanco," which was 570 miles from the Canaries. The waters were dangerous because of the shoals and strong currents, and Cadamosto remarks that "one navigates only by day, with lead in hand." Two ships had already been wrecked in this region. He does not make clear just when. Inland from Cape Blanco some 350 miles to the east was Wadan, "frequented by Arabs

[2] The European of the fifteenth century thought of any direction south, east or west as "down," "Lower," or "under;" whereas we think of east or west as "out," south as "down," and north as "up."

[3] Cadamosto, Voyages, chap. 2. The various editions divide the text in different ways. For ease of consultation, the chapters referred to here are those of the English translation published by the Hakluyt Society, though all citations have been compared with the Portuguese text in Godinho, Documentos, III, 98–228, with the Italian and Portuguese in Silva Marques, Descobrimentos, I, suplemento, 164–248, and with my own translations. The earlier editions do not contain some matters found in the Ramusio edition of 1550, particularly Henry's learning. See Leite, Descobrimentos, I, 131–134, and the edition by the Academia Portuguesa de História, 1948.

[4] Godinho, Documentos, II, 114 and note 29, p. 187, discusses the doubts about date of sailing. See also, for the second voyage of Cadamosto, note 1, p. 210, where the same question of a March or May sailing arises, and Cadamosto, Voyages, chap. 1.

[5] Cadamosto, Voyages, chaps. 3–8, discusses the products of Porto Santo and Madeira; Godinho, Documentos, III, 118, note 9, summarizes the economy of Porto Santo and Madeira in the mid-fifteenth century.

who sent caravans from Timbuktu and other places in the Land of the Blacks." These merchants were Muslims, "hostile to Christians." Very numerous, they had many camels which they used to "carry brass and silver from Barbary . . . to Timbuktu . . . and to the Blacks." From the nomadic merchants Cadamosto bought Malagueta pepper.[6]

He mentions that Henry had established a trading post (*feitoria*) in the island of Arguim "and nobody . . . can trade there with the Arabs except those who hold a license." Arguim traded in a variety of merchandise, "especially wheat, of which they are always short," for blacks and gold. Henry was building a fort in Arguim "to guard this commerce forever. . . . Every year caravels come and go from Portugal to Arguim."[7]

Of the natives along the coast Cadamosto says "you should remember that these people have no knowledge of any Christians, except the Portuguese."[8] Arguim was a center of flourishing trade for the Portuguese throughout the second half of the fifteenth century and the beginning of the sixteenth.

Slaving: Ten Men for a Horse

The Arabs had many "Berber" horses which they exchanged in the "Land of the Blacks" for slaves — at a ratio of ten to fifteen slaves for one horse. Other items traded for slaves and gold were the Moorish silk from Granada and Tunis, and silver. "Every year," Cadamosto said, "the Portuguese take from Arguim 1000 slaves." Before the traffic was organized, "Portuguese caravels . . . descended on the land at night . . . [and] took men and women . . . to Portugal as slaves. Now for some time all have been at peace and have conducted trade. . . . The said Prince will not permit any further injury. . . . He hopes that by mixing with Christians they may . . . be converted."[9] The transformation from raids and piracy to a more legitimate commerce without the disappearance of either the raids or piracy may be seen in what Cadamosto relates.[10] Azurara

[6] Cadamosto, *Voyages*, chaps. 9–10.
[7] *Ibid.*, chap. 9; Godinho, *Documentos*, III, 125, and note 16, p. 179, discusses the possible dates for the beginning of *feitoria* and Fort Arguim, placing it not before 1455 and not after 1461.
[8] Cadamosto, *Voyages*, chap. 11.
[9] *Ibid.*, chap. 9.
[10] *Ibid.*; Godinho, *Documentos*, III, 127 and notes 18 and 19, pp. 180–181.

placed this change at about 1448, explaining as the reason for ending his work there that "the affairs of this area were thereafter always conducted more with commerce and mutual agreements than with force and feats of arms."[11]

Cadamosto described the salt-for-gold trade of the interior of Africa, which he heard of but did not see, in about the same way as Herodotus had. The traders on each side alternately piled up their offering and retired out of sight while the other side heaped up the amount they would exchange; the process was repeated until one of the trading parties accepted the exchange and carried away his "purchase." In a situation where a mutual language was not known and where neither party fully trusted the other, this was perhaps as good an arrangement as could be found. This was in the territory forbidden to whites which Ibn Battuta visited from 1352 to 1354.[12]

The gold gathered in the empire of Mali was divided into three portions: one went by caravan to Cairo; the second and third portions went to Timbuktu where they were again divided, one part going to Tunis and the Mediterranean coast, and the other to Oran, Fez, Safi, and Messa, where, says Cadamosto "we Italians and other Christians buy it from the Moors . . . and it is the best thing bought from the said land." The Portuguese *feitoria* on the island of Arguim was able to trade for part of this gold as well as for other products, thus depriving the Mediterranean of part of the Sahara caravan commerce.[13] Beyond Cape Blanco, Cadamosto sailed to the Senegal River, previously discovered by the Portuguese, to which he says "year after year the ships have continued to go to my time."[14]

Cadamosto's Admiration for the Africans

He was struck with the appearance of the people of "lower Ethiopia," i.e., the Senegal and beyond. "It seems to me a marvelous thing that beyond the river the people should be extremely black, tall, and have large,

[11] Azurara, *Crónica da Guiné*, chap. 96.

[12] Cadamosto, *Voyages*, chap. 11; and Godinho, *Documentos*, III, 129–131, note 23; E. W. Bovil, *The Golden Trade of the Moors*.

[13] Godinho, *Documentos*, III, 133–134.

[14] *Ibid.*, 136–137; the distance given by Cadamosto from Cape Blanco to the Senegal is 380 miles; Pereira's *Esmeraldo* gives 93 leagues or 372 miles, thus showing substantial agreement.

well-formed bodies, and the country is green, fertile, and heavily tim-
bered [while to the north the people are] mulatto colored, lean, dried up,
and short, and the country desert and poor." [15] He thought of the Senegal,
as did Azurara and others, as "a branch of the Gion [Nile]. . . . It flows
through all Ethiopia . . . [and]passing through Cairo it irrigates
. . . Egypt. This river has many very large branches . . . great rivers
on this coast of Ethiopia." [16] This erroneous geography had not been
entirely rejected a century later when Ramusio published Cadamosto's
manuscript and interpolated a section on the four rivers of the Terrestrial
Paradise. But in this green and rich land that Cadamosto calls "lower
Ethiopia," its people, the Jaloffs (Wolof), lived in "poverty and poor
culture" in "huts of straw." The king of this region "maintains himself with
robberies he orders of people, of his own as well as his neighbors . . . for slaves he sells to . . . Arabs who exchange them for
horses . . . and to Christians since they began trading here." [17]

Sailing beyond the Senegal southward in the direction of Cape Verde,
Cadamosto came to the territory of a chieftain he called Budomel
(Damel). Here he disembarked, "having been informed by certain Portuguese" about the friendliness and possibilities of trade with Budomel,
"a person in whom one could have faith and trust." Cadamosto gave him
the horses he had brought for trade and was invited to go to the king's
house twenty-five miles inland. He was promised 100 slaves for "seven
horses . . . which cost 300 ducats" and other merchandise. The going
rate was nine to fourteen slaves for a horse. The king presented
Cadamosto with a gift Cadamosto prized very highly, a girl of twelve to
thirteen, "very beautiful for being so black." [18]

Traveling a few miles inland with Budomel, Cadamosto found the king
installed without much wealth but with great ceremony, surrounded by
his wives, slaves, and subjects, in a village of grass huts where Budomel
lived. [19] His subjects were treated with great haughtiness, being allowed
to approach him only nude, prostrate, and throwing dirt over their heads
and backs. For the slightest offense they and their families might be
seized as slaves. Cadamosto spoke of Christianity to Budomel, who was a
Muslim. Budomel thought both religions were good. He consulted

[15] Cadamosto, *Voyages*, chaps. 12–14; Godinho, *Documentos*, III, 135–137.
[16] Cadamosto, *Voyages*, chap. 14, p. 28, note 2, of Hakluyt translation and chap. 15.
[17] Cadamosto, *Voyages*, chaps. 16–20; Godinho, *Documentos*, III, 138–142.
[18] Cadamosto, *Voyages*, chap. 20; Godinho, *Documentos*, III, 143–145.
[19] Cadamosto, *Voyages*, chap. 21.

Cadamosto who, "being a Christian," knew so many things and was so wise, as "the Christians were," about how to satisfy his many wives. Cadamosto does not record his answer for the benefit of Budomel, nor, alas, for us.[20] In the local market Cadamosto was struck by the general poverty, the lack of things for which he could trade, and particularly the absence of gold. Men and women crowded around him wondering if his whiteness was paint, touching him and rubbing him with spit to see if it would come off. Finding it would not, "they were amazed."[21]

The ability of Europeans to sail over the water appeared to the blacks to be diabolical because they did not understand "the art of navigation, the compass, nor the chart" — a statement that has caused much debate about how much was then known of the astrolabe and the quadrant, which Cadamosto does not mention. This may be considered an indication that as of 1455 these instruments were not yet in use by sailors — for the navigators on his voyages were Portuguese.[22]

Usodimare Joins Cadamosto: Maritime Insurance

Cadamosto decided to sail further south. At the moment of sailing he saw two ships and knew they could be "nothing other than Christians." One of the vessels belonged to, or was freighted by, Antoniotto Usodimare (1416–62?), a Genoese merchant who was making a desperate effort to recoup his finances and pay his creditors, and the other to one of Henry's retainers. The next day the three ships reached Cape Verde, which Cadamosto estimated to be thirty Italian miles from where he had stopped with Budomel. The ships dropped anchor just beyond Cape Verde at three small uninhabited islands, which did not have fresh water. The following day they sailed on "always in sight of land," and they saw "numerous green trees, large and beautiful, growing . . . along the beach as if they had come down to drink from the ocean, which is beautiful to see." Cadamosto's pleasure in what he was observing was limitless. "In spite of having voyaged to many areas of the Levant and the West, I never saw a more beautiful land." Still further on, the coast was inhabited by people who had no king or lord, "because they did not want their women and children sold for slaves as is done by the kings and lords of

[20]*Ibid.*, chap. 22.
[21]*Ibid.*, chap. 31.
[22]*Ibid.*, chap. 33.

other Negro lands."[23] The thick forest in which they lived and the poison-ous arrows which they used had enabled them, according to Cadamosto, to remain free in spite of efforts of the surrounding kings to capture them.

As Cadamosto sailed southward he came to a large river, which was perhaps the same one discovered in 1446. He estimated his distance from Cape Verde at sixty miles "as noted on the navigation chart made in that country [Portugal]."[24] To get a better view of the coast and to ensure their safety, the caravels often sailed only during the day and anchored at night. He sent an interpreter ashore "because every ship had Negro interpreters brought from Portugal . . . sold by the lords of the Senegal to the first Portuguese . . . Christians . . . who knew the Spanish [sic] language well." The unfortunate interpreter was slain by the natives soon after he landed. With this impolite reception "we hoisted our sails . . . following our route south," keeping in sight of the shore which "was ever more beautiful" until they reached what was perhaps the Gambia River. Up river they found natives "who were surprised at something their ancestors had never seen — ships with white men." Cadamosto could have found natives who had not seen Europeans, even if there had been previous visitors who landed even a short distance away. Cadamosto makes it clear the Portuguese had already been along this coast. Vallarte may also have visited this river before 1455.[25] They were surrounded by blacks, with whom they fought, killing a great many. After the battle they asked why the blacks fought and were told, "We have heard of you . . . and know for certain that Christians eat human flesh and buy Negroes for no other purpose but to eat them."[26] The commanders of the ships wanted to sail on but were forced by a sailor's mutiny "to return, in God's name, to Spain [Portugal]."

The few remarks that Cadamosto made concerning astronomical mat-ters and navigation indicate that his navigators used neither astrolabe nor quadrant. "We did not see the North Star more than once during the days we were in the mouth of this river; it appeared very low over the sea, seeming to be about a lance-length above the horizon; and to see it the

[23]*Ibid.*, chaps. 34–35.

[24]The same distance given in Pereira's *Esmeraldo*, chap. 28, 15 leagues (60 miles).

[25]However, Valentim Fernandes attributes this discovery to 1455. Historians who seek to find "exactly" where Cadamosto and others touched on this coast, and to determine if any explorers arrived before Cadamosto, find this statement disturbing. The Portuguese explorer Nuno Tristão had reached this coast and had been killed by the natives but pre-cisely where is a matter of dispute.

[26]Cadamosto, *Voyages*, chaps. 36–38.

weather had to be very clear." The *Carro do Sul*, or Southern Cross, was also seen, consisting of six bright stars, in the shape of a cross lying on its side. Cadamosto made a drawing, but there is no mention of the position in degrees.[27]

Antoniotto Usodimare made a few additional comments of value.[28] In a letter he wrote to his creditors in Genoa, he made it appear that he was alone and does not mention Cadamosto. He said he was given forty slaves by a Negro noble as well as some elephant tusks, parrots, and a little musk, from which perfume is made. He shared the geographical misconceptions of the times, stating that "it was only 300 leagues . . . to the boundaries of the territory of Prester John."

The most interesting information in Usodimare's letter, perhaps, is his request that his creditors have patience with him for six months, "more so because I have taken out insurance."[29] Such casual mention of sea insurance indicates how customary this must have been in Portugal in the mid-fifteenth century.

The Cape Verde Islands

In 1456 Cadamosto and Usodimare, each with a caravel and accompanied by another sent by Henry, sailed from Lagos in the beginning of May.[30] They passed the Canaries with favoring winds, and pushed by "a current of water which flows with impetus toward the southwest," they passed Cape Blanco. On the following night they were caught in a storm which blew from the southwest. "In order not to turn back we stood out to sea,

[27] *Ibid.*, chap. 39; Godinho, *Documentos*, III, 174–175 and note 50, p. 191. Polaris is difficult to see owing to its low altitude and to the haze along the coast at times. Some Portuguese historians use Cadamosto's words as an indication that he was not a navigator, which was perhaps true. He was primarily a merchant. Today the Southern Cross has five stars, one of which is very dim.

[28] Antoniotto Usodimare was a member of a seagoing and merchant family in Genoa. He is not to be confused with the man of the same name who lived in Lisbon as early as 1442, nor with António de Noli who also made an expedition along the African coast and discovered some of the Cape Verde Islands. Godinho, *Documentos*, III, 98, notes 1 and 2.

[29] Godinho, *Documentos*, III, 98–104.

[30] Cadamosto, *Voyages*, chap. 40. The starting date for Cadamosto's second voyage is given as May 1 in the Ramusio edition and in the sixteenth-century copies of Cadamosto, but as the beginning of March in the oldest known text of Cadamosto, *Viagens de Luiz de Cadamosto e Pedro de Sintra*, edited by Machado and Peres, p. 60 in the Italian text, p. 157 in the Portuguese text. Godinho, *Documentos*, III, 193ff., discusses the confusion surrounding the sailing date, citing various views, but he accepts May as being in accord with the early Cadamosto manuscripts. Crone in his introduction to the Hakluyt edition, p. xxvi and p. 63, note 4, prefers March.

WNW if I am not mistaken, to skirt around and withstand the weather, two nights and three days" (*per costegiare e parare il tempo*).[31] The third day they sighted land. The islands they found fit the description of the Cape Verdes, but the direction sailed from Cape Blanco, if Cadamosto was "not mistaken," would not have brought them to these islands nor to other land. The storm that has raged among historians about Cadamosto's narrative is far greater than the storm the caravels encountered. Cadamosto's storm ended in three days; the storm over what he discovered has lasted five centuries. Many suggestions have been proposed to make his statement sound more reasonable. If we could assume a misprint and substitute Cape Verde for Cape Blanco,[32] the west and northwest direction Cadamosto thought they sailed would make sense. The question is still without a firm answer; but inasmuch as his description of the islands discovered fits the Cape Verde Islands, the weight of the reasons for considering him the discoverer outbalances that against.[33]

The Cape Verde Islands were not inhabited, and Cadamosto made no effort to explore them. "I wished to . . . continue my voyage." Afterward when others were attracted there by the news of the four he had found, ten islands were discovered. Sailing south from Cape Verde he reached the Gambia River again. He ascended it "sixty or more miles," where he established trade with the local king named Batimança, and obtained some slaves, but only small amounts of gold "in comparison with what we hoped to find."[34] Remaining there some days[35] they traded with the Negroes and obtained "cotton thread and cloth . . . very well made, . . . shells, parrots, civit cats, skins and fruits . . . at very low price."[36] The natives killed an elephant and gave it to Cadamosto. He

[31] Cadamosto, *Voyages*, chaps. 40–41; second voyage, chap. 1, in Silva Marques, *Descobrimentos, suplemento*, 231. This text was taken from the Rinaldo Caddeo edition.

[32] The desire to discredit Cadamosto has been strong since 1884 when José Joaquim Lopes de Lima published the first volume of his *Ensaios sobre a statística das posessões portuguêzas na África ocidental e oriental*. Some historians deny that Cadamosto made a second voyage. There are enough discrepancies in Cadamosto's writings, as in those of every other chronicler or historian of discoveries, to warrant skepticism. For example, there are no islands off Cape Blanco that fit the description. If we admit a slip of the pen and substitute Cape Verde for Blanco, what Cadamosto wrote seems more reasonable. See Godinho, *Documentos*, III, 194, note 2, for a long discussion on Cadamosto and his commentators.

[33] See the Machado-Peres edition of Cadamosto for reasons to reject Cadamosto as the discoverer of the Cape Verde Islands.

[34] Cadamosto, *Voyages*, chap. 40; Godinho, *Documentos*, III, 189–199.

[35] The number of days is given as two, eleven, and fifteen in different copies of the Cadamosto manuscript.

[36] Cadamosto, *Voyages*, chap. 42.

tried it "baked and stewed" in order "to be able to say that we had eaten an animal that nobody in my country had tried."[37] He did not find the "delicacy" very good. He took one of its feet, the trunk, a lot of the hair, and some of the meat "that I had salted," to Prince Henry, "who received it all as a great present because it was the first thing he had received from that land discovered through his initiative."[38] Cadamosto describes in detail the birds, fish, snakes, and other animals of the African coast.

Leaving the Gambia and sailing southward along a dangerous coast, "navigating only by day . . . and dropping anchor at night," he reached the Casamansa(?) in two days and further on a cape he named "red Cape." Still farther he encountered the São Domingos (Cacheu? Monsoa?) and the Rio de Santa Ana (Geba?). Here natives in dugouts (almadias), one of which "was almost as large as our caravel but not as high" and carried thirty blacks, came alongside Cadamosto's caravel. All efforts of the Europeans and Africans to find a common language failed. The expedition decided to return to Portugal. Here, says Cadamosto, "the North Star was seen very low."[39]

This was the limit of Cadamosto's second voyage. On the return they found the Bijagós Islands, inhabited by blacks. This is the first known reference to the archipelago of Bijagós commonly known in the fifteenth century as the Ilhas of Baum.[40]

Who Discovered the Cape Verde Islands?

Some have thought it somewhat strange that Cadamosto, who clearly believed himself the first to see the Cape Verde Islands, made no claims to nor asked for a grant to any of the Cape Verdes. It must be noted, however, that he was a merchant on a trading expedition, primarily interested in making a fortune that would enable him to return to Venice

[37]*Ibid.*, chap. 43. The English Hakluyt version leaves out "It was not on this voyage that I saw them [elephants], rather in another on which I entered the Gambia river aboard a caravel." This statement is found in fifteenth-century manuscripts but not in later versions. From it can be inferred a third Cadamosto voyage not indicated elsewhere. See Machado-Peres, *Viagens de Cadamosto*, and Godinho, *Documentos*, III, 203, note on pp. 219–220.

[38]Cadamosto, *Voyages*, chap. 43.

[39]On the dangerous waters here, see Avelino Teixeira da Mota, "A descoberta da Guiné," in *Boletim Cultural da Guiné Portuguesa*, I, 1946, quoted in Godinho, *Documentos*, III, 206, note 22, p. 220; Cadamosto, *Voyages*, chaps. 46–47; Peres, *Descobrimentos portugueses*, p. 135.

[40]Pereira, *Esmeraldo*, chap. 31; Godinho, *Documentos*, III, 226, note 28.

(which he did in 1463) to take part in the public life of his city, and that he never manifested any desire to become a donatary, as did António de Noli, who was later to discover and hold Santiago in the Cape Verdes.[41]

The account given by Cadamosto quite clearly shows the regularity of trade along the Guinea coast. In fact, steady trade and small additional coastal discoveries were the rule. An illustration of this may be seen in a letter of Afonso V, 1456, concerning a caravel that was to go to Guinea. It was to pick up clothes in Odeana in Portugal for shipment to Safi in Morocco to be traded for cloaks (*alquices*) which in turn were to be taken to Guinea.[42] This episode helps to establish two points: the Portuguese customarily traded with the Muslims in certain products, and a regular trade with Guinea had been established. The connection between expansion in Morocco and exploration along the coast is also evident.

The first official document relating to Cape Verde Islands is dated December 3, 1460, by which Afonso V gave to his brother Fernando, the adopted son of Henry the Navigator and Henry's heir by his last will and testament, the known islands of Cape Verde.[43]

A *carta régia* (royal letter) of September 19, 1462, attributed the discovery of the Cape Verde Islands to the Italian António de Noli. Diogo Gomes in his memoirs, told to Martin Behaim and preserved in the manuscript of Valentim Fernandes, attributes the discoveries to himself and to Noli. He says they were sailing in two caravels and returning from the "Terra dos Barbacins" (region of the Gambia River) to Portugal, at a long distance from the coast, when they saw the islands. Gomes relates that his caravel was swifter; "I arrived first at one of those islands."[44] Gomes does not indicate clearly the year of his voyage. Having stated that his voyage to Guinea was made in 1456, two years before the conquest of

[41] Almeida, *História de Portugal*, II, 99, attributes the discovery of the Cape Verde Islands to António de Noli and discusses the sources at length. Godinho, *Documentos*, III, 272ff., discusses the claims of Cadamosto, Diogo Gomes, and António de Noli to the title of discoverer. The suggestions made by F. C. Wieder that Vincente Dias discovered the Cape Verde Islands in 1445 and that they are the mysterious islands on the Bianco map of 1448 are discussed and dismissed as unproven by Godinho, *Documentos*, III, 272–276. Crone, in his introduction to the Hakluyt edition of Cadamosto, holds there is no reason to reject a Cadamosto discovery of 1456 and to accept a later Noli voyage, perhaps accompanied by Gomes. Damião Peres says Cadamosto *could have* included Noli's voyage as his own.
[42] Godinho, *Documentos*, III, 95–97.
[43] A document dated September 18, 1460, allegedly mentioned the Cape Verde Islands, but this document contains no reference to the Cape Verdes. Oliveira Boleo cited it without having read it and drew erroneous conclusions. Peres, *Descobrimentos portugueses*, p. 189, notes 2 and 3; Godinho, *Documentos*, III, 276–281.
[44] Cited in Peres, *Descobrimentos portugueses*, p. 195, note 1.

Alcácer-Seguer, he adds that in 1458 there was sent to King Nominans, whom he does not identify but who no doubt was one of the several Negro kings in the Guinea area, a priest and an assistant to instruct him. Gomes then follows this with an account of the death of Henry in 1460. Next he treats the voyages in which he says he discovered the Cape Verde Islands. "Two years later King Afonso outfitted a large caravel of which he made me captain." This leaves possibilities of the two years being counted from 1456, 1458, or 1460, making his discovery in 1458, 1460, or 1462. The grant to Noli in September 1462 is a strong indication that the Gomes-Noli discovery was in that year.[45] Would Noli have waited two (or four) years to make his claim? The Spanish chronicler Alfonso de Palencia, however, writing some twenty years later than the discovery, attributes it to Noli.[46] The seven western Cape Verdes were discovered by the Portuguese Diogo Afonso, a squire of the household of Prince Fernando, brother of King Afonso V, as shown in a *carta régia* of September 19, 1462, and another of October 28 of the same year. Prince Fernando was granted the government of the islands by the king.[47]

Portugal and the Fall of the Byzantine Empire

During the years the Portuguese were developing their trade and exploring the African coast and the Atlantic islands, they were confronted with a European situation which offered both a problem and an opportunity — the fall of Constantinople to the Turks in 1453. The standard interpretation of this event is that it "sent a stream of refugees and tremors of fear, shock, and despair throughout Christendom. The permanence of Ottoman conquest in Europe was now guaranteed by the elimination of the only strategic base which Christendom could use against the Turks."[48] That Europe felt tremors of "fear, shock, and despair" there is no doubt. But the experience did not shake the European nations from their centuries-old division and bring them to a unified opposition to the Ottoman Empire.[49] Rather, the continued expansion of the Ottomans into the

[45]*Ibid.*, p. 203.
[46]Alonso de Palencia, *Crónica de Henrique IV*, tr., Paz y Melia, IV, 215–216, quoted in Peres, *Descobrimentos portuguêses*, p. 203. For a good discussion see Peres, *'Descobrimentos portuguêses*, pp. 189–205.
[47]Godinho, *Documentos*, III, 279–281, 295–298.
[48]Paul Coles, *The Ottoman Impact on Europe*, p. 26.
[49]The kings of England and France, and the Emperor of Germany showed no interest in

Balkans and the throttling of Greek and Genoese merchant colonies in the Black Sea, diverting a profitable trade in grain, horses, fish, lead, and south Russian slaves into Turkish channels, served mainly to stimulate Christian traders to attempt to make a better deal with the Turks. The end of the Hundred Years War between England and France in the same year could have released experienced Christian fighting men to go against the Infidels, but it did not. England became embroiled in a destructive civil war, the War of the Roses. The French monarchy was absorbed in intrigues against powerful vassals within the country and against its neighbors as well. French merchants engaged in trade in the Mediterranean as usual. France was more often allied with than against the Ottomans.

The fall of Constantinople was to have a lasting effect on Portugal's future. In an effort to end the normal relationship among the Italian cities, which was rivalry and warfare over trade, Pope Nicolas V brought about a temporary peace signed in Lodi in April 1454 and later was able to form a league with the objective of defending Italy from the Turks and avoiding French intervention in the Italian peninsula.

The first direct influence of the events in the eastern Mediterranean on Portugal came from the call of Pope Calixtus III in bulls issued February 15, March 12, and 23, 1456, and April 10, 1457, for a united front of Christians against the Muslim advances.[50] In February 1456 Calixtus authorized Afonso V to raise money for the war against the Turks by granting him the tithe of "all ecclesiastical revenues." Afonso also struck off a new gold coin which he named the cruzado. He promised to send 12,000 troops at his own cost, which demanded heavy expenses — "not," says Rui de Pina, "without great lamentations in the kingdom."[51] The death of Calixtus III, August 8, 1458, ended the efforts to organize a Crusade. Inasmuch as the other Christian kingdoms had not responded favorably,

the Crusade. The German clergy refused to contribute anything. Philip the Good of Burgundy promised an army, and the kings of Aragon and Portugal promised fleets. Godinho, *Documentos*, III, 232, notes 2, 3, quoting Henry Pirenne, et al., *La fin du Moyen Âge*. Portugal had sent fifteen vessels which returned when it became evident there would be no Crusade.

[50] Almeida, *História de Portugal*, II, 104, note 1. Afonso V began preparing an army at least as early as 1456. One interpretation of Afonso V's intention is that he already had in mind an attack in Africa and used the call to Crusade as a convenient way to raise money and armed forces while at the same time diverting the Moroccans from his real purpose. Godinho, *Documentos*, III, note 5 on p. 232 and p. 260.

[51] Almeida, *História de Portugal*, II, 104–106; Peres, *História de Portugal*, III, 107–114; Godinho, *Documentos*, III, 231–244, note 5 citing Pina, *Crónica Affonso V*, chaps. 135–138.

the army Afonso V had raised for the Crusade was now turned toward an attack on Alcácer-Seguer in Morocco.

Thus the fall of Constantinople became for Portugal one of a series of events that led to the affirmation of Portugal's ambition to establish itself firmly in Africa. Whether Portugal could or would have renewed its own African campaign at this time without the assistance rendered by Pope Calixtus III in his efforts to stimulate a Crusade is not certain; but in any case Portugal was alert to take advantage of the situation to pursue its own policies.

Capture of Alcácer-Seguer, 1458

Rui de Pina (1440–1522), chronicler of Afonso V and other Portuguese kings, was the first to mention the fear in Portugal of the Turkish advance in the eastern Mediterranean. If it cannot be proved that the Portuguese actions in northern Africa and along the coast resulted from the fear of Turkish advances, nor that Portugal was directly affected by it after this time, it is not difficult nevertheless to imagine that the Portuguese, conscious of Muslim power in Granada and Africa and in constant fear of the Muslims, would see the capture of Constantinople as one more threat to themselves. The Portuguese concept of a Crusade was to fight the Muslims near at hand, combining the religious motive with their own strategic and economic objectives. Afonso V would have participated in a general attack on the Turks if it had developed; but when such an attack did not come, he was quick to use his forces in North Africa.

Some twenty years had elapsed since the disaster at Tangier in 1437, and Muslim pressure on Ceuta had not let up. At some time between 1456 and 1458, Afonso V had decided to direct his efforts toward the conquest of another city in Africa. A small incident revealed the royal plans. On February 26, 1456, Afonso ordered the confiscation of the goods of Davy Maalom, a Jewish resident in Lagos, because Davy had allegedly sent a letter to the *alcaide* of Safi warning him that the Portuguese were sending a caravel to scout the fortifications. It was, according to the king, "a great lie in our disservice." Whether it was, as the king stated, a falsehood, or whether, as some modern historians say, it merely forced the Portuguese to change the objective of the attack, the letter does correctly portray the state of Portuguese thinking.[52]

[52] Godinho, *Documentos*, III, 228–229.

The most likely points of conquest in Morocco were Safi, Tangier, and Alcácer-Seguer. Ceuta was reinforced in 1457 to ward off a threat of attack by the king of Fez. Alcácer-Seguer was finally chosen. King Afonso embarked in Setúbal at the end of September 1458, stopped over in Sagres where Henry awaited him, paused again in Lagos for a few days to wait for the fleets from Porto and the Mondego, and sailed on October 17. The fleet, estimated by Rui de Pina at 220 sails and 25,000 fighting men, arrived before Alcácer on October 21 and captured the city two days later. The Portuguese were now well situated to guard their line of communications southward.[53]

Henry petitioned the king on December 26, 1457, to grant to the Order of Christ the spiritualities and patronage from Cape Nun south, in accordance with the bull of Calixtus III, dated March 13, 1456, to which reference has already been made. He requested that a tax of a "Twentieth" be paid to the Order on all "the slaves, male and female, gold, and fish, as well as all other goods and merchandise." The king made the grant by royal letter on January 4, 1458.[54]

Portuguese Expansion to the Death of Henry, 1460

Portuguese discoveries during the last year of Henry's life, or immediately following his death, were carried as far as Sierra Leone. Cadamosto writes: "After me others went, principally two caravels outfitted by the king which he sent after the death of Prince Henry, the captain of which was Pedro de Sintra, squire of [Henry] . . . to discover new lands."[55] Not all agree that Sintra sailed for the first time after Henry died. He made two voyages, on one of which he was accompanied by Soeiro da Costa. The first, according to modern investigation, could have been January 1460, before Henry died on November 13, of that year, and the second in July or August 1461.[56] The farthest point he reached was somewhere along the coast of Sierra Leone or slightly farther south. The exact point is impossible to locate with existing information. A contention

[53] Damião de Gois says "280 ships (naus), galleys and other vessels (navios) for supplies and service," and 26,000 men; Godinho, Documentos, III, 240–245. All statistics of this type should be regarded as estimates only. The figures agree closely but seem extremely high.
[54] Godinho, Documentos, I, 147–152.
[55] Ibid., III, 305.
[56] Cadamosto, Voyages, chap. 47; Godinho, Documentos, III, 210, 312, and note 21 on page 317.

based on complicated reasoning that Henry's caravels had attained a point in lower Angola or southwest Africa, sustained principally by Jaime Cortesão, has not gained the support of leading Portuguese historians.[57] The most defensible position is that of Damião Peres: "We can accept no other conclusion than that Sierra Leone was the farthest limit of African discoveries in Prince Henry's lifetime."[58]

Henry had granted two of the Azores, Terceira and Graciosa, to his nephew Fernando on August 22, 1460. Afonso V approved this grant on September 2. Fernando had in 1457 been conceded the possession of islands he "might discover."[59] Fernando was Henry's chief heir. After Henry died on November 13, 1460, the king specifically gave to Fernando the Madeiras and the Azores as well as Santiago, Fogo, Maio, Boa Vista, and Sal in the Cape Verdes. There is nothing specific in Henry's will ordering further explorations or mentioning any search for Prester John or India.[60]

When the seven western Cape Verde Islands were discovered in 1462, Fernando received those by a *carta régia* of September 19, 1462. Two captaincies were established in the island of Santiago at this time. On the south side, Ribeira Grande was ceded to António de Noli. The north side went to Diogo Afonso for finding the seven western islands. To encourage settlement, Fernando obtained from the king on June 12, 1466, a charter (*foral*) for the inhabitants of the Cape Verdes and Guinea, with fiscal, civil, and judicial powers. On payment of stipulated royal taxes the Capeverdians could trade freely in their own merchandise, both in the islands and outside. They were free from customs duties on their goods sent to the homeland and were to have a monopoly of the commerce of the African coast in the areas already discovered, approximately from the Senegal River to Sierra Leone.

Both António de Noli and Diogo Afonso, with the inducements they could offer settlers under the terms of their captaincies, established colonies of Europeans in Santiago. Later other colonists came. This was the first colony of Europeans established in a tropical region. The Portuguese by this time had been some twenty or more years in the wet tropics. Their

[57] J. Cortesão, *Descobrimentos portugêses*, I, 360–384; Leite, *Descobrimentos*, I, 323–339, 411–449, rejects with solid documentation the Cortesão position; Godinho, *Documentos*, III, 305; Peres, *Descobrimentos portuguêses*, pp. 139ff.

[58] *Ibid.*, pp. 152–166.

[59] Godinho, *Documentos*, I, 217–220.

[60] Almeida, *História de Portugal*, II, 106–110.

success in settling the Cape Verde Islands at this time and parts of the African coast later shows an adjustment by the Portuguese to the blacks (who were also brought into the Cape Verde Islands as slaves) not equalled by any other Europeans. Along the African coast they traded goods of European origin, mainly cotton cloth, beads, gewgaws, dyes, soaps, horses, burros, metals, and salt from their own salt pans, in exchange for black slaves, ivory, malagueta, wax, hides, and gold (in small quantities). This part of the coast never supplied the Portuguese with the great amounts of gold believed to exist in the interior around the legendary Timbuktu.

The natives of this area of Africa were in fact extremely poor and had neither much to sell nor, therefore, the means to buy. They, themselves, as slaves, became the most valuable commercial product. Slave trade was normal among the African natives, and Christian traders were able to divert to themselves a portion of the trade which had for centuries been carried overland by Muslim merchants. The Christians justified their actions by believing that they were saving the souls of the enslaved people.[61]

[61] João Barreto, *História da Guiné*, pp. 64–68.

CHAPTER 7

Henry "The Navigator" Who Followed His Stars

Was Henry a Learned Man?

So great were the accomplishments of Portugal between 1415 and 1460 that some historians have sought to reconstruct the period in a rational way and ascribe it all to a plan. So great was the contribution of Henry that many have given to him sole credit for Portuguese expansion and called him "The Navigator." He has become an untouchable, almost a sainted figure not to be criticized. Yet the facts seem to be that Portugal's expansion was no more the result of a "plan" than was the national expansion of other nations and that Henry was the most important but by no means the only person pushing expansion. For many, understanding Henry has necessitated viewing him as a learned man of vast reading and study, and as an inspired man who in his youth established himself in Sagres, had the Villa do Infante built, gathered round him learned scientists, established a school of cosmography, astronomy, and navigation, designed new types of ships and navigational instruments, founded the first astronomical observatory in Europe, and with single-minded determination sent his men to seek far-away India.[1] Perhaps Henry was greater

[1] Works about Henry include: Fortunato de Almeida, *O Infante de Sagres*; Charles Raymond Beazley, *Prince Henry the Navigator*; Joaquim Bensaúde, *A cruzada do Infante D. Henrique*; Mendes de Brito, *O Infante D. Henrique*; José Moreira de Campos, *O Infante D. Henrique*; Maria Alice M. Côrte-Real, "As Índias Orientais no plano henriquino"; António Dominguez de Sousa Costa, "O Infante D. Henrique na expansão portuguêsa"; A. Fontoura da Costa, "Vila do Infante"; Costa Brochado, *Infante D. Henrique*; Francisco Fernandes Lopes, *A figura e a obra do Infante*; Cândido Lusitano, *Vida do Infante D. Henrique*;

as a man because none of these things were true; if they were true, there is insufficient evidence to prove them so.

Charles Raymond Beazley, Luciano Pereira da Silva, and, most recently, Jaime Cortesão, are three writers among the many who have lauded Henry's learning.[2] Nevertheless such learning is not attested to by his contemporaries or near contemporaries. For example, Cadamosto, Azurara, Mateu de Pisano, and Diogo Gomes, all contemporaries, and Duarte Pacheco Pereira and Rui de Pina, who lived a generation later, "do not confirm the high culture of the Prince. They held this culture in such little esteem that they pass it over in silence, where it would be expected they would exault it."[3]

Cadamosto is usually cited as lauding Henry's erudition. The earliest texts of his works, however, do not contain the praise found in the sixteenth-century editions, which have interpolations, made perhaps by Ramusio, the sixteenth-century editor who sometimes amended what he published.[4] The *Chronica de Guiné*, a work in which Henry was extravagantly praised by Azurara, should contain, if anything does, information about his learning; "There is not found, nevertheless, one single word of his love of books, neither in this chronicle nor in other chronicles by [Azurara]."[5]

No contemporary mentions Henry as an inventor of astronomical instruments, nor as an improver of the astrolabe, quadrant, or compass, all known long before his time. Nor does any contemporary praise his knowledge of astronomy. All these attributions came from later times, not earlier than seventy years after his death. Henry was not learned in geography nor was he a mathematician. Those who knew him confirmed that he introduced no new navigational skills. If he passed long nights in

Richard Henry Major, *The Life of Prince Henry of Portugal*; T. O. Marcondes de Souza, "O Infante D. Henrique"; Elaine Sanceau, *Henry the Navigator*; A Moreira de Sá, *O Infante Dom Henrique e a universidade*. Henry made a small contribution to the University of Coimbra for the teaching of theology but not for mathematics or science.

[2] J. Cortesão, *Descobrimentos portugueses*, I, 227–249; 295–317; 390–400. For the most realistic view of Henry, see Leite, *Descobrimentos*, I, 67–237, and *passim*. Leite is very caustic in writing about the "Lenda Henriquina" as supported by such historians as Jaime Cortesão, Costa Brochado, and others of the "romantic" school, but basically he is an admirer of Henry's great accomplishments. The origin of the romantic school may be seen in João Pedro de Oliveira Martins, *Os filhos de Dom João I*. See also Francis M. Rogers, *The Travels of the Infante Dom Pedro*, pp. 242, 250–266, for comments.

[3] Leite, *Descobrimentos*, I, 131.

[4] *Ibid.*, I, 133–134.

[5] *Ibid.*, 141.

scientific reading or quiet meditation, or if he was of a contemplative nature, the records do not tell us so.[6]

Statements that he read Strabo, Edrisi, and Ptolemy or the "two" Arabic mathematicians Al Hazin and Alboacim (who are the same person) are not substantiated. He is sometimes credited with having read the works of little known authors such as Rabi-Zac, the geography of Avicenna (who wrote on medicine), the geography of Ptolemy (of which there was no known copy in Portugal in his time), Regiomontanus (who wrote after Henry died), Cicero, Seneca, Caesar, Vasco de Lobeira, the Count of Lucanor, *The Confessions of St. Augustine*, romances of chivalry such as the *Amadis de Gaula*, and the *Libros del saber da la astronomia* of Alfonso the Wise, of which no copy was known in Portugal until the sixteenth century.[7] He could have read the copy of *The Book of Marco Polo*, said to have been brought from Venice by his brother Pedro in 1428. There was a copy of *Marco Polo* in Duarte's library; whether it was the same copy or another is not known.

The "School" of Sagres

If Henry's personal erudition cannot be verified, what of the school of Sagres and the scientists said to have taught and studied there? Azurara does not mention a school. One of the most careful modern historians, Duarte Leite, speaks scornfully of the "famous nautical school of Sagres, which even today, in spite of mortal blows, continues to live in the belief of legions of people."[8] "Among the numerous legends which embellish our history," says the same historian, "this one stands out for two characteristics: it is exotic, it came to us from England via France, and it contains not one whit of truth whatever in essentials or details."[9] The first to mention a school was the English historian Samuel Purchas in the seventeenth century, who quoted João de Barros with reference to Jacome de Mallorca. But Barros says nothing of a school. The legend grew in the seventeenth and eighteenth centuries. In 1836 the Portuguese government erected a plaque at Sagres: "The great Prince Henry founded

---

[6]*Ibid.*, 141, 160–161, 225–226, 245.

[7]Albuquerque, *Descobrimentos*, pp. 233–244, believes that an incomplete fourteenth-century copy found in Portugal shows it might have been accessible to Henry.

[8]Leite, *Descobrimentos*, I, 161. For a defense of the "school" see Alexandre Gaspar de Naia, "Não é um mito a escola náutica Henrique."

[9]Leite, *Descobrimentos*, I, 161–162.

here . . . a palace, the famous school of cosmography, the astronomical observatory and the naval arsenal." [10] In 1868 the English historian Henry Major, noted that he accepted the belief in the school but indicated that "some doubted." The Marquis de Souza Holstein introduced a serious caveat when in 1877 he rejected the belief that a school had existed but suggested that a scientific academy had. By 1894 Brito Rebello rejected the academy idea, Henry's mathematical learning, and marine studies of any kind. The doubts increased thereafter, though the idea of a "school", i.e., men gathered to consult, persisted and still persists in popular concepts and among some historians. It is the kind of legend that is too romantic to be relinquished. [11]

For those who want to imagine Henry with his school and astronomical observatory, there is at Sagres a great stone circle some 180 feet in diameter with forty-two stone spokes, somewhat like a gigantic center from which one might cite compass directions. But no known compass has forty-two points, the spokes are not all the same distance apart, and no document justifies saying it was part of an observatory.

Was Henry Surrounded by "Scientists"?

The existence of scientists who supposedly gathered around Henry is equally difficult to verify in evidence contemporary with Henry or close enough to his time to be considered reliable. Always mentioned first is Jacome de Mallorca (supposedly Jafuda Cresques), son of Abraham Cresques, author of the Catalan map of ca. 1375. Converted to Christianity, he was known as Jaime Ribas. [12] Duarte Pacheco Pereira in the *Esmeraldo* says that Henry "sent to the island of Mallorca for a Master Jacome,

[10] *Ibid.*, 162.

[11] *Ibid.*, 186–187, 246; Marquês de Sousa Holstein, *A escola de Sagres*. S. E. Morison, who directs a devastating hurricane against the imaginary voyages to imaginary islands in the Atlantic Ocean (*European Discovery of America*), still writes: "Prince Henry the Navigator established around 1420 a center for exploration and hydrography at Sagres on Cape St. Vincent" (p. 94), although there is no evidence whatever of such a center nor of Henry's activity there before about 1437. Morison does not mention the Valsequa map of 1439 which credits Portugal with the discovery of the Azores in 1427 (p. 95).

[12] Gonçalo de Reparaz, Junior, identified Henry's cartographer as Jacome or Jaime Ribas, son of Abraham Cresques, and placed the date of his coming to Portugal between 1420 and 1427. See Reparaz, "Mestre Jacome," in *Biblos*, Coimbra 1930 (there seems to be no firm basis for the Reparaz dates 1420–1427). Leite says Jaime would have been 73–76 years old in 1443, *Descobrimentos*, I, 177. See also Rolando A. Laguarda Trias, *La aportación científica de mallorquines y portugueses a la cartografía*.

expert in making navigation charts, in which island such charts were first made, and with many gifts and rewards induced him to come to this kingdom; and it was he who taught the making of those maps which those in our time learned."[13] Duarte Pacheco gives no date for the arrival of Jaime in Portugal. Half a century after this, João de Barros also records the presence of Jaime in words that might indicate he copied from the *Esmeraldo*; but perhaps not, for he credits Jaime with qualifications not mentioned by Duarte Pacheco — he was a man "very well-versed in the art of navigation, who made navigational charts and instruments . . . who taught his science to Portuguese artisans of that occupation."[14] Barros does not state when Jaime came to Portugal. There is no other contemporary word about Jaime, and he is unknown to official records. Azurara does not mention him.

Nor is there any reliable knowledge of the other "scientists" so often, so freely, and so vaguely mentioned. There is no reliable evidence of Portuguese scientists or technicians attached to the prince. This would not prevent belief in the collaboration of anonymous experts, if there were traces of their passing; but there are none. It might be believed that Jaime brought technical advances to Portugal if Henry's men had practiced the art differently from other mariners. But the prince's men sailed their routes using Genoese, Catalan, and Flemish compasses; and there is no evidence of specifically Portuguese compasses or magnetic needles.[15]

Of other alleged advisers of Henry, the Spanish pilot Morales was a legendary character out of the story of Robert Machim and Ana de Arfet; Mestre Pedro was only an illuminator; Patricio de Conti was a Venetian who exercised the function of consul in Lagos and also collected a stipend from Henry, according to Cadamosto who gives us the only information known about him. There is nothing to connect him to Nicoló de Conti who traveled in the East. As for Friar Egidio, supposedly a professor of mathematics in Bologna, Italy, the only indication that he worked with Henry is in a book by Friar Santa Maria written in 1697 — 250 years after Henry's time.[16]

The records do show that Henry had five "physicians" (físicos). Jaime Cortesão says they were almost all Jews who probably also practiced

[13] Pereira, *Esmeraldo*, bk. I, chap. 33; Leite, *Descobrimentos*, I, 174–175.
[14] Barros, *Ásia*, Dec. I, bk. 1, chap. 16.
[15] Leite, *Descobrimentos*, I, 163 and 187.
[16] *Ibid.*, 240–242; Costa Brochado, *Infante*, pp. 147–223, citing Padre Francisco de Santamaria, *O céu aberto na terra*, Lisbon, 1697.

astrology, which in that period was closely linked to medicine.[17] The conclusion drawn by some is that the astrologers were advisers to Henry on astronomy and hence on navigation. This can be sustained only on the basis that anything that cannot be proved false is true. Only one of the men named may have lived in Sagres or Lagos; the others were in various parts of Portugal where Henry had extensive properties. One lived in Évora, another in Santarém, a third in Leiria, and a fourth, in Oporto. The fifth, having left no proof that he lived at the center of Henry's maritime activities, cannot be traced. At the most, the documents justify the suggestion that they may have been astrologers; but they do not justify that assumption that they advised Henry on navigation.[18]

The Ships of Discovery

Did Henry make improvements in ship styles? The period of exploration witnessed a change in the types of ships used on long voyages. Reliable information about ship types is, nevertheless, very scanty. Azurara does not enlighten us concerning the ships used in Henry's time or about instructions given to his pilots. Though Azurara mentions that after 1441 the caravel was the chief vessel of exploration, he does not explain the advantages of this type of ship nor does he describe its structure. Cadamosto, however, notes the superiority of the caravel in his writings, calling it, as we have seen, "the best of all sailing ships."

There is no information about the ships used in the voyages preceding the passage of Bojador in 1434, but according to Azurara those used from 1434 to 1441 were the *barcha* and the *barinel*, both small, and three of nonspecified type. After 1441 caravels are always mentioned with the exception of one pinnace (*fusta*) of Palenço in the Lanzarote expedition of 1445. Between 1448 and 1460 no other type of vessel is mentioned. Occasionally at other times the *urca*, a heavy vessel, was listed.[19] The caravel was derived, some have suggested from the *caravo* or *carib* of the Arabs, which had two or three masts with lateen (latin) sails, a castle only in the stern, and was slender with a proportion of about 3 × 1 length for breadth. Of shallow draft, it was light and sensitive and could easily be sailed inshore or close to the wind. Only a few unsatisfactory pictures of

[17] This is the view of J. Cortesão in Peres, *História de Portugal*, III, 374–375; Fernando da Silva Correia, "Um notável médico conselheiro do Infante D. Henrique."
[18] Leite, *Descobrimentos*, I, 169–170.
[19] On ships see Leite, *Descobrimentos*, I, 138–139, 181–182, 231.

the caravel are extant. Nothing is known about its appearance or exact dimensions. No architectural plans remain, if such ever existed — ship carpenters of the time were more empirical than scientific.

The caravel evolved; it was not invented at one stroke. The type was known before 1415. Other ships like the *coque* (*coca*) of northern Spain and France could sail the high seas and did. Duarte Leite points out that the caravel was used by both Portuguese and Spaniards — for it was known along the coast from Sagres to Gibraltar. "It is inexact," he says "that the caravel of Henry's times was a type of embarkation exclusively Portuguese, seeing that there were always caravels simultaneously in Spain." Although many want to believe that Henry invented the caravel by deliberate planning, there is no evidence to prove this. The caravel was first mentioned in English sources in 1448, when "a ship of Portugal called a caravel" was captured off the Isle of Wight.[20] To the end of the fifteenth century the caravel and explorers went together. In the sixteenth century the caravels still sailed, though by the end of the fifteenth heavier ships, for larger cargo, were used by explorers also — but in some sense they were a union of the caravel and the stubbier *nau*. The caravel had increased in size, used both lateen and square sails (*velas redondas*), and was closer on the one hand to the lighter caravel in sailing qualities and on the other to the *nau* in capacity.

Navigation and Maps

What of navigation and maps in the first half of the fifteenth century? These will be discussed more fully later. A few observations will suffice here. As I said before, it is evident that mariners who could reach Madeira by 1418, or a bit later, and the Azores by 1427 had solved the essential problem of how to sail the ocean out of sight of land and return home. With what instruments? The compass alone? Sighting on stars and sun? Certainly, they had at least a rudimentary knowledge of celestial navigation.[21]

[20]*Ibid.*, I, 182, note 1.

[21]J. Cortesão, in Peres, *História de Portugal*, III, 374–375; Leite, *Descobrimentos*, I, 169–170. Jaime Cortesão held that in Henry's time navigators could determine latitude by observation of the Pole Star, basing this on the testimony of Nikolaus Lanckmann von Valckenstein who wrote an account of the voyage from Lisbon to Pisa of two ambassadors sent to accompany the princess Leonor of Portugal to Italy to marry Emperor Frederick III. Leite points out that von Valckenstein was not a navigator and not necessarily capable of a scientific description of navigation (Leite, *Descobrimentos*, I, 169–170). Leonor's itinerary is

The argument that by 1460 and before navigators could determine latitude at sea by observation of the Pole Star is based on the statement of Nikolaus Lanckmann von Valckenstein, who accompanied a Portuguese fleet from Lisbon to Pisa in 1450. He could not have observed carefully how the mariners navigated; or if he did, he did not record it well. He was not a navigator. In any case, mariners had sailed the route for centuries without benefit of anything but a compass, and after ca. 1300 they had sea charts drawn on rhumbs, or direction lines.

Diogo Gomes in his account of his life taken down by Martin Behaim in the last quarter of the fifteenth century speaks of using an astrolabe in about 1460 for navigation, whether on land (which was customary among astrologers) or on the sea is not clear. Nor is it certain that Gomes was speaking of himself; perhaps Behaim was talking of a later period, in which case the year was 1484 or after.[22] Cadamosto mentions the North Star, the Southern Cross, the compass, and the sea chart in 1456 but not the astrolabe — his navigators were the Portuguese pilots of his ships.

As the Portuguese moved down the coast of Africa, they were able to substitute "what the eye had seen (*visto por olho*)," in Azurara's phrase, for what was drawn on maps up to that time "by hazard" (*a capricho*). The Catalan maps showed some relatively accurate knowledge of the interior of Africa but not much of the coast south of Bojador. Maps mentioned by Azurara have not survived. Most mapmakers were struggling to reconcile the traditional view of Africa, handed down from ancient times, as receding in a curve southeast or even east with the new knowledge that the coast stubbornly ran southwest for hundreds of miles before turning south; only at the end of Henry's life was it seen as trending southeast again. We can get a rough, and only a rough, idea of the evolution of their knowledge by examining the maps of the time, for example those of André Bianco in 1436 and 1448 and Fra Mauro in 1459. Whatever new knowledge the mapmakers gained came from the Portuguese mariners. There are no reliable records of other mariners to whom the new knowledge on the maps can be ascribed.

There can be only surmise about what was shown by the map Prince Pedro brought from Venice (1428?) because there is no known original or

---

in Luciano Cordeiro, *Portugueses fora de Portugal: uma sobrinha do Infante, Imperatriz da Allemanha e Rainha da Hungria* and in Caetano de Souza, *Provas*, I, 601–633. See Francis M. Rogers, *The Travels of the Infante Dom Pedro*. p. 53.

[22] Leite, *Descobrimentos*, I, 243.

copy. Nothing justifies believing it contained anything very different from the maps of Villadestes (1413) or Bianco (1436). Nor can there be more than uninformed guesses about the relationship of Jaime de Mallorca to mapmaking in Portugal because none of his work remains. As late as 1457 Henry showed himself ignorant of Catalan cartography, which may indicate that Jaime de Mallorca had had little if any effect in Portugal. Speculation on what maps the Portuguese made before the last third of the fifteenth century is fruitless.[23]

What Sort of Man Was Henry?

If Henry himself was not a man of scientific learning, if he was not advised by men of cosmographical and navigational skills, if there was no school of Sagres, if no maps survive to show the cartographic skill of the Portuguese in Henry's time, (and the answer to all these questions is negative), what qualities did Henry have to make him a leader of men, and why did Portugal become the leader of discoveries?

Henry was described by Azurara as a man of strong physique, energetic and curious about the world if not bent toward scientific study, a prince fond of having a large retinue (which, more than the cost of explorations, explains his constant demand for revenue), a man with an affable and communicative nature, who welcomed both Portuguese and foreign visitors (with whom he apparently often talked all night, though there is no evidence that he consulted them on scientific subjects).

It is obvious that Henry lost no opportunity to promote his own and Portugal's interests. Third in line among the living legitimate sons of João I, he was too energetic and too ambitious to be content with a passive role in life. He aspired to set himself up in North Africa, to conquer Granada from the Muslims and rule it, to play a role in the dynastic confusion of Castile, to gain the Canary Islands, and to explore and trade along the known and unknown coast of Africa. His new projects and his demands for favors from king and pope were unceasing. Henry controlled more wealth than any other man in Portugal, with the possible exception of the king. He acquired the Madeiras, the Azores, and the Cape Verdes; he held monopolies on dye and soap manufacturing, on river and tuna fishing, on fishing on the Atlantic and African coasts, and on coral gathering — a list

[23]*Ibid.*, 176, 229.

which by no means includes all Henry's holdings. He was Duke of Vizeu, among his other titles, and governor and administrator of the Order of Christ.[24]

That he took more interest in African conquest and exploration than any other one person of importance in Portugal is clear. He gained concessions from his father João I (to 1433), from his brother King Duarte (1433–38), from his brother the Regent Pedro (1438–48), and from his nephew King Afonso V (to 1460). But Pedro also pushed exploration and development of the African coast and the islands, he fostered Henry's ambitions, and, because of his extensive travels when young, had far more knowledge of the affairs of the world than did Henry.

Henry's Legacy to Portugal and the World

Henry harnessed his own talents and energies to those of his family and country. He did not need to invent ships, train sailors, educate pilots, or give courage to his men. He found all these at his command. What he needed to do, and what he did, was to give a focus to Portuguese energies — and he did it with only a small part of his own energies, most of which went to govern his large estates and to further his economic interests. Exploration was a small part of his activities, though in the long run it was to make the rest of his life seem unimportant and to ensure that it would be largely ignored by most who hear his name. Henry "The Navigator" he has become, though not so known to his contemporaries, for he made but three brief voyages to Morocco. The legends that have grown up around him and have gained acceptance as history by the public and by some historians are in a sense more true of him than the truth. No other one name has the importance of Henry's in the history of the world's greatest exploring nation — Portugal.

[24] António J. Dias Dinis, "O testamento do Infante D. Henrique"; "Reflexões do segundo testamento henriquino"; and *Estudos Henriquinos*, chap. 1.

CHAPTER 8

Navigation: Portuguese Haven-Finding in the Ocean Sea

Navigational Science about 1415

It is evident that from the time (ca. 1420) Portugal began colonization of the Madeira Islands, some 400 miles in the ocean west of Africa, and the Azores, (ca. 1427) 745 to 1000 miles west of Portugal, the problem of sailing in the open Atlantic had been at least partly solved.[1] Coastal navigation from city to city in the Mediterranean and the Atlantic offered no further major obstacles at the beginning of the fifteenth century. The Mediterranean was a long, narrow, enclosed sea in which sooner or later a familiar landmark would come into view. Sailing the coasts of Europe and Northwest Africa was facilitated by the prevailing westerly and northwesterly winds, which would almost consistently bring a lost sailor back eastward anywhere between the Madeiras and the British Islands. Storms

---

[1]The following discussion is based principally on E. R. G. Taylor, *The Haven-Finding Art*, for the general development of navigation, and Albuquerque, *Descobrimentos portugueses*, pp. 43–83, 129–181, 233–400; Leite, *Descobrimentos*, I, 375–410, II, 455–511; Peres, *Descobrimentos portugueses*, pp. 227–245, unless otherwise indicated. The staunchest defenders of Portuguese priority in navigation and ship construction are: Gago Coutinho, whose two-volume *A náutica dos descobrimentos* gathers the extensive studies of a man who was an experienced mariner and aviator, and J. Cortesão, *Descobrimentos*, I, 88–128 and *passim*, II, 263–349. See also António Barbosa, *Novos subsídios . . . da ciência náutica portuguêsa*; Joaquim Bensaúde, *Histoire de la science nautique portugaise*, and other works by Bensaúde listed in the bibliography; Abel Fontoura da Costa, *A ciência náutica dos portuguêses*; Gago Coutinho, "A astrologia na Península" in *A náutica dos descobrimentos*, I, 119–126; George H. T. Kimble, "Portuguese Policy and Its Influence on Cartography"; M. M. Sarmento Rodrigues, "Prioridade portuguêsa das invenções científicas no Ultramar"; Frazão de Vasconcelos, *Pilotos das navegações portuguêsas dos séculos XV e XVII*.

could take the mariner temporarily astray, and there are many romantic stories of discoveries made by ships blown off route; but on the whole the mariner had only to follow the wind to arrive at some point of the coast with which he was familiar, or at least which he could follow north or south to his destination. If coastal sailing was never quite so simple as this sounds, it is easy to see that sailing hundreds of miles from land and returning to the desired port demanded learning new wind patterns and the flow of ocean currents, as well as acquiring sophistication in sailing techniques and ship construction not hitherto known.

There has been a tendency for historians of different nations to claim as their own the honor of scientific advances in navigation. It is not possible to attribute to any one nation, however, all navigational progress, nor to credit any one group of sailors with all the improvements made during the thirteenth to sixteenth centuries. Certainly it seems that the navigators and the astronomer-astrologist of the Mediterranean were in the forefront of this development. It is just as evident that most of the high-seas sailing in the fifteenth century that resulted in discoveries was done by the Portuguese and that logically it is to them that we should attribute practical application of sailing techniques and shipbuilding. Andalusian sailors and Spanish scientists shared in this development. There may have been northern European contributions from time to time, but in no way were the men of the Iberian Peninsula dependent upon outsiders to teach them how to sail the Atlantic.

The use of the moon, stars, and sun by observation without instruments has long been a rough way of guiding direction and keeping time, both on land and by sea. The accumulated knowledge passed on from seaman to seaman, or in the desert areas from caravaneer to caravaneer, was an elementary form of celestial navigation. Sailors who customarily voyaged between northern and southern Europe knew their approximate latitude without instruments, although they may have used the compass. Because the east-west longitudinal position had no natural fixed point from which to measure, it was not scientifically determined at sea until 1762.

The northern seamen (the Irish and the Norse sailors) could orient themselves by the heavenly bodies sufficiently, it is evident, to make voyages from Norway to the Faroes, Iceland, and Greenland, and to return home.[2] The relation of change in the length of day to latitude could

[2] Heinrich Winter, "Who invented the Compass?" in *Mariner's Mirror*, 23:95–102 (1937),

hardly escape the notice of those who spent their lives on long sea voyages. It was discovered that the Pole Star, which the Norsemen called the "ship star," was the most reliable observation for direction; and the circling of the Little Dipper (Lesser Bear) and the Big Dipper (Greater Bear) was a measurement for time at night. No document establishes how early there were instruments for observation. It was considered "scientific" that about 1000 Gerbert (Pope Sylvester II) advocated looking at the stars through fixed tubes to determine whether or not they were motionless.

Mediterranean Navigation in the Early Middle Ages

Developments that first made sailing a more exact art and eventually a science can be seen most clearly in the Mediterranean as early as the eleventh century. Two events helped mariners of Europe pass beyond the utilitarian skills of navigation: one was the revival of mathematics and astronomy after 1000, the other the use of the magnetic stone. Revival of interest in the natural world came about partly through the Syrians who translated Greek works into Syriac. One of these was a treatise on the astrolabe. The Arabic conquerors took over Greek learning both via Syria and directly from the Greeks. The reconquest by Christians of areas occupied by Muslims and Jewish scholars put Christians in contact with ancient learning and facilitated translations of Euclid and other Greek scientists into Latin. Although orthodox Christians regarded such knowledge as semiheretical, it did introduce such useful instruments as the astrological-astronomical astrolabe for timekeeping and calendar making.

The rise of the Mediterranean port cities in the eleventh and twelfth centuries, in which Amalfi, Italy was one of the leaders, brought renewed interest in methods of navigation. William of Puglia, a poet who wrote ca. 1109–11, hailed Amalfi as famous for showing sailors "the paths of the sea and skies," which would support the tradition that the practical use of the magnetic needle was discovered by this date. Since ancient times it had been known that an iron needle floating on water would turn in the direction of the magnet. Magicians used this for their tricks. Someone eventually noted that when a magnetized needle was left without a magnet to attract it, it would continue to point north.

concludes: "It is . . . a strong probability that it was the Vikings who introduced the pristine forms of the compass to the Italians" (p. 102).

Among attempts to account for the use of the magnetic needle at sea is the tradition that it was Chinese in origin and was transmitted to the West by Arab sailors. There is no evidence whatever to support this belief. A south-pointing needle is recorded in China between A.D. 1086 and 1093, and between 1101 and 1103; and its use on shipboard is mentioned in Chinese annals. But the Arabs' use of it is not recorded until 1243. The Arabs, in fact, borrowed the name of the magnetic compass from the Italians.[3]

Treatises on the Compass and Navigation

In 1180 Alexander of Neckam (1157–1217), English scholastic, made the earliest recorded European reference to the use of a magnetic compass by seamen in his *De utensilibus*. He noted that among ship stores he saw "a needle" which when "turned and whirled around" would point the direction, permitting sailors to steer their course when the "Cynosura" was hidden by clouds. It is certain, judging from his remarks, that the magnetic needle was used at sea before he wrote. An indication of how well known the magnetic needle was at the beginning of the thirteenth century comes from the poet Guyot of Provins who ca. 1200–05 wished irreverently that the "Holy Father" was as unchanging as the "star that never moves," by which sailors "keep course" and which they call the Tramontane, standing still while around it circle other stars (Big and Little Bear). The sailors "touch a needle with an ugly stone," put the needle through a straw, and thus it floats on water pointing always to the star. In 1218 Jacques de Vitry, bishop in Acre, reported "an iron needle" which, once it had made contact with the magnet stone, turned toward the North Star, which lay "motionless while the rest revolve." The needle, he said, was "a necessity" for travelers by sea.

Two Dominican friars, Thomas of Cantimpre, ca. 1240, and Vincent of Beauvais, slightly later, recorded "a needle pressed against a magnetic stone," which was then inserted through a straw and placed in a basin of water. When the stone was moved over the basin faster and faster, the needle whirled swiftly until the stone suddenly was snatched away; then the needle turned toward the North Star (*Stella Maris*).[4]

[3] Taylor, *Haven-Finding*, pp. 95–96.
[4] *Ibid.*

No close readings could be made with the needle floating in water. Only when the instrument makers put the needle on a pivot, drew a precise wind rose, and placed the needle in a box to protect it, could approximate directions be found. In some places the mariner's compass was called the box (bussola), rather than the needle (aguja), as in the Iberian Peninsula where it may have been invented. As time went on improvements were made probably in the Mediterranean and in northern Europe by the English, Dutch, and Germans, who used the terms compass, mariner's compass, sailor's compass, or *Stella Maris*, rather than the "needle." On the mariner's compass the horizon was divided into thirty-two points, rather than into the 360° used by astronomers. The first recorded division of the eight-point wind rose into subdivisions was made by Matthew Paris about 1240 in England. The scientific study of the principle of the compass began in the thirteenth century with such men as Peter Peregrinus and Roger Bacon, who pointed out that it was not the Pole Star which attracted the needle.

For the practical sailor these scientific efforts were largely immaterial at first, inasmuch as his compass was made to point to magnetic north and his observations were noted accordingly. This was sufficient until later when the determination of latitude made greater accuracy both possible and necessary.

A Norse sailing handbook, *The King's Mirror*, appeared about 1250 and probably before the magnetic compass was used at sea, for it does not mention the lodestone. In it a father advises his son that he should know arithmetic, the length of daylight in relation to his latitudinal position, how to observe the heavenly bodies, the progression of the tides, and the division of the horizon into eight winds forming a wind rose. He should also have a knowledge of the habitats of various fish and other sea animals, such as the whale, the walrus, and the seal, as a help to practical navigation.[5]

Italian, Spanish, and Muslim Treatises

Improvements in the thirteenth century made it possible to gather into one book the sailing directions known for the Mediterranean and the Black Sea. In this period there was a scale chart, used with the magnetic

[5]*Ibid.*, pp. 80–85.

compass and an arithmetical method, by which the pilot could work out his course. All this seems to have been of Italian origin.[6]

The first known comprehensive work was *Lo compasso da navigare*, written about 1250. It contains directions for sailing from port to port beginning at Cape St. Vincent in Portugal, passing through the Strait of Gibraltar along the north coast of the Mediterranean to the eastern end and returning westward along the southern Mediterranean coast into the Atlantic and south along Africa as far as Safi in Morocco. The measure used is the Roman (Italian) mile, equal to approximately 4100 English feet or about four-fifths of a statute mile.

In *Las sietes partidas del Rey Alfonso X* ("El Sabio") of Castile, the pilots are told they should know "all the moods of the sea, where it is stationary and where there are currents; the winds and all their changes, as well as all other sea-lore; and furthermore, they should know the islands and ports . . . entrances and exits, in order to steer a ship safely."[7] There is a reference to navigation by the stars: "The mariners guide themselves on dark nights by the needle, the mediator between the stars and the lodestone, which shows them where to go in foul weather and fair."[8]

The outstanding example of a compilation of astronomical information from the Arabs is the *Libros del saber de la astronomia* prepared at the direction of Alfonso X in the mid-thirteenth century by Christian, Jewish, and Muslim scholars.[9] It includes minute descriptions of astronomical instruments with instructions for their construction and use. The method for fixing the position of the sun in all the signs of the zodiac is described, i.e., determining the sun's celestial longitude and the relationship of this coordinate with the latitude of the observer. Frequently more than one method of solving a problem is indicated, as for example how to determine latitude by the sun at true midday, given the sun's declination on the day of the observation. The process that later Portuguese mariners used as an adaptation of information gained from the *Libros del saber*.[10] The most convenient way of determining latitude was to have prepared

[6] *Ibid.*, 98–104; Heinrich Winter, "The Origin of the Sea Chart."
[7] *Siete Partidas*, pt. II, tit. XXIV, ley 5.
[8] *Ibid.*, tit. IX, ley 28.
[9] Manuel Rico y Sinobas, ed. 5 vols.
[10] Albuquerque, *História dos descobrimentos*, pp. 268–270, says some of the tables included in later publications were Portuguese though attributed to Alfonso X; J. K. Wright, "Notes on the Knowledge of Latitude."

tables of solar declination, known as Alfonsine tables, which accompanied the *Libros del saber*, including "ephemerides" of sun, moon, and planets. The ordinances of Jaime I of Aragon, 1258, also contain legislation concerning navigation.[11]

What was needed for the development of navigation was a scholarly man who was also a mariner. There must have been such, for the Italian sailors of the period of the Crusades were using the mariner's needle with the wind rose attached. By the thirteenth century when Venice and Genoa were the foremost trading cities, the navigation instruments in use were sufficiently complicated to make it desirable to have men of some education as pilots or ship captains.[12]

The First Maritime Charts

One necessity was a maritime chart which would contain accurate sailing directions. The first mention of a chart of this type used on shipboard was in 1270, when St. Louis of France sailed from Aigues-Mortes to Tunis with his Crusading fleet. The oldest chart known is the *Carta Pisana*, made about 1275–1300 by someone who knew both navigation and mathematics. It showed compass bearings according to wind roses, distance, and scale. Maritime charts like this were perhaps the first made to scale since those of ancient times, which were astronomers' maps not sea charts and were unknown in medieval Europe. Both the rulers and dividers (also known as the compass) were employed for making and using the sea chart, which required knowledge of elementary arithmetic. The *Carta Pisana* shows the Mediterranean and the Atlantic as far as Cape St. Vincent; but later when Italian sailing to the north became customary, charts were extended to show accurately the English Channel, Flanders, the North Sea, and parts of Scotland.

The eight-point wind rose was developed in the Mediterranean into a sixty-four-point instrument. The names of the eight winds were retained in Italian, and combinations of these were used for the fifty-six additional winds. In northern Europe sailors used a total of thirty-two points. Four basic winds were indicated, as for example, *tramontane*, N; *ostro*, S; *levante*, E; and *ponente*, W. To these were added *greco*, NE; *sirocco*, SE; *maestro*, NW; and *libeccio*, SW. In areas long occupied by Arabs the term

[11] Antonio Ballesteros, ed., *Historia de América*, III, 389.
[12] Taylor, *Haven-Finding*, pp. 96–100.

garbino, derived from *El Gharb*, which meant west, was used instead of libeccio. The thirty-two-point compass is first mentioned in Chaucer's treatise on the astrolabe in 1390 but was probably developed earlier. It was painted and highly decorated. The Pole Star, toward which the sailor directed his course at night as the star stood motionless like a fixed hinge of the turning sky, was compared to the Virgin Mary — "Mary is like a Pole Star."[13]

Raymond Lully, the Catalan encyclopedic scholar, refers ca. 1300 to "instruments, chart, compass needle, and Sea Star."[14] Lully accompanied his text with figures to illustrate the nocturnal astrolabe which gave the hour according to the position of the Smaller Bear. The observer was required to know the mid-night position of the guards for each month, or better for each fortnight of the year, which shifted about an hour every two weeks.[15] Lully also included a "numerical table" (*quadro numérico*), useful in determining the route sailed by the ship, this being similar if not identical to the *Toleta de Marteloio*.[16]

The *Toleta de Marteloio*, or tables for navigation, probably date back to the thirteenth century, as may be judged from the writing of Lully, though the term has no satisfactory explanation. The tables helped a mariner determine his course, or if he was tacking (zigzagging), they indicated how far off course he was and enabled him to return to it. A knowledge of elementary trigonometry was necessary for the preparation of the tables which first came perhaps from Jewish scholars but were known to Leonardo Piza and Lully. To use the tables, the navigator needed only to multiply and divide.[17] They may be the origin of the traverse tables used by modern navigators.

Chart Makers

Some chart makers of the fourteenth century are known through their signed charts, as for example Petrus and Perrinus Vesconti of Genoa. An atlas of Vesconti maps was included with Marino Sanuto's book sent to the

[13] For information on the compass, sea charts, celestial navigation, and descriptions of the principal charts and maps of the fifteenth and sixteenth centuries, see the excellent article by Isa Adonias, "A cartografia vetustíssima do Brasil até 1500."

[14] Albuquerque, *História dos descobrimentos*, p. 57.

[15] Taylor, *Haven-Finding*, pp. 145–147, describes the method in considerable detail.

[16] Albuquerque, *História descobrimentos*, pp. 58–59.

[17] Taylor, *Haven-Finding*, pp. 112–121.

pope in 1320; the atlas contained a nautical chart and a map of the world. The charts in the present volume are examples of other fourteenth-century works which, owing to a high attrition rate among sea charts, are few in number. There is an order for payment for a *livro de navegar* by the king of Aragon in 1323. Martin de Aragón wrote a *Livro sobre la carta de navegar* in the first years of the fourteenth century.[18] The king of Aragon, in 1352, required all ships to carry two maritime charts.

Charts were produced in Mallorca, Venice, Ancona, and Montpellier, as well as in other cities during the fourteenth century. In Mallorca many of the chart and instrument makers were Jews who had lived there under Arabic domination. In 1373 Prince Juan of Aragon ordered made a navigational chart (*carta de navegar*), which was to show as much as possible of the areas west of Gibraltar. In 1379 Juan ordered a *mappa mundi* from Mallorca where Jewish cartographers had introduced the scale chart, known first in the Mediterranean, to world maps. In 1381 Abraham Cresques was described as "Master of maps and magnetic compasses." He was dead by 1387, and his *mappae mundi* were ordered finished by an unnamed "Christian master." Evidence that sailors came to use tables as aids is an order to pay Cresques for "certain tables" he had provided in 1382. Two years later Juan of Aragon ordered from Cresques navigational tables, *taules de navigar*.

Navigation in Fourteenth-Century Portugal and Spain

When did the Mediterranean navigational science reach Portugal? Did Manuel Pessanha, the Genoese merchant and sea captain put under contract by King Dinis, bring new knowledge to Portugal in 1317? There are no precise answers to these questions though it can be taken for granted that Pessanha and his twenty captains were acquainted with navigation as it was then known in the Mediterranean. The discovery of astronomical tables of Portuguese origin shows that at the time Pessanha arrived in Portugal knowledge of astrology was very advanced.[19] "It is well known," says a modern scholar, "that during the fourteenth and fifteenth centuries the best doctors as well as some royal councillors . . . came from the Israelite minority . . . as may be seen in 1383, when there was momen-

---

[18] Albuquerque, *História dos descobrimentos*, pp. 60–61; Heinrich Winter, "Catalan Portolan Maps."

[19] Albuquerque, *História dos descobrimentos*, p. 76.

tary danger of an attack on the Jewish colony which passed quickly, . . . the Jews living in a relative security to the end of the fifteenth
century."[20] In the first work in which astronomical knowledge was
adapted to navigation, two Jews at least, José Vizinho and Mestre Rodrigues, used the work of another Jew, Abraham Zacuto. "We see," says
Luis Albuquerque, speaking of the thirteenth-century work of Robert
Anglès, "how in the *Almanach perpetuum* of Zacuto and in the *Almanach
Português* which antedated it almost a century and half, there are found
tables which are perfectly analogous."[21]

The navigational skill of the Iberians was recognized early. In the *Book
of the Canarien* about the Jean de Bettencourt expedition to the Canaries
in 1402, the authors refer to "Portugal, Spain, and Aragon" as having
"pilots who know the ports and these regions (*paragens*). [22] In the Atlantic
Ocean, the Iberian pilots slowly learned new methods of navigation.
Meanwhile the Mediterranean pilots continued to follow their usual
rules.

Iberian astrologer-astronomers were leaders in discovering the new
scientific navigation. The exact times at which such practical knowledge
was first put to use are difficult to ascertain and are the subject of much
disputation among scholars and among nations, each nation claiming the
honors of the new science. There seems little reason to doubt that the
nation that contributed most was Portugal, the nation that contributed
most to the discovery of the Atlantic Ocean. The problem was to use
the celestial bodies as a means of fixing position at sea, as could be done
on land, i.e., to establish longitude and latitude.[23]

Longitude and Latitude

Longitude could not be measured from any natural fixed point but only
from some arbitrary place, much as the Romans used the Fortunate Is-

[20]*Ibid.*, pp. 273–274, and Luis de Albuquerque, *A determinação da declinação solar*.
[21] Albuquerque, *História dos descobrimentos*, p. 273, and other works listed in the bibliography; Arthur H. Robinson, *Marine Cartography*.
[22] Albuquerque, *História dos descobrimentos*, p. 82.
[23] Albuquerque, "Sôbre a determinação de latitude," and Gago Coutinho, *A náutica dos
descobrimentos*, I, 132–149. LaGuardia Trias, Uruguayan historian, presents one of the best
expositions of the development of celestial navigation, holding that there was no true celestial navigation until latitude could be determined at sea and that there were no known charts
with accurate indication of latitude until after 1500. He rejects Portuguese claims for pre-
1500 celestial navigation but emphasizes Portuguese leadership over all other navigators,

lands (the Canaries) or, in modern times, most of the world uses Green-wich.[24] Discovering the positions of heavenly bodies in relation to exact positions on the earth was the difficult problem. From the spherical earth the sky afforded 360 points on the celestial equator from which to make east-west measurements; these are the places at which the sun path cross-es the celestial equator, or equinoctial, in spring and autumn.

Fixing latitude did not prove difficult when measuring from a stationary earthly point of observation on the Pole Star or the sun. However, it did require that the observer be on a steady platform, the land itself, so that he could use his astrolabe to get a sight on a star or the sun and relate the position of the heavenly body to his distance from the earthly equator. Obviously on an unsteady surface, such as a ship at sea, this could not be done precisely and could be inaccurate up to several degrees. When it first became possible to measure latitude on a ship at sea and by whom it was first done is still disputed. It was not simple to teach astronomy and the calendar to a sailor, although it became desirable in the fifteenth century to do so — for the small world was expanding fast and voyages were becoming correspondingly longer.[25]

A comparison of navigation in the East and West is interesting. Nicoló de Conti, an Italian who lived in the East during the early fifteenth century, stated that the Indians navigated chiefly by the southern stars, inasmuch as the north Pole Star was scarcely visible. Marco Polo had observed the same thing in the late thirteenth century. Conti also re-ported that they did not "navigate by the needle." Fra Mauro, who made a map for the Portuguese in 1459, obtained the same information from some unknown source. Both Conti and Mauro were mistaken, though it is true that the sailors of the Indian Ocean placed less emphasis on sailing by the compass.[26] They did, however, have the kamal, an instrument for sighting celestial bodies to measure the altitude of the stars from the horizon. It was a board attached to a cord with knots at desired intervals. The cord was held in the mouth and extended to a point where the horizon could be seen exactly at the bottom and the star at the top of the board. Each knot had a known reference point on the coast, thus giving

including the Spaniards. See Rolando A. LaGuardia Trias, "Elucidario de las latitudes colombianas," *Boletín de la Real Sociedad Geográfica*, and "Importancia de las mas antiguas latitudes de la costa brasileña."

[24]"O velho problema da longitude," in *A náutica dos descobrimentos*, II, 230–237.
[25]Taylor, *Haven-Finding*, p. 154.
[26]*Ibid.*, pp. 127–129.

the latitude, though it was not expressed as such. This same principle was known in the cross-staff of the West, first described in 1342 but not commonly used until the age of great discoveries.[27]

The discovery of Ptolemy's geography in the early fifteenth century was to bring great benefits to sailors who had never heard his name. Ptolemy listed the latitudes and longitudes of the world as they were known to him. The geography was translated from Greek into Latin in 1409, and copies were available throughout Europe. Learned men were soon convinced that the best way to describe a given position on the globe was by stating altitude (distance from the equator) at a point on the earth where it crossed a given longitude (distance from any place east or west of a chosen point, i.e., Greenwich in our present-day reckoning). Such a system of coordinates was analogous to that used to map the skies, from which any point could be described in degrees, minutes, and seconds, north or south, east or west, as for example $10°,5'4''$ W by $°,16''$ S.[28] This idea was not new to astrologer-astronomers, who were adding to the list of longitudes and latitudes used with the ephemerides in an astronomical almanac which gave the positions of the heavenly bodies for each day of the year. Such tables were useful to astronomers, but not to laymen, nor at first to seamen. The application of this revived knowledge to navigation required the interest of men who combined learning with practical seagoing experience.

Portuguese Knowledge of Nautical Instruments

The problem is to find evidence of the instruments and knowledge the Portuguese used for their long voyages, which are sufficient proof in themselves of the Portuguese ability to sail anywhere on earth and return home. Besides the compass for direction, they used the astrolabe, the quadrant, later the cross-staff (balestilha), and maps.

The study of astrology-astronomy in Portugal, though not at the university, was sufficient for the development of navigation.[29] The first document that expressly refers to the use of the mariner's needle (agulha de marear) in Portugal is dated 1416. It is in a list of ship's stores which

[27] Ibid.
[28] Ibid., p. 151
[29] António José Saraiva, Para a História da cultura em Portugal, II, 379, cited in Albuquerque, História dos descobrimentos, p. 238.

includes "three navigational needles, a clock (hourglass) and two sounding-leads."[30] The astrolabe with which the altitude of the sun or a star was measured was a round instrument with a movable alidade, like the hand on a clock. The astrolabe was suspended or merely held up by the observer. The alidade turned around the center and served as a sight rule, which allowed the light of the sun or a star to shine through two pinholes. The alidade turned on two scales from zero degrees (horizontal position) to ninety degrees (vertical position). A mariner's astrolabe consisted only of the main circular plate, on which was engraved the scale of degrees, a swivel suspension ring, and the alidade. There was also a "nocturnal astrolabe" which was intended only for keeping time by the stars at night.[31]

That the knowledge of keeping time at night was known in Portugal in the fifteenth century is indicated by the remark of King Duarte in his *Leal conselheiro* where he lists the rules and indicates the convenience of knowing them by heart, "as in fact in these realms so many know that I do not believe there are so many in any other country."[32] The rules given by Duarte are similar to those in the Catalan map of ca. 1375.

The art of navigation needed by Portuguese mariners at the beginning of the fifteenth century was that of the Mediterranean in the twelfth to fourteenth centuries. It can be summarized as "choice of the desired route on a map, steering the ship on the chosen route, and an estimate of the distance sailed." But when sailing in unknown seas without sea charts or rutters to guide the pilots, it was necessary to sail the bays and river mouths almost foot by foot, avoiding the promontories, observing the winds, seeking shelter, and noticing the break of waves to avoid shallows.[33]

Portuguese Maps

Such information was reported by the pilots on returning home and noted on the charts that were prepared in Henry's time. Once beyond Bojador, or sailing to and from the islands, the sailors met conditions that forced

[30] Silva Marques, *Descobrimentos*, I, 241.
[31] Taylor, *Haven-Finding*, p. 158; R. T. Gunther, "The Astrolabe."
[32] Quoted in Albuquerque, *História dos descobrimentos*, p. 77.
[33] As mentioned by Cadamosto when he was on the African coast, in Godinho, *Documentos*, III, 167.

them to find ways to make the return journey. It was discovered at some date that from the region of the Canaries they could sail northward to the Azores and catch the westerly winds into Portugal when conditions did not permit a return directly from the Canaries or Madeira to Portugal along the African Coast.[34] The Spaniards used the same route to the Canaries. This has been called "return by the circle route" (*volta pelo largo*) by some modern Portuguese scholars. It cannot be established exactly when the *volta pelo largo* was first used,[35] but after the discovery of the Azores in 1427, it was possible. When return voyages from south of Bojador became more frequent, and in the period in which the *Crónica da Guiné* was written, approximately 1450 and later, there are references to such a route.[36] In 1446 Dinis Dias sailed without stopping "until he passed the land of the Moors and reached the Negro lands."[37] At the same time Álvaro Fernandes sailed "straight to Cape Verde." Cadamosto indicates that for days at a time he sailed out of sight of land.[38]

Sailing to Madeira and the Azores by dead reckoning, checked by instrumental observation of the altitude of the sun or a star (*altura*), was a technique developed in the fifteenth century. There was no mention of latitude in the earlier part of the century. Ports were then described as being located at a given altitude.

When Portugal advanced along the African coast, maps were made of the discoveries. Duarte Pacheco Pereira does not, as some authors have stated, say that the mariners of Henry's time learned to use nautical charts

[34] Albuquerque, *História dos descobrimentos*, pp. 246–247, citing Gago Coutinho, *A náutica dos descobrimentos*, I, 87–88; Harold L. Burstyn, "Theories of Wind and Ocean Currents."

[35] Gago Coutinho, "Açores. A volta do mar largo," in *A náutica dos descobrimentos*, I, 197–233. See Albuquerque, *História dos descobrimentos*, p. 247, note 25, citing A velino Teixeira da Mota, "Historiographia da expansão portuguêsa," in *Anais do Clube Militar Naval*, p. 255, 1949. This has been called *Volta pelo largo* by some modern scholars. When return voyages from south of Cape Bojador became more frequent, and in the period in which the *Crónica da Guiné* was written, we have a reference to such a route, i.e., by ca. 1450. Diogo Gomes noted that being in Madeira and "wishing to return to Portugal, the winds being contrary, I went to the Azores Islands" but that Noli waited for favorable winds and "arrived in Portugal before me" (quoted in Albuquerque, *História dos descobrimentos*, p. 249 and Godinho, *Documentos*, I, 94). Albuquerque concludes that by the middle of the fifteenth century sailors could use the winds to sail into the Atlantic and take the indirect route home. It should be noted, however, that in most cases no mention is made of the *Volta pelo largo*. The winds do blow from the west or southwest at times and perhaps most voyages went directly to the northeast and home from Madeira and the Canaries.

[36] Albuquerque, *História dos descobrimentos*, p. 248.

[37] Albuquerque, *História dos descobrimentos*, pp. 248–249, quotes, the 1949 edition of Azurara's *Crónica*, p. 149.

[38] Cadamosto, *Voyages*, cited in Albuquerque, *História dos descobrimentos*, p. 249.

from Jaime de Mallorca. He says only that Jaime was called to prepare charts, an art that existed in the early sixteenth century.[39] Azurara refers to the maps of the African coast before the passage of Bojador as being drawn "only by guess," but indicates that in his time the maps were based on "what the eye has seen."[40] When Henry received his charter of exclusive rights of navigation south of Bojador in 1443, the charter stated that until then "nobody in Christendom knew anything about it . . . for neither directly in the navigation charts, nor in world maps, were the areas drawn except at the fancy of somebody." Henry "ordered navigation charts made."[41] It is thus clear that sea charts were known in Portugal when the Atlantic voyages first began.

Portuguese Scientific Interests

Portugal's scientific interests are indicated by a number of works translated into Portuguese in the fifteenth century, those done by Prince Pedro from Latin being an example. Both João I and Duarte manifested their interest in astrology-astronomy and other scientific works. Until recently, for lack of sufficient documentation, some historians held that interest in scientific works was nonexistent in fifteenth-century Portugal. There is now enough evidence to show this was not true. A number of astrological-astronomical works have turned up in Portuguese libraries in circumstances that indicate they were there in the fifteenth century.[42] There is now a strong tendency to attempt extremely broad conclusions that strain the evidence. Portugal's contributions are over emphasized, causing some writers, in reaction, to deny unjustifiably Portugal's lead in navigation.[43]

The earliest reference to astronomical observation aboard a Portuguese ship was made by a German ambassador in the middle of the fifteenth century. Praising the equipment of the Portuguese ships, he mentioned

[39] Pereira, *Esmeraldo*, bk. I, chap. 33.
[40] Azurara, *Crónica da Guiné*, p. 348, 1949 ed.
[41] Godinho, *Documentos*, I, 142; Albuquerque, *História dos descobrimentos*, pp. 80–81.
[42] Albuquerque, *História dos descobrimentos*, pp. 273–278.
[43] For evidence, see Albuquerque, *História dos descobrimentos*, p. 278–300. Among such works are the *Libro Comprido* of Aben Ragel; the *Tratado da Esfera* of Sacrobosco (Hollywood); the *Tabulae Astronomicae and Almanacques portugueses*, written in Portuguese but found in Madrid. Albuquerque says that the finding of part of Sacrobosco's *Tratado* shows Duarte Leite was wrong in saying it was not known in Portugal until the sixteenth century.

that there were "in addition to the pilots . . . master astrologers, very knowledgeable of the routes according to the stars and the Pole."[44] This phrase is not explicit. It could be interpreted to mean that the astrologers observed the stars to determine the time of night or the altitude of the Pole Star in order to fix course. It is rather risky to assert on the basis of this quotation that latitude could be set on board ship in 1450. Cadamosto, who was a contemporary, speaks of "the art of navigation, the compass . . . and the map," but he does not refer to latitude.[45]

The reference made by Gomes to the use of a quadrant about 1460 is too suspect to justify claims that it is an example of determining latitude. Until a map of that date drawn with latitudes is found, the proof is inconclusive. Some historians doubt that the statement was made by Gomes; instead, they attributed the claim to Behaim and suggest that he was referring to a date of about 1484.[46]

Whether or not Gomes used the quadrant to get the altitude of the stars or the sun, it was used a short time later. When one was too far south to shoot the Pole Star, either the southern stars or the sun had to be used. This would suggest that the sun might have become more useful after 1472 when Portuguese explorers reached the equator.

The Astrolabe and Latitude

In the late fifteenth century and during the sixteenth, the astrolabe became the most important instrument for taking the altitude of the sun and the stars. The question as yet unanswerable is the date when the classical astrolabe used by astrologers was simplified sufficiently to become a nautical astrolabe. Obviously, aligning the astrolabe in such a way that the

[44] Quoted in Albuquerque, *História dos descobrimentos*, pp. 250–251, note 31, who cites Sousa, *Provas de história genealógica*, I, bk. III, 346; and Cortesão in *História de Portugal*, Peres, ed., III, 375.

[45] Albuquerque, *História dos descobrimentos*, pp. 251–252, and Godinho, *Documentos*, III, 162.

[46] Diogo Gomes cited in Godinho, *Documentos*, I, 94, and Albuquerque, *História dos descobrimentos*, pp. 252–254. The collection of maps made by Armando Cortesão and A. Teixeira da Mota in *Portugaliae monumenta cartographica* is the most complete work on maps related to explorations. The use of the Pole Star did not necessarily imply latitude; it could also be used to tell the approximate distance made good by a ship. See Albuquerque, *História dos descobrimentos*, pp. 253–254; Luciano Pereira da Silva, *Obras completas*, II, 175; and Valentim Fernandes, *Repertório dos tempos*, which has instructions on "How to navigate by any star known to man in the sky" in the facsimile ed. of Joaquim Bensaúde, p. 142. See also, Albuquerque, "O primeiro guia náutico português."

light of a star or the sun shines through the pinholes of the alidade is hard on stable land. From the deck of a small ship tossing at sea, it was quite a different and more difficult matter. The latter years of the fifteenth century were clearly times of experimentation to find the best instruments and the best science for the long voyages.

The use of the astrolabe in the late fifteenth century is indicated by various contemporaries or near contemporaries, but it was not yet very satisfactory and accurate at sea. João de Barros states that when Vasco da Gama arrived at Santa Helena Bay after ninety days at sea "they debarked to take on water as well as to take the altitude of the sun, for since the navigators of this kingdom had been using the astrolabe for only a short time for navigation, they did not have much faith in sighting the sun aboard ship because of its heaving."[47] A correct reading of the astrolabe depended upon fixing on exact midday, otherwise considerable errors could be made. Mestre João, who accompanied Cabral in 1500, wrote to King Manuel from Brazil that he found it impossible to take the sights at sea. Errors of four or five degrees were made, he wrote, however little the ship rocked; therefore, accurate sights could not be taken except on land.[48] Duarte Pacheco Pereira, writing between 1505 and 1508, recommended that "the altitude of the sun should be taken precisely at midday with the astrolabe or the quadrant."[49] The most famous of Portugal's scientific navigators in the sixteenth century, João de Castro, emphasized that a correct reading of the astrolabe depended on doing it at precisely midday. He complained that pilots did not know how to take the sun's altitude correctly and placed the blame largely on "the clocks" which varied too much.[50] Columbus spoke of using an astrolabe and reported that Bartolomeu Dias measured latitude with one. The error of 10°, i.e., 45°S instead of 35°S., which Columbus reported that Dias found for southernmost Africa, may have occurred because Columbus recorded the information incorrectly. The mistake can be accounted for either as an example of the inaccurate use of the astrolabe or as an example of accurate

[47] Barros, *Ásia*, Dec. I, bk. 4, chap. 2.

[48] Mestre João to King Manuel in William B. Greenlee, ed. and trans., *Cabral*, pp. 34–39; Albuquerque, *História dos descobrimentos*, p. 304.

[49] Pereira, *Esmeraldo*, bk. I, chap. 10; Albuquerque, *História dos descobrimentos*, pp. 299–300.

[50] João de Castro, *Roteiro de Lisboa à Goa*, ed., Andrade Cario, pp. 182–184, quoted in Albuquerque, *História dos descobrimentos*, p. 303, note 128.

use, if the 45°S apply to the farthest point south reached by Dias (45°?) rather than to Africa itself (ca. 35°). [51]

Once transatlantic sailing had started, mariners were forced to deal with a problem known before but which became more serious — variations of the compass. It had long been recognized that the magnetic needle did not point precisely at the North Star. Thus compasses from different centers of manufacture varied from one another, and pilots sometimes carried several compasses. Columbus noticed a westward variation on his first voyage. But a pilot could not know without long experience with his own compass how much to allow for error. Furthermore, the compass varied more or less the farther the ship sailed east or west. It "northeasted" or "northwested," leading the mariner off course. Only later improvements helped to solve this problem.

Tables of Solar Declination

Closely connected with the use of the astrolabe for navigation was the preparation of tables of solar declination (known and used in astrology for centuries before). According to the historian João de Barros, João II "entrusted this task to Mestre Rodrigo and Mestre José, a Jew, both his physicians, and to a Martin Behaim . . . who boasted that he had been a student of Regiomontanus, famous astronomer among the professors of this science. They found this method of solar navigation, for which they made tables of declination of the sun like those now used by navigators." [52]

At one time the tendency was to accept Barros's statement as evidence that Regiomontanus was the author of the tables of solar declination used in Portugal. It has now been demonstrated, however, that the tables prepared by Regiomontanus and published in 1474 differ in a slight but significant way from those prepared in Salamanca and Portugal by Abraham Zacuto in his *Almanach perpetuum*, first printed in 1496 but existing in manuscript form before that time. The tables used by the Iberian navigators were of Iberian origin, the work of Zacuto which came to Portugal by way of his student José Vizinho. He and Zacuto represented the common Iberian astrological-astronomical tradition. [53]

[51] Albuquerque, *História dos descobrimentos*, pp. 374–375; Pereira da Silva, *Obras completas*, II, 315.
[52] Barros, *Ásia*, De. I, bk. 4, chap. 2.
[53] Albuquerque, *História dos descobrimentos*, p. 383, citing Pedro Nunes, *Obras*, 1, 199.

When Alexander von Humboldt suggested that the *Ephemerides* of Regiomontanus was the origin of the tables of solar declination used in Portugal, there was an outburst of Portuguese indignation. It was not necessary to bring from outside the Iberian Peninsula what had existed there long before. The navigational advance needed in the fifteenth century depended on preparing men who were competent in both astronomy and practical navigation. But "the practical men of navigation were not recruited from among the erudite."[54]

The tables of solar declination were prepared in Portugal perhaps in 1485. Christopher Columbus is our witness: "The king of Portugal sent Mestre José, his physician and astrologer, to Guinea in 1485, to observe the altitude of the sun in all of Guinea."[55] The *Regimento do astrolabio e do quadrante*, published in Lisbon about 1509, but dating to a period as far back as 1480, is the oldest existing navigation manual. It essentially shows the regiment (*regimento*), the guide-rules of the North Star for raising the Pole, the guide-rules for shooting the sun, and the altitudes (*alturas*) for a list of positions from the equator northward, as well as the table of declination of the sun.[56] The reading of latitude in the *Regimento* is correct to within half a degree in most cases and sometimes within ten minutes. João de Castro in the sixteenth century estimated a maximum error of two degrees in a tossing sea or half a degree in a calm sea when determining latitude by the sun.[57]

Once mariners had gone beyond where the North Star could be used, they needed a new heavenly body as a guide. This was found in part in the Southern Cross sketched by Cadamosto, as previously noted. Mestre João also drew a picture of it and sent the drawing to Manuel in 1500. As early as 1503, and not later than 1506, Pedro Anes taught the *Regimento do Sul* (i.e., sailing by the Southern Cross) to other mariners "as a sidereal clock" (*como relógio sideral*).[58]

The *balestilha* (cross-staff), known to the Arabs, was used for a time by the mariners of Portugal in the sixteenth century. The first mention of it in Portugal was by João de Lisboa, in the *Livro de marinharia*, about 1514. At this date Portuguese mariners would have used all three instru-

[54] Albuquerque, *Descobrimentos*, p. 236.

[55] *Ibid.*, p. 374, note 230; Pereira da Silva, *Obras completas*, II, 315.

[56] Taylor, *Haven-Finding*, pp. 152–165.

[57] Albuquerque, *História dos descobrimentos*, pp. 304–305, citing Castro's *Roteiro de Lisboa à Goa*. p. 63.

[58] J. Cortesão, in Peres, *História de Portugal*, IV, 222.

ments — the balestilha, the astrolabe, and the quadrant.[59] João de Castro advised the use of the balestilha for sighting stars rather than attempting to shoot the sun at its zenith near the equator. The *Tabuas da India*, or *taboletas da India* (the Kamal), which works on the same principal as the balestilha, was introduced for a time after Vasco da Gama's voyage but was found to be less accurate than the astrolabe.[60]

Formal Instruction in the Science of Navigation

How much formal instruction did the pilots receive in the new navigational methods? There is no indication that a position as elaborate as Spain's *piloto mayor* (a post occupied by Amérigo Vespucci), who set sailing instructions and prepared maps, existed. The pilots, cartographers, and instrument makers did attend a class, however, created especially for them in Lisbon, where the *cosmographo mor* taught by contract a "mathematics class" which presumably included elements of cosmography. At the conclusion, an examination was required for a certificate.[61] The document on which this statement rests dates from the seventeenth century, but it refers to the payment of twenty *mil reis* and three *moios* of wheat "just as Pedro Nunes had." In the early sixteenth century, Pedro Nunes (1502–78), the most famous professor of mathematics and cosmography of his time in Portugal, was frequently called to Lisbon from his teaching in Coimbra to teach and consult on maritime affairs. From 1557 onward his absences from Coimbra were more prolonged, sometimes two or more years.[62]

Possibly in connection with this course Pedro Nunes wrote his epitome of cosmography taken from the *Tratado da esfera* of Sacrobosco. Latin, in which it was written, was certainly not known to most of the would-be pilots and cosmographers. So Nunes translated it into Portuguese. "It is almost certain" says a modern scholar, "that the use of astronomical instruments such as the quadrant, astrolabe, and the balestilha was taught here also, along with the knowledge of the tables of declination of the sun and the reading of the nautical charts."[63] The instructions were composed

[59] Albuquerque, *História dos descobrimentos*, p. 306, note 132.
[60] *Ibid.*, pp. 307–309.
[61] Francisco M. de Souza Viterbo, *Trabalhos náuticos*, I, 171, cited in Albuquerque, *História dos descobrimentos*, p. 240, note 12.
[62] *Ibid.*
[63] Albuquerque, *História dos descobrimentos*, pp. 238–241.

of a few "elementary facts which the pilots could not forget during the voyages." But the complaints made in the sixteenth century about the "inexpertness" (*impericia*) of some pilots indicates that the instruction may not have been thorough nor the certificate of pilotage difficult to obtain. It should be noted, however, that astrology-astronomy was never precisely a university study until the seventeenth century. Experimental science in Portugal in the sixteenth century brought the knowledge of navigation to a limited sector of the university but did not expand it widely outside learned circles.[64]

On the high seas, where it counted, the Portuguese led — and northern Europe lagged. "At the very time that the Portuguese were laying the foundation of our astronomical navigation, an experienced French sailor, Pierre Garcie, was writing *Le grand routier et pilotage*," about 1483, using traditional navigational methods. His book was standard in northern Europe for fifty years and was translated into English.[65] Meanwhile the Portuguese and Spaniards dominated the science of high-seas sailing to past the middle of the sixteenth century.

[64] Saraiva, *Para a história da cultura em Portugal*, II, 379, cited in Albuquerque, *História dos descobrimentos*, p. 238.
[65] Taylor, *Haven-Finding*, pp. 167–168.

CHAPTER 9

Dividing the Land and the Waters: the Treaty of Alcáçovas, 1479–80

Death of Henry: the Dual Policy of Expansion Continued

On the death of Henry in November 1460, the rights he had held reverted to the crown. No one was a successor to Henry in the legendary sense of a man devoted to exploration. On August 22, 1460, Prince Fernando, his nephew and adopted son, had received Terceira and Graciosa in the Azores. Shortly after Henry's death the three archipelagos of the Azores, Madeiras, and Cape Verdes were granted to Fernando by the king on December 3, with "income, taxes, and jurisdiction . . . exactly as Prince Henry held them from us."[1] The Western Cape Verde Islands also went to Fernando on September 19, 1462.

Trade and navigation along the African coast continued as before. Soeiro Mendes was appointed captain of the trading post at Arguim in 1461. Freedom of navigation and commerce for the Portuguese along the coast was granted on payments of the stipulated duties and taxes to the crown. The rights thus granted were often abused by merchants through avoidance of duties and smuggling of prohibited articles, such as arms, iron, and other merchandise.[2] Afonso V was thinking more about further conquest in Morocco, however, than he was about additional exploration. Inspired by his conquest of Alcácer-Seguer in 1458, he decided on new attacks. He was in the midst of preparations in 1460 when illness stopped

[1] João Barreto, *História da Guiné*, pp. 59–63; Peres, *Descobrimentos portugueses*, pp. 189–205; Blake, *European Beginnings in West Africa*, pp. 26–40.
[2] Barreto, *Guiné*, pp. 59–63.

144

him momentarily. As soon as possible he renewed the project and embarked with his brother Fernando on November 7, 1463. A storm sank some of his ships and forced him to Ceuta instead of to Tangier, which was his destination. The campaign continued to go wrong, and two attacks failed in the fall of 1463. A third attack on January 19, 1464, resulted in a disastrous failure.[3]

For a time the king gave his attention to exploration while planning his next effort in Morocco. To promote the colonization begun by António de Noli and Diogo Afonso, Fernando obtained special privileges for the settlers of the Cape Verde Islands from the king on June 12, 1466. They could trade in Guinea, except in Arguim, and on payment of duties of 25 percent, they could sell their "merchandise and slaves" in the Cape Verdes. They were also allowed to export their products, with some tax exemptions, to Portugal.[4]

In 1470–71 Afonso V was again preparing for African conquest, and again he thought of Tangier; but he decided rather to attack Arzila. Prince João, later to be João II, participated in this attack. On August 24 the Portuguese captured the city killing some 2000 "infidels" and taking 5000 captives.[5] The capture of Arzila spread fear throughout the surrounding regions. The inhabitants of Tangier, to avoid similar fate, abandoned their city to the Portuguese who entered without a fight. Afonso V now entitled himself "King of Portugal and of Algarve on this and on the other side of the sea in Africa," a title which was preserved even after the loss of Algarve in Africa, in the same way that the sovereigns of England kept the title granted to Henry VIII, "Defender of the Faith," long after they had broken with the Church of Rome. Further south in Morocco the cities of Azemmour and Safi petitioned the protection of Portugal and recognized Portuguese authority. Larache also passed into Portuguese control.[6]

Further Discoveries: Fernão Gomes

Meantime discoveries and development were progressing along the Gulf of Guinea, though beyond Cape Verde and the Cape Verde Islands sailing

[3] Almeida, *História de Portugal*, II, 113–116; Rui de Pina, *Crónica Affonso V*, chaps. 147–156.

[4] Barreto, *Guiné*, p. 66; John W. Blake, *Europeans in West Africa*, pp. 64–67.

[5] Almeida, *História de Portugal*, II, 113–116; António Baião, *Documentos relativos a Marrocos*; Damião de Góis, *Crónica Dom João*, chaps. 18–31; David Lopes, *História de Arzila* (1471–1550); Rui de Pina, *Crónica Afonso V*, chaps. 162–167.

[6] David Lopes in *HEP*, I, 150–153.

conditions were much more difficult. Instead of reliable northeast winds there were variable winds and often dense fog and calms which detained ships. The heavy swells far out at sea breaking on shallow shores and the often sudden and violent rain storms and tornadoes were among other dangers. Such sailing conditions hindered, but did not stop, the Portuguese.[7]

Further discoveries came after the royal contract made with Fernão Gomes in November 1469. João de Barros, our only source of information since the contract itself has not been found, says: "At this time the commerce of Guinea went along very smoothly among our [mariners] and the people of those lands traded with one another in peace and love without the sallies and armed assaults which there were at first." He said that things probably could not have been otherwise at the beginning, owing to the "aggressive and barbarous" nature of the people. But after they had learned the "truth" and received the benefits of "salvation of the soul and of understanding," they became very "domesticated," so that when ships arrived in their ports many people came from the interior "to trade for our merchandise" in exchange for the souls that came to receive "salvation in captivity."

And things going along thus, normally and regularly along the coast already discovered, the king, occupied with affairs of the realm and not wishing himself to carry on commerce and even less let things go on as they were with respect to the taxes paid . . . in November, 1469, contracted for a period of five years with Fernão Gomes, an honorable citizen of Lisbon, for 200 *milreis* a year. The condition set was that every year of those five years he was obligated to discover 100 leagues along the coast . . . 500 leagues in total. This discovery was to begin in Sierra Leone where Pedro de Sintra and Soeiro da Costa ended, before this the last discoverers. . . . He could not trade on the coast opposite the Cape Verde Islands, as this was the right of the colonizer of the islands . . . nor was he permitted to trade at the castle of Arguim, for the king had given this to Prince João, his son.[8]

The contract was renewed for an additional year on June 11, 1473, having been so profitable that Gomes was required to pay 300 milreis a year over the entire life of the contract, i.e., 1800 milreis. Gomes carried

---

[7] Peres, *Descobrimentos portugueses*, pp. 139–164, who rejects the Jaime Cortesão thesis of discoveries beyond Sierra Leone in Henry's time. See Cortesão, *Descobrimentos portugueses*, I, 361–364; Ernst Gerhard Jacob, "A descoberta da África sudoeste pelos portugueses."

[8] Barros, *Ásia*, Dec. I, bk. 2, chap. 2; Peres, *Descobrimentos portugueses*, pp. 145–152; Blake, *Europeans in West Africa*, pp. 67–69.

out his obligations and by the end of the contract had discovered the Guinea coast to the point where it turned southward and extended to Cape Catarina, beyond the equator.

The first expedition equipped by Fernão Gomes was that of João de Santarém and Pero Escobar (or Escolar), so far as incomplete records indicate. In January 1471, this expedition discovered the "gold trade" (Shama Bay, later the Gold Coast) to Cape Three Points.[9] This would place the first discovery about half way along the Guinea coast and far beyond the last point attributable to Pedro de Sintra. A map of anonymous authorship assigned to a date near 1471 shows discoveries to approximately Rio do Lago (3°E).[10] São Tomé and Príncipe were also discovered, apparently between 1471 and 1475; but there is no clear record of the date.[11]

To Soeiro da Costa, another of Fernão Gomes's captains, is attributed the discovery of the river bearing his name. It is to the west of Cape Three Points and could have been discovered earlier by Santarém and Escobar. It does not, however, appear on the maps of that time and was probably discovered later. Fernão do Pó coasted the area of the Bay of Biafra to the limits of the Gulf of Guinea and discovered the island he called Formosa, later named for him.[12] Lopo Gonçalves sailed as far as the cape first called Cape de Lope and today called Cape Lopez. Rui de Sequeira, about 1471 or 1475, continued on as far as Cape Catarina. There is no record of further discoveries along the coast until the time of João II.[13]

When Prince João became nineteen in 1474, he was granted a lifetime concession to the king's rights to "the commerce of Guinea and the fisheries of the Guinea seas of both Mina and Arguim."[14] This concession gave to João the income that was due the crown for these areas, but it did not cancel commercial concessions such as those of Fernão Gomes. The advent of João marks a new period in Portuguese expansion. Already at nineteen a veteran of the battlefield and a young man of "strong purpose,"

[9] Pereira *Esmeraldo*, bk. II, chap. 4; Barros, *Ásia*, Dec. I, bk. 2, chap. 2.

[10] Abel Fontoura da Costa, *Uma carta náutica portuguêsa anónima* de *"circa" 1471*; and Costa, *Descobrimentos portuguêses no Atlântico*, pp. 277-278; Peres, *Descobrimentos portuguêses*, p. 99, note 1, and p. 210.

[11] For the uncertainties on the dates, see Peres, *Descobrimentos portuguêses*, pp. 210-211, who shows that Lopes de Lima and Fontoura da Costa, who follows him, have no firm basis for the exact date of discovery.

[12] Pereira, *Esmeraldo*, bk. II, chaps. 4 and 10; Barros, *Ásia*, Dec. I, bk. 2, chap. 2.

[13] Peres, *Descobrimentos portuguêses*, pp. 211-212.

[14] Peres, *Descobrimentos portuguêses*, pp. 152-166; Joaquim Bensaúde, *Astronomie nautique*, pp. 271-273; António Brásio, *Monumenta missionária africana*, IV, 12-15.

he had demonstrated his determination, vigor, and ability. Afonso V said of him in 1481 "we know for certain that he himself and his officials govern very well the navigation and commerce of Africa and keep them in good order." [15]

The Rivalry of Portugal and Spain

During the years between 1474, when João received his powers, and 1481, when they were again confirmed and clarified, there was an intensification of Portuguese-Castilian rivalry in both domestic affairs and African commerce and expansion. The intertwined marriage relations of Portugal and Castile helped to bring them into conflict once again.

The marriage in 1455 of Juana, sister of Afonso V of Portugal, to Enrique IV, who ruled Castile from 1454 to 1474, had placed a Portuguese queen on the Castilian throne. This was neither the first nor the last of a long succession of intermarriages between the royal families and nobilities of the two countries. Living in a court which even by the royal standard of the times was reckoned as unusually licentious, Juana had allegedly participated in the freedoms the king allowed himself and his courtiers. One result of this was to cast doubt on the paternity of her daughter, also named Juana, heir to the Castilian throne. She was derisively known as "Juana la Beltraneja" because according to the prevailing gossip she was the child of Juan Beltrán de la Cueva rather than of Enrique IV himself, who agreed at one time that he was not the father.

The reign of Enrique IV was one of continual civil war, at the end of which his opponents sought to block the accession to the Castilian throne of Juana la Beltraneja and her Portuguese husband, King Afonso V. The rival claimant to the Castilian throne was Isabella, Enrique's sister, who had married Ferdinand of Aragon in 1469, contrary to the king's will. In 1473 Afonso V and Enrique IV had agreed on the marriage of Afonso to Juana, his own niece. Ferdinand and Isabella had objected strenuously.

When Enrique IV died in December 1474, Isabella was immediately proclaimed queen of Castile. Afonso V, early in 1475, prepared to invade Castile to uphold Juana's rights to the throne and by sending a diplomatic mission to France to propose an alliance with Louis XI. In May 1475, Afonso entered Spain and married Juana in Placencia. The two now called themselves king and queen of Castile, Leon, and Portugal. The marriage

[15] Peres, *Descobrimentos portuguêses*, pp. 247–250.

was not in accordance with canonical laws, and the papacy never granted the necessary dispensation.[16]

Isabella chose this moment to renew Castilian claims to the African coast, which had been neither abandoned nor pursued after 1454 when her brother Enrique IV came to the throne. On August 19, 1475, Isabella directed to her nobles, authorities, and other subjects a letter stating that it was well known that her predecessors "had made conquests in Africa and Guinea" and collected the Fifth from all the merchandise that came from there until Portugal "intervened with the consent of King Enrique, my brother," to the detriment of Castile and of its income. Her letter appointed collectors for the Fifth and forbade anyone to go "to the said ports of Africa and Guinea" without special permission of the collectors that she had appointed "under penalty of death and loss of all your goods." The division of prizes captured at sea between the crown and sailors was specified.

The Andalusian mariners from the Atlantic coast of southern Spain were not happy with this royal decision to place controls over commerce on the African coast. They had obviously been trading there without royal consent and without respecting Portugal's monopoly, as the Castilian chronicler Hernando del Pulgar (1436?–93?) makes clear. "In those times," he says without making reference to specific years, "in an area that . . . might have been as much as 1000 leagues of sea," lands had been found with barbaric people, "black men who lived nude in huts," but who possessed great mines of gold. The news soon spread among the mariners of the Andalusian ports. "Some outfitted a caravel and ventured to go on that voyage. They obtained a great deal of gold in exchange for old clothes and old brass and copper." There was so much excitement that "everybody was scheming to go to that country! Some made 10,000 *pesos de oro* on a voyage, each *peso* being worth two gold florins of Aragon." Pulgar's account is more picturesque than precise, but it has the value of bringing to our attention the rivalry of the Andalusian and the Portuguese merchants for profits to be made in the African territories.[17] Portugal and

---

[16] Almeida, *História de Portugal*, II, 117–137; Pedro Aguado Bleye, *Manual Historia de España*, 8th ed., I, 797–811, II, 29–40; J. H. Elliot, *Imperial Spain, 1469–1716*. Isabella and Ferdinand opposed the marriage and presented their objections to the papacy. After several years of tribulations Juana entered a convent where she remained until her death in 1530. Almeida, *História de Portugal*, II, 117–137.

[17] Pérez Embid, *Descubrimientos*, pp. 179–184, citing Pulgar. *Crónica de los Reyes Católicos*, ed., Carriazo, I, chap. 81; Blake, *European Beginnings*, pp. 41–78. Other merchants also found the Guinea trade attractive. At about the time of the Castilian voyage to

Castile were thus arrayed against each other in a domestic and colonial war that was to last for several years.

War: 1475–79

The war between Portugal and Spain that began in 1475 with border raids by forces of both countries resulted in the Battle of Toro in March 1476. Afonso V and Prince João opposed Ferdinand of Aragon. Both sides claimed victory but Afonso and João were forced to abandon Spain; and the claim to the Castilian throne was definitely lost. Afonso V went to France to solicit the aid of Louis XI and entrusted the government of Portugal to João.[18]

There is reference to a Castilian expedition of late 1475 or the beginning of 1476 concerning caravels "which Your Highness ordered outfitted to send to Guinea." There is also a record of at least two and perhaps three expeditions to Guinea from Puerto de Santa Maria and Palos in 1476, one or maybe two of them by individuals who ignored the royal controls, and another by Carlos de Valera, undertaken with the knowledge of the throne. The Castilian chronicler Alonso de Palencia (1423–92) speaks of two expeditions, one with two caravels and another with three, which brought back slaves, some of them noble or royal. Ferdinand intervened to restore the important captives to their homes.

The expeditions of Carlos de Valera, son of Mosén Diego, which sailed in 1476 with some twenty to thirty caravels and three *naus* from the Biscay area, were seven months on the voyage, returning early in 1477. Palencia relates that the Castilian monarch knew of a large fleet in Lisbon bound for Guinea, as was accustomed, and that there were difficulties in "readying thirty light ships, the large ships not being appropriate for navigation in those waters which the caravels reach quickly."[19] Valera raided thirteen of the islands off the coast of Guinea, and captured António de Noli on Santiago, one of the Cape Verde Islands, "for whom the Genoese merchants agreed to pay a thousand *doblas* within four months." They also brought back some 400 slaves. On December 6, 1476, the

---

Guinea in 1475 and 1476, a Flemish vessel piloted by a Castilian sailed to the Portuguese Mina coast where it took on a rich cargo, but it sank at the Praia dos Escravos on the return journey. This episode shows that the road to Guinea was no secret.

[18] Almeida, *História de Portugal*, II, 128–137.

[19] Unless otherwise noted, the following is from Pérez Embid, *Descubrimientos*, pp. 186, 196–210, 323.

Catholic kings issued regulations for the system of navigation to be followed by their subjects in commerce with Guinea. In 1477 there were three or four expeditions with an unknown number of ships, from which we may conclude they were not on the order of Valera's in 1476, that sailed to or received a license to sail to Guinea, Pedro de Covides fitted out a fleet of thirty-five vessels in 1478 which Pulgar calls caravels (*caravelas*) in one place and ships (*naus*) in another. The lot of this expedition was not a happy one, Pulgar records. The Portuguese captured the entire fleet and the large cargo of gold. A happy result was that the prisoners of this Castilian fleet were exchanged by the Portuguese for those taken by the Castilians in the Battle of Toro.

Apparently not daunted by this disaster, early in 1479 the sovereigns of Spain gave orders "to put more expedition into the preparation of an armada of twenty caravels to go to the Mine of Guinea." The expedition was to leave in June. Nothing is known for certain of the results. A memorandum sent by Mosén Diego to the queen in 1482 is seemingly a reference to it. By this time Ferdinand and Isabella made individual contracts (*capitulaciones particulares*) with each of the navigators, the method used in the conquest of America after 1492. Some mariners of Spain had gone to the African areas, "to the gold mines," in 1480 after the treaty had been made in Alcáçovas in 1479 but before it had been ratified in Toledo in March 1480 and had not yet returned. They were given "special passes" (*seguro especial*) for safety.[20]

The reaction of Portugal to the Castilian efforts to trade in waters Portugal considered reserved to her by both papal bull and treaty was naturally not kindly. A *carta régia* of April 6, 1480, ordered the Portuguese mariners to capture "ships of any peoples of Spain or any others whatever [and] . . . without any further order, and without any trial whatever . . . throw the prisoners into the sea."[21]

This, fortunately for the historical record, was not done to the *Mondanina*, a Castilian vessel captured January 6, 1480, in which the Frenchman Eustache de la Fosse was taken. Later he wrote an interesting and informative account of his experience in which he gave the name of the captain, Diogo Cão, who took his ship, later to be one of the foremost discoverers of the African coast.[22] Owing to the difficulty of identifying the

---

[20] Pérez Embid, *Descubrimientos*, p. 212, cites Rui de Pina, *Crónica Afonso V*, chap. 208; see also Joaquim Bensaúde, *Lacune et surprises*, p. 287; Góis, *Crónica De. João*, chap. 103.

[21] Peres, *Descobrimentos portuguêses*, p. 250, citing *Alguns documentos*, pp. 45–46.

[22] Peres, *Descobrimentos portuguêses*, pp. 249–250, citing R. Foulche-Delbosc, in *Revue Hispanique*, 4:174 (1897).

various expeditions and reconciling the Portuguese and Spanish accounts of events, the only thing that is entirely clear is the deadly rivalry between Portugal and Spain in Africa. In a war in which the Castilians were victorious on land and the Portuguese at sea, the Treaty of Alcáçovas was negotiated.

Treaty of Alcáçovas-Toledo, 1479–80

The Treaty of Alcáçovas was signed by the respective ambassadors on September 4, 1479, ratified by Queen Isabella on September 27, and by both Spain and Portugal in 1480. There were, in fact, two separate treaties. One, known as the Treaty of Las Terçarias de Moura, regulated the matrimonial affairs of the two royal families.[23] The other, more important for understanding the expansion of Portugal, adjusted the rival claims of Portugal and Castile in the Atlantic and incorporated a treaty made between the two in Medina del Campo in 1430 and ratified by Portugal October 3, 1431.

The division of territories gave to Portugal the Azores, the Madeiras, the Cape Verde Islands, and the "lands discovered and to be discovered, found and to be found . . . and all the islands already discovered and to be discovered, and any other island which might be found and conquered from the Canary Islands beyond toward Guinea . . . excepting [Canary Islands by name] and all the other islands of Canary, conquered and to be conquered, which remain to the kingdom of Castile."[24] Furthermore, Castile agreed to forbid her own subjects or foreigners to sail to the Portuguese possessions from her territory without Portuguese license, thus leaving to the Portuguese exclusive rights to navigate to Guinea. Nevertheless, when the Americas were discovered the phrase "and all the other islands of Canary, conquered and to be conquered" gave Castile the claim that Portugal's lands were limited to areas "toward Guinea" (contra Guinea). This will become clear when their respective spheres are defined in the Treaty of Tordesillas in 1494. A papal blessing was given to Alcáçovas by the bull Aeterni Patris, June 21, 1481.

With the Treaty of Alcáçovas signed and approved by the papacy, Portugal was now ready to resume the development of trade and ad-

[23] Pérez Embid, Descubrimientos, pp. 214–215; Almeida, História de Portugal, II, 132–134.
[24] Pérez Embid, Descubrimientos, pp. 214–220; Peres, Descobrimentos portuguêses, pp. 250–251.

vancement along the coast of Africa, which had been interrupted after 1475 when Rui de Sequeira sailed to Cape Catarina, one degree below the equator. The death of Afonso V on August 28, 1481, left the affairs of Portugal entirely in the hands of João II, who had in fact been more in charge than had his father for five years past.[25]

[25] F. G. Davenport, ed., *European Treatise Bearing on the History of The United States*, has the text and translation into English; Garcia de Resende, *Crónica d'El-Rey D. João II*; J. P. de Oliveira Martins, *O príncipe perfeito*; Elaine Sanceau, *The Perfect Prince*.

CHAPTER 10

João II: the "Perfect Prince" Who Looked South and East

João II's Vigorous Policy: São Jorge da Mina, 1482

João lost no time in securing physically the land to which the Treaty of Alcáçovas gave him a free hand. A fleet of ten caravels and two *urcas* commanded by Diogo de Azambuja left Lisbon for Guinea December 12, 1481, with 500 soldiers and 100 skilled workmen.[1] Arriving at the chosen place on the Gold Coast, he established a *feitoria* and began building a fortress which was named São Jorge da Mina, near what is today Cape Coast a little more than 1°W. Among those who participated in this voyage was Christopher Columbus, who had arrived in Portugal in 1476. São Jorge da Mina long served the Portuguese as a commercial center for trade with the various areas of the coast — called Malagueta, the Ivory Coast, the Gold Coast, and the Slave Coast — as well as the islands of São Tomé and Príncipe. It also became a point of supply for expeditions exploring further south along the African coast.

Diogo Cão, descendant of a family which had fought in the War of Independence from Spain in 1385, was the first explorer to advance Portugal's flag south of Cape Catarina.[2] As indicated before, he had served the king along the coast of Africa during the war with Spain ending in 1480

[1] Luciano Cordeiro, *Diogo D'Azambuja*; Frazão de Vasconcelos, *A fortaleza de S. Jorge da Mina*; Alberto Iria, "Da Fundação de . . . São Jorge da Mina"; Manuel Nunes Dias, "A organização da rota . . . da Mina"; Blake, *Europeans in West Africa*, pp. 18–63, 70–78; Blake, *European Beginnings*, pp. 79–105.

[2] Luciano Cordeiro, *Diogo Cão*; Viriato de Sousa Campos, *Viajens Diogo Cão e de Bartolomeu Dias*; Irisalva da Nóbrega Moita, "Os portugueses no Congo."

and had captured the Spanish vessel *Mondanina*. Cão left Portugal in 1482 before August 31, probably in the spring. After coasting Africa he stopped at São Jorge da Mina, "a place where he could obtain some necessary provisions."[3] As far as Cape Catarina, he was in territory already known. Beyond there he was exploring new lands. He found a very large river "which enters the sea with such a rush that twenty leagues from the coast its waters are sweet."[4] This was the Rio Poderoso — known later as the Zaire, then as the Congo (the Portuguese changed it to Congo, the name of a king there), and now again as Zaire — where he planted the pillar (padrão) de São Jorge on the left bank of the estuary, a site still known as the Ponta do Padrão. He reached Cape Santa Maria in about 13° S latitude where he planted a second pillar and named the place Santo Agostinho. From a point a bit further south he started on his return journey. It was now perhaps September 1483. He reached Lisbon sometime shortly before April 8, 1484.

Cão brought back some natives of the Congo region, taken as hostages when the men he had sent inland to contact a powerful chieftain did not return. He promised to restore the captives to their homeland. In doing this he was following what Barros pointed out was the custom of the Portuguese. The Portuguese who were left behind could learn the language and gather knowledge of the customs of the country; "the Negroes could learn our language, so thus the king could get information of what they were like."[5] João II was overjoyed at the news he received from Diogo Cão. He heaped honors on Cão and lifted him to the nobility.

The reason for the king's pleasure was revealed in the "Oration of Obedience," which Dr. Vasco Fernandes Lucena, Portuguese ambassador to the papacy, made on December 11, 1485, to Pope Innocent VIII. The Portuguese ships had traveled, said the ambassador, "to near the Promentory Prasso at the beginning of the Arabian Gulf."[6]

The mistake the Portuguese made in believing themselves to be near the Arabian Sea can be understood by consulting André Bianco's map of 1436 or Fra Mauro's map of 1459, the latter drawn specifically by Portuguese order with data furnished from the voyages made to that time. That other Europeans, who knew only what had been learned from the Portuguese,

---

[3] Barros, *Ásia*, Dec. I, bk. 2, chap. 3; Peres, *Descobrimentos portugueses*, pp. 253–286.
[4] Barros, *Ásia*, Dec. I, bk. 3, chap. 3.
[5] *Ibid.*
[6] Quoted in Peres, *Descobrimentos portugueses*, p. 270; Abel Fontoura da Costa, *Às portas da Índia em 1484*; Francis M. Rogers, *The obedience of a King*.

shared such beliefs goes without saying. Cão's discoveries were soon revealed in the Cristóforo Sóligo map (about 1485–90).[7]

Reports concerning Diogo Cão's first and second voyages are extremely contradictory. Most of the chief sources of information, as for example Rui de Pina and Garcia de Resende (chroniclers of João II), Duarte Pacheco Pereira, João de Barros, and António Galvão, give extensive details, yet they are not clear about the number of voyages, their dates, or their extent. Only the discoveries in the nineteenth century of pillars (*padrões*) set up by Cão and the map drawn by Sóligo have afforded a reasonably accurate knowledge of Cão's voyages.[8]

Diogo Cão and Martin Behaim

Diogo Cão left Lisbon on his second voyage in the autumn of 1485, taking back to their homeland the hostages he had previously brought from the Congo. The details of his voyage along the coast are not well established. Barros says he stopped in the Congo to exchange his prisoners.[9] Beyond the point where he had planted the pillars on the first voyage, that is Cape Santa Maria at Monte Negro (Cabo Negro), he planted another pillar on January 18, 1486, according to a notation by Behaim on his globe of 1492. Still farther south at a place called Cabo do Padrão (Cape Cross) he set up another pillar, the farthest point being apparently Ponta dos Farilhoes, 22°10'S (Walvis Bay), a little short of the Tropic of Capricorn, midway along the coast of what is now South West Africa. This point is marked on the map of Martellus (ca. 1489), with a long notation ending, *hic moritur*. Whether Cão died at this point, as some have interpreted *hic moritur*, or whether this expression merely means that the voyage terminated here is not known.[10] Barros says that Diogo Cão again visited the king of the

---

[7] Some have held that Cão reached the Indian Ocean. For a convincing refutation, see Peres, *Descobrimentos portuguêses*, pp. 270–272.

[8] See Peres, *Descobrimentos portuguêses*, pp. 253–272, for an acute examination of the evidence.

[9] Barros, *Ásia*, Dec. I, bk. 2, chap. 3.

[10] For various translations of *hic moritur*, see Peres, *Descobrimentos portuguêses*, pp. 274–277, and Américo da Costa Ramalho, "Sôbre a data da morte de Diogo Cão." Damião Peres cites an example of the kind of "evidence" sometimes used to show that Cão lived to return home — the finding of Cão's alleged tomb in the church of São Domingos in Villa Real. This report published in 1931 by Ruella Pombo merely repeated what had been said by António Barros in his "Memórias de un vencido," p. 107. It was repeated in the chapter on Diogo Cão in the *História da Expansão Portuguêsa*, I, 372, note 5. However, there is no tomb of Diogo Cão known anywhere, and the tomb referred to is actually that of a Pero

Congo on his return to Portugal on the second voyage.[11] Rui de Pina and Garcia de Resende both emphasize the cordial interview between Cão and the Congolese king, who resolved to send more of his subjects, children as well as adults, to Lisbon; but they are not definite about the sequence of events.

There is confusion about whether two other voyages were made during the years of Cão explorations or if these were the same as Cão's.[12] Martin Behaim placed a legend on his famous globe of 1492, which gave a brief account in Latin of two caravels sent by João II, early in 1484, on a commercial voyage. "The royal ships carried various types of merchandise for trade and eighteen horses . . . as gifts for the Black kings, so that they might think well of us and give us samples of the products of the land." The ships passed the Gambia River and reached a region 2000 "miles or leagues [one league equals three or more miles] . . . distant. . . . We returned and in nineteen months we reached our king."[13] This somewhat indefinite statement does not say clearly that Behaim claimed to have made this voyage himself, nor, as some have wanted to believe, that he accompanied Cão on the second voyage. Though the shift from the third to the first person in the Latin original of this legend makes it appear that Behaim claimed to have been on the voyage, it is nevertheless possible that he was quoting someone else when he shifted to the first person. Some have portrayed Behaim as providing a kind of scientific liaison between the northern European studies of the school of Johann Müller, Regiomontanus, famous German astronomer (Barros notes that Behaim boasted of being his student) and the navigation practiced by the Portuguese. That Behaim was educated is indicated by his knowledge of

Domingues. See Peres, *Descobrimentos portugueses*, pp. 276–277. Peres suggests that João II was highly displeased by Cão's inadvertent deception ("Dom João II was not a man to forgive mistakes like the one of Diogo Cão"), and Cão was left in disgrace and not honored for his great discoveries.

[11] Barros, *Ásia*, Dec. I, bk. 3 chap. 3. The inscription of Ielala has been accepted as evidence that Diogo Cão was on the Congo river. Near the cataracts, about 100 miles from the mouth of the river, are some rocks carved with a shield of Portugal, a cross, and a legend listing the names of Cão and a number of his crew. Cão drops mysteriously from history at this point, adding one more enigma to the list of those endlessly debated by historians. Peres, *Descobrimentos portugueses*, pp. 282–286.

[12] La Roncière says of the first Diogo Cão voyage: "Here for the continuation of the Diogo Cão voyage a difficulty presents itself. The route crosses that of another expedition. A duality of expeditions explains it seems the differences in the maps of Henricus Martellus (1489) and the globe of Martin Behaim (1492)," *Afrique*, II, 72–73, citing Luciano Cordeiro, *Diogo Cão*, p. 63.

[13] Cited in Peres, *Descobrimentos portugueses*, p. 279, and in Luciano Cordeiro, *Diogo Cão*.

Latin; also he was sufficiently competent to make his globe — though there are many errors of a strange kind if he indeed had sailed as far along the African coast as he is reputed to have done. It has not been established that he contributed to Portuguese navigational science. He was twenty-five years old when, perhaps as early as 1482 (but probably in 1484) he first came from Nuremberg to Portugal where he lived, except for visits to his homeland, until his death in 1507. It is doubtless true that he might have been principally interested in commerce, which can be said of most of the Portuguese explorers, as well as of Henry and João II. That he was motivated by desire for adventure likewise equates him with the discoverers. He was knighted (*cavaleiro*) in 1485 and was married in 1488, or before, to the daughter of the Fleming Jobst Hurter (Joz or Josse d'Utra), captain of the islands of Faial and Pico.[14]

In the *Liber chronicarum* compiled by Hartman Schedel and published in 1493 in Nuremberg, the same city in which the Behaim globe was constructed, there is a statement similar to the legend on Behaim's globe: "About 1483, the King of Portugal, João II, . . . sent certain galleys (*galés*) . . . southward toward Ethiopia. The captains were Diogo Cão and the German Martin Behaim of Nuremberg . . . highly expert in the geography and persevering at sea," who sailed southward to where "they opened up a new world[15] until then unknown. . . . After twenty-six months [sixteen months in the German version], many having died of the heat, they returned to Portugal bringing pepper, grains of paradise and many other things too numerous to mention."[16]

Schedel made the further statement that Behaim was sent "to determine the latitudes" according to the Ptolemaic system, which can only deepen our mystification. If Schedel meant latitudes determined from a land basis, there was no need to summon help for this from outside the Iberian Peninsula. If he meant the determination of latitude by celestial bodies from a ship at sea, he demonstrated no evidence of how this could be done at that date.[17] Neither the date 1484 on the globe nor 1483 in the

[14] Luciano Cordeiro, *Diogo Cão*, p. 49; Ernst Gerhard Jacob "Quelques points controversés . . . Colomb, Magalhães et Behaim"; G. H. T. Kimble, in "Some Notes on Mediaeval Cartography . . . Behaim's Globe," holds Behaim "ignorant" and his coast of Africa "falsified"; E. G. Ravenstein, *Martin Behaim*, chap. VII, and *passim*.

[15] The Portuguese is "Novo Mundo"; thus the concept "New World" was applied to Africa before the discovery of America.

[16] Quoted in Peres, *Descobrimentos portuguêses*, pp. 279–80.

[17] Peres holds that though it is uncertain that Behaim accompanied Cão, he might still have made the voyage with João Afonso Aveiro in 1484–85 as far as Benin. Peres, *Descobrimentos portuguêses*, pp. 277–282; Ravenstein, *Martin Behaim*, pp. 26–30.

Chronicarum accords with the belief that Cão's first voyage was in 1482 and his second in 1485.

João II's Triple Play

In 1487 João II started a three-pronged effort to solve the problems presented by Portuguese discoveries — his plan was to push further into the interior of Africa, to send out a new sea voyage (commanded by Bartolomeu Dias) that would go beyond the explorations of Cão and around Africa, and to establish contact with the East via the Mediterranean and the Levant.

Many Portuguese had gone some distance into the African interior by 1487 only to find that the desert region of the Sahara was dangerous and difficult, and more easily reached by the old caravan routes from Morocco and the Mediterranean than from the Atlantic coast. Inland from the rivers Senegal and Gambia, the tropical forest, some jungle, and some heavily settled lands offered both natural and human obstacles. Not much had been done to verify the loose estimate of Antoniotto Usodimare that about 300 leagues inland the lands of Prester John began. João was resolved to find out what the geography was really like, but because the maps he had to work with still erroneously showed the rounding coast receding toward the east, he failed in his attempts.

The news brought back about 1485 or 1486 by João Afonso Aveiro from Benin about an emperor named Ogané who held as high a position among the African people as the pope did among the Christians, and whose approval had to be won for the selection of lesser rulers, seemed to confirm earlier information. The journey to reach Ogané, mistaken by the Portuguese and Usodimare for Prester John, was said to be twenty moons, or about 250 to 300 leagues.[18] Though Ogané was not Prester John, he was a real ruler and may be identified as the Oni of Ife to whom the rulers of Benin in the fifteenth century accorded, and modern inhabitants still accord, a loose spiritual allegiance. João sent several emissaries inland to Timbuktu, to Takrur (Tucural), and to the rulers whose king João de Barros calls Mossi (king of the Moses). Whether these people were the Mossi of the Upper Volta River, who warred with Askia rulers of Songhai (to whom the Portuguese also sent emissaries) is not clear. João

[18] Prestage, *Portuguese Pioneers*, pp. 212–214; Barros, *Ásia*, Dec. I, bk. 3 chap. 4; Peres, *Descobrimentos portuguêses*, p. 315; Blake, *Europeans in West Africa*, pp. 78–79.

also sent along with Bartolomeu Dias several natives of Africa, previously brought to Portugal, to be left ashore to make inquiries. Only sketchy knowledge of the results survives.

Dias Discovers the Cape of Good Hope

Bartolomeu Dias sailed in early August 1487 and returned in December 1488.[19] The date of his return is verified by Columbus who was present in Lisbon and witnessed the arrival. He left a marginal note attesting to this in two works he used for his own education, the *Imago mundi* of Pierre D'Ailly and the *Historia rerum ubique gestarum* of Pope Pius II. Dias on his outward voyage passed beyond the point previously touched by Diogo Cão. Barros says he "named the capes, bays, and other landmarks, some for the saints day they reached a given place, some for other reasons."[20]

By December 4, 1487, Dias had gone beyond the last pillar implanted by Diogo Cão, passing Walvis Bay on December 8, and Hottentot Bay, December 23. Some days later, it is not clear when nor from what point, "putting out to sea, the weather forced them to run thirteen days with sail at half mast," according to Barros.[21] After thirteen days and when he had sensed the atmosphere to be distinctly cooler, he sought the coast again "taking care to run still north-south but, as they had run several days without seeing land, they turned to a northerly direction, coming to land at a bay they named Bahia dos Vaqueiros," possibly Mossel Bay about 23°E 35°S on the southeast coast of Africa.[22]

The great feat had been accomplished. What had been sought by many of the Portuguese mariners of Henry the Navigator's time, by the mariners of Diogo Gomes and by Diogo Cão, had now been found — the passage from the Atlantic to the Indian Ocean around the south of Africa. The distance sailed was some 70°S and 33°E of Lisbon.[23] According to the

[19] Peres, *Descobrimentos portuguêses*, pp. 287–314, discusses the difficulty of identifying who among the three or more men named Bartolomeu Dias was the discoverer, and which of two possibilities is the correct date of the discovery. Barros, *Ásia*, Dec. I, bk. 3 chap. 4, who gives the date as 1486–87, is now considered to be in error. See also, Peres, *Uma prioridade portuguêsa . . . incontestável* and A. Teixeira da Mota, "A viagem de Bartolomeu Dias."
[20] Barros, *Ásia*, Dec. I, bk. 3, ch. 4.
[21] *Ibid.*
[22] *Ibid.* The exact places and dates of this voyage are also disputed. *Descobrimentos portuguêses*, p. 298.
[23] Barros, *Ásia*, Dec. I, bk. 3, chap. 4 Ravenstein, Fontoura da Costa, and Eric Axelson have all attempted to identify places and dates of discovery, but they have been unable to agree with one another. Peres, *Descobrimentos portuguêses*, p. 297.

Columbus note mentioned above, they had reached 3100 leagues from Lisbon, "verified by the astrolabe that they were 45° beyond the equator." These measurements are roughly correct if we consider them applicable to the farthest point south reached by Dias (in which case he could measure latitude by astrolabe at sea), rather than to the south coast of Africa. Some students of the subject, above all those who seek to belittle Columbus, have considered the 45°S as an error made by Columbus himself, taking the 45° as meaning the southern point of Africa (which is actually approximately 35° degrees).

Stopping for a few days in the Bahia dos Vaqueiros to take on water and supplies, Dias found that the native Africans had kinky hair like those in Guinea, but that they spoke none of the languages known to his interpreters. They were intermittently friendly and hostile (one native was killed in combat) to the Portuguese.

After a few days, of sailing eastward, Dias passed what is today Cape Seal, Cape Recife, and Algoa Bay. Farther east, he reached a point identified by most modern historians as the Great Fish River (Rio do Infante). A few days later and farther along the coast, Dias was forced by the crew of his ships to start his return home from the area where the coast of Africa turned northeastward. Like Moses, says the chronicler António Galvão, "he was permitted to see but not to enter the promised land."[24] Returning westward, on May 16 he reached False Bay where he gave the name Cape of Good Hope to the great promontory overlooking it.[25] Coasting northward, on July 24 he again entered Angra das Voltas, where he had stopped outward bound. From here on he touched, according to Barros, three places: the island of Príncipe, where he picked up Duarte Pacheco Pereira, the Rio do Resgate, of unknown location, and Mina. He arrived in Lisbon on December 1488.[26]

There is no logbook, no chronicle, no diary of his voyage — only the sketchy account written by João de Barros sixty years later and other even less satisfactory histories. As little is chronicled about the reception of Dias on his return as about the voyage. He apparently received no honors

[24] Quoted in Peres, *Descobrimentos portugueses*, p. 300, from António Galvão, *Tratado dos descorbimentos*, 1st. ed., p. 26.

[25] Barros says he named the Cape *Tormentoso* (Cape of Storms) and that João II changed it to Cape of Good Hope. Duarte Pacheco, who made a part of the return journey with Dias, says that it was Dias who named it Cape of Good Hope.

[26] Peres, *Descobrimentos portugueses*, pp. 304–311; Gago Coutinho, "Cabo de Boa Esperança. A volta do Cabo," in *A náutica dos descobrimentos*, I, 271–299.

comparable to those heaped on Diogo Cão. The pension of twelve *milreis* which the king gave him from the revenues of the Casa da Guiné was a modest reward for one of the most important geographical discoveries ever made by man. Nor did João II manifest great interest in what Dias had done. He made no immediate efforts, so far as records show, to send out another expedition. The next voyage of importance was made by Vasco da Gama, almost nine years later.

Attempts to Penetrate the Interior of Africa

João was still determined to make discoveries in the interior of Africa and to assert his claims firmly. One effort was made to establish a fort at the mouth of Senegal River, similar to that of São Jorge da Mina, with various objectives in mind: to protect the area from interlopers, to use the post as a base from which to push up the Senegal River, still believed to be a branch of the Nile, and to reach the land of Prester John. At the least, he could tap the commerce of the interior of Africa and obtain information about a route to the Orient, the distance across Africa still unknown and greatly underestimated.

When in 1486 in a contest over the throne of one of the Jaloff (Wolof) peoples of the Senegal region, African King Bemoin asked for help, João II granted it on condition that the king and his subjects convert to Christianity. João sent missionaries and officials who, meeting with delaying tactics by Bemoin, were ordered home a year later. Alarmed by this order, Bemoin sent João II a hundred slaves, accompanied by the king's nephew, who, as Bemoin's representative, was to ask João II to continue his aid. Forced to flee by his enemies, Bemoin took refuge in the fort of Arguim, from which with twenty-five followers he embarked for Portugal, where he was received with great pomp and ceremony. After being instructed in Christianity, he was baptized December 3, 1489, with the Christian name of João, in honor of João II, as well as being knighted and given a coat of arms.

He was returned to Senegal with a Portuguese fleet of twenty-five caravels, under the command of Pedro Vaz da Cunha, with men, ammunitions, and supplies to establish a fort. Soon after reaching Bemoin's land again, Cunha accused him of treachery and assassinated him. Cunha then returned to Portugal without establishing the projected fort.[27]

[27] Barreto, *Guiné*, pp. 68–72; Blake, *Europeans in West Africa*, pp. 80–87.

Envoys to the East: Paiva and Covilhã

While João's several efforts to penetrate Africa were in progress, and while Dias was skirting the African coast, others were en route to the East and to Prester John (Ethiopia) by way of the Mediterranean and the Red Sea. The first chosen for this difficult task were Friar Antonio of Lisbon and Pero de Montarroio. They went first to Jerusalem because João "knew that many religious came as pilgrims to that sacred place" from Prester John's land. They got no further than Jerusalem. "Because they did not know Arabic" says Barros, "they did not dare go with the religious they met in Jerusalem."[28]

Two new emissaries were chosen who started the same year that Bartolomeu Dias initiated his voyage. They were Afonso de Paiva, who carried letters from João II to Prester John, and Pero de Covilhã, who was to gather information about the ports and navigation of the Indian Ocean. Of the qualifications of Paiva for this journey nothing is known.[29] Covilhã, however, was an adventurer who had grown up in Spain in the house of Ponce de León and was hardened by the rough-and-tumble fighting in the streets of Seville. He was a veteran of wars in Castile and had participated in the Battle of Toro. He had been present with Afonso V in the courts of Louis XI of France and the Duke of Burgundy, and had gone as a secret agent for Portugal to the court of Ferdinand and Isabella. He had twice been in North Africa where he had learned Arabic and accustomed himself to wearing desert clothing.

The two men left Santarém May 7, 1487, with 400 cruzados, part in cash and part in letters of credit provided by Bartolomeu Marchioni. They were also given instructions concerning the itinerary, according to the account of Father Francisco Álvares who heard the story from Covilhã in Ethiopia some thirty years later.[30] Traveling by way of Valencia, Barcelona, Naples, and Rhodes, they reached Alexandria disguised as merchants. From here they continued by way of Cairo in the company of Moors from Tremecem and Fez [Morocco] en route to Aden, where they arrived in the summer of 1488, a year after leaving Portugal. Here they parted, Afonso de Paiva for Ethiopia and Pero de Covilhã to India. Paiva

[28] Barros, Ásia, Dec. I, bk. 3, chap. 5.
[29] Ibid.; and C. F. Beckingham, "The Travels of Pero de Covilhã."
[30] Padre Francisco Álvares, Verdadeira informação das terras do Preste João das Índias, 1st. ed., 1540, and Barros, Ásia, are the main sources of information concerning Paiva and Covilhã. Barros wrote after the publication of Álvares's work; see Barros, Ásia, Dec. I, bk. 3, chap. 5.

died before he was able to carry out his mission; Covilhã shipped to Cannanore, from there to Calicut and Goa, and perhaps retraced some of his steps to Ormuz, from which he returned to Cairo in late 1490 or early 1491, and learned of the death of Paiva. João II had at this time known for two years or more the results of Bartolomeu Dias's voyage, which for the first time gave him and Europe a relatively accurate picture of what sailing around Africa meant.

In Cairo, Covilhã found two Jews who carried letters from João II ordering him to return if he had completed his mission; otherwise he was to continue. One of the men was Rabbi Abraham. The other was José de Lamego, said to be a shoemaker who had been to "Babylonia" [Baghdad?], where he had heard stories of Ormuz which he had related to João II before coming to search for Paiva and Covilhã. José was sent back to Portugal with a letter to João II, telling of the cinnamon and pepper of Calicut, of the clove that came from farther east, and of the importance of Calicut as a center where all spices could be obtained. Of greatest importance was Covilhã's report that it was possible to navigate to India by "the Guinea Sea" to Sofala, "to which he had also gone," on the east coast of Africa. Father Álvares does not state when Covilhã had been in Sofala. Barros says: "Covilhã embarked in Goa for the Mine of Sofala, which is in Ethiopia above Egypt," but it is not certain whether this means the city of Sofala or the general area.[31]

Rabbi Abraham of Beja went with Covilhã to Aden where they embarked to Ormuz. The rabbi was left there, and Covilhã proceeded to Ethiopia where he lived for the rest of his life, honored, married, and endowed with estates, but prevented from leaving by the Ethiopian emperor.

The Results of the Paiva-Covilhã Mission

What did João learn from this mission? A modern, respected Portuguese historian remarks that "João II must have been very happy" to receive the letter sent to him from Cairo by Pero de Covilhã.[32] The same historian remarks that meanwhile Bartolomeu Dias had long since returned, and the king "knew now from the information sent by Covilhã that the difficul-

[31]*Ibid.*, Dec. I, bk. 3, chap. 5.
[32]Peres, *Descobrimentos portuguêses*, p. 320.

ties offered by the route of the Indian Ocean to India were few — the maritime way to the Orient was open to the ships of Portugal."[33]

Proof that Pero de Covilhã's letters reached the king is inconclusive. The way in which Vasco da Gama conducted his voyage makes it difficult to believe that Covilhã's news of the East ever reached João II or Manuel. Gaspar Correia, not always considered a reliable source, remarks that "a long time intervened before [José] went to Portugal, the ships that went to discover Indian already having left."[34] Fernão Lopes de Castanheda, a more reliable source, says: "If the King Dom João received the letters Pero de Covilhã entrusted to the Jews, I did not know of it."[35]

About a year after Covilhã had left on his trip in 1487, an Ethiopian priest named Lucas Marcos came from Rome to Portugal. João II provided him with various letters for Prester John stating "the desire he had for his friendship and of how he had explored the whole coast of Africa and Ethiopia." By this means João hoped to come into closer association with Ethiopia. In 1492 Rui de Souza left the base at Pinda near what is today Santo António do Zaire and traveled inland to make a treaty of alliance with the Mani-Congo. Several priests and soldiers were left to convert the natives and seek Prester John. They penetrated some 200 miles up the Congo.[36]

The road to the East was not through Africa — a fact that Europeans only very slowly came to realize. In the late sixteenth century, and still later, men were seeking an easy land road across Africa from the Altantic to the Indian Ocean.

[33] The conclusion of Peres, *Descobrimentos portugueses*, p. 320. The Conde de Ficalho, in his *Viajens de Pedro de Covilhã*, p. 121, assumed the letter arrived because the Mediterranean was well traveled and the voyage easy.

[34] Gaspar Correia, *Lendas da Índia*, I, 6, 7, and 688; II, 325; III, 27–32, and *passim*, in Almeida, *História de Portugal*, II, 160, note 1.

[35] Fernão Lopes de Castanheda, *Descobrimento da Índia*, bk. I, chap. 1. João de Barros assumes the arrival of the letters.

[36] Francisco Leite de Faria, "Uma relção de Rui de Pina sôbre o Congo 1492"; António Silva Rêgo, *Portuguese Colonization*, pp. 23–41.

CHAPTER 11

Christopher Columbus: a Genoese Who Made a "Portuguese" Voyage for Spain

Columbus in Portugal: 1476–84

In the interval between the voyages of Bartolomeu Dias and Vasco da Gama, Portugal and the world were struck by the news that, as Rui de Pina wrote, "Columbus came from the discovery of the islands of Cipango [Japan] and the Antilles, where he went by order of the kings of Castile, from which land he brought the first examples of the people, and gold, and some other things."[1] What Columbus himself thought he had discovered is indicated by the papal bull of May 3, 1493, in which Castile was granted "in the ocean sea, in western waters, as is said, toward the Indians, . . . certain very remote islands and even mainlands, that hitherto had not been discovered by others."[2] The Portuguese attitude toward Columbus is characterized by a modern writer who says "the enterprise of Christopher Columbus, without any new concept thought up by him, can only be seen as an episode in the whole system of Portuguese attempts toward the west."[3] If this sounds like a Portuguese version of the fox's

---

[1] Rui de Pina, *Crónica João II*, chap. 46; Ferdinand Columbus, *Columbus*, chaps. 5, 6, and 11 (for objectives of his father); Barros, *Ásia*, Dec. I, bk. 3, chap. 11; Las Casas, *Historia*, bk. I, chap. 28.

[2] Davenport, *European Treaties*, pp. 58 and 62 (the Latin is *per partes ocidentales, ut dicetur, versus Indios, in mare oceano navigantes, certas insulas remotissimas, et etiam terras firmas. . . .*").

[3] Almeida, *História de Portugal*, II, 181–182; Arthur Lobo de Ávila, *Cristóbal Colón: Salvador Gonsalves Zarco*; Gago Coutinho, "Cristovão Colombo" in *A náutica dos descobrimentos*, I, 337–348; Las Casas, *Historia*, bk. I, chap. 29; Patrocínio Ribeiro, *A nacionalidade portuguêsa de Christóvam Colombo*.

sour grapes, it may be asked if there is not some justice in the belief that Columbus made a successful "Portuguese voyage to the west."

Columbus first arrived in Portugal in May 1476. As a result of a sea-fight off the southern coast of Portugal in which his ship was sunk, he swam ashore to the port of Lagos. He was en route to England at the time he was shipwrecked. From Lagos he went to Lisbon where his brother Bartolomeu was living. Before Columbus arrived in Portugal at about the age of twenty-five, he had had some seagoing experience in the Mediter-ranean, though not as a navigator. Inasmuch as he made no known voy-ages from the time he reached Spain nine years later, 1484–85, until his world-shaking voyage of 1492, it is evident that what he learned about navigating the Atlantic he learned in Portugal. In Lisbon he and his brother were partners in a chart-making and bookselling business. It is surmised that he thus encountered the books that were to influence him. In Portugal he learned Portuguese and Spanish, the latter becoming his principal tongue, which he spoke and wrote with a Portuguese admixture. He also wrote commercial Latin, then widely used in the Mediterranean and Atlantic.[4]

It has been mistakenly believed that he claimed to have made a voyage to Bristol, England in 1477 and then gone on to Iceland. But if the statement on which this belief is based is properly interpreted, it is clear that Columbus made no such claim.[5] In 1479 he was back in Genoa where he stated that the year before he had been in Lisbon and in Madeira to buy sugar, and that he was returning to Portugal. Columbus was closely associated with the chief Italian merchants, and those living in Portugal introduced him quickly into his new environment. Among his business associates were such important families as the Spinola, the Paola Di Negro, the Centurione, and the Jeronimo de Medicis, all of whom carried on business in Madeira where Columbus was at one time a resident. In 1479 or 1480 Columbus married Felipa Perestrelo e Monis, the daughter of Bartolomeu Perestrelo, an Italian of noble origin and captain of Porto Santo, and on her mother's side the granddaughter of Gil Aires Monis of Algarve, who fought at Ceuta. Columbus was thus well connected in

[4] Samuel Eliot Morison, *Columbus Mariner*, pp. 6–10, and *Admiral of the Ocean Sea*, I, 36; T. O. Marcondes de Souza, *O descobrimento da América*, pp. 102–111; Jean M. Mariejol, *The Spain of Ferdinand and Isabella*: Charles Verlinden and Florentino Pérez Embid, *Cristóbal Colón, passim*; H. Vignaud, *Historia de . . . Christophe Colomb*.

[5] Some have held he went as far as Iceland, though with little evidence. See Alwyn A. Ruddock, "Columbus and Iceland: New Light on an Old Problem," who says: "In conclu-sion, therefore, it seems clear that Columbus never went to Iceland" [nor to Bristol].

Portugal. In 1480 he moved to Porto Santo, a good position from which to learn about Portuguese voyages. In 1482 he accompanied Diogo de Azambuja in the settlement of São Jorge da Mina on the Guinea coast of Africa. His son and biographer Ferdinand Columbus says "it was in Portugal that the admiral began to surmise that if men could sail so far south one might also sail west and find lands in that direction."[6] Columbus's mother-in-law allegedly gave him her husband's charts and notes. What these contained can only be surmised, for certainly there is nothing to justify the belief that the papers revealed a "secret" voyage to America as has been alleged.

Speculation about Land to the West

While in Portugal, Columbus became acquainted with a letter, in which a map was enclosed, written by Paolo dal Pozzo Toscanelli on June 24, 1474, to the Portuguese cônego Fernão Martins, councillor of King Afonso V. Toscanelli wrote: "Although I have on many other occasions mentioned the very short distance from here to the places where the spices grow, by sea shorter than the way you go by Guinea, the Serenissimo Rey asks me to describe how even the least informed can understand and follow that road; and though it could be done using a globe, showing the configuration of the world, I decided to show the said road on a map similar to those made for navigation, and so I send it to Your Majesty, drawn by my hand, in which are represented your shores and islands where you began to navigate toward the west, and . . . the number of miles you must go to reach the places of the spices and precious stones."[7]

Failure to find the original of the letter or the map caused some historians to question their authenticity. The letter is now generally accepted, but no authentic copy of the map has been found. Some Portuguese

---

[6] Morison, Columbus Mariner, p. 13; E. G. R. Taylor, "Ideas of the Shape and Habitability of the Earth." The idea of finding lands to the west had been encouraged by the freedom taken by cartographers in strewing the Atlantic Ocean with islands. The known existence of the Canaries, plus the settlement of Madeira during the 1420s and the discovery of the Azores from about 1427, were proof enough to many mariners that other lands existed to the west. The map of 1424 as well as maps bearing dates 1435, 1446, 1448, and later showing such islands as Antillas, Satanaz, Brazil, as well as many others, could hardly fail to whet the appetites of those who would emulate the adventures which had made captains of João Gonçalves Zarco, Tristão Vaz Teixeira, Bartolomeu Perestrelo, Jós de Hurtere, and Diogo de Teive in the Madeira and the Azores islands.

[7] Quoted in Peres, Descobrimentos portuguêses, pp. 322–323.

historians deny that Toscanelli's theory had any influence in Portugal, noting that it was rejected by King João II (1481–95). One historian remarks: "The only plausible explanation of the disinterest is to admit that there was already knowledge of the geographical realities in Portugal about the western Atlantic, or, at least, a more exact evaluation than Toscanelli's of the dimensions of the globe."[8]

Columbus had more faith in Toscanelli's idea than did the Portuguese. In 1483 or 1484 he petitioned King João II to finance him in a venture to the west. The Portuguese historian João de Barros gives a version of why João II rejected Columbus's proposals to him: the king seeing that "Columbus was very talkative and vain (*glorioso*) in showing his capacity and more fanciful and imaginative with his island of Cipango than correct in what he said, paid little heed to him."[9] João submitted the Columbus project to his advisers and, as Barros reports, "all held what Columbus said to be nonsense."[10] Columbus then left Portugal for Spain either late in 1484 or early in 1485.[11] Though Columbus was rejected, on June 1484, Fernão Domingues do Arco was promised the captaincy of an island which he proposed to discover toward the west, "after the said island has been found."[12]

Among the serious proposals for discoveries to the west was one made by Fernão Dulmo (Van Olmen), described as knight and captain in the island of Terceira, who, the king noted, "wishes to find a large island or islands or mainland (*terra firme per costa*) which is presumed to be the Island of the Seven Cities, and all this at his own cost and expense."[13] As historians have loved to point out, the terms of this grant are similar to those Columbus was later to receive from Spain, except that the Spanish crown contributed to the expense of the voyage of discovery. It should be remembered, however, that the provisions of the grant to Dulmo did not differ greatly from those of previous grants except that the words "*terra firme per costa*" were added, presumably meaning mainland as opposed to island, and held by some to show that a discovery had already been made. Dulmo was to be given the hereditary captaincy of the lands he might discover "with all the income and rights," including "criminal

[8]*Ibid.*, p. 325.
[9]Barros, *Ásia*, Dec. I, bk. 3, chap. 11.
[10]*Ibid.*
[11]Juan Manzano Manzano, *Cristóbal Colón.*
[12]Peres, *Descobrimentos portuguêses*, p. 329, citing *Alguns documentos*, p. 56.
[13]*Ibid.*, pp. 329, 345–346, citing *Alguns documentos*, pp. 58–59.

jurisdiction with power to garrot and kill and administer all other penalties."[14]

Dulmo took as his partner and co-captain João Afonso do Estreito of Madeira. They agreed on a division of the expenses and proposed March 1487 as the date of departure from Terceira. Each would command a caravel, and for the first forty days Dulmo would be in charge of the expedition; thereafter for a projected six-month voyage João Afonso would be in command. João Afonso obtained for himself the captaincy of the lands that might be discovered during the time he led the expedition.

Nothing further is known about this expedition, which perhaps never was organized as planned. In June 1487 Dulmo was still in Terceira. It seems exaggerated to regard this as a pre-Columbian voyage. But it is to be noted that the demands Columbus made of João II and Ferdinand and Isabella were clearly similar to those already made by other explorers in Portugal. "In conclusion, everything leads to the belief that the initiative of Fernão Dulmo did not go beyond a project which circumstances prevented him from converting into an actual voyage."[15]

Columbus was back in Lisbon in December 1488, when Bartolomeu Dias arrived after discovering the Cape of Good Hope.[16] Columbus had returned to Portugal at the urgent request of João II. However, João employed neither Columbus nor any of his own seamen to make further immediate discoveries. Thus it was that Columbus, an Italian by birth, though Portuguese by seagoing experience and navigation, made a voyage in Spanish service, which was essentially like several already made by Portuguese seeking land unsuccessfully in the Atlantic Ocean. It was painful then for the Portuguese to learn of his success and is still painful in retrospect for modern Portuguese to contemplate what might have been if João II's advisers had not found Columbus's proposal "nonsense."

[14]*Ibid.*, p. 330, 345–346, citing *Alguns documentos*, pp. 62–63; Peres finds it greatly significant that the grant to Fernão Telles in 1475 said nothing of *terra firme* but the grant to Dulmo did.

[15]Peres, *Descobrimentos portugueses*, p. 334. Peres shows conclusively that the effort of André L'Hoist in 1933 to prove this voyage reached Brazil is based on alleged "Lisbon Archives" without specifying which archives and which documents. He apparently relied on Serpa for his information, but Serpa nowhere says Dulmo discovered Brazil. Arthur Davies also alleges a Dulmo discovery, using the Juan de la Cosa map of 1500(?), and the Cantino and Canerio maps of 1502, as well as the Waldsemüler map of 1507. His reasoning is not generally accepted. Peres, *Descobrimentos portugueses*, pp. 329–334.

[16]One of the curious coincidences of history occurred when Columbus, driven by storm into Lisbon on March 4, 1493, anchored at Belém, and the commander of a large ship anchored alongside was Bartolomeu Dias.

First Voyage: Columbus Driven by Storm into Portugal

When Columbus returned from his first voyage driven by storm to the island of Santa Maria in the Azores, members of his crew were held prisoner for a short time before being allowed to sail on. When he reached Lisbon on March 4, 1493, [17] in another storm which had almost sunk his ship, he presented a grave problem to João II. "The King Dom João hearing the news of the location where Columbus said the discovered land was, became very confused and believed really that the discovered land belonged to him, and gave the members of his council to understand so." [18] João informed Columbus that he believed he had intruded on the areas that belonged to Portugal according to the Treaty of Alcáçovas in 1479. Columbus was aware of the significance of the treaty for he refers in his diaries to the "convention existing between the kings." [19] João II accused Columbus of poaching in his territory. But since the Indians Columbus brought back were clearly different from the blacks of Guinea, João was in serious doubt. Barros says João "was very upset to see that the people who came with him did not have black, kinky hair like those of Guinea, but rather resembling the color of hair which he was informed was like that of India over which he had labored so hard." [20]

Columbus conducted himself before the king with his accustomed self-confidence (arrogance, as the Portuguese saw it), and some of the courtiers offered to see to it that he never reached Castile to tell his story. Rejecting such advice as both unchristian and undiplomatic, João II, greeted Columbus with courtesy, clothed him and his followers, refitted his ship, and allowed him to sail to Spain.

Barros's assessment of Columbus was very likely the one that prevailed when Barros wrote in the mid-sixteenth century. "According to what all say, he was of the Genoese nation, a skillful man, eloquent, a good Latinist, and very honorable in his undertakings (*muy glorioso em seus negocios*)" [21]

João II ordered a fleet prepared under the command of Francisco de

---

[17] Peres, *Descobrimentos portugueses*, pp. 349–50.
[18] Barros, *Ásia*, Dec. I, bk. 3, chap. 11; T. O. Marcondes de Souza, "A divulgação . . . do descobrimento."
[19] Martín Fernández de Navarrete, *Colección de los viajes*, I, 310.
[20] Barros, *Ásia*, Dec. I, bk. 3, chap. 11.
[21] *Ibid.*

Almeida to seek the land Columbus had visited. Spain protested this project, requested that João II not send a fleet until a determination could be made of the area of the discoveries with respect to existing treaties of territorial division, and invited João to send ambassadors. Thus began the negotiations which were to lead to the Treaty of Tordesillas.

The arrival of Columbus liberated Castile from the narrow strip of sea along the Atlantic coast defined in the Treaty of Alcáçovas. As one modern Spanish historian has said: "In strong contrast [with what Spain possessed by treaty] all the riches of the mines, all the roads of the ocean, all the possibilities of the Indies had fallen to the Lusitanian crown."[22] Suddenly, in the seas in which Portugal had had no rival, it was faced with Spanish claims.

The Papal Bulls and the Treaty of Tordesillas

In the negotiations that now began, in which both nations made polite representations that were threats of war, João II first claimed the land to the south of an east-west line drawn from the Canaries, leaving for Spain only the lands north of this line.[23] An ambassador, Rui de Sandi, was sent to Barcelona where Ferdinand and Isabella then were. Before he reached Barcelona, a Spanish ambassador, Lope de Herrera, had left for Portugal to make it clear that Spain now claimed the ocean north or south of the Canaries, except that part defined in Alcáçovas as "below the Canaries, toward Guinea." As Spain saw it, the treaty in which it had lost all except the Canaries now became a claim to a vast ocean with unknown possibilities. It was urgent that Portuguese and Spanish spheres be redefined. New embassies were exchanged. But Spain had not delayed in putting forth claims with the chief seat of international authority — the papacy. Inasmuch as the Treaty of Alcáçovas had been ratified by the papacy in 1481, only the pope could define the new status of the rivals.[24]

---

[22] Pérez Embid, *Descubrimientos*, p. 234.

[23] Soon after the arrival of Columbus in Portugal, João II sent his ambassador Rui de Sandi to the Castilian court with instructions to say that "as he understood that the Castilian kings wished to continue discoveries westward from the Canary Islands, without going south, he [João] requested them to order the Admiral [Columbus] to observe this order and he [João] would command his ship in their voyages of discovery not to sail to the north." Cited in Peres, *Descobrimentos portuguêses*, p. 350, note 3, from Herrera, *Historia general de los hechos de los castellanos en las islas y tierra firme del mar y océano*; Barros, *Ásia*, Dec. I, bk. 2, chap. V. For the relation of Portugal and Spain under Ferdinand and Isabella, see the two works by Antonio de la Torre cited in the bibliography.

[24] Pérez Embid, *Descubrimientos*, pp. 237–238, citing Ruméu de Armas, *Colón en*

The first news of Columbus's discovery reached Rome from Lisbon April 11, 1493, a week before Columbus himself arrived in Barcelona.[25] The Spanish ambassador to the Holy See since 1484 was Bernardino de Carvajal. He communicated the news officially to the Vatican in time for the first bull *Inter Caetera* to be issued by Alexander VI, May 3, according to which the sovereigns of Castile were granted lands discovered and to be discovered if not possessed by any Christian power. Portugal's previous rights were protected by the statement that "no right conferred on any Christian Prince is hereby to be understood as withdrawn or to be withdrawn." This vague division satisfied neither Spain nor Portugal. It drew no set boundaries in the Atlantic between the claims of the two nations. A second bull *Eximiae Devotionis* bore the same date but apparently was not expedited until July.[26] It reinforced the Spanish claim. A third bull, also named *Inter Caetera*, bears the date May 4 but was actually expedited in June.[27] It is worthy of note that though *Eximiae Devotionis* was issued first, it was expedited later than the second *Inter Caetera* of May 4.

The second *Inter Caetera* made a fundamental change in the division of territory. It set a line one hundred leagues west of either the Azores or the Cape Verde Islands, thus imposing a limitation on Spain not in either of the other bulls. An interesting question is who caused this change which was not to the interest of Spain. One suggestion is that Pedro da Silva, Portuguese envoy to the Vatican, objected to the vague terms of the first bulls and suggested the third.[28]

Negotiations, details of which unfortunately have been lost, were continuing meanwhile between Spain and Portugal. Spain sought to make its claim even more secure and obtained a fourth bull, *Dudum Siquidem*,[29] September 26, 1493. It confirmed the *Inter Caetera* of May 4 and ex-

---

Barcelona, pp. 45–47, who cites Zurita, *Anales de Aragón*, V. chap. 25, and Fernández de Navarrete, *Colección*, II, 123; Davenport, *European Treaties*, pp. 56–63; Edmundo Genofre, "Cristóvão Colombo e a ação papal."

[25] Henry Harrisse, *The Discovery of North America* (reissued by Israel, Amsterdam, 1961), pp. 54ff., cites Domenico Malipero in *Annali Veneti* which gives an extensive description of Columbus's voyage under date of April 11; see also Henry Harrisse, *Christophe Colon*, II, 117; Gago Coutinho, "Henry Harrisse e a descoberta da América," in *A náutica dos descobrimentos*, II, 238–249.

[26] Davenport, *European Treaties*, p. 64–70.

[27] *Ibid.*, pp. 71–78.

[28] Harrisse, *Discovery*, pp. 54–58; Harrisse, *Christopher Colon*, II, 117ff. For a contrary view, see Peres, *Descobrimentos portuguêses*, pp. 351–360. Marcondes de Souza holds Harrisse's view, see *Descobrimento da América*, 102ff. and *passim*.

[29] Davenport, *European Treaties*, pp. 79–83.

tended its meaning to cover any lands discovered by Spain in her westward navigation, even in the eastern regions of the Indies, excluding all other crowns, which meant Portugal, from navigation, fishing, or exploring without the license of Spain. The bull even revoked earlier papal grants which had given Portugal a claim to lands not actually in its possession in those regions. Portugal was now limited by papal pronouncements to the regions between the African coast and one hundred leagues west of the Azores or the Cape Verdes. Spain had seemingly reversed the situation with regard to possession of new discoveries. However, João II was not the sort of monarch who would permit himself to be thus deprived of what his nation had struggled so long to procure. In negotiations which made it clear he would resort to war to assert his claims, he forced on Spain the Treaty of Tordesillas on June 7, 1494.[30] By this treaty a line of demarcation was set 370 leagues beyond the Cape Verde Islands, giving Portugal claim to Brazil which was yet to be discovered. Any land found by either country in the bounds of the other was to be surrendered. The line was to be established by a commission of representatives of the pilots, astrologers, and mariners of the two nations. The commission was to sail westward to two caravels within ten months until they had found land or had determined the line. Since contemporary methods of establishing longitude were insufficient, the proposed demarcation was at first postponed and later abandoned. The two nations disputed the issue until 1777.[31]

[30] Davenport, *European Treaties*, pp. 84–106; Carlos Coimbra, "Os objetivos portuguêses do Tratado de Tordesilhas"; Gago Coutinho, "Tratado de Tordesillas," in *A náutica dos descobrimentos*, I, 300–314; Manuel Múrias, "Legitimidade do direito de Portugal às terras descobertas: Tratado de Tordesillas."

[31] Pérez Embid, *Descubrimientos*, pp. 245–248.

CHAPTER 12

Vasco da Gama: "May the Devil Take You! What Brought You Here?"

Why No Explorer Immediately Followed the Dias Discovery

The return of Bartolomeu Dias from the discovery of the Cape route to the Indian Ocean and the reception of the report of Pero de Covilhã, if that report indeed reached the king's hands, should have signalized, it seems, vigorous action in following up these two encouraging leads. Instead, more than eight years elapsed before the next known expedition, Vasco da Gama's, which reached India. Why the long delay, especially when in 1485 João II had informed the pope, and thus all Europe, that he was at the doors of India?

Various explanations have been offered.[1] The king was preoccupied with many problems: the Moroccan campaign in which there was hard fighting in 1487 and 1488; the two fleets João sent in 1489 in an unsuccessful effort to construct a fort on the island of Graciosa, a few leagues from Larache; another fleet sent to Morocco in 1490; the death of the king's son Afonso, heir to the throne, killed when his horse fell in July 1491; the expulsion of the Jews from Spain and their flight into Portugal in 1492, a situation to which João had to devote considerable time; and Columbus's discovery of America and the need to secure Portuguese rights. If the Covilha report did not reach João in time for him to take

[1] Almeida, *História de Portugal*, II, 162–170, 186; David Lopes, in Peres, *História de Portugal*, II, 450–452; also Lopes, in *HEP*, I, 153–154; Elaine Sanceau, *The Reign of the Fortunate King*, pp. 1–25.

175

advantage of the information it contained, this too would have delayed him. The death of João in 1495 and the accession of Manuel have also been considered causes for delay. The marriage negotiations between Manuel and the Catholic kings for the marriage of their daughter who demanded the expulsion of the Jews and Muslims from Portugal required Manuel's attention during the latter part of 1495 and down to the year 1497. Some historians have suggested that the royal counselors thought Portugal too weak and too poor for long sea ventures, and saw the Dias trip as a discouraging rather than an encouraging event. João de Barros reports that King Manuel held a council concerning the da Gama voyage "in which there were many different opinions, the majority holding that India should not be discovered."[2] The majority did not prevail and the preparations for the voyage continued.

A number of historians have rejected all these explanations of why there were no expeditions and have alleged that there were successful expeditions which sailed the Atlantic in secret to gather evidence concerning ocean currents, wind patterns, and sailing conditions generally. One such voyage at least was said to have reached America before Columbus. During these secret sailings, new types of ships were said to have been built and tested. There is some logic to, but no proof of, the alleged experimentation in shipbuilding and neither logic to nor proof of secret voyages. In fact, if the reasons given above for the delay between the Dias and the da Gama voyages are valid, they would be equally so for secret voyages.[3]

Vasco da Gama: 1497–99

Vasco da Gama embarked in a fleet of four vessels on July 8, 1497, and sighted India on May 18, 1498.[4] The first of his ships returned to Portugal in July 1499. He sailed around Africa and returned, a distance greater than that around the world at the equator; twice he had been out of sight of land for ninety days; and he completed the first voyage ever definitely known to have been made by sea between the West and the

[2] Barros, Ásia. Dec. I, bk. 4, ch. 1.

[3] On "Secrecy" see Jaime Cortesão who summarizes his writings between 1928 and 1960 in Descobrimentos, I, 92–118, 211–249, 256–269, 360–390, 477–500; II, 9–145 and passim; Gago Coutinho, Á náutica dos descobrimentos, bears heavily on "secrecy."

[4] K. G. Jayne, Vasco da Gama; Elaine Sanceau, Good Hope; Augusto C. Teixeira de Aragão, Vasco da Gama.

East. The economic and social life of the world were to be profoundly changed by the new trade route opened up by his voyage. The grandiosity of what he did is indisputable. However, many of the details concerning his voyage are uncertain. The only eyewitness account is an anonymous chronicle (or diary) kept by one of the participants in the voyage, sometimes identified as Álvaro Velho.[5] Other information is gained from letters written by Italian merchants in Portugal, from letters sent by King Manuel to announce the discovery, and from the sixteenth-century historians. Much contradictory information about what are essentially minor aspects of the expedition has caused some modern historians to lose sight of the great significance of the expedition as they debate among themselves the disputed details.

Hardly any of the details are generally agreed upon. It is not known for certain when the voyage was first planned, why Vasco da Gama was chosen to lead it, when the ships were built, what the names of all the ships were, what types of ships there were, how many men were in the crews, or how many died on the voyage (two ships of the four were lost). The diary states that the fleet sailed on July 8, but this too is somewhat uncertain since other dates are given by early historians. What route they sailed from Santiago in the Cape Verde Islands to Santa Helena Bay, more than ninety days out of sight of land, is unknown; but it has been imaginatively reconstructed by various historians on the basis of ocean currents and wind conditions. Finally, it is not known if Vasco da Gama returned to Lisbon in August or September of 1499. That his return began a transformation in world economic history, to which only a generation later the effects of Columbus's voyage began to contribute fundamentally, is certain.

Da Gama's Objectives, Ships, and Men

When Vasco da Gama sailed, his objectives were clear. He was ordered to find the way to India, tap the spice markets of the East, and make contact and possibly treaties of peace and alliance with Christian rulers who

[5]*Diário da viagem de Vasco da Gama.* Also José Pedro Machado and Viriato Campos, *Vasco da Gama e a sua viagem de descobrimento.* For a good account see Peres, *Descobrimentos portugueses,* pp. 361–406, and Sanceau, *Good Hope.* For an interpretation by a mariner, see Gago Coutinho, "O diário da primeira viagem de Vasco da Gama à Índia," in *A náutica dos descobrimentos,* I, 440–514, and "O descobrimento do caminho marítimo para a Índia," I, 385–402.

supposedly lived there. His mission was essentially exploration, not commercial venture. He carried few trade goods and those he did take, as it turned out, were appropriate only to the simple economy of western Africa and not at all to the sophisticated society of the East. He was commissioned with letters of accreditation to Prester John and to the Samorin of Calicut, but he had not been informed about Eastern customs and therefore was not properly prepared. In the West the kings gave presents to their retainers; in the East, as Vasco da Gama found out in a painful way, the custom was for the visitors to bring rich gifts to the monarchs.

Of his four ships, two were described as *naus* newly built for the voyage, one was possibly a caravel, and the other a supply ship, presumably another *nau*. His ships, whether they are described as *naus* or caravels, were built with the benefit of the experience that almost a century of high-seas sailing and explorations had given to Portuguese ship carpenters and mariners.

His crew may have numbered as many as 170, of which only fifty-five(?) were to return. Vasco da Gama, born to a family of minor nobility in the fishing village Sines on the Atlantic coast 100 miles south of Lisbon, was described by Damião de Góis as "an unmarried man of the right age to bear up under the strains of such a voyage,"[6] and by Lopes de Castanheda as "experienced in sea going and who had done many services for King João."[7] The other ship captains were da Gama's brother Paulo, Nicolau Coelho, and Gonçalo Nunes. His pilots, i.e., navigators, included the most experienced men in Portugal, among them Pero de Alenquer, Pero Escobar, João de Coimbra, and Afonso Gonçalves.

"We left Restelo a Saturday the eighth day of the month of July of the year 1497," says the anonymous diarist.[8] They were accompanied by Bartolomeu Dias in a caravel bound for São Jorge da Mina. On July 27 the ships, which had become separated en route, rejoined in Santiago, in the Cape Verde Islands, where they remained for a week putting things in order. They sailed from Santiago on August 3, and for the next ninety days they were at sea out of sight of land. The route taken can only be conjectured on the basis of wind patterns in the South Atlantic; it cannot be known for certain with information now at hand. Many historians

[6] Damião de Góis, *Crónica do D. Emanuel*, pt. I, chap. 23.
[7] Lopes de Castanheda, *Descobrimento da Índia*, bk. 1, chap. 11.
[8] All quotations, unless otherwise noted, are from the *Diário da viagem de Vasco da Gama*.

nevertheless have drawn lines through the Atlantic showing the supposed sailing route and have defended their ideas with fervor.

From Santiago "we left in an easterly direction," says the diarist, which would have taken them along the well-known coastal route of Africa. But the one thing that can be said positively about their route is that it was not along the coast. On August 18, sailing in a "southerly direction," Vasco da Gama's ship, the *São Gabriel*, suffered a small accident. "This would be 200 leagues from Santiago," where they were delayed for two days and a night. On August 22, they sailed through the sea a "south quarter southwest" direction and encountered many birds similar to herons, "which at nightfall flew in a S.S.E. direction and this," says the diarist, "a good 800 leagues at sea." Reckoned from where? Many have guessed; nobody can say for sure. Some have tried to solve the mystery by finding an appropriate point of land 800 leagues (i.e., some 2400 miles) distant, and others have guessed that the diarist skipped August and was writing in September or October. Whether Vasco da Gama was caught in the belt of weak and variable winds, the doldrums that separates the northeast trades from the southwest trades, is not known. The assumption made by many that trade winds blow so true they enable a ship to sail its desired course like a train running on a track is false and therefore it would be incorrect to postulate da Gama's route on the basis of this assumption. Trade winds can and do temporarily vary greatly from their general direction, and many tropical storms originate in the area west and southwest of the Cape Verde Islands.

In any case, Vasco da Gama was sailing in a vast ocean where no one is known to have sailed before and was depending on his pilots to navigate to the known land of South Africa, already touched by Dias in 1488. His great gamble paid off, for his pilots carried him south and east, with winds which later experience showed to be westerly, to the coast of Africa approximately at Santa Helena Bay, 100 miles north of the Cape of Good Hope. Sailing directions down to the present day are for ships to hit the equator, ideally between 25° and 30°W, and to sail south or a little southwesterly until they find the westerlies to take them around Good Hope.

From the East Coast of Africa to India

They were not lost. Pero de Alenquer estimated correctly their distance from the Cape. Resting eight days to take on water, wood, and whatever supplies were available, they sailed on and passed the Cape November 22, with the wind astern, reaching the Angra de São Braz on November 25. Here the cargo of the supply ship was distributed among the other vessels, the ship was broken up, and a pillar planted (which the natives destroyed before da Gama was out of sight of land). They sailed December 6 and headed north along Africa's east coast. Both the winds and the currents were against them. Not until December 25 did they reach the point still called Natal (Christmas). On January 11, 1498, being short of water they put in to shore at a place which they called "land of the good people" and "River of Copper" in southern Mozambique. On January 24 and 25, they reached the "River of Good Omen" (Rio dos Bons sinais), probably at Quelimane, where they planted another pillar. They had not touched Sofala, the future center of gold trade, because of the westward indentation of the coast from Inharrime to Cape Quelimane. The condition of the crew was now pitiful; scurvy had struck them. "There were many with swelled feet and hands, the gums growing over the teeth to such an extent they could not eat." After a month spent restoring their health, they continued to the island of Mozambique March 2.

Here Vasco da Gama received good news. Further up the coast at Melinde, he was told, he could find pilots who could guide him across the Indian Ocean. Here also he met the first of the Muslim merchants who dominated the trade of that ocean. Taking on a pilot, they sailed March 11. Adverse currents of water, calms, and contrary winds held the ships in check, and only on March 27 were they able to sail north.

After a day and half of sailing north they came to Melinde where the ruler was also Muslim but was friendly and became a firm ally of the Portuguese. They also found the pilot they were seeking, Ahmed Ibn Madgid. Some modern historians believe he was the most famous pilot and authority on navigation of his time; but this is not sufficiently documented to be accepted as fact.[9] It was, fortunately for them, the period of the southwestern monsoon which blows in the spring and summer. This took them across the ocean in a generally northeasterly direction. They sighted India on May 18, 1498 and dropped anchor a few miles north of Calicut at the port of Capocate on May 20.[10]

[9] T. A. Chumovsky, Três roteiros; Costa Broachado, O piloto Árabe de Vasco da Gama. See Luis de Albuquerque, "Quelques commentaires sur la navigation orientale" for doubts about the identity of da Gama's pilot.

[10] On India at the time of the Portuguese arrival, see Romila Thapar (and Percival Spear),

Da Gama's First Experiences and Surprises in India

The long-sought goal had been reached — the West had found the East.[11] Da Gama had proved that Ptolemy's classical geographical concept that India and Africa were joined by land, with a lake between, was wrong; but during the hazardous journey it had also been discovered that André Bianco and Fra Mauro had on their maps incorrectly placed the tip of Africa approximately at the Gulf of Aden. Da Gama and his crew had made what seems in retrospect to have been an impossible voyage. They would encounter equally great problems in their relationships with the people of newly found India and in their return voyage to Portugal.

The day after they reached Capocate, a party was sent ashore and was greeted by two Moors from Tunis, one of whom spoke to them in Castilian: "May the Devil take you! What brought you here?" The answer to this was "Christians and spices." Back aboard ship, another of the Moors greeted the captain with "good luck, lots of rubies, lots of emeralds!" The Portuguese were "greatly astonished to hear our tongue (*sic*) spoken so far from Portugal." They found the men to be poorly dressed and the women "as a rule ugly and of small stature." But more important, they wore "many jewels of gold . . . bracelets . . . rings set with precious stones, on their toes."

Da Gama was asked to come to Calicut to see the Samorin. The trip into the city was by boat and by land, and throughout the journey the Portuguese were surrounded by thousands of curious people, who "had all come to see us." On the way they came to what they thought was a Christian church, inside of which "stood a small image which they said represented Our Lady." The Portuguese were so anti-Muslim that, not daunted by the Hindu images, they worshipped them as Christian. The "saints" with protruding teeth and several arms looked strange; but because the Muslims had no images, the Portuguese assumed that the statues and those who worshiped them were Christian. The crowds became so dense the Portuguese could hardly move.

At last they were in the palace and at the door of the room where the Samorin awaited them. Now began the unpleasant episodes. "Several men were wounded at this door and we got in only by force." They were

A *History of India*; K. M. Panikkar, *India and the Indian Ocean*; Lopes de Castanheda, *Descobrimento da Índia*, vol. 1.

[11] K. M. Panikkar, *Asia and Western Dominance*.

awestruck by the sight of velvet, fine cotton cloth (finer than any linen,"), large gold cups (in fact, spittoons for the disposal of betel nuts), silver jugs, a gilt canopy, and the jewels worn by the Samorin. They withdrew to a separate room, where da Gama explained the long Portuguese search for the road to India and declared that their objective was to find Christians like themselves, rather than to search for gold and silver since they had in Portugal "such abundance that they did not need what was to be found in India."

The next day, Tuesday, May 29, da Gama got ready gifts for the Samorin, which were poor indeed in comparison with the finery and riches they had seen the night before. The Indians "laughed at him," and the Samorin's agents refused to present him to their ruler with such poor stuff. Da Gama was kept waiting all day and night, and finally left the palace. But on May 30 he was again taken to the palace, now crowded with armed men. Here he was again kept waiting and treated with little respect. When he was finally received, the Samorin scoffed at him for the poor gifts but seemed pleased at the contents of the letters he had brought.

When the Portuguese attempted to return to their ships, they became embroiled in almost constant misunderstandings and quarrels with the Indians. It seemed to them that they were caught in a trap. The Indians sought to have da Gama's fleet sail closer to shore, but the Portuguese feared the fleet would be captured. Da Gama and his men were in effect prisoners. The Indians ordered da Gama to have his merchandise brought ashore for sale. "The merchants sent by the king remained eight days but instead of buying, belittled the merchandise." Da Gama now requested that his merchandise be sent to Calicut, which the Samorin ordered done "at his own expense as nothing belonging to the king of Portugal was to be burdened with charges . . . but this was done because they intended to do us harm . . . for the king had been told that we were thieves who went about stealing."

Relations with the populace, the "Christians," were still good. The Portuguese came ashore freely, and swarms of people went over the ships, though the hungry masses robbed the Portuguese of their food. Da Gama left a factor ashore with the merchandise and men to assist him. The Portuguese sold their trade goods cheaply in order to bring home small supplies of cloves, cinnamon, and precious stones. It was now mid-August; the Portuguese had been in the country for three months and were anxious to sail for home.

When the Portuguese approached the Samorin for permission to leave and requested that he send presents to the king of Portugal, he showed a "bad face," held some of the Portuguese prisoners, and prohibited all boats from approaching the Portuguese ships. "We felt grieved," say the diarist, "to think that a Christian king . . . should treat us in such a bad way." The treatment was blamed on "the Moors of the palace" who were seeking to discredit the Portuguese. When a week later, August 19, things had eased up a bit and many people were coming aboard the Portuguese ships, "six persons of quality" and twelve others were taken prisoners. Bargaining began for exchanging the men for the Portuguese on shore. The Samorin sent a letter intended for the king of Portugal and drawn up by Diogo Dias, in which he offered cinnamon, cloves, ginger, pepper, and precious stones for gold, silver, coral, and scarlet cloth.

On August 29 the prominent hostages were released, but the others were kept. When Vasco da Gama finally had all his men back aboard, he sailed and fought a brief battle with the ships of the Samorin on August 30. Among those who accompanied him was Moncaide, a Moor who had served the Portuguese so well that his life would be in danger if he remained in Calicut.

The Agonizing Voyage Home to Portugal

The voyage home was even more difficult than the one out, and nearly disastrous. Leaving Calicut they coasted northward with weak winds. The season of the northeasterly monsoon had not arrived. On September 10 Vasco da Gama sent a last message to the Samorin; and on September 15 he planted another pillar in the S. Mary Islands, 13°, 22°N. At Angediva (meaning the five islands), the Portuguese were joined by a glib-talking individual, who told them he was a Christian feigning to be a Muslim, in the service of Yusuf Adil Khan, the Turkish ruler of Bijapur in western India. Suspecting treachery, they whipped him until he confessed he was a spy for the Adil Khan, who was preparing a fleet to attack the Portuguese. The spy was in fact a Polish Jew who had been for years an adventurer in the East. He now converted to Christianity and was given the name Gaspar da Gama, his godfather being Vasco da Gama. As Gaspar da India, the name usually given him, he was very useful to the Portuguese thereafter.

The Portuguese rested until October 5 in the Angediva Islands and then began what was to be a horrible voyage. The winds were either contrary or absent. Fresh food and water became scarce. Scurvy reappeared. The diarist repeats his description of the nauseous disease, gums growing over the teeth, bodies swelling until men died. "Thirty died. . . . An equal number had died before." The rest were so weak they could scarcely man the ships. The pilots resolved to force Vasco da Gama, who was determined to proceed to Portugal, to return to India, but fortunately a favorable wind caught them. The time of the northeasterlies had come. They sighted the first land of Africa on January 2, 1499, but passed it up to sail on to the friendly Muslim town of Melinde, which they reached February 7.

Melinde had white houses, as did their own Portuguese towns, and the land was green with groves of oranges. They were welcomed by the sultan with gifts of water, live sheep, poultry, eggs, oranges, and other fruits.

They had been almost ninety days at sea, and not a man of those still living could have endured any longer. Vasco da Gama made the best gifts he could to the friendly religious enemy and five days later sailed on. Too few were left to man all the ships. The *São Rafael* was intentionally burned after her stores had been transferred to the *São Gabriel* and the *Berrio*. They sailed past Zanzibar, rich trade center of Arabs and Persians, past Sofala from which the gold came, and stopped on the island of Mozambique to set up their last pillar. On March 3 they reached São Braz where they killed sea lions and penguins to provision their ships. Now they were all "hale and well," said the diarist, as they went around the Cape into the Atlantic Ocean. They neared the Cape Verde Islands twenty-seven days later and were caught in a calm.

The diary ends here, and we can only guess whether the author died or the copy we have is incomplete. They ultimately reached Santiago in the Cape Verde Islands from which Vasco da Gama took a caravel to hurry his dying brother Paulo to the Azores in the hope of saving his life. The trip was in vain. Captain Nicolau Coelho in the *Berrio* reached Cascais, Portugal, on July 10. Vasco da Gama did not come to Lisbon until the end of August or the beginning of September.

Home: Results of the Voyage

The news of the return of the expedition produced a fever of excitement and activity. There were doubters until the *São Gabriel* arrived, for it contained what little had been brought back from the East to prove that they had been there. The rich Italian merchant Sernigi immediately spread the news by letter to his homeland. The exultant King Manuel wrote a letter to his royal in-laws, Ferdinand and Isabella, the day after Nicolau Coelho arrived, informing them, not perhaps without malice, that "God had been pleased in his mercy" to bring the search for the East to a successful conclusion. Now India had been "found and discovered," as had other kingdoms, where there were "great populations where all the trade of spices and precious stones is carried on."[12] They had brought back cinnamon, cloves, ginger, nutmeg, and pepper, as well as other spices, woods, and precious stones (though in small quantity since the voyage had not carried much trade merchandise). All this, said King Manuel, he informed them of "because we know what great pleasure and satisfaction this will be to Your Highness." King Manuel predicted that the fruits of this voyage would be many, for the "Indian Christians" (i.e., Hindus) would be confirmed in the true faith and aid in the "final destruction of the Moors in those parts." Furthermore the trade would be diverted from the Muslims to the Christians, which "May God in his mercy bring to pass."[13]

When Vasco da Gama arrived from the Azores, he was welcomed by the king, highly honored, and enobled. The few but precious stones, porcelains, silks, and spices were spread before the royal family. Sernigi wrote that they had brought back "little and nothing of value." But the king, at least, understood the great significance of Vasco da Gama's voyage. To his existing title of "King of Portugal, and of the Algarve, Lord of Guiné," he now added "and of the Conquest, Navigation, and Commerce of Ethiopia, Arabia, Persia, and India." Portuguese kings never assumed the special title of "king" or "emperor" over these eastern areas (as, for example, the English kings called themselves emperor of India), though they were urged by their viceroys to do so.

[12] Letter of Manual to Ferdinand and Isabella, in Greenlee, *Cabral*, pp. 41–52; Sérgio J. Pacifici, ed. and trans., of *Copy Letter of King of Portugal to King of Castile, concerning India*.
[13] Letter of Manuel, see note 12 above. For the reaction of the Venetians see P. Sardella, "Nouvelles et speculations a Venise", and Donald Weinstein, ed. and trans., *Ambassador from Venice: Pietro Pasqualigo in Lisbon, 1501*.

The pope, of course, was informed of the return of Vasco da Gama.[14] Manuel reported that the Samorin was a Christian, as were the other "Christian" rulers of India, though the form of Christianity seemed heretical. Some time would have to pass before the Portuguese, who for centuries had fought the Muslims in Portugal and in Africa, could understand that not all non-Muslims were Christians. The great opportunities for Christian conquest in the East were laid before the pope, and he was requested to repeat for the East those grants of power made so many times to the Portuguese for Atlantic lands.

[14]Vsevolod Slessarev "Raphael Maffei's Contribution to the History of Portuguese Discoveries," CIHD, Actas 3:551–576 (1961). Slessarev calls attention to a channel of communication between Rome and Portugal hitherto overlooked, i.e., the Cardinal of Lisbon Jorge da Costa (also known as Alpedrinha). Manuel informed him of the return of da Gama on August 28, 1499. Slessarev calls the cardinal the best informed man in Rome on Portuguese affairs.

CHAPTER 13

Cabral: the Captain Who Touched Four Continents

The Prompt Organization of a Second Voyage to India

The first news of Vasco da Gama's success was the signal for the immediate organization of a second expedition. This time there was no delay and no hesitation. The difficulties that Vasco da Gama had encountered in the East called for a fleet strong enough to show off Portugal's power, to establish commerce with the East, and to open diplomatic relations with the Samorin and other rulers. On February 15, 1500, Pedro Álvares Cabral was appointed to command this fleet. He was described as a "nobleman (*homen fidalgo*) of good education and competent for the task."[1] No records indicate that Cabral was a mariner experienced in long voyages. He was appointed for other qualities. King Manuel had at his disposal an abundance of pilots who could navigate the route to India.

An armada of thirteen ships[2] was quickly organized, showing Portugal's

[1] Quoted from Gaspar Correia, *Lendas da Índia*, I, 146, in Peres, *Descobrimentos portugueses*, p. 431.

[2] The number of ships has variously been given as from 12 to 14. However all of the chief historians, Castanheda, J. de Barros, Damião de Góis, and Gaspar Correia, say 13. The contemporary accounts about the types of ships vary sufficiently for Manuel in his letter of 1501 to the Spanish monarchs to say "treze náus" and Damião de Góis to note merely "13 velas," in *Crónica Manuel*, I, chap. 54. Other accounts say only that "seven caravelas" arrived in India. The weight of evidence is on the side of 13 at the start, as shown by Damião Peres in *Descobrimentos portugueses*, pp. 433–444, which includes an extensive bibliography and a critical analysis of the chief sources of information concerning Cabral's voyage.

capacity for sea ventures.[3] Some of the thirteen vessels were described as *naus* and others as caravels, though by 1500 advances in ship construction had made the distinctions in the sailing qualities of seagoing ships less pronounced than it had been. The caravel and *nau* were not always distinguished from each other by the chroniclers of the period.[4] Frequently the same vessels were called *naus* in one place and caravels in another. Gaspar Correia spoke of *navios pequenos* and indicated that perhaps size rather than construction was the most important difference among ships.

Estimates of the number of people in the expedition varied between 1200 and 1500. Among the most notable Portuguese ship captains who began the new voyage were Nicolau Coelho, who had just returned with Vasco da Gama, Bartolomeu Dias, and his brother Diogo, who were veterans of the Atlantic. Among the pilots (i.e., navigators) were Afonso Lopes and Pero Escobar.[5] One of the official scriveners (*escrivães*) was Pero Vaz de Caminha, whose account of the voyage as far as Brazil was to become the most important single source of information concerning that discovery, because it is both a historical and a literary masterpiece.[6]

For his sailing direction, Cabral had the advantage of Vasco da Gama's

[3]The basic documents concerning the Cabral voyage are in A. Fontoura da Costa and António Baião, eds., *Os sete únicos documentos de 1500*, and Greenlee, *Cabral*, the most extensive collection in English translation. A Portuguese version was published in Oporto in 1951. Alexandre Marques Lobato, "Dois novos fragmentos do regimento de Cabral para a viagem da Índia em 1500"; *História da colonização portuguêsa do Brazil*, Malheiro Dias, ed., *HCPB*; J. Capistrano de Abreu, *O descobrimento do Brasil*; Katia Maria Abud et al., "O descobrimento do Brasil"; Ana Maria de A. Camargo, "O descobrimento do Brasil"; J. Cortesão, *A expedição de Pedro Álvares Cabral*; Didio J. da Costa, *O Brasil e o ciclo das grandes navegações*; Gago Coutinho, "Influência que as primeiras viagens portuguêsas à América do Norte tiveram sôbre o descobrimento da Terra de Santa Cruz," in *A náutica dos descobrimentos*, II, 11–26; "Descobrimento do Brasil," in *A náutica dos Descobrimentos*, II, 33–78; "A descoberta do Brasil em 1500 e o seu estudo no volume publicado em 1938 pela Hakluyt Society," *A náutica dos Descobrimentos*, II, 302–325; Hélio Dantas, "Pedr'Alvares Cabral"; Manuel Nunes Dias, *O descobrimento do Brasil*; Myoko Makino, "O descobrimento do Brasil"; Leite, *Descobrimentos*, I, 507–712, II, 11–256; T. O. Marcondes de Souza, *O descobrimento do Brasil*; *O descobrimento da América*, "A viagem de Cabral," and *Algumas achegas à história dos descobrimentos*; C. E. Nowell, "The Discovery of Brazil"; Damião Peres, *O descobrimento do Brasil por Pedro Álvares Cabral antecedentes e intencionalidade*; Peres, *Descobrimentos portuguêses*, pp. 430–472.
[4]The difference in the types of ships has become a matter of considerable importance to some historians, as seen in Peres, *Descobrimentos portuguêses*, pp. 439–441.
[5]Among the important navigators who did *not* make the trip was Duarte Pacheco Pereira, though it is frequently said he did so, following Góis, *Crónica Emanuel*, pt. I, chaps. 54–58. See Duarte Leite, *Descobridores do Brasil*, pp. 25–27.
[6]Carta de Vaz de Caminha. There have been numerous editions of this letter. See Greenlee, *The Voyage of Pedro Álvares Cabral*, in English; Dias *HCPB*, vol. II, chapter 7; Jaime Cortesão, *A carta de Pero Vaz de Caminha*; and T. O. Marcondes de Souza, "A carta de Pero Vaz de Caminha"; and *O descobrimento do Brasil*.

experience. Only a brief rough draft of what was doubtless a more extensive document prepared for Cabral has survived. Da Gama advised that
after they passed the Cape Verde Islands the wind would be behind them
and they should make their way toward the south. If the course had to
vary, let it be in a "southwesterly direction"; and as soon as they met with
"scant wind (*vento escasso*)" they should continue on through the sea (*ir
na volta do mar*) until the Cape of Good Hope was directly to the east.[7]

Sailing Instructions: Discovery of Brazil

The departure was made an occasion of great ceremony. After a solemn
mass which King Manuel himself attended, a procession led Cabral and
other leaders of the voyage to the embarkation. The next day, March 9,
1500, when a favorable wind arose, the anchors were weighed. They
passed São Nicolau in the Cape Verde Islands on the 16th, and on the
23rd, as Vaz de Caminha says, the vessel of Vasco de Ataide was lost from
the fleet, without rough weather to account for the loss.

Failing to find the lost ship, Cabral sailed on, carried by the northeasterlies until, supposedly according to da Gama's instructions, he crossed
the equator, and reached the area of the "scant winds," i.e., the southeasterlies. With these winds on his bow, he sailed a generally southwesterly
course with the intention of making a position with the Cape of Good
Hope directly to the east where he could pick up westerly winds to take
him around the Cape.[8]

The sailing route taken by Cabral and Vasco da Gama was approximately the route recommended for sailing ships to the end of the
nineteenth century. To avoid the doldrums lying just to the north of the
equator and roughly west of 20°W, sailing ships had to cross the equator at
not more than approximately 30°W, bearing southward until they sailed
beyond the easternmost point of Brazil lest they be caught, as many ships
later were, by ocean currents and the southeasterlies, and forced along
the north coast of Brazil and to the area of the Antilles. Once within the
influence of the southeast trade, they were carried westward by the wind
on their bow, and the problem was to avoid being forced by both wind

[7]Published in Greenlee, *Cabral*, p. 167. Found by Varnhagen in the mid-nineteenth
century and published in his *História geral do Brasil*, 1854. Given to the Torre do Tombo it
was misplaced and rediscovered in 1934 by Director António Baião. Published by Fontoura
da Costa and Baião in *Os sete únicos documentos de 1500*, pp. 15–20.

[8]Greenlee, *Cabral*, discusses the reason for the westerly diversion on pp. xlviiff.

and southbearing Brazil current on to the Brazilian coast. The success of this maneuver depended less on the skill of the pilot than it did on the luck of catching just right the sometimes shifting winds or storms. Experience was later to show that as long as the ships sailed this route, no art of the navigator, however highly developed, could guarantee that the ship might not be drawn either too far to the east into the doldrums or too far to the west and into the Antilles or Brazil.[9] Cabral hit the route just right to avoid the alternative dangers, but the ships were carried further west than was necessary. If all later voyages to Brazil and India had sailed the course as fortunately as did Cabral, it might be accepted as fact that the art of navigation had solved the problems of sailing the high seas; but we know this was not true. Few voyages to Brazil and India were so well executed as Cabral's.

As Vaz de Caminha expressed it, "we continued our way through this sea (seguimos nosso caminho por este mar de longo)" until on April 22, 1500, land was sighted in what later was called Brazil.[10] Gradually there appeared "a huge mountain, high and round," which Cabral named Monte Pascual (Easter Mountain). The name he gave the discovery was "Land of the True Cross" (Vera Cruz), changed by King Manuel to Santa Cruz, and in time to Brazil, for the wood which was its first profitable product. This was "660 or 670 leagues" (ca. 2000 miles) from the Cape Verdes. Caminha wrote to Manuel of "the news of the finding (achamento) of this new land of yours, which was just found (achou) on this voyage." When they had found a safe port (porto seguro), they captured two "well-built" natives who were taken to the flagship amidst much pleasure and festivities. Caminha describes them as dark, rather reddish, having "good" faces and well-shaped noses, and naked. There were also women who were naked and not displeasing to the eye; one painted her thighs and buttocks with black paint and left "her shameful parts (sus vergonhas) nude and exposed with such innocence that there was no indecency whatever."

Caminha saw a purpose in the discovery. "And since Our Lord, who gave them fine bodies and good faces as to good men, brought us here, I

---

[9] Morison, Portuguese Voyages, p. 99. Modern Portuguese historians, of whom Gago Coutinho is an example, have sought to show that Vasco da Gama and Cabral were sailing a route previously known from secret voyages. See Gago Coutinho, A náutica dos descobrimentos, I, 271–300, and passim.

[10] Unless otherwise identified, quotations about the discovery of Brazil to May 2 are from Vaz de Caminha.

believe it was not without purpose. And so Your Highness, who so much wishes to expand the Holy Catholic faith, should take measures for their salvation." After the first mass was said ashore, the priest preached a sermon at the end of which he spoke of "our coming and the discovery (*achamento*) of this land, following the sign of the cross" which Caminha considered was "very much to the point (*a próposito*)."

Description of the Brazilian Indians

Efforts to communicate with the Indians were largely futile. When Cabral showed them a gray parrot, they pointed toward the land, as if to say parrots were found there. They paid no attention to a sheep. But they were afraid to touch a hen, though they afterward took it. A short distance inland the Portuguese found a village to which some twenty or thirty Portuguese went with the Indians and traded with them. Those who went there said they "had a lot of fun together." The Portuguese traded bells and "other trifles" for "large and beautiful red parrots" and caps and cloth of feathers "woven in a very beautiful way." The Indians did not till the soil, breed stock, or have ox, cow, goat, sheep, hen, or any domestic animal. "They eat only manioc . . . which was in abundance" and fruits. Nevertheless, Caminha saw them as stronger and better fed than the Portuguese with "wheat and vegetables."

Caminha described the bay in which they lay as "large . . . some twenty or twenty-five leagues of coastline" and the interior extending "as far as the eye could reach . . . land and forest." Still "the best profit" from it would be to save the souls of the people, which would be "the principal seed which Your Highness should sow there." "And if" says Caminha, "Vera Cruz [Brazil] should turn out to be nothing more than a stopover en route to Calicut, that would be enough!" Manuel in his letter to Ferdinand and Isabella mentioned Brazil as a stopping place to Calicut, without suggesting that there had been a prior discovery.[11]

What and Where Was Brazil?
a Message to King Manuel

It was important that they find out where they were. Mestre João, the Galician astrologer-astronomer who accompanied Cabral, reported to

[11] Manuel's letter to Ferdinand and Isabella, July 29, 1501, in Greenlee, *Cabral*, pp.

King Manuel.[12] His is the first document containing a design of the Southern Cross seen from the New World, though Cadamosto had mentioned it and drawn a design with six stars. Mestre João wrote in Spanish. "Senhor: Monday 27 of April . . . on shore, I and the pilots of the chief captain and . . . of Sancho de Tovar took the height of the sun at midday . . . fifty-six degrees, and the shadow was north. By the rules of the astrolabe, we judged . . . 17°S. . . . Your Highness should know that all the pilots [estimated more than I]. Pero Escobar says 150 leagues more than I, some more and some less. . . . The truth cannot be ascertained until we reach the Cape of Good Hope and there we shall know who calculates more exactly, they with their chart or I with the chart and the astrolabe."

There is no hint of a previous visit by anybody or of the location of Brazil; so Mestre João suggests to the king that he ask for "a *mappa mundi* which pero Vaz Bisagudo has," which shows the location but does not indicate whether it is inhabited. "It is an old *mappa mundi*, and there . . . also find La Mina marked."[13] Caminha says they "almost understood by signs" that they were on an island, of which there were four; people from the other islands came to fight them. Since Mina is on the Guinea coast of Africa and was founded in 1482, a map made before 1482 would not show it. If the map were newer, it is strange that the king should have to ask one of his mariners for it; and it could hardly be described as old.

The astronomical observations were a problem: "I have not been able to learn . . . which degree each star is" says Mestre João. "Rather it seems impossible to me to take the altitude of any star at sea for . . . however little the ship rolls one is wrong four or five degrees." It could be done only on land. "At sea it is better to navigate by the altitude of the sun rather than by any star, and better with the astrolabe than with the quadrant or with any other instrument."[14]

Cabral had to consider what to do about the newly discovered land. He held a council, ordering "all captains" aboard his ships, and asked them

41–52; *Os sete únicos documentos*; and Marcondes de Souza, *Descobrimento do Brasil*, pp. 331–339.

[12] Mestre João's letter to King Manuel, May 1, 1500, in Greenlee, *Cabral*, pp. 34–40; Marcondes de Souza, *Descobrimento do Brasil*, pp. 299–300; Fontoura da Costa and Baião *Os sete únicos documentos*.

[13] Mestre João to Manuel, May 1, 1500, in Greenlee, *Cabral*, pp. 34–40.

[14] Mestre João to Manuel, May 1, 1500, in *ibid.*

MAPS

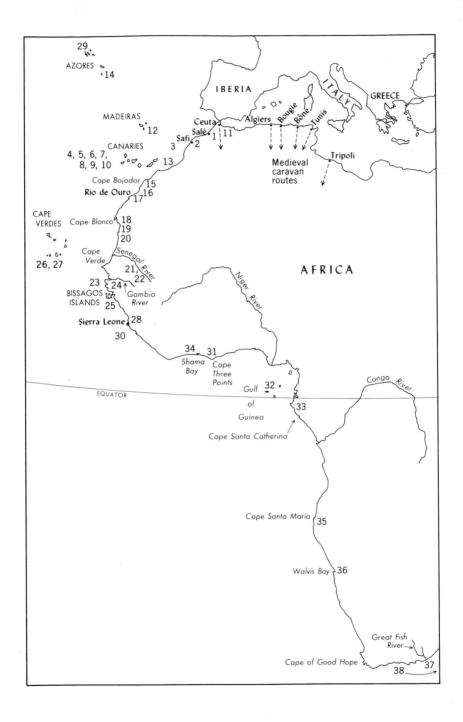

29

AZORES
·14

IBERIA

ITALY

GREECE

MADEIRAS
12

CANARIES

Ceuta
Salé
1   11

Algiers Bougie Bône
Tunis

4, 5, 6, 7,
8, 9, 10

Safi
3   2

13

Tripoli

Cape Bojador
15
Rio de Ouro
16
17

Medieval
caravan
routes

CAPE
VERDES

Cape Blanco
18
19
20

Cape
Verde

Senegal River

Niger River

AFRICA

26, 27

21
22

23
24
BISSAGOS
ISLANDS
25

Gambia
River

Sierra Leone
28

30

34   31
Shama   Cape
Bay   Three
Points

Gulf   32
of
Guinea

Congo River

EQUATOR

33

Cape Santa Catherina

Cape Santa Maria
35

Walvis Bay
36

Great Fish
River

Cape of Good Hope
38
37

1. 1162 Salé: Genoese
2. 1253 Safi: Genoese
3. 1291 Vivaldi brothers; lost
4. 1312(?) Lanceroto Malocello discovers Canaries
5. 1336 or 1341 Portuguese-Italian expedition(s)?
6. 1342, 1346, 1369, 1389 Mallorcan and Catalan expeditions to Canaries
7. 1344 Canaries granted to Luis de España by the Pope
8. 1393 Castilian expedition to Canaries
9. 1393–1402 Other expeditions from Andalucia and Cantabria(?)
10. 1402 Spain grants Canaries to Jean de Bettencourt with occupation thereafter
11. 1415 Portugal captures Ceuta
12. 1418–20(?) Portuguese settle in Madeiras
13. 1426(?) Gonçalo Velho sails beyond Cape Nun
14. 1427–32(?) Portugal discovers and settles Azores
15. 1434 Gil Eanes sails beyond Cape Bojador, the fifteenth Portuguese attempt
16. 1435 Eanes and Baldaia reach Angra dos Ruivos
17. 1436 Baldaia to Rio de Ouro and Pedra da Galé
18. 1441 Nuno Tristão to Cape Blanco
19. 1443 Nuno Tristão to Arguim and Garças
20. 1444 Lanzarote to Naar and Tider
21. 1444 Nuno Tristão to Terra dos Negros
22. 1444 Dinis Dias to Cape Verde
23. 1445 Álvaro Fernandes to Cabo dos Mastos
24. 1446 Nuno Tristão killed at Gambia(?) River
25. 1455 Cadamosto and Usodimare reach Portuguese Guinea and Bissagos Islands
26. 1456 Cadamosto and Diogo Gomes in separate expeditions to points further south? Cadamosto in Cape Verde Islands
27. 1460 António de Noli and Diogo Gomes in Cape Verde Islands(?)
28. 1460–61 Pedro de Sintra to Sierra Leone
29. 1462 Concession to João Vogado to search for islands of Capraria and Lovo; not found
30. 1469 Concession to Diogo Gomes to sail beyond Sierra Leone for five years
31. 1471 João de Santarém and Pero Escobar to Guinea Coast as far as Shama Bay
32. 1472–74(?) Fernando Pó, São Tomé and Príncipe in Gulf of Guinea
33. 1474 or 1475 Rui de Sequeira to Cape Santa Catharina
34. 1482 Construction of Feitoria-Fort of São Jorge da Mina on Guinea Coast
35. 1482–84 First Voyages of Diogo Cão beyond Equator and Congo River to Cape Santa Maria 13° S
36. 1485 Second voyage of Cão to approximately 22° S at Walvis Bay
37. 1487–88 Voyage of Bartolomeu Dias around Cape of Good Hope to east coast of Africa to about present-day Great Fish River
38. 1497–99 Vasco da Gama to India and return

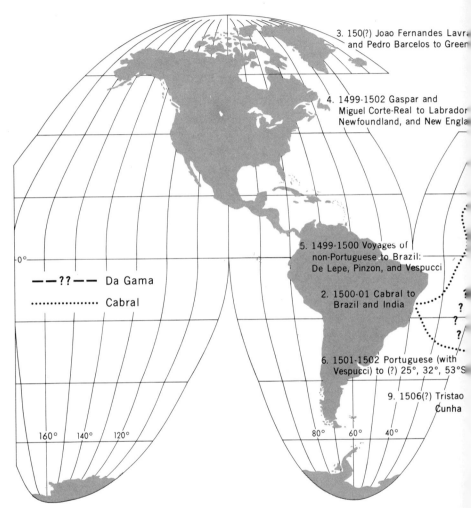

3. 150(?) Joao Fernandes Lavr
and Pedro Barcelos to Green

4. 1499-1502 Gaspar and
Miguel Corte-Real to Labrador
Newfoundland, and New Engla

5. 1499-1500 Voyages of
non-Portuguese to Brazil:
De Lepe, Pinzon, and Vespucci

2. 1500-01 Cabral to
Brazil and India

6. 1501-1502 Portuguese (with
Vespucci) to (?) 25°, 32°, 53°S

9. 1506(?) Tristao
Cunha

—— ?? —— Da Gama

·············· Cabral

Portuguese Explorations in the Sixteenth Century

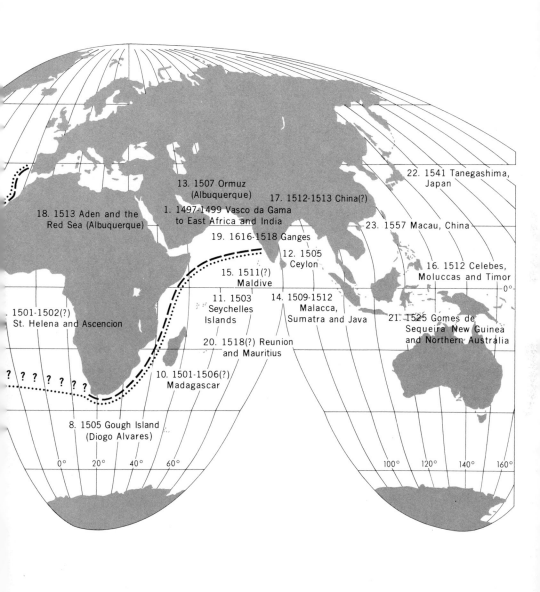

22. 1541 Tanegashima, Japan

13. 1507 Ormuz (Albuquerque)

17. 1512-1513 China(?)

18. 1513 Aden and the Red Sea (Albuquerque)

1. 1497-1499 Vasco da Gama to East Africa and India

23. 1557 Macau, China

19. 1616-1518 Ganges

12. 1505 Ceylon

15. 1511(?) Maldive

16. 1512 Celebes, Moluccas and Timor

0°

1501-1502(?) St. Helena and Ascencion

11. 1503 Seychelles Islands

14. 1509-1512 Malacca, Sumatra and Java

21. 1525 Gomes de Sequeira New Guinea and Northern Australia

20. 1518(?) Reunion and Mauritius

? ? ? ? ? ?

10. 1501-1506(?) Madagascar

8. 1505 Gough Island (Diogo Alvares)

0°   20°   40°   60°   100°   120°   140°   160°

Winds and Currents in the Atlantic Ocean

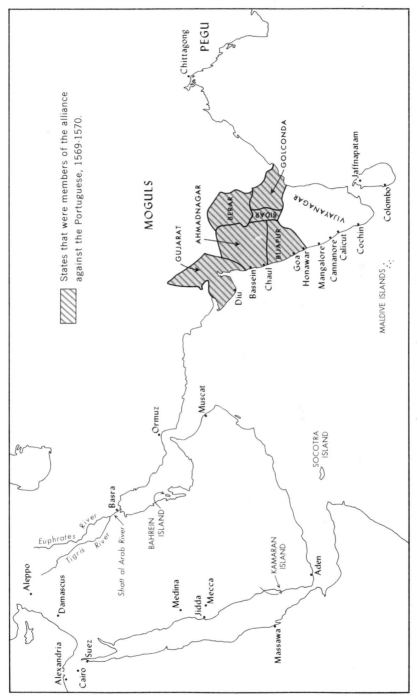

States that were members of the alliance against the Portuguese, 1569-1570.

The Portuguese Theater in India

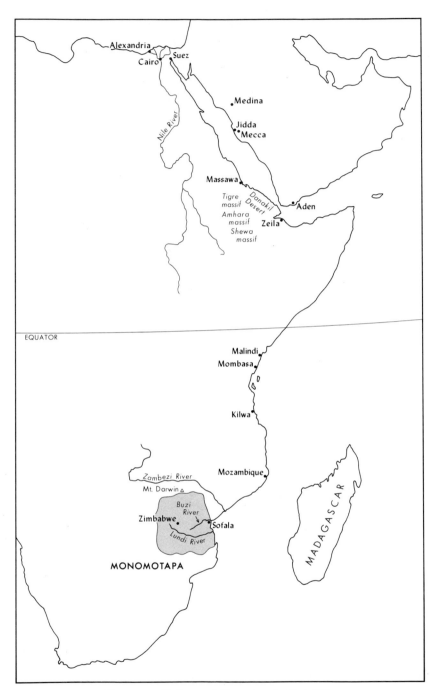

Portuguese Stations and Campaigns in East Africa

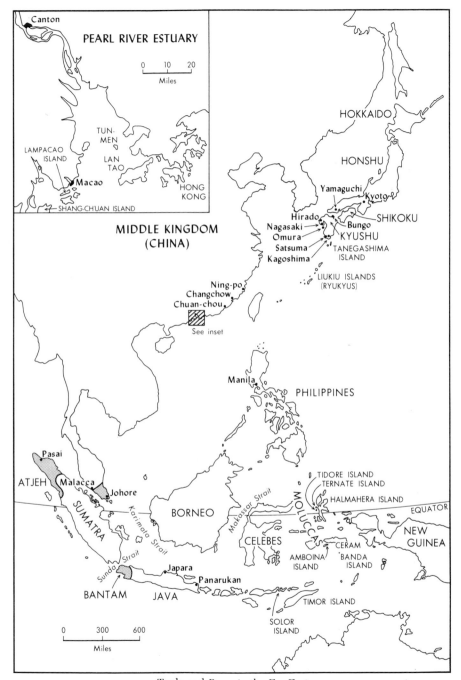

PEARL RIVER ESTUARY

Canton

0   10   20
Miles

TUN-
MEN

LAN
TAO

LAMPACAO
ISLAND

Macao

HONG
KONG

SHANG-CHUAN ISLAND

MIDDLE KINGDOM
(CHINA)

HOKKAIDO

HONSHU

Yamaguchi

Kyoto

SHIKOKU

Hirado

Nagasaki   Bungo

Omura   KYUSHU

Satsuma   TANEGASHIMA
                ISLAND
Kagoshima

LIUKIU ISLANDS
(RYUKYUS)

Ning-po
Changchow
Chuan-chou

See inset

Manila

PHILIPPINES

Pasai

ATJEH   Malacca

Johore

SUMATRA

TIDORE ISLAND
TERNATE ISLAND

HALMAHERA ISLAND

BORNEO

Makassar Strait

MOLUCCA

EQUATOR

NEW
GUINEA

Karimata Strait

CELEBES

CERAM

AMBOINA   BANDA
ISLAND   ISLAND

Sunda Strait

Japara

Panarukan

BANTAM   JAVA

TIMOR ISLAND

SOLOR
ISLAND

0   300   600
Miles

Trade and Bases in the Far East

ILLUSTRATIONS

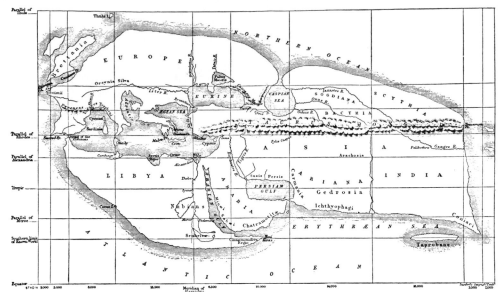

Eratosthenes' world: third century B.C. Africa is shown
trending east and ending at the Red Sea.

Cosmas's design ridiculing
the concept of
a spherical world.

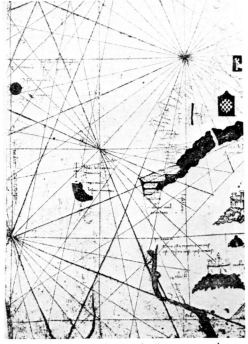

The Dulcert map of 1339, the first map to show
the island of Lanzarote with the Cross of Genoa.

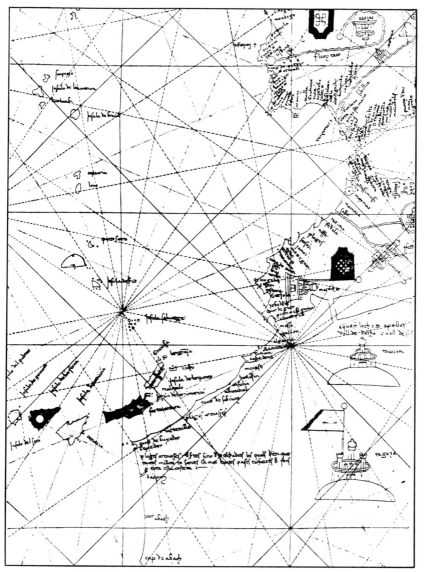

A Catalan map of ca. 1375, showing the False Azores
and Lanzarote with the Cross of Genoa.

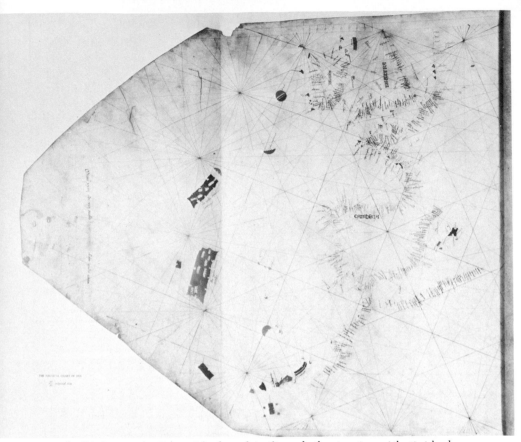

A map of 1424 showing the Canary Islands, and Antilia and other imaginary Atlantic islands.

The André Bianco map of 1436, showing Africa trending east and ending near the tip of India.

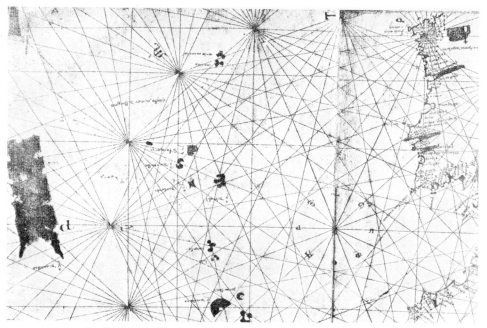

A detail of the André Bianco map of 1436, showing
the False Azores and an imaginary Antilia.

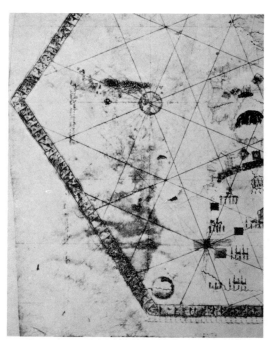

The Valsequa map of 1439, attributing discovery
of the Azores to the Portuguese in 1427.

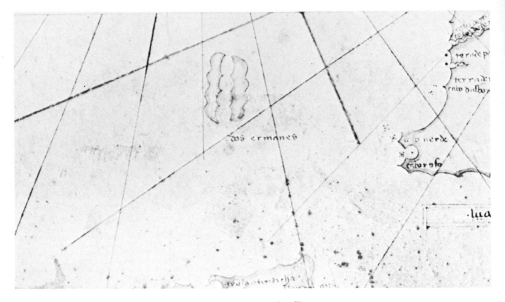

The André Bianco map of 1448, showing an "Authentic Island" southwest of Cape Verde.

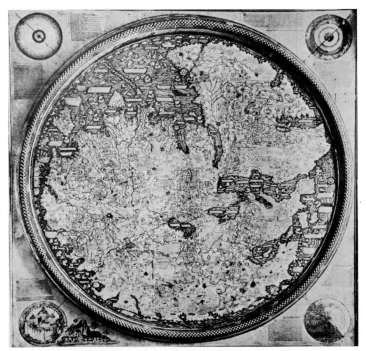

The Fra Mauro map of 1459. This was drawn for the Portuguese and shows Africa trending southeast but ending farther south than it did on previous maps.

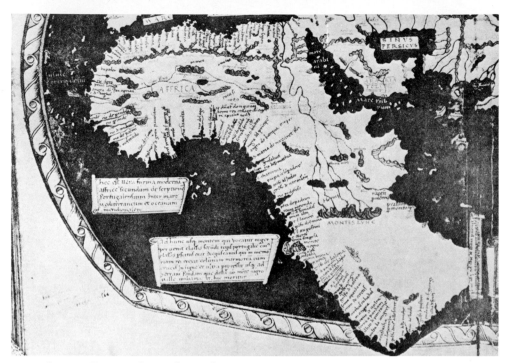

The Martellus map of 1489, drawn after
Dias's voyage beyond the Cape of Good
Hope. Africa extends many degrees too
far east.

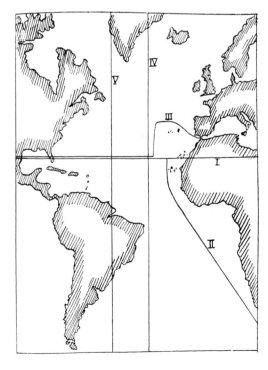

The division of claims in the Atlantic
Ocean after Columbus discovered
America: I. the division proposed by
Joao II; II. the Spanish counteroffer; III.
the second Portuguese proposal; IV. the
papal line drawn in the Bull of *Inter
Caetera*, May 4, 1493; V. the line of
demarcation drawn in the Treaty of
Tordesillas, June 7, 1494.

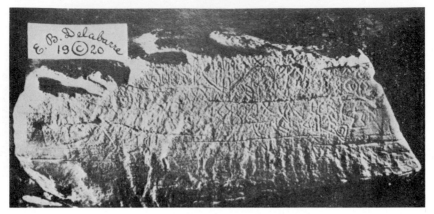

Dighton Rock, believed by some to show that
Miguel Corte-Real was in New England in 1511.

A *barcha*. This type of vessel was used in discoveries before
1441; in that year the first known caravel was sent out by Henry
the Navigator. From João Braz de Oliveira, *Os navios da
descoberta*.

A fifteenth-century caravel. This type of ship, with many subsequent improvements, was used in discoveries after 1441.

A late fifteenth-century caravel of the type used by Columbus.

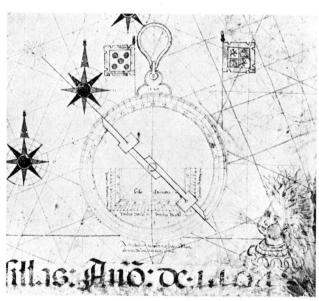

A mariner's astrolabe, sixteenth-century.

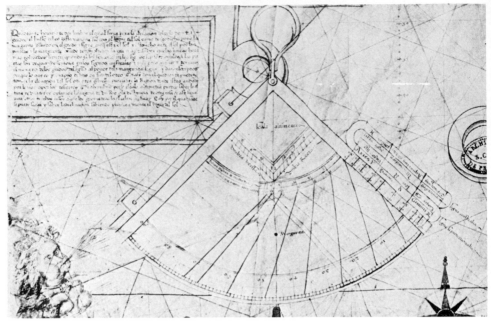

A mariner's quadrant, sixteenth century.

The stone circle at Sagres, about 180 feet in diameter, with 42 or 43 irregularly spaced spokes. The date of construction is unknown and its purpose has never been satisfactorily determined. Photograph reproduced with the permission of Professor Shozo Masuda, University of Tokyo.

all if he should "send the news of the finding (*achamento*) of his land" to the king by the supply ship so he could order that it be better explored (*mandar descobrir*) and they could thereby "gain more knowledge about it than we now had time to learn because we were going to continue our voyage."[15] A ship was sent home, possibly under command of Gaspar de Lemos, though others have been named. The sailing route home, its arrival in port, and all other information concerning the ship is lacking in official records. That it returned to Portugal is certain, for the letters reached the king. Manuel acted in 1501, before Cabral returned from India, by sending out a fleet of three ships, which encountered two of Cabral's homebound fleet at Cape Verde.

First Reports about Brazil

One of the accounts of the Cabral voyage is by an anonymous chronicler. He reported of Brazil that when it was sighted, "we went to see what land it was" and that Cabral wanted "to see what people they were." He found them "between black and white [and] nude as they were born, without shame. No one understood their language." There were many kinds of trees. The water was excellent. They did not know if it was an island or mainland, but because of its size they judged it to be *terra firma*. He also reported the decision to inform the king "of the finding of this land . . . we have seen and discovered."[16] He said that when they returned from India they found on the coast of Africa three small ships which the king "sent to discover the new land."[17]

Giovanni Camerino (known as Il Cretico), a Venetian in Lisbon, wrote home that the voyage to Calicut was "more than fifteen thousand miles, but by cutting across they shorten it somewhat. . . . Above the Cape of Good Hope and [toward the west they had discovered a new land] which they call the Parrot Land . . . because some are found there. . . . They judge that this was mainland."[18] Another Venetian, Marino Sanuto, whose diary covers the turn of the fifteenth century re-

[15]Vaz de Caminha's letter, in *ibid.*
[16]The anonymous writer, in Greenlee, *Cabral*, pp. 53–93; Marcondes de Souza, *Descobrimento do Brasil*, pp. 301–330.
[17]The anonymous writer, in Greenlee, *Cabral*, pp. 53–93.
[18]Giovanni Camerino or Giovanni Matteo Cretico, known as Il Cretico, in Greenlee, *Cabral*, pp. 119–123. He states that Bartolomeu Marchioni owned one of the ships in the Cabral fleet. See also Marcondes de Souza, *Descobrimento do Brasil*, pp. 340–343.

ported on the three ships sent out in 1501 "to discover the Land of Parrots, or rather, Santa Cruz . . . more than 2500 miles of new coast, [without] end . . . filled with brazil wood and cassia."[19] In September 1501 Girolamo Priuli of Venice reported "four caravels which had returned with three thousand cantara of spices. . . . The said king is preparing twenty-four caravels . . . for India."[20] In a letter written from Lisbon immediately on the return of Cabral's first ship, Bartolomeu Marchioni, the Florentine merchant, reported that Cabral "has discovered a new world," but that it was a very dangerous voyage. "The king," he added, believed the voyage "a marvellous thing."[21]

Vespucci, in the fleet on its way to explore the land Cabral's ship had reported, repeated what the crews of the ships told him of "a land where they found white people, naked, belonging to the same land I discovered for the King of Castile, except that it is farther east, of which by my other letter I wrote you."[22] Manuel wrote to Ferdinand and Isabella that Cabral "reached a land which he newly discovered," which he named Santa Cruz. Manuel felt the "Lord wanted it found," for it is "very convenient and necessary for the voyage to India." But because Cabral was bound for India, "he did not stay over to obtain more information. . . . He sent only to notify me, then continued by the way of Good Hope."[23]

Cabral sailed from Brazil on May 2 and reached India on September 13. He was never to return to Brazil, as indeed he never returned to India. But his voyage tied together the trade of four continents — Europe, America, Africa, and Asia. The sequence of his voyage was the establishment immediately of a Portuguese seagoing empire from Africa to the farthest East, and slowly of a land empire in Brazil. The story of Portuguese activity in the East is continued in this volume in the next and succeeding chapters. Portugal's development of Brazil is the subject of volume III of this series.

[19] Marino Sanuto, in Greenlee, *Cabral*, 138–141.
[20] Diary of Girolamo Priuli, in Greenlee, *Cabral*, pp. 131–138.
[21] Marchioni's letters to Florence of June and July 1501 in Greenlee, *Cabral*, pp. 145–150.
[22] Vespucci to Lorenzo de Medici, June 4, 1501, in Greenlee, *Cabral*, pp. 151–161; Roberto Levellier, *Amérigo Vespucci: Cartas*, pp. 126–141, 283–289; Marcondes de Souza, *Descobrimento do Brasil*, pp. 348–354.
[23] In Greenlee, *Cabral*, pp. 41–51; Marcondes de Souza, *Descobrimentos do Brasil*, pp. 331–339.

CHAPTER 14

Preconditions to an Asian Empire

It has usually escaped notice outside Portugal that the fifteen-year burst of national activity that followed the return of Vasco da Gama was one of the most purposeful and decisive in the history of the Western world. No one, except the Portuguese, ever dreamed that less than a generation after da Gama's weather-beaten ships turned up in the roads of Calicut, his small but determined nation on the western rim of Europe could establish itself firmly as master of the Indian Ocean, twelve thousand sea miles from home. This feat, together with the equally decisive Spanish exploits of Cortés and the Pizarro brothers, forever linked Europe with Asia and the Americas.

Spain's conquests in America, heroic as they were, were accomplished at the expense of peoples who, technologically, had barely emerged from the Stone Age. To create its Asian empire, Portugal had to travel three times as far, strain national resources, and thwart peoples as well armed as its own fighting men, in some cases, better armed. Probably no nation so tiny has ever established its influence more widely or against greater odds — nor done so more deliberately.

The conditions preceding Portuguese expansion into Asia were extraordinary. The only visible assets of the Portuguese were the determination of Manuel, their king, and their new and unique expertise of reaching India by water. The factors opposing them appeared insurmountable. The ocean passage was treacherous and uncertain, and da Gama's and Cabral's first voyages served Portugal notice that it would

195

exact a heavy toll of ships and sailors. Moreover, the Portuguese, by the very act of sailing over it to India, not only threatened Venice, the most powerful maritime state in contemporary Europe, but incurred the hostitility of the whole Muslim community involved in East-West trade. This community was not only wealthier and more numerous than the Portuguese; it also traversed a much shorter route to India. Both the Muslim community and Venice could be expected to do everything possible to thwart the newcomers — and indeed they did so.

To enumerate all these visible aspects of the problem, however, is not to tell all of the story. For although the sea route around Africa was long and terrible, the older trade routes, the Venetian position, and the Muslim political organization all had grave defects. The Venetians, though powerful, were afraid to back the infidel against their Portuguese fellow Christians. The Muslims were in a better place to make trouble, but they lacked any tradition of government interference on behalf of private merchants and had no navy immediately available. And, finally, the Portuguese were backed by Genoese and Florentine investment money, they were ferocious fighters, and they possessed superior armament. In the balance, they overweighed the forces against them and created an empire.

The National Effort

Little is known about how or why decisions were made during Portugal's thrust into the Indian Ocean, but there is some evidence, chiefly in the *Crónica de Dom Manuel* of the humanist Damião de Góis and secondarily in the *Da Ásia* of João de Barros, that the basic resolution to persevere in the establishment of contact with India was made more than a year before da Gama's departure — not, as one would expect, only after his return. In a debate which Góis reports to have taken place at Monte-mór O Novo in the Alentejo during the month of December 1495, some councillors of the new king, Manuel, are said to have expressed fear not that the Indian expedition then under consideration might fail, but that it might succeed in arousing toward Portugal the hostility of every monarch then involved in the Indian trade. It would be far wiser, this faction felt, for Portugal to remain content with the comparatively peaceful exploitation of what had already been discovered in Africa.[1] Góis indicates, however, that the

[1] Damião de Góis, *Crónica do Felicíssimo Rey D. Manuel*, I, 48 (of 1949–1955 edition).

young King Manuel, fresh upon his throne, was eager to distinguish his reign by culminating the efforts of his antecessors. Voting with his councillors who wished to pursue the Indian enterprise, he launched Portugal upon its imperial track. Then and there the orders were given to outfit ships, and the search, which ended in the selection of da Gama, was begun for a suitable commander. Once da Gama returned from India, there seem to have been no further debates over Portugal's imperial future but only one over the best way to follow up the discovery and assure royal control of the wealth da Gama had sampled. Barros does not contradict Góis but merely shifts the emphasis slightly: the opposing councillors, he indicates, were fearful of the expense involved rather than of any jealousy Portugal might incur.[2]

Whatever the true reasons might have been — it is likely both Barros and Góis were correct — the Portuguese were evidently laying the foundations or, rather, the keels of a new expedition to Calicut and the Malabar Coast even before da Gama returned from his first voyage. Otherwise, it would not likely have been possible to send out a thirteen-vessel, 1200-man expedition under Pedro Álvares Cabral only five months after da Gama returned. In the next five years, the Portuguese outdid themselves in building and launching every ship their economy and effort could provide to ensure the success of a death struggle far from their shores, farther than any European nation had ever attempted to work its purposes.

What seems most remarkable of all about the Portuguese national effort is that not the king nor da Gama nor anybody else in the country could have had much advance information about the place toward which all their efforts were directed. One might read into Góis's account of the Monte-mór O Novo conference a preknowledge of the actual political and economic situation in Asia, but it is just as likely that the reluctant councillors had Venice and the Mamelukes in mind as probable enemies — even granting that Góis himself did not alloy his reportage with forty years of hindsight. More certainly, da Gama did not behave as though his superiors had communicated to him the kind of knowledge Pero de Covilhã must have included in his intelligence reports — that is, the ones entrusted to Rabbi Abraham of Beja and José of Lamego in Cairo. For no informed person seeking the real Samorin of Calicut amidst all his plumage and jewels would ever have offered him red-cloth caps, bells, and

[2]Barros, *Da Ásia*, Dec. I, bk. 4, chap. 1.

little mirrors in exchange for his pepper — or failed to bestow upon him rich presents of ivory and gold made to order for him in Portugal. Da Gama and his men had to scrounge up makeshift gifts for him — at which he sneered — out of their personal possessions. It is even odder that Covilhã's report, if it ever did arrive at King João's court, had not told da Gama about the Hindus. He actually believed, as did King Manuel, that everyone who was not Muslim in India was some unorthodox sort of Christian. He and his men even mistook statues of the Goddess Dewaki nursing the Infant Vishnu for the Virgin Mary.[3]

There was nothing strange about the way Portugal reacted to India thereafter. All told, the Portuguese appear to have sent out eighty-one ships from Lisbon among six annual convoys in the years 1501 through 1505, if the three chroniclers, Castanheda, Barros, and Corrêa, plus Duarte Galvão and one or two other existing sources, are correct. The sailors and soldiers aboard them must have numbered around 7000 since the contemporary writers tell how many men went along with three of the six expeditions and it is easy enough to project the rest.[4]

Royal policy is plainly reflected in the year-by-year pattern: the fleets were smaller in the early years before the Portuguese fully realized that in order to trade, they must first conquer. Hence Cabral's expedition of 1500, though much bigger than da Gama's pioneering fleet, was of medium size — thirteen ships (of which only six actually reached India) — but the fleet of João da Nova in 1501 contained only four vessels. After Cabral's return and his report that opposition to the Portuguese in India was growing, the fleets increased in number; the voyages of 1502, 1504, and 1505 were each composed of upward of twenty vessels, some of them intended not to carry spices home to Portugal on the return monsoon but to remain in India as warships.

The Carreira da Índia

It had taken Prince Henry and his heirs eighty years to develop the route around Africa to India, and although this knowledge may be accounted

---

[3] E. G. Ravenstein, ed. *A Journal of the First Voyage of Vasco da Gama*, pp. 53–54.

[4] The number of men carried on three of the larger convoys, Cabral's own in 1500, Lopo Soares de Albergaria's in 1504, and Francisco de Almeida's in 1505, ranged between 1200 and 1500 apiece; da Gama's second fleet of 1502 contained about the same number of vessels as Almeida's. Some of the remaining thirteen ships which comprised the two other expeditions are known to have been caravels; so it is unlikely that all together held more than 900.

Portugal's greatest national asset in the year 1500, one must remind one's self constantly that the actual practice of traveling it put men and ships to the severest tests ever devised for them. Since the latter part of the nineteenth century, governments have been able to transport men and material across great distances with ease, and the very humdrum of this modern accomplishment tends to diminish the wonders of the great navigational feat which had to be repeated throughout the history of sail each time Portugal dispatched a ship to India.

The most direct passage between Lisbon and Goa or Calicut via the Cape is just under 10,000 statute miles, but no ship driven by canvas could ever take this route because the prevailing winds and currents would not permit it. Vasco da Gama's first voyage will serve as an introduction to what was involved; the only difference between this journey and the later ones was that da Gama did not begin in the proper season to take advantage of the monsoon winds and that he seems to have had extraordinarily bad luck with stormy seas in the South Atlantic while on his way to the Cape. And Cabral, of course, showed how easy it was to make an involuntary landfall in Brazil.

All navigators who traveled the Indian route over the three centuries following those epic voyages kept approximately the same route; but they knew the vagaries of wind and current far better by then, and they were able to make the trip in six to eight months. Half a dozen *roteiros* or rutters (sets of sailing directions) exist from the sixteenth century for the *Carreira*; these make it plain that a captain could expect a wide variety of weather conditions, that changes in wind or current might occur much earlier or later than expected, and that these would alter the course and duration of a voyage.[5]

Ships outbound from Lisbon nearly always hoisted anchor between February and April, aiming to round the Cape of Good Hope between June and August in time to catch the southwest monsoons. Sailing southward toward Madeira and the Canaries, they soon picked up the northeast trade winds and the Canary current, and rode a divergent of this almost to Sierra Leone where it joins the Guinea current and rounds the bulge of Africa. But pilots did not follow it beyond the equator; instead they turned southwest and made their way across the equatorial low pressure

[5] Notably, those of João Baptista Lavanha and João de Lisboa as reprinted in Humberto Leitão, pref. and ed. *Dois roteiros do século XVI, de Manuel Monteiro e Gaspar Ferreira Reimão atribuidos a João Baptista Lavanha.* See also Henrique Quirino da Fonseca, ed. *Diários de navegação da Carreira da Índia nos anos de 1595, 1596, 1597, 1600 e 1613.*

zone, or doldrums, on fickle but generally easterly winds until they neared the South American continent and picked up the South Equatorial and Brazil currents within a few hundred miles of Pernambuco. This vast detour is made necessary by the fact that all subequatorial winds and currents off the west coast of Africa move northward, leaving sailing ships no alternative but to cross the South Atlantic and follow the Brazilian coast inside Trinidad and almost to the latitude of Rio de Janeiro.

Only then could sails be expected to billow with the prevailing westerlies of the southern hemisphere and move ships in a great arc to the southeast toward the Cape of Good Hope. Upon reaching the vicinity of the Cape, depending upon a variety of factors from stormy weather to their orders from Lisbon, the navigators might choose between beating their way around Cape Agulhas and up the Mozambique Channel, calling at Mozambique Island, or continuing below the Cape and Madagascar, afterward bending north-northeast into the Indian Ocean and east again to India. If ships preferred to call at Mozambique, which was common, they followed the contour of Africa to a point near Cape Gardafui before falling off eastward to cross the Indian Ocean.

The homeward passage from Goa or Cochin was somewhat more direct, but it had sweeping detours, too. To utilize the reversal of the monsoons — between October and December they blew from the northeast toward the African coast instead of away from it — ships had to depart between Christmas and April. In this season, pilots were able to beat approximately the same courses back toward the Cape which they had taken on the outward trip. But once they had rounded it, they aimed their prows directly northwest, pushed by the southeasterly winds along the Benguela and South Equatorial currents to a point near the equator, where their courses crossed at right angles the track of the outbound *Carreira*. It was at this stage, however, that the pace ordinarily became tedious. First, vessels encountered the low pressure area of the doldrums and frequently lost all speed for days on end; then somewhat farther to the north the winds and currents picked up again; but the winds were out of the northeast, and progress frequently had to be made by zigzag tacks. Finally, with some luck pilots could find a suitable if tricky wind in the high-pressure system some seven hundred miles west of the Canaries and sail into the Azores. From there, it was a relatively simple matter to ride the Portugal Current east to Lisbon. By this time a ship completing the circuit had been away from home for a year and a half and had logged about 23,000 statute miles, roughly equivalent to a circuit of the globe at the equator.[6]

What the long voyage meant in human terms is expressed by the Portuguese proverb, "If you want to learn how to pray, go to sea." The trip Spanish imperialists took between Seville and the Isthmus or Vera Cruz was a mere lark by comparison; their galleons seldom required more than six or eight weeks sailing time in either direction, driven as they were before the steady winds helped by the currents of the Great Circle Route. For the India-bound Portuguese, the outward portion of their voyage was similar and only a pleasant beginning; the supply of fresh food still held out and no scurvy had developed. But before they had reached the howling storms of the Cape of Good Hope, provisions were stale, sailors' joints and gums had already begun to swell, and dysentery had broken out. It must have seemed that the only thing worse than being becalmed was the prospect of enduring another mast-bending gale; no wonder the religious processions on deck and the litanies were interminable whenever priests were aboard. The route was too long and too taxing — it was not uncommon for a third of a ship's passengers and crew to die at sea. Only too often, of course, the ship itself failed to survive the *Carreira*: Cabral's expedition lost seven of thirteen vessels on the way to Calicut, and this presaged what a normal experience on the *Carreira* would be.

The Old Trade Routes

Perilous and roundabout as the *Carreira* was, however, its development dramatically outflanked the Muslim world and broke the monopoly of its established trade routes between Europe and Asia. We have already remarked that the traditional routes were very ancient and that they had served to link the two continents commercially, though not culturally, because few Europeans were able to pass along them. What the Muslim system had thwarted, the Portuguese discoveries made possible.

Some writers had assumed, rather hastily, that the Portuguese route doomed the older passages as soon as it was discovered — this was the common error of textbook writers a generation or so ago. More recently, others have half-blamed the "failure" of the Portuguese empire upon the superiority of the shorter routes of supply. Now that the *Carreira* has

---

[6]There are many accounts of the *Carreira* in print. Among the best is Charles R. Boxer's preface to *The Tragic History of the Sea*, pp. 1–30.

been described it is informative to compare it with the older passages through the Middle East — even though precise comparison is made impossible by the totally different economic organizations of the competing traders.

All Araby is in reality a vast wasteland; the late Sir Halford MacKinder identified it as the western portion of what he called the "Great Poverty Steppe" — a tremendous arid belt that stretches accross the entire land mass of Africa and Asia between the Straits of Gibraltar and the Sea of Okhotsk near Sakhalin Island.[7] Over this whole belt, rainfall is scarce; and in fairly predictable cycles it is virtually nonexistent — which meant in historical times that its population was never far from nomadism; whole communities frequently had to uproot themselves and their sheep, goats, and, in Africa, camels in order to survive droughts. In the process, they became specialists in mobility. The Ottomans to a large extent possessed the characteristics of nomads, certainly in their ability to move swiftly and flank their enemies. It is ironic that discovery of the *Carreira* outmaneuvered the maneuverers, for soon after the Ottomans had captured Constantinople and were advancing through the Balkans, the Portuguese turned the Cape of Good Hope in their sailing ships.

The Great Poverty Steppe was of little intrinsic interest to most Europeans before the nineteenth century. Aside from Christian yearnings for the Holy Land, only the Iberian peoples showed much interest in capturing or colonizing any part of it. What drew most Europeans to the region was neither the desire to conquer nor the desire to preach, but the merchandise offered for sale in Aleppo, Cairo, and Alexandria — the spices and silks of the Orient. Exactly how much the Portuguese knew in detail of this Muslim-to-Christian Eastern trade is not known. It was the Italians, principally the Venetians, who did most of the business with the Muslim traders, and they were jealous of their prerogatives, just as the Muslims in turn were not willing to have the Europeans pass through their lands and trade in Persia or India. A few adventurers had done so during the late Middle Ages, between the time of Marco Polo in the thirteenth century and Lodovico di Varthema in the fifteenth; by the sixteenth century, a few representatives of the great Venetian trading houses had traded in Persia or India. Covilhã and Paiva had done it, too, and the vicissitudes they encountered were typical, though recorded in much less detail than those of some later travelers.

[7] In his *Democratic Ideals and Reality*, published in various editions.

Between Marco Polo's day and Vasco da Gama's discovery of the way around Africa, there had been six major routes connecting Asia and the Mediterranean. Of these, two need not concern this narrative, since they had come into existence during the Mongol Peace after 1268 and virtually ceased to exist after its collapse in the 1340s — the northerly route from the mouth of the Don River at the top of the Black Sea that led eastward above the Caspian and a medial route that began in Trebizond on the south shore of the Black Sea and led through Tabriz to Central Asia. A third, from Ayas in the Gulf of Alexandretta to Tabriz, though passable, was of minor importance. The other routes, making use of the Persian Gulf and the Red Sea, bore the lion's share of the traffic.[8]

Traders who used the Persian Gulf traditionally dealt more in silks than in spices because Persia itself was an important producer of silks and the expensive 800-mile portage across the Syrian Desert from Bassorah to Damascus or Aleppo only made sense when most of a trader's goods originated in a region to the north of the Indian Ocean. Otherwise, although Persian Gulf navigation (in spite of the Noutek pirates) was less hazardous than that of the Red Sea, the Red Sea lay on a more direct line from Calicut to the Mediterranean, and its principal portage across the desert from Suez to Cairo was about 700 miles shorter — and thus enormously cheaper — than the long desert trek from Bassorah to Aleppo, which by 1500 had been all but abandoned. Hence, virtually all of the spice traffic was carried via the Red Sea, and it is likely that any spices which did find their way to Europe via the Persian Gulf and Bassorah were handled as sidelines by the few silk merchants who sporadically used the route or by those who at least had begun their careers in the Persian silk trade.

The difficulties of the *Carreira da Índia* in terms of the hazards and the great distances it represented have been mentioned. What usually escapes notice is that the Middle Eastern routes were almost equally disadvantageous in spite of their vastly shorter traverse. If in preference to the Carreira one chose the Red Sea route between Calicut and Europe (Venice in this case), the startling decrease in distance of nearly 7000 miles tended to be canceled out by the expensive transfers and portages involved, together with seasonal and dangerous navigation of the Red Sea itself.

[8] For a fuller discussion of routes see A. H. Lybyer, "The Ottoman Turks and the Routes of Oriental Trade."

Walled on both sides by rugged, granite mountains, the Red Sea is a 1400-mile-long gash in the desert whose navigation can be practiced only by men who have spent their lives in its study. For the most part, in the words of one eighteenth-century traveler, it is "full of sunk rocks, very dangerous to sailors, and innumerable islands."[9] These submerged reefs were so perilous between Leet (about ninety miles south of Jidda) and the island of Kamaran (opposite Massawa) that a mainmast lookout had to give constant instructions to the helmsman. Even so, Westerners were always astonished at the apparently close chances the navigators took. The navigators, however, incurred no more than the necessary risks: they never traveled at night, but anchored securely into a convenient harbor if possible.

In spite of all care, the unexpected and vicious squalls of the Red Sea exacted their tolls of ships and merchandise. Vessels which had no room to maneuver were frequently driven onto submerged rocks, and crewmen had to cast into the waves all or most of their precious cargoes to save themselves. At other times even mooring lines snapped in gale winds, and the Arabs' *dhows* and *baghlas*, lightly constructed for maneuverability and because timber was scarce, were swiftly dashed to pieces.[10]

Another drawback of the Red Sea for sailing vessels was that Arab navigators plying it were at the mercy of the alternating monsoons no less than were the Portuguese crossing the Indian Ocean. The only difference was that the parallel mountains which marched down either shore of the Red Sea funneled the regular monsoon patterns (which blow from the quarters of the compass) into north or south winds, according to the season. Consequently, ship owners could make only one return trip each year. In view of the fact that their vessels were small, the profits from each lading had to be unusually high.

Difficulties in navigation were only one obstacle. It was the tedious transshipment of the cargoes at various points which ran up overhead. Because vessels suited to the Indian Ocean had to be larger than those practicable on the Red Sea, it was customary for traders to discharge cargo at Aden or Mocha for lading into the smaller Red Sea ships; once these vessels reached Suez, the same cargo had to be portaged across to Cairo by animal back and then loaded again onto river vessels for ferrying up to

[9] William Daniel, in Sir William Foster, ed. *The Red Sea and Adjacent Countries at the Close of the Seventeenth Century*, p. 65.
[10] *Ibid.*, pp. 73, 156, 181.

Alexandria. The cost of these transfers from ship's hold to mule or camel back were extraordinarily high, though perhaps not as great as on the Persian Gulf route, where scholars estimate that in the seventeenth century, at least, freightage from Bassorah to Aleppo was more expensive than the comparable charges from India all the way around the Cape to Europe.[11] It was therefore perhaps not entirely attributable to Arab greed that spices which had sold for 2½ to 3 ducats per hundredweight in Calicut were resold in Cairo for as much as 68.[12]

In the years immediately preceding the Portuguese arrival in the East, and during the period when da Gama and Cabral were establishing their initial contacts in India, it would appear that Arab trade with the Orient was at its zenith.[13] The Mediterranean entrepôts for silk, dyes, and spices were growing swiftly in the face of lively demand from Europe. This provided every incentive for the Muslim merchant class to procure an increasing supply. Perhaps because they were essentially nomads, the Arabic peoples were attracted to trading and travel, especially when they could combine with it the observance and propagation of their religious beliefs — *hadjdj wa-hadjah* (pilgrimage combined with business), as they called selling their wares while visiting the holy city of Mecca.[14] This style of life had carried them into the Malay Archipelago and to the China coast by the ninth century according to most authorities. By the time the Portuguese arrived in Malacca, Java, and the Moluccas, they found Islam already well established and growing fast. In fact, when the Spaniards moved into the Philippines years after the initial Portuguese conquests in Asia, they prided themselves upon having stopped the spread of Mohammedanism beyond Mindanao Island.

For all their commercial and missionary thrust, however, Muslim traders operated almost exclusively as individuals, without very much supervision by their rulers in the Middle East or elsewhere. Trade was mostly organized around partnerships and families. Although simple *commenda* arrangements had tended to evolve into more sophisticated *societas maris* relationships, wherein the owners hired vessels and agents to handle their

[11] P. Masson, *Histoire du commerce français dans le Levant au XVIIᵉ siecle*, p. 545.

[12] For pepper prices at Cairo see: Wilhelm von Heyd, *Histoire du commerce vénétien et egyptien du Levant au Moyen Age*, II, 565; Ravenstein, ed. *The First Voyage of Vasco da Gama*, pp. 103–104; Vitorino Magalhães Godinho, "Le repli venetien et egyptian et la route du Cap."

[13] R. B. Sergeant, *The Portuguese off the South Arabian Coast*, p. 5.

[14] For example see George F. Hourani, *Arab Seafaring in the Indian Ocean*, pp. 69–73.

merchandise, it would appear that credit mechanisms and accounting procedures were nowhere near as complex as they were in contemporary Italy or Flanders. On the other hand, Muslim traders were not beset by at least one worry that plagued their European counterparts, who were constantly regulated, restricted, and fined by their own and rival monarchs. For the most part, Arab businessmen merely paid the tolls, fees, and port charges levied upon them by the Mamelukes or by the petty sultans or other rulers whose lands they passed or in whose entrepôts they traded. Sometimes these approached 10 percent (as with the Mamelukes), but the merchants mostly passed the costs on, ultimately to the Venetians. For the rest, except perhaps for the Chinese, there were no rulers in all Asia with fleets sufficient to have controlled the Arab traders' activities to any great extent even if they had so desired. This freedom from political meddling, however, revealed its bad side when the Portuguese arrived: since no Asian government was in a position to dominate them, none was in a position to protect them from the Europeans.

Perhaps the real lesson to be drawn from comparison of the *Carreira da Índia* with the Middle Eastern route is not that one was really cheaper or safer than the other, once allowance was made for tolls, shoals, and cartage in the Arab route, or a high death rate, circuitous passage, and stormy seas in the Portuguese. Rather, what emerges is that the Arab system was highly vulnerable to the concerted action of an outflanker who used the Cape route and possessed the armament and unified command the Arabs lacked. The Portuguese may not have had more than a handful of men and ships in comparison to those of the Arab traders, but their unexpected arrival and concerted movements magnified their superior armament a hundredfold in what was virtually a vacuum of naval power. This enabled them quickly to interdict Muslim trade and block for a season its source of supply and its markets.

Venice and the Portuguese Discovery of India

So far, the narrative has made frequent mention of the Genoese and Florentines in their dealings with Portugal, but has said little of the Venetians. With a few exceptions, such as Alvise da Cadamosto, the Venetians in fact hardly interested themselves in Portuguese affairs until the time of Vasco da Gama. This was mostly because they considered Portugal to be a backwater and were content to leave to others the relatively minor pickings afforded by the Portuguese African trade before the discovery of India.

In their own sphere, they were nearly supreme. Their round ships dominated the trade of the Mediterranean Sea, freighting cotton and alum from Syria and Egypt, wine from Crete to England, slaves and grain from the Black Sea, and salt, oil, and wine between the ports of the inland seas and even as far as Flanders. If taken alone, this commerce in staples and bulky commodities would have made Venice wealthy but hardly grand.[15] Above all other things, its grandeur can be ascribed to the fact that it once "held the gorgeous East in fee," at least so far as Asian commerce with Europe was concerned, buying, carrying, and distributing nearly all the spices and oriental luxury goods that Christians received from the eastern Mediterranean entrepôts of Aleppo and Alexandria.

Venice had been prominent in this commerce since the time of the Crusades, but it had been only in the past century that the Adriatic oligarchy had triumphed completely over its erstwhile rival Genoa in the competition for trade supremacy of the eastern Mediterranean. For although both city states had lost forward bases to the advancing Ottoman Turks, it had been the Genoese who suffered most and who thereupon had focused their efforts on the western end of the sea. The Venetians, on the other hand, had accommodated themselves to the new realities, paid tribute to the Ottomans wherever their outposts (as at Cyprus) were most vulnerable, and concentrated on the undiminished commerce from the Orient that flowed through the nonaggressive Mameluke Empire in Syria and Egypt.

Perhaps because they had demonstrated to themselves the value of remaining calm in the face of calamity, or because they had been absorbed so fully by the Ottoman menace, the Venetians had not paid much attention to the Portuguese national effort to discover a direct maritime route to India. Even in 1500, almost a year after they had received the first garbled news about Vasco da Gama's return from India, King Manuel's own report of it to the Signoria apparently went largely unnoticed amid new hostilities and the loss to the Turks of Coron, Modon, and Lepanto. But when Cabral's spice-laden fleet returned to Lisbon in 1501, the implications finally seem to have struck home. Then a wave of pessimism set in. One writer, the merchant-diarist Girolamo Priuli, darkly

---

[15] It was this trade that allowed Venice to weather the temporary loss of the Oriental trade. See Frederick C. Lane, "Venetian Shipping during the Commercial Revolution."

forecast that "if this voyage from Lisbon to Calicut continues as it has begun, there will be a shortage of spices for the Venetian galleys, and their merchants will be like a baby without milk and nourishment. And in this, I clearly see the ruin of the city of Venice."[16]

For the time being, the Venetians were quite unable to do anything effective to counter the sudden Portuguese competition. In fact, even verbal expressions of hositility or disapproval would have been misplaced. For since Venice most urgently needed to enlist help against the encroaching Turks, its councils had determined that the most likely way to achieve this was through a call upon the emperor, the pope, the king of Spain, and any other Christian rulers who would listen, to join Venice in a holy league. Indeed, rather than fulminating against him, the Venetians slyly called upon King Manuel for help. Any Portuguese ship tied down in the Mediterranean, they must have reasoned, could hardly be used to compete with them for the oriental trade.

To the Venetians' surprise, Dom Manuel appeared to be the most receptive of all the monarchs whom they approached with their scheme. Though pleading that poverty and taut commitments precluded his contributing the splendid armada against the Turks he might wish to send, he nonetheless offered thirty-five stout ships to the eastern Mediterranean for defense against the Turks. The Venetian ambassador Pietro Pasqualigo professed himself to be moved and delighted.[17] But in the end, the joke was on Venice. The promised armada arrived too late to be of real help and was acting under orders to engage none but Turkish fleets in the open sea. Since the Turkish navy made it a point to avoid such engagements, the Portuguese naval force was all but useless to the Venetians, who wished to recapture strongholds recently fallen to the enemy. About all the Venetians could do to spite their upstart trade rival was to spread the rumor among some Indian representatives then visiting Lisbon that Portugal was far too poor a country to become a good customer. This could hardly have been very convincing to the Venetian merchants themselves: beginning about 1503, the Arab merchants in Cairo and Syria had far fewer cloves and peppers to offer, in fact only about a quarter of their fifteenth-century supply.[18] Not only had the Venetian diplomatic mission to Portugal failed, but Priuli's gloomiest forecast seemed to have come true.

[16] Quoted in Donald Weinstein, *Ambassador from Venice*, p. 30.
[17] *Ibid.*, p. 21.
[18] Heyd, *Histoire du commerce du Levant*, II, 508.

For more than a century Portugal and Venice remained outwardly friendly rivals who continued to pursue the same oriental commodities along separate routes of supply. Had they been physically nearer or had their two trades actually touched one another at any point save at the sources, the two commercial rivals would almost surely have fought in spite of the similarity of their culture and religion — as did the Dutch and the English in the next century. But even though no war between them was feasible, the whole flow of oriental goods to Europe, and to some extent the relocation of its marketing patterns, was conditioned by their competition from the opposite fringes of Christendom. Each power had allies of sorts. In spite of the underlying differences and mutual exclusivity of Christian and Muslim cultures, the Venetians ultimately collaborated with the Turks and Arabs. The Portuguese leaned for technical and financial support upon the Venetians' old rivals, the Florentines and, particularly, the Genoese.

The Genoese, Florentines, and Other Foreigners as Portuguese Commercial Allies

The caravan routes across the Sahara from Jenné and Timbuktu terminated in Morocco and the North African ports as far east as Tripoli, and the gold and slaves they channeled to the Mediterranean had attracted Italian merchants to Ceuta and the Mahgreb by 1162. Whether any of these went the short extra distance and crossed the straits to do business in the ports of the Algarve, then still Muslim, is not known; but it is probable that a few did call there. In the next century, however, Italian merchants made their first voyages to far-off Flanders in big merchant galleys, and these certainly stopped over at Lisbon on both the outward and return voyages. By this time, Italians were clearly doing business in Portugal, for a document of 1278 indicates that a Genoese, Don Vivaldo, had become a citizen of Lisbon and was active in civic affairs.[19] Thereafter, the Italian community grew apace, until by the fifteenth century it was numerous and flourishing.

One of the striking characteristics of this colony was that it was largely Genoese and Florentine; only a minor part of it appears to have been Venetian, even at the beginning. What few Venetian merchants there were seem to have been on a cordial enough footing with the Portuguese

[19] Bailey W. Diffie, *Prelude to Empire*, pp. 50–51.

for the most part. But aside from the use of Lisbon as a regular station en route to Flanders, the Venetians hardly figure at all in Portuguese affairs. Until recent research demonstrated their continuing residence in Lisbon after the opening years of the fourteenth century, it was even supposed that the Venetian colony had been banished by King Dinis after 1309 when the Venetians were allied with his enemies.[20] Most likely the real reason for the relative scarcity of Venetian merchants in Portugal is that their own commercial interest lay in the eastern Mediterranean, and to a lesser extent in northern Europe, whereas the Genoese had increasingly specialized in North Africa and the Iberian Peninsula, especially after their loss of Chios and their expulsion from the Black Sea.

At the very time when the Venetians were thought to have been expelled by King Dinis, that monarch was busy making important concessions to a Genoese merchant sailor that virtually institutionalized the presence of Venice's Ligurian rivals in Portuguese national life. As indicated earlier, in 1317 Manuel Pessanha concluded a pact with Dinis which made him *almirante-mór*, or admiral-in-chief, of the Portuguese navy and granted him a subsidy and trade privileges between Lisbon and his native city in return for twenty warships and their crews.[21] Thereafter, the names of scores of other Genoese families appear in the commercial and maritime history of Portugal — the Doria, the Lomellini, the Grimaldi, and the Catanei, to mention only four of the most prominent. Over the next four centuries, the financial experience and enterprise of these Ligurians influenced all phases of Portuguese economic and colonial development. In the fifteenth century, they played a major role in the discovery of the Cape Verde Islands, and they were of prime importance in the development of the Madeiran sugar industry. They also acted as *feitores* (factors) and as creditors to the *Casa de Guiné e Mina* and later, in the sixteenth century, to the same body when known as the *Casa da Índia*.[22] (See chapter 18.)

The Florentines were also active as merchants and bankers on the Portuguese scene. Only twenty-one years after the naval contract made with Manuel Pessanha, the Portuguese crown conceded its first of many

[20] *Ibid.*, pp. 103–104, n. 5.

[21] *Ibid.*, p. 54.

[22] For a brief general description, see the article by Domenico Gioffre in *DHP*, 11, pp. 338–340. Throughout the same period there was also a large and active Portuguese colony in Genoa, an important market for colonial products. See also Virginia Rau, *Estudos de história*, I, *passim*.

charters containing purely commercial privileges to the famous Bardi family of bankers. Thereafter, the Florentine community became second in importance only to the Genoese. In the course of time, the Flemings, the French, and the famous German banking houses of Welser, Fugger, and Höchstetter were granted privileges in Portugal roughly similar to the ones long held by the Genoese and Florentines. In general, these accorded grantees the right to trade between their home territories and Portugal or its possessions, the right to own property, bear arms, and obtain redress. Residents from the same nation were also frequently conceded the right to settle disputes among themselves under their own legal codes.

In modern times, writers have frequently misunderstood, neglected, or misemphasized the nature and role of these foreign enclaves in Portuguese economic and maritime life, and the result has been that general readers can only with difficulty form a balanced idea of their relation to Portuguese maritime expansion. It is certainly far from true that the Italians taught an unsophisticated Portuguese nation of crusading warriors the arts of banking and navigation, as some have asserted; the Portuguese merchants had already gained much experience in both areas before the Italians were granted concessions. In fact, the crown's highly sophisticated levying of compulsory maritime insurance upon merchants engaged in the Flanders trade seems to have been a Portuguese innovation.[23] It would be more nearly true to assess the Italian role as one of providing the additional expertise and, especially, the capital and credit that the small and relatively new nation needed to expand its trade suddenly in response to the new opportunities opened through discovery in Africa, Brazil, and Asia.

What actually did occur was a collaboration between a growing crown monopoly and foreign capital seeking an outlet, and it would not be far from true to say that the monopoly was made workable by the infusion of foreign capital and by numerous contractual relationships between the crown on one hand and the foreign merchants on the other. Foreign ships and *feitores* (factors) traveled to India with Cabral, João da Nova, and da Gama on his second voyage; and the crown frequently granted permission for its clients to make solo trips to Brazil for the purpose of trading there. Often the real impediment to such participation was the

---

[23] Diffie, *Prelude to Empire*, pp. 44; 69–70.

preference of the Genoese, Florentines, and Germans merely to contract for certain amounts of merchandise and allow the Portuguese to take the risks. In many ways, however, the Portuguese were probably better suited to do so. For when those risks meant cutting Muslim throats or fighting at sea, the Portuguese of the era could have had few rivals.

Morocco: A School for Cutthroats

The Portuguese had fought Muslims on and off during nearly all their national history, but it was not until the conquest of Ceuta that they carried this rivalry into the Islamic home territory of North Africa. When they did, it was the Moors' turn to feel as if expulsion of the intruders was a holy mission, while, indeed, the Portuguese had never lost their sense of the Crusade. The result was a century of furious stalemate — from 1415 when Ceuta was captured until João III was forced to abandon Safi, Arzila, Alcácer Seguer and Azemmour, keeping only Mazagão, Tangier, and Ceuta itself. During all this time, the Portuguese had been able to capture some cities along the shoreline, but they failed completely, at Graciosa, Marrakech, and elsewhere, to extend their rule very much inland, let alone, as they had hoped, to capture Fez and any real share of the elusive trans-Saharan gold and slave trade. At most, Portugal may have derived a slight advantage commercially through trading for cereal grains in the intervals between fighting — even though the exportable surplus was precarious and dependent on good years.

The drawbacks of this Moroccan enterprise will be discussed more fully in chapters 16, 17, and 22; but the point to be made is that its contribution to Portugal on the eve of expansion overseas lay in the training of commanders and in the hardening of soldiers. The great Afonso de Albuquerque, Duarte Pacheco Pereira, and Diogo Lopes de Sequeira were among the most notable of those who learned their trade in this peculiarly vicious fighting, where mistreatment and slaughter of prisoners and even the mutilation of corpses was at least as common as the more civilized practice of holding prisoners for ransom or exchange.[24] There can be little doubt that much of the barbarous treatment the Portuguese accorded Muslims in India during the first years of their conquest there had been learned at Tangier and Alcácer-Seguer; even among those who had come fresh from

[24] Gomes Eanes de Zurara (Azurara), *Crónica do Conde D. Duarte de Menezes* in *CIHP*, III, 38.

Portugal with no experience, the example set by the veterans was contagious.

It was this very ferocity of the Portuguese soldiers in Asia which cowed even the boldest of their adversaries: at Diu, a contingent of Muslim soldiers on board an enemy ship threw themselves overboard in their mail, apparently preferring to drown rather than face a far more horrible demise at the hands of Christian devils. Obviously, the demonic fury of the Portuguese in Asia was misplaced: the Asian Muslims had never been close to North Africa. But the Portuguese had only one term — *mouros* or moors — and one treatment for them all.

Exactly how high the percentages were of Moroccan veterans fighting alongside Albuquerque and Almeida in the Indian Ocean is impossible to know, but their number was probably high during the first decade or so of the conquest era, just as veterans of the fighting in Granada were common among the Spanish adventurers in America — and for the same reasons. The conquest of Granada was completed in 1492, just as Columbus was discovering America, while fighting in Morocco slacked off only shortly before — and perhaps partly because of the Indian discoveries. Seasoned manpower thus became available to pursue colonial ventures in both Portuguese Asia and Spanish America.

In his *Books of the Brave*, Professor Irving Leonard has suggested that conquistadores in America fought with much the same spirit as did their heroes of chivalric romance, and he cites instances where soldiers actually seemed to behave like the supermen in *Amadís de Gaula* (1508), whose origin, incidentally, is thought to have been Portuguese.[25] Soldiers in the vanguard of the Portuguese expansion would not have been familiar with this particular work, but Leonard proves that the Spanish conquistadores of a decade later both knew it and took it with them to the New World. Certainly, exploits like Pedro de Alvarado's famous pole vault at Tenochtitlán in 1522 were fantastic enough to make it seem as though Amadís had been the inspiration.

Be this as it may, it is surely true that the Iberian martial ideals expressed by the author or authors of *Amadís* and the group psychology that animated the armies of Almeida and Albuquerque or Cortés and Pizarro were of the same tradition.[26] It must have been demoralizing for the

[25] Irving A. Leonard, *The Books of the Brave*.
[26] At least one Spaniard who accompanied the Portuguese to Asia was steeped in Amadís's exploits and compared the deeds of the Portuguese to them. See James B. MacKenna, ed. *A Spaniard in the Portuguese Indies*, pp. 136–137.

opponents of Portugal to discover that the men whom they faced actually seemed to fight harder when injured than when unscathed. Battle wounds, in fact, were considered a mark of distinction, as in the case of a man who Couto reports to have been injured in a tiff with the king of Jaffnapatam's forces in Ceylon. This chronicler remarks that "a good deal of blood ran down his fine long beard, which made him even a handsomer and more noble-looking gentleman."[27] So eager were the Portuguese to prove their prowess, in fact, that at the first siege of Diu, when a Portuguese grew impatient at having to wait in a queue to have his wounds bandaged, he ran back into the fray and returned only when he had received a more severe injury. Even the dying, it would seem, did not ask special privileges when a fight hung in the balance. At the conquest of Goa, one soldier, João de Lima, found his brother, Jerónimo, mortally wounded. As he bent over Jerónimo's prostrate form, the dying man whispered, "Brother, you have your way to go and I have mine." When he returned, he found Jerónimo dead.[28] If isolated, the incidents would not be significant. However, the chronicles are filled with such stories —men who attempted to scale walls after losing both hands, or men who refused to wear armor in order to mock their enemies and show their disdain for death. Taken together, these stories provide the most convincing evidence of why small numbers of Portuguese regularly fought much larger enemy forces, as well armed as themselves, and defeated them. Only their brutality, learned in Morocco, and their reckless disregard for personal injury can account for their regular — and baffling — successes. Probably only at sea were they demonstrably superior to their enemies in any other respect.

The Naval Superiority

The reasons for the sweeping Portuguese naval superiority over the Muslim forces may be clear enough in outline, but the details remain murky. It is plain enough that the Portuguese routinely demolished Arab, Egyptian, and Gujarati vessels during the first years of their activity in India partly because these were flimsily made and manned by demoralized crews. Less sure is whether Portuguese fighting men or their technology

[27] Diogo de Couto, Da Ásia, Dec. VII, bk. 4, chap. 5.
[28] Gaspar de Corrêa, Lendas da Índia, II, 150; also, Fernão Lopes de Castanheda, História do descobrimento e conquista da Índia, II, 104.

— their ships and cannon — were primarily responsible for the near-invincibility, and in what degree.

The Muslim princes whose lands bordered the Indian Ocean had never built quantities of naval vessels for service there because they paid little attention to their merchants and had no maritime enemies in the Indian Ocean region save for pirates. Moreover, what war vessels they did possess were not stoutly put together: both the Indian and Arab shipbuilders had the peculiar habit of lashing a ship's planking together with ropes instead of using iron spikes as Europeans did — an excellent way of preventing corrosion and saving metal, scarce in the Arab world, but not a sturdy method of construction. Quite aside from the flimsiness of Muslim-built vessels, when the enemies of the Portuguese did commission war vessels for use in the Indian Ocean, they built mostly galleys and only a few round ships. Because galleys were propelled primarily by oars and depended largely on speed for their success, they had to be long, narrow, and lightly constructed.[29] They fought one another by maneuvering to ram an adversary amidships with their armored beaks, whereupon the crew and archers from the successful galley would throw grappling hooks into the disabled one and embrace it as a spider embraces a fly. The presence of so many banks of oarsmen side-by-side did not permit guns to be mounted broadside and restricted armament to a few light pieces in the bow or perhaps in the stern. The real might of a galley lay in the manpower available to clamber aboard enemy ships and overcome their crews. As it turned out, there was no worse way to deal with the Portuguese challengers. Attempting to board a well-gunned and sturdily constructed round ship was asking to be massacred.

Before the sixteenth century, round ships in the Mediterranean were usually freight vessels, veritable tubs whose beams were often a third or more their length. These had existed since ancient times in much the same form — high sides, a single mast, and typically only a single sail. There was not much beating to windward in this primitive vessel: because the ship had only one mast, the pilot could generally hoist anchor only when he had obtained a following wind.

Ships of this type were mostly used for transporting bulky commodities of relatively low intrinsic value, such as grain, dried fish, or lumber. Highly prized silks or spices were usually carried in large galleys, espe-

[29] M. P. Nougarède, "Qualités nautiques des navires arabes."

cially like those developed by the Venetians around the thirteenth century, which were driven primarily by sail but maintained oarsmen for limited use and as defenders.[30] Typically the round ships were not heavily armed. They were built with high decks fore and aft, whose purpose was defensive; but their owners mainly relied on small crews to cut transport costs and on their bulky cargoes of low value to make piracy not seem worth the effort. Mediterranean round ships were usually small; in only a few notable instances were they both large and heavily armed — for example, the *Roccaforte*, a huge Genoese ship of 1260 designed to transport Crusaders and their steeds to the Holy Land. In most instances fortified ships were built for use in the English Channel and the Baltic area, where cold winds and stormy seas had discouraged all but the superhardy early Vikings from favoring oar-propelled ships. The northern European monarchs had round ships constructed for their navies, ships that looked like little castles afloat, with crenellated towers built into their hulls both fore and aft. One imagines that in a fight, ordinary galleys could have done these vessels no fatal harm, but that armored round ships before the days of cannon would also have lacked the punch to threaten galleys, much less afford any protection to other round ships in a convoy.

The Portuguese often used galleys in the Orient, but they did not depend on them as a primary naval force until their conquest of the Indian Ocean was complete.[31] Rather, they had adopted the round ship which featured all the improvements of the fifteenth century — elongated hulls and additional masts with smaller but more numerous and handy sails. Stoutly constructed to stand the pounding of heavy Atlantic seas, their ships could not easily be sunk by ramming attacks, and the multitiered fore and after structures of the larger vessels must have glowered down ten or more feet above the decks of enemy galleys either when the galleys attacked the round ships at sea or were trapped by them in harbors, as at Diu. About the only thing a round ship could not do was to overtake a galley, unless its rowers were exhausted. But it so happened that most of the naval fights between the Portuguese, the Turks, and Samorin, and the Gujarati were under conditions favorable to the Europeans.

How many pieces of artillery a heavy round ship commanded by Al-

---

[30] Frederic C. Lane, *Venetian Ships and Shipbuilders of the Renaissance*.
[31] Henrique Lopes de Mendonça, *Estudos sôbre navios portuguêses*, p. 34. This book possibly provides the best description of the types of Portuguese vessels in use at the time of the conquest of the Indian Ocean.

meida or Albuquerque actually did carry and how effectively these could be put to use smashing Arab-style galleys is no more than a matter of conjecture. There exist few documents that tell how many guns ships of the era carried, and shipwrights did not make architectural drawings — at least none have been preserved. Moreover, all but a few depictions made in the early sixteenth century are hopelessly untrue to scale — people the size of giants bulge over the railings, and the hulls themselves are far too tublike. When guns are represented, they are grossly oversized, protrude too far, and the artist has room for only a few of them. No doubt most of these limitations were forced on the contemporary artists by the scale or material in which they were working. For example, many ships appear in minuscule, as on parchment maps or manuscripts, or vastly simplified, as in funerary sculpture. Until the Dutch artists of the seventeenth century made the marinescape a permanent part of their repertory, neither was there a market per se for paintings of ships, nor must the painters have been sufficiently aware of how ships were constructed to be able to draw them faithfully.

The only extant reasonably accurate rendering of early sixteenth-century Portuguese *naus*, or heavy vessels, is in a panel now in the National Maritime Museum at Greenwich, England, which is attributed to the Portuguese artist Gregório Lopes, or to the Dutch artist Cornelis Anthoniszoon. It depicts five *naus* transporting the marriage party of the Infanta Beatriz of Portugal to Savoy in 1521.[32] The lead ship is thought to have been none other than the *Santa Maria do Monte Sinai*, a vessel constructed in India around 1512, which Vasco da Gama sailed back to its place of origin when he returned in 1521 as Portuguese Asia's second viceroy. The most cursory look at the ships reveals that even the stern galleries carried guns and that other guns were actually mounted in the sides of the forecastles facing the waists of the vessels — presumably to be loaded with grapeshot if hostile borders ever clambered over the railings and occupied the lower decks. But more striking than this are the two to three tiers of gun embrasures in the sides of both the sterns and the forecastles and a long row of embrasures, apparently for mounting heavy pieces, on the lower decks. If these were similar to the vessels Cabral,

[32] The painting passed in this century from a Portuguese collection to one in Germany and then to the National Maritime Museum in Greenwich, England, where it was reattributed to Anthoniszoon. Here researchers are likely to become confused if they come across earlier references to it.

Albuquerque, and Almeida sailed — and they probably were not greatly different — then each large one could have carried thirty to forty guns, not counting light swivel pieces which could be mounted on the railings of the open decks. If this is so, then there cannot be much question why the Portuguese, though greatly outnumbered, so thoroughly shattered their opponents at Diu. The poet Gil Vincente apparently read the message aright as he viewed the departure of Dona Beatriz in the same five *naus* depicted in Gregório Lopes's painting:

> Leva gente muita fina,
> Poderoso artilheria
> Que vai por graça divina.
>
> [The fleet]
>
> Carries people in all their finery,
> With *powerful artillery*,
> And travels with divine grace.[33]

Arming ships with many guns, nearly all short and light by later standards, appears to have been a widespread practice in the first decades of the sixteenth century. To cite only an instance or so, Henry VIII of England had two very large ships built, the *Henry Grâce à Dieu* of 1514 and the *Great Galley* of 1515 which, because much larger, carried a far greater number of guns than it is likely the *Santa Catarina do Monte Sinai* did — the *Henry*, 184 guns and the *Galley*, 147 iron and 70 brass guns! Moreover, a huge Portuguese galleon, the *Botafogo*, loaned to Charles V during his assault on Tunis in 1535, was said to have mounted a grand total of 366![34] All these ships must be considered extraordinary, but they do show that the age was anything but reluctant to commit artillery to naval use.

Since the time of João II, the Portuguese had been accustomed to mounting bombards even in the hulls of their caravels. Both that king and his successor, Manuel, were good customers not only of the German bronze cannon makers but also of a small home industry. The German nonferrous guns were the best, though very expensive; even the wealthiest monarchs were not able to afford as many as they wished. Instead, they increased their firepower with cast-iron guns, even though these were heavier and more prone to explode or crack. They also utilized

---

[33] Henrique Quirino da Fonseca, *Os portugueses no mar*, I, 257.
[34] Damião Peres, ed. *História de Portugal*, III, 624.

crude small cannons, mostly breechloaders, which had been made by annealing iron rods around a cylindrical core of wood. They were usually swivel-mounted on the railings of ships. Some fired stone balls, others cast ones; none set records for safety. It required as much courage as it did skill to become a gunner.

When the Portuguese ships first arrived in India, they no doubt carried a host of these short pieces. Europeans tended to discard these later in the century in favor of fewer, but longer and heavier guns of greater range and accuracy, which worked best against other round ships. But the shorter, more primitive guns of the early Portuguese could be reloaded more quickly and no doubt proved ideal against galleys and their crews. When one notes that the largest galleys and even the galleasses lacked the firepower to sink a round ship, but had to close with it in preparation for boarding, it becomes clear that the smallness and inaccuracy of the Portuguese guns were not really a hindrance. For when the galleys ventured to within perhaps 100 feet, or were trapped in a harbor, they must have faced a deadly, continuous fire at almost point-blank range on their open decks. It is true, as Professor John H. Parry remarks, that the guns and shot with which da Gama and Cabral bombarded Calicut could not have done much real damage to the town,[35] but when directed in broadside at a fragile galley, the results might have been quite different.

The actual establishment of Portuguese power in the Indian Ocean occurred in definite stages, but this is not to say that these were in any way planned or foreseen, either by the king and his council or by the conquistadores themselves. They can be discerned only in retrospect, and the next chapters will essay such an analysis.

[35] J. H. Parry, *The Age of Reconnaissance*, p. 122.

CHAPTER 15

From Discovery to Conquest

In the ten-year span between the arrival of Cabral at Calicut in 1500 and the beginning of Afonso de Albuquerque's governorship, the Portuguese discoverers mastered the Indian Ocean. This evolution from visitor to conquistador was startlingly rapid, but it was pragmatic rather than premeditated. The indications are that at first Cabral and the king were only interested in filling ships with spices and sailing home to make the greatest possible profit. Moreover, until Cabral's return, King Manuel still nourished a hope that the Samorin might turn out to be some sort of Christian who had merely fallen out of touch with Rome. But Cabral had quickly learned otherwise, just as he had soon perceived that the Arab traders had not been hostile to da Gama by chance in 1499: they regarded the Portuguese as trespassers on their preserves.

As matters had developed, the Samorin of Calicut, though a Hindu, was perfectly willing to add the Portuguese to his list of customers. His older and more numerous Arab clientele, however, did everything possible to thwart the sale of pepper to Portugal. When Cabral attempted retaliation, the Muslims stirred up a riot against the Portuguese who had gone ashore. Cabral had then opened fire on Calicut and literally blasted the Samorin into the enemy camp. This camp soon came to include the Egyptian Mamelukes, the Gujarati of Cambay, and, less visibly, the Venetians.

Even before the Portuguese had arrived in India, while at Mozambique and Mombasa on da Gama's first voyage, they had demonstrated how readily they would turn to violence against Muslims. Hence, it would appear that a clash was inevitable as soon as Moorish traders showed their hand. Otherwise, the Portuguese seem to have come to India with peaceful enough intent. When Pedro Álvares Cabral arrived before Calicut in 1501 Lisbon seems to have had no notions of conquest and indeed no particular strategy in mind beyond the hope of forging a close alliance with the Samorin and, if possible, loading their ships ahead of their Muslim competitors. Cabral's instructions are filled with commercial information, apparently dictated by da Gama, but there is little, at least in the parts of his *regimento* that survive, to indicate that his superiors foresaw anything quite like his attack on Calicut and his alliance with the king of Cochin.[1] To the contrary, it would seem that King Manuel and his counselors still thought that the Samorin might turn out to be a non-Catholic Christian after all, and the *regimento* alludes to the Samorin as "being very firm in matters which relate to our faith."[2] Moreover, the letter King Manuel addressed to the Samorin makes the offer of "religious persons . . . and also church ornaments, so that you may be able to see the doctrine of the Christian faith which we hold."[3]

Even though the Samorin turned out to be a "pagan," this need not have led to hostilities with him, for he was pleased with the elaborate gifts sent him by King Manuel, he welcomed the Portuguese warmly enough, and things seemed to be off to a promising start. But before Cabral had succeeded in establishing a very firm relationship at court, the friction that arose between the Portuguese and the Muslims had so poisoned the relations between Calicut and Portugal that Cabral ordered bombardment of the city in retaliation for the attack on his *feitoria* (see chapter 13).

Then after he had sailed out of its roads, he learned that Trimumpará, the kinglet of Cochin farther south along the Malabar Coast, hated the Samorin and was eager to do business with the Europeans. Cabral had thereupon called in Cochin, established friendly relations there, and loaded a cargo of pepper. Until that time Cochin had been unknown to the Portuguese, who had heard only about the more famous Calicut; but

[1] William B. Greenlee, ed. and trans. *The Voyage of Pedro Álvares Cabral to Brazil and India*, pp. 163–190. He was specially told to avoid hostilities with the Moors at Calicut but was allowed to take Moorish prisoners at sea.
[2] *Ibid.*, p. 182. King Manuel seems not to have envisioned a fight to eject Muslim competitors in 1500, although in his instructions to Cabral, he foreshadows it by asking him to urge the Samorin that his Christian duty was to send the Muslims away.
[3] *Ibid.*, p. 189.

Cochin was actually much more conveniently situated to the pepper fields, and it possessed an infinitely superior harbor — or rather one should say that Calicut really had no harbor at all and owed its fame as a market more to its rulers' commercial policies than to its location. Before departing for Lisbon, Cabral also called upon the raja of Cannanore, a pepper principality north of Calicut, because he had learned that this ruler also wished to escape the Samorin's domination. The Raja thereupon aligned Cannanore with Portugal.

The Decision to Pursue Empire

It was Cabral's report to King Manuel and the council which ended any illusions that the Samorin was a Christian and signaled the change in Portuguese objectives from peaceful to martial ones, Naturally, Cabral tried to play down his own rashness, and he counseled the use of intimidation and force to achieve Portugal's goals. For the rest, King Manuel and his counselors were confronted with their first accurate picture of what faced Portugal if they wished to continue the Indian enterprise. Barros wrote that they raised anew all of the questions considered five years previously at Monte-mór O Novo, in light of the realization that on the stretch of Indian shoreline between Goa and Cochin alone "there were more Moors than all those facing us on the coast of Africa between Ceuta and Alexandria . . . all of whom plotted our destruction."[4] King Manuel, however, was not to be easily dissuaded, and he overruled his more timid counselors a second time, among other reasons because he had a full sense of history. Both Góis, in his account of the original Monte-mór O Novo meeting, and Barros, who reported this one, stressed King Manuel's feeling that he was obliged to crown with final achievement the efforts inaugurated by his ancestors. As a renaissance prince, Manuel wished to add undying luster to his reign with such a great deed, "holding in mind," as Barros observed, "the tenet of that most wise Solomon that an illustrious name is worth more than all the riches on earth." "Regarding kings," Barros continued, "of all the things they can do, whatever these might be, nothing imparts to them a greater name than to add to their crown some just and illustrious title."[5] Indeed no other title ever adopted by a Euro-

---

[4] João de Barros and Diogo do Couto, *Décadas da Ásia*, (*Dos feitos que os portugueses fizeram no descubrimento e conquista dos mares, e terras do Oriente*, Dec. I, bk. 6, chap. 1.
[5] *Ibid.*

pean sovereign has become half so famous as the one Manuel claimed for himself no sooner than he had decided to push ahead with the new challenge (see chapter 12).

It is curious that Barros makes only oblique reference to economic considerations. Obviously, King Manuel's more cautious counselors not only brought up the argument made at Monte-mór O Novo in 1496 that Portugal could profit with less investment and more peacefully from the trade with Guinea and even Ethiopia, but they now argued with complete certainty that to pursue the Indian market would only result in the same sort of confrontation with Moorish resistance that Portugal had long experienced in North Africa, only now it was vastly farther away. Yet, if Barros's sentiments reflect Manuel's at the fateful meeting — and they probably do — the only answer to this was that worthy princes must act from higher motives than do mere moneygrubbers, whose moneys perish with them, "even if princes' acts at times cause them to lose substance, and at times, everything; while few men who act only to get rich can enrich themselves without infamy."[6]

Perhaps because the king and his staff were displeased with Cabral's performance, he seems to have been set aside as the logical commander to return in 1502 with the most powerful fleet sent to Indian waters since the Chinese fleets of the fifteenth century. Instead, Vasco da Gama was chosen again, and twenty vessels, fifteen under him and five under his brother Estevão, set sail in February and March of that year, obviously not bent on a course of appeasement. Unfortunately, the *regimento* for da Gama's second voyage has never been found, for in it one might expect to find Portugal's first blueprint for the establishment of its Indian empire. But certainly da Gama's actions indicate that he returned to India as a warrior, determined to exact revenge for the murder of the Portuguese *feitor* and his men in Calicut the year before, and to capture the Malabar pepper trade for his country. As a curtain raiser, his fleet captured and burned a large and richly laden Moorish vessel of Calicut, apparently en route home from a pilgrimage to Mecca and filled with wealthy merchants and their families. Then his fleet descended upon Cochin. There followed the cordial exchange of presents between da Gama, on behalf of King Manuel, and the king, whose friendliness toward the Portuguese had already involved him in hostilities with the Samorin. While in Cochin, da

[6]*Ibid.*

Gama established a *feitoria* and induced the king to agree to a fixed price for the sale of spices to Portugal, the first of many such arrangements that the Portuguese and the Dutch after them concluded in Asia with their various client states (see chapter 18). Next the fleet proceeded to Calicut for a showdown.

It is interesting as a measure of the Samorin's flexibility and his eagerness for trade that he decided to give the Portuguese a second chance, in order to stop them from doing business with his rival Cochin. He chose to be conciliatory. He could hardly have failed to be menaced by da Gama's powerful squadron, and he could scarcely have yet forgotten the bombardment meted out to him by Cabral two years before. But he was obviously not so cowed by the Portuguese that he would agree to anything. He offered to deliver up the dozen Moors who were chiefly responsible for the conspiracy against Cabral's *feitoria*, together with the 20,000 pardaus he had fined them. But he refused to yield to da Gama's demand that all Muslims be expelled from Calicut and all those guilty be delivered up to the Portuguese for punishment. Calicut, he insisted, must remain open to all customers. A day later he forwarded the news that the Moors held responsible for the massacre had offered to double their 20,000 pardau payment in ransom for themselves. Da Gama's response must have taken the Samorin completely by surprise: the admiral suddenly gave the order to hoist anchor, swung his ships in close to shore, and opened fire, hurling stone and metal cannonballs into the city's streets for an entire day before sailing off toward Cochin. In addition to this inexplicable and barbarous act, which killed indiscriminately, he committed one even more appalling: he butchered or burned alive several hundred innocent fishermen who had assumed that peace was in the offing and had sailed out beyond the Portuguese fleet to pursue their day's catch. No one has ever attempted to defend his action — and few have even tried to explain it. Da Gama's orders must have been to punish Calicut as he saw fit and to pursue a policy of intimidation aimed at terrifying the other Malabar rulers into expelling their own Arab colonies. Da Gama and Cabral, too, for that matter, may have been slightly quicker to anger and more extreme than others of their contemporaries, but it is wise to remember that Europeans of the age were almost completely without feeling for non-Christian peoples and had little interest in or understanding of cultures other than their own. For the Portuguese especially, nearly a

century of vicious fighting in Morocco had brutalized attitudes and probably made the soldiers who journeyed to the Orient even less humane than
the Spaniards who dealt with the Indians in America, where at least there
was no overtone of bitter religious rivalry or conspiratorial opposition.
The Portuguese actions could hardly have served their cause very well
either, for they prompted the formation of an Indo-Egyptian alliance
against Portugal and the construction of the fleet which six years later, in
1509, challenged Francisco de Almeida off Diu. Da Gama and Cabral
thereby became doubly important in history: after finding the way to
India for the Portuguese, they determined that King Manuel had no
option but to dominate its oceanic commerce.

Meanwhile, Portuguese ships continued to be dispatched to India; in
1503, three squadrons of three ships each sailed within a short time, the
first under the command of Afonso de Albuquerque; then in 1504 thirteen
more sailed, and in 1505, twenty-two, under Francisco de Almeida.
These enabled Portugal to continue the carrot-and-stick policies da Gama
and Cabral had begun, for in sixteenth-century practice the larger vessels
were equally adapted for hurling cannonballs into a port or loading profitable quantities of its spices. One thing at least is certain: the Portuguese
were as eager to cultivate the friendly rulers as they were to punish the
Samorin and avenge themselves upon the Mohammedans who attempted
to block them, and to this extent their policy was successful. Most of the
Malabar rulers — those of Cannanore, Cochin, Quilon, Calicoylan, and
Travancore among others — were under the suzerainty of the Samorin
and distinctly inferior to him commercially. Cochin had led the others in
breaking away at the earliest moment, and Cannanore had quickly followed. Next, the queen of Quilon had welcomed da Gama, no doubt at
once fearing his might and being eager to increase her revenues.

The gratuitous destruction visited upon Calicut swiftly caused the Portuguese more inconvenience than they need otherwise have experienced.
The naval bombardment had done the Samorin no military damage at all,
and as soon as da Gama sailed for Portugal in 1503, this ruler of course set
out to punish the king of his former tributary Cochin and uproot the
Portuguese *feitoria* there. Fortunately for the Portuguese, the king of
Cochin remained steadfastly loyal to them, despite their failure to protect
him on that occasion. It seems the squadron commander, Vicente Sodré,
whom da Gama had left behind to defend Cochin, instead set out to

plunder Muslim shipping and was lost in a sudden storm. Forced to withdraw to an island with the Portuguese *feitores*, the king suffered his city to be burned rather than yield up the Portuguese. Later in the same year, another fleet, under Francisco de Albuquerque, arrived from Portugal; after importunement, this captain did loan a tiny Portuguese army under Duarte Pacheco Pereira, the author of the *Esmeraldo de situ orbis*, to protect Cochin. For their lack of foresight, the Portuguese deserved being pushed into the sea; but Pereira turned out to be a formidable commander, in fact one whom fate dealt the ultimate indignity of not allowing him a role in history commensurate with his abilities. When the Samorin vigorously renewed his attempt in 1504 to conquer Cochin, Pereira so skillfully deployed his men and vessels that for five months the forces of the Samorin were bloodied, ambushed, and baffled at every turn by Pereira and a mere handful of soldiers. Finally, they retired in defeat and exhaustion. This action of Pereira served to protect Portugal's other allies, too, for the attack on Cochin absorbed the Samorin's armies until Portugal was able to bring more forces into the Indian Ocean. Pereira returned to Portugal soon afterward and never assumed another command. He was a man of great integrity and talent, literary as well as military, and he possessed the same sure touch for command of Eurasian armies that later distinguished the Frenchman Dupleix. Portugal was fortunate in having him available to offset the immediate consequences of da Gama's rashness.

King Manuel, meanwhile, showed his continued resolve from the Lisbon end of the *Carreira* to make the Portuguese enterprise in India succeed. Even as Duarte Pacheco Pereira successfully pitted his wits and forces against the Samorin, a new thirteen-ship fleet sailed from Lisbon. When its commander, Lopo Soares de Albergaria, heard of Pereira's difficulties, he hurried to his aid. It must have been Albergaria's show of force on the Malabar Coast that caused the Arab merchants to despair of their future there, for soon afterward, most of them gathered their belongings and crowded into a refugee convoy bound for the Red Sea. As luck would have it for the Portuguese, Albergaria's force, laden with spices for the return journey, just then turned up off Calicut and caught the Arabs in the act of departure. After a sharp fight, Albergaria annihilated their whole fleet and thereby delivered a coup de grace to the Samorin's commercial allies. The scene was now fully set for permanent Portuguese establishment on India's west coast.

Almeida and the Beginnings of an Imperial Strategy

Until this point, the Portuguese do not seem to have begun the formulation of strategic policy designed to gain control of the Indian Ocean. But in 1505, six years after their first arrival in Calicut, the rudiments appear in the *regimento* given to Francisco de Almeida. This veteran of both the Battle of Toro in 1479 and the siege of Granada (where he served the same Catholic Kings he had opposed under Afonso V) was seemingly chosen only after temporary blindness had prevented another trusted *fidalgo*, Tristão da Cunha, from assuming the supreme command. But King Manuel obviously placed the highest confidence in Almeida's abilities, at least initially. He set sail in March of that year with the largest force yet assembled for service in the Orient: twenty-two ships and 1500 fighting men.

His instructions have been preserved; they embody an amazingly sophisticated grasp of what moderns have identified and christened as "geopolitics," and have even fancied that no one understood before the nineteenth century. First of all, Almeida was appointed for three years, rather than being put in command of a fleet only for the duration of its round trip. This clearly indicates that King Manuel and his council had faced the need for a continuity of leadership in Asia. Second, Almeida was instructed to capture and fortify Kilwa and Mombasa on the East African coast and to build a fortress in the Angediva Islands off the west coast of India between Goa and Honavar — moves which were obviously designed to secure friendly stepping-stones for Portuguese vessels between India and the Cape of Good Hope. Then, under the heading "Red Sea," King Manuel's instructions propose the most daring concept of all:

It seems to us that nothing would serve us better than to have a fortress at the mouth of the Red Sea or near to it — rather inside it than outside might afford the better control — because from there we could see to it that no spices might pass to the land of the sultan of Egypt, and all those in India would lose the false notion that they could trade any more, save through us. . . . You should collect our ships after accomplishing all you are commanded to do at Quilon . . . and when these are collected, it would please us for you to pass to the mouth of the Red Sea.[7]

Moreover, a year later Almeida was instructed, if possible, to capture and fortify Ceylon and Malacca.[8]

[7]Raimundo de Bulhão Pato, ed. *Cartas de Affonso de Albuquerque, seguidas de documentos que as elucidam*, II, p. 311.
[8]*Cartas de Albuquerque*, III, 268–276.

Almeida's *regimento* in effect sets forth most of the "geopolitical" elements governing the formation of the Portuguese empire in the decades that followed. It renders totally inaccurate the view presented by the British writer G. A. Ballard, who would have one believe that the great Afonso de Albuquerque, a full five years later, was "the first man in history to evolve an organized system of trade on an oceanic scope and to arrive at an understanding of the proper principles of its defence as a special branch of naval science."[9] The fact is more nearly that Almeida did not act on the advice forwarded by the crown as fully and perfectly as Albuquerque did, after he had succeeded to Almeida's job. And the real question involves not how Albuquerque but how Lisbon came to conceive the ideas in the first place. King Manuel, naturally, never once visited Asia; and, furthermore, in 1506, only a year after the *regimento* just quoted was written, he was suggesting that Almeida capture or fortify Malacca or Ceylon — places which until that time, to his knowledge anyway, no Portuguese had yet visited! Most certainly, Manuel did not possess a crystal ball and was not a genius. As will presently be seen, he was not even capable of forwarding consistent advice to his viceroys and governors.

It must be remembered that Muslim traders had been sailing freely about the Indian Ocean since the tenth century and that there was little they did not know about its geography. Besides this, the Portuguese by 1500, after nearly a century of coastal exploration in Africa, had become expert geographical observers and missed little of possible interest. Few nations have produced such expert and judicious descriptions of hitherto unknown lands as *The Book of Duarte Barbosa* and *The Suma Oriental* of Tomé Pires, both written by 1518. The astuteness with which the authors analyze such locations as Ormuz, Aden, and Malacca leaves little doubt that the strategic insight long credited to Albuquerque alone was actually common to many Portuguese engaged in the overseas enterprises.[10] It is most probable — in fact almost certain — that all the Portuguese had to do to find out what cities and sites were valuable in the Orient was to ask the right questions in the Arabic language many had learned while serving in Morocco. That not all the Arabs and other navigators were reluctant

[9] G. A. Ballard, *Rulers of the Indian Ocean*, p. 51.

[10] For an example, see Armando Cortesão, ed. and trans. *The Suma Oriental of Tomé Pires and the Book of Francisco Rodriques*, I, p. 15. The second work in the title could also have been mentioned, as might Duarte Pacheco Pereira's *Esmeraldo de situ orbis*, except that it deals only with Africa, where the Portuguese had much longer experience.

to part with such geographical information is indicated by the fact that the Portuguese never found it hard to locate pilots to take them wherever they wished to go — Sequeira to Malacca or Albuquerque into the Red Sea, not to mention da Gama to Calicut on the original voyage from Malindi in 1499.

As for Almeida himself, only two letters by him to the king survive. The first is a very long one written upon his arrival in India and hence not very instructive. But the second goes far to explain why Almeida was not more active in carrying out King Manuel's instructions. This document is dated by António Baião as late 1508. It contains a brief passage which suggests why Almeida did not attempt to establish his country's presence even in the ports and places where he bore standing orders to do so, including Aden, Malacca, and Ceylon. Regarding the establishment of a fortress in Quilon (Coulão), he wrote the king:

As for the fortress here in Quilon, the more fortresses your Majesty might possess, the more your power will be divided: all your forces should be on the sea, because if there we should not be powerful (which Your Majesty forbid!), everything would be against us. . . . In so far as you are powerful on the sea, all India will be as yours, but if you do not possess this kind of power on the sea, fortresses ashore will do you precious little good.[11]

Francisco de Almeida's reputation was made as a ferocious fighter and not as an empire builder, but his outward journey did at least create the beginnings of a new imperium to match Manuel's ambitious titles. Probably because last-minute adjustments had been made at Lisbon after his *regimento* had been drafted, he did not stop at Sofala, but left its fortification to Pedro de Añaya, a Spaniard who sailed in command of six ships after Almeida's departure. The new viceroy instead stopped at Kilwa, where he set upon its throne a king friendly to Portugal. After erecting a fort there, he proceeded to Mombasa, a place not mentioned in his existing *regimento*. Greeted by artillery fire, he captured the city, burned it to the ground, and destroyed all vessels found there. Next, he crossed the Indian Ocean and fortified Angediva as instructed, meanwhile receiving embassies from the ruler of Honavar and an Arab community at Chitakal, both eager to escape his wrath. He then proceeded to Quilon and Cochin, where he strengthened their defenses. Thereafter, despite this active beginning, the dispatch of his son Lourenço to the Maldives and

[11] Quoted by António Baião in *HEP*, II, 112.

Ceylon was his only other move toward the creation of an imperium. (And even that episode was probably not motivated by much more than a desire to track down some enemy traders.)

As matters developed, Almeida was soon obliged to defend the Portuguese presence in the Indian Ocean from fleets sent against him by a Turco-Indian alliance formed by the linchpin of the older trading system, the Mameluke sultan of Egypt. This alliance seems to have been backed, at least tacitly, by the Venetians themselves.

The Response of the Sultan

While the Portuguese were busy assembling fleets and fighting men for service in the Indian Ocean, the Venetians had fought listlessly on against the Ottoman Turks in the disastrous Second Turkish War. Finally, in 1503, they signed a dreary seven-year truce which required them to give up as the price for this respite the possession of their lone conquest in the war, the island of Santa Maura in the Ionian Sea. It was only after the negotiations for this unhappy arrangement were well under way in 1502 that they began to think again about the condition of their Eastern trade. By this time, they must also have scarcely been able to tolerate the irony of their attempt to enlist King Manuel's help against the Turks. For all the while this king was busy wrecking their Levantine trade at its source, he feigned his cordiality by knighting Ambassador Pietro Pasqualigo and making the Signoria godfather to his baby son. This was apparently more than the Venetians could bear. Abruptly, in the spring of 1502, the Signoria recalled Pasqualigo and broke diplomatic relations with Portugal, apparently even forgetting amid the stress of other events that an embassy in Lisbon would provide a prime listening post.[12]

Not long after their termination of this pretended cordiality toward Portugal, the Venetians further altered their course and appointed a commission of fifteen notables in December 1502, whose job it was to consider what might be done to oust Manuel's ships from the Indian Ocean, or at least prevent them from doing further damage. At the behest of this group, the Signoria lost no time in hurrying off a new ambassador to Egypt to voice the commission's concern over what Portugal was doing to the oriental trade. He first suggested to the Egyptians that duties on

[12] Weinstein, *Ambassador from Venice*, pp. 75–76.

spices and Indian goods be lowered to make the Venetians competitive with Portuguese prices in Europe. Then he proposed discreetly that means be found to discourage the return of the Portuguese to Indian waters. The phrase used by the Signoria was "rapid and secret remedies" — sufficiently vague so that if news leaked out to the Christian world, no one could maintain that Venice necessarily supported the downfall of a fellow Catholic power at the hands of the infidel.[13] The sultan, however, was left free to draw his own conclusions.

When it came to actual "remedies," the sultan had no better idea how to stop the Portuguese than did the Venetians in the summer of 1504. He frightened Franciscan prior Fra Mauro into hurrying from the Holy Land to report in Venice and Rome that Egypt had threatened to destroy the Holy Sepulcher and other places unless the Portuguese withdrew, a scheme which was little more than an indication of how much da Gama's discovery took by surprise the Muslim world. The Mamelukes, however, had no monopoly on the contemplation of desperate measures: for a time the Venetians even appear to have entertained the possibility of digging a Suez Canal.[14]

Ultimately, however, Venice went back to its information gathering in Lisbon — this time clandestinely and without the expense of an embassy — while the sultan took the only course open to him and prepared an armada to do battle with the Portuguese interlopers. But an attack on the Portuguese at sea entailed no little trouble and preparation for a ruler who had hitherto only milked his merchants and never thought of defending them. His realms totally lacked suitable timber, for one thing, and this had to be obtained from the Black Sea in twenty-five rented vessels. Moreover, even before he received his raw materials, the weather and the Crusaders combined to favor Portugal. While sailing in the vicinity of Rhodes, the Egyptian convoy encountered unexpectedly a fleet of the Hospitalers of St. John, commanded quite coincidentally by a Portuguese, who laid into the convoy with a will and sank or captured eleven vessels. Later, the weakened remnant ran into a fierce storm and lost another four ships. Only two-fifths of the original lumber ever reached Alexandria. By the time it had been freighted overland and built into ships at Suez, it was 1507. The original order might have built thirty or

[13] Weinstein, *Ambassador from Venice*, p. 77.
[14] *Ibid.*

more large galleys; as it was, the commander, Amir Hussain, left port in February 1507 to join his allies in India with only a dozen large vessels and about 1500 combatants.[15]

Whether or not the Venetians took any part in these preparations remains unknown. The Portuguese were quick to accuse them, which is not surprising, but there appears to be no conclusive evidence in the matter.[16] If the Signoria did participate, its stake would have been limited to a payment or two, carried out in the utmost secrecy. It is far more certain that the Venetians wished the sultan well and were at first elated and then more deeply pessimistic than ever when they heard the results.

The Viceroyalty of Almeida, Continued

For the first two years of Francisco de Almeida's viceroyalty, the Portuguese held firm in the Indian Ocean despite continued troubles with the Samorin and the fact that after his first conquests, Almeida confined his fleets to convoy duty and his men to defense. By April 1506 the Samorin had outfitted a fleet of over two hundred ships, many of whose gunwales sported bales of cotton for protection against Portuguese gunfire. In addition, the Hindu king now possessed some ordnance of his own, thanks to the defection from Portuguese ranks of two Milanese armorers who entered the Samorin's service. Before being killed on his orders for allegedly wishing to turn coat once more, these brothers were reported by another Italian, Lodovico di Varthema, to have supervised the casting of four or five hundred assorted cannon, many for naval use.[17]

The first trial of this fleet in March 1506 resulted in a disaster for the Samorin; off Cannanore, it ran afoul of a small Portuguese squadron commanded by the viceroy's son Lourenço. There followed a protracted engagement in which one gathers the Hindu, Arab, and Turkish crews were totally untrained and uncoordinated. Many of their largest vessels were sunk and their crews killed or drowned. Much of the fleet must have escaped, however, for despite high Portuguese estimates of the damage done, it would have been all but physically impossible for the three *naus* and a caravel, plus some foists commanded by Lourenço, to have sunk

[15] Heyd, *Histoire du commerce*, II, pp. 534–538.
[16] See Weinstein, *Ambassador from Venice*, pp. 104–105, n. 14.
[17] Lodovico di Varthema, *The Travels of Lodovico di Varthema in Egypt, Syria, Arabia Deserta and Arabia Felix, in Persia, India and Ethopia, A.D. 1503 to 1508*, p. 262.

more than a few dozen. Moreover, the Samorin was able to float an even bigger fleet less than a year later.

Following this victory, the Portuguese enjoyed but a brief respite from trouble. Soon their friend the king of Cannanore died and was succeeded by a monarch who hated the Europeans and fell to intriguing with the Samorin. The Samorin sent him some mercenaries and twenty-one pieces of artillery; in 1507, he laid siege to the Portuguese in the makeshift fortress they had built, which consisted of little more than a wall across a promontory. Beleaguered and battered, the Europeans were awaiting a final assault when Tristão da Cunha sailed in from Socotra and broke it up. Meanwhile, pressed for men and supplies, the viceroy had to abandon the fortress on Angediva after it had been similarly attacked by a Goan fleet in the pay of Calicut.

But the most ominous development of all escaped the attention of the Portuguese. In the months since his armada's defeat at the hands of Lourenço de Almeida, the Samorin had stealthily rebuilt this navy, and sometime in 1507, it had slipped past Cochin and Cannanore without detection. Its destination seems to have been none other than a rendez-vouz with the Egyptian fleet of the Mameluke Admiral Amir Hussain near Chaul.

The outward-bound Portuguese fleet under Tristão da Cunha and Afonso de Albuquerque which departed from Lisbon in 1506 naturally could have had no knowledge of this impending junction of enemies, and it proceeded according to its own plan. Hoping that the island of Socotra would provide them with a suitable base from which to choke off Red Sea commerce to and from India, Albuquerque and Cunha had captured its main port, Soko, after a stiff fight and set about to build a fortress there. Then the commanders had split up. Cunha in five ships continued on to India where, as just remarked, he found Cannanore in distress and relieved its garrison before going on to Cochin, loading spices, and departing for Portugal. Albuquerque, meanwhile, remained for a time at Soko and then set off toward the Persian Gulf, where he remained for many months before Ormuz.

In the meantime, the Calicut-Egyptian plan unfolded in the leisurely way characteristic of an epoch when concerted activity between distant allies was hampered by sailboat communication. Amir Hussain seems to have taken more time in descending upon India than the Samorin had anticipated, stopping off twice in Arabia to settle old scores with the

Mameluke sultan's enemies. Apparently, the Samorin's fleet had expected him in 1507, at Chaul, and was waiting in the vicinity when Lourenço de Almeida, its old nemesis, sailed up the coast on a mission to protect friendly shipping from pirates. Off Dubal, Lourenço was told of the Calicut fleet tucked away in its estuary, but it is doubtful that he suspected the true purpose. More likely he thought its mission was merely to harass the merchants of Cochin and Cannanore. He wished to attack, but his captains were unanimous in their advice that the narrowness of the harbor entrance would put them at too great a disadvantage. After a few lesser actions, he returned to Cochin, where, characteristically, his fire-eating father, the viceroy, dismissed the reluctant captains.

The Rivalry with Gujarat

It was at about this time that the Portuguese became aware of a potentially dangerous new rival in the Indian sultanate of Gujarat, whose merchants and port officials seem all the while to have been more alert to Portuguese intentions than the Portuguese were of any potential rivalry. Probably this was because Calicut, as the center of the all-important Indian pepper trade to the Red Sea and Europe, had wholly absorbed Portuguese attention and held it during their first few years in India. Calicut, however, was but a single large port with a few satellite harbor towns, and its pepper commerce lay wholly in the hands of Arabian and Egyptian foreigners. Gujarat, or Cambay, as it was then called, was much larger in area and population — it covered the entire Kathiawar peninsula, together with the eastern shore of the Gulf of Cambay — and its territories and ports so hummed with activity that the sixteenth-century Portuguese geographer Tomé Pires likened its populace to the Italians.[18]

There were about fifteen important cities in Gujarat, of which the ports of Cambay, Diu, Surat, Bassein, Mangalore, and Render, and the inland cities of Andava and Champanel, were the principal. Its sultan and ruling classes were Muslim, but a considerable proportion of both its population at large and its merchantry remained Hindu. The countryside abounded in wheat and legumes, which were available for export; but, above all, the area was famous for its textiles, both cotton and silk, in all qualities from the roughest to the most splendid. In addition, its workshops produced carpets, silver jewelry, and cut gemstones.

[18] Pires, *Suma Oriental*, I, 41.

According to Pires, its trading pattern could be likened to two out-
stretched arms, "with her right arm . . . [reaching] out towards Aden
and the other . . . towards Malacca."[19] For it was the Gujarati, excellent sailors as well as fabricators and merchants, who completed the link
between the Levant and Malacca, not the Arabs. The cloves, mace, and
nutmeg of the Moluccas, the silks, musk, and sandalwood of China were
nearly all fetched to India by Gujarati vessels in barter for their textiles,
grains, and other items; and they were sold to the Arabs and Egyptians,
and to the Ormuz merchants who wanted to purchase them in Cambay
and the other ports of Gujarat.[20]

It is therefore obvious enough that any growing Portuguese pretensions
to control the Indian Ocean would be bound to menace Gujarat's very
existence as a commercial power. The capture of Socotra by Cunha and
Albuquerque could hardly have gone unheeded by the Gujarati merchants, for the Red Sea was as important for their trade as it was for
Calicut's. That Socotra soon proved to be too far out in the Gulf of Aden
from the Straits of Bab el Mandeb for the Portuguese to monitor the Arab
traffic effectively was certainly less important than the Portuguese intent
to do so, which its conquest almost certainly revealed. It could only have
meant that the Portuguese were out to cripple or lay under tribute the
whole established commercial system.

The Gujarati, on the other hand, were anything but foolhardy in their
opposition to the Portuguese. About all Viceroy Almeida might have
suspected in 1508 was that Malik Ayaz, a former Russian slave who had
become naval chief and master of Diu for the sultan of Cambay, had been
in touch again with the Samorin. This in itself was nothing new; in 1506,
the Samorin had tried and failed to coax him from his neutrality. But this
only seems to have been because Malik Ayaz had little confidence in the
Samorin's navy, little, if any, support from his sultan, whose interests
were only concerned with campaigns inland, and was waiting to see what
the Egyptians might bring with them from Suez. However, Malik Ayaz
must have known that no help arrived from Lisbon in 1508, and word
must have been given him by the Samorin that a large fleet from Egypt
was on the way.

[19]*Ibid.*, p. 42.
[20]See Maria Antoinette Petronella Meilink-Roelofsz, *Asian Trade and European
Influence in the Malay Archipelago between 1500 and about 1630*, pp. 61–66.

The Showdown Fights

When Amir Hussain and his fleet finally did arrive in India in 1508, he made straight for Diu. Happily for Portugal, the Samorin's fleet had apparently tired of waiting for him and gone home — it is likely that Malik Ayaz denied the fleet use of his port facilities. The Egyptians, however, were much more formidable, and the shrewd Russian haggled with them, setting a high premium on his availability as an ally.

Just then, word seems to have arrived that Lourenço de Almeida was anchored in the harbor at Chaul, not many leagues to the south, and that his force was inferior to Amir Hussain's. Amir Hussain possessed six large round ships and six galleasses, great galleys which ordinarily had guns mounted on a deck above the banks of rowers.

Lourenço had set out with a light force, mostly of galleys, to convoy friendly shipping north from Cochin and Cannanore, and only while en route does he seem to have been warned by his father that some arrangement was in progress between Malik Ayaz and the Egyptians. But no additional help accompanied the warning, and he seems to have discounted it. The whole Egyptian fleet sailed into Chaul and surprised the Portuguese completely.[21] Even as the enemy fleet appeared, it was thought for a moment that the ships might belong to Albuquerque's expedition bound for Cochin from Persia.

In the melee which followed, both sides fired hotly at one another as the Egyptian vessels bore in. But the Portuguese seem to have been the better gunners, and the Egyptian attempt to board the Portuguese ships was thwarted bloodily. Until near nightfall on the second day of battle, the Portuguese seemed to be gaining the upper hand over Amir Hussain's forces when Malik Ayaz sailed to his aid with a large number of galleys. Accounts differ at this point about whether Lourenço de Almeida was now willing to withdraw, or whether the rebuke his father had delivered to him the year before was still stinging in his ears. At any rate, powder supplies were dangerously low, and a fighting retreat became necessary on the third morning. Unfortunately for the Portuguese, the tides in the Gulf of Cambay are exceptionally swift, so much so that one traveler reported watching a fleeing dog drowned by an insurging wall of water. Lourenço's ship attempted its departure from Chaul harbor too late and

[21] Barros, Da Ásia, Dec. II, bk. 2, ch. 7.

then sailed too close to a row of pilings erected at the entrance when pursued by Amir Hussain's squadron. Almost simultaneously, the vessel sustained a direct hit at waterline and was rammed against the pilings by the ebb tide until the Egyptians caught up to it. One Mameluke cannonball carried away Lourenço's leg; he then had himself lashed to a mast so that he could continue to give orders. But moments later, a second projectile hit him squarely, while still others sank the ship. The remaining Portuguese vessels, by then safely out of danger, bore the news to Viceroy Almeida.

By all accounts, the viceroy showed no grief at these losses in public. But revenge for his son became his most fervent concern. "Who ate the young rooster must now taste the old rooster," he was said to have muttered.

When the sad news arrived of the death of Lourenço and perhaps 140 other Portuguese, the elder Almeida had taken sides in a bitter dispute between Afonso de Albuquerque and Albuquerque's captains. Albuquerque's role in the controversy was exacerbated by the fact that the king had given Albuquerque orders when he left Portugal which nominated him in Almeida's stead, as soon as Almeida's three-year term expired. That time had now come, but Almeida was determined not to give way to Albuquerque or anyone else until he had personally smashed Amir Hussain.

After their capture of Socotra, Tristão da Cunha and Albuquerque had parted company. Cunha, it will be remembered, went on to India, where he relieved Cannonore, while Albuquerque took seven ships and no more than 500 men to attack Ormuz, an independent Persian sultanate based on the island of the same name whose strategic location near the mouth of the Persian Gulf made it the entrepôt for all the Indian Ocean traffic to and from Safavid Persia proper and from Persia across the desert to Aleppo and the Mediterranean (although by 1500 this caravan crossing was infrequently made). Its control by Portugal would not only shut off enemy commerce with Persia, but would give Portugal a major source of Persian silver by enabling it to replace Arab and Indian commerce with its own. Albuquerque's original instructions had been to capture Aden. Apparently, he deviated from them only because he lacked the forces to carry so strong a citadel and reasoned that it made more sense to shift operations to the waterless and not as strongly fortified island controlling the Persian Gulf. In this move he was undoubtedly correct, but the undertaking was only less ambitious than the assault on Aden would have been, and this without express royal orders. In spite of everything, Albuquerque nearly achieved his objective and through sheer determination at that. Although he never possessed enough men to capture or occupy Ormuz in house-to-house fighting, he did possess a fleet with formidable firepower and, even more important, a reputation for ferocity and ruthlessness which had preceded him along the Arabian coast as he stopped to sack and destroy all cities that refused to put themselves under his protection. Once before Ormuz, he boldly demanded that Ormuz's twelve-year-old sultan and his governor, Khwaja Atar, make themselves vassals of the king of Portugal. When Khwaja Atar temporized, Albuquerque picked a fight with his navy and utterly wrecked it, thereafter renewing the Portuguese demands. This time they were accepted, and Albuquerque set about to erect a stone fortress next to the city.

Albuquerque's own captains were not happy at this development, for toiling in the hot sun was hardly the pastime they had envisioned for their commands. Prowling about the Indian Ocean and grabbing off richly laden Arab vessels would have made them all wealthy, and it must hardly have mattered to them what their commander so obviously had in mind: the strategic and economic value to their country.

As subsequent events were so clearly to demonstrate, Albuquerque was not a man who placed selfish interest above service to his monarch, and he displayed scant patience with those who did. He angrily ignored all his subordinates' mounting protests and persevered in his design to finish the fortress. Thereafter, everything went wrong. Four sailors deserted to Khwaja Atar and revealed the dissension in the Portuguese squadron. The Ormuz governor refused to hand the men back, whereupon Albuquerque blockaded the island city (and thereby stopped the importation of its water supply from the mainland). By then he suspected that his own captains were in illicit communication with Khwaja Atar; in any event, three of them suddenly deserted him in their ships to take their case to Viceroy Almeida in Cochin. Albuquerque was then forced to give up the struggle temporarily and sail off to Socotra where he relieved the garrison before returning to Ormuz once more, bombarding the city, and then sailing on to India in 1508.[22]

[22] For the inquest held by Almeida into Albuquerque's conduct before Ormuz see *Cartas de Albuquerque*, II, 159–231. See also, III, 283–297.

When Albuquerque arrived in Cochin, Viceroy Almeida, flanked by all Albuquerque's insubordinate captains, was waiting for him. Albuquerque showed Almeida the royal patent authorizing him to take over; but Almeida refused to honor it and instead put his rival under house arrest. Civil war might have ensued in Portuguese India had not Albuquerque shown admirable forbearance and submitted to the indignity until the king's will could be manifested again.

The chroniclers and even recent historians have spent much time embellishing their stories of the bitter quarrel between these two leaders, but it would seem most interesting as an illustration, not of how petty a great commander like Almeida could be at his worst, but of the intense fear that the "new monarchs" of early modern times had of delegating any but the most limited power to their nobility. If Gaspar Corrêa's account can be trusted, King Manuel had appointed Almeida as his chief officer in India and given him the title of viceroy as a great mark of his affection and unlimited confidence, explaining "I give you power, as though it were in my own person, with the title of Viceroy of India, which in my days no other person will hold."[23] But when Almeida's sailing orders were issued, they read that Almeida had been appointed "for three years."[24] Finally, Almeida had hardly become acquainted with his new position of "unlimited confidence" when (in 1506) King Manuel appointed Albuquerque to the governorship of India two years hence, as soon as Almeida's term was due to expire. The transaction was supposed to have been a closely guarded secret, but secrets have a way of leaking out; in this instance, Almeida quite obviously was party to it long in advance. Manuel indeed earned his sobriquet *O Venturoso* ("The Fortunate") when matters did not grow worse than they actually did between the two. For in effect they were simultaneous governors.

The story has its counterparts in the developing Spanish empire in this very same era: one has only to consider the speed with which Columbus was removed from his "perpetual" viceroyalty, the way in which his son Diego's rights were abridged, and the way in which Cortés was treated. All of those men also fought a losing battle against the inevitable royal jealousy of their independence. To Almeida's credit, he at least used his borrowed time to Portugal's advantage.

[23] Corrêa, *Lendas*, I, p. 532.
[24] Bulhão Pato, ed. *Cartas de Albuquerque*, pp. 269–271.

The Great Victory at Diu

In the autumn of 1509, determined to avenge his son, Almeida gathered a force of some nineteen ships, twelve of them large, and 1200 men, representing nearly all the Portuguese strength in the Indian Ocean, and set out for Diu, where Amir Hussain and his fleet remained the guests of Malik Ayaz. The Gujarati and Egyptians knew Almeida was coming, for the Samorin had kept watch over the outfitting of his fleets in Cochin and Cannanore and even managed to send Amir Hussain a number of light ships to bolster his forces. Apparently deeply impressed with the Egyptian victory over Lourenço de Almeida the year before, the ruler of Calicut embraced Amir Hussain with much less reservation than did Malik Ayaz, his host, and he planned to follow Almeida up the coast and fall on the Portuguese ships from behind during their forthcoming battle with Amir Hussain.

For reasons not very clear today, Almeida and his fleet paused before Dabul to attack and destroy this rich city on the Deccan coast which was in league with the Samorin. By this time, Malik Ayaz had learned of the formidable naval power Almeida had amassed and again decided to temporize, lest Almeida succeed in beating the Mameluke fleet. In fact he seems to have wagered on both sides in the game, for he contacted Almeida secretly in Dabul, even while a number of Gujarati vessels, including four heavy ones, joined Amir Hussain's navy. Among other things, he tried to placate Almeida by offering to release the prisoners he had captured from Lourenço's ill-fated vessel.

Whatever transpired between Almeida and Malik Ayaz's emissary in Dabul, however, the viceroy sailed boldly into the harbor at Diu in February 1509. The battle that followed was one of the most decisive in maritime history; it dispersed for a century any serious threat to Portugal's control of the Indian Ocean, and, in a wider sense, established Western naval supremacy in the Indian Ocean until this day. Tactically speaking, however, it was less than epochal; the existing accounts by Barros, Castanheda, and Corrêa indicate that little more than a free-for-all took place. After posting three or four vessels outside Diu which successfully frustrated the Samorin's armada, Almeida sailed straight into Diu's small and shallow harbor as though he owned it. According to all reports, the ramparts surrounding it were bristling with artillery, and no doubt Amir

Hussain could not believe that the foe would make what seemed to him such a foolish move. Possibly because of double-dealing by Malik Ayaz, Amir Hussain's fleet remained at anchor, conveniently clustered together. Once Almeida's navy was inside, one gathers that the Gujarati gunners ashore could not be sure whom they were hitting in the narrow harbor, while the Egyptian, Gujarati, and some Calicutian vessels had no room for maneuvering and could be fired upon at point-blank range by Portuguese gunnery. In the bloody hand-to-hand melee of broadsides, grapplings, and boarding, the Portuguese demoralized and butchered the enemy. In a scene obscured by acrid smoke from the booming ships' guns, Corrêa claims that one large Portuguese ship fired more than 600 large cannonballs alone within a half day on June 20. Amir Hussain himself was soon badly hurt and managed to escape ashore amid the terrible carnage. The Portuguese lost over a hundred men themselves, but they completely destroyed the enemy fleet and dyed the whole harbor crimson it is said, as the Egyptians and Gujarati tried to break loose and run their ships around to safety.[25] Malik Ayaz skillfully made his peace with Almeida, released the prisoners from Lourenço's sunken flagship, attired and well fed, and promised to become a humble subject of King Manuel. The viceroy, feeling himself avenged, then withdrew and sailed for Cochin, stopping only to collect tribute from Dabul and intimidate the inhabitants of hostile cities along the coast by firing the arms and legs of Egyptian captives onto their roofs and streets.

Not long after his victory, Almeida was obliged to give way to Afonso de Albuquerque. His unique achievement was that he held the line, that is, he staved off the greatest challenge of all to Portugal's nascent power in the Indian Ocean. But he appears to have done little else.

There is a curious parallel between him and the first Dutch East India Company governor-general, Pieter Both, who was appointed in 1612 and occupies the same sort of transitional position in the Dutch East India Company's empire as does Almeida in the Portuguese. Each leader was the first appointee in the East with a status more permanent than that of mere commander of an annual fleet, and each seems to have been highly reluctant on principle to commit his superiors and nation to holdings ashore which entailed administration, fortification, and expense. But their policies were reversed by successors who were convinced these very

[25] Corrêa, *Lendas*, I, p. 914.

things were necessary if their empires were to grow and achieve permanence. Almeida was succeeded by Albuquerque and Both (though not
directly) by Jan Pieterszoon Coen; the two were empire builders.

In Almeida's defense, it is safe to say that eventually the proliferation of
fortresses proved a weakness in the Portuguese empire. But it is probably
also safe to say that Almeida would not have provided quite enough of
them.

CHAPTER 16

The Shape of Empire: the Nucleus, 1509–15

Portugal was now too firmly settled in India to be dislodged by any but the unanimous — and therefore unlikely — efforts of its native rulers. At sea the "Franks," as the Muslims called western Europeans, were practically unbeatable. Their naval power not only enabled them to triumph over maritime opposition; it cast their shadow over the beaches and harbors of India as well. By then, too, the Portuguese had come to understand that no rival Indian state could prosper against their will if its prosperity depended upon water transportation. Moreover, they realized that no matter how much power any sultan possessed on land, he could not capture a stout Portuguese fortress well provisioned from the ocean.[1]

In 1509, if there was indeed any real disagreement within the Portuguese camp, it was not over the principle, but over how far it should be applied. Almeida, apparently, did not think it necessary to fasten Portuguese power to more than two or three bases on land. Albuquerque quite clearly saw that possession of Cochin and Cannanore alone did not give King Manuel's fleets a strategic enough position in the Indian Ocean to enable them to monitor and supplant the competition, whose navies Almeida had defeated. As already noted, the royal council had conceived the idea of closing off the Red Sea, and the capture of Socotra had been a

[1] The Venetians had known all about such applications of seapower for centuries, but the Ottomans had learned from them the hard way; the sultan was forced to build a superior tactical navy in order to uproot his Italian rivals from Modon, Choron, and Lepanto. See Andrew C. Hess, "The Evolution of the Ottoman Seaborne Empire in the Age of the Oceanic Discoveries, 1453–1525."

243

false step in that direction. In addition, Albuquerque's attempt on Ormuz had been designed to capture the commerce of the Persian Gulf for Portugal. Almeida, however, had not furthered these designs — perhaps because of the sentiments already noted. Beyond this, it is also quite possible that, had he stayed on as viceroy, his backing of Albuquerque's captains in the quarrel already described would have prevented him from reestablishing the discipline needed to carry out any future projects that demanded a comparable self-sacrifice.

It must be remembered that what had caused the dispute between Albuquerque and his captains was the short-term interests of subordinates who were more concerned with pillage than with imperial strategy. This self-aggrandizement at the expense of the crown in fact proved to be a constant throughout the history of the Portuguese Asian empire; but it is suggestive in this connection that, if only to confound Albuquerque and block his appointment as governor, Almeida had sided with the rebels against him. Had Almeida indeed succeeded in downing Albuquerque with their help and so remained in command, he might well have been obliged to set his future course in deference to their wishes. These did not include toiling under the hot sun when entrepreneurship blended with piracy might pay far more attractive dividends. Critics like Diogo do Couto toward the end of the century accused all too many viceroys of giving way to the prevailing ethos and losing the ability to lead.

Although Almeida may have done little deliberately to post the *Quinas*, or royal coat of arms, upon new outposts east of Cape Comorin, the period of his viceroyalty provided some of the necessary reconnaissance for Albuquerque. Almeida's own son, in fact, had inaugurated the process in 1506.

Hearing, apparently, that traders from farther east were filtering through to Calicut via the Maldive Islands and hoping to intercept them, the viceroy sent Lourenço de Almeida in search of this archipelago and of Ceylon, which was known to lie in the same general direction. According to Barros, the Portuguese motives were at least partially commercial, for he mentions that the Maldives afforded a hemplike fiber called *cairo*, or *coir*, used in the manufacture of rope for ships' riggings.[2] Ceylon was also well known as the prime source of cinnamon, although at this time its use was not as widespread in Europe as it later became and it was then freely obtainable in Cochin.

[2] Barros, *Da Ásia*, Dec. I, bk. 10, chap. 5.

Soon after the young commander had turned south, his vessels were caught up in the Southwest Monsoon Drift, as the seasonal current is called that sweeps along the Malabar Coast in late summer; before they realized it, the Portuguese had been carried around Cape Comorin and brought to a landfall in Ceylon. The Maldives remained undiscovered for the time being, but the Portuguese thus found their way beyond the Indian subcontinent, just as Dias had earlier passed around Africa. Lourenço remained, apparently, only long enough to visit the king of Kotte, make an agreement with him involving a tribute of cinnamon and elephants in return for protection against his enemies, and accept some cinnamon bales from frightened Muslim merchants. Then he returned to India, where struggles with the Samorin diverted his father's attention.

Four years later, in 1510, the Portuguese discovered Malacca, the strategic entrepôt city between the Pacific and the Indian oceans and the wealthiest trading center in the Far East. This discovery, however, was not to Almeida's credit at all, but to that of King Manuel and his council in Lisbon. Except for the fact that the expedition sent from Portugal stopped off in Cochin en route (where, incidentally, Almeida was in the midst of his bickering with Albuquerque) its commander, Diogo Lopes de Sequeira, was in no way subordinate to Almeida, but was given an entirely independent jurisdiction over the seas east of the Indian subcontinent. Manuel had received glowing reports of Malacca based upon what the Portuguese had learned in India from Gujarati merchants. He had also been told by the returning Tristão da Cunha that Madagascar (which Cunha, it seems, had just discovered) possessed many spices of great value. King Manuel thereupon dispatched Sequeira, a *fidalgo* of his household, with four ships to look into the matter, instructing him that if he could not relocate Madagascar or if it proved unpromising, he should proceed past Cape Comorin to Malacca and try for an agreement with its sultan like those made with the more friendly Indian port cities. If this was accomplished, he was to stay on as Portugal's governor in the region east of India. Sequeira indeed rediscovered Madagascar, but when he learned Cunha had been wrong about its worth, he went on. Then, after calling at Cochin, he turned the Cape Comorin — the first time it had been done since Lourenço de Almeida's voyage — skirted Ceylon, and easily located Malacca with the help of experienced Muslim pilots.

When he arrived, the history of the initial Portuguese visits to India was virtually repeated. He was greeted cordially enough by the sultan, who allowed the Portuguese to send some thirty men ashore under Rui Araujo to establish a *feitoria*, but then the Muslim merchants of the city had their inning. They convinced the ruler, Sultan Mohamed, that the Portuguese meant no good. Suddenly, he made an about-face, wiped out the infant *feitoria*, killed several men, captured Araujo and some others, and even tried to attack Sequeira's vessels, which escaped after firing a few salvos into the town. After this misadventure, Sequeira directed two of his ships to Cochin and returned to Lisbon with his tale of woe, but also with exciting reports of Malacca's importance as an entrepôt and of its vast wealth.

Aden, Ormuz, and Malacca had thus all come to official attention during Almeida's term (1505–09) as the strategic cities of the Indian Ocean. When Albuquerque came to power, he provided exactly the leadership and dedication necessary to win these for his king. That he can no longer be credited, as Ballard credited him, with some kind of prophetic geographical vision in inventing the strategic concept that underlay their selection hardly detracts from his stature. Albuquerque's real distinction lies in his vision and determination to carry out his superiors' rough design at a time when Portugal's opportunity was great but totally dependent upon inspired and aggressive leadership so far from home.

Incidentally, had Manuel's wishes regarding the structure of command in Asia been carried out, Albuquerque might never have had the chance to accomplish what he did. Just as the king was lucky that Almeida and Albuquerque did not come to blows as a result of his ambiguous directions, so he was fortunate that events frustrated his intent to create three independent areas east of the Cape of Good Hope, instead of leaving Albuquerque with supreme power. It has been noted that the king had given Diogo Lopes de Sequeira what could have proved to be an independent satrapy east of Cape Comorin; in addition he had appointed still another *fidalgo*, Jorge de Aguiar, as commander of the area from the Cape of Good Hope to Cambay. Purely by circumstance, neither appointment actually worked to divide Albuquerque's authority; Sequeira only occupied his command long enough to confirm the importance of Malacca and furnish some sailors who could act as guides to it, and Jorge de Aguiar soon drowned. Aguiar's successor, Duarte de Lemos, possessed only a second-hand nomination, owing to the death of his superior, and some bad ships. As it was, he sailed to Cochin and was subsequently recalled to Portugal, leaving Albuquerque with as much effective power as Almeida had possessed.[3] It is ironic that for perhaps the only time in Portuguese Indian history the vast distance between Lisbon and India actually proved beneficial to the crown.

An Initial Failure

Fernando Coutinho was a member of the royal household immediately identifiable as the lusty Falstaffian courtier of the renaissance, who was strong of arm, great of belly, but weak of brain. This man, as the marshal of Portugal, was not only Albuquerque's cousin, but the highest officer ever to visit Portuguese India, at least in early modern times. His single, inestimable service to his country was performed on his arrival at Cochin in November 1509, for he dislodged the stubborn viceroy, Almeida, and installed Albuquerque in his stead. Almeida, incidentally, thereupon set sail for Portugal, but died in Africa near the Cape of Good Hope when a surprise attack by natives with poisioned arrows caught him and his landing party too far from their boat.

Coutinho brought with him fifteen ships and about 3000 men in a force that King Manuel had assembled for a Portuguese offensive against Calicut. The move in itself was logical enough, and Albuquerque agreed wholeheartedly. Intelligence reports indicated that the Samorin was absent with most of his armies; so, Albuquerque and Coutinho lost no time at the end of 1509 to strike at his capital.

Had Albuquerque been in sole command, the attack would probably have carried. But Coutinho, despite repeated warnings from Albuquerque, plunged deep into the city from the Portuguese beachhead and was happily pursuing his goal of prying loose a pair of famously ornate doors from the Samorin's palace when a counterattack cut him off. Then in the narrow streets, he and his lieutenants had cast aside some of their armor and were panting for breath under the weight of souvenirs when they were overwhelmed and killed. In attempting to relieve the marshal, Albuquerque himself suffered a painful arrow wound from a rooftop sniper. Thereafter, he could only organize an orderly retreat and leave the Samo-

[3] But not his title of viceroy. Albuquerque and all his successors who were noblemen, but not entitled by custom to call themselves "Dom," were merely designated as "governor." On the other hand, in the first decades some men who did possess the title were merely designated as "governor" by the king. The only invariable rule seems to have been that anyone nominated as an alternate in the "vias," i.e. to take office in case of the death of the governor or viceroy nominated in the first instance, was merely titled "governor."

rin's palace and some of the waterfront in flames. Perhaps the main significance of the fiasco is that it marks the end of Albuquerque's apprenticeship, one of the longest on record.

Albuquerque as Governor

Excepting Francisco Pizarro, Albuquerque at about fifty was to become the most venerable and remarkable conquistador and empire builder of all.[4] As the second son of an important nobleman, he was early sent to the royal court for service and training. He served under both Afonso V and João II before being sent off to do garrison duty in Arzila, that place so well suited for the tempering of soldiers. Later, as has already been remarked, he held important naval commands before being given a patent to govern India on the king's behalf.

Aside from the fact that he had been made *estaleiro-mór*, or equerry, to King João II, nothing is known of what other important positions he might have held while still in Portugal. His son Braz claims he took part in all the crown's military adventures from Toro on.[5] (The Battle of Toro in 1476 ended King Afonso V's hopes of claiming the Spanish throne.) He must have occupied positions close to the king and inspired his confidence, because there is no other explanation for his sudden rise to prominence. One might even speculate that he convinced the king early in Almeida's tenure that this viceroy did not have sufficient vision or aggressiveness to ensure permanent Portuguese control of the Indian seaways to Europe. Aside from the general indisposition of early modern monarchs to endow their subordinates with anything akin to permanent or independent power, it is also possible that King Manuel early began to doubt Almeida's suitability to carry out his council's design for empire.

Whatever did go on in King Manuel's mind or in his council regarding Almeida may never be known, but it is certain that Albuquerque took office with a mandate to carry out an aggressive policy. Besides the scheme to plunder Calicut (and carry off the Samorin's doors), Coutinho bore with him orders for Albuquerque to capture Goa. This is either

---

[4] Barros and Albuquerque's son Braz put his age at fifty-seven at the time of his governorship, but Corrêa, one of his personal secretaries, makes him five years older. Albuquerque speaks of himself as fifty in 1512, if the transcription of a letter written to Dom Manuel in that year is correct. See *Cartas de Albuquerque*, I, p. 34.

[5] Braz de Albuquerque, *Comentários de Grande Afonso de Albuquerque, Capitão Geral que foi das Indias Orientais em tempo do Muito Poderozo Rey D. Manuel*, pt. IV, chap. 50.

entirely overlooked or not clearly stated by historians, if only because the three chroniclers and Albuquerque's son Braz all tell a different tale regarding the immediate circumstances of Goa's capture, which is made to look as if it happened on the spur of the moment and hardly by pre-design. Actually, Albuquerque seems only to have been watching for the right moment, and what passes for coincidence was the transmission of a last-minute clearance between Albuquerque and his spy.

Fernão Lopes de Castanheda, the earliest chronicler to publish a history of Portuguese India, reports Albuquerque's first days in office, before the attack on Calicut:

And in this time the governor, Afonso de Albuquerque, commanded that the bar of Goa be fathomed because the Marshal brought orders from the king to do so, and to determine whether large ships might enter there. But the bar having been fathomed, nothing was done about it because those who were in Cannanore with the viceroy (before Almeida's departure) scoffed so loudly and found fault with the scheme, maintaining it would be impossible to capture Goa, a place of such magnitude and so strongly manned.[6]

Albuquerque himself fully confirmed this predesign in a letter to the king, and he added some interesting details. He wrote: "Sire, I captured Goa because Your Highness ordered me to, and the Marshal had orders to take it in his instructions."[7]

[6] Fernão Lopes de Castanheda, *Historia do descobrimento e conquista da Índia pelos portugueses*, I, p. 482. Opposition to Albuquerque's policy of conquest and fortress building in Asia continued throughout his governorship. One can recognize Almeida's thinking in it, but it becomes increasingly hard to distinguish the theoretical from the personal. This is well illustrated by the case of António Real. Some time following the capture of Goa, Real, the captain of Cochin and one of Albuquerque's principal enemies, wrote to him that he opposed the acquisition of such places as Goa, Dabul, Diu, Mangalore, etc. because "Your Mercy knows full well that in those far away places, it is extremely tiresome even to sustain gatekeepers on the job, yet you understand how to support these abovementioned fortresses four thousand leagues from Portugal. My counsel would be that the King, our Lord, should trade in India and not concern himself with war. . . ." *Cartas de Albuquerque*, II, 37–43. But Real also blocked Albuquerque's orders and attempted via misrepresentation, lies, and intrigue to discredit him with the king. See Corrêa, *Lendas*, II, 197, 271, 320, 333.

[7] He adds: "I also took it because it was chief headquarters of the league which was set on foot in order to cast us out of India; and if the armada which the Turks had prepared in the river at Goa (with plenty of men, artillery, and arms for this undertaking) had been brought to completion, and if the fleet of the Rumes (Turks from Egypt) had come at this juncture as expected, we would have lost everything. . . ." Brás de Albuquerque, *Comentários do Grande Afonso de Albuquerque*, II, pp. 207–211. See also Barros, *Da Ásia*, Dec. III, bk. 6, chap. 3. Oddly, the three chroniclers do not cast much further light on this league, which Albuquerque says was composed of refugees from Amir Hussain's flotilla, who, after Diu, had taken refuge and service with the Adil Shah. Corrêa, *Lendas*, II, 86–87.

Immediately after Albuquerque's retreat from Calicut, all the accounts then record his feverish outfitting of a large fleet — twenty-three vessels and 1200 men — in only four weeks. His ostensible purpose, according to Barros and Castanheda, was to carry out a raid on Suez and the Red Sea, although Corrêa, who was one of Albuquerque's secretaries, believed he actually planned a return visit to Ormuz.[8] Certainly, Albuquerque was eager to settle accounts with Khwaja Atar, and it might have been desirable to teach the Egyptians a lesson by scourging the Red Sea. But since it is known that the governor was already investigating the possibilities of striking at Goa, it is hard to believe that the death of the Bijapurese ruler Yusuf Adil Shah and its advantages for Portugal were unknown to him all during his preparations of January. This formidable Muslim sultan may not have possessed much of a maritime personality as lord of Hindu Goa; but his armies dominated the Deccan, and his demise was a major event. His successor, Ismael Adil Shah, immediately set out into the interior parts of his realm to fight off neighbors who wished to test this new ruler's mettle. It was the big news of the moment in India. It was also obviously the moment for the Portuguese to strike at the virtually undefended island of Goa while he was away. The sultan's Hindu subjects were eager to cast off the Muslim yoke. Had Albuquerque made such unusually speedy preparations in ignorance of this opportunity, it would have to be maintained that he rejoiced in day-and-night exertions for their own sake.

The official story told by the chroniclers is that he had weighed anchor with his squadron and was en route to the Red Sea or Ormuz when the friendly Indian pirate Timoja hailed him off the Goan coast and proposed the joint capture of Goa, citing both the advantages to be gained from its occupation — ships were being built there to fight the Portuguese — and the disunity in the enemy camp. Albuquerque is then supposed to have taken council among his officers and decided to attack on the spur of the moment. If Albuquerque's letter and Castanheda's story of the scoutings before Goa are true, however, it would seem that the meeting was merely staged by Albuquerque to establish that the conditions were in fact right. He may have consciously kept both the Red Sea expedition and Goa open as alternatives, and then decided to attack Goa. But Goa must have been his real concern.

[8] Corrêa, *Lendas*, II, 44. Albuquerque might well have advertised either as his destination to give himself an excuse for taking along Duarte de Lemos's vessels; Lemos, after all, had been given an independent command in that area. Also, he probably realized that the best way to deceive the Adil Shah was to mislead his own subordinates.

Although it was King Manuel and his advisors who had selected Goa, its conquest was in keeping with Albuquerque's ambitions for creation of a powerful and permanent Portuguese imperium in India. He would not have remained content to appear as a guest at Cochin permanently, even though the Portuguese were its real masters. To have done so would, at the least, not have allowed Portuguese governors to cut the figures of oriental potentates, but would have left them perpetually in the demeaning posture of being the boarders of a second-rate Malabar ruler. Appearances were of prime importance in the Orient, and Albuquerque understood this well. Moreover, Goa itself was of great value.

Its harbor was superior even to that of Cochin, for it was not in a bay of the ocean, but five miles up a broad estuary of the Mandovi River, where only storms of hurricane force could menace shipping. Moreover, Goa was an island, formed by the convergence of the Mandovi and another broad river, the Rachol, which like the Mandovi rose in the Western Ghats to the east. It was easily defensible, for the narrow channel, the Combarjua, that joined the two rivers and divided Goa from the mainland was marshy, infested with crocodiles, and normally both too deep for fording and too shallow for vessels of any utility as troop transports. Cochin could not be securely held without help from native armies; Goa could be defended by the Portuguese alone. Moreover, its position midway up the Indian peninsula probably appealed to Albuquerque as affording Portugal a better position for keeping an eye on potential opposition than did Cochin, and its location farther from Cape Comorin was better suited for navigation on the monsoon wind system. Its rich trade in Arabian horses doubtlessly offered some attraction to Albuquerque, but hardly enough to make one believe that he would have thought of conquering the city solely for that reason.[9]

Albuquerque's initial capture of the city was even easier than Timoja had led him to believe, but the problem lay in holding it. Leaving his biggest ships outside the Mandovi bar, he stormed the lightly held fortress of Panjim, halfway upstream to Goa. At this, the Hindu inhabitants ignored their hated Muslim masters and negotiated directly with the invaders. Upon a promise of clemency from Albuquerque they threw open one set of gates while the Bijapurese garrison escaped from another. The Portuguese were soon in firm control of Goa and its rich booty.

[9] For background information on Goa, see João M. P. Figueiredo, "Goa pre-portuguesa," pp. 145–151 and 227–259.

Albuquerque wasted no time inaugurating a Portuguese administration, issuing a new golden coinage, and feverishly trying to repair the thoroughly dilapidated Goan defenses, sadly neglected by the Muslims.

Albuquerque was soon forced to abandon the city precisely because its bastion walls were in tumbledown condition. Before his men could make them tenable, Ismael Adil Shah returned with a force which contemporaries estimated at 50,000 men, among them many contingents of Turks, fighters whom the Portuguese feared far more than they did Indian troops. By his own indirect admission, Albuquerque deployed his forces badly along the Combarjua, which at the change of monsoons was shallow and fordable at many points. Then to make matters worse, differences of opinion between Albuquerque and his captains further reduced Portuguese strength. Burning for revenge, the Adil Shah himself took charge of the attack, and with zeal uncharacteristic of an Asian commander of the period, forced a crossing under cover of darkness and rain and took a quantity of cannon protecting the fords. Meanwhile, Muslims within the city led an uprising there, quite obviously by predesign. The Hindu populace, as if to pave the way for their forgiveness by the Bijapurese, joined with gusto in harrying the Portuguese troops. After seizing a number of Muslim hostages, Albuquerque fought a rearguard action and reached his ships with considerable loss. By then, he could not escape to Cochin because heavy weather from the oncoming southwest monsoons bottled up his ships in the Mandovi roads (it was May 1510) and left them exposed to artillery from ashore. It was the darkest moment of his entire career and apparently the ultimate failure after Ormuz and his fiasco before Calicut. Albuquerque himself, however, probably wasted little time in so thinking.

The Portuguese have characteristically not been introspective people. As their enemies frequently discovered, they were never less prone to introspection than when cornered. For them, there was no such thing as defeat in a just cause; even to entertain the idea would unsettle them far more than the prospect of annihilation. Albuquerque's extraordinary behavior at this time seems odd only to foreigners — it baffled the Adil Shah. Having Albuquerque at his mercy, or so he thought, he offered to make peace on what seem even today to have been generous terms: he promised Portugal the right to build a fortress at the extreme western end of the island. Albuquerque astonished him with the rejoinder that Goa was now Portuguese and that peace was out of the question until it was handed over.[10]

Plagued by batteries, naval attacks, near-starvation, and insubordination reminiscent of that before Ormuz, and despite the death in battle of his favorite nephew and self-designated successor António, Albuquerque desperately frustrated the Adil Shah's every attempt to destroy him. By the end of July, the Adil Shah was eager to be rid of the Portuguese and to return to the unsettled interior. Albuquerque must have given him great satisfaction, then, when he was forced to sail off in the middle of August; the Adil Shah departed Goa almost immediately, leaving perhaps a fifth of his best forces to guard it.

When Albuquerque abandoned Goa, his ships were leaking and rotten, the ruler of friendly Cochin was threatened by a palace revolt, and no reinforcements from Portugal were in sight. Besides this there were persistent rumors that the sultan of Egypt had dispatched a new fleet to India. When fresh ships did come from Europe, they were intended only for Malacca upon king's orders and were placed under a *fidalgo*, Diogo Mendes, who had been given a rival command over that region. Yet only three months later, Albuquerque reappeared almost miraculously at the bar of Goa, his Cochinese trouble settled, his fleet completely refurbished, and Diogo Mendes grudgingly at his side with all the Malaccan reinforcements. On Saint Catherine's Day — November 25, 1510 — he stormed the city for a second time, despite the fact that his forces were outnumbered by about one-to-four, forced open the gates at dawn, and fought ferociously against the Turks defending it. By noon the city was his. Captured Muslims, soldiers and residents alike, were hacked to pieces with the help of a willing Hindu population, whose self-preservative reconversion to the Bijapurese cause the preceding May was speedily forgiven.

Goa had to be defended almost constantly over the next two years, for the Adil Shah was almost as determined to have it back as Albuquerque was to hold it. Luckily for the Portuguese, the impetus of their second attack, together with the fact that the Adil Shah's main forces were engaged far inland, allowed them more opportunity for the construction of proper fortification. This time there came no full-scale counterattack before the Portuguese were prepared.

[10] Corrêa, *Lendas*, II, 86–87.

The establishment of the Portuguese in Goa was no less a milestone than their great naval victory at Diu. Not only did Goa afford them a port and base of operations better situated than Cochin, but the fact of its conquest totally changed the attitudes of Indian rulers. India had witnessed so many truly overwhelming conquerors in its long history that, no matter how spectacular Almeida's naval victories might have been, neither potential friends nor bitterest enemies probably regarded the Portuguese as permanent on the Indian scene until they had defeated the powerful Adil Shah and occupied some of his territory.[11] Thereafter, both the king of Cambay and the Samorin sent embassies to Albuquerque and offered alliances, concessions, and fortress sites. As Albuquerque himself wrote to King Manuel, "The capture of Goa alone worked more to the credit of your Majesty than fifteen years worth of armadas that were sent out to India." By dint of this conquest Portugal was established as an Asian imperial force. It would even appear that the Mamelukes in Egypt were powerfully discouraged when they heard the news.[12]

Malacca

Albuquerque had only succeeded in recapturing Goa through the preempting of Diogo Mendes's forces bound independently for Malacca under crown orders to capture it. He was thereafter faced with another dilemma of an Asian command divided between himself and Mendes like that of the previous year when he had been confronted with Duarte de Lemos's authority in matters pertaining to Ormuz and the Red Sea. Quite clearly Lisbon had erred in giving either Lemos or Mendes a direct responsibility, above all when it could not furnish them with forces powerful enough to carry out the charges it laid upon them. This mistake can best be understood both as an underestimation of the forces actually needed and as the king's acceptance of the prevalent belief that to create overmighty subordinates far from home was to court rebellion. But from Albuquerque's point of view, division only spelled disaster. He clearly grasped the need to keep available the few Portuguese forces in Asia for concerted assaults upon the major objectives the crown itself had specified. For example, he had already resisted one move by the king to divide Portuguese efforts when he absorbed Duarte de Lemos's sup-

---

[11] *Comentários do Grande Afonso de Albuquerque*, II, 208.
[12] Castanheda, *Historia do descobrimento e conquista da India*, II, p. 116.

posedly independent forces before the first assault on Goa. Lisbon had given Mendes only four ships with which to attack Malacca, and he could scarcely have succeeded. Albuquerque now moved to incorporate Mendes's forces into his own, a move less legal, perhaps, than it was necessary.

At this point Albuquerque sought next to assault Aden, to follow up his victory against the potential Cairo-Cambay-Bijapur-Calicut axis by cutting Cairo off from possible future concert with the Indian powers. But the monsoons were against him. By the time he had fortified Goa and prepared a fleet, it was April 1511, and he decided instead to undertake Mendes's Malaccan enterprise himself. Mendes, who was almost as strong-willed as Albuquerque, protested violently that Albuquerque was rather to lend him aid than usurp his command. When this did no good, he tried to escape. Albuquerque thereupon imprisoned and banished him, explaining to King Manuel that Mendes had been completely unhelpful in the conquest of Goa and had later caused "the most thoroughly shameful episode I have ever seen."[13] Later on in the same letter, however, Albuquerque makes it clear that he did not dislike the man, but rather intimated that they might have got on well together under other circumstances. The hint is, of course, that Manuel had been mistaken in giving Diogo Mendes an independent command in the first place. "I pray, Sire," Albuquerque wrote, "that for Mercy's sake you look after the affairs of India carefully, for these are very delicate, and the slightest error can do you much damage there."[14]

In April 1511, Albuquerque added the four ships of Diogo Mendes to thirteen or fourteen of his own, including three heavy galleys; and after the false start toward the Red Sea, the fleet sailed around the Cape of Comorin and made for the coast of Sumatra and the Strait of Malacca. As the principal entrepôt between India and the Far East, the city which awaited him and his 1200 men was by far the richest prize that the Portuguese had yet attempted to take in Asia or Africa. It has already been mentioned as the principal eastern terminus for the wide-ranging and influential Gujarati merchants. But this was only one of the many ethnic groups that thronged to Malacca and did business there: Chinese, Japanese, Javanese, Klings, Bengali, Peguans, Persians, and the Arabs themselves squeezed through the narrow streets along with the indige-

[13] *Cartas de Albuquerque*, I. p. 59.
[14] *Cartas de Albuquerque*, I, p. 60.

nous Malay population, mostly fishermen. Here every kind of oriental and western produce changed hands; as Tomé Pires expressed it: "Men cannot estimate the worth of Malacca, on account of its greatness and profit. Malacca is a city that was made for merchandise, fitter than any other in the world; the end of monsoons and the beginning of new." [15]

In spite of its enormous wealth and size — Malacca stretched for a league along the straits dividing the Indian and Pacific oceans — the city was neither particularly old nor especially beautiful. Its dwellings and even the royal palace were wooden, with thatched roofs, and almost the only stone structures in the city were the principal mosques and the tombs of its fifteenth-century kings. The fact that it totally lacked masonry walls and bastions for defense was largely compensated for by a large garrison of mercenaries, perhaps 20,000 strong, and copious amounts of artillery — Braz de Albuquerque swears that there were over 3000 pieces, and Castanheda 2000, nearly all of them bronze. [16]

Beyond its lack of European-style fortifications, Malacca's greatest weakness in 1511 lay in the unpopularity of its sultan's rule. This had not always been true; in fact, the city, founded in a real sense shortly after 1400 by a prince from Sumatra (who settled among fishers and pirates already on the site), had grown to its present size under wise government. Sultan Mohamed's predecessor, the great Tun Perak, had ruled over fifty years (1446–98) and had largely made the city what it was. But Mohamed himself proved capricious and his justice corrupt toward both the native population and the merchant community. The first news that greeted Albuquerque upon his arrival was the complaint from Chinese junks in the harbor that Mohamed was mistreating them.

The capture of Asia's greatest trading city by a mere 900 Portuguese and 200 Indian mercenaries must rank as an event in the history of Europe expansion no less stunning than the better-known conquest of Tenochtitlán by Hernando Cortés. The Aztecs possessed no artillery; the sultan's forces had more pieces than the Portuguese. Moreover, they did not stand in awe of the invaders as did Montezuma and the Aztecs. In fact, what seems to have worked against Malacca's ruler more than anything

[15] Pires, *Suma Oriental*, II, 286. On the origins of Malacca, see Fr. Manuel Teixeira, *Portuguese Missions in Malacca and Singapore, 1511–1958*, pp. 7–34.
[16] Castanheda, *Historia do descobrimento*; Albuquerque, *Comentarios*, III, 128. Brás says that the city was a league in length and, that there was plenty of tin and copper in the area, and that Malacca possessed skilled metal casters. Even so, the number must be considered figurative.

else was his inertia and indolence in the face of the Portuguese threat. It would seem that he waited far too long to take Albuquerque and his men seriously, and that when he finally did hurl his fearsome secret weapon, his elephant brigade, at them, the total backfiring of this strategy unnerved and ruined him. It is a pity that no nineteenth-century historian of Prescott's stature ever told the tale.

Albuquerque had by this time discovered that decisive action made up for small numbers of fighting men. Upon his arrival at Malacca, he tried immediately to cow Sultan Mohamed by sailing his ships boldly into Malacca's roads with pennons flying and artillery booming in salute. Then he proclaimed himself master of all shipping before the city (it was at this point, incidentally, that the Chinese approached him). He next demanded of the sultan that the captives from Sequeira's ill-fated attempt to found a *feitoria* be released and reparations be paid. Mohamed appears to have been worried by this only at the beginning — before his observers had reported to him that the Portuguese ships held far too few men to endanger his position. Then he resorted to stalling on both prisoner and peace demands while he strengthened his defenses. Realizing his need to act, Albuquerque retorted by burning some Gujarati ships and four waterfront buildings. The sultan then released the Portuguese prisoners, a move apparently designed to buy more time. It must have indicated to Albuquerque that the sultan was unready or unwilling to take stern counter measures and therefore might be vulnerable. He did not assault the city recklessly; rather, he deliberately carried out a limited invasion at a vital point to see how effectively the Malaccan forces could be used against him in the crowded areas of the city.

In the early sixteenth century, Malacca was divided approximately in two by the Malacca River and consisted of quarters — crowded groups of dwellings and warehouses joined by shaded roads. Albuquerque identified the bridge connecting the halves of the city as the logical place to find out what a full-scale assault might hold in store for his men. The proximity of the bridge to the straits made it easy to attack with landing boats and easy to abandon. On July 25, at dawn, his men landed on either side of the bridge and charged it. Fighting was fierce: besides artillery fire, the Portuguese were vexed by clouds of poisoned arrows. But by early afternoon, the bridge was theirs. For a time, the Portuguese governor ordered it held, as if waiting to see whether Mohamed would give way and accede to Portuguese demands. But it would seem Albuquerque had not really made serious plans to remain ashore, and as sundown approached, he reluctantly gave orders to withdraw.

Thereafter, Sultan Mohamed continued to arm; but Albuquerque by now sensed that, despite his superiority in men and weaponry, the Malaccan ruler had little stomach for a real showdown. After a conference with his captains, Albuquerque outfitted a high-decked Chinese junk which had been offered him, filled it with men, guns, and barrels of sand, and floated it up to the bridge on a high tide. The stratagem was completely successful; by the following day the entire Portuguese contingent had landed. Late that afternoon, they charged the barricades, which had been erected since the first assault, with a fury that astonished and routed the defenders. The Portuguese attackers next shoved the barriers aside, and guns were landed from the ships to sweep down the open streets. On one side of the bridge, a mosque was taken after heavy fighting, and the attackers pursued the defenders through the empty streets.

Then, suddenly the sultan appeared in person with his full force of war elephants to crush the invaders. As the huge beasts bore down on the astonished Portuguese, a certain Fernão Gomes de Lemos frantically jabbed the lead animal in the eye with his pike, an instrument developed originally to halt cavalry charges in Europe. As the animal screamed and reared, he jabbed it in the tender parts; other Portuguese quickly emulated his tactics and wounded the other lead elephants. Trumpeting wildly, the animals wheeled and trampled the armies behind them, hurling the sultan himself to the ground and turning what was to have been the doom of the Portuguese into Malaccan pandemonium.

For a week, there was a strange lull in the battle. Twenty-eight Portuguese had been killed outright and many more wounded, some fatally with poisoned arrows. Albuquerque seems to have wished to rest his army and wait for an overture from Mohamed, but none came. On the other hand, merchant after merchant appealed to the Portuguese for protection and were given flags to post on their dwellings as a signal that their possessions were not to be looted. Then, on August 24, the Portuguese attacked again. It developed that the sultan had fled. The Portuguese, under stern orders from Albuquerque, were granted permission to loot the city in an orderly manner, respecting the previously distributed flags. Malacca's golden pillage rivaled and possibly surpassed in sheer weight and magnificence that of Cortés and Pizarro in the New World, even though Albuquerque's restraint left most of the city's wealth in the hands of its native owners.

The capture of Malacca strongly suggests that the brilliant Portuguese military feats ashore in Asia were due less to the superior armament or technology the Europeans possessed at sea than to a superior tenacity and coordination. As at Goa, the Portuguese soldiers in Malacca were experienced in fighting as a team; they cut throats with a joy no Asians could match (save perhaps the Bandanese), and their group psychology made it a point of pride to vie with one another in discounting their injuries and fighting on. For example, the commander of the fortified junk, António de Abreu, was struck in the mouth by a shot that knocked out half his teeth and carried away part of his tongue; yet he was indignant that Albuquerque should wish to relieve him of command. The chronicles are full of such tales, and they can hardly be without significance in explanations of how the Portuguese conveyed an impression of demonic invincibility. In hand-to-hand combat both around the walls of a fortress and in the streets of Malacca itself, a large army like the sultan's could engage the Portuguese with only a small proportion of its total mass, and defeat of these forward forces in the bloody brawls which followed was enough to demoralize the reserves to the rear and send them streaming off in retreat. Men, like the Portuguese, who tore into their enemies with a ferocity and an obvious relish, were a novelty in Malacca and in most of the Indian states, and they proved nearly invincible in a limited, amphibious operation where they could chose the *point d'appui* for their peculiar talents.

After the capture of Malacca, Albuquerque set his men in round-the-clock shifts to build a fortress capable of resisting a counterattack like the one that had temporarily deprived him of Goa the year before. The mosques of the city and the tombs of the former sultans provided a convenient quarry in an area where stones were scarce. Malaria and heat delayed the work for months, but by November 1511, it was complete. Meanwhile, Albuquerque had established a Portuguese administration for the city and set an example for those who might be tempted to work against Portuguese rule by seizing and executing a powerful Javanese merchant, Utimuta Raja, who had been in secret correspondence with the exiled ruling family.

Albuquerque was by now restive about Goa's fate and prepared his return in the *Flor de la Mar*, a large but wormy carrack he had preempted from Duarte de Lemos who had been afraid to sail in it. Portuguese-built vessels had a short life-span in southern waters because shipwrights had not yet learned to sheath them in copper or lead alloy below the waterline to keep out wood-eating crustaceans. Indian built vessels of teak were far less palatable to the pests, but the Portuguese were then just beginning to act on Almeida's observation of 1505 that they should avail themselves of the local shipbuilding facilities.[17] Unfortunately for the Portuguese returning from Malacca with their plunder, the *Flor de la Mar* was the most capacious ship in the return fleet, although slaves had to man the pumps continually to keep it afloat. Into its hold on Albuquerque's command went all the opulent booty from the sack.

Near the time for his own departure, Albuquerque sent out three ships to continue eastward and find the Molucca or Spice Islands, the source of nutmeg, cloves, and mace. He also left a squadron to patrol the straits and protect Malacca. Then he set out in the spongy *Flor de la Mar* for India with two smaller vessels and a junk. Unhappily for the passengers, the owners of the loot, and posterity, a great storm arose while the squadron was still sailing off the Sumatran coast. The *Flor de la Mar* began to cave in at the seams and afterward struck and was ground to bits on a reef. But it stayed afloat until Albuquerque and most of the crew escaped into the ship's boat or onto a hastily improvised raft. The whole cargo of spoils was lost, including gifts for King Manuel that would have made him the envy of all the monarchs in Christendom. Albuquerque, who had packed aboard four handsome stone lions to decorate his tomb, escaped only with the pants and shirt he was wearing.

The raft with the governor and the boat were found the next day by one of the other ships of the squadron, and all the occupants were taken aboard for the return voyage to Cochin. Albuquerque thus returned ignominiously from his greatest exploit. The booty which alone could have impressed King Manuel and the renaissance world with Malacca's magnificence lies soaking at the base of a coral reef, perhaps forever.

Firepower at Benasterim

Upon Albuquerque's return to India, he learned that Goa was again under siege, but that there was no immediate danger. The most awkward aspect

---

[17] In Almeida's letter to Dom Manuel of 1505, reprinted in *HEP*, II, 105–110. Within a few more years, they were building excellent ships in India.

of the predicament was that Rodrigo Rebelo, the commander of Goa, had neglected his governor's orders to fortify Benasterim, a strongpoint commanding a strategic portion of the Combarjua channel between the island of Goa and the mainland. The Adil Shah's general, Rassul Khan, had quickly moved in and strongly fortified it, deploying his heavy artillery to protect his passage to the mainland and driving pilings across it. Then he had concentrated his efforts on recapturing Goa. To make matters worse, when Albuquerque finally arrived before the city in August 1512, he heard that the Mamelukes were threatening India with another fleet, supposedly even then in the vicinity of Gujarat.[18] This did not materialize, however, and the governor instead utilized his forces to drive the Bijapurese back from Goa into Benasterim. Then he attacked by land and by water, utilizing every spare soldier he could muster in India — including those who had just arrived in the yearly fleet from Portugal, bringing his strength to about 3000 by Castanheda's estimate. It was not until September that Benasterim surrendered, as good fortune would have it, just before the Adil Shah arrived with reinforcements, surveyed the situation, and withdrew.

Although made necessary only by a subordinate's carelessness, the siege of Benasterim holds considerable interest for modern readers because of the portentous role massed artillery duels played in determining the outcome. Both the (Turkish) Bijapurese forces and the Portuguese were well equipped with powerful cast-metal guns. The Portuguese artillery was seemingly not transplanted naval ordinance dragged with tackle, for Castanheda specifically mentions that these guns — or at least some of them — accompanied the troops in line of march between the walls of Goa and Benasterim. Albuquerque also armored and towed six small ships into the narrow Combarjua to bombard the wall of Benasterim facing the mainland and to prevent the enemy from obtaining reinforcements. The principal attack, however, was on the other side of the fortress facing Goa. So fierce was the firing that Albuquerque himself states unequivocally that the ships poured 4000 rounds into the waterside alone over the space of eight days.[19] The ships in turn were so riddled from powerful counterbatteries that they came to resemble Swiss cheese, their hulls resting on the shallow bottom. The main Portuguese concentration of fire, however, was on the landside, where the attackers opened gaping

[18] Corrêa, *Lendas*, II, 271, and Castanheda, *Historia do descobrimento*, II, 216.
[19] *Cartas de Albuquerque*, 1, 107.

breaches in the walls with their big pieces. The accounts read more like those of seventeenth- or even eighteenth-century sieges than of a siege in the opening years of the sixteenth. It is evident that both Turkish forces in Asia and the Portuguese were outfitted with better weaponry than was current among European armies of the time. (Most European sieges of the period were fought with lighter cannon with barrels built up of welded rods, and they depended more upon scaling operations than upon heavy gunfire.) Ultimately, Rassul Khan decided to surrender when his walls had been badly broken by the Portuguese barrages and his gunpowder had run low, and Albuquerque (over objections from his bloodthirsty subordinates) accepted the surrender rather than waste his men in hand-to-hand fighting.[20] The lesson is plain enough that the heaviest Portuguese fighting in Asia was seldom over the initial conquest of a city or fort, but usually over holding it afterward against counterattack. And, as at Benasterim, nearly all the greatest Portuguese victories in Asia, unlike the Spanish conquests in the Americas, were won only through the use of the most modern armament and tactics of the period, and against adversaries hardly inferior to themselves. The Portuguese of the period, incidentally, loved to point this out.

The news of Malacca's fall had undoubtedly reached India long before Albuquerque's return, and the wily Gujarati naval commander and governor of Diu, Malik Ayaz, had no doubt been reflecting on it while the Portuguese blasted Rassul Khan from Benasterim. The capture of their major client city on the Malay Peninsula dealt a severe blow to the Cambayan trading system, and it was no coincidence that it had been the Gujarati who had counseled Sultan Mohamed to resist the Portuguese — or that the ships Albuquerque had first destroyed upon his arrival there in 1511 were theirs. Malik Ayaz, however, was far too wise to reveal his hand. It is plain that the Portuguese regarded him as an enemy, and all the rumors and speculations in India over the arrival of a new Mameluke fleet raised the possibility of another league between the Turks and Malik. Given Malik's duplicity, however, it was hardly surprising that after the recapture of Benasterim by Albuquerque, he was among the first to send an ambassador, Ali Sid, to proffer Cambayan congratulations and almost certainly also to assess the Portuguese strength. None of this was lost on Albuquerque, who went out of his way to demonstrate Portuguese

[20]The best coverage of the siege is in *Cartas de Albuquerque*, I, 102–110. See also Castanheda, *História da India*, II, 217–221; Corrêa, *Lendas*, II, 306–312.

pyrotechnical might by showing warehouses and guns to Ali Sid. At one
point the poor emissary was even buckled into a breastplate and scared
half out of his wits when a Portuguese harquebusier fired a big ball of wax
against it.[21] The lesson was almost certainly not lost on Malik, and it was a
decade before the Gujarati again stirred against the Portuguese.

Failure before Aden

Almeida's original standing orders had instructed him to capture Aden if
he was able, "because from there we could see to it that no spices might
pass to the land of the sultan [of Egypt]."[22] During his years as viceroy,
however, Almeida showed no sign of planning to attack Aden, even
though it was becoming increasingly obvious to all that Sofala was nearly
useless as a plug for the Red Sea. Albuquerque had wished to storm Aden
immediately after Fernando Coutinho, the marshal, was out of the way.
However, contrary winds and Diogo Mendes's charge to capture Malacca
had prompted Albuquerque to carry out that enterprise first. Rassul
Khan's siege of Goa had next interfered with Albuquerque's plans. But,
finally, in February 1513, he assembled twenty war vessels, with perhaps
1700 Portuguese and 800 Malabar auxiliaries, and sailed off via Cape
Guardufi to attempt capture of the strategic city.

Aden was the most important trading city of the western Indian Ocean,
just as Malacca was the hub of its eastern perimeter. In both places there
was the exchange of goods from East and West, and the same mingling of
peoples, though mostly Levantines and Malabars were seen in Aden. The
spices and silks, sandalwood and ginger root from Malacca and farther east
were usually transshipped at least once before they reached Aden —
usually at Gujarat. Once in Aden, the products of East and West were
sold and freighted aboard other vessels. If westbound, the spices and silks
were loaded into the narrow, shallow-draught vessels that plied the Red
Sea; if eastbound, the gold, copper, woolen cloths, wheat, and rice were
put aboard the more substantial and capacious *baghlas* of the Gujarati for
transport to India. In addition, Aden was a center for the trade in Arabian
horses to the Indian subcontinent, mostly via Goa before the Portuguese
captured it.[23]

[21] Corrêa, *Lendas*, II, 323.
[22] See chapter 15.
[23] See Pires, *Suma Oriental*, I, 15–18; Barbosa, *The Book of Duarte Barbosa*, I, 55–57.

Both Malacca and Aden were independently ruled cities, not beholden to any great power such as China or Egypt, and both were more nearly entrepôts than great distribution centers because neither had much of a hinterland. But there the similarity ended. Malacca scarcely had a stone within its boundaries, was surrounded by marshes, and like most East Asian cities had never been walled. Aden, on the other hand, sat on a rocky promontory and was so protected on three sides by jagged and precipitous peaks, one 1800 feet tall, that to fortify the town, it was only necessary to build a stout wall with bastions across the face of the city at the water's edge. The sultans and their stonemasons did not stop there, however — it puzzled and faintly amused the Portuguese in 1513 to see the jagged hilltops behind the city festooned with neat, crenellated towers, showy, but useless because they were too high and too far away.

Unlike the plan at Malacca, where Albuquerque moved so cautiously, his strategy at Aden was to fall on the city with a minimum of preliminaries. From the start, however, everything went wrong. Harquebusiers being landed from ships' boats had to jump out and wade in the surf when the place chosen for their landing proved full of submerged rocks; in doing so, they wet their powder supplies. Gunners discovered that cannonballs from the fleet merely bounced off the walls and bastions. Finally, when Albuquerque decided to scale the walls without further delay, the ladders brought along from Cochin, though amply wide, proved too short. The few men who finally did reach the top were soon either killed or driven back. About all the Portuguese did accomplish was to storm a fort protecting the harbor and prevent its artillery from harassing the fleet at anchor. Aden, in sum, was stronger and better fortified than the Portuguese had hoped, its Arab defenders tougher and more experienced than any they had encountered at Malacca. The reason for this, incidentally, seems not to have been that the sultan had specifically wished to guard himself against a Portuguese incursion, but that he greatly feared the masters of Egypt and held himself perpetually in a state of readiness. This will become fully apparent presently.

Following his repulse before the city, Albuquerque sailed through the Strait of Bab al Mandeb with all his fleet and became the first Portuguese to command a naval squadron in the Red Sea. It is odd that neither the chroniclers nor modern writers speculate much about this visit, but in fact treat it as a passing event even though Albuquerque's own letters are filled with the most minute information about it.

The journey into the Red Sea and the attack on Aden must have been conceived as alternatives. To judge from his actions, Albuquerque was not so stubbornly determined to capture Aden as he was Goa or Malacca, and when one stiff assault failed to produce the desired results, he withdrew. The reason for this could only have been that the Portuguese were not wholly convinced at the time that Aden was essential and thought that some other port inside the Red Sea might serve just as well to block off commerce to Suez. It must be remembered that this idea was written into Almeida's *regimento* in 1505.[24] It would therefore not have been worth the effort to sacrifice the soldiers and supplies an all-out attack to carry Aden would have required — providing another place inside the Red Sea might serve the same purpose and perhaps later weaken Aden for a successful assault. Hence, mindful that the monsoon season was drawing to an end in the narrow sea, which facilitated northbound sailing, Albuquerque disengaged his troops and, after briefly considering Ormuz as an alternative, went to have a look.

Short of the Mameluke sultan of Cairo, there was no opponent on the Red Sea capable of challenging the Portuguese. Perhaps for this reason Albuquerque had no desire to remain inconspicuous. To the contrary, he flew all his fleet's pennons while passing the strait and fired all his guns in salute.[25]

It is uncertain just what actions the governor might have taken against ports or shipping, let alone the sultan's fleet, had he been able to locate it. Unfortunately for the Portuguese, the northerly winds of the monsoon season failed earlier than anticipated, before their armada even reached the Farasan Islands, a third of the distance between the strait and Suez. Thereafter, Albuquerque had to content himself with sending out reconnaissance vessels while laying over for two months on the island of Kamaran, where water, if not food, was plentiful. Many men died here of fevers and dysentery, while Albuquerque refitted his fleet and awaited the change of the monsoons which would return him to India.

Much has been written about two favorite projects of his concerning the Red Sea, one to raid Medina and steal the body of Mohammed, and another to ruin Egypt by diverting the Nile into the Red Sea. Letters he

[24] See chapter 15.
[25] He was probably aware that the news would soon reach Cairo by camel; according to João de Barros, word reached the sultan in only fifteen days and set off a paroxysm of repercussions, including the execution of three of the sultan's chief lieutenants. See Barros, *Da Ásia*, Dec. II, bk. 8, ch. 3.

wrote to King Manuel four months after his return, however, do not suggest that he intended to carry out either of them, at least in the immediate future. Instead, the letters propose a far less visionary but a more practical course of action. If the Mameluke fleet was to be sought out and destroyed, Albuquerque wrote Manuel on December 1, 1513, the sultan would be unable to build another so long as the Portuguese remained vigilant, for Suez was the sole port near enough Cairo on the whole sea to be available to him. The fleet having been destroyed, the Portuguese then had only to choose a port like Jidda, on the opposite side of the narrow sinus, fortify it heavily, and establish a naval base there. Land armies from Egypt could never survive the long march through the desert to attack it, and from its vantage point the Portuguese forces could construct a powerful galley fleet and do exactly as they pleased with all the area and its commerce.[26] Alternately, he considered fortification of Dalaca Island or Suakin (which he mistakenly also believed to be an island).

Albuquerque's letters to King Manuel were written four months after his return to India, and it is hard to divine from them whether he had originally planned to capture Jidda on his recent expedition. One would guess, however, that he had and that when he wrote, he wished to conceal his failure by convincing the king that his sole purpose in entering the Red Sea was reconnaissance. The letters abound in minute descriptions of everything that grew, crept, crawled, or walked along the Red Sea shores and with connective phrases like "having gathered this information. . . ." But, despite this overenumerative framework, he never mentions how many hundreds of his men had died on Kamaran Island, an omission which is highly suggestive of Albuquerque's embarrassment. His enemies, of course, were quick to inform the king of his empty-handedness upon his return, and no doubt their interpretation that the expedition had been a total failure was believed by the king, to judge from the fact that Albuquerque's dismissal followed closely upon the arrival and analysis of the news in Lisbon. It would seem that no matter what his own strategy or reasons, it was his bad luck with the Red Sea monsoons which gave his enemies their final ammunition.

Albuquerque had vowed to return to Aden, and the fact that he carried out a raid on it and burned a number of ships in its harbor on his exit from the Red Sea demonstrates that he had not lost interest in that citadel.

[26]*Cartas de Albuquerque*, I, 169–170.

Most probably, had he lived and remained in command beyond 1515, he would have returned in great force, captured the city, and then taken up his scheme to establish Portuguese power at Jidda or in one of the other places he had proposed.[27] Perhaps the true significance of the Red Sea expedition is that it suggests the direction Portuguese imperialism would have taken under his leadership. As it was, Albuquerque's scheme actually survived him, for his successor and bitter rival, Lopo Soares de Albergaria, also planned to attack Jidda in 1516 before he lost his nerve. Had Jidda actually been captured and held, it is possible that the whole course of Portuguese imperialism would have been altered — for as historian Frederick Lane has implied, it was Portugal's ultimate failure to close off the Red Sea to a revival of Arab commerce that opened one of the most obvious ways to the decline of its Asian empire.[28]

After his return from Aden to India in August of 1513, Albuquerque embarked upon a round of negotiations with Calicut, Cambay, Ormuz, Narsinga, and the Adil Shah. In many ways this was merely the result of a postponement occasioned by the expedition to Aden and the Red Sea, for after the capture of Malacca and the siege of Benasterim, Albuquerque had not taken the time to realize all the diplomatic benefits for Portugal to which his victories had entitled him. On the other hand, it is apparent that his failure to capture Aden worked against him. What he most wanted was permission to erect fortresses at Diu and Calicut — and in Ormuz to repossess and complete the one he had begun five years earlier. None of the kings involved were exactly stupid, however; and although none of them said "no," or dared defy him, all of them dragged their heels. Portuguese fortresses in their harbors would have amounted to permanent blockades, allowing in and out of their kingdoms only shipping taxed and authorized by Portugal. All of the produce of Calicut was destined for Aden and much of Cambay's, as well, hence, so long as Aden was still outside the Portuguese orbit, neither the Samorin nor the sultan of Cambay was quite willing to put himself under Portuguese suzerainty and allow the Europeans to determine with whom he should trade and to what extent.

[27] *Cartas de Albuquerque*, I, 278–283.
[28] See Frederick R. Lane. "The Mediterranean Spice Trade." The only trouble with this line of reasoning is that if the Portuguese could not profit from their Asian empire before the revival of Muslim commerce via the Red Sea to the Mediterranean, it is unlikely that preventing this trade after 1540 or 1550 would have solved the basic Portuguese deficit. See chapter 22.

With the Samorin, Albuquerque neatly — if unscrupulously — solved the problem by inducing the Samorin's ambitious brother to poison him, thereby becoming Samorin himself. The new potentate was favorably disposed toward the Portuguese and somewhat dependent upon them; he signed a treaty with them, granting full trading privileges and the right to erect their fortress — which was soon rising on a submerged reef just off this principal anchorage.

Albuquerque knew very well that Malik Ayaz was behind the sultan of Cambay's unwillingness to allow a Portuguese fortress at Diu. The sultan, however, professed himself willing to allow erection of a fortress elsewhere, at Chaul or Surat, and matters remained at an impasse for the time being.

The Conquest of Ormuz

The governor spent thirteen months at Goa in all, his longest stay in any single location during his governorship. During this time, he gave shape to the government of Goa (to be discussed in chapter 18) and carefully practiced his troops, no doubt either to assault Aden once more or settle his old score with the sultan of Ormuz. As matters developed, it was at Ormuz that the situation became most favorable for direct intervention.

Albuquerque's interest had turned toward the Persian Gulf in 1513, when an ambassador from the Shah Ismael of Persia had sent a messenger, begging him to return an ambassador to Tabriz. The shah, it seems, felt increasingly isolated in the Islamic world, both as the hereditary rival of the Turks and as a kind of protestant among the orthodox, or Sunnite, Muslims. The differences between the Persian Shi-ite Muslims and the rest of the Islamic world are too complex and numerous to mention here, but it is probably enough to say that the Persian dynasts maintained that only descendants of the Prophet (like themselves) could be considered authentic religious leaders among the Islamic heads of state, and they denied the validity of mere tradition, insisting upon the sole authority of the Koran in matters of faith. Shah Ismael had apparently sent his ambassador to India chiefly to proselytize its rulers, especially the sultan of Cambay. But he also wished to make friends with the Portuguese, the new power on the Indian seas who hated the Turks as much as he did. As it turned out, his religious mission produced little more than an exchange of presents and courtesies. But the Portuguese were eager to impress his emissaries with their wealth and power, and Albuquerque lost no time sending an ambassador of his own, Miguel Ferreira, to Iran.

By this time, Albuquerque had received news that his old adversary at Ormuz, chief minister Khwaja Atar, was dead. So was the youthful sultan himself, whose younger brother, Saifu-d-din now reigned in his stead. What mattered most was that a new minister, a Persian named Reis Hamed, had seized real control of the state and was almost certainly in league with Shah Ismael to make Ormuz a tributary of Persia. Albuquerque must have decided that he should finish his business at Ormuz post-haste before a developing friendship with Shah Ismael might force him to watch helplessly as Reis Hamed steered Ormuz into the Persian orbit.

It could scarcely have been a coincidence, then, that Albuquerque appeared suddenly before Ormuz in late March 1515, with some twenty-seven ships and 3000 men, just as Ferreira was returning from his embassy to Tabriz laden with embarrassingly rich presents from the shah. The diplomatic confusion was compounded (and Albuquerque's darkest suspicions confirmed) by the presence of the shah's own ambassador in the city, there to lay plans with Reis Hamed.

What followed was surely one of history's most masterful and ruthless one-man performances. Albuquerque did honor to the Persian emissary and even gave him a ringside seat. First he built a stockade. The Persian was all the while proposing that the shah should give the Portuguese permission to establish a *feitoria* in Ormuz. Albuquerque turned to deal with Reis Hamed in his own way. He had learned that the young sultan, Saifu-d-din, greatly feared the minister and would scarcely protest if he were murdered. To accomplish this Albuquerque invited the sultan to visit him in the new stockade. Reis Hamed was leery of meeting Albuquerque under any condition save one in which he could cut his throat. But when Saifu-d-din accepted the governor's invitation, Albuquerque reasoned that Reis Hamed was bound to follow, lest the sultan be induced to make a deal with the Portuguese. The best the minister could do was to insist that the sultan's retainers and Albuquerque's captains come to the parley unarmed. Both sides, of course, violated this agreement — for although Albuquerque and his captains seem to have been without weapons, the meeting room was surrounded by his own armed soldiers ready to fall on Reis Hamed and his men from only yards away. Reis Hamed was not only armed, but he left more armed men at the gates of the stockade before he and his cutlery-laden entourage ventured inside. They were immediately reprimanded by Albuquerque for violating the agreement, and when Reis Hamed cursed him and went for his sword, he was mobbed by Portuguese soldiers and stabbed to death so eagerly that some of the stabbers wounded one another. At first frightened out of his wits, the young monarch was reassured that no harm would befall him and that he had been liberated. He then happily cried out that he would accept King Manuel as a father. Thereafter, a great Portuguese fortress was constructed in the harbor, paid for by the sultan. Reis Hamed's relatives and retainers were chased off the island, and with a final display of courtesy, the Persian ambassador was sent home with gifts and a friendly Portuguese mission to accompany him back to Tabriz. (Needless to say, it was coldly welcomed by the shah.)

The actual construction of the fortress, however, proved an unhealthy task, just as it had at Malacca and at Goa, where Portuguese toiling in tropical climates had sickened and died. This time it was Albuquerque himself who was affected, apparently with a form of dysentery. By the time for his departure for Goa, he was too feeble to take a formal leave of the sultan. To compound his misery, vessels from India intercepted his fleet off Muscat and delivered dispatches containing his dismissal as governor of India and appointing Lopo Soares de Albergaria in his stead, together with Albuquerque's bitterest enemies as Albergaria's lieutenants. Thereafter, Albuquerque lost the will to live, dictated his testament, and specified the places and mode of his burial — first at the chapel he had established in Goa and afterwards, when only his bones remained, at the Igreja da Graça at Lisbon where they rest today. He clung to life until his fleet had passed the Mandovi bar. Borne to the doorway of his cabin to gaze for a last time upon Goa, he beheld it for a moment and died at the age of about 56, in December of 1515.

To retell the exploits of Afonso de Albuquerque as governor of Portuguese India is to recreate the essential shape of the Portuguese empire as it endured until well into the seventeenth century, or indeed until Ormuz fell in 1623, which created the first major rent in its fabric. By his own criteria and in the judgment of historians, his work was incomplete without the capture of Aden, which, as will be seen below, his successor, Albergaria let slip through his fingers. Otherwise, almost nothing was later added to the Portuguese empire in Asia that was not prepared for by Albuquerque's reconnaissance or anticipated in his diplomacy.

Imperial conquerors are not in great historical repute today: Cortés, Pizarro, Albuquerque, and Clive may have some admirers throughout the world, but they have as many or more detractors, chiefly because the colonial cause for which they fought is not in fashion and their tactics were better designed to achieve certain objectives than to imbue later generations with a sense or patriotism or sportsmanship. Albuquerque was frequently cruel and ruthless by modern criteria — few contemporaries can resist imposing mid-twentieth-century standards upon the past — but his enduring achievement is that he gave a form to Portuguese (and therefore European and Western) power in Asia that lasted until other Europeans arrived, notably the Dutch and the English. As such, he is perhaps the most important architect of the bridge built between East and West. Had the Portuguese experiment collapsed in Asia during the sixteenth century, it is doubtful whether the British or Dutch would have attempted to build their own empires there early in the seventeenth, for both were only emboldened by the Portuguese success in Asia. This was especially true because the entrepreneur in each case was not royal but commercial. Both British India and Dutch Indonesia were erected on a Portuguese foundation, and that foundation was laid by Afonso de Albuquerque.

CHAPTER 17

The Shape of Empire, Continued:
the Nucleus, 1515–80

Over the next sixty-five years, or until the temporary end of Portuguese independence under Philip II in 1580, Albuquerque's successors added territory and fortresses here and there. But most of the additions were the result of actions initiated by the great governor (for example, Diu), or they lay well inside the lines of Portuguese force which Albuquerque had established (for example, Ceylon, along the main line of the communication among Goa, Cochin, and Malacca). Even Portuguese stations in the Malay archipelago were results of his reconnaissance expeditions, like the one of 1511 dispatched from Malacca. (On the other hand, the stations in China and Japan were founded by wide-ranging merchants and churchmen; they did not result from royal or viceregal initiative, nor were they centers of Portuguese power.[1])

A change for the worse came over India almost immediately after the death of Albuquerque, and it was inaugurated by his immediate successor, Lopo Soares de Albergaria (1515–18). One might even believe that Portuguese Asia never recovered from it. Albergaria was the leader of the clique that had formed around Almeida in opposition to Albuquerque, and like many whose skills lie with intrigue, he made a weak and negative leader once he actually came to power. Resistance to Albuquerque's firm

---

[1] There is some reason to believe that Albuquerque did not favor an extension of Portuguese power into the China sea. But, in a real sense, the conventional power of the Portuguese military and bureaucracy never was attempted there — except in the limited and temporary office of the captaincy-general of the Japan voyage (see chapter 21). See *Alguns Documentos*, pp. 194–195.

discipline was widespread even from the days when he had first besieged Ormuz in 1509, and it must be remembered that Almeida had never indicated how he proposed to master Albuquerque's dissident captains who absconded before that city. The faction opposed to Albuquerque survived and over the years was enlarged with new dissenters, and it continually fed back a stream of tales and distortions to the court of King Manuel. His court in turn abounded with intriguers, chief of whom seems to have been the Baron of Alvito. The king, like most renaissance princes, including his neighboring monarchs Ferdinand and Isabella, was exceedingly susceptible to any representations that his colonial rulers had ambitions of their own, did not follow orders, or behaved recklessly. Moreover, Manuel was less sure of himself, and hence less trusting of others, than were the Catholic Kings. The result was that he allowed himself to be influenced by Albuquerque's denigrators and dismissed the man who had brought him so many victories. Then having done so, he put power into the hands of an incompetent.[2]

Almost immediately, Albergaria relaxed the rule established and rigorously enforced by Albuquerque that prohibited private trading by Portuguese subjects. Henceforth, the divergency in Portuguese Asia of private interests and those of the crown became a permanent cleft. Such a relaxation was in the spirit of the disobedient captains who deserted before Ormuz. Quite apparently, Albergaria was not strong or resolute enough to resist the pressure upon him. For it is obvious that the captains' real quarrel with Albuquerque was that he made them serve King Manuel's interests instead of their own (though, of course, their rationalizations indicated otherwise). Allowing Portuguese subjects in India to fill their own purses, however, could only have disastrous consequences in an empire whose very character was military. As the late Richard S. Whiteway was the first to suggest in his *The Rise of the Portuguese Power in India* (1899), the piracy and disorder that one hears about almost

[2] The sudden dismissal of Albuquerque is similar to that of Almeida and illustrates how Dom Manuel could completely reverse himself. He repented when news arrived of Albuquerque's success at Ormuz and, simultaneously, of the new Egyptian fleet about to descend on India and challenge Portuguese power, again. In a letter of March 20, 1516, not yet having heard of Albuquerque's death, Manuel commanded him to remain in India and take charge of the fleet to repel the invader. Later he brought Albuquerque's bastard son Bráz to his court and insisted that he legally change his name to Afonso, so that he might have Albuquerque's name ever at his side. This peculiar and belated action at least gave Bráz the leisure to write the biography of his father (or, rather, of his exploits in Asia) called the *Comentários*, a prime source.

overnight thereafter was almost surely a direct result; for greedy soldiers, hijacking is easier and more natural than commerce, or at any rate it blends well with it.[3] Officially, no ship was allowed to pass along the Indian coast whether Muslim or Hindu, without a Portuguese *cartaz*, or license. Thereafter these vessels were frequently hijacked even if they had one.[4]

Albergaria proved no more competent as a commander than he had as a disciplinarian; thanks to his poor judgment, Portugal let slip its sole opportunity to subdue Aden. In 1516, the last and greatest Egyptian fleet descended the Red Sea, a formidable force of twenty-seven ships and 6000 men under the command of a Turk named Sulaiman Reis, although Amir Hussain himself was along. Portuguese India received news via Lisbon and Rome that the expedition was planning to attack Goa and Cochin. A dispatch instructing Albergaria to intercept it arrived in January 1516, and the governor set out in February at the head of a powerful Portuguese armada — thirty-seven ships and 5400 men in all, counting Portuguese, Indian auxiliaries, and slaves.[5] No head-on collision of the antagonists took place, however. For the Egyptian sultan had mistakenly directed Sulaiman Reis to stop along the way and punish the recalcitrant potentate of Aden, who had many times exchanged insults with him. Combining divergent objectives in a single military campaign is seldom wise, and the Mameluke sultan miscalculated. Indeed it was only Aden's strong walls which allowed its sultan such intransigence. Moreover, ever since Albuquerque's attack of 1513, Aden had been brought to a state of extrareadiness. Sulaiman, therefore, received the surprise of his career when he assaulted the place. Aden gave back far better than it received, and instead of sailing on to accost the Portuguese, as planned, Sulaiman had to withdraw into the Red Sea with heavy loss.

Just then, Albergaria, fresh and ready for action, sailed up to the newly battered city. It was the chance of his lifetime. Knowing that Aden could not oppose him, its governor, Amir Amrjan, offered the Portuguese

[3] Richard S. Whiteway, *The Rise of the Portuguese Power in India*, p. 180.

[4] For example, during a siege of the Portuguese fortress at Pasummah in Sumatra in 1522, even the relief vessel sent to its commander, André Anriques, was hijacked by Portuguese pirates.

[5] News of Turkish shipbuilding and other potentially hostile activities in the Gulf of Suez frequently came from the Portuguese ambassador in Rome, who kept in touch with clergy and lay visitors arriving from the Eastern Mediterranean. For example, see L. A. Rebello da Silva, *et al.*, eds. *Corpo Diplomatico Portuguez*, III, 396–397; IV, 14–15; VII, 35, 153, 201, 234; VIII, 115, 364.

an opportunity to build a fortress in his city if only they would afford him protection against a fresh attack expected from the Mamelukes. Albuquerque would have leaped at the opportunity, but Albergaria opposed all his captains' counsel to do so, saying he had orders only to fight a naval engagement with the Egyptians — besides which, he reckoned that the city would be available when he returned.[6] He then set out up the Red Sea in pursuit of the Egyptian fleet.

What he did not realize was that rumors had just reached his enemy of the death of their Mameluke sultan in a great battle with the Ottoman Turks. Thereupon, Amir Hussain had mutinied with a large part of the fleet and sailed into Jidda. Sulaiman Reis followed him into the port, got his hands on the rebel, and sent him back toward Egypt with instructions to the captain of the vessel that he should see to it that Amir Hussain never arrived.[7] Meanwhile, discontent bubbled among the native inhabitants of the city, restless over their uninvited guests, and between the Amir Hussain and Sulaiman Reis factions.

When Albergaria arrived outside Jidda, he learned of the dissension and at first seemed determined to take the city. Then, in spite of the counsel of all his captains that a dangerous fight was preferable to want of supplies and the deadly inactivity they would face between the Red Sea monsoons, he lost his nerve, apparently because of some huge Turkish cannon and the large contingent of fighting men inside the city. After hesitating a precious eleven days, he then hoisted anchor and sailed away, lamely citing his *regimento* to the effect that he was only supposed to fight Egyptians on the sea and that he had been cautioned not to take unusual chances.[8] Besides this, he said, the death of the Egyptian sultan per se would put an end to future incursions into India.

By this time it was June. The Portuguese were short on food, and Albergaria found himself trapped by the same summer doldrums that had blocked Albuquerque's departure from the narrow sea three years before. It was perhaps only fitting that the experience his faction had used against Albuquerque at court now exactly repeated itself under his command. His fleet put ashore at Kamaran Island, where Albuquerque had languished, and before the winds permitted Albergaria's departure at the end of July,

[6] Barros, *Da Ásia* Dec. III, bk. 1, chap. 2; Corrêa, *Lendas*, II, 490.

[7] Barros, *Da Ásia*, Dec. III, bk. 1, chap. 3.

[8] *Ibid.*, p. 44; Corrêa, *Lendas*, II, 497. Corrêa adds that a Christian fugitive who escaped to the fleet from ashore said that the Turks had exhausted their powder supply at Aden and could not have fired more than a few rounds before surrendering.

800 Portuguese and practically all the slaves had died. Even worse, on his exit he discovered that all the walls of Aden had been rebuilt and that Amir Amrjan now had no intention of renewing his offer to allow the Portuguese a fortress in his city. Moreover, Albergaria's fleet was so weakened by his Red Sea stopover and so torn by faction that any attack was out of the question. In fact, he was reduced to the ignominy of having to purchase drinking water from the citadel he might have humbled.

Thereafter, Albergaria remained the butt of ridicule and withdrew into himself. He dined with only a few intimates, refused all gifts, even the most trifling, and brooded over the memory of his great predecessor to the extent that Corrêa says he even wished to destroy the chapel of Nossa Senhora da Serra which Albuquerque had built and where he was buried.[9]

Albergaria therefore became the diametrical opposite of the great conqueror, and, unfortunately, future viceroys and governors resembled him rather than his dead rival. Diogo Lopes de Sequeira (1518–21), who succeeded Albergaria, had already proved himself a timid bungler in his visit to Malacca more than a decade before, and he had learned little in the meantime. Ordered to capture Diu from Malik Ayaz, he twice lost his nerve when it appeared he would face a nip and tuck fight. In the first instance, Barros says, his forces were much superior in armament, but he was bluffed by the wily Russian.[10] Upon the second forgone attempt, he decided to fortify Chaul instead and then failed to hold it because he had by then dispersed his fleet on a variety of other assignments. He didn't try to impose discipline on his captains, but rather allowed them to pillage mercilessly the natives who were subject to their commands. Complaints even reached Lisbon from the merchants of Cannanore and elsewhere that vessels issued Portuguese *cartazes* were seized hours later by the very captains who had issued them. Sequeira himself was the first among many chief officers to return to Portugal, staggering under the weight of riches acquired illegally while in office. It was therefore only partial retribution that he was obliged to slip large chunks of his new wealth to members of the royal court who threatened to expose him.[11] This, how-

[9] Corrêa, *Lendas*, II, 472. He claimed that its position prejudiced the defense of the city.
[10] Barros, *Da Ásia*, Dec. III, bk. 4, chap. 7.
[11] In one instance he is said to have entered into an illegal partnership with a Muslim merchant friendly to the Portuguese, helped him while he loaded a vessel with pepper for sale in the Red Sea, then confiscated it and pocketed the proceeds. In retribution the merchant turned corsair and plagued the Portuguese for years.

ever, did not deter his successor, Duarte de Menezes, the fifth governor (1521–24), from likewise enriching himself. Neither governor had any instinct at all for keeping Portugal's important tributaries in line. Sequeira foolishly allowed the sultan of Cochin to attack the then quiescent Samorin, even lending him a tiny contingent of harquebusiers. The attack failed and the Samorin once again became a belligerent. Likewise, relations deteriorated with Ormuz. Albuquerque had commanded the sultan's respect, but Albergaria had not. Under Sequeira's slipshod handling, the city revolted, and it was neither to his credit nor to Menezes's that the Portuguese commander and troops there defended their fortress brilliantly. Menezes, in fact, even lost some outlying territories of Goa to the Adil Shah.

Lopo Soares de Albergaria, Diogo Lopes de Sequeira, and Duarte de Menezes were the last three appointees of King Manuel I, and they are eloquent testimonials to his lack of judgment in selecting lieutenants. The three successors to Albuquerque can be credited with only two accomplishments to offset their deficiencies. Albergaria can best be remembered as the founder of the Portuguese fortress *feitoria* at Colombo, Ceylon, in 1518, a deed he undertook only at the eleventh hour of his term so that he might leave behind him something worthy of recall — in fact, he sailed out of Goa for that island only when his successor was expected momentarily on the monsoon. Diogo Lopes de Sequeira, on the other hand, achieved his only good mark early in his tenure when he made the first return contact with Ethiopia and Prester John by sending home the emperor's emissary Matthew, together with Rodrigo de Lima and Father Francisco Álvares, in 1519, during Portugal's third naval incursion into the Red Sea (see chapter 19). His overdeveloped sense of caution at least stood him in good stead on this expedition, for no sooner had he delivered the ambassadors at Massawa than he beat a hasty retreat from the Strait of Bab el Madeb, thereby avoiding the doldrums which had entrapped Albuquerque and Albergaria.

The three fumbling governors who followed Albuquerque suggest strongly that King Manuel earned his sobriquet, "The Fortunate," because events were kind to him rather than because he created his own success. He became king only because João II had executed his relatives for treason. He inherited the Indian enterprise when only a single voyage was needed to complete the work of Prince Henry and João II; and despite their shortcoming, Vasco da Gama and Cabral had not failed him.

Then Almeida and Albuquerque had won him an empire. Apparently, however, he could not tell the difference between a Diogo Lopes de Sequeira or a Duarte de Menezes and a Duarte Pacheco Pereira. At court, his policies seem to have been determined by factionalism and politics; Manuel appears to have been all too readily influenced by what he had been told by the latest *fidalgo* arriving from Asia on the last ship.

The result was haphazard: incompetents followed geniuses and royal dispatch followed royal dispatch, sometimes bearing sound advice and often abrupt changes of plan. Because Albuquerque had a strong sense of purpose, he followed only the orders that suited him, and once, in 1513, he even went so far as to rebuke his royal master for his inconsistency. "I must say to you, sire," he wrote, "that you must be careful of the orders and directions you send, for each year ones arrive which contradict the others, and each year you change your mind and have new counsel. India is not like the Castle of São Jorge da Mina, something you can play around with, because it has many great kings and rulers with multitudes of cavalry and footsoldiers and plenty of artillery."[12] One can imagine that the net result of such confusing leadership was as if there had been no direction at all, and it is easy to see how Albuquerque's successors could have fallen prey to inertia and self-serving.

Morocco versus India

To make matters worse, by the middle of Manuel's reign the Portuguese had resumed their military activity in North Africa, and it is obvious to anyone who compares the chronicles of Portuguese bloodletting there with the pleas for additional military assistance from Albuquerque and others in India that Manuel's interests had become divided even before Albuquerque had finished his conquests and passed from the scene. The men and ships that ought to have rounded the Cape of Good Hope and been sent to attack Aden in 1513 or 1515 instead were used to capture Azemmour and El-Mehdiya and initiate another quarter century of struggle against Moors close to home.

It is traditional to open histories of European expansion at the date 1415, when the Portuguese under King João I captured Ceuta. Thereafter, because moderns trace from this event the interest of Prince

[12] *Cartas de Albuquerque*, I, 165.

Henry the Navigator in African and Atlantic exploration, they tend to overlook the fact that, as indicated earlier, Ceuta was stormed for its own sake and was followed by a series of other Moroccan operations throughout the fifteenth century. In fact, to Portuguese minds, it is likely that the discovery and conquest of India was seen more as a twin to the Moroccan enterprise than as their kingdom's bravest achievement. For a century, whenever an opportunity presented itself to expand their holdings across the Strait of Gibraltar, they had quickly taken advantage of it. Moreover, there were elements of the Moroccan situation that appealed far more to the *fidalguia* than did service in far-off India. Given the urge to fight or loot, or to Crusade, one did not first have to undergo the terrors of the *Carreira da Índia* to reach the enemy, but could shuttle across the strait, clash arms with the infidel in a matter of days, and then return to one's hearthside in time for Christmas or Easter. Heroic deeds were immediately visible, pensions flowed, and promotions could be granted before the king and court had been distracted by intervening concerns. It is also most likely that India's identification with commerce in Portuguese minds put it far lower on the list of prestigious activities fit for gentlemen than was quasireligious service in North Africa.[13]

King Manuel had inherited four fortresses in Morocco, namely Ceuta, Alcácer-Seguer, Tangier, and Arzila, and he persuaded himself that he might go beyond the purely shoreline operations of his antecessors and extend his power inland toward the sultanate of Fez. In 1506 he quietly had a huge fortress constructed near Safi in a deserted bay. Then it was suggested to him that the Berber emirs of Marrakesh, weaker rivals of the great sultan, might welcome Portuguese protection. There followed a secret mission, encouragement from the emir, but nothing solid. The Portuguese did make friends with Yahya Bentafufa, the Berber chieftain of Safi, and together they reduced the neighboring tribes to submission.

This success encouraged King Manuel to besiege Azemmour in 1513 with 18,000 men under the command of his nephew — this was eighteen times as many men as Albuquerque had led against Malacca and six times as many as he had had before Aden the same year. Azemmour fell and another expensive and gigantic Portuguese fortress arose. Then, in 1515, as Albuquerque took over Ormuz, Manuel sent 200 ships to Mamora, a place

[13] See Couto, *Da Ásia*, Dec. V, bk. 3, chap. 8.

near the site of modern El-Mehdiya, which the Portuguese selected because of its convenient location for mounting an attack against Fez. He sent along scores of Portuguese families to colonize it, and once landed, the expedition set about the task of erecting yet another huge fortification to protect the new town then being established. Suddenly, before it was completed, the sultan of Fez appeared with 30,000 fierce tribesmen and drove the Portuguese out in utter disorder, killing perhaps 4000 of them and capturing all the families, who later had to be ransomed at enormous cost lest they be sold into slavery. The following year the Portuguese ally Yahya Bentafufa was assassinated by rivals, the dominion over Safi collapsed, and King Manuel was set back in Morocco almost to where he had started.[14]

There can be little doubt that India paid for all this activity in North Africa, either directly or indirectly. It coincided with the period of Almeida's and Albuquerque's empire building in India, and the moneys and manpower spent in one theater could not be spent in another by a small nation, limited in population and resources. It is true that many of the Portuguese personnel available for Moroccan service were feudal levies (the Duke of Bragança alone contributed 3000 men) and might not have been available for service in India, but the matter is only one of degree. Had the profits from India merely been plowed back into the conquest of Aden or of Jidda, enough men and ships could surely have been recruited and enough armament supplied to close the Red Sea and complete the Asian empire. In fact, forces comparable to the losses at El-Mehdiya alone would have been sufficient for this task. João de Lima, the captain-general of Calicut, complained in a letter to Manuel dated 1518: "India is badly off in artillery. Here in Cochin, I see no more than 15 pieces, and these are not sufficient (even) for a galleon, which requires 35 guns. All the other ships have no more than two or three (pieces). It behooves Your Majesty to assist us with artillery now more than ever."[15]

The Ruinous Reign of João III

King Manuel died suddenly at the close of 1521, and his nineteen-year-old son by Maria of Spain ascended the throne as João III. According to his

[14] See HEP, II, 153–167.
[15] Letter of D. João de Lima to D. Manuel I, Cochin, 22 December, 1518, quoted in Frederick Charles Denvers, The Portuguese in India, I, 343–344.

chronicler, Father Luis de Sousa, João as a boy was perhaps intelligent enough, but he was self-indulgent — or at least his tutors never made him apply himself sufficiently rigorously even to learn Latin.[16] In his teens, he appears to have become a dutiful apprentice in the arts of government, and on the whole he seems to have been as conscientious and prepared to rule as any monarch of the time. None of his ruling practices were at radical variance with his father's. Rather, with a few exceptions, he ran his country and empire much as Manuel might have had he been alive — except perhaps that João was a better patron of letters.

Continuance of Manuel's Moroccan policy alone would have been enough to deprive India of men and arms. But it was not João's daily rule per se which made his reign such a disaster for Portugal (though he could be rapacious and petty); it was his dynastic politics, the cost of which was absurdly out of proportion to the Portuguese ability to pay. The evidence for this is contained in a document entitled "Extraordinary Expenses wich King D. João III made from the time that he began his rule until he called the third cortes in Almerim in the year 1544," in reality little more than a listing, item-by-item, which indicates how the king made his "despezas extraordinarias" (or nonroutine expenditures) over the twenty-two-year period, 1522–44, no doubt with moneys borrowed or representing proceeds from the oriental trade which were operating capital rather than profit. It shows an overall debit of 1,946,000 cruzados, enormous for a small country of the time.

An inspection of the listing soon reveals that, in the tradition of old-regime monarchies, dynastic expenses are mingled with purely governmental expenses, and that the royal marriage costs roughly equal all expenditures for the country's defense. In fact, if one counts the 350,000 cruzado sum shown as having been paid to the Spaniards in settlement of their Moluccan claims as an outgrowth of João's marriage — and hence as a dynastic expense rather than a defensive one — it becomes obvious that João's debt of 1,946,000 cruzados, or gold ducats, by 1544 closely resembled his cost of doing family business with the Spaniards: 1,790,000 cruzados. This includes the return of his stepmother Dona Leonor's dowry to Spain, the marriage of his sister Isabella to the emperor, which

[16] Father Luís de Sousa, *Anais de Dom João III*, I, 12–13. Father Luis's tongue-in-cheek style is full of double entendres, however, and in this instance he may merely be encouraging the perceptive reader to draw personal conclusions.

alone cost 950,000 cruzados, and the marriage of his daughter Maria to Philip of Spain. In contrast, the cost of defending India in the same twenty-two-year span since his accession amounted to 610,000 cruzados, the fighting in Morocco 450,000, and the defense of Brazil, 80,000. In all, the sum of 1,140,000 was spent for military operations — only two-thirds of his Spanish outlay.[17]

Thus the king expended far more on his family's personal business than on his country's essentials, although the distinction can be made this sharply only in light of today's democratic standards. And of the "essential" money, as much was dissipated on fighting losing battles in profitless Morocco as in defending Portugal's prime source of revenue in India. João had merely inherited the Moroccan mirage from his father, and he is usually credited with having had the sense to disengage his country from its fruitless role there. But before he accepted the abandonment of Safi and Azemmour in 1542, Alcácer-Seguer in 1549, and Arzila in 1550, he had spent twenty additional years, thousands more lives, and as much money as on India in pursuit of his dynasty's vanishing illusion of North African empire.

It is too much to ask of a sixteenth-century government like Portugal's or even a twentieth-century government like the United States' that it set a system of long-range priorities and then hold to it rigidly. This might be ideal in any age, but it is hardly possible in light of all the pressures that are brought to bear by divergent interests and circumstances. Rather, what João III seems really to have lacked is any sense of relative values or of shrewdness — like that possessed in abundance by his namesake, João II (1455–75), whose reign preceded King Manuel's.

In 1529, for example, when the negotiations for the double marriage of the emperor to João's sister Isabella and João to Charles V's sister Caterina were in progress, the emperor and the king were already at odds as a result of Magellan's circumnavigation (see chapter 20). The issue had not been resolved at that time over the longitude of the Moluccas, in a day when longitude was almost impossible to determine with any certainty. But the Spanish stubbornly claimed what the Portuguese had discovered first, and their claims were based on their interpretation of where the Tordesillas line fell on the other side of the world.[18]

[17] Document printed in Sousa, *Anais de D. João III*, II, 272–275.
[18] Armando Cortesão "O Descobrimento da Australásia e a 'Questão das Moluccas'," pp. 147 and 147, n. 6.

Charles, meanwhile, had offered a dowry of 200,000 gold ducats for his sister Caterina's marriage to João. But apparently he then had the gall to propose to João that the amount instead be foregone at the rate of 40,000 per year by the Portuguese king in return for only six years of Portuguese undisputed access to the Moluccas. (It is ironic that modern geometric science has vindicated the Portuguese in their ownership.) All this while, Charles was sending out expeditions to try to duplicate Magellan's voyage of circumnavigation, thereby keeping up the pressure on his future brother-in-law. This was clearly not a courteous thing to do or a way to treat relatives, but it was statecraft.

By the same token there can be little doubt about how João II would have reacted in similar circumstances: it is in fact a matter of record. In 1494, when the Tordesillas treaty was being worked out, he insisted to the Catholic kings that the demarcation line be drawn 400 leagues west of the Azores and Cape Verdes rather than 100 as Pope Alexander VI had proposed. When the Spanish balked, João garrisoned the border forts and prepared for war — knowing full well that Ferdinand had his eyes on Italy and that he would not fight a war over what might prove to be a great quantity of empty sea, just at the moment when bigger things occupied his thoughts. Ferdinand had promptly backed down and settled for 370 leagues.

In the 1520s, Charles faced far greater problems than had Ferdinand in 1494. He could not afford trouble with Portugal; it is likely that a repetition of João II's garrisoning trick, plus the offer of a much smaller amount, would have cured Charles's bullying quickly. But instead of so maneuvering, especially in the year 1529 when Charles was exhausted from a war with Francis I and eager to settle the Lutheran question, João III must have thought himself businesslike for inducing Charles to waive his Moluccan claims *in perpetuum* — and for 350,000 cruzados, less than twice the amount Charles had demanded for only six years.

João III appears to have been too easily intimidated by his imperial brother-in-law, in fact almost pitifully eager to part with the Portuguese patrimony in his behalf. As mentioned earlier, Charles was willing to provide a dowry of only 200,000 cruzados for his sister Caterina, in her royal marriage with João — and then did not even intend to pay it, at that. In 1526, João actually paid Charles 900,000 cruzados in cash as Isabella's dowry, certainly the largest dowry in European history. Moreover, he sent after it only three years later the 350,000 cruzados just mentioned, to buy off Spain's shadowy claim on the Moluccas. Finally fifteen years later he endowed his daughter Maria for 400,000 cruzados in her marriage to his nephew Prince Philip of Spain.[19]

Portugal, in effect, defrayed a substantial part of Spain's war expenses at a time when Charles's needs were like a bottomless pit. The Portuguese people seem to have sensed what was in store for them in 1524, for they sent João a letter, or at least the letter was signed "Your Loyal and Obedient people of this very Noble City of Lisbon and thus in the Name of all the Cities, Villages and Councils of those Kingdoms." It quite literally asked the king to "hold his horses" (*Leixe pacer mais dias as bestas nas suas cárregas.*) while he reconsidered his oncoming union with Caterina. The people instead asked him to marry her sister and his father's young widow, the dowager queen, Leonor, who, as rumor had it, was to have been João's bride until King Manuel had taken a fancy to her. The petition carefully explained that the people knew and loved Leonor, and that the expense of sending her home, refunding part and forgoing the rest of her as yet largely unpaid dowry, would only be replaced with staggering new expenses which would have to be redeemed "by us poor artisans and laborers."[20] João, of course, did not listen at all and went on to provide his sister with a dowry almost five times the size Leonor had brought. Famine was already prevalent at the time, taxes soon increased just as predicted, and within a decade, scores of people had disappeared from the realm — either through death or migration into Spain to escape just the sort of levies predicted by the petition.

João himself did not keep a lavish court or household. His personal tastes were simple and frugal in comparison with his father's circuslike entourage, and most of his days were spent in the careful, if sometimes short-sighted, exercise of his duties in attending to realm and empire. His one extravagance involved his predatory brother-in-law, who knew how to fleece him.

João must have felt inferior in every way to Charles, and it is most likely that lavish gifts were his one way of compensating, as if he could find only indirect ways of showing his real feelings. Clearly, he resented Charles's

---

[19] Much of the known material involving the negotiations is reprinted in *GTT*, VII (1968). It is scattered throughout the volume, but see pp. 627–631 of the index.

[20] Printed in Francisco de Andrade, *Cronica do muyto alto e muyto poderoso rey destas reynos de Portugal Dom João III deste nome*, 17v-18-18v. This work is really an imperial history. It is unfortunate that Andrade dismisses the other events of João's reign as "too well known" to merit his writing about them.

imperial title, for, peevishly, he let it be known that on the peninsula at least, he considered his brother-in-law as no more than king of Spain and as his equal. When Charles decreed that João's ambassador must stand before the emperor, João commanded that the emperor's ambassadors be received in the same manner.[21] But in all other ways, the ways that counted, Charles clearly had João's number.

The splash João made was not that of a Mycenas, but of a millstone tied around Portugal's neck. It was even plainer in João's reign than it was in his father's that Portuguese Asia never received enough men and ships to change the status quo following the death of Albuquerque or, otherwise stated, to complete the strategic design to which Albuquerque was so dedicated by mounting a major campaign to capture Aden or to close the Red Sea. Conditions were promising during much of João's reign, and it might have been done if even an additional 350,000 cruzados — the amount of the Moluccan payment — had instead been spent to assemble and ship men and supplies to an Asian governor like João de Castro, Estevão da Gama, or Nuno da Cunha, all of whom could have provided the leadership.[22] The ability of the Portuguese to hold on in India without this massive help should not disguise the fact that their once formidable offensive capacity was all but a memory. Instead, the characteristic situation of Portuguese India during João's whole reign, in fact, was sustaining one siege after another. Its one major acquisition, Diu, was made only in circumstances which no one could have foreseen. The moral is that Goa had not lost all its fighters, but it lacked offensive punch. All the money for that had gone to Spain.

The Acquisition of Diu

So much had happened in the quarter of century since the Portuguese had first arrived in India that João's appointment of Vasco da Gama as viceroy of India in 1524 seems almost like the invocation of a hero from some

---

[21] Sousa, *Anais de D. João III*, I, 86–87.

[22] When Philip II took over the Portuguese empire in 1580, he lost little time in striving to close off the Red Sea to Turkish and Arab commerce. He failed, of course, because even more than João III, he lacked capital and personnel for such enterprises. But he surely possessed the right instinct, and he shows that contemporaries indeed acknowledged the rival Red Sea-Mediterranean route's damaging effect on Portuguese commerce. See M. A. Hedwig Fitzler, "Der Anteil der Deutschen an der kolonialpolitik Philip II von Spanien in Asien," p. 249.

golden age. This, in fact, was the whole idea. The king and his council were perturbed by the scandalous behavior of Manuel's last gubernatorial appointees, and it is amply clear that by their selection of a great national hero and his investiture with the full viceregal title (not used since Almeida's appointment) they intended to punish the malefactors and effect a thorough colonial housecleaning. They had certainly picked the right man. For whatever else one might say of the old count-admiral, he was dynamic and rigorously honest.

Upon his arrival at Goa, he lay about him with the zeal of an Old Testament prophet, flogging harlots, claiming back goods (and even cannon) which had been expropriated from the crown, purging incompetents, and, true to his past, attacking Muslim trading competition with great energy. Then, his health already failing from the too swift pace he had set for himself in a tropical climate, he descended upon Cochin, arrested the retiring governor, Duarte de Menezes, and ordered him back to Portugal. Duarte's brother, Luis, it is said, became so upset over da Gama that he and a priest, who was a trusted crony, personally dug a hole in the sandy beach by night to bury a chest of his ill-gotten treasure.[23] A week later, however, he was reported to have been digging it up again: on Christmas eve of 1524, da Gama died. When the royal orders of succession were opened, the appointee was Henrique de Menezes (1524–26), who, though a kinsman of Duarte's, was a staunch follower of da Gama. He proved honest enough personally, but was a poor administrator and a worse diplomatist. In fact, his only forte was as a warrior, especially against Gujarat and the Samorin. Before he had even finished his term, a leg wound proved fatal. His successor, Lopo Vaz de Sampaio (1526–29), a loyal captain of Albuquerque's, was an improvement, but had his own defects. Perhaps the greatest was that he had to be selected from among the alternate nominations provided by Lisbon because the actual nominee, Pero Mascarenhas, was governing Malacca and could not be reached in time. Although capable and honest, Sampaio could accomplish little but the destruction of the king of Cambay's fleet (in 1528) because Mascarenhas and his followers stubbornly contested his right to hold office after Mascarenhas's return to Goa.

Thus it was not until the nine-year gubernatorial term of Nuno da Cunha (1529–38), son of the doughty Tristão da Cunha, that the Portuguese returned to the attack and gave Portuguese India its final

---

[23] Corrêa, *Lendas*, II, 841–842.

strategic form. Commanding one of the stronger armadas sent to India by João III, Cunha first stopped in Africa to capture Mombasa, whose ruler had long been a nuisance to the Portuguese. Then, once he had arrived in India, he addressed himself to the perennial quest for Diu, this time amid favorable auguries. The first was that Sampaio had left a trim but powerful navy to augment Cunha's striking power brought from Portugal. Even more auspicious was the fact that the wily Malik Ayaz had died in 1523. His sons, much less able than he, had quarreled among themselves and with the king of Cambay over who should rule the city. Nuno da Cunha carefully stalked his prey. In 1530, he moved the seat of Portuguese Asian government from Cochin to Goa to be closer to his quarry, and in 1531, after carefully assembling his forces, he attacked. In spite of all the promising signs the assault miscarried. Diu had just been reinforced by a nephew of the Mameluke admiral Sulaiman Reis, who had inherited what was left of the fugitive (from the Ottomans) squadron after his uncle's murder two years before. His 2000 men and prime artillery succeeded in repulsing Cunha's 400-ship attack, in part thanks to Cunha's own dalliance when he wasted time and troops in assaulting a nearby fort of secondary importance. Thereafter, Cunha contented himself with gaining permission to fortify Chaul and storming Daman, Pate, Mangalore, and Patam. All the while Cunha kept his eye on Diu and tightly blockaded it.

Three years later, Diu was actually presented to him through the working of events that had been taking place inland. In 1524, the great Mogul conqueror Babur had descended from the Khyber Pass into the Indo-Gangetic Plain and defeated a massed army levied by Islamic powers previously established there. Babur died in 1530, but not before he had established his capital at Delhi and begun to move southward. His son Humayun continued the Mogul expansion and in 1533 came into collision with the sultan of Cambay, then the Shah Bahadur. Bahadur was forced to choose between a lesser and a greater evil — the Portuguese, who were a nuisance but no threat to Gujarati existence, and the Moguls, who were obviously bent on his destruction. The choice was obvious, or seemed so at the time. In 1534, he concluded peace with the Portuguese and gave Cunha permission to build a fortress at Diu in return for his help against Humayun. Cunha says that he threatened Bahadur at the moment of decision with joining forces with the Moguls and pillaging Cambay. This, he thought, brought Bahadur around to his point of view.[24]

[24] Luciano Ribeiro, "Documentáno preâmbulos do Primeiro Cêrco de Diu," p. 174.

Diu was a great prize because it commanded the gateway to India from the Red Sea and stood watch over the shipping of the Cambayan Gulf. The Portuguese had long wanted it precisely for these reasons, and while he lived, the crafty Malik Ayaz, the sultan of Cambay's port commander, had opposed all Portuguese attempts to gain any sort of foothold there because he realized how heavily their exactions would bear upon the Gujarati merchant classes. Unfortunately for the merchant classes, however, the Cambayan sultans were leaders of a military caste whose main interests lay in aggression and expansion inland. They taxed their merchants lightly — only about 6 percent of their total income came from customs duties — but probably also for this reason, they hardly seemed aware of them. Bahadur's concession to the Portuguese of a fortress site at Diu appears to have been a prime example of just this indifference to all but the military concerns of the moment; it scarcely must have occurred to him that he was delivering his entire mercantile and shipping interests into foreign hands. In contrast, as will be explained in chapter 18, the Portuguese were then able to make the levying of port duties on the ubiquitous Gujarati the mainstay of their customs houses and a major part of their revenue in the *Estado da Índia*. Besides this, the acquisition of Diu came just in time to provide Portuguese India with a shield against the Ottoman Turks.[25]

The First Siege of Diu

Bahadur soon came to regret his generosity, for, as it turned out, the Portuguese help provided by Governor Cunha proved ineffectual — only a hundred harquebusiers or so — and was soon routed along with the rest of the Cambayan forces. Thereafter, Humayun and the Moguls reduced the pressure on Gujarat, shifting their offensives to the East. The Portuguese by this time had nearly finished their job of throwing up heavy walls around their prize.

The dislike presently grew so intense between Bahadur and the Portuguese that war was declared. Bahadur, who was careless and, unlike a good Muslim, drank too much, was killed at the outset, in 1537, during a curious skirmish between the rivals.[26] He had heard that the Ottomans

[25] M. N. Pearson, *Merchants and Rulers in Gujarat: the Response to the Portuguese in the 16th Century.*

[26] Whiteway, in his *Rise of the Portuguese Power in India*, pp. 243–250, has tried to untangle and reconcile the accounts of Corrèa and Couto regarding the incident.

had prepared a great fleet — their first — against Portugal in the Red Sea and were preparing to descend into the Indian Ocean with it. It seems Bahadur had even dispatched an ambassador to Suez before he was killed.[27] The Turks needed his strategic alliance to provide a base of operation and probably would have called on him whether invited or not.

The following year, in the fall of 1538, the Turkish armada, commanded by a terrible eunuch of Greek parentage, Sulaiman Pasha, appeared before Diu with seventy-two ships, about 6500 men, some of the world's finest artillery, and a number of siege experts. He was joined opposite the Portuguese fort by Khwaja Safar, an Italian renegade who served as governor of the still Gujarati city of Diu, and a Gujarati general, Ali Khan, whose combined armies, exclusive of Sulaiman Pasha's, were estimated by Couto at 19,000.[28] Barely 800 Portuguese were in the fortress to defend it. Once the battle began, they fought ferociously; but toward the end of October, wall after wall had been knocked down by the powerful Turkish artillery and the end appeared near. In November, deliverance came from an unexpected quarter, the Gujarati themselves. Just as a relief armada under Cunha's successor, Viceroy Garçia de Noronha (1538–40), neared Diu, the Turks suddenly embarked and sailed away because their Gujarati hosts and allies had become deeply suspicious of the Turks and Egyptians, and stopped supplying them with provisions.[29]

Diu had thus proven its worth to the Portuguese almost immediately, acting as a kind of lightning rod to attract and ground the attacks of the Turkish before these could be directed toward Goa and Cochin.

Toward a Portuguese Ocean and a Turkish Sea

Diu was never needed to repel a Turkish invasion of Portuguese India again because the Gujarati and the Ottomans had fallen out. This rift between the Muslim besiegers had not only saved the Portuguese, but had deprived the Ottomans of any future chance to operate against the bases of Portuguese power in India, for the Turks themselves now possessed neither bases nor strategically placed allies there. Goa lay between the Red Sea and their only other possible Indian friend, the Samorin of Calicut. Hence the Turks were effectively put in check.[30]

[27] Castanheda, *História do descobrimento*, IV, 504.
[28] Couto, *Da Ásia*, Dec. V, bk. 3, ch. 1. For an account of the siege, see also Lopo de Sousa Coutinho, *Livro primeiro do cerco de Diu, que os Turcos poseram a forteleza de Diu*.
[29] Couto, *Da Ásia*, Dec. V, bk. 5, chap. 3.
[30] The fact that they besieged Muscat and Ormuz in the next decade only goes to show

How the disenchantment between Cambay and Turkey came about is curious. It would appear that a side action Sulaiman Pasha had made on the way to besiege Diu was instrumental in ruining any chances for Ottoman success in India. True to the tradition of their predecessors, the Mamelukes, the Ottoman forces of Sulaiman had made the usual Turkish stopover at Aden on their way out of the Red Sea. This time the aging Amir Amrjan had been caught totally unprepared, and the unusually violent and cruel Sulaiman Pasha had been able to do what Sulaiman Reis had not nearly a generation before: he occupied the city by treachery and had Amir Amrjan executed, after receiving magnificent gifts from him. Then he had virtually bludgeoned the frightened sultan of Aden into becoming an Ottoman creature.[31] The political trouble with this was that Amir Amrjan and Aden, his victims, had been on very good terms with the Gujarati. When once in India, Sulaiman mistreated his Gujarati hosts, who became convinced that what had happened to their friends at Aden was more than likely to be in store for them. Hence Sulaiman Pasha's victory over Aden was Pyrrhic because it sowed the suspicion among his Indian allies that the Turks might prove worse than the Portuguese if installed at Diu as their successors.

Although it worked to the ultimate disadvantage of the Ottomans in the Indian Ocean, their capture of Aden, their levying of a heavy tribute, and their imposition on it of a *sanjak bey*, or Ottoman governor, did presage the end of Portuguese designs on the Red Sea.

Following the Ottoman navy's withdrawal from the Indian Ocean to Suez, the Portuguese, after 1538, made but one major attempt to pay it a return visit in its own waters. This was in 1541, when Estevão da Gama (1540–42), Noronha's able successor and son of the great discoverer, set out personally at the head of a sizable naval force (some seventy-odd vessels) to track down the Ottoman Red Sea navy and, if possible, to destroy it. But even before Lepanto it was characteristic of the Ottomans (and of all Turks, for that matter) that they disliked open-sea engagements. Unable to tempt them into battle, Estevão sailed far up the Red Sea and then tried a commandostyle raid on the enemy fleet in the Suez

---

that their desire to hurt the Portuguese was undiminished but that they were unable to find any Indian powers to act as hosts and provide forward bases.

[31] According to an account written by a Venetian captain impressed by Sulaiman Pasha, the commander had 200 galley slaves put to death when he suspected them of rowing less hard than they might have. See O. K. Nambiar, *Portuguese Pirates and Indian Seamen*, p. 135.

dockyards where the fleet was berthed. Unfortunately, word had leaked out beforehand and the would-be commandos in their light galleys were unable to do any more than show the flag before rejoining the main armada and returning to India.[32] Today most interest in the expedition has been aroused by Estevão's dispatch overland of his younger brother Cristovão and 400 soldiers for service with the Christian Ethiopians against a Muslim Somali onslaught (see chapter 19). In a strategic sense, it is more significant because it was the last Portuguese invasion of any size into a sea Abuquerque and King Manuel had once planned to dominate.

Taken together, the first siege of Diu in 1538 and the 1541 expedition into the Red Sea mark the close of an epoch in European expansion — the period in which the Mediterranean interests and the Portuguese, their outflankers, vied to displace one another and control all the trade between Asia and Europe. Both failed to erase their rivals, but each maintained its own routes and a share of the East-West trade. Until the coming of the English and Dutch at the end of the century, Portuguese power went unchallenged on the Indian Ocean, even though it was impossible to control all the rival shipping there. As will be observed in chapter 22, a significant amount of Muslim commerce continued to leak in and out of the Red Sea, along the Malabar Coast and beyond. Moreover, although the Portuguese may have lorded it over the Indian Ocean militarily, as masters of Diu, Chaul, Daman, Cannanore, Goa, Cochin, and Ceylon, Ormuz to the north and Malacca to the east, they paid dearly for this shape of empire over the next thirty years.

India under Siege

After Sulaiman Pasha's frustrated departure from Diu in 1538, the Goan viceroyalty weathered three decades of major and minor crisis — these complicated twists and turns fill the sole comprehensive narrative of the period, the *Decadas* of Diogo do Couto. Then, suddenly, in 1570 the

---

[32] There is a recently published contemporary account of this expedition, with discussion by Elaine Sanceau. See "Uma narrativa da expedição portuguêsa de 1541 ao Mar Roxo," pp. 199–234. Couto and Corrêa also cover the expedition, although not at first hand. Castanheda's narrative, incidentally, ends at Book IX, Chapter XXXI, immediately before this incident. The best description of the places visited in the course of the round trip is that of the famous scholar-governor João de Castro, in his *Roteiro em que se contem a viagem que fizeram os portugueses no anno de 1541 partindo da nobre cidade de Goa atee Suez que he no fim do Mar Roxo.*

Portuguese found themselves fighting for their very existence as Goa, Chaul, Honavar, and Malacca were beleaguered simultaneously by a coalition of Asian sultanates — Bijapur, Ahmadnagar, Achin, and Calicut — in the greatest concerted attack of the sixteenth century on Portugal's empire. Thanks to the bold leadership of Viceroy Luís de Ataíde, the defenders hurled back wave after wave of attackers for almost a year before wearing them out. Upon this climax there came an anticlimax: the Moguls, this time under the leadership of Humayan's successor, Akbar, resumed their southward march, crushed the sultanate of Cambay, and conquered half of Ahmadnagar. At first, the battle-weakened Portuguese were genuinely dismayed. But then they discovered that the mighty Akbar, descended from a long line of Central Asian rulers, was neither commerce-oriented nor sea-minded. Although he indeed possessed the urge to throw out the Portuguese initially, he had no intention of wasting large amounts of men and money to remove them from bits of (to him) worthless territory like Diu, Bassein, and Daman. The Portuguese even came to realize that Akbar played an important role in preventing further assaults on Goa and the other forts by giving the Adil Shah and his colleagues a healthy new preoccupation.[33]

To provide even a condensation of developments between the first siege of Diu and the great sieges of 1570 would be to give readers the same feeling of confusion they might experience when trying to read the synopses of three Verdi operas simultaneously. If anything, the tangle of events and circumstances is even worse. It is therefore perhaps wiser to organize the period around certain generalizations and to suggest that readers of Portuguese consult the *Decadas* of Couto just mentioned. Other readers can at least follow Couto's outline in F. C. Danvers's *The Portuguese in India* (1896, reprinted in 1966), although they will miss the old chronicler's observations and descriptions, which alone make the effort worthwhile.

As already stated, the Ottomans had no further success in renewing their axis with Gujarat or Calicut, although at the beginning of the epoch, in 1551 and 1553, they did send fleets into the Indian Ocean, whose goal it was to despoil, punish, and make trouble for the Christians. Even when these forces did succeed in capturing Portuguese-held Muscat in 1551,

---

[33] At leaat Couto did. In his *Dialogo do soldado prático*, he has the soldier say that only their fear of Akbar's attacking them kept the sultans from overrunning the Portuguese. See Diogo do Couto, *O soldado prático*, pp. 113–114.

they merely enslaved the defenders, wrecked the place, and then abandoned it. No talented Muslim admiral like Barbarossa or Dragut ever commanded a Turkish squadron in the southern seas. Piri Reis, the Turkish geographer and commander who took Muscat, was certainly the best of the Muslim admirals, and his only recognition was to be beheaded at Cairo upon returning. His successors Moradobec and Ali Bey were no more than clumsy hacks whose only accomplishment was to oblige the Portuguese to turn out and chase them.

Although the Ottomans did not make much headway in the Indian Ocean, they did thwart Portuguese control of the Persian Gulf. In 1546, their armies conquered far enough southeastward to capture Basra, the gate to the Tigris and Euphrates valleys and the eastern terminus of the desert route to Aleppo. There ensued an intermittent struggle between the two antagonistic empires, mostly focused on Bahrein Island, the control of which each side regarded as necessary for outright domination of the sinus. The Ottomans hoped to facilitate their aims by using their subjection of Aden as means of reinforcing their naval presence in the Gulf. But their naval power was too scanty and unreliable, and the Portuguese were too vigilant for them to achieve any positive results; the Portuguese got the better of nearly all the fights.[34] The Ottomans may well have won the economic war, though. For although they did not greatly interfere with the Portuguese trade in Arabian horses (some 600–800 per year) or Persian silk, neither did the Portuguese much hamper Ottoman-sponsored commerce in the region, which was doubtless aided by resuscitation of desert travel between Basra and Aleppo. Through their renewal of this separate avenue to the Mediterranean, the Turks probably made it more difficult for the Portuguese to maintain any pretense of cutting off all Muslim intercourse along the traditional routes to Europe (see chapter 22).

The Indian rivals of Portugal had not yet fully learned the lessons of land-based sea power — that waterside fortresses were almost impossible to capture with armies alone. Gujarat, Bijapur, Calicut, Achin, and even Sitawaka in Ceylon, among others, commanded sufficient subjects and revenues to field formidable armies. They were continually bridled by the Portuguese, and they were ever tempted to strike at them because the Portuguese fortresses appeared to be chronically undergarrisoned. The

[34] See Salih Özbaran, "The Ottoman Turks and the Portuguese in the Persian Gulf, 1534–1581."

few Portuguese in them, on the other hand, loved to fight and could hold out against tremendous odds until relieved by water from Goa or other posts. To cite a classic example, only eight years after the first Siege of Diu, in 1546, the Gujarati, driven by Governor Martim Afonso de Sousa's (1542–45) excesses, tried again to capture the Portuguese forces, this time without Ottoman help (if not without Turkish help, for the Gujarati, like other Muslim powers in India, favored Turkish mercenaries because they were such fierce fighters). They mounted a furious seven-month siege which nearly achieved its goal. But in the end, through the heroic and sacrificial efforts of one of Goa's greatest governors, João de Castro (1545–48), they were repulsed and taught a bloody lesson through a surprise Portuguese counterattack. The story is celebrated in Portuguese secondary school books, and every educated Portuguese adult at least remembers Castro's pledge of his beard to the Goan moneylenders to finance Diu's relief expedition.[35] Its real lesson is not that the circumstances were unique. On the contrary, they were part of a pattern: witness, among others, the sieges of Cannanore in 1546 or Bassein in 1569, when help provided from Goa turned the tide, and the defenders, at first weak, ultimately swarmed out and slaughtered the besiegers.

Such ordeals no doubt ultimately enfeebled the Portuguese, but no one would have suspected this from observing them at the time. Far from playing matters safe and dreading to provoke their enemies, they were never loath to seize an opportunity or play a dangerous game, and this aggressiveness in itself frequently invited trouble. One case in point is the dubiously justified revenge Viceroy Francisco de Coutinho (1561–64) took on the Samorin's shipping in 1564, thereby provoking renewed hostilities with Calicut. A better example is the attempt Viceroy Pero Mascarenhas (1554–55) made to depose the Adil Shah of Bijapur and replace him with the ruler friendly to the Portuguese. The Adil Shah, who was quiescent at the time, naturally sent an army against Goa.

During this era, the Portuguese also gained outposts and territory: in the coastal strip south of the Gulf of Cambay they acquired Bulsar and Daman, and in 1554, they captured the whole island of Diu beyond the

<hr/>

[35] For a full account in English, see Elaine Sanceau, *Knight of the Renaissance, a Biography of Dom João de Castro, Soldier, Sailor, Scientist and Viceroy, 1500–1548.* See also J. B. Aquarone, *D. João de Castro, Gouverneur et Vice-Roi des Indes Orientales (1500–1548); Contribution à l'histoire de la domination portugaise en Asie et à l'étude de l'astronomie nautique, de la géographie et de l'humanisme au XVIe siècle.*

fort in the confusion following Sultan Mahmud III's murder. In Ceylon, the highly religious Viceroy Constantino de Bragança (1558–61), though suffering a bloody setback, subdued the king of Jaffnapatam in the island's north (where, incidentally, he came upon and ground to powder, or thought he had, the sacred tooth relic of the Buddha). Under Viceroys Antão de Noronha (1564–68) and Luís de Ataíde (1568–71) Mangalore, Honavar, and Barcelor were all captured. What the ultimate Portuguese advantage or disadvantage actually was in these actions is hard to assess; for once taken, nearly all these places became hot spots from time to time and had to be defended with men and money.

It was only in Ceylon that the Portuguese became the rulers of extensive new territory before 1580, at least within their Asian viceroyalty, and even this rule was pragmatic and circumstantial before 1594. After 1518, when Lopo Soares de Albergaria established Portuguese rule at Colombo, the role of the Portuguese there had grown beyond the point, as at Cochin, where they merely intervened occasionally to help preserve a friendly ruler. Admittedly, the difference was only a matter of degree; but in Ceylon the "emperor" of Kotte, on the island's southwest coast, had become so totally dependent on Portugal to prop his rule that he became no more than a front for the Portuguese captaincy-general.[36] After the middle of the century, moreover, the Portuguese had come to consider their commitment in the island's affairs as akin to a sacred trust: not only had St. Francis Xavier visited the north of the island and made many converts, but in 1557, King Bhuwaneka Bahu's son and successor as king of Kotte and nominal suzerain of the entire island embraced the Christian faith and was baptized as "Dom João Dharmapala, by Grace of God Perea Pandar." This conversion of a king undoubtedly appealed to the Christian sentiments of the Portuguese, but it lessened the loyalty of his predominantly Buddhist nation and presented his rivals with a new weapon. Chief among his rivals at the outset of his nearly half-century reign was King Mayadunne of Sitawaka, a small principality just inland from Kotte; the dazzling shifts, assaults, and intrigues of this clever, unscrupulous champion of the old faith continually bloodied and bewildered both João and his European masters. Mayadunne's son Raja Sinha I, was, if anything,

[36] Pending completion of the official history of Ceylon, there is still no coverage of the period 1518–80 better than the *Conquista de Ceilão (Espiritual e temporal)* by Father Fernão de Queiroz, S. J. (1617–1688), translated and published as the *Conquest of Ceylon (Spiritual and Temporal)*, 3 vols., tr. S. J. Perera, S. J., especially I and II.

even more troublesome and made the Portuguese captains-general pay dearly for every *bhar* of cinnamon they exported to India and Europe. Long before João's death in 1597, the Portuguese were even obliged to move his capital from its traditional seat at Kotte somewhat inland to the protection of their stronghold at Colombo.

Despite an occasional reverse on land or at sea, the Portuguese empire in Asia showed remarkably few outward signs of decline until the 1580s and after, at least in its military posture. To be sure, as will be seen in chapter 22, the time had passed, probably before the 1540s, when the crown could claim to break even, let alone show any profits, on its operations between India and Portugal. Couto complained bitterly of cracking fortress walls and chronic shortages, while manpower, never plentiful, had grown critical in every category. Added to this, there had not been a strategically important new acquisition since Diu, and those forts that had been added only put new strains on already meager reserves. In the face of all these liabilities, the Portuguese continued to hold their own against the most determined opposition Asian rulers could muster.

In 1570, the Goan viceroyalty surmounted its severest challenge since 1509, when Sulaiman Reis, Malik Ayaz, and the Samorin met Francisco de Almeida at Diu. It is clear from the logistics of the engagement alone that Goa was not at its peak in soldiers or in ordnance — the Portuguese, according to Couto, had no more than thirty cannon, not counting those aboard ships, barely more than 1500 or 1600 soldiers available to defend the capital city, plus some auxiliaries and slaves, and were spread thinly elsewhere. But they fought off four simultaneous attackers at Goa, Chaul, Malacca, and Honavar.[37] And in doing so, they probably faced greater numbers of their enemy in each siege than all the soldiers Portugal had sent to India since the first voyage of Vasco da Gama.

There can be little doubt that some Portuguese actions like those already cited had added tinder to the fire that had always smoldered against Portugal on the Malabar and Deccan coasts, and it is certain that the league formed to cast them out of India was in part a result of their own sins come roosting home. For example, the cruel actions of the piratical Diogo de Mesquita against Malabarese shipping were certainly fundamental in stirring the Samorin to take part in the league, and Mesquita's actions were all but openly condoned by the viceroys.[38]

---

[37] Couto, *Da Ásia*, Dec. VIII, chap. 34.

[38] A definite, but highly elusive, feature of the period is the all-pervading piracy on the

If Diogo do Couto's information is correct, the alliance against Portugal was a logical outgrowth of — and indeed was financed by — the defeat of the Hindu kingdom of Vijayanagar in 1565, principally by the Nizam Shah of Ahmadnagar, the Adil Shah of Bijapur, the Kuth Shah of Golconda, and the Barid Shah of Bidar.[39] In fact, according to Couto, the plan began at a Muslim service of thanksgiving for their great victory over Vijayanagar at Talikota and was religiously inspired, even though the Hindu Samorin was subsequently included in their new cause. The sultans could by then hardly have been unaware of the benefits to be won

Malabar Coast, in the Bay of Bengal, and in the Strait of Malacca. Every chronicle and every contemporary account involving travel on the Indian Ocean refers to it; yet by nature, it is an extremely diffuse subject. The Portuguese dominated the Indian Ocean in this period, but they were scarcely numerous enough to monitor more than a proportion of either the long- or short-distance traffic involved. From the very beginning, when commanders like Dom Lourenço de Almeida were assigned to convoy friendly merchants as well as to intercept the enemy, and throughout the entire sixteenth century, Portuguese shipping and that of client states sailed in *cáfilas*, or convoys, accompanied by armored galleys. In addition, Goan governors sent out search-and-destroy armadas to raid the pirate lairs in Calicut and Kanara that enjoyed the secret support of Calicut. If this were its only dimension, the subject would be simple enough, but in fact it has many others. For the Portuguese treated as corsairs not only real ones like Ali Ibrahim and Kuti Ali but persons like Kunhale, the Samorin's naval chief. The Samorin was an avowed enemy of the Portuguese, and Kunhale's job was not only to convoy *cáfilas* originating or trading with Calicut but to strike at Portuguese shipping whenever he saw it underprotected. In effect, Kunhale was a belligerent; but from the Portuguese point of view, his status or irregular style of warfare did not distinguish him from any other kind of cutthroat. The Portuguese viewpoint, of course, was that they were the rightful rulers of the seas and as such the keepers of the peace. They could hardly have entertained the notion that others like the Samorin might consider them the real interlopers for preying upon Indian shipping. Yet today, Indian historians see things precisely this way, as for example Dr. O. K. Nambiar, who entitled his 1955 study on the subject *Portuguese Pirates and Indian Seamen*. Whatever one's definition of piracy, no one can deny that among the Portuguese community at large there were, by any criteria, real corsairs, chief among them the horrible Diogo de Mesquita, whose terror and rapine was winked at by many viceroys and governors. And, as in the Bay of Bengal, there were Portuguese sea-brigands who lived entirely beyond the pale of any allegiance, tacit or otherwise, and preyed on all comers, even the Portuguese themselves. Finally, there were the occasional filibusters — usually legitimate Portuguese traders — who could not resist a fat prize if it passed too close to their gunwales, particularly when commercial pickings were too slim to keep them honest. The Portuguese in truth neither succeeded in stopping piracy nor were guiltless of it themselves. As the late W. H. Moreland pointed out, piracy was only one of the hazards of doing business. There were plenty of other equally grave hazards involved in making a living out of Indian Far Eastern commerce — typhoons, shipwreck, and changing market conditions were among them — and even the high "fees" the Portuguese officials often took to permit infringement on the monopoly trade, or simply to allow merchants to go in peace. See W. H. Moreland, *India at the Death of Akbar: an Economic Study*, pp. 222–224. All one can safely say is that the Malabar Coast, Chittagong, and Malacca were dangerous places for nearly all comers at one time or another because in reality no one power or party could keep them from being that way. One might as well write the same thing of the Caribbean in the next century.

[39] Couto, *Da Ásia*, Dec. VIII, chap. 33.

by concerted action, and the element of *jihad*, or religious war, could have been applied with even greater cogency to the Christian Portuguese than to the Hindu Vijayanagari. The allies were even said to have divided up their anticipated spoils in advance of the campaign: Goa, Honavar, and Barcelor to the Adil Shah, Bassein, Chaul, and Daman to the Nizam Shah, and Cochin, Cannanore, Mangalore, and Chalé to the Samorin.[40] Then, to embarrass the Portuguese further and to increase their effectiveness, the allies approached another old Portuguese enemy, the sultan of Atjeh in Sumatra, and proposed he levy another of his sieges on Malacca to coincide with the concerted assaults in India.

The mighty preparations of the coalition were impossible to conceal completely, especially since Portuguese horse traders circulated frequently between Goa and Bijapur; likewise, the news leaked out to Chaul, as well, and its captain lost hardly a moment in setting its soldiers and inhabitants to erect fortifications of logs, stones, and earth, even demolishing their own homes and garden walls to gain building materials quickly (for unlike most Portuguese sites in Asia, the town of Chaul stood outside the fort and until then possessed no walls or bulwarks). As time went on, Viceroy Ataíde gained more exact knowledge of what was brewing: he enlisted in his pay an uncle of the Adil Shah's principal wife, who had access to the most intimate secrets of the alliance.[41]

The sieges began late in 1570 and in the first weeks of 1571, when the Adil Shah had assembled 30,000 men around Goa and the Nizam Shah perhaps an equal number before Chaul. A month later, he brought up twice as many men and horses. At this point, it would have been difficult to know whether Luís de Ataíde was a madman or a genius: when counseled to dismantle Chaul and bring its garrison of something less than 1500 men back to Goa to help with its defense, he instead sent Chaul 600 of his own force of perhaps 2200 available soldiers. Then coolly, he astounded his own command by sending off to Portugal and Ormuz the accustomed fleets — he explained that the cargoes were needed there and that otherwise the enemy might think the Portuguese considered themselves to be in trouble.[42]

Ataíde, however, knew what he was doing; for as the months wore on,

[40]*Ibid.*
[41]*Ibid.*, chap. 37.
[42]*Ibid.*, chap. 34. At all times the Portuguese were aware that one of their best weapons in Asia was psychological.

the men he had placed at the forts held off the enemy, and a number of small ships sailed up and down the rivers, peppering the enemy and sometimes even carrying out commando raids on Bijapurese batteries. These vastly outnumbered those of the Portuguese in quantity and over-shadowed them in size. At Benasterim, enemy ordnance made rubble of the walls. At Chaul, the enemy host pounded the Portuguese jury walls day after day with seventy cannon; but after four months of furious seesaw fighting, it had only succeeded in capturing a monastery at one end of the town together with a few buildings. The Nizam Shah meanwhile had sent forces to attack Daman and Bassein. Then, in April, the Hindu queen of a minor Kanarese state called Gersoppa besieged Honavar at the Adil Shah's bidding and with his reinforcement. Ataíde promptly sent some relief and it held. In fact, the harder the Nizam and Adil Shahs tried, and the more men they threw into battle, the more bloodily they were re-pulsed. Only the Samorin remained inactive at first. His job had been to provide fleets to invest Goa and Chaul from the sea, but his efforts proved tardy and ineffective. Ultimately, he furiously invested a relatively minor and vulnerable Portuguese fort at Chalé. His was the only success of the great war, for he did capture it, but only after his colleague sultans had given up and retired from Goa and Chaul in June 1571. The fourth origi-nal partner in the alliance, the sultan of Atjeh, who had to sail across the straits from Sumatra to beleaguer Malacca, had proved to be the most unsuccessful of all. On his way there, he had run afoul of a Portu-guese fleet, been defeated, and was forced to limp home.

Thus ended the great Indian war against the Portuguese Asian empire. Luís de Ataíde sailed home in triumph a few months later to receive the accolades of a Christendom still basking in the great victory against the Turks at Lepanto. The defenses of Goa and Chaul only served to confirm Europe's impression that the tide was turning against Islam, and Ataíde's brilliant role as their author was quickly celebrated in poetry and prose.[43]

Were it not for all the economic ills that had beset it, it could be said with justice that Portuguese power in Asia had now become more stable than ever. Two years later, the Great Mogul, Akbar, conquered Gujarat and gravely menaced the Nizam Shah, who barely managed to hold out until overrun at the end of the century. This new Mogul threat to the

---

[43] Of the most value today is the work of António de Castilho, *Comentario do cerco de Goa e Chaul no anno de MDLXX Viserey Dom Luís de Ataíde.*

Central Asian sultanates, together with the recent lessons meted out at Chaul and Goa, provided security for Portugal, at least so far as the Indian powers were concerned, until well into the seventeenth century. Akbar may have disturbed the Portuguese at first, but they soon perceived that the Moguls did not share their interests in the spice trade and did not covet the vest-pocket-sized territories they held.

The story of the periphery — Portuguese Asian holdings and exploits far from their seats of power in India, Eastern Africa, and the Far East — remain to be narrated separately. Meanwhile, the following chapter will consider how the Portuguese overseas empire was organized.

CHAPTER 18

Institutions of Trade
and Government

The Portuguese colonial institutions that were created in the century between the conquest of Ceuta and the death of Albuquerque — or a little after — were designed to serve entirely dissimilar circumstances and fall into two distinct patterns. The first of these patterns was royal, authoritarian, and commercial; the second emphasized private capital, delegated authority, and agriculture. In the first, the crown itself became a giant mercantile corporation, as along the African coast and in Asia. In the second, it became a colonial franchiser which entrusted the management of its assets to others and allowed them the greatest share of the profits, as in the Atlantic islands and later in Brazil.

The two patterns evolved out of two older traditions, both rooted in the Iberian past at the time of the *Reconquista*. The crown as a commercial and capitalistic entity probably began before 1250 in Portugal itself, though the circumstances are unknown. Thereafter, it was developed into a coherent system in conjunction with the medieval Flanders trade and with the African ventures of Prince Henry. The crown as a franchiser of others to rule in its stead had quite another origin — probably among the Genoese outposts of the Mediterranean in the Middle Ages — but the spirit is apparent in the numerous grants with extensive governmental and economic privileges which were awarded by medieval Iberian rulers because they needed help from their wealthier subjects to hold and assimilate newly won territories and so had to make the terms attractive.

Although the two patterns of direct crown capitalism and colonial franchising were developed and applied simultaneously by Prince Henry and the Portuguese monarchs, it is advisable to discuss them separately in the interests of clarity. The Atlantic-island pattern will be described in the pages that follow. But it must be remembered that this priority in sequence is merely an editorial convenience, in consideration of the fact that the Atlantic insular development was perfected in the fifteenth century and the capitalism of the crown did not reach its epitome until the sixteenth. Strictly speaking, there is no clear-cut chronology involved: the Portuguese crown began its career as a capitalist in Flanders even before the discovery era, and the settlement of Brazil was promoted according to a reapplication of the Atlantic-enfranchisement pattern some years after the Afro-Asian coastal pattern had assumed its final form.

Capitalism among the Islands

There were immediate opportunities for trading along the African coast almost from the moment of discovery, but the Madeira Islands, the Cape Verde Islands, and the Azores were all uninhabited when Portuguese navigators found them. Hence, the system of *feitorias* and licenses to carry on commerce even then being worked out by Prince Henry was not of much use because virgin land required another kind of approach to make it yield something of value. The answer was obviously colonization directed toward the development of agriculture; but aside from their being no inhabitants, either slave or free, to clear land, almost nothing grew on the islands that was of any use to contemporaries. Suitable crops had to be determined, and the plants or seeds had to be brought in from outside.[1]

Prince Henry had received the rights to Porto Santo, Madeira, and Deserta from his brother King Duarte in 1433 (see chapter 4), and it was in regard to these territories that the pattern evolved which was later applied to the other islands and, of course, ultimately to Brazil. It was not

[1] The materials in this section are based, unless otherwise noted, on João Barreto, *História de Guiné*; Maria de Lourdes Esteves dos Santos de Freitas Ferraz, "A Ilha da Madeira na época quatrocentista"; Francisco Paulo Mendes da Luz, *O conselho da Índia*; José Ferreira Martins, "Casa da Índia"; Armando Castro, *A evolução econômica de Portugal*; Herbert Heaton, *The Economics of Empire*; Virginia Rau and Jorge de Macedo, *O açucar de Madeira*; and the article "O açucar na Ilha de Madeira," José Gonçalo de Santa Rita, "O govêrno central e o govêrno local"; "Uma carta de quitação do Infante D. Henrique mencionando productos obtidos nos tractos de Guiné"; Vitórino Magalhães Godinho, *História econômica e social da expansão portuguesa* and *Economia dos descobrimentos*.

Prince Henry who invented the solution; rather, it should only be said that he made formal what a trio of his enterprising retainers had already undertaken. It will be recalled from chapter 4 that two of these, João Gonçalves Zarco and Tristão Vaz Teixeira, discovered or rediscovered Porto Santo, perhaps in 1418, and were deeply impressed by its possibilities. After reporting their find to Prince Henry, they returned with another of their number, Bartolomeu Perestrelo, and the three of them divided among themselves their original find and the greater island of Madeira, which they seemingly discovered only on this return journey. Perestrelo took Porto Santo; Zarco and Teixeira divided Madeira; all three of them began to colonize. When Prince Henry received the royal rights as donatary fourteen years later, he eventually drew up letters patent recognizing the division and designating the possessors as his captains, or, in effect, donataries of the donatary, with similar rights. The document concerning Perestrelo at Porto Santo is dated November 1, 1446. It is so important as a model for similar grants which followed that it will be quoted in toto:

I, Prince Henry, administrator and governor of the Order of Knights of the Mastership of Our Lord Jesus Christ, Duke of Vizeu, Lord of Covilhã, make known to all who receive this my letter and to whom the contents are pertinent, that I give in charge to Bartolomeu Perestrelo, knight of my household, my island of Pôrto Santo in order that the said Bartolomeu Perestrelo keep it for me in justice and law; and on his death, it is my pleasure that his first or second son, if there be such, take charge in the manner stated herein . . . and so on in direct line of descendants; and if the said son is too young, I or my heirs will name a person to rule until he is of age. Item: it is my pleasure that he hold in the said island jurisdiction for me in my name in both civil and criminal matters, except the death penalty or severance of a part of the body, which shall be brought before me; nevertheless notwithstanding such jurisdiction, it is my pleasure that all my orders and decisions on appeals shall be carried out there as a right that belongs to me. Furthermore, it is my pleasure that the said Bartolomeu Perestrelo have for himself all grain mills in the said island, which I hereby give him in charge; and no one but he or whoever he permits may construct mills, except hand mills which may be built by anyone who wishes, but not for the purpose of milling for others, nor may anyone build a horse or water-powered mill (*atafonas*) except he himself or whoever has his approval. Item: it is my pleasure that he may collect water rights of one mark of silver or its equivalent yearly from everybody or two planks every week of those customarily sawed, paying to us, however, the tenth of all such lumber, in the same way as is paid for other products of the said sawmill, and that Bartolomeu Perestrelo have also the same rights from any other mill (*engenho*) that may be built there, excluding veins of iron ore or other metals. Item: it is my pleasure that he have all baking ovens that are equipped with vats; however notwithstanding that anyone who wishes may construct his own bread oven, but not to make bread for anyone else whosoever. Item: it is my pleasure that if he has salt for sale nobody else but he may sell salt; selling it at half a *real* of silver an *alqueire* or its just price and no more; and when he has no salt, others on the island may freely sell it until he obtains a supply. Furthermore, it is my pleasure that he have the tenth of everything that is owed to me as income from the island, or which may in the future be owed to me, as is stated in the charter (forral) which I ordered prepared for him. And likewise it is my pleasure that his son, or other direct descendant, to whom the position passes, may also enjoy this income.

Item: it is my pleasure that he may give to whomever he wishes grants of land on this island by his letters-patent according to the charter of the island, on condition that he to whom the said land be given shall improve it within five years; and if not improved, it may be given to another; and if after it has been worked it should again fail to be worked within five years, it may likewise be granted to another; this does not prevent me from granting land to whomever I please if there should be land for development not previously granted; and it also pleases me that his son, or heirs and descendants who may hold the post make grants. By this letter I charge all my heirs and successors and ask all who may follow me to hold to this my letter and carry it out and see that it is carried out and kept in everything and in every way in the manner stated, because I made this grant (*mercê*) to the said Perestrelo because he was the first who on my order settled the island, and because of many other services he did for me, in reward for which I made this grant to him and his successors, as has been stated. And furthermore, it is my pleasure that the said residents may sell their improved properties to whomever they please. Furthermore, it is my pleasure that the inhabitants of the island may kill the unclaimed cattle (*gados bravos*) without interference, except the cattle running on the small islands or some other enclosed place where the landlord of the island puts them. In witness whereof I ordered him to be given this my letter signed by my hand and sealed with the seal of my Coat of Arms. Granted in my Vila the 1st of November. Prepared by Gil Fernandes, 1446, Anno Domini.[2]

Working within the terms of this and similar contracts, the captains granted in turn large portions of their territories to other developers large and small, both Portuguese and foreign. It is hard to trace exactly the

[2] Godinho, *Documentos*, I, 189–192.

sequence of who got what originally and why, but after a generation or two, a general configuration of ownership and land exploitation emerged. For the most part, small farms and small economic activities predominated; these tended to remain family operations, or nearly so, and in the hands of colonists from Portugal. For the relatively few large operations slaves were imported to work them almost from the outset; and in addition to the Portuguese, these were owned by Genoese, Florentines, and Flemings. So many Flemings, in fact, went to the Azores that they became known as "The Flemish Isles" because outside Portugal the erroneous idea was bruited about that they were Flemish discoveries.

Madeira is the prime early example of what would later be the familiar colonial export economy based on the produce of the soil. By 1461 Madeira had achieved a prosperous and growing economy, and it will be used to illustrate how the economy of the Portuguese Atlantic islands flourished under the donatary system. Along the coast in that year, according to Azurara, there were "crops, threshing floors, grain mills, cane fields, sugar mills, both arbor and bush grapes and wine presses." In the interior, the island was covered with forests of cedar, yew, and other kinds of trees which were cut to supply wood for carpenters and furniture makers. The population was growing, wrote Cadamosto in 1455, amounting to "800 men total, among whom 100 work with horses." Azurara, writing at about the same time or a bit later, said "there were in Madeira 150 inhabitants (*moradores*), not counting others who were there, such as merchants, single men and women, young men, boys and girls who had already been born in the island, as well as priests and friars, and others who come and go for merchandise and things necessary from that island." If the word *moradores* as used by Azurara means "households," the estimates of Azurara and Cadamosto are about the same, some 800 people of all ages. About forty years later at the beginning of the sixteenth century, an estimate placed the population at 15,000 to 18,000 European inhabitants (of whom many were foreigners) and 2000 slaves. The inhabitants gave the impression of being conscious of their rights and "full of initiative." The economy was well balanced with a considerable export of its products. This export consisted principally of wine, sugar, wood, and wheat, though the proportions of these are difficult to establish. Wheat production in 1455 was reckoned at 3000 *moios*; the *moio* was as much grain as a mill(*mo*) could grind in a day, reckoned at 60 *alqueires*, also an indefinite quantity which varied from place to place, but perhaps about 8,4 to 18 liters or more. (Thus the 3000 *moios* could be 1,500.000 to 3,000.000 liters). Five or six years later the exportation to Guinea alone was 1000 *moios*. It has already been noted that some of the caravels in the Guinea trade provisioned in Madeira or were sent out initially from that island on their double mission of exploration and commerce. Wheat was exported to Portugal itself, as it was also to the *feitoria* of Arguim where it bought gold and slaves. This pattern, however, was short-lived. After the middle of the century, sugar and wine increased in importance and wheat declined. Soon, the island was importing breadstuff and exporting sugar. During the sixteenth century, in fact, the Azores became the breadbasket for Madeira.

The Sweet Taste of Success

The first sugar mill was installed in 1452 by Diogo de Teive under Prince Henry's authority. Three years later the island produced a minimum of 6000 arrobas, about 150,000 pounds or more. By 1460, the production had doubled.[3]

Where the first cane grown in Madeira came from is not known for certain. It may have been Sicily, Valencia in Spain, or even Portugal itself. According to Duarte Pacheco Pereira in his *Esmeraldo de situ orbis* "Henry sent to Sicily for sugar canes and planted them in Madeira and for skilled men (*mestres*) to teach the Portuguese how to make sugar."[4] Barros said the same thing in 1552.[5] But Valentim Fernandes wrote, between 1505–08, "The Prince sent to Valencia for sugar cuttings."[6] And certainly, in 1478, a Valencian named James Timer, *mestre de açúcar*, did receive privileges in Madeira.[7] Valencia, even while under Muslim rule, had been known as a center for sugar production. Moreover, after the capture of Ceuta in 1415, the Portuguese came into contact with still other sugar-producing regions along the coast of Africa. Cane cuttings, and the knowl-

[3]Virginia Rau and Jorge de Macedo, on sugar in Madeira, see footnote 1 this chapter. Godinho, *Documentos*, I, 171–192; III, 347–362; Duarte de Leite, *Descobrimentos*, 1, 455–464.

[4]Duarte Pacheco Pereira, *Esmeraldo de situ orbis*, tr. George H. T. Kimble, p. 100.

[5]Barros, *Da Ásia*, Dec. I, bk. 1, chap. 16.

[6]Quoted in António Baião (ed. and ann.), *O Manuscrito de Valentim Fernandes; Oferecido à Academia por Joaquim Bensaúde*, p. 111.

[7]Silva Marques, *Descobrimentos*, II, 178.

edge of cane growing and the making of sugar, could also have come to Madeira from all these areas. And it would even appear that Portugal itself might have produced sugar in Algarve.[8] As early as the twelfth century, there is a record of sugar sent to Flanders in a Portuguese ship.

The official records of sugar production for Madeira for 1494 show 80,500 arrobas, and production was on the increase. In 1498 Madeira exported to Lisbon 7000 arrobas of sugar, to Flanders, 40,000, and to Constantinople, 15,000. A decree of August 21, 1498, limited the annual export of sugar from Madeira to 120,000 arrobas. Most of the sugar was produced by owners of small or medium-sized farms whose production was on the order of 250 arrobas; a production of 1500 was considered very large indeed. Probably only a limited number of these producers could afford slaves, most of whom seem to have worked on the ten large plantations. Of those, the largest produced only about 6.5 percent of the total crop, and the smallest produced only 2.3 percent.

The presence of foreigners in Madeira may have been welcomed by the donatarios, but for a time in the latter fifteenth century, at least, it appears to have been a hot issue among the colonists of Portuguese origin. Complaints were made in the town council of Funchal in 1472 and in the Cortes of 1472–73 that the Genoese and the Jews controlled the sugar trade. In 1481–82, the inhabitants asked that foreigners be expelled from the island. Their request was of course not met. Some of the foreigners, however, were sufficiently concerned — and sufficiently influential — to get themselves declared as "natives of these parts." Among the important foreigners in Madeira or the Madeira trade were João António Cesare, a Genoese; Paulo de Negro, residing in Lisbon (who sent Christopher Columbus to Madeira to buy 2000 arrobas of sugar for Luis Centurione in 1478); Luis Doria; Urbano and Bautista Lomelino; and António Spínola (naturalized in 1490), to list only the principal names.

By the end of the fifteenth century, foreign participation in this production, though frequently mentioned, seems to have dwindled considerably. The exporter of sugar was, however, frequently a foreigner who had contacts with the markets of Flanders, Italy, England, the Netherlands, France, and elsewhere. This brought about clashes between native producers and foreign traders. When in 1498 King Manuel gave preference to Por-

[8]There is a record of a land rental (aforamento) in *Loulé*, dated May 8, 1409, and signed by King João I, which authorizes three individuals to grow sugar cane. See Silva Marques, *Descobrimentos*, I, 221.

tuguese exporters, he permitted two Florentine merchants, Bartolomeu Marchioni and Jerónimo Sernigi, to be considered as "native merchants." The Genoese Lourenço Catanio bought 50,000 arrobas of sugar at 400 reais an arroba from the king in 1500, which made sugar thirty to sixty times the price of wheat. In 1503, still other Italians formed a trading combine for this most profitable of all agricultural commodities, as well as for other Madeiran exports. Cabral's discovery, however, was soon to dilute Madeira's sweet taste. Over the next half century, the island lost to Brazil its position as the prime producer of cane, sorghum, and refined crystals for the European market.

The donation and development of the Azores Islands closely paralleled that of Madeira, except that they were discovered and settled at a somewhat later date and never became as prosperous. São Miguel and Santa Maria were the first to be peopled, soon before 1439, through the efforts of the man thought to have been their first captain-donatary, Gonçalo Velho Cabral; it is said that he brought families thence from Estremadura, the Alto Alentejo, and the Algarve. The westernmost island of the archipelago, Corvo, apparently was not even discovered until 1452 (see chapter 4), and the last island, Graciosa, was still being populated through the efforts of its captains, Pedro Correia and Vasco Gil Sodré, in the early years of the sixteenth century. None of the islands seem to have been agriculturally important so far as export was concerned until well after the middle of the fifteenth century, when the easternmost islands began to export wheat (as already noted), both to Portugal proper and to Madeira. Sugar was never an important commodity, though it was grown, and if the islands were ever known for any speciality, it was for production of blue and purple dyestuffs. Aside from providing a jumping-off place for New World expeditions (as with Labrador and the Corte-Real brothers) and a returning place from India and Brazil, their role is not as interesting in the expansion economically, geographically, or governmentally, as that of the Cape Verde Islands.

The Cape Verde Islands were the last of the Atlantic Old World archipelagoes to be discovered, and because they lie so much closer inshore to Africa than do the Azores or Madeira, their relationship to the mainland was far more intimate from the beginning. Though no copy of the original donation from King Afonso V to Prince Henry survives, it was surely made soon after Cadamosto's return voyage with news of his find in

1455, for Henry left it in his will to the Infante Dom Fernando in 1460. Prince Fernando then created captains of his own, including António de Noli, a Genoese who may have visited the islands in the year of their discovery.

Although specific information is scanty, from all appearances the captains had no trouble finding colonists. Prince Henry's construction of a *feitora* in Arguim at about the same time the islands were discovered must have given both legitimate concession merchants and interlopers the idea that a base of operations sufficiently nearby might yield rich dividends. As early as 1462 and 1466 they were given important rights to trade on the mainland opposite the islands, and they were already sufficiently influential in 1469 that when Fernão Gomes was given his contract to trade and explore along the African coast in 1469, the trading zone and prior rights of the Cape Verdians were specifically excluded from it.

These traders were primarily slavers, and they would hardly have descended upon the islands so rapidly if their motives had been purely agricultural. But agriculture in the form of cotton growing quickly began to make sense to them. Cloth was one of the prime barter commodities for slaves among the African chieftains, and the semiarid nature of the Cape Verdes was well suited for cotton, if not for sugar. Slaves were already on hand, and it was but a simple step to divert them to the production of the plants, the thread, and the cloth itself. It was even discovered that a lichen called *urzela* would flourish there; this yields a purple dye, which was used both to dye textiles and for export. King Afonso V in 1469 even went so far as to make this export a monopoly by granting it to two Spaniards, Juan and Pedro de Lugo.

Still another boon for the new insular economy was the discovery that even the handsome shells strewn about the isolated beaches were valuable, at least in the eyes of the African mainlanders. They used as money one particular variety, a species relatively scarce on the continent but one which proved plentiful in the Cape Verdes. Naturally, the Portuguese lost little time in combing the beaches when they learned that good specimens would buy ivory, slaves, and even gold. In 1480, King Afonso V took cognizance of this bivalvular currency as a vital part of the insular economy when he attempted to prevent its inflation resulting from too much export to the African continent. He decreed on July 24 that unlicensed persons exporting these shells should suffer the punishments reserved for counterfeiters: whipping, confiscation of goods, and loss of all civil rights.

The Cape Verdes retained jurisdiction over their assigned strip of the African coast until well into the nineteenth century. But in the fifteenth and sixteenth, it was not inhabited by many, save for the *lançados* (or as they were later known, the *tangomaus*), outcasts whose nucleus may have been formed by men who had lost their status as Portuguese free citizens after conviction as criminals. King João II had the intelligent, but perhaps not ultimately successful, idea for the state that prisoners might be given the chance to leave jail and ultimately redeem themselves through dangerous and unpleasant service around the fringes of empire. Some of these may have been dumped ashore to act as intermediaries between the Cape Verdian Portuguese and the tribes. But they never seem to have attempted to rehabilitate themselves, if indeed they were involved in King João's scheme, and they were soon joined by others of uncertain origin who chose to escape the pale of Europeanization. Nearly all of those who managed to survive learned the native languages, took African wives, often in platoons, shed their Christianity, ignored Portuguese ordinances, and acquired such riches as their relations with the Cape Verdian traders and the African tribal chiefs would permit. They so vexed the crown in 1518 that it attempted unsuccessfully to end the problem of these floating outcasts by sending a ship to the area and proclaiming that all who considered themselves Christians should board it if they intended to maintain any vestige of legal status under Portuguese law and wished their possessions to be transmissible to their heirs. But the *lançados* remained an annoyance to Lisbon until the nineteenth century.

Madeira and Porto Santo, the Azores, and the Cape Verdes were all settled under the captain-donatary system during the middle fifty years of the fifteenth century, and there can be no better commentary on the effectiveness of the system than to note that in 1530 the royal government in Lisbon turned to it again in a more sophisticated form when confronted with the need to people the wilderness of Brazil. Not the least among its virtues in the eyes of the king and his councillors must have been their experience by then that the privileges and powers bestowed upon the captain-donataries, even though most could be willed to their heirs, showed no danger of leading to permanent alienation of the prerogatives or territories involved. Instead, within a generation or two it nearly al-

ways happened that all that had been given away had been recovered by
the king, with interest. First of all, the crown had always retained the
ultimate right to modify the terms of the contracts unilaterally, if necessary. In the case of the first-instance donataries — Prince Henry and his
heirs — the circuit was brief: the islands were transmitted from Prince
Henry, who died in 1460, by will to his nephew the Infante Fernando,
who died in 1470, and were inherited by Fernando's widow, who in turn
willed them to Manuel who became king. For the captains who received
their endowments from the donataries, the crown discovered that most of
their rights reverted when their heirs failed to maintain them, or else
their lines died out. Even when this did not happen, however, it was not
hard to reclaim their jurisdiction piecemeal. After 1481, for example, the
captains in the Cape Verdes were told to obey and lend aid to the royal
examiner sent out to review their legal practices and their books — upon
no less pain than the forfeit of their captaincies. This was made to stick,
and therefater the captaincies were subject to supervision, control, and
retribution from Lisbon. Then four years after the creation of the Brazilian captaincies, King João III in 1534 sent out to the islands his first
corregidores, judicial officers whose job it was to rule upon all cases that
might be of interest to the king. Hence it was that although the islands
still possessed much of their original proprietary character, the central
government had already placed its mark on them. It was only a matter of
time thereafter until it reclaimed them — as it did in 1600, by sending out
royal governors.

As useful as was the donatary system for populating uninhabited lands,
it could not have served the kings of Portugal in situations where coordinated military and commercial undertakings were required to exploit
overseas discoveries. For these, the other system evolved by the Portuguese monarchy was required, that of monarchical capitalism.

Capitalism and the Portuguese Crown

Probably no other European power at the beginning of the sixteenth
century could have accomplished as much in the Indian Ocean as Portugal
did, not even Spain. Columbus's four voyages not excepted, Ferdinand
and Isabella did not finance the conquest of America but merely provided
the *capitulaciones*, or licenses, to do so and allowed Castilian or Genoese
bankers or private individuals to put up the money. Once the route had

been pioneered, navigation to the Americas was not difficult. Manned by competent sailors most any ship would arrive there on the prevailing winds, and a daring and resourceful Cortés or even an Alvarado could set out to overcome Aztec, Inca, or Mayan opposition with little help from the king. This is not to belittle the Spanish achievement but to illustrate that it required far more than private conquistador finances to develop and travel the long *Carreira*, and once having done so, to disrupt the trading pattern of an ocean area comparable in breadth to the present-day Soviet Union. Neither the Spanish nor the French, constantly at war with one another, could have attempted it during the first half of the sixteenth century, nor could the early Tudors, who lacked the capital, let alone the commercial experience or the navigational expertise. Had it not been for the peculiar royal capitalism of Portugal, the task would have been beyond the compass of any individual or combine extant in the year 1500. By then, the kings of Portugal had had more than a century of experience at creating useful commercial institutions to follow their explorers and exploit their discoveries.

The state capitalism of the Portuguese was one of the most unusual experiments of early modern Europe. Western governments had licensed and regulated trade, and it was by no means unknown for them to make a discreet commercial investment or two, or, toward the seventeenth century, to dabble in the monopoly of salt or of tobacco. But never before or since has one of them become the entrepreneur of an entire imperial undertaking and thrown its whole resources into the creation of profits from a trading monopoly on its overseas discoveries. This was facilitated through the use of a pattern that emerged from earlier medieval practice, was perfected in the course of African trading, and ultimately came to be applied on a vast scale to the Indian Ocean. To see how this pattern originated, a quick review of the relationship of Portugal to northern Europe is necessary.

Mention has already been made of Portugal's status as a "wharf between two seas" during the development of medieval maritime trade between the channel ports and the Mediterranean, and it has been shown how the Portuguese early took advantage of their location as the nearest country by water that could supply northern Europe with such typically southern products as wine, salt, almonds, dried fruits, and olive oil. After the Crusades, the demand for these products grew swiftly, and soon the merchants, the nobles, and even the crown were busy constructing vessels and establishing commercial liaisons with England, France, and, especially, Flanders. By the end of the fourteenth century, this overseas enterprise had so grown in complexity and volume that the crown found it necessary to establish a permanent representative at Bruges, which had become the principal distribution point for Portuguese produce. The task of this representative, called a *feitor* or factor, was both to deal with foreign governments as the king's ambassador and to rule the Portuguese merchant community. He also acted as the royal business agent. In Bruges, foreigners were not permitted to own property outright, but the factor was allowed to rent warehouses and living accommodations for the Portuguese in a designated quarter, and he was awarded certain privileges by the city fathers in their behalf, chiefly those regarding import concessions and the right to adjudicate disputes under Portuguese law within his community. The Portuguese community, which the factor ruled, was called in Portuguese a *feitoria*,[9] and it was self-contained even to the point of being assigned a parish church and a burying place. Other national groups in Bruges and elsewhere, notably the Spanish, French, Venetians, English, Milanese, and Scottish, had similar enclaves with their own factors. Sometimes the term "factor" was also applied in a rather different sense to the private representatives of great commercial and banking houses, chiefly Italian.

What distinguished the medieval Portuguese *feitoria* from all the other national operations, such as the *fondachi* of the Italians, was the active interest the crown had long possessed in its own trading. The Portuguese *feitor* was not only the referee among quarreling merchants of his nation and the impost collector for the crown. Important as these public functions were to the *feitoria*, he was, above all else, the king's own commercial agent, buying on his account everything from baubles for the queen's adornment to copper for the mint and arms for waging war.[10] In any case, the king found it natural to be both father and competitor to his merchants. Then, in the course of the fifteenth century, he swiftly outdistanced them.

Henry the Navigator remains enigmatic even in minor matters, and it is

---

[9]This is frequently translated as "factory," but this translation lends itself to confusion with the modern sense of "manufactory," which the "feitoria" was not. For further information about the Portuguese *feitoria* in Bruges see A. H. de Oliveira Marques, "Notas para a história da feitoria portuguêsa na Flandres, no século XV," and also reprinted in the author's *Ensaios da história medieval.*

[10]Diffie, *Prelude to Empire*, pp. 69–70.

uncertain whether he foresaw that his efforts might turn the crown into an outright monopolist of the African domain his efforts had created. Certainly, he established his claims to the exclusive propriety of his discoveries, even if he did lack adequate capital of his own and had to license the participation of others. For a time after Henry's death in 1460, King Afonso V continued this policy: he licensed the area south and east of Sierra Leone to Fernão Gomes in 1469. Gomes received a five-year concession, later extended by one year to six. But King João II, while still a prince, reversed the trend: he asked for and received control of the entire African enterprise in 1474. When he ascended the throne in 1481, the two tendencies came together, the crown as business entity and the crown as imperial monopolist. As a result of Prince Henry's African discoveries, the king now had enormously augmented the amount of trading goods at his disposal: ivory, ostrich plumes, hides, gum Arabic, and some malagueta or guinea pepper. He also derived an immediate supply of hard cash from African gold dust and from the sale of slaves to the sugar-producing islanders of the Madeiras. The royal windfall certainly must have affected the *feitoria* as an institution. Even before the *feitoria* was moved from Bruges to Antwerp at the end of the fifteenth century, its *feitor* was busy around the clock with the king's accelerated buying and selling. Except in theory, perhaps, he had divested himself of his original role as chief of the Portuguese business community. (Since 1438, incidentally, a pair of annually elected consuls had taken over the magisterial functions of the *feitoria*.)

Another consequence of its utility to the king was that the *feitoria* had become exportable. Or, rather, one should say that because it had evolved into the prime instrument of the crown's commercial dealings abroad, the king saw fit to create new *feitorias* wherever they served his purpose. Naturally, the first outside Europe were in Africa.

Prince Henry had established his customs agents and representatives around 1456 in a fort he built at Arguim Island, located on the far side of Cape Branco. It is perfectly correct to call this operation a *feitoria*, and it was no doubt modeled to a large degree upon the one at Bruges. A second royal *feitoria* was not founded in Africa until 1482, when King João II sent out his trusted knight Diogo de Azambuja to build a new one far beyond Cape Branco at São Jorge da Mina (Elmina) on the Gold Coast. This new installation was housed in a European-style castle, whose stones were precut in Portugal and shipped down for assembly in hulking *urcas*. Its stout walls were designed to protect it from native attack, but they also served notice on would-be traders. King João II commanded the financial power which Prince Henry had lacked, and he had no love for concessionaires, Portuguese or otherwise. None were allowed near the place until late in the sixteenth century.[11] The only personnel authorized to trade there for the principal commodities — gold dust and slaves — were the king's own employees, as Duarte Pacheco Pereira put it, "our people who are sent out by the most serene king in his ships."[12]

In addition to founding this new *feitoria* at Elmina, King João II established royal control over the older one at Arguim, where he fixed the buying and selling prices for the gold and malagueta pepper (but not the slaves) bartered there. A third *feitoria*, according to Barros, was opened during King João's reign some seventy leagues inland from Arguim, at a place called Wadan. This was so located to facilitate trade with Timbuktu and provide intelligence about lands further to the east. But the rigors of the desert climate soon obliged its closing.[13]

By then the *feitoria* pattern was thoroughly established, and thereafter, as the Portuguese moved down the African continent and around the Cape of Good Hope, they opened *feitorias* on the Swahili coast, as at Sofala, Mozambique, and Malindi. Once the Portuguese reached India, *feitorias* were established wherever they wished to buy and sell. The first was created by Cabral in 1500 at Calicut, and as will be recalled from his brief and tumultuous visit there, it was short-lived because the *feitor*, Ayres Corrêa, and most of his staff were murdered. Later on the same voyage, however, Cabral encountered the friendly ruler of Cochin, and in 1502, on his second voyage, Vasco da Gama left a second *feitoria* behind him there, which was to endure. Within a generation after that, the crown had installed a score more in the various trading centers and *conquistas* where the Portuguese focused their activities — at Goa, Malacca, Ormuz, Ceylon, and Ternate, to name but a few. Usually, but not always, (as at São Tomé de Meliapur or Hugli) these were in cities under direct or indirect Portuguese rule; although even then (as at Cannanore in 1506 and later at Calicut) a sudden change in the host's policies could leave the *feitoria* stranded and fighting for its life. In India, all the *feitorias* came under the supervision of the chief royal fiscal officer known as the *vedor geral da fazenda*.

---

[11] Godinho, *Descobrimentos e económia mundial*, I, 188.
[12] Duarte Pacheco Pereira, *Esmeraldo de situ orbis*, p. 121.
[13] Godinho, *Descobrimentos e económia mundial*, I, 163.

In Brazil, among the new Portuguese acquisitions the *feitoria* played a negligible role, and the institution's brief history there illustrates how completely it depended on service to the crown. Almost as a matter of course Manuel indeed saw to it that one was inaugurated soon after Cabral had visited Brazil — in fact during the visit by Gonçalo Coelho and Amerigo Vespucci in 1502–3. But it was India and not "Santa Cruz Island," as Brazil was originally called, which had captured Lisbon's imagination; and the new *feitoria*, probably located in the vicinity of modern Cabo Frio, was soon leased out to its *feitor*, Fernão de Noronha, and a group of New Christians for the space of three years. Even so, it is clear that during the first years the crown considered the cession only temporary and meant to enforce the monopoly on behalf of its lessees so that royal control could one day be reclaimed in toto: for example, the *regimento*, or sailing orders, given to a Portuguese ship bound for Brazil in 1511 proclaimed that no one must trade there "without license of the feitor."[14] In fact, crew members were not even to set foot outside the island where the *feitoria* was located. But the king's enthusiasm for Brazil declined as the years passed, and it became obvious that the South American *conquista* was more suitable to the captain-donatary system than to direct royal exploitation. It is worth mentioning, though, that the captains-donatary themselves sometimes used the *feitoria* after they were established by the crown in 1534.

Aside from the *feitoria*, there was one other institution of great importance which served to implement Portuguese crown capitalism, the *Casa de Guiné, Mina e Índia*, or, as it came to be called, simply the *Casa da Índia*. Its lineage, if not its unbroken physical existence, stems from the chandler's warehouse, storage sheds, and customs post which had been established in Lagos as the *Casa de Guiné* to outfit and receive caravels returning from Africa and to collect the percentages Prince Henry imposed upon merchants he had authorized to traffic with the new discoveries. Shortly after his accession, João II had adapted the arrangement for royal use and perhaps even taken over Henry's original buildings. Then in 1481 or 1482, following the establishment of São Jorge da Mina, he moved the *Casa*, by then called the *Casa de Guiné e Mina* to Lisbon, where it continued to act as a kind of home-office *feitoria*, a clearing and accounting house for goods received from its overseas

14 Peres (ed.) *História de Portugal*, IV, 141–143.

branches. It also set prices and made sales and disbursals. In addition, the *Casa* readied fleets for departure, received incoming ones, issued certificates and licenses to incoming and outbound personnel, and even acted as a postal bureau. Just as its names were changed periodically, the *Casa's* functions varied from era to era. Before 1506, the king allowed some private and foreign merchants to finance a portion of his cargoes, whereupon the *Casa* invested their monies for them and distributed their share of spices. Later in the century when the royal monopoly was relaxed in regard to some spices, it again acted as an intermediary for the procurement of pepper, nutmeg, and ginger in contracted amounts, upon payment of bullion. Needless to say, the *Casa da Índia's feitor*, or, as he was later called, *provedor*, was one of the king's most important and trusted officials, as was the institution's chief treasurer.[15]

From the foregoing description of the *feitoria* and the *Casa de Guiné Mina e Índia*, it is evident that, even before Vasco da Gama rounded the Cape on his way to Calicut, he was in effect the advance agent of a powerful royal corporation whose operating and marketing system was already well established and ready to expand. In contrast, the Spanish had only limited experience overseas, and there were none of the convenient and well-oiled institutions available to Queen Isabella after Columbus's first voyage which would allow the crown of Castile to begin building an empire immediately. All these had to be worked out in the years that followed. In fact, one of the first steps Spain took to facilitate the development of its new territories was to copy and adapt the *Casa de Guiné Mina e Índia* to its own needs — as the *Casa de Contratación*.[16]

The Trading Monopoly in Action

Once the Portuguese reached India, their empire, like the Venetian trade with Islam, rested on a foundation of pepper. This wonderful spice not only improved the frequently rancid meats and monotonous dishes of the

[15] See Maria Emilia Cordeiro Ferreira, "India, Casa da," II, 505–513; José Ferreira Martins, "Casa da Índia." Originally, there also was a *Casa dos escravos* to handle the buying and selling of slaves. See also, Marcello Caetano, *O conselho ultramarino* and Damião Peres, *Regimentos das casas de Índias e Mina*.

[16] For a comparison of Spanish with Portuguese colonial institutions, see Eduardo Ibarra, *RIM*, II (1941), 19–36. The Genoese had evolved a similar institution in their medieval Mediterranean empire, but it is most logical that the Spanish borrowed the nearer and more up-to-date Portuguese example.

sixteenth century, but, according to contemporaries, it bettered people's eyesight, cured dropsy, and eliminated liver pains.[17] As living standards rose during that hundred-year span, fewer and fewer townsmen and nobles went without its habitual use, and consumption more than doubled. This meant an assured market for virtually all the pepper the Portuguese *feitores* could procure at the seven main and secondary *feitorias* along the Malabar and Kanarese coasts: Cochin, Honavar, Barcelor, Mangalore, Cannanore, Quilon and Calicoylan.

In the very first years, the Portuguese had mostly bought their pepper via native intermediaries who were members of the *sudra*, or commercial caste, and had merely waited for them to show up at a *feitoria* with a quantity of it for sale. Such passivity proved uncertain and costly. Not only did the Indian middlemen require a profit, but the ships of the *Carreira* could not wait upon another's whim. They had to have ladings waiting for them when they arrived from Portugal. The obvious solution was foreshadowed by Vasco da Gama's treaty of 1503 with the king of Cochin: upon the Portuguese guarantee of his royal duties and rights, the king in turn had fixed the sale price for pepper within his domains and undertaken to supply it to the *feitorias*. In 1508, Viceroy Francisco de Almeida proposed similar arrangements to all the other Indian suppliers of Portugal, offering them 2 ½ cruzados per quintal, ¾ in gold, ¼ in copper. What arrangements he did not close on this basis, his successors, especially Albuquerque, did, under prodding from Lisbon.[18] The crown then knew, or thought it did, exactly what its specie would buy and felt it had assured itself of a steady supply at the cheapest price. To a large extent this was true, but the bargain, however expedient it may have appeared to be from Portugal, was only made at the expense of a certain commercial flexibility. Since the owners of the pepper-producing lands were mostly Brahmans, culturally and religiously disdainful of business, few of them would accept bolts of cloth or measures of rice for their pepper, as the *sudra* middlemen often would. Hence, by deliberately eliminating the broker, the crown limited its *feitores* to a style of trading which, although initially cheaper, precluded their use of the Asian interport trade as a source of payment. It made future procurement of pepper dependent upon the export from Portugal of precious metals, most of

[17] Jan Huighen van Linschoten, *The Voyage of Jan Huyghen van Linschoten to the East Indies*, II, 75.
[18] Vitorino Magalhães Godinho, *L'economie de l'empire portugais*, pp. 631–632.

these earned from previous sales of pepper in Europe. Once this cycle became firmly fixed, of specie-for-pepper-for-specie, even the original proportion of copper (or sometimes of coral or lead) disappeared — certainly by the middle of the sixteenth century. Thereafter, any shortage of specie brought out from Portugal in the fleets made the procurement of pepper dependent upon the *feitores'* uncertain ability to obtain credit in a market where the producers themselves were dependent upon cash to pay their workers.[19] There also proved to be another joker in the fixed-price arrangement, one which could have been anticipated by inflation-conscious moderns; the suppliers, when unable to raise their prices, simply debased the quality.

Pepper was by far the most important of the monopoly items because it was traded in such huge volumes. But there were many other drugs and spices of higher intrinsic value which the *feitorias* either bought or acquired by tribute or levy. In general, the drugs, or *drogas*, as they were called in Portuguese, were distinguished from *especiarias*, or spices, in that they were consumed entirely as medicines, for example, as aromatics (benzoin, camphor), as ointments (musk, garu), or as digestives (betel). The spices, too, were believed to have medicinal value; but they were far more profitable because they were consumed as concomitants of foods and hence were used in far greater quantities. They alone were "big business."

Besides pepper, South Asia produced only two, perhaps three major spices: ginger root,[20] cinnamon, and cardamon — the last of little importance in Europe before the end of the sixteenth century. All of these were purchased on fixed-price contracts, although cinnamon — prime quality cinnamon grew only in Ceylon — was obtained as well through an annual tribute from the Sinhalese kings of Kotte, whose yearly share of 300 bahars (each of about 550 lbs.), plus some elephants, was increased by the Portuguese to 400 bahars, minus the elephants, as the European consumers demanded more of it.

In value per given weight, however, both pepper and cinnamon ran far behind the "luxury spices" — cloves, nutmeg, and mace. All three (although nutmeg and mace are merely separate parts of the same fruit) came from the diminutive Molucca and Banda island groups, thousands of

---

[19]*Ibid.*, p. 651.
[20]In recent times, China has been the more familiar source of ginger, but in the sixteenth century, little, if any, of the European supply was obtained outside the Indian subcontinent.

sailing miles to the east of India, and were, perhaps for that reason alone, worth three times as much as the Indian condiments. At first, these were merely bought on contract by *feitores* on Ternate and Amboina, much as were the Indian spices. But the crown changed its approach when it began to appoint concessionaires who made annual voyages from Goa after 1523 (see chapter 20). It also began to exact tributes from the sultans of Gilolo and Tidore. Thereafter, the local *feitores* in Indonesia acted mostly as customs officials who collected either royal percentages in kind from various traders or yearly tributes from rulers and then shipped them on to the *feitorias* in Malacca and Goa under the royal seals.

Beyond India, wherever Portuguese administration thinned out, the crown did not long attempt to enforce its monopoly in the sense that it procured its own spices and other monopoly goods. Instead, each year it licensed an individual Portuguese to make a single trading voyage to a certain area, originally as a reward for past service, but later in the century for a payment. In return, the entrepeneur of this annual voyage paid the crown all customs duties on his eventual cargo, plus a percentage of his profit, as well. Two of these voyages, those to the Moluccas and to China and Japan, are described in detail in chapters 20 and 21. Others were chartered to Ceylon, to Malacca, to Mozambique, to Pegu, to the Banda Islands, to Sunda, to Tenasserim (in present-day Burma) and to East Bengal. By 1600, however, all but those to China and Japan, to the Moluccas and Mozambique had become extinct.

Cartazes, Customs, and Convoys

Once the Portuguese had ousted their Muslim competitors from the Indian Ocean, they considered it their own preserve and tried to order its trade according to their profit. Practically speaking, though, the only regions where they possessed sufficient naval power to monitor and tax native shipping were along the western coast of India and (at times) the Straits of Malacca. In both areas, they held the major strategic ports as bases — Goa, Cochin, Diu in India, and Malacca — and could control the flow of shipping that passed by them (or in Malacca's case, through the Straits). The means used were ingenious. Each year they sent out armadas northward and soutward from Goa between May and September — the season when the monsoons allowed coastal sailing. Those fleets obliged all private merchantmen plying the coast, Portuguese or native, to purchase

Portuguese *cartazes*, or passes, themselves of negligible price. The real object of the *cartazes*, however, was not what they cost per se, but what a bearer of one was required to do as a consequence: to call in Portuguese ports and pay customs duties on goods he was either exporting to or importing from other sources. At Goa, these were 6 percent ad valorem until 1569 and 7 ⅛ percent thereafter, at Chaul, 8 percent on imports and 6 percent on exports, and at Diu, only 3 ½ percent, and later 4 percent. The Portuguese also collected a 7 percent tax in Malacca on traffic passing through the Straits. Beyond the two regions (and for a short time, a part of India's Coromandel Coast) the Portuguese did not seriously attempt the *cartaz* system. Moreover, they never enjoyed any success with their squadrons dispatched to sail near the Stait of Bab el Mandeb and keep Arab traders from filtering through to the Indian Ocean.

In return for the native merchants' bearing of *cartazes* and payment of duties, the Portuguese undertook to provide convoy protection against pirates and those enemies like the Samorin who considered the acceptance of a *cartaz* by a merchant as evidence of collusion. After 1569, when the Indian states hostile to Portugal stepped up their attacks on Goa and Diu, the Portuguese intensified their convoy activity — and hence charged higher duties.

The Gujarati merchants had long been obliged to accept the *cartaz* system and its consequent tariffs on their commerce, even though these were far heavier than those of their own rulers. These merchants in fact appeared virtually to have supported Goa with their payments, in spite of the fact that Cambay was so powerful a state that it could easily have pushed the Portuguese out of Daman, Chaul, and probably Diu itself if it had really wanted to do so. But as M. N. Pearson points out in his study on the subject, Cambay was not a modern state which followed an integrated military and commercial policy. Even the great sieges of Diu had not been supported by the inland nobility, which remained aloof. The only link, in fact, between the merchants and the rulers in Gujarat was the customs revenues the rulers collected from them. These were much lower than the Portuguese rates and made up only some 6 percent of Cambay's total income. This sum was too little to excite the Gujarati ruling classes, who in effect hardly cared at all whether their merchants were happy or sad because the revenues they provided were negligible. Abandoned by their own government, the Gujarati then turned to the maritime Portuguese and obeyed the *cartaz* system because they had little choice to do otherwise.

Since the Gujarati were so industrious — they were the principal maritime traders in the Orient — they were also the prime suppliers of tariffs and fees to the Portuguese customs houses. It has even been estimated that these amounted to perhaps 45 percent of the total revenues of the *estado da Índia*.[21]

Royal Administration in Asia

Rule over the Portuguese holdings in Asia was through a simple military government which makes the organization of the Spanish New World look complex by comparison. This was not because the Portuguese in Asia were simpleminded or backward, as critics from the late R. S. Whiteway to the contemporary historian D. R. Sar Desai have believed.[22] Rather, the reason appears to be much less abstract: there were so few Europeans in the Portuguese Asian empire at any one time that they simply did not require a more elaborate government. According to Professor Boxer's estimates, there were probably never more than 6000 to 7000 Portuguese in or subject to military service in all the Orient at any one time during the sixteenth and seventeenth centuries; and if one adds generously to this another 6000 to 7000 clerics, European dependents, servants, and half bloods who lived wholly according to European law, the figure still can come to no more than 12,000 or 14,000 at the most optimistic.[23] And those were widely scattered, from Mozambique to Macau.

Many more persons than this lived within the confines of Portuguese rule, namely the indigenes who remained in their homes and lands after the Portuguese conquests. But for the most part they continued to be subject to their own headmen and laws, their taxes tended to be self-collecting through their own systems, and their only direct contact with Portuguese rule over a lifetime might be in legal, commercial, or religious matters when their affairs meshed with those of the Europeans. All of this

[21] M. N. Pearson, *Merchants and Rulers in Gujarat*, chaps. I, II, and IV.

[22] Whiteway, *Rise of the Portuguese Power in India*, pp. 12–13, and D. R. Sar Desai "The Portuguese Administration in Malacca, 1511–1641" p. 504. What Dr. Sar Desai says of Portugal is equally applicable to the Spanish, French, Austrian, or Russian monarchies of the same era.

[23] Charles R. Boxer, *Four Centuries of Portuguese Expansion, 1415–1825*, pp. 19–20. Meanwhile, Portugal itself was such a small nation that, until its absorption by Spain in 1580, the king and his council of state handled all colonial affairs without assistance from a special colonial council.

reduced the need for Portuguese-style government to the simplest of dimensions.

There are really three types of administration of which one must speak in Portuguese Asia: the viceregal, the local, and the native. In practice, these were overlapping; but they are distinct enough to be treated separately.

The Viceroyalty

Much has already been written here in a circumstantial way about the governors and viceroys of Portuguese Asia, the nature of their administrations, and the extent of their jurisdictions. In general, this highest managerial post seems to have been derived from Mediterranean models, via Aragon, and it is interesting that among Christopher Columbus's titles in his original *capitulación* from Queen Isabella was "Viceroy of the Indies" — thirteen years before the title was created in Portugal. This would indicate that the precedent and title were already close at hand in 1505, or, rather, close to King Manuel's environment. This monarch just might have meant to add a touch of irony in bestowing the title on Francisco de Almeida at that time; for in 1505, it must have begun to dawn on nearly all concerned — even without the *Mundus novus* letter attributed to Vespucci — that the true claim to the title lay with the Portuguese and not the Castillians.

Although the two highest titles, of viceroy and governor, later came to carry identical powers in a practical sense, it is apparent from the context of affairs in 1509, when Almeida departed from office, that the governorship of Portuguese Asia was not originally meant to be equivalent to the viceroyalty. For after Almeida's dismissal, Albuquerque was originally to be only one of three governors, whose territories had been carved from Almeida's unitary jurisdiction. But he had assumed the powers of the other two, and King Manuel let this de facto adjustment become permanent — in effect allowing Albuquerque and his successors to remain as plenipotentiaries under the less prestigious title. It was not until King João III's appointment of Vasco da Gama in 1523 that the actual title of viceroy was revived, and thereafter it was reserved for the higher nobility.[24]

[24] See chapter 16, n. 3.

Whether called viceroy or governor, however, the appointee seldom served for more than three years in his office. In fact, only six of thirty-four in the sixteenth century did so. Three years was the term assigned by the Portuguese and the Spanish monarchies to their viceroys, as well as to all their other officeholders; and both crowns considered a longer period to be both dangerous and unnecessary. They obviously reasoned that if the viceroy became too used to commanding in a region so far from home, and if his subordinates identified too many of their jobs and favors with him, he might try to pursue his own policy and perhaps even scheme toward independence. On the other hand, it seems never to have occurred to the Iberian kings that any special experience in any post was either desirable or necessary, that is, experience aside from general service to the crown and ability to command. This was perhaps because lower officials were expected mostly to follow their orders, and a viceroy was to refer all questions of even the slightest importance to his king and the royal councils. The approach would have worked better had the radio or telegraph existed, for no allowances ever seem to have been made for the great distances, the time, and hence the information lag, or for the local conditions and possibilities. But the system was poorly adapted to an era when sailing ships were the standard means of communication. Once in India, a viceroy could dispatch requests for guidance only in his first year and hope to receive a reply before his term ended. Queries sent off in his second year resulted in royal orders for the desk of his successor, who more than likely ignored them.

In practice, however, viceroys did pretty much as they pleased during their tenure. The only real limits to their power were that they and their judges could not pronounce a sentence of death or of mutilation over *fidalgos* without permission from the king and that they had no power over the hiring and firing of his higher public officials (although they could refuse to instate or suspend them with cause, and they could influence the crown over whom to appoint or not to appoint in the future). Otherwise, the king was obliged to give them enormous latitude as a matter of necessity, whether he liked to or not. He also had to magnify the viceregal grandeur and appearance of power, because neighboring Asian potentates were at least as impressed by opulence and grandeur as they were by navies and guns. Whenever a viceroy set foot outside his palace, he went about in an ornate sedan chair, escorted by halberdiers and gentlemen and heralded by trumpeters.[25] He was probably more meticulous in his observance of folderol than ever was his master in Europe, for, after all, the king did not need to dazzle his subjects and fellow monarchs daily to maintain his role in European affairs.

Although the Portuguese monarchs did not get around to establishing a *counselho do estado*, or council of state, until 1563, the viceroy in Goa seems to have maintained an advisory council from an earlier date, and its chief participants were the main royal officers, the archbishop of Goa, and any other *fidalgos* deemed to be of sufficient standing and experience.[26] Their decisions were not incumbent upon the viceroy, but if the records of their deliberations in the seventeenth century (which alone have been preserved) are any criterion, all viceroys thought more than twice before disregarding them.

Aside from the vast army of scribes, inspectors, judges, and other functionaries who ran the state, viceroys (and governors) had their own personal staffs, of which the post of *Secretário da Índia* was the most important. This official also served as the secretary of the *conselho*, managed the viceregal correspondence and drafting of orders, and sometimes acted as a go-between vis-à-vis the other officials and his chief. Viceroys also had a chaplain, a barber, an interpreter, a chief investigator, a captain, and sixty guards, as well as their musicians and manual servants. For all of these they were given a certain allowance, but it seldom sufficed because most viceroyal appointees brought out large entourages of relatives and adherents from Europe who had to be supported out of the viceroy's own pocket.

Beneath the viceroy were the departments of the judiciary and finance, both of which evolved into their characteristic forms only around the middle of the sixteenth century. Before 1544 or 1545, the viceroys (or governors) and their councils, aided by a few *desembargadores* and *juizes*, or judges, were in effect their own judiciary. But in the administration of João de Castro, or perhaps the year before his arrival in 1545, the crown created a *mesa de relação* at Goa, staffed it with its own *ouvidores*, or justices (six, in later years), and empowered it to act as a supreme court

---

[25] Linschoten, *Voyage*, I, 218–219.

[26] The royal *conselho do estado* was established by the Cardinal-Infante Henriques; before his time, the monarchs had merely charged various of their councillors with the task of helping them into the overseas territories. See Francisco Paulo Mendes da Luz, *O conselho da Índia*, pp. 22–23.

for all of Portuguese Asia. There was no other judicial institution in the whole viceroyalty with a panel of judges, and the *mesa de relação* was the one place where relief could be sought from the rulings of fortress commanders and their local courts. Each of these justices, save for the *ouvidor geral da Índia*, or chief justice, incidentally, had a separate descriptive title because he headed his own judicial department independent of the *relação*; for example, the *chançarel* also acted as the head judge of the chancery, and the *provedor mór dos defuntos da Índia* acted as chief probate judge.

Just as the judiciary received its form a few years before the middle of the century, the financial structure underwent a similar reorganization in 1549. Until then, the head fiscal officer in India was the *provedor mór da casa dos contos*, or chief of the treasury, called the *casa dos contos*. But in that year King João III became deeply disturbed at reports of its irregularities and created a comptroller-general, the *vedor da fazenda da Índia*, as the oriental state's chief financial officer and downgraded the *provedor mór* to the mere status of a bureau chief, at least to judge from the fact that the salary of the *vedor* was eight times as great.[27] The *feitor* of the city of Goa should also be mentioned as an important royal officer here, for although his title might suggest that he was a member of the administration intermediate between central and local, in fact he was one of the chief royal officers by merit of Goa's importance as both the capital and the concentration point for all sailings and shipments to Lisbon of royal monopoly goods.

The *alfândega*, or customs house, was an institution which predated all the more recent colonial ones and even the *feitoria* itself. The model for it was drawn from the Portuguese and Moorish Middle Ages and from native customs houses in Asia, and its imposts were regulated according to local usage and royal pleasure. At Goa, it paid most of its tolls and duties on incoming and outgoing goods into the *casa dos contos;* however, it differed from the other bureaus of the viceroyal administration in that it did not draw its pay from the central treasury, but retained a percentage of its tolls as remuneration. Its head, called a *juiz* or an *almoxarife* (a term of Arabic origin, as is *alfândega)* was royally appointed and served under the *vedor da fazenda.* In accordance with the standard Portuguese administrative policy of disturbing native legal and commercial patterns as

[27] The financial system was not permanently cleansed, however, and in 1589 King Philip I (II of Spain) was busy again at reform.

little as possible, most of the duties and port charges it levied were close to the charges the Portuguese had found in effect when they took over.[28]

Royal administration in the other cities and fortresses of Asia subject to Portuguese rule was really little more than a miniaturization and simplification of the central viceregal machinery in Goa. At Diu or Malacca, for example, the captain, the *feitor,* who also acted as chief of the *feitoria,* an *ouvidor,* or judge, and a battery of scribes, market inspectors, and constabulary officers collected the money, dispensed the justice, and effected the royal will.

The main variations on this general scheme were in Macao and, indeed, in Goa. In Macao (see chapter 21), there was no resident captain-general until the seventeenth century, but the city was subject to the rule of the captain-general of the Japan voyage. Goa had its own municipal captain under the viceroy, much as an admiral's flagship is captained by another officer, who concerns himself exclusively with local management. In addition, the island of Goa had a captain for each of its main fortresses.

Officially, aspirants could be appointed to posts in this bureaucracy only by the king, although obviously the monarch and his advisers could hardly show much personal knowledge or interest in any save nominees for the most important positions, such as that of the viceroy, the *vedor da fazenda,* the main fortress captains, factors, treasurers, and justices. For the rest, excepting some jobs that inevitably were wangled by outbound viceroys and other influential people for their retainers or relatives even before they left Lisbon, it was the incumbent viceroy or governor and chancery in Goa who made most nominations to vacant posts or to occupied ones whose terms were due to expire. Then all these had to be confirmed by the king. Meanwhile nominees either starved or occupied positions on a de facto basis before the royal confirmation arrived. Since all the better posts had long waiting lists of persons nominated three, six, nine, or twelve years and even decades in advance, the delay did not matter much. Once an appointee had managed to squeeze into one job, he sought a string of appointments to others, preferably at better pay. Then he merely moved sideways or upward every three years.

[28] The papers of an early royal comptroller, Afonso Mexia, show how much of the *alfândega's* practices in Goa were based upon Bijapurese customs usages. See Joaquim Heliodoro da Cunha Rivara (ed. and comp.) *Archivo Portuguêz Oriental,* V, doc. 5 and 53. The same was true in Malacca. See *Regimentos das fortalezas,* pp. 255–256. In Macao, the duties were Chinese as well as Portuguese, and Cantonese customs officers were actually in attendance to salt their share away.

The entering ploy for a candidate who wished a career in the Indian bureaucracy was either a certificate issued in Lisbon before embarkation which showed that the bearer possessed some noble blood, or else a number of them issued by various officials in Portuguese India showing that the aspirant had served the crown honorably as a soldier for a certain number of years, usually twelve. Then the candidate, if lucky or well connected, would be given a beginning job on a level of service commensurate with his blood and education. The trouble with the system, even when it worked smoothly, was that it preserved the rigid class distinctions of Europe in a tropical environment where experience and ability should have been the chief criteria. As it was, a literate common soldier with years of service was fortunate to get a petty job in an outlying customs post, and a teen-aged fourth or fifth son of a poor but noble family, fresh from Portugal, was likely to become an assistant treasurer or a constable.[29]

Least favored among royal employees, the *soldado*, or common soldier, was the most in need of bettering himself and therefore the most likely among the Portuguese in Asia to innovate — or else to sink into poverty and even beggary. When there were not sieges to relieve, annual convoy duty and attacks on pirate strongholds provided almost the only employment. The duration of this employment was entirely up to the viceroy and crown; but usually in the fall, the government would beat a drum in the squares of the principal Portuguese Asian cities and enroll soldiers for a few months of actual duty. They would thereupon collect their annual pay in a lump sum and have their service certificates duly inscribed with the facts of their enlistment.[30] If they gambled their money away or spent it too fast, they faced hard times as soon as the government released them. But they could not hope to overcome this basic insecurity until they had served for twelve years and could prove it with the necessary credentials. If discouraged, they were hardly in a position to go back to Portugal; for although the crown had brought them to Goa at royal expense, they had to pay their own way home and seldom could afford to do so.

They did have two legal alternatives.[31] One was to accept the hospitality of a wealthy *fidalgo* who wished to have an assured command of

---

[29] For a fuller discussion of some of the abuses in the system, see George D. Winius, *The Fatal History of Portuguese Ceylon; Transition to Dutch Rule*, chapter 6; or better, See Diogo de Couto, *O soldado práctico, passim.*

[30] See Linschoten, *Voyage*, I, 189–191.

[31] They also had an illegal one. Many *soldados* went a.w.o.l. and became mercenaries in the armies of Asian rulers.

soldiers able-bodied and completely loyal to him, and this meant enlistment only when and where he himself served. The other option was to retire, take a wife, whether European or Asian, and become reclassified as a *casado*, or married man, subject to military service only in emergency. *Casados* commonly took this status to open a shop or to trade in commodities, like foodstuffs, spices, or textiles, with other cities of the empire or with cities wholly under Asian rule. Of the *casados* and the influence they possessed, more will be said in chapters 21 and 22.

Civilian Administration: the Municipality

Throughout the Iberian world, no institution was more persistent or more typical than the municipal council, or, as it was variously known according to time or place, the *consilium*, the *consejo*, the *ayuntamiento*, the *cabildo* or, in Portugal, the *senado da câmara*. Before the end of the sixteenth century, Latin America had dozens of them. In contrast, by 1580 Portuguese Asia had only two — at Goa and Cochin — although additional ones appeared at Macao, around 1582, and at Colombo and Malacca soon after the opening of the seventeenth century. The explanation for this lag in forming civilian municipal governments among the Portuguese east of the Cape of Good Hope undoubtedly lies in the crown's military and monopolistic administrative design. Apart from Goa itself, where Afonso de Albuquerque established a *senado da câmara* in late 1510 or early 1511[32] as a first step toward creating a truly Portuguese colony, the other cities, fortresses, and *feitorias* of the Asian viceroyalty were either founded later or took more time to develop a civilian, or *casado*, population. Some of them never did organize a *senado da câmara*, but remained under military rule. And at least one city, Diu, organized and then lost its *câmara*.

In many ways, however, the Portuguese municipal bodies which did exist enjoyed a richer and more independent existence than did their Spanish-American counterparts. The sole reason for this appears to have been that the Portuguese crown, unlike the Spanish, did not deliberately encourage their subservience by selling the offices of their regents, or aldermen, and then allowing the incumbents to make their posts hereditary. Instead, the kings of Portugal, to their everlasting credit, kept out of

---

[32] According to Boxer, in his *Portuguese Society in the Tropics; the Municipal Councils of Goa, Macao, Bahia and Luanda, 1510–1800*, p. 12.

civic governmental affairs once they allowed the *câmaras* to be organized. The *senado da câmara* then scrupulously maintained its heritage of honest elections and, consequently, its independence from viceregal and royal domination.[33]

Aside from this major difference, however, students of colonial Latin America will find the Goan *senada da câmara* familiar because its functions closely resemble those of the *cabildo:* it levied and collected city taxes, leased out municipal lands and concessions, maintained public bridges, streets, and fountains, issued licenses to build, certified weighing and measuring instruments, and fixed the prices of staple foodstuffs. In composition, it consisted during most of the sixteenth century of three *vereadores*, or aldermen, one a *fidalgo* and two merely "noble" (a vaguer term which allowed much latitude), two *juizes ordinários* (civic magistrates, one civil and one criminal in jurisdiction), a *procurador da cidade* (a city attorney), and between four and twelve *procuradores dos mesteres*, (representatives of the leading guilds). These officers each had the right to cast a vote. In 1572, a modification was imposed by the crown which increased the number of *vereadores* to four, three of whom now had to be qualified lawyers, and the president was required to be a leading *fidalgo*. Then there were other slight modifications under Spanish rule beginning in 1585, but none of them altered the *câmara's* essential nature.

The *câmara* of Goa and the ones which followed it in Portuguese Asia were eager to obtain full municipal status under the crown, and they quickly applied, Goa as early as 1516, for the privileges citizens enjoyed under Lisbon's own charter. Nearly all of these were granted, and the main difference between the governance of the Asian cities and the cities of Portugal lay in the right the captains of Indian cities possessed, via royal stipulation, to attend the *câmara* meetings whenever they saw fit and to cast a double vote.[34] This did not signify, however, that the central government sought to domineer the *câmara*, and, indeed, the Goan *câmara* freely criticized the viceroys and governors whenever it felt its prerogatives were being abridged by the crown officers. It often did valiant

[33] *Ibid.* See pp. 5–7 for electoral practices.

[34] *Ibid.*, p. 13. Many of the existing documents pertaining to the Goan *senado da câmara* have been reprinted in the *Archivo Portuguez Oriental*, fascículos I and II. These are called "Livro lo das cartas que os Reis de Portugal escreveram á cidade de Goa," the "Cartas da câmara de Goa a sua Magestade, 1595–1609," and "Livro dos privilegios da cidade de Goa." Please be warned, however, that only sets of the *Archivo* which contain the second (1877) edition of the first fascicule contain the "Cartas da câmara de Goa a sua Magestade."

service to the state, incidentally, as when it lent João de Castro the money he needed to relieve the second great siege of Diu in 1545.

Rule over the Indigenes

The capture of Goa and Malacca near the beginning of the sixteenth century, the acquisition of Bardes and Salcete in 1543, and the Portuguese crown's inheritance of Kotte in Ceylon by degrees after 1580 brought thousands of native peoples under the rule of Lisbon. The exact number, even in the capital of Goa itself, is elusive. The only estimate which seems based on more than a vague impression is António Bocarro-Pedro de Resende's, and it was made not during the sixteenth century, but in 1635 or thereabouts. Even then it is useful to establish only a rough proportion of Portuguese to Indians, for the writer estimates that there were 3000 hearths in the city, excluding convents, of which 800 were Portuguese.[35] Although there is no telling how many souls there were on the average to a Portuguese-Indian hearth of the time (Bocarro-Resende's further breakdown adds up to 3200, not 3000 hearths, which diminishes confidence in its objective accuracy), one can surmise that the European Portuguese were in the decided minority — especially if, as the document indicates, not all people in service to the purely Portuguese families were themselves white. Furthermore, it would not appear from the text that any of the thirty-one or so native villages on the Goan island, which do not form part of the city of Goa proper, were taken into account. Hence, if there was such a preponderance of Asians in Goa, where the Europeans were most numerous, it only stands to reason that the indigenes were even more heavily in the majority in Malacca and Ceylon or in Bardes and Salcete, where there were never more than a few hundred whites in residence, either as soldiers or as *casados*.[36]

Of the indigenes, who must therefore have formed 75 to 90 percent of the king of Portugal's Asian subjects, a certain percentage (especially in Goa) were Christianized and, hence, subject to European, rather than Asian, laws.[37] But this still left the greatest number of the inhabitants of

[35] In the *Livro das plantas de todas as fortalezas, cidades e povações do estado da Índia Oriental*, as printed in the A. B. Bragança Pereira (ed.) *Arquivo portuguêz Oriental, nova edicão*, tomo IV, vol. II, parte I, pp. 222–223.

[36] See Tikiri Abeyasinghe, *Portuguese Rule in Ceylon, 1594–1612*, pp. 115–116, and I. A. MacGregor, "Notes on the Portuguese in Malaya," p. 6.

[37] The Bocarro-Resende document claims that of 3000 households (or 3200 if one holds

most any region in Asia in a category neither Christian nor European, and accustomed to legal codes and taxes totally alien to their conquerors. The Portuguese solved this dilemma in the simplest and most direct way: they merely grafted the older Asian administration, together with its customary laws, onto their own system. This allowed those Asians who maintained their own religion and who did not deal directly with the Portuguese to till their lands, sell their fish, and pay their tithes exactly as their forefathers had. All the Portuguese had to do was to make certain that the go-between offices were satisfactorily filled.

The originator of this system, as one might expect, was none other than Afonso de Albuquerque, who, by merit of his conquests of Goa and Malacca, was the first administrator actually faced with the need to rule directly over Indian and Malaysian peoples. Whether or not, as the late British historian and archivist F. C. Danvers suggests, Albuquerque fused Western and Eastern systems of government in emulation of Alexander the Great — one must never underestimate the power of antiquity in the Renaissance — it is just as likely that Albuquerque was the first modern European to realize that he had no other alternative.[38] For the Dutch, who were hardly slavish imitators of their Portuguese predecessors, did precisely the same thing at a later date, both in Java, where the Portuguese had never settled, and in Ceylon.

Although the archives contain hundreds of fragmentary references indicating the survival of native rule under Portuguese administration, no sources provide a better picture of how it operated than the *Foral dos usos e costumes* of 1526 and the much later reports of Antão Vaz Freire, not completed until about 1613. The earlier document concerns the thirty-one villages that preexisted the Portuguese conquest of Goa and was drawn up only sixteen years afterward by Afonso Mexia, the chief fiscal aide to Governor Nuno da Cunha. The later documents were the work of another *vedor*, a special agent sent to Ceylon at royal command in 1609.

---

the writer(s) to literal addition) 2500 were "cazados, pretos christãos, canarís, e de outras nações da Índia." But this would hardly have held true for the peoples living on the rest of the Goan island or on the mainland territories of Bardes and Salcete. Moreover, Christianity does not seem to have made much headway in Malacca or to have comprised more than a small, if significant, minority among the Ceylonese. It should also be mentioned that the Portuguese had pulled down the non-Christian mosques and temples of the Goan lands around the middle of the sixteenth century; probably more natives called themselves Christians in the seventeenth century, when the Bocarro-Resende inventory was taken, than in the sixteenth century, under consideration in this work.

[38] Danvers, *Portuguese in India*, I, pp. 328–329.

Though they deal with different eras, they have certain features in common. They show that the Portuguese in both cases placed the responsibility for the collection of tithes or services, together with the administration of justice, in the hands of headmen of districts or villages. They were called *tanadars* and *gancars* in Goa, and variously, *disavas, mudaliyars, aratchis,* and *vidanas* in Ceylon.

On the island of Goa (and later in its surrounding territories of Bardes and Salcete), there was a developed money economy, and the Portuguese, who held their fortresses securely, did not interest themselves in the military service of the Konkani peoples. Rather, they contented themselves, as the Bijapurese had, with collecting mostly cash from the *gancars,* who acted as tax collectors and also dispensed justice. In Ceylon, where wars were numerous, Europeans few, and money not in general use outside Colombo, the capital city, the Portuguese took a different approach, but one also in accordance with local custom: they accepted the traditional military service from the *disavas, mudaliyars,* and *aratchis,* who, feudal style, held their lands in return for it. In addition, the Portuguese accepted bundles of cinnamon from another kind of officer, a *vidana,* who supervised a district of *chaleas,* or members of the cinnamon-picking caste. Both the *gancars* and the *vidanas* could be held personally responsible for the full amounts due their masters from their districts; but, otherwise, they were legally privileged. In Goa, *gancars* could keep for themselves any amounts collected in excess of their allotments, but they could also be ruined if they did not produce their quotas.[39]

Outside Goa and Ceylon, much less is known about customary rule under Portugal, but what has been studied indicates the same general

[39] The *Foral dos usos e costumes* has not only been published in its full Portuguese text, but it has been translated into English and widely excerpted. The original text can be found in the Cunha Rivara (ed.) *Archivo portuguêz Oriental,* fasc. 5, doc. 58, pp. 118–133, but it was translated by B. H. Baden-Powell in "The Villages of Goa in the Early Sixteenth Century," pp. 262–277. Extensive excerpts were also reprinted in the more recent Donald F. Lach and Carol Flaumenhaft (jt. eds. and comps.) *Asia on the Eve of Europe's Expansion,* pp. 52–60. R. S. Whiteway also published a very incomplete abstract in Appendix II of his *Rise of Portuguese Power in India,* but it is so sketchy that one would do better to consult one of the other versions mentioned.

No printing of Antão Vaz Freire's *Tombo* (or, rather, the part of it that survives) has ever been made, but its contents have been skillfully analyzed and the information it contains made available to readers by Tikiri Abeyasinghe, in his *Portuguese Rule in Ceylon,* pp. 100–166. He also uses many additional sources. The original documents survive as codices 280, 484, 221, and 222 of the Arquivo Histórico Ultramarino, Lisbon.

pattern. For example, in Muslim Malacca, native officials known as *shahbandars* had originally both collected port duties from native traders and ruled portions of the city. The Portuguese soon did away with these offices, apparently; but they kept intact the positions of the *temmengong* and the *bendahara*, the chief financial and ruling posts of the native administration.[40]

Although the foregoing sketch of Portuguese imperial operations has been brief, it has perhaps indicated that its institutions were compact and — in theory, at least — well designed to accomplish the things they were meant to do, at least until more modern structures were innovated by the Dutch and the English in the seventeenth century. The crown early made the necessary distinction between agricultural and commercial spheres in its empire, and because commerce was closest to its heart, it successfully found deputies to promote and develop colonies whose worth, at least in the beginning, was purely agricultural. Then it set out to create a commercial Asian empire under the aegis of royal absolutism.

From beginning to end, the Asian empire belonged to the Old Régime, as opposed, for example, to the British or Dutch empires; and as will be remarked in chapter 22, its organization was more a mirror of early sixteenth-century royal practices in Europe than it was of the commercial realities under which it operated. At the time it was conceived, however, no one could have understood this; even Holland and England had not yet evolved as societies whose bourgeois interests could have set the tone for an imperial government. As such, the organization of the Portuguese Asian empire was antiquated by 1600 or 1602, when its rivals created their own blueprints for colonial government. But it must also be remembered that the Portuguese empire in Asia endured as an important entity for about as long a time as the Dutch and British empires did — each for approximately 150 years.

Whether the failure can be blamed on the malfunctioning of its administrative system per se is not demonstrable. The most that can be said is that, like so many other things in life, it appeared more workable in the abstract than it proved to be in practice and this in fact is the fatal weakness of all absolutisms of whatever form. The main trouble with the Portuguese Asian system seems to have been that the crown presupposed a loyalty and a dedication of its subjects that most of them did not possess

[40] See D. R. Sar Desai, "Portuguese Administration in Malacca," p. 509.

so far from home. Then, unable to supervise them, the crown was perhaps unaware to what extent they operated the system to their own advantage.

The Church as an Arm of the State

Although this book remains close to the problems directly involved in empire building — navigation, conquest, administration, and economics — a few words must be written about the church in order to explain its presence in the vanguard of imperial development, a subject which figures prominently in the next three chapters. The church and religious ideals played such an important role in the crown's expansion into Africa, Indonesia, and Japan that it seems almost essential to tell why and under what circumstances the clergymen involved came to be there. This is not wholly out of place in a chapter such as this, for in a real way, they were as much ministers of the government as they were ministers of the faith.

The Portuguese, like the Spanish, had a long history of conquest behind them on the Iberian Peninsula before they ever embarked on their expansion overseas, and in its middle and latter phases, this conquest had been motivated in part by the desire to bring Christianity to Muslim populations. This urge to proselytize had become so ingrained in both nations that the missionary aspect of their expansion overseas came virtually as second nature to them. Many even believed that the papal bulls consigning the hemisphere exclusively to penetration by Spain and Portugal might be invalidated unless the two countries actively sought converts in their zones. Finally, the Spanish and Portuguese (and later the French) kings became the effective heads of the Catholic churches within their colonial boundaries. They nominated the bishops, they endowed the convents out of royal revenues, they licensed both the orders and the individual clergy who sought passage there, and they frequently sent them packing home if the fathers displeased them or they discovered that they were present illegally. And they often used the clergy for diplomatic missions and occasionally even as secular administrators.

Although there can be little doubt about their zeal in attempting to spread the Christian faith, the Portuguese in Asia never enjoyed the wholesale missionary success of the Spanish in the New World or even a repetition of their earlier success in the Congo, if mostly because, unlike the Spanish, they never conquered widely enough to subject large numbers of native peoples to their total control, nor did they set themselves to uproot and destroy the societies that they did come to dominate, as in Ceylon or the Goan lands. There was therefore no "shortcut" to bringing Asian peoples to the baptismal font. Indeed, the problem in Asia and East Africa was far more complicated than making conversions in Europe or West Africa because, for one thing, the Indian caste system made a pariah, or untouchable, out of any Indian, even a Brahman, who did not keep the Hindu observances. And, for another, it goes almost without saying that the Muslims on the Swahili coast of East Africa and in Asia were highly resistant to conversion. After all, Christianity was for them an incomplete revelation, and the Portuguese had learned long before that efforts to convert them were wasted. Before 1542, about the only mass conversions the Portuguese made in Asia were among the Hindu *Paravas,* or fisherfolk, who lived near the Cape of Comorin, perhaps 20,000 or even 40,000 in number. They were of low caste and almost a people apart in India; so it probably did not greatly matter to them if they did suffer an additional stigma by embracing the alien creed. Besides which, their fisheries had recently come under Portuguese control. The other Asian converts were mostly slaves, servants, concubines, and merchants closely associated with the Europeans. Their proselytization was encouraged, as in the Goan lands, by a barrage of laws which provided greater civil liberties and commercial privileges to those who became Christian.

In 1542, the Jesuit cofounder Father Francisco Xavier arrived in India from Lisbon and gave new impetus to the Portuguese missionary effort, hitherto forwarded chiefly by the Franciscans and Dominicans. João III had been one of the original sponsors of the Jesuits in their campaign for papal recognition, and so when he requested that Xavier and another Jesuit be sent to the Portuguese Indies, the Society of Jesus saw its new opportunity as God-given. In the ten years before his death in 1552, Xavier, "The Apostle of the Indies," taught and made conversions in India, Ceylon, Japan, Malacca, and Indonesia. He died on the threshhold of China. Today the Portuguese missionary activities in Asia are largely associated with his name, at least popularly, and with the Jesuits. Meanwhile Goa had become the first bishopric in Aia in 1534, and Cochin, Malacca, and Macao followed in 1556 and 1557. In addition, the Jesuit emissary to Ethiopia in 1557 was given the title of bishop, and later

"Patriarch," but since the Ethiopians never adopted Catholic Christianity, the appointment was more wishful than real.[41]

[41] No comprehensive work on the Portuguese Asian Church has ever been published, although Father António da Silva Rêgo has begun one on its missionary activities, only a single volume of which has been published to date. It is called *História das missões do padroado português do Oriente; Índia (1500–1542)*. This is not to be confused with his documental series entitled *Documentação para a história das missões do padroado português no Oriente, 1499–1582*, which is much too extended for general reading. There are also histories which are more nearly contemporaneous with the era under consideration, namely the Jesuit Father Francisco de Sousa's *Oriente conquistado a Jesu Christo*, and the Franciscan Father Paulo da Trindade's *Conquista espiritual do Oriente*, written about 1630–36 but published only in 1962–1967. Both essentially concern themselves only with the affairs of the orders to which they belonged, but since the Jesuits and the Franciscans were among the most active of the orders in Asian missionary efforts under the Portuguese, their works give a fair idea of what took place.

CHAPTER 19

The Shape of Empire:
the Western Periphery

The Indian empire of Almeida and Albuquerque has already been described, and it formed the nucleus of *Ásia Portuguesa*. But its governors and viceroys ruled in a much vaster area than this, one that sprawled from the Cape of Good Hope eastward to the China Seas and terminated at a point where the Tordesillas line was thought to fall as it circled the other side of the globe.

To either side of this central system of fortresses — Ormuz-Diu-Goa, Cochin, Ceylon, and Malacca — there lay two peripheral regions of Portuguese activity, one in South-East Africa and one in the Far East, each different from the central system and from one another.

The first of those regions, the South-East African coast, lay along the sea routes from Lisbon to India, and its basic function for the Portuguese was indeed as a way station. Its intermediate position meant that the Portuguese could bring considerable naval and amphibious power to bear on hostile East African cities like Mombasa or Kilwa, and in fact they did so periodically. (The Portuguese cause, incidentally, was aided by the fact that none of the East African cities was really very powerful.) Such logistics alone were enough to guarantee that coastal Eastern Africa would not be a typical peripheral area, for the common denominator of the other outlying region, the Far East, was Portuguese military weakness.

Accordingly, on the other side of India away from the path of the *Carreira*, the area to the east of Malacca was obviously very distant from the centers of Portuguese might — so far, indeed, that even a feeble

338

sultanate like Ternate in the Moluccas was capable of ejecting the Portuguese when their captains-general misbehaved to the point of enraging the ruler and populace. Under the circumstances, there could be no serious question of the Portuguese dominating or opposing the Chinese or Japanese, the most powerful nations in Asia. The result was that the Portuguese presence beyond Malacca bore little if any resemblance to their presence in India — so little in fact that it might be argued that it really represented the empire of an empire, a spare room tacked onto an existing house.

This thinning out of military power east of Malacca also meant that the number of administrators and officers was greatly reduced, and in turn that the crown's ability to extract money from the periphery was greatly restricted. But perhaps this approach to the "empire's empire" is a negative one — for to describe it in a different way, its chief characteristic was that a new class of Portuguese, the *casados*, acting as private merchants, and the *fidalgos*, acting as concessionaires, built the China and Japan trade. In fact, they and not the crown discovered Japan and created Macao.

Some Technical Considerations

Before proceeding further, a few words seem necessary to explain why subchapters on Ethiopia and the Japanese missionary efforts of the Jesuits have been included in this survey of the peripheral areas of the Portuguese empire, even though neither area was ever under Portuguese rule. In truth the choice has been more or less arbitrary.

Moderns are well schooled in contemporary definitions of imperialism, and these usually require that to be considered a component part of an empire, a territory must be controlled either directly or indirectly by the empire-building country. Any application of this twentieth-century measuring stick would automatically exclude Ethiopia and Japan from consideration, even though the Portuguese engaged in intensive and purposeful activities there according to their own standards.

The Portuguese of the sixteenth century were ignorant of our concepts regarding empire — a word they used only in its Latin sense of "dominion" and seldom applied to describe overseas possessions. To them, their territories in Asia were their *conquistas*, and as late as the 1680s a Jesuit historian entitled his book on Ceylon *A conquista (espiritual e temporal) de Ceilão, (The Spiritual and Temporal Conquest of Ceylon)*, meaning that the Portuguese had conducted both spiritual and political activities there.

As remarked in the last chapter, the Portuguese sponsored Christianity everywhere in their African and Asian hemisphere, mostly within areas under their direct rule but frequently outside them — and they did so to render a kind of heavenly tax on their enjoyment of the papal donation. Ethiopia and Japan were among the major targets of their Christian concern, and they expended much money, anguish, and human lives there without hope of any gain except spiritual. (In Japan, the Jesuits actually went into business to support their missions.) And, as will be seen, they achieved spectacular results, at least within the time span under consideration in this volume. Indeed the Portuguese of the era would have been shocked had they learned that their presence in Asia had been under scrutiny without due consideration of those two spiritual "conquests" in areas where they stood to gain little for having performed them. They may rest assured that the areas of their striving, not for Mammon, but for God, have been included here even at the expense of the more modern viewpoint. For their spiritual "conquests" reveal fully as much of their natures as do their temporal ones.

Historical narrative is nearly always more informative than abstractions about history, and in turning from these panoramas to the particulars, it is apparent that there is a good deal more to the landscape when viewed from close at hand than from high above. For example, South-East Africa may have been atypical of some of the other peripheral areas because it was a way station. But upon scrutiny, it is obvious that this characteristic only applied to the coastal strip and not to the hinterlands.

South-East Africa

Among the outlying territories and regions so variously subject to Portuguese influence, it was only in coastal East Africa that the royal hegemony was absolute and Portuguese policy consistent during the first decades of empire. From the beginning da Gama and the government alike realized that fleets needed a convenient haven and stopover when traveling between Lisbon and India, and that this must be beyond the Cape, since outwardbound vessels did not make a landfall on the Atlantic side of Africa at all. Thereafter, it did not take da Gama or his successors long to observe that the area was at once wealthy (it traded in gold for all the goods of the Orient), predominantly hostile (it was solidly Muslim), and eminently conquerable (because it contained no native powers of any consequence). The result was that Portugal quickly moved in and remained the dominant power in the region at least throughout the sixteenth century.

At the time of the Portuguese arrival, the Swahili coast of Africa, as that two-thousand-mile-long stretch of coast between Sofala and Mogadishu has become known, consisted of a string of oligarchic Arab and Afro-Arab city statelets sandwiched between a hostile interior and the sea. The more sophisticated and powerful of the towns — among them Pate or Patta, Sofala, Malindi, Kilwa, and Mombasa — were peopled with a mixed breed of Bantu, Hamitic, Arab, Indian, and even Persian stock, but with a prevailing Arab culture. To the Portuguese, these civilized peoples were simply known as *mouros* or Moors, in contradistinction to the wild pagan peoples of the interior, whom the Arabs called Kaffirs and the Portuguese *cafres*. Present-day writers substitute the term "Swahili" for "Moor" to denote the Islamized East African, but the name "Kaffir" is still used to denote the less civilized. Finally, inside the cities there were small groups of Indian traders called Banyans.

The coastal towns were frequently located on islands or in harbors chosen for their defensibility from the mainland as well as from the sea, for the Bantu tribes of the interior were both the source of their wealth and of potential trouble when on the warpath. In times of peace they afforded slaves, gold dust, and ivory in return for glass beads and cotton cloth; in times of trouble, they frequently surprised and slaughtered the Swahili townsmen. Otherwise, the cities occupied their time in quarreling among themselves and in trading their wares in the monsoons across the Indian Ocean. These brought them in return Gujarati textiles, Malabar spices, and Persian silks and rugs, and also great wealth and a high degree of sophistication, both economic and cultural. The more important coastal towns coined their own money and built stately houses with richly carved doors and opulent hangings inside.

Such wealthy cities so strategically located on the sea road to India were highly interesting to the Portuguese, and it was not long before they took full advantage of their opportunities.

It has already been shown in chapter 12 that the initial utilization of Malindi as a port of call and jumping-off place for Calicut was purely

circumstantial and came about because Malindi extended the only welcome that da Gama and Cabral received along the Swahili coast during
the first Portuguese voyages to India in 1498 and 1500. But Malindi was
farther north than was convenient for India-bound vessels, and it cannot
have been coincidental that da Gama made peace with the ruler of
Mozambique on his second voyage in 1502, . . . "leaving a factory
(feitoria) there so that ships going there might find supplies."[1]

Three years later, in 1505, India-bound Viceroy Francisco de Almeida
moved into the region with decisive force. As remarked in chapter 16, it
was in this first viceroy's regimento to establish fortresses at Sofala and
Kilwa as he passed en route to India — in a polite way if the sheiks
welcomed them, by force if they did not.[2] For although the Portuguese
might have been willing to forgive these port cities for their inhospitality
to da Gama and Cabral a few years before, they could not easily forget that
the Sheikh of Kilwa was suzerain over most of the towns of the Swahili
coast and that Sofala and Kilwa were fabulously rich.

As it turned out, Sofala was spared for the time being, apparently
because a last-minute change not shown in Almeida's regimento had assigned its conquest to Pedro de Añaya.[3] But after reuniting his fleet (scattered by Cape storms) at Mozambique, Almeida sailed north along the
coast to take over Kilwa. Despite a certain pretense of diplomacy manifested on the occasion, it is clear enough that the viceroy was only looking
for an excuse to depose its sheikh and would not allow him a hairbreadth
of latitude for bargaining.[4] The sheikh, no doubt sensed this, for when he
saw that his every evasion and polite excuse only led to a new demand, he
abdicated and fled before Almeida's vastly superior power. Then, after
appointing an ambitious but pliant adviser of the former ruler as his
successor, the viceroy went about his business of occupying and fortifying
the city, and relieving it of its excess wealth.

Mombasa seemingly came next on Almeida's revised agenda, and although it was smaller and less influential than Kilwa, it was prouder and
less willing to submit to Portugal. In fact, when a pair of Portuguese ships
ventured in to fathom the harbor in August 1505, they were fired on by a
shore battery which they soon silenced. Thereafter, the Portuguese

[1] Castanheda, História do descobrimento, I, 96.
[2] See Cartas de Albuquerque, II, 281–289.
[3] See chapter 16.
[4] See Eric Axelson, South-East Africa, 1488–1530, pp. 62–67.

spurned a bribe to desist, brought up the whole of their forces, and pillaged the rich town, leaving it in smoldering ruins and carrying off all its gold and silver, cloth and jet from Cambay, and silk, rugs, and camphor from Persia. Thereafter, Almeida abandoned Mombasa and continued on to India.

By then, the only thing that stood between Portugal and complete supremacy in East Africa was the rich city of Sofala, whose conquest had for some reason first been assigned to Almeida and then given to the smaller fleet or the Castilian Pedro de Añaya, who was to follow later the same year. Añaya in fact did not sail from Lisbon until Almeida had virtually completed his operations in Africa. However, when the Spaniard finally arrived before the city in September 1505, he did not storm it as Almeida had stormed Mombasa. Instead, he entered cautiously, was politely greeted by its sheikh, and he professed that Portugal wished to live in peace with the city, establish a *feitoria*, and trade normally. He wished to build a fortress, he said, only to help defend Sofala from the recurring attacks of Kaffir tribesmen. Thereupon the sheikh granted permission, the Portuguese paid compensation to the owners of buildings on the site, and the fortress was completed by November, though, owing to the scarcity of stone in the region, it was chiefly of humble adobe and less than formidable.

Such a peaceful contrast to the overthrow of Kilwa and the destruction of Mombasa was not destined to persist. Before many months had passed, it seems that the one faction of the Sofalans that had favored war from the beginning had been joined by other traders and by the Arab community, once the lucrative Portuguese trading activities had cut into their profits.[5] Thereafter, this war faction had gained the ascendancy and the sheikh (who secretly had counted all along on the Portuguese falling prey to fevers) threw in his lot with those plotting a surprise assault on the garrison.

Añaya, however, learned of the cabal from a turncoat Sofalan, and despite the sickness prevalent among his men, he not only beat off the attackers, many of whom had been borrowed from the inland tribes, but he sallied out of his fort, butchered a number of the local inhabitants, and wound up finding and slaughtering the sheikh himself. Following this, the Sofalans asked for peace and the Portuguese gladly granted it, naming

[5]*Ibid.*, p. 85.

as their puppet sheikh a friend of their informant. A few days later, Añaya fell sick and died, while the Portuguese gathered every stone they could find in the region and built a stronger fortress than ever for themselves.[6]

Although the Portuguese now had their choice of any anchorage along the entire coast, they continued to prefer their original stopping place at Mozambique, apparently because it was the most conveniently located. There, by the orders of King Manuel, the first hospital was built in 1507–8, together with a larger *feitoria* and warehouse. Thereafter, the city — located on a small island just off the coast, but with a fair harbor — became the main port of call for vessels traveling either to or from India and Lisbon.[7] The captain of Sofala was instructed to ship his gold dust up the coast to Mozambique's *feitoria* to coincide with the arrival of the India-bound fleet.[8] Almost at the same time, by 1509, Albuquerque had lost interest in Kilwa, and in 1512 orders came through from King Manuel to abandon it.

Although Mozambique continued to be the chief stopover for Portuguese Indiamen until the end of sailing operations, there is overwhelming evidence that it proved far from ideal. Almost from the beginning, complaints flowed into Lisbon that malaria and other diseases carried off more crew members during the last stop there than did the rigors of voyaging, and there were schemes and proposals put forward as late as the middle of the next century that other ports be designated instead.[9] In response the crown sometimes changed the *regimentos* of India-bound vessels to sail outside of Madagascar and avoid the Mozambique Channel entirely, changing their courses from north to east in the mid-Indian Ocean. This solution, however, was employed only at intervals, for the most part, the stopover at Mozambique remained in vogue.

Whether Mozambique was so inherently unhealthy, or whether the troubles encountered there by crew members were the result of other factors, is hard to say. Some contemporaries claimed that the island produced barely enough food to take care of the year-round inhabitants — who did not seem to be particularly unhealthy — and that

[6] Axelson's account incorporates those of all the chroniclers and other sources, save that of Martín Fernandez de Figueroa, for which see: James B. McKenna, *A Spaniard in the Portuguese Indies: the Narrative of Martin Fernández de Figueroa, passim.*

[7] Axelson, *South-East Africa, 1488–1530*, p. 96.

[8] *Ibid.*, p. 97.

[9] Inter Alia, see *Documentos remetidos da Índia*, bk. 61, folios 331–332; also, Charles R. Boxer and Carlos de Azevedo, *Fort Jesus and the Portuguese in Mombasa* p. 43.

the problem lay in the contamination of the extra food supplies imported from the mainland to take care of the transients. Alternately, they swore that supplies were good enough but that the water was bad.[10] It would seem more likely that men weakened by the long sea voyage who had not had time to produce antibodies to the local microbes — fecal- and mosquito-borne alike — were the most afflicted by them.

In the longer view, most students of European expansion have wondered at one time or another why the Portuguese did not do as the Dutch later did and found a station instead at the Cape of Good Hope. No doubt this would have been the wisest solution of all in one sense, for the Cape possessed a far healthier climate and was so located that all ships might have utilized it, no matter which side of Madagascar their routings might have specified. In the context of the sixteenth century, however, such a course would have been most unlikely. For there were no existing settlements near the Cape and no agriculture on a scale that could have supported a large garrison of Portuguese. To have settled Portuguese farmers and established a self-sustained agricultural colony there might have been possible under the captain-donatary system, but considering that Mozambique was already there and only 600 miles up the coast, it must have seemed preferable (if the sixteenth-century Portuguese ever really considered a Cape colony) to lavish their main resources on India. Beyond this it is interesting that more than a century and a half later, the Dutch, with far greater resources, struggled mightily before their Cape settlement became a success and even then did not think seriously of attempting it until long after they had twice failed to capture Mozambique Island!

Next to seeking a way station to India in South-East Africa, the Portuguese were attracted to the region by its trading resources, chiefly its gold. The purely economic aspects of empire will be discussed in chapter 22, but it should be mentioned here that the quest for the source of South-East Africa's mineral wealth preoccupied the Portuguese throughout the sixteenth and the seventeenth centures, especially when it became apparent that proceeds from the Asian revenues and from the spice trade would not pay the costs of maintaining *Ásia Portuguesa*. Direct contact with the interior was prompted by their desire to do away with intermediates, to occupy the producing areas themselves, and, if possible, to increase production.

[10] See Charles R. Boxer, "The Carreira da India (Ships, Men, Cargoes, Voyages)," in *O centro de estudos históricos ultramarinos e as comemorações Henriquinas*, p. 57.

In spite of their oft-stated goal, however, the Portuguese made only two important series of trips into the interior during the sixteenth century. The first of these, and by far the most remarkable, was made between 1512 and 1515 by António Fernandes, who was most probably an illiterate *degredado*. As mentioned earlier, from the reign of João II, who conceived the idea, until well into the reign of Manuel, *degredados*, or convicts, were given a chance of serving out their sentences in shorter time or even of escaping the death penalty by cooperating with explorers and navigators to undertake missions that would otherwise have been deemed too hazardous to ask of an ordinary subject.

Fernandes was sent out from Sofala, seemingly with only a few native companions, to determine the source or sources of the gold which found its way to Sofala from a region called Monomotapa to the northwest. In the first of these journeys (two of which are known), he seems to have penetrated well into the area, first to a point west of Mt. Darwin and present-day Salisbury, discovering in the process most of the major rivers before his return and describing the main chieftains and tribes dwelling near them. He even provided the first known description of the aboriginal bushmen. To have accomplished all he did, he must of necessity have commanded the Bantu language — if only to judge from the elaborate interviews he reported with the various headmen along his way. As professor Eric Axelson of Witwatersrand University suggests, he was most certainly the same António Fernandes, named by João de Barros, who had been set upon the deserted shores of South-East Africa by Almeida in 1505. At that time he had probably learned all the necessary techniques of survival including how to speak the native tongues.

In his second journey, he apparently retraced his steps directly back to the Monomotapa region, then traveled south to the Lundi River, and followed it in an easterly direction before bearing north to the Buza River and returning to Sofala. Of Fernandes's third journey and his ultimate fate, nothing is known; all the definite information about him is embodied in two reports from officials of Sofala to King Manuel.[11]

Fernandes described the whereabouts of the gold fields in adequate enough detail to provide a routing for contemporaries, but of course his

[11] Those of Gaspar Veloso and João Vaz de Almeida, whose letters to Dom Manuel I are reprinted in *Documentos sobre os portugueses em Moçambique e na África Central 1497–1840 (Documents on the Portuguese in Mozambique and Central Africa)*, II, 180–189, and IV, 282–288.

efforts were of little use to Portugal until such time as authorities could assemble enough men, arms, and supplies for a major expedition into the interior which could assume direct royal control over the region.

Unfortunately, however attractive such a project might have appeared, it was something that could wait — while new threats of Turkish incursions, sieges in India, struggles over Morocco, dynastic marriages, and renewed interest in Brazil all assumed a higher priority or represented a more pressing need. The move to conquer Monomotapa, in fact, did not get underway until 1571 and probably was intimately connected with the move of King Sebastião and his advisors in 1569 to divide Portuguese Asia into three jurisdictions, one for India, one for Malacca and the Far East, and one for East Africa, all virtually equal and independent.[12]

Creation of the new African entity at any rate was well designed to expedite a major campaign, for it removed the Asian governors and viceroys as intermediaries between the crown and any actions taken in Africa. In a time of shrinking Portuguese resources, these chief colonial officials had consistently tabled projects to be undertaken far from Goa and favored those closer to home (and likely projects that filled their own purses, since no doubt a worldly Goan governor would be quick to calculate that if he financed the capture of mines in Africa, his own arm would not be long enough to reach the till, and commanders on the scene would have prime opportunities for graft virtually under their noses).

If Diogo do Couto is correct, it would appear that the rationale for the whole scheme lay in the Asian empire's increasing failure as a trading operation — which led Portuguese mercantilists to promote the idea that the possession of mines à la Spain was a necessity if the Asian empire was ever to become profitable.[13] If so, the project had a certain logic and urgency. And certainly, it died hard — fresh proposals to master Monomotapa and its gold fields were still being weighed after the Portuguese Restoration of 1640.

The first *fidalgo* appointed to the new African captain-generalcy was none other than the successful ex-governor of India, Francisco Barreto, whom it seems King Sebastião had personally selected as the commander most likely to succeed.[14] Governor Barreto was given 1,000 men for the

---

[12] See Couto, *Da Ásia*, Dec. IX, chap. 1.

[13] Couto, *Soldado prático*, p. 224.

[14] In fact, as suggested in chapter 22, giving him a suitable command was the probable guiding factor in the whole arrangement. Only the title of captain general endured, for after

purpose, but these were hardly adequate to capture and hold an entire region comprising hundreds of square miles. As it was, Barreto began his campaign successfully enough by defeating the Monga tribesmen on the Zambezi and was eager to journey on southward to Monomotapa for a military showdown there. Unfortunately his warlike approach aroused the objections of a priest accompanying the expedition, Father Francisco de Monclaros, S.J., whom the Jesuit-ridden King Sebastião had nominated to be his adviser. Monclaros, it seems, wished the conquests to be made with love and not pikes. As this impasse continued, Barreto received word that a former protégé-turned-enemy, one António Brandão, had lied to the king and was making big trouble for Barreto in Mozambique. Agonized by his double frustration, Barreto moved toward the coast, still listening to the remonstrances of Father Monclaros that he would pay God dearly for his sins. If so, he had not long to wait, for on the way insomnia, loss of appetite, and depression so weakened him that he suddenly took ill and died.[15]

In 1574, under a new commander, the same Portuguese troops made a new and more successful sortie into the gold region which at last reached the city of Zimbabwe, near its center. The reality, however, was far different from the Midas-like visions the Portuguese imagination had conjured. It was too bad that councillors far from the scene presently forgot the truth. The mines indeed yielded their gold, but, as the expedition discovered, only in modest amounts and only after the natives had expended tedious and backbreaking labor and endured constant danger of cave-ins. Soon the expedition was obliged to return home, leaving 200 men behind as a token occupational force. Within a year or so, they had all been massacred. Thereafter, the same sequence was repeated sporadically over the next half-century, so persistent was Portugal's desire to become a mining proprietor in its own right.[16]

In sum, it is clear on both counts — the need to possess a stopping point between Portugal and India, and the desire to win riches in trading — that the Portuguese gained less than they had sought in South-East Africa. For although Sofala's gold production appears to have increased in yield during the next century, it never caused the royal treas-

---

Barreto's death, the incumbent became clearly subordinate to Goa once more. The Malaccan captain-generalcy was not filled and the whole scheme did not outlive Sebastião himself.

[15] Couto, Da Ásia, Dec. IX, chap. 23.

[16] For basic information see Justus Strandes, The Portuguese Period in East Africa, pp. 121–122.

ury to glitter, and Mozambique (and its cemetery) remained not the temporary but the final resting place for hundreds of sailors.[17] The best to be said of Lusitanian imperialism in the region is that until well beyond 1580, at least, it was one of Portugal's more peaceful overseas theaters. Only in the 1590s, when Mombasa had to be reconquered and occupied, was its peace disturbed. Otherwise, East Africa was only noteworthy for the degree of harmony that prevailed between the Muslim Swahili and their Christian overlords. The worst to be said is that the establishment of Portugal in East Africa reduced to near poverty the once prosperous coastal city states.[18]

Ethiopia

Ethiopia was never part of *Ásia Portuguesa* in an administrative or commercial sense, but it does deserve a place in any treatment of Portuguese imperialism. Not only did the search for Prester John play an important role in setting Portuguese expansion in motion, but in their subsequent dealings with the ruler and peoples of Ethiopia, the Portuguese went far to belie their image as harsh and rapacious. Rather, in this semimythical land, they showed quite another side of their natures, one which indicates that their standards of conduct were relative to the kind of situation they faced.

Conquistadores, whether Portuguese or Spanish, have enjoyed a good deal of attention in our own times but seldom much repute. Especially in the closing years of the nineteenth century writers from F. C. Danvers and R. S. Whiteway in England to Justus Strandes in Germany wrote in tones of chronic indignation over Portuguese cruelty and greed. They however, failed to recognize in a day before cultural anthropology that such brutal qualities were hardly predominant in sixteenth-century Portuguese, but actually represented an extreme among their many modes of conduct, in this case, the response evoked by opposition from peoples Portugal identified as its bitter hereditary enemies, the Muslims, or "mouros." Because Muslims held most of the commercial and military power in South Asia and East Africa, the Portuguese typically collided with them. When thus hindered or provoked, it has already been ob-

---

[17] See Vitorino Magalhaẽs Godinho, *L'economie de l'empire portugais au^x XV° et XVI° siècles*, pp. 265–275.

[18] See G. W. F. Stripling, *The Ottoman Turks and the Arabs, 1511–1572.*

served that the Portuguese were capable of almost any atrocity. Even the word "mouro" evoked in the humblest Portuguese soldier an urge to buckle on his sword. On the other hand, the Portuguese almost never multilated or mistreated Hindus on the few occasions when they fought them (as at Calicut). Finally, as in Ethiopia, far from seeking to move in upon and exploit the Abyssinian Christians as outsiders, the Portuguese displayed a different, but equally vivid facet of their natures, a sacrificial and heroic one, faithful unto death and with no expectation of material reward. Just as their Crusading spirit made them brutal toward those whom they identified as enemies of their faith, it made them act nobly toward those they recognized as its friends.

The Cross in the Mountains

Considering that a modern commercial aircraft can fly from Lisbon to Addis Ababa in a little over six hours, it is remarkable that the Portuguese sought Prester John fervently for a century before locating him, or, rather, what passed for him.[19] Aside from the one-way trek of Pero de Covilhã to the Lion of Judah's court in the late fifteenth century, the Portuguese had created their entire empire in India, Africa, and Malaya before any contact was made with Ethiopia.

Ethiopia was so hidden away from the Christian world in the first centuries of the modern era — or even until the inauguration of the Suez Canal in 1869 — that it is hardly surprising the Portuguese failed to locate it much sooner than they did. Ethiopia was hard to approach from any direction through its narrow, forty-mile corridor of Red Sea coastline around Massawa that connected it to the outside world in the early sixteenth century. From this bottleneck the country extends southward across a string of high plateaus for more than 1,000 miles, sandwiched between the burning plains of the Sudan on one side and the deserts of the Somali peninsula on the other. In the sixteenth century the journey down from the sea was not to be lightly undertaken for the country was rough and what constituted a road was often only a matter of opinion. On the coastside, along a series of fault lines, the massifs rose abruptly 7000 to 8000 feet above the Danakil desert. The western slopes of those massifs were somewhat gentler (their rivers drained off into the Nile system), but the difference was only one of degree and not of much help to the

[19] See Francis M. Rogers, *The Quest for Eastern Christians*, *passim*.

traveler, whose best chance was to take the direct route and accept the difficulties. Of the tablelands he would have encountered, the Amhara is the most famous and in fact lends its name to the Semitized Hamitic peoples who live in the Ethiopian highlands and to the language many of them speak. Most of the Amhara massif is above 8000 feet and enjoys a temperate climate much like that of Kenya. Altitudes of 10,000 feet are common on this and the other plateaus like the Shewa, and the highest peak in the country, Mt. Bajeda, rises 15,158 feet.

It is hardly puzzling that the inhabitants sought by the Portuguese in so isolated an area should have differed racially and religiously from the pagan negroid peoples to the west and the Arabs to the east. Introduced to Christianity by Greco-Roman merchants of late classical times and wholly converted by St. Fromentius in the fourth century, the Amharic plateau dwellers and their kings steadfastly resisted all subsequent armies and missionaries from the Islamic world, especially from the Somali Muslims in the desert country to the east. Only some Tigré-speaking Abyssinians dwelling in the extreme northern plateaus, some lowland peoples around Massawa, and the inhabitants of the southern part of the country actually embraced the Muslim faith.

During the expansion of Islam, Ethiopian Christianity came under grave pressures from the Arab world to the north and east, but its Aksumite and Abyssinian kings meanwhile did succeed in expanding their realm and their faith southward, as far as the Shewa massif. Their church never fell out of contact with the Christian patriarchate at Alexandria, and the Ethiopian kings always obtained their *abuna,* or metropolitan, from among the monks of the Coptic monastery of St. Antonio's. In addition, their church maintained a monastic community at Jerusalem, and in 1441 at the invitation of Eugenius IV this community even sent delegates to a council at the Vatican. It is also possible that the "Jorge" referred to in the chancery papers of Afonso V as having visited Portugal in 1452 as an emissary of Prester John was in reality a monk from this house.

In any event, it was not until 1487 that the Portuguese sent Paiva and Covilhã in search of Prester John and not until 1508 that they attempted another embassy. This one, blessed by Albuquerque, seems to have been murdered by Muslims while on the way back from Abyssinia. But at least the embassy succeeded in drawing a response from Ethiopia a few years later when the Ethiopian regent Queen Elena wrote a letter full of pieties to King Manuel and sent it to India through her own representative, an

Armenian named Matthew, who traveled with his brother-in-law, wife, servants, and a piece of the Holy Cross.[20] The group made it to Goa in December 1512, after being robbed at Zaila and detained in Bijapur. Albuquerque received the party with every honor and dispatched it to Cannanore, whence, according to orders, Matthew was to be transported to King Manuel. He was so sent, but only after Albuquerque's enemies had tried to prove him an impostor and a Muslim spy. Manuel received him and the piece of cross with tears of joy.

While Matthew was in Portugal, Albuquerque made his abortive attempt on Aden and his expedition into the Red Sea. No doubt the contact he had already made with Queen Elena was responsible for his suggestion that Massawa would make a good station for Portuguese establishment within the Red Sea.[21]

It was not until 1515 that King Manuel sent Matthew back to India, together with his own ambassador, a pious and enthusiastic septuagenarian named Duarte Galvão, who bore with him a panoply of magnificent gifts for Prestor John. Unfortunately, the two emissaries were dispatched with the fleet bringing Lopo Soares de Albergaria to Goa, where that arch bungler was to take over Albuquerque's job. By Albergaria's twisted logic, any friend of Albuquerque's was an enemy of his; thereafter he made life miserable for Matthew and Galvão. (Albuquerque, as noted in chapter 17, died before entering Goa on his return from Ormuz.) The embassy languished in Goa until 1517 and then was taken with Albergaria on his dismally mismanaged Red Sea expedition. He, however, refused to let them land at Massawa. Galvão died on Kamaran Island and Matthew was returned to India to wait again.

Finally, early in 1520, Albergaria's successor, Diogo Lopes de Sequeira, determined to drop Matthew off at Ethiopia's lone port during the third Portuguese sweep into the Red Sea. As matters developed, Sequeira did not accomplish much of value beside this overdue act of diplomacy during his incursion. No correspondence has survived between Lisbon and Goa on the subject of Matthew's embassy, and it is difficult to know whether in delivering Matthew, Sequeira was acting upon the express orders of Lisbon or merely contriving to rid himself of a nuisance — rumors were even spreading once more that Matthew was an imposter.

[20] Brás de Albuquerque, *Comentários*, pt. II, chap. 49.
[21] See chapter 17.

Sequeira had planned to attack Jidda first, but he was obliged to sail directly into Massawa when the expected Red Sea monsoons failed to appear. There, after a short wait, he made contact with the *Bahr Nagas*, the governor of Ethiopia's maritime marches for the Christian emperor. The *Bahr Nagas* and the other Ethiopians all recognized and did homage to Matthew, whereupon any doubts about him that Sequeira and the others might have entertained disappeared. It was only then that the Portuguese leader decided to improvise an embassy to accompany him. This did not prove difficult; for although Galvão was dead, Father Francisco Álvares, the original chaplain King Manuel had assigned as a principal in the 1515 embassy, still remained faithfully at Matthew's side. He reported his desire to get on with the mission, and because of the fascination of Prester John, a number of *fidalgos* quickly volunteered.[22] From among these, Rodrigo de Lima was chosen as ambassador, and three others were given lesser roles. All Manuel's lavish presents for Prester John had by then long since rotted or disappeared in India; the richest items available were gathered up from the ships and sent along with the embassy which departed in April 1520. Unhappily, Matthew fell ill en route and died in less than a month, long before the Portuguese had even finished traversing the initial, the Tigré, massif. Thereafter, they were on their own, and they labored up rocky mountain passes and down, through jungle and scorching desert for five months — amid varying degrees of hostility and cooperation from the natives. It was not until October that they reached the province of Amhara and espied the tent city of "Prester John" far in the distance "which seemed to cover the whole countryside."[23] (Like the Spanish monarchs of the same epoch or the Mongol rulers of Central Asia, the royal capital was located wherever the emperor, or Negus, as he was called, happened to pause.)

Lebna Dengal Davit, the twenty-four-year-old Ethiopian Negus, expected total obeisance from his subjects, and he remained so aloof from them that, except for two or three personal appearances per year, he even held his audiences with them from behind a curtain. Although he housed his Portuguese guests in a tent reserved for exalted persons and quickly demanded to see his presents (he had heard in a roundabout way some years before of the original ones), he seemed disappointed with their

[22] See Padre Francisco Álvares, *The Prester John of the Indies*, eds. C. F. Buckingham and G. W. B. Huntingford, 1, p. 61.
[23] *Ibid.*, 1, p. 265.

makeshift offerings and in no hurry to grant an interview. Rodrigo de Lima had first to answer endless questions about Portugal, its royal family, and, above all, about the Christian religion. He even had to fire a harquebus, sing and dance for Lebna Dengal in front of his curtain, and send him a pair of European breeches before the Negus summoned them to a direct audience, "sitting in majesty, as they paint God the father on a wall,"[24] wearing a blue taffeta veil and a high, dome-shaped, gold and silver crown. In contrast to all the preliminary trivia they had endured, however, the interview was businesslike — about fortress building in the Strait of Bab el Mandeb, a project which Rodrigo de Lima represented as only the strategic beginning of a master plan to capture the main ports of the Red Sea and ruin Muslim prosperity.[25] Lebna Dengal showed great interest in this and promised to supply ample provisions to the fort when it was established. On that note their interview was closed.

Returning to India, however, proved far more difficult than the outbound journey. After receiving a gold and silver crown for King Manuel, together with laboriously composed and ornately decorated dispatches in three languages, Amharic, Arabic, and Portuguese (which version, incidentally, was created with the help of Pero de Covilhã), Lima, his men, and a new Ethiopian ambassador hurried to Massawa — only to find that no Portuguese fleet had entered the Red Sea that year. Nor was there any in 1522. Then they arrived too late to catch the one sent the following year; but it left behind word that King Manuel was dead. This news made necessary a second tedious drafting session, this time to produce a letter for King João III, after which Lebna Dengal decided to write a second for the pope. The Portuguese then hurried off to the sea again but missed the fleet sent in 1524. In fact, they did not catch another until 1526 and did not reach Portugal until July 1527 — twelve years after Manuel had sent out Duarte Galvão and twenty-one since the first embassy of João Gomes to Ethiopia.

The Expedition of Cristóvão da Gama

The very year of the Portuguese embassy's return to Lisbon, a serious menace arose for Lebna Dengal Davit in Ethiopia. The Somali Arabs to the east had made war on and off with the highland Christians since 1332; then in 1517, three years before Rodrigo de Lima's arrival, an attack by

[24]*Ibid.*, 1, p. 304.
[25]*Ibid.*, 1, pp. 305–306.

the Somali Emir of Harar, Mahfuzh, had come to naught when Mahfuzh had been slain. In 1527, his son-in-law Ahmed Ibn Ibrahim el Ghazi, determined to avenge this loss, tried his own hand at invading the Christian territory. He proved far more formidable than Mahfuzh; for not only had he obtained the backing of all the Muslim tribes in Somaliland, but he solicited and received firearms, troops, and alliances with the Red Sea Arabs and with the Ottomans as well. Thereafter, his raids and battles gradually eroded Lebna Dengal Davit's position until he lost province after province to Ahmed Ibn Ibrahim, whom the Portuguese called "Granyé" (or "the left-handed"). Granyé, in fact, struck such terror into the hearts of the Ethiopian chiefs that a number of them deserted Lebna Dengal each time he lost a battle and joined the winning side. The Christian monarchy had been reduced to all but a shadow when Lebna Dengal died in 1540.

It is obvious that the royal interest in closing off the Red Sea had waned greatly since the days of Albuquerque and Lopes de Sequeira, and when the ambassador of Lebna Dengal arrived in Lisbon with Rodrigo de Lima, King João kept him waiting there for over a decade. Impatient, the Ethiopian monarch sent a second ambassador, the vain and boastful Portuguese physician João Bermudes, who had accompanied the Lima embassy in 1520 — and who, oddly enough, had been appointed *abuna*, or head of the Abyssinian Coptic church by Lebna Dengal, apparently because he had been unable to obtain an *abuna* from Egypt and Bermudes coveted the job. Bermudes took the dangerous Mediterranean route and seems to have arrived in Portugal in 1536 or early 1537. Then both ambassadors set out in 1540 for India; the original one died at Goa, and João Bermudes was dropped off at Massawa in 1541, from Estevão da Gama's fleet.[26]

It was only at this stopover that the Portuguese received news of Lebna Dengal Davit's death and the pitiful state of his kingdom, which Granyé had all but finished conquering from the new Negus, Galadewos. The notion that Prester John was in trouble might well have seemed anticlimactic to men who so long had dreamed of seeking his aid to overcome their own enemies. But Portuguese of the era were geniuses of action who wasted little time in musing over the absurd. It was enough for them to learn that Moorish devils were threatening to snuff out a

---

[26] João Bermudes's own account of his adventures is printed in *The Portuguese Expedition to Abyssinia in 1543–1591, as Narrated by Castanhoso, with Some Contemporary Letters, the Short Account of Bermudes' and Certain Extracts from Corrêa*, pp. 129–257. Bermudes, however, was so self-laudatory that he cannot be taken too seriously.

kingdom of fellow Christians. Estevão da Gama could spare only 400 men, but it would seem that virtually the whole complement of his armada volunteered. He appointed his younger brother Cristóvão commander and sent them off with eight small pieces of artillery. It is clear that not Cristóvão nor any of the 400 expected to return alive, let alone to profit. Rather, they thought of themselves as Christian soldiers marching onward to holy war.

It was not for the first time in the century that small European armies had marched into the highlands of unknown continents and fought heroically — Cortéz, Pizarro, Valdivia, Almagro, all had done it. But their motives were to subjugate, not aid, the native population. It is significant that Cristóvão had borne at the head of his column not a royal banner, but a white flag embroidered with the red cross of the order of Christ. It was the first and last holy mission of its kind following the Crusades, and even worthier than the Crusades because the object was to defend fellow Christians and not gain back mere real estate.

The little Portuguese army remained intact only for about a year and a half — from June 1541 until February 1543. During this whole time it did not find Galadewos, but instead encountered Granyé and interposed itself between the Ethiopian Negus, his shrunken army, and the Muslims. Twice in April 1542 the outnumbered army of Cristóvão defeated but failed to capture the Muslim aggressor. By August, however, Granyé had brought up massive reinforcements which included 1,000 experienced Turkish musketeers lent by the Pasha of Zebid, the commander of the Strait of Bab el Mandeb, and outfitted with a quantity of artillery superior to that of the Portuguese.[27] Cristóvão's men, at the time numbered less than 350, had four horses and were supported, somewhat dubiously, by less than 1,000 of the *Bahr Nagas's* troops. The value of these was negligible, if only because of blood of Ethiopian troops ran cold whenever they had to face artillery. As the battle began, they stole away and joined Galadewos. Miguel de Castanhoso, one of the few men to survive all the bloody campaigns, wrote that the Portuguese, who fought on disadvantageous ground at a place south of present-day Wolfa, could hold off the enemy host only by making repeated assaults on it — each one of which cost a number of lives.[28] As night fell, those Portuguese who were still

[27] Couto, *Da Ásia*, Dec. V, bk. 8, chap. 13, and *The Portuguese Expedition to Abyssinia*, p. 161.
[28] *The Portuguese Expedition to Abyssinia*, pp. 61–63.

able to walk retreated; his arm shattered, Cristóvão became separated from the main body of survivors, was captured, and quickly beheaded.

Granyé and the Turkish troops must have decided at this point that they had already killed most of the Portuguese and that the rest were disarmed and dispirited. Hence he allowed most of the thousand Turks to return to the Pasha of Zebid and retained only his usual contingent of 200 Turkish soldiers, probably thinking them sufficient to finish off Galadewos and his followers.[29]

He was mistaken. About 170 of the Portuguese had survived, and they soon located and joined Galadewos's army, which had been bivouacked in mountains to the south of the Portuguese. Galadewos appears even to have been on the way to rendezvous with Cristóvão's forces when news arrived of the young commander's defeat and death. (Diogo do Couto believed, and probably with reason, that it was Cristóvão's youthful inexperience and zeal which had betrayed him, and that he should have resisted the urge to do battle until the Negus's army and his own had thus united.[30])

The Portuguese ranks may have been decimated, but they burned for revenge on Granyé; four months later they achieved it. In February 1543, the two forces met in the war's decisive engagement. This time the Portuguese, though fewer, had plenty of horses and could charge their enemy more effectively than in the previous November. Granyé rode at the vanguard of his armies, and if Corrêa is to be believed, the Portuguese made straight for him. A certain João Galego is said to have pushed his way through the enemy ranks and fired a ball through Granyé's chest before himself being killed.[31] Shortly thereafter, the captain of Granyé's 200 Turks was slain, and the whole campaign against Galadewos collapsed overnight.

Ethiopia was to be sorely vexed by the Muslims in the future. In 1559 another Muslim chieftain, Nur-Ibn-Mudi, invaded Ethiopia's heartland and killed Galadewos, together with a few Portuguese followers; but this Moor never lived to enjoy his victory. On his way home, a fierce heathen hill tribe of Abyssinia, the Galla, ambushed his army and literally hacked it to pieces. Thereafter, the Gallan peoples had their own fling at conquering the Christians; but ultimately the Ethiopian monarchy cast them out

[29] *Ibid.*, p. 69.
[30] Couto, *Da Ásia*, Dec. V, bk. 8, chap. 13.
[31] Corrêa, *Lendas*, IV, p. 390.

without foreign help, probably because the Gallans themselves did not have access to any.

A Question of Orthodoxy

Having preserved "Prester John" from his Muslim enemies, the Portuguese then set about to save him from his own heresies. Rodrigo de Lima's chaplain, Father Francisco Álvares, had years before detected some irregularities in the Ethiopian mode of worship; but he was by nature a tolerant Christian. When his book describing Ethiopia and its customs appeared in 1540, however, it was read with great interest by the gimlet-eyed theologians of the Inquisition, who detected in his accounts of the Ethiopian church no less than forty-one grossly incorrect propositions, chief among them the Coptic Monophysite heresy that Christ's nature was wholly divine and not partly human, condemned by the Latin Church at the Council of Chalcedon in A.D. 453.[32] Moreover, after the return of the Rodrigo de Lima embassy, Portuguese theologians had examined the beliefs of the new Ethiopian ambassador sent along with Lima, one Saga Zaab, who was also a churchman, and found them tainted with similar errors.

Miguel de Castanhoso, the survivor and chronicler of Cristóvão's campaigns in 1541–43, had been allowed to leave Ethiopia by Galadewos and then was lucky enough to hail a lone Portuguese vessel at Massawa in February 1544. Upon his return to Portugal in 1545, he transmitted a letter to King João from the Ethiopian monarch which, among other things, complained of the physician João Bermudes's incompetence and irresponsibility as his *abuna*. This appeared to provide an ideal occasion for the orthodox Portuguese Catholics to correct the errors that had crept into the Ethiopian rite.

João III wasted little time in writing several letters — one to Galadewos suggesting that Bermudes be relieved of his *abunaship* and promising to supply Ethiopia with a more worthy candidate. Then, he sent dispatches to the Holy Father and to Ignatius Loyola in Rome, requesting that the Jesuits set matters straight in the Abyssinian church.

Communication in the sixteenth century was slow at best, but in this case it inexplicably took the Jesuits until 1555, or nine years after João III's request, to deliver a priest to Ethiopia, one Father Gonçalo Rod-

[32] Elaine Sanceau, *The Land of Prester John*, p. 169.

rigues, whose job it was to prepare the way for a new patriarch supplied by Rome. By then, Galadewos already had fetched a new *abuna* of his own from Alexandria, and he showed his annoyance with Father Rodrigues's untactful allegations that the Ethiopian church was doctrinally unsound. About all Father Rodrigues accomplished during his advance mission was to compose a pamphlet on Ethiopian doctrinal shortcomings and argue with some monks. In 1557, a new Jesuit bishop of Hierapolis, so consecrated solely to give his mission the greater authority, appeared with five more of his order. This man, André de Oviedo, was well received, if only because Galadewos was a cautious man and because he was never certain when he might again require help from Portugal. Besides, he loved to dispute theology with Oviedo and even developed a certain liking for him. When Galadewos was killed in 1559, his successor, Adames, treated the Portuguese coldly and at one point even imprisoned Oviedo. But soon rebellion flared among his subjects. This time the seaside governor, the *Bahr Nagas*, allied himself with the Turks, and Adames had to enlist the support of the remaining Portuguese once more. But it did him no good: he was killed fighting in 1562. His son Malac Segued, who had no liking for religious controversy, merely banned the Catholics from court and left them to shift for themselves elsewhere in the country. Oviedo lived an austere and saintly life. Before his death in 1577, he made scores of converts among individual Ethiopians, but neither he nor the fathers who followed, like the saintly Jesuit Pedro Pães, who became a great friend of the Negus, actually succeeded in uniting the Abyssinian church with Rome. Finally, in 1634, all Catholic priests were ordered expelled by the Negus Fasiladas, who then executed their closest associates among the Abyssinians and a few years later caught several more Jesuits secretly ministering to their converts and hanged them.

The story of the Portuguese association with Abyssinia has an unreal quality because it smacks more of chivalric romance than of motives people of today can understand. The mentality of sixteenth-century men was much more akin to that of medievals than of moderns and so they were capable of greater simplicity of mind than are people today. The Portuguese conquistadores made far better thieves — and also far better saints — than we.

CHAPTER 20

The Periphery: Indonesia

The Malay Archipelago came closest to resembling the world's treasury of spices and spicy woods. It produced, among others, nutmeg, mace, pepper, cloves, and sandalwood. If the Portuguese had possessed a hundred years of hindsight in 1500, they could have done no better than to bypass India and settle in Malaysia, as the Dutch did a century after da Gama's discovery.

The Portuguese were exceedingly interested in the area, and they demonstrated this interest as soon as Albuquerque had conquered Malacca. But their ability to exploit it was limited by the heavy commitments they had already made to the garrisons and *feitorias* in India. The result was that they had to forgo many of the potentially profitable areas — like Java — and concentrate on the commodities that paid the largest immediate dividends and on the relatively tiny areas in which they were produced. These largely consisted of the nutmeg and mace of the Banda Islands and the cloves of the Moluccas (two groups of islands rather close together) and only at the end of the century, the sandalwood of Solor and Timor, which lay en route to the other islands from Malacca.

The Portuguese crown tried to monopolize these products, as if they were from Africa or India, but it held only one real fortress, at Ternate in the Moluccas, and possessed only a part-time fleet. Moreover, its subjects smuggled spices flagrantly for their own profit. The chief officers, the captains-general of Ternate, were so far from Goa and Lisbon, and so eager to get rich in a single term of office, that they comported themselves like criminals rather than responsible administrators. João de Barros wrote that the Moluccan Islands were the "dwelling place of all evil and have no merit save for cloves. Because God made them we have to call them good — but so far as [cloves] are the stuff for which our people came here, they are the apple of all discord and bring down more curses than ever did gold."[1]

The Archipelago before Portugal's Advent

If superimposed upon a map of North America, the islands and seas of the Malay Archipelago would stretch from San Fancisco to Bermuda and from Buffalo, New York, to Key West.[2] The area they occupy on land and sea is about four million square miles, or approximately the equivalent of the continental United States and Alaska combined. In contrast, the heartland of Portuguese Asia, the Indian coast from Diu to Cochin, was but a single strip of shoreline extending over a distance comparable to the North America coast from Portland, Oregon, to Los Angeles. It is well to keep these comparisons firmly in mind, for they suggest that the handful of Portuguese men and ships who sailed past the Strait of Malacca could not have created any but the most isolated and local centers of power, and that these would be subject only to the loosest possible control either from Goa or Lisbon.

As one might expect from reading about the political disunity the Portuguese found in India, the indigenes of the Malay Archipelago were as ethnically and religiously diverse as the Indians, and like them had no feeling of nationality and no idea that they comprised a special geographic entity of any kind. It is significant that the term "Indonesia" was not applied to the area until 1850 — and this by an English scholar. About 170 languages were spoken there — often three or more on the same islet — and in all the greater land masses, highly civilized peoples shared living space with the most backward savages. Also, all the advanced peoples had experienced diverse cultural influences imported from areas thousands of miles distant: Java, Sumatra, Bali, and the ports of Borneo and Celebes had at different times and to various degrees, become Hindu, Buddhist, and, most recently, Muslim. All the civilized areas contained to some degree a mixture of the three elements.

[1] Barros, *Da Ásia*, Dec. III, bk. 4, chap. 2.
[2] We are indebted for this comparison to Professor B. H. M. Vlekke, in his *Nusantara*, a *History of Indonesia*, p. 1.

Among these regions, eastern Java was the cradle for the most sophisticated cultures, and from there the arts and political influences spread
outward — to nearby Bali first and then westerly toward Sumatra and the
Malay Peninsula. During most of the fifteenth century, for example, the
dominant cultural and political power in this region was the Hindu-
Buddhist kingdom of Majapahit, whose rulers had extended their
sovereignty over Java and Bali, and finally all the way to the Strait of
Malacca. Then Majapahit went into a rapid decline during the fifteenth
century, a process simultaneous with, but probably not closely related to, a
swift growth of Islam throughout Malaya and the archipelago.[3] In the
vanguard of this Muslim faith were the Gujarati who traded Indian textiles for Indonesian spices, and who made converts in the course of their
commercial travels on the monsoons.[4] Only much later were they followed by full-time missionaries. The nature of the conversions they effected, however, is somewhat open to question, at least so far as or-
thodoxy is concerned. For the canny Javanese and Sumatrese traders
seem to have been less moved by a genuine love of the Prophet than by
feelings that it was good business to adopt the religion of their customers
and that any new source of magic would increase their inner strength and
luck. Hence they did not cast out the old beliefs but merely blended the
new with them. Some of the oldest Muslim gravestones found in Java are
improbably adorned with a mixture of Arabic inscriptions and Shivaitic
symbols.[5]

The rapid spread of Islam in the course of the fifteenth century suggests
that the volume of trade among Indonesia, the Middle East, and India
had grown commensurately, and that traders from Gujarat were doing
business everywhere in the archipelago. This was no doubt partly because
the European market was burgeoning in this period, but it was also
because the Chinese traders had shifted their business from the Javanese
ports to Malacca in the same era and left their old trade to the Muslims as
well.[6]

[3] The original spread of Hinduism to Indonesia was no doubt via Indian merchants, but
some writers believe the Hindus had come to regard oceanic travel as religiously
contaminating and had left their routes in the hands of the Muslims — who in turn
began to propagate their own religion in the course of their travels. About the only
Hindu merchants still active in the textile-for-spice trade between India and Indonesia when the Portuguese arrived were the Klings from Coromandel.
[4] Pires, *Suma Oriental*, 1, p. 200.
[5] Vlekke, *Nusantara*, p. 86.
[6] See Meilink-Roelofsz, *Asian Trade*, pp. 26, 82; also Pires, *Suma Oriental*, 1, p. 179.

Before Vasco da Gama reached India in 1499, the Portuguese could hardly have discovered where cloves, nutmeg, and mace came from, because all these luxury commodities among the spices were funneled through Indian markets after transport from Indonesia. But once the Portuguese had arrived on the Indian scene, they surely learned the facts very quickly and decided that if the nutmeg, mace, and cloves on sale there fetched such an enormously higher price per hundredweight than pepper did, then it would be profitable to trace them directly to their places of origin. Albuquerque lost so little time in seeking the Moluccas after his conquest of Malacca that it is logical to assume the Portuguese had pieced together a fairly complete picture of Southeast Asia and its trading patterns even before he left Goa. Undoubtedly Muslim pilots and traders were the best source of information, among them those who had either guided Diogo Lopes de Sequeira to Malacca or talked to him after he had arrived there two years before.

It was in November 1511, only three months after Malacca had fallen, that Albuquerque dispatched an expedition of three ships to seek the Moluccas under his captain, António de Abreu, and with another officer, Francisco Serrão, as commander of one of the vessels. Significantly it not only bore Javanese pilots to show the way, but was preceded by a native merchant ship and a rich Malaccan Muslim, Nehoda Ismael, to make sure the Portuguese would be well received.[7] Abreu reached Amboina and the Banda Islands safely, filled his holds with cloves, nutmeg, and mace, and returned to Malacca. Serrão and eight of his men, however, became shipwrecked on the reefs of an island, probably Giliang, whose only inhabitants were sea turtles. Fortunately, the Portuguese wreckage was spied by a band of Malaysian pirates, who specialized in exploiting just such distress. Serrão and his sailors saw them coming and merely lay low, waiting for the cutthroats to come ashore. Then they sprang up behind them and commandeered their vessel to the Moluccas.[8]

The Portuguese captain and his men were stranded there for three years, and, having little else to occupy them, they began supporting the sultan of Ternate, the Kechil Boleif, against his local enemy, the sultan of Tidore. By 1514, when a new Portuguese expedition arrived, Serrão and a few of his companions had so ingratiated themselves with the sultan and had become so adapted to their new life-style that they chose to remain

[7] Barros, *Da Ásia*, Dec. III, bk. 5, chap. 6.
[8] See Humberto Leitão, *Os portugueses em Solor e Timor de 1515 a 1702*, pp. 39–41.

after their countrymen's ships had returned to Malacca. They were not likely to have craved the companionship of their countrymen, however; there were subsequent, albeit small Portuguese expeditions from Malacca to the Banda Islands and the Moluccas in 1516, 1517, 1518, and 1519.[9]

Spain versus Portugal: the Moluccas Question

Although Serrão stayed on after the Portuguese ships had sailed away, he sent dispatches and letters by them to his superiors and closest friends. One of his missives almost certainly went to an intimate of his, a youngish captain (aged about thirty) named Fernão de Magalhães, better known by the Hispanicized Magellanes or Magellan. By the time this communication reached him, Magellan had served seven or eight years in minor posts in the Orient and had been a participant in many of the noteworthy events there, including the capture of Malacca. More recently he had served King Manuel at Azemmour in North Africa.

It is not known how or when Magellan actually received his great inspiration that the Spice Islands, or Moluccas, were accessible from South America, nor is it known whether he spelled it out to Manuel or anybody connected with the Portuguese court or councils. But it is known that he was in disfavor, at least temporarily, because while in charge of dividing up the spoils from a victorious clash near Azemmour he had been accused by dissidents of keeping the lion's share for himself. Magellan had bitterly denied this.

Had he mentioned his idea to any of his Portuguese superiors, it is extremely likely that he would have incurred further disfavor — since the sole consequence would have been to call Spain's attention to something which could cause trouble for Portugal. For it will be recalled that the Tordesillas Treaty of 1494 drew an Atlantic line of demarcation at about 46° west latitude, but did not make explicit that the knife that slices through one side of an orange from stem to navel will emerge to halve it precisely on the opposite side, 180° away, or, in this instance, at 134° east latitude. This extension, however, was implicit, and Portugal had nothing to gain by putting the idea in Spanish heads that the eastern part of the Indonesian Archipelago and with it the Moluccas, might be within the Spanish hemisphere. Geographers and statesmen of the era were acutely

[9] Leitão, *Portugueses em Solor e Timor*, pp. 53–54.

conscious that there yet existed no precise method of determining longitude. Moreover, the vague and inaccurate maps based on Ptolemy placed the Golden Chersonese, or Malay Peninsula, too far to the east. The Portuguese always suspected darkly that the Spanish would seize on any pretext to claim the Moluccas for themselves — which in fact they did.[10]

Whatever the origins of Magellan's difficulty, he would have been compelled to take his idea to the Spanish because they alone stood to gain from it. In many ways, Magellan is the spiritual successor to Columbus. For not only was he similarly obliged by circumstances to take service with Spain, but his idea and its successful execution actually accomplished what Columbus had failed to — that is, finding Asia by sailing to the west. The only difference is that Portugal might have profited if it had sponsored Columbus, but it stood only to lose had it underwritten Magellan.

The magnificent voyage of Magellan, undertaken for Charles V, belongs to a history of Spain and Spanish expansion. Perhaps the only thing to be said about it from a Portuguese viewpoint is that the Portuguese cartographer Rui Faleiro lent his salesmanship and learning to the task of convincing the Spaniards that they should underwrite the journey; Magellan led it and his brother-in-law Duarte Barbosa, author of the first European description of the ports and lands of maritime Asia, went along. In addition, a Portuguese writer, the Visconte de Lagôa, has reckoned that some 40 of the approximately 240 crew members were Portuguese.[11] The outcome, however, was totally Spanish: both Charles of Spain's discovery and claim to the Philippines (named for his son) and his counterclaims to the Moluccas were based upon Magellan's achievement.

Enough has already been said about the interaction between the emperor and João III (in chapter 17) to suggest that, ultimately, the "Moluccas Question" was decided not so much on the basis of the practical limits of each monarchy's power as it was on the willingness of João III to accommodate himself to the emperor's bullying. All that remains to be described is the short-lived Luso-Spanish rivalry in the Indonesian Archipelago and the actual terms of the settlement between the two Iberian monarchies.

[10] See Almeida's orders of 6 April 1507(?) as reprinted in *Cartas de Albuquerque*, III, pp. 268–276; also reproduced in Artur Basilio de Sá, *Documentação para a história das missões do padroado português do Oriente; Insulíndia*, 1, pp. 3–15.

[11] Visconde de Lagôa, *Fernão de Magalhães (A sua vida e a sua viagem)*, I, 265–315.

Portuguese countermeasures began almost immediately after Magellan's departure from Spain, for King Manuel's informants in Seville sent word to Lisbon as soon as the fleet had hoisted anchor. Quickly, orders were sent via India that a Portuguese squadron should be dispatched to build a fortress in the Moluccas and prevent the renegade from proclaiming the area a Spanish possession. As events actually occurred, the Portuguese arrived and departed six months ahead of the Spanish who were long delayed in the Philippines and Borneo. But in June 1522 a Portuguese commander, António de Brito, had been sent out to fortify Ternate, and he heard there that Magellan's two surviving ships were still lurking in the vicinity, at Tidore. He succeeded in capturing one of them, the *Trinidad*, at Tidore before it could elude him.[12] The other ship, the *Victoria*, had already departed. It arrived in Spain that September, laden with enough cloves to allow Charles V a huge profit, enough to pay for the whole expedition several times over.

João III, when he heard late in September 1522 that the *Victoria* had evaded all of the traps his father had set for it and had arrived safely in Spain, sent a vehement protest to the emperor that Spaniards had poached deliberately on territory that had been discovered and occupied by Portugal. The emperor, always measured in his handling of others, did not hurl an angry counterprotest at João, which might have provoked an explosion. Instead, he proposed to join João in appointing a Luso-Spanish study commission that would arbitrate the matter and send two ships to the Malay Archipelago to fix the line in its proper position. He further proposed that the papacy should send a third vessel to arbitrate and, if the commission members could not agree, then the Holy See should impose its own conclusions.[13] The proposal sounded reasonable enough on the surface.

The snare, however, was that by suggesting that the matter be submitted to joint study and arbitration, Charles was in effect asking João to recognize that Spain had a serious claim. The pope at that time (December 1522) was Adrian VI, Charles's old tutor — which could hardly hurt the Spanish cause. And the very fact that half the commission, the

[12] His account survives and is reprinted in José Ramos Coelho (ed.), *Alguns documentos do Archivo Nacional da Torre do Tombo, acerca das navegações e conquistas portuguêzas*, pp. 464–476.

[13] *Ibid.*, p. 462.

Spanish side, were to be Charles's appointees, meant that they would certainly find in his favor and keep the combined body from making any decision until it gave the Spanish at least something of what they wanted.

João III eventually accepted the proposal — no doubt his double-marriage plans with the Hapsburgs, even then being arranged, had a good deal to do with his willingness — and the commission met on April 11, 1524, between Elvas and Badajoz in the middle of the bridge that crossed the Caia, the tiny stream dividing the two countries. Its deliberations fill exactly 100 solid pages of a modern folio-size volume of printed documents.[14] This is no wonder at all, since there were almost enough delegates, advisors, geographical experts, and hangers-on to comprise a small army; they included, among others, Sebastiano del Cano, the captain who brought the *Victoria* home, Sebastian Cabot, Fernando Colón, or Columbus, and Diogo Lopes de Sequeira.

The illustrious names of some of the commissioners, however, did not assure the production of illustrious arguments: before its inconclusive adjournment on May 31, the commission labored mightily without having decided what Atlantic base line should be selected as the proper prime from which to calculate the Pacific meridian in question — or even the length of a degree of longitude. Naturally the Spanish followed Ptolemy as closely as possible, for a smaller earth and consequently width of a degree meant a better chance of keeping the Moluccas in their hemisphere. The Portuguese, of course, held out for a larger earth and a longer degree.[15] To this kind of argument there was really no solution save with tools more sophisticated than those the age possessed. Ultimately, the Portuguese, who commanded much greater experience in navigation than the Spanish, were proved much more nearly right in their calculations. But the only practical benefit from the deliberations accrued to the Spanish: they gained a podium from which to publicize their ideas and bring pressure on Lisbon.

Nothing came of the emperor's suggestions that representatives of both parties should repair to the actual site of the disagreement or that the pope should send a delegation. Probably nothing would have been settled had an on-site inspection materialized, for neither celestial sightings nor

[14]*Cartas de Albuquerque*, IV, pp. 73–173.

[15]For an account of the negotiations, see Armando Cortesão's chapter "O descobrimento da Australia e a 'questão das Moluccas,'" pp. 129–150.

dead reckoning are useful in determining questions of longitude. The midstream meetings doubtlessly served Charles's purpose just as well. He had now created a bargaining position for himself, and he could not help but win something if he kept up the pressure, for example by sending out subsequent expeditions in Magellan's track as he did the following year, 1525.

Ultimately, as already recounted in chapter 17, he offered the Portuguese a six-year "lease" on his Moluccan pretensions for an exorbitant sum, and then, when they did not rise to the bait, he sold all his claims to them outright for the 350,000 gold-dobra price already discussed. Spain and Portugal signed a treaty to this effect at Zaragoza on April 22, 1529. Portugal now possessed unchallenged access to the Moluccas. The only portion of the treaty recognizing that Portugal might have been right in the matter all along was a proviso stating that if the Molucca Islands were proved clearly to lie within the Portuguese hemisphere, the emperor must return the payment, since his claims would have been shown to be invalid. Otherwise, the Portuguese held "all right, action, domain, propriety and possession, or semi-possession and all right to navigate, contract and trade in any manner desired [in the Moluccas.]" There then followed a formula designed to set the longitudinal meridian dividing Spanish and Portuguese hemispheres far enough to the east so that the Moluccas would lie within Lisbon's domain whether by Portuguese or Spanish computations.[16]

Thus ended, officially at least, the aftermath of Magellan's circumnavigation and the unfinished business of the Tordesillas Treaty. Unofficially, the Spanish continued to take liberties with the arrangement, both because they felt they had been deceived by the Portuguese and because, having discovered the Philippines, they felt they should keep the de facto right to occupy them.[17] Their real stumbling block was that no one had managed to sail back across the Pacific from Indonesia or the Philippines, and that most Spaniards had been captured by the Portuguese before returning home via the Cape of Good Hope. Until the monkish navigator Andrés de Urdaneta beat his way back across the Pacific in 1565, there could have been no serious Spanish ideas of Pacific settlement.

[16]*Alguns documentos*, pp. 500–502.

[17] A good deal of the sentiment on both sides seems to have ignored the question of where the meridians actually divided the world and merely emphasized the primacy of discovery. For example, see the testimony of Diogo Lopes de Sequeira in *GTT*, III, p. 20.

The Pattern of Exploitation

The initial passage of António de Abreu from Malacca to Amboina, as already described, had been led by a Malaccan merchant ship and aided by Malay pilots. They followed a course used by virtually all native shipping that plied between Malacca and spice islands to the east. In fact, this course was made so inevitable by the direction of the monsoons in the area and the shapes and locations of the islands, great and tiny alike, that any alternate routes were almost impossible — or at least not worth the roundaboutness and difficulty.

A glance at the simplest map of Southeast Asia will show that western Sumatra overlaps the Malay Peninsula so far to the northwest that any Moluccan-bound sailing vessel setting out from Malacca in August must necessarily travel southeast either through the Karimata Strait or more likely through a more southerly passage between Borneo and Sumatra and into the Java Sea. It would have been foolish to go any other way. For example, not only is the western shore of Sumatra a lea shore and dangerous for navigation, but it would require a 1200-mile detour from Malacca to pass around the north end of Sumatra and sail back on the west side to the same litilude, let alone the fact that half of this detour would have to be against the wind! Similarly, there was hardly much more reason for anyone's wishing to make the long detour around the north of Borneo, though it was done occasionally, and as early as 1526. Not only would the northerly extension of this large island necessitate an extreme detour similar to the detour around Sumatra, but the pattern of the winds would render such a passage very difficult. These blow down the South China Sea out of the northeast, then bend almost like a fishhook, and flow into the Java Sea from the west. Since the same pattern prevails in the Makassar Strait, there is no possible reason to detour around the north end of Celebes either.

In March or April, the return passage from the Moluccas to Malacca on the southeast monsoons is only possible if one takes the same passage in reverse, for it might then be easy enough to reach the northern extremes of Borneo or Celebes. But it would prove extremely laborious to sail back to Malacca without waiting for another season's reversal of winds, although on very long trading voyages, this was sometimes done. Even the preferred direct route was littered with dangers similar to those of the Red Sea; all the early authorities from Francisco Rodrigues and João de

Lisboa to the Frenchman François Pyrard de Laval speak of the navigational perils to be encountered in the Java Sea, where hundreds of isles and reefs blocked the way and made sailing at night impossible. Even by day, Pyrard says, one went nowhere, except with plumb line in hand.[18] Much of the time, vessels plying between Malacca and the Moluccas called at other points on the way — in Java, for example, and in the Banda Islands. In those instances, passages took more than a single seasonal cycle of the monsoon winds, and vessels were often twenty or more months at sea completing their round trips.

What these conditions, wind patterns, and hazards signified for Portuguese navigation between Malacca and the Moluccas is that for all practical purposes it was restricted to a single track prescribed by nature — and it only stands to reason that the sole Portuguese settlements of any consequence outside the Moluccas — in Amboina, in the Bandas, and much later in Solor and Timor — lay near the well-traveled route.

The sequence of Portuguese settlement and administration in Indonesia is revealing. For the first sixty years or so, there were only four *feitorias* and one fort in the whole archipelago: the fort, São João on Ternate, which together with its settlement resembled a European colonial town in architecture and plan, and three very much smaller unfortified or only lightly stockaded communities, one in Amboina and two in the Bandas on Lontar and Neira. All originated in the 1520s: for example, the fort in Ternate dated from the presence there first of Serrão and after 1521 of António de Brito, a newly appointed captain-general of the Moluccas; and the *feitoria* in Amboina had resulted from the solicitation in 1522 of the native population who sought Portuguese protection from nearby enemies.[19] From these bases in the years that followed, trade expanded among the islands while Portuguese administration did not.

There are several plausible explanations for this. One is that the states to the east of Sumatra, though nominally Muslim were mostly producers, not middlemen, and were less concerned with trade competition than with getting a good price.[20] Hence the Portuguese freely bought nutmeg

---

[18] François Pyrard de Laval, *The Voyage of François Pyrard de Laval*, 2, chap. 12.

[19] This is not to count a fort constructed in 1521 at Pacem, as the Portuguese called Pasummah, in Sumatra. It was forced to surrender to Atjeh the following year.

[20] Gujarat, for instance, was bound to be a competitor of the Portuguese because Portugal strove to displace its trade with an alternative system. This was also true of Atjeh and Johore, but it was not so with the states that merely grew or made something to trade or sell.

and mace in the Banda Islands (and even settled there), sandalwood in Timor, cloth in Java, and many other commodities like sulphur in Solor — without ever having to level their guns. Under those trading conditions, there could have been little motive for the Portuguese to employ their Malabar and Deccan strong-arm tactics, especially when they were so far from their own power bases. But whatever the cause and effect, the Portuguese behaved more like ordinary merchants in much of Indonesia than they did anywhere except in Bengal and the China Seas.

A second likely reason why the Portuguese did not enter more ambitiously into the establishment of *feitorias* and fortresses in Indonesia is that Malacca, upon which they would have had to depend for the supplies of manpower and munitions to undertake such enterprises, no doubt had little of these to spare because of its continual and debilitating fights with its neighbors, Atjeh across the strait in Sumatra and Johore, the state near Singapore which had been founded by the heirs of Sultan Mohamed of Malacca. In fact, this rivalry during the sixteenth century sometimes makes it difficult to tell whether the Portuguese were dominating the strait or the strait was bottling up the Portuguese. As Professor Meilink-Roelofsz points out, the basis of this hostility was competition for the same markets and involved quite the opposite of what has been spoken about in connection with the producers of spices and other commodities.[21] Johore and Atjeh both sought to displace Malacca as the warehouse and interchange point between East and South Asia. They frequently besieged it, the Portuguese retaliated with raids and expeditions against their capitals, and the two native principalities scrapped with one another. The strait never remained at peace for more than a few years.

In 1513, for instance, Atjeh's fleet challenged the Portuguese and was destroyed in battle; in 1517 Johore unsuccessfully besieged Malacca; and in 1525 did so again, whereupon captain-general Pero Mascarenhas of Malacca paid Johore a return visit. Then there were subsequent sieges of Malacca in 1550, 1567, and 1571, when Atjeh consorted with Bijapur to besiege the city and was beaten off. Thereafter, the area quieted down, but only until 1586. Matters would have been worse still for Portugal had not Johore and Atjeh been mutually at odds. The whole situation bore constant watching by the Portuguese, and they could hardly have used Malacca all this while as an effective arsenal for the supply of additional forts in Indonesia.

[21] Meilink-Roelofsz, *Asian Trade*, pp. 139–146.

In fact when the Portuguese finally did find some new outposts there — and this was not until after 1561 in the Solor group and after the 1580s in Timor — it was not the military who led the way, but the missionaries, whose presence and need for protection gradually involved officialdom and led to the appointments of captains and other officers and to the erection of strongholds.[22] That Portuguese economic patterns in Indonesia did not any longer hinge upon fortress building or actual possession is suggested by the fact that before a captain was appointed whose charge extended over Timor — in 1593 — the Portuguese had been trading there for white and yellow sandalwood for about fifty years; and it was not for another seventy years that they actually made up their minds to erect a permanent settlement and dominate the region.

In contrast to the Dutch seventeenth-century empire in Asia which made Java the very heart of its operations, the Portuguese had very little to do with this important island. Probably this was partly because they did not need its pepper and partly because they lacked the naval power to challenge its native principalities on the seas. For the most part they skirted all but the eastern end, where they used Hindu Panarukan as a way station between Malacca and the Moluccas. They also bought much of Malacca's rice supply from one Javanese region or another in the sixteenth century; they bought some pepper intermittently from Bantam; and toward the end of the era, they traded for some Javanese cloth to use in barter for sandalwood and spices elsewhere in the archipelago. Otherwise, aside from a few skirmishes at sea the Portuguese had with Japara in the second half of the sixteenth century, next to nothing is even known about their official relations with Java. It appears that, so far as Portugal was concerned, it merely lay along the route to the Spice Islands, where the important trading activity was concentrated on obtaining the cloves, mace, and nutmeg which were uniquely available there. For the Portuguese, these were the cargoes that brought the highest prices per hundredweight in Europe and that repaid best the limited amount of capital and manpower that could be devoted to Indonesia.

Of these prime luxury spices, most of the nutmeg and mace (products of the same plant) was obtained from the two Portuguese *feitorias* in the Bandas, and cloves came from all five of the Moluccan Islands, but principally from Ternate and Tidore. Amboina, located between the Moluccas

---

[22] Leitõ, *Os portugueses em Solor e Timor*, pp. 75–205.

and Bandas, raised cloves and nutmeg and mace, apparently not indigen-
ously but in response to a growing demand from foreign traders. In nearly
all instances, the exchange commodity was cotton cloth from India.

From the early years of the sixteenth century, the Portuguese intent in
the Spice Islands was to operate a tight crown monopoly where the *feitor*
alone handled all transactions at fixed prices (see chapter 18). This was
eventually liberalized to include some private trading after the royal ships
had been served — among other reasons, probably to provide an incentive for *casados* to move in from Malacca and India and help forestall
further Spanish attempts at occupation via the New World.[23] Under this
modification of 1535, private traders were required to register their
purchases with the *feitor*, who would thereupon claim a third part for the
crown at a fixed price, always lower than that of the free market. Finally,
the spices had to be transported to Malacca in royal ships, for which the
feitor charged an additional three-tenths of the private cargo. In 1537,
however, the crown tried to revert to the older strict monopoly system
save for some exceptions made in favor of Ternate's crown officials and a
small amount of personal trading by crew members of official ships. This,
of course, was an impossible move, and it was only in effect while the
rigidly honest captain-general António Galvão remained in office.
Thereafter, the rules were unenforceable: Gonçalo Pereira, the only other
captain who seriously attempted to do his duty, was murdered by his
subordinates. Even the captains-general and high officers of Malacca undertook illicit voyages, mostly to the Banda Islands, where they kept out
of sight of Ternate while they bought nutmeg, mace, and some cloves
(which had been smuggled over from the Moluccas).[24] And, finally, even
the original native trade in spices continued to thrive: the islands were so
numerous and the passages so myriad that it was all but impossible to
keep it down.

The crown's actual role in the trade after 1523 consisted of two large
ships per year which plied between Goa and Cochin and the Spice Islands. One was a cloves ship which went to Ternate, the other a nutmeg
and mace ship which put in at Lontar and Neira in the Bandas. The
concessions for both were granted to *fidalgos* in return for services or
favors, or to influential merchants. In both instances, the appointees
acted as their own *feitores* and were usually allowed to borrow a ship from

[23] Vitorino Magalhães Godinho, *L'Economie de l'empire portugais*, pp. 794–795.
[24] Magalhães Godinho, *L'economie de l'empire portugais*, p. 806.

the *Carreira*, and often even to outfit it on royal credit.[25] After all the expenses were paid — including government tonnage charges, the cost of provisioning the fortress at Ternate, and the royal share of the spices (about one-third) — the appointees were still assured of a profit of about 15,000 cruzados, while the government cleared about 20,000.[26] Those arrangements saved the crown a good deal of expense in outfitting the vessels, no doubt; but they also paid the grantee a fortune for his services. Probably, it was the best that could be expected, since, had the government done the outfitting and sailing, graft on the part of its officials would have taken the same amount or more.

The most conspicuous breakdown of royal authority in Indonesia appears not to have been so much economic as political. The Portuguese captains-general of the Moluccas were not eager to travel so far and to such a fabled region merely out of devotion to royal service, or to satisfy a romantic curiosity about tropical sunsets. They came to get rich, and their appointments lasted but three years. Typically, they arrived hungrily on the scene with all their relatives and hangers-on, and they worked frantically — but not for the king. Their activities give Luso-Moluccan relations a flavor all their own.

Portuguese Rule in the Spice Islands

Just as it seemed that only saints went to Ethiopia, it would appear that mostly sinners went to Amboina, Ternate, or the Banda group, the only spice-producing islands on which the Portuguese settled to any extent during most of the sixteenth century. Contemporaries who could assess the situation better than anyone today ascribed the prevailing wickedness on Ternate to "captains, who, being so far from authority's reach, pursue their own whims rather than your [Majesty's] service, because we have the kind here who do not follow their orders either in whole or in part, nor allow the other officials to follow theirs — not even their magistrates [to enforce] the ordinances."[27]

In addition to this penchant for wickedness on the part of the Portuguese, the comparatively primitive native inhabitants were not exactly

[25] See Sá, *Insulíndia*, IV, pp. 41–42 and 52–53. Also, Panduronga Pissurlencar, *Regimentos das fortalezas da India*, pp. 468–474.
[26] Magalhães Godinho, *L'economie de l'empire portugais*, p. 811.
[27] In a letter to João III from Ternate. See Sá, *Insulíndia*, I, 475.

innocent themselves. For one thing, they had a long history of headhunting which had only recently disappeared. For another, the Blessed Francis Xavier, who struggled hard and persistently but did not succeed in reforming either the captains or the indigenes during his sojourn there in 1545–46, observed of the Moluccans that "they are a people who poison those whom they don't like, and in this manner they kill one another aplenty."[28] He also complained that although the sultan of Ternate spoke Portuguese very well and felt himself honored to be a vassal of João III's, he didn't become Christian, not because he was especially devoted to the Muslim religion, but because "of not wanting to give up his carnal vices." The Amboinese he described as "very barbaric and full of treasons."[29]

None of these statements appear to have been far from wrong, because the sixteenth-century Asian chronicles and documents of the Portuguese occupation of Ternate and Amboina tell of little else than a steady succession of internecine rivalries, double crosses, murders, and even mass acts of criminal violence. In comparison, the story of Portuguese India, or even of nearby Timor and Solor in later times, seems almost tame. To begin with, about 1521 Francisco Serrão, the shipwrecked (1511) friend of Magellan who had become the bulwark of the Ternatean throne, was reported to have been poisoned along with his friend the sultan by the sultan of Tidore.[30]

The following year, António de Brito, the first *fidalgo* who formally took charge as captain-general of the Moluccas (previously mentioned as having seized the Spanish vessel *Trinidad* near Tidore), discovered how difficult it was to carry out his duties in the Moluccas. Not only was the fortress he was to build on Ternate delayed when scores of his men sickened and died, but his attempts to get rid of Tidore's ruler were all sabotaged by a powerful wife of the deceased sultan of Ternate who acted as regent for the boy king, the Kechil Daroez, and who happened to be the daughter of the sultan he sought to depose.[31] Then a few years later when his successor Garcia Henriques finally succeeded in making peace with Tidore, the Kechil Daroez became so enraged at not having been consulted that he himself ostentatiously made peace with his bitter rival. Henriques became so worried that the real aim of both rulers was to expel

[28] In a letter to his order in Rome, *Ibid.*, pp. 536–537.
[29] In an addition to a letter sent to his confreres in Europe, *Ibid.*, p. 498.
[30] In a letter by King Aby Hyat to João, in Sá, *Insulíndia*, I, 123.
[31] Barros, *Da Ásia*, Dec. III, bk. 5, chap. 7.

the Europeans that in 1526 he reversed himself by surprising Tidore and burning it.

As if the Portuguese were not frustrated enough by the Moluccans, within weeks after this fiasco, Martín Yanez, the surviving leader of the Spanish expedition sent in the wake of Magellan by Charles V, sailed into Tidore with some 300 men and was warmly welcomed when he let it be known that the Spaniards opposed Portugal. The Tidoreans swiftly helped him construct a fort, and when Henriques and the Portuguese attacked it, they were twice repulsed with losses.

As Henriques pondered what move to make next, the whole situation became further — and almost hopelessly — complicated by the arrival of his successor, Jorge de Menezes, who had been appointed by Lopo Vaz de Sampaio. It will be recalled from chapter 17 that the governorship of India underwent a disputed succession at this time between Pero Mascarenhas and Sampaio, when Mascarenhas, who had been appointed by the king, was unable to sail from Malacca to Goa in time. Captains in Asia were notoriously unwilling to give up their appointments under any circumstances, and this time a nasty struggle broke out between the two men which gave the Spaniards on Tidore a respite until 1528, or the year when Menezes finally sent Henriques to Malacca in chains. After one more repulse by the Spaniards, Menezes finally forced their surrender, whence some of them eventually returned to Spain via Goa.

Menezes, so far from any surveillance by his superiors, turned out to be a devil in the flesh. He poisoned the sultan of Ternate and beheaded the regent before he was arrested. His successor as captain of the Moluccas was one Gonçalo Pereira, who was murdered when, with honest intentions, he tried to investigate the smuggling of cloves, in which practically all his subordinates were implicated. His successors were no better than Jorge de Menezes, and after the next one, Tristão de Ataíde, arrived, he falsely imprisoned the Kechil Aeiro, on charges of killing Pereira, sent him in chains to Goa, raised a bastard to the throne,[32] and, in reward for his efforts, saw a league of the surrounding island peoples raised against

[32] The bastard, Kechil Pucaraga, became a convert to Christianity and reigned as King Manuel. At his early death, he donated his kingdom to João III and for good measure threw in Amboina for his spiritual mentor, the captain-general of the Moluccas, Jordão de Freitas. The arrangements were annuled, however, when João de Castro exonerated Kechil Aeiro as the rightful ruler of Ternate and returned him to the Moluccas with Bernardim de Sousa. Freitas was arrested. See Sá, *Insulíndia*, I, 550, and IV, 31–40; also *Gavetas*, IX (1971), pp. 305–306. Tristão de Ataíde's letter to João III also contains information about the Spanish incursion under Martín Yanez. See pp. 307–312.

Portugal. It was not until 1536 that a captain arrived who was both honest and successful. He was António Galvão, the son of the deceased ambassadorial appointee to Abyssinia. He was both a gentleman and a scholar (years later in Lisbon he wrote the celebrated *Tratado dos descobrimentos*), and he was able not only to break up the league against the Portuguese but to win the respect of the Moluccans by treating them justly and even founding a seminary for them. After the expiration of his term in 1538, however, Ternate never again received a worthy captain, and all the dismal patterns established before António Galvão's advent were repeated with few variations until in 1576 the Portuguese were expelled from Ternate.

In 1542, four years after Galvão's departure, incidentally, some 300 more Spaniards sailed into the Moluccas from the New World, this time under Captain Ruy Lopes de Villalobos. Immediately, they headed for Tidore and fortified themselves. For almost three years they resisted all attempts to capture them made by two Portuguese officers, one of whom, Jordão de Freitas, was even obliged to sign an agreement with Villalobos in 1545 permitting him temporary occupation of his island stronghold. But by the end of that year, sickness and privation finally caught up with the Spaniards and they surrendered to the next captain-general, Bernardim de Sousa, on the option either of taking service with Portugal or of being transported — eventually — back to Europe.[33] For modern readers, the real significance of the incursion is that it provides another link between Magellan's original expedition, its visit to the Moluccas, and the actual Spanish settlement in the Philippines in 1571. It shows that in spite of King João's huge payment in 1529, the Spanish were unconvinced that they had forgone all claims in the Pacific and that they intended to pursue them.

This third Spanish incursion may have created some problems for the Portuguese, but these were minor beside the corrupt and irresponsible leadership that continued to plague them in the Moluccas.

The great Portuguese Asian governor João de Castro had exonerated and sent home (with the outcoming captain, Bernardim de Sousa) Sultan

[33] Couto, *Da Ásia*, Dec. V, bk. 8, chap. 10; bk. 9, chap. 6; and bk. 10, chap. 5, is the major source for these details, but see also the *História das Ilhas de Maluco escripta no anno de 1561*, as reprinted in Sá, *Insulíndia*, III, 193–218. There is also another work on the subject which may have been written by António Galvão himself. It is edited by Hubert M. Jacobs, S. J. as: *A Treatise on the Moluccas (c. 1544); Probably the Preliminary Version of António Galvão's lost História das Moluccas*. See especially pp. 317–326.

Kechil Aeiro, whom Captain Tristão de Ataíde had falsely accused of murder and shipped to India, and for a few years afterward there were at least no sensational injustices in Ternate. But in 1565, the new captain, a repulsive character named Duarte de Deça (or Eça), not only had imprisoned the sultan and his family unjustly, but tried to poison them as well. Finally, his own men became so fed up with his tactics that, in face of a new native uprising, they arrested him.[34]

Duarte de Deça, however, was only an amateur and a bungler as an evildoer. Unfortunately for the Portuguese and the Ternateans, a really vicious commander came on the scene in 1567 in the person of Diogo Lopes de Mesquita, a *fidalgo* of the king's household and a scoundrel whom Couto alone has exposed.[35] This man contrived to increase the Ternatean sultan's personal tribute in cloves until it amounted virtually to the whole supply, except for that share required by the royal Portuguese monopoly; then he mulcted it all for himself. When the Kechil Aeiro, an amiable man completely loyal to the Portuguese, became angry in 1568, Mesquita apologized elaborately and was forgiven. Then, when the Kechil's guard was down, he had him stabbed to death. Not even the smallest cruelty escaped this captain-general. The sultan's family desired to give the body a decent burial; Mesquita had it cut in pieces and thrown into the sea.[36]

Nobody could blame the new sultan, the Kechil Babullah, for swearing to exact vengeance on the murderers of his father. He called upon his people and his allies to wage a war and throw the Portuguese out of the Moluccas. He could hardly have picked a better time — or a worse one for the Portuguese — for in 1570 and thereafter, the allied assault on Goa, Chaul, and Malacca (see chapter 17) not only kept the viceroy from sending adequate relief but left Portuguese India considerably weakened. Other events worked against them, too.

At the same time that the Portuguese were wearing out their welcome on Ternate, a different upheaval against the Portuguese took place on Amboina and created a serious diversion from the affairs of Ternate, although in this instance, the provocation offered the natives by the Por-

[34] Couto, *Da Ásia*, Dec. VII, bk. 4, chap. 7 and bk. 5, chap. 2. When he was returned to Portugal from Goa, however, he went unpunished.

[35] The chronicler António Bocarro, in his manuscript *História geral de Maluco*, mentions that Mesquita ordered the king's death, but says he doesn't know why he did it. See Sá, *Insulíndia*, IV, 210.

[36] Couto, *Da Ásia*, Dec. VIII, chap. 26.

tuguese does not appear to have been of the same magnitude. In fact, one readily recalls Xavier's observation made twenty-one years before that the Amboinese were "barbaric and full of treasons." During a banquet given in appreciation for a successful joint victory, the supposedly Christian (a result of Xavier's own preaching) Amboinese took umbrage at a drunken Portuguese who tried to seduce the beautiful young daughter of Chieftain Jemelio or Genullio. When Jemelio came on the scene to protest, the drunk struck him. That was all the Amboinese needed. They expelled the Portuguese, who protested that the rudeness was only of one man, not of the whole group. The Amboinese, however, were barely getting underway. Seething, they attacked a nearby Christian people still friendly to the Portuguese, and merely because they remained steadfast, they not only tortured and put them to death, but were even said to have reverted to cannibalism.[37]

All this was too much for the Portuguese to handle at once. The arrival at Amboina of the experienced naval commander Gonçalo Pereira Marramaque with reinforcements soon quelled the trouble and restored the Portuguese garrison. But by the time Marramaque had returned order to Amboina, he no longer had the strength to squelch Babullah's army fighting the Portuguese on Ternate. Seven years later, in 1575, the army had closed in on the Portuguese fortress itself and laid it under siege. Marramaque was expected again; but this time news arrived instead that all his ships had gone down in a storm.

Sultan Babullah then pressed home his attack, a native ally on whose help the Portuguese had counted deserted them, and the Jesuits urged surrender; Ternate capitulated in 1576.[38] Although the sultan of Tidore, always jealous of Ternate and fearful of its power, invited them to fortify Tidore in 1578, the Portuguese were never as well situated as on Ternate. When the Dutch arrived at the turn of the century, the natives of the Moluccas and of Amboina all willingly lent a hand to expel them.

[37] See Couto, *Da Ásia*, Dec. VIII, chap. 25; also compare Sá, *Insulíndia*, IV, 197–202.
[38] For the fall of S. João de Ternate, see Fr. Francisco de Sousa, S. J., *Oriente conquistado a Jesu Christo*, II, 327–330.

CHAPTER 21

The Periphery: China and Japan

Each time the Portuguese turned a corner of the great Eurasian land mass, they seem to have changed their style completely. In the Atlantic they were explorers, in the Indian Ocean they were conquerors, and in the Far East they were businessmen.

Another less epigrammatic way of expressing the reality would be to say that the little country first aimed at India in its outreach from Europe and that once it achieved Calicut, it committed all its resources to southwestern India. Then, with the characteristic restlessness of the age, even before settling down, it began the whole process over again by penetrating the Far East.

This time, the few adventurers who had traveled halfway around the globe from Portugal were not followed by a wave of national enterprise and conquest directed from Lisbon or Goa. But, just as this was hardly possible over such enormous distances, oddly enough it also proved unnecessary. Unlike the intense jealousies the Portuguese had aroused in India as interlopers, they encountered a fortuitous and untapped market for trade between China and Japan — and despite their initial mistakes, they evolved a new style of empire and moved to take advantage of it. They founded a new city on Chinese soil, a new station in Nagasaki, and then they made up for their lack of missionary success in India by converting perhaps 150,000 people to Christianity in Japan.

China

When Vasco da Gama's fleet first arrived in Calicut, crew members were told by the natives that about eighty years before some white sailors who resembled the Portuguese had visited their city almost annually for more than a generation. They had worn armor, the Indians said, and came in great vessels with four masts. But when the Portuguese pressed them for the nationality of the former visitors, the Calicutians were at a loss — whereupon the Portuguese imagined that they had been Slavs or Germans.[1] At the time, of course, they could hardly have guessed that the sailors of old had been none other than the Chinese of Admiral Cheng Ho.[2]

Within eight years, however, the Portuguese had expanded their knowledge of the Orient until not only did King Manuel dispatch Diogo Lopes de Sequeira to Malacca in 1508, but in his *regimento* he asked him to be on the lookout for the Chinese and learn anything he could about them.[3] The correct identification of Malacca as a place where one could expect to meet Chinese suggests that the Portuguese had been conversing with Gujarati sailors, for indeed the whole reason that those Indian merchants went to Malacca in the first place was to trade spices and cloves with their Chinese counterparts. And, of course, one of the first sights that both Sequeira and Albuquerque saw when they sailed into Malacca's roads were junks from Canton. It will also be recalled that the Chinese were immediately friendly and even lent the Portuguese the junk Albuquerque and António de Abreu had used to capture Malacca's famous bridge.[4]

Albuquerque had dispatched Abreu to explore the Moluccas in 1511, but he does not seem to have initiated a similar expedition to China. Instead, it appears to have been his nephew Jorge de Albuquerque, then captain of Malacca, who actually sent (or perhaps collaborated in sending) what must have been the first European maritime expedition to the Middle Kingdom in 1514. Only Barros, among the chroniclers, mentions it; but it is alluded to by two Italian contemporaries in Portuguese service.

[1] Ravenstein, *Journal of First Voyage of Vasco da Gama*, p. 13.
[2] The first Portuguese translation of *The Book of Marco Polo* was not published until 1502, and even then it was not until a century later, in 1607, that the Jesuit Bento de Gois crossed over the Himalayas and demonstrated that Polo's Cathay and China were identical.
[3] *Cartas de Albuquerque*, II, p. 416.
[4] See chapter 16.

All that is known of the mission is that Jorge Álvares, the ambassador, left a *padrão* at Lintin Island in the Pearl River estuary between Canton and modern Hong Kong, where his son died and where he himself was later buried.[5] The Italians, who have both left accounts, made it seem as if Álvares brought trading goods as well as presents for the emperor along with him, and they indicate that although the Chinese never allowed him to land on the mainland, he and his party disposed of their goods at a tidy increase in value and discovered that "there is as great a profit in taking spices to China as to Portugal."[6]

The reasons for this new commercial opportunity were opaque to the Portuguese, for they then knew nothing at all about the Middle Kingdom. However, what they did not know of China hurt as well as helped them.

In the first place, the commercial possibilities would hardly have been so rich as they were had not the Chinese merchant classes previously developed an extensive foreign-trading network between the ninth and the fifteenth centuries and then been forced by their government to reverse themselves and restrict their dealings in Southeast Asia to Malacca. This seems to have made room for Portuguese enterprise by reducing the volume of trade considerably and leaving an unfulfilled demand for additional products, especially pepper and other spices, ivory, and sandalwood. But on the other hand, the same xenophobia and bureaucratic highhandedness which had been a major factor in banning the Chinese from foreign trade and travel were also capable of making life difficult for the Portuguese and making them pay dearly for their ignorance of imperial protocol.

It is likely that a variety of factors combined to shut down most of the direct Chinese trade with Java and India before the second quarter of the fifteenth century. Most were political, but there appear to have been some purely competitive aspects as well, such as the slowness of the Chinese junks which were not nearly so efficient as the smaller and faster (but far flimsier) Muslim vessels based on Arab designs.[7] The most important piece in the Chinese puzzle seems to have been a Ming policy born of a combined dislike of foreigners and a desire to stop the extensive piracy along China's southeast coastline by the Japanese.[8] This policy was effec-

---

[5] In Barros, *Da Ásia*, Dec. III, bk. 6, chap. 2.
[6] Quoted in T'ien-tse Chang, *Sino-Portuguese Trade from 1514 to 1644*, pp. 36–37.
[7] Meilink-Roelofsz, *Asian Trade*, pp. 74–75.
[8] And, almost equally important, to keep the Chinese from joining them in the illegal

tive but commercially disastrous: it forbade Chinese nationals from carrying on any navigation save that along their own coastline.[9] Only Malacca appears to have been an exception — perhaps because it was a state under China's suzerainty and because it did much to eliminate piracy in its own region.[10] But the net effect was to force many traders out of business or into exile.

The Troubled Embassy of Tomé Pires

This Chinese loss of trade was the Portuguese gain; but as the Europeans soon discovered, dealing with the Chinese without knowledge of their habits could lead to unpleasant consequences. In 1521, when they became deeply offended, it took years before they would allow the Portuguese to deal with them again, at least openly. In 1515, King Manuel sent three captains along in the retinue of Lopo Soares de Albergaria, who were to proceed to China and negotiate trading arrangements.[11] In 1516, after arriving in Goa, Albergaria picked one of the captains, Fernão Peres de Andrade, to command the new expedition and Jorge Álvares, the original emissary, to captain one of its seven ships. Andrade, after many delays, reached a base of the coastal guards in the mouth of the Pearl River in 1517 and after a long wait, received a de facto, but not wholly official, permission to proceed to Canton and obtained some pilots to guide him. Once there, he fired a booming salute — which nettled his hosts, who believed guns should be discharged only in anger. Andrade, however, apologized, was somewhat grudgingly forgiven, and then got down to the business of making a commercial pact, the first between China and a western power.

So far things were under control, and Andrade even went so far as to obtain Chinese leave to send an ambassador to Peking — the same Tomé Pires who a few years before had written a useful description of the Orient as the Portuguese found it about 1513, the *Suma Oriental*. Pires, however, was to become the innocent victim of indiscretions on the part of Fernão Peres de Andrade's brother Simão.

From the beginning Tomé Pires faced maddening delays. Fernão Peres

---

pursuit. See Chang, *Sino-Portuguese Trade*, p. 95; also see C. R. Boxer (ed.), *South China in the Sixteenth Century*, p. xxiv.

[9] Chang, *Sino-Portuguese Trade*, pp. 94–95.

[10] Meilink-Roelofsz, *Asian Trade*, p. 75.

[11] Barros, *Da Ásia*, Dec. III, bk. 7, chap. 6.

de Andrade disposed of his cargoes at handsome profits while one of his captains, Jorge Mascarenhas, sailed north and traded equally profitably in what must have been the Bay of Amoy.[12] Then both Peres de Andrade and Mascarenhas returned to Malacca. However, Tomé Pires, who remained in Canton, did not receive permission from the imperial court to depart for Peking until 1520.

By this time, Simão Peres de Andrade had made his disastrous appearance at Tun-Men in the Pearl River estuary, where he arrived in the summer of 1519. This *fidalgo* was self-seeking and arrogant, unlike his brother who was considerate and tactful, and he soon gave the xenophobes among the mandarin ruling classes all the pretext they needed to crack down heavily upon the fo-lang-chi[13] or "Franks" — as the Portuguese were called. If one can imagine that the Chinese had still not forgiven Fernão Peres for his semiofficial entry or his salute, it is easy to see that his brother Simão had it in his power to spoil Sino-Portuguese relations for decades. Without receiving permission, he ordered that a fort be built on Tun-Men and impressed Chinese into labor gangs to do the work; he built a gallows and hanged a sailor; and he forcibly hindered Siamese, Cambodian and other foreign traders from landing their cargoes until the Portuguese had sold theirs. Finally, he even appears to have bought some Chinese children offered to him as slaves.[14] This kind of conduct might have been appropriate for the Swahili or even the Malabar Coast; but the Chinese had very well-developed ideas of their own sovereignty and saw Andrade's conduct as massive lèse majesté.

Inappropriately, the whole weight of the imperial wrath fell upon Tomé Pires, for when he reached Peking, he was denied an audience with the emperor. Instead, charges were brought against him which specified not only Simão Peres de Andrade's misconduct, but Fernão Peres de Andrade's illegal entry and the cannon salute.[15] It also appears that some misunderstanding arose over King Manuel's letter, which addressed the emperor as an equal and not as a superior. And matters were scarcely aided by the sudden death in April 1521 of the Emperor Wu-tsung, who, more charitably than his courtiers, attributed most of the foreigners' failings to ignorance.[16] Rebuffed, Pires and his party returned to Canton in

---

[12] Boxer, *South China*, p. xx.

[13] Or, more properly, the "fo-lang-chi," the Chinese ear's rendition of the Arab term, "Frangue" which the Muslims had applied to Europeans from the time of the crusades.

[14] Chang, *Sino-Portuguese Trade*, pp. ·97–98.

[15] *Ibid.*, pp. 50–51.

[16] The Portuguese in Canton also failed to realize that Chinese etiquette required a

September 1521, where they were arrested. This was because in that same month an order had arrived from the imperial court that all Portuguese must leave China; when those trading at Canton and Tun-Men had replied casually that they had not yet finished their business, all Europeans ashore were arrested and their ships on the Pearl River were hemmed in by junks.[17] But the trapped Portuguese vessels had suddenly fought their way to safety and escaped.

Pires and his embassy were held hostage, apparently with the idea that this would not only prevent a repetition of Portuguese misconduct but would reinforce the chances of the Chinese protectee, the sultan of Malacca, to get his capital back. Little did the Chinese know that the Portuguese did not even ransom the Infante Fernando in 1437 by returning Ceuta. Like that unfortunate prince, Pires was never delivered from his bondage.

In 1522 matters worsened still more for Ambassador Pires and his men, who were, if only briefly, put into chains and suffered the confiscation of their goods, perhaps, as Chinese historian T'ien-tse Chang speculated, in retaliation for a sharp naval engagement fought between the imperial fleet and a Portuguese squadron under Martim Afonso de Mello Coutinho.[18] This captain had come from Portugal via Cochin on something of a diplomatic mission of his own, charged by King Manuel (not long before that monarch's death in 1521) with making a treaty of friendship with the emperor and obtaining permission to build a fortress on Tun-Men, Shang-ch'uan or elsewhere. Coutinho heard of the troubles with China in Malacca, but he decided to press on anyway in hopes both of trading and of smoothing things over.

Instead, he ended up in a fierce battle in which two of six Portuguese ships were lost and forty-two Portuguese sailors were captured. Among these about half were executed out of hand. Thereafter, both sides feared a renewal of the fighting, and the Chinese not only built up their navy, but they closed the port of Canton completely. Pires appears to have died in prison by 1524.[19]

Chang also suggests, with some plausibility, that Portuguese behavior

cessation of trade during a period of imperial mourning like the one that followed Wu-tsung's death.

[17] Chang, *Sino-Portuguese Trade*, pp. 54–55; cf. Barros, *Da Ásia*, Dec. III, bk. 6, chap. 2.

[18] Chang, *Sino-Portuguese Trade*, p. 56.

[19] Armando Cortesão, in his introduction to his edition of the *Suma Oriental*, claims he lived in exile until 1540, but see Boxer's note in *South China*, p. xxi.

between 1517 and 1522 at Tun-Men and the city of Canton was strongly similar to that preceding the capture of Goa and Malacca, and he also suggests that the Portuguese meant to seize Canton just as they had fallen upon these other cities.[20] This idea did cross the mind of Christovão Vieira, one of the captives of the Pires mission, in 1527, but it is not likely that it would have gone beyond the talking stage in Lisbon or Goa.[21] When one considers that post-Albuquerquian *Ásia Portuguesa* could not even carry Diu by storm — and it was close to Goa — it seems unlikely they could ever so delude themselves. Malacca appears to have been about the limit of either their military capabilities or their ambitions for anything but trade. More likely, they acted as they did because they knew little of China's immense size and power, and because the king and governors had too little control over some of their rapacious and arrogant subordinates, who were thousands of miles from any kind of supervision. A character like Simão Peres de Andrade differs little from one like Diogo de Mesquita on Ternate: both were lawless Renaissance noblemen who only sought to exercise arbitrary power and enrich themselves in any way possible. One can only observe that China received from the Portuguese *fidalgos* about the same treatment Ternate had — the only difference being that Ternate had far less to say about it.[22]

The Smuggling Persists

China was too huge to be governed effectively from Peking, justs as Portugal's empire was too far-flung to be administered effectively from Lisbon. The comparison is valid enough, for in China as in the Portuguese empire, the provincial viceroys acknowledged full enough obedience to their supreme ruler. But in practice they were too far away to consult him on every decision — besides which they had private concerns of their own, either regional or personal in nature, which led them on divergent paths.[23] In the case of the Cantonese governors and those of China's other port provinces, much of their income, both public and private, came from

[20] Chang, *Sino-Portuguese Trade*, pp. 63–68.

[21] See Donald F. Lach, *Asia in the Making of Europe*, I, 735–737.

[22] It is only fair to point out that from the beginning the crown always enjoined its captains and ambassadors to conduct themselves with the utmost tact and courtesy.

[23] China was clearly beginning to decline during the Ming Dynasty, but whether this condition helps explain how and why the Portuguese were received or treated is doubtful. Rather, it seems profitable to choose decentralization as the simplest explanation for things as they were.

duties and tolls levied upon import and export goods. Hence the imperial judgment against foreign trade meant money out of their treasuries, as well as a general depression of their bourgeois gentry's wealth. This class had largely made its money from maritime commerce, and it was not about to see itself ruined.

For a time Canton was too hot a place for the Portuguese to risk being seen in — even after 1530 when its port was again opened to shipping — because the officialdom there could not ignore a specific imperial ban against the fo-lang-chi. But in China's other major ports, Changchou, Chüan-chu, and Ningpo in Fukien and Chekiang provinces, the Portuguese merely remained below deck and hired Malays or Siamese to front for them, and Chinese customs never manifested undue curiosity so long as dues were paid.

It is interesting in this connection that almost the only high official who took seriously the imperial ban on trading by the Portuguese was obliged to pay for his zeal with his life. The new viceroy of Fukien Province, Chu Wan, sent coast guard ships out to look for Japanese buccaneers in 1548–49. These eluded him, but he captured two contraband-laden Portuguese junks instead and imprisoned their (mostly Asiatic) crews, executing many of them summarily. When the wealthy trading families in Fukien learned of this, families whose incomes depended upon the continuation of smuggling, they contrived to get Chu Wan arrested and tried for his life on the grounds that he had executed the foreigners without the emperor's express consent. Almost everybody knew that the real reason for the trial was Chu Wan's vigorous maritime law enforcement; and so, when the judgement went against him (he committed suicide in prison ahead of the executioner) and when the Portuguese still alive were given token sentences, the message was not missed by other provincial officials.[24] Thereafter, they failed to distinguish Portuguese fo-lang-chi from Malaccan Malays. The Portuguese, however, steered shy of Fukien just in case and again turned their interests to the Canton area.

The Haven at Macau

For trading operations on any major scale in China, the Portuguese needed a place to store and display their wares; and for some years they

[24] See Boxer, *South China*, pp. xxviii–xxxi, and Chang, *Sino-Portuguese Trade*, pp. 82–84.

had to be content with temporary shacks and tents on coastal islands such as Shang-Ch'uan and Lang-pai-kao, both off the Pearl River mouth and about thirty miles apart. But this expedient was unsatisfactory and precarious for the Portuguese merchants even though it was favored by the Chinese bureaucrats. It was during this interim period, incidentally, that the Jesuit Father Francisco Xavier sought to enter China, and it was on Shang-Ch'uan Island (or "São João") that he died of fever in 1552. The Portuguese continued to press the Chinese for a trading center all their own, and eventually they were heeded. Five years later they were allowed to occupy a new and more permanent site near their original landing place at Lintin Island. In Chinese this was usually known as Ao-Men (meaning "Gate of the Bay"), but the Portuguese preferred A-ma-ngao (meaning "Bay of the goddess Ama"), perhaps because its final vowels "ao" sounded familiar to their ears and because their own geographical nomenclature was so studded with holy names. The place, to all intents, soon became "Macao" — or more piously and officially Povoação do Nome de Deus na China, or "Community in the Name of God in China."

There is some mystery surrounding the original arrangements made between the Portuguese and the Chinese which allowed permanent occupation of the site. The Portuguese of later times liked to claim that the permission was granted as a result of their having driven away pirates who occupied the place — hence that they had rendered a service in return. The Portuguese colonial historian José M. Braga argues this, and it may actually be true; but his evidence is more traditional than contemporaneous.[25] Moreover, it is hard to imagine that the Chinese Wei, or military guards, really depended upon a handful of Portuguese from the other side of the globe to expel a few hundred corsairs from a small piece of land. It is much more probable that because Portuguese trade was so urgently desired by the Cantonese government and the merchant community alike, China had finally decided simply to give the Portuguese a permanent place they could use as a trading station. Obviously, both the administration and the traders could expect to profit most if the fo-lang-chi were happily situated and in a position to expand their operations, attract their friends, and thus do more business than ever.

That pure economics and not Portuguese police service was at the basis of the bargain is suggested by a surviving letter of Leonel de Sousa, then

[25] José Maria Braga, The Western Pioneers and Their Discovery of Macao, pp. 102–139.

captain-major of the Japan voyage,[26] who seems to have treated with Cantonese officials and naval officers about this time to put Luso-Chinese trade on a firmer footing. Sousa's letter was written in January 1555 — only months after he probably accomplished this — and although it is specific enough about some things, it makes no mention of any Portuguese "rights" accorded by the Chinese for any reason. The only real stipulations were in the form of Portuguese promises to pay all duties to the viceroy's custom agents and not to fortify themselves.[27]

By 1560, a simple government had been formed, consisting of a *capitão da terra*, or captain, and an *ouvidor*, or judge, both of whom were subordinate to the annually appointed *capitão-mór da viagem do Japão*, or captain-major of the Japan voyage, who spent some months in Macao each year en route to and from Japan and Malacca. A generation later, by 1583 or 1585, Macao achieved full city status when these officials were joined to a *senado da câmara* with aldermen and other officials. It did not receive a full-time *capitão geral*, or captain-general, until the seventeenth century; throughout the sixteenth, the captain-major of the Japan voyage continued to rule the city, if only during the period of his stay.[28]

Macao's relationship with the Chinese authorities was peculiar. These officials erected a gate across the isthmus connecting Macao with the mainland (the so-called Porta do Cêrco) upon which they placed the admonitory and more than faintly patronizing inscription "Dread Our Greatness and Respect Our Virtue."[29] Through it the Chinese passed the foodstuffs needed by the inhabitants, but at other times they sealed it with strips of paper and allowed inside China proper only those very few Portuguese who had express authorizations. Of the Portuguese officials, the only one in contact with the Chinese provincial authorities was the *procurador* of the *câmara*. The Chinese in turn were represented in Macao only by customs officers. In other respects, until 1582, the Chinese higher authorities took no official cognizance of Portuguese Macao's exist-

[26] See the section on Japan for this title.

[27] This is reprinted in *Gavetas*, I, 909–915; also see the narrative of Gaspar da Cruz in Boxer, *South China*, p. 190. See also Boxer's introductory essay in the same volume, pp. xxxv–xxxvii.

[28] See A. Ljungstadt, *An Historical Sketch of the Portuguese Settlements in China. A Supplementary Chapter Entitled Description of the City of Canton*, pp. 30–46. See also Boxer, *Fidalgos in the Far East*, pp. 8–11. The *senado da câmara* was the Portuguese version of the Iberian municipal council, in Spain called the *ayuntamiento* and in the Spanish colonies the *cabildo*. See chapter 18.

[29] Chang, *Sino-Portuguese Trade*, p. 98.

ence; for almost a decade at its beginning, in fact, the Portuguese mission bearing tribute was turned back at the Porta do Cêrco.

But in 1582, the new Chinese viceroy of the provinces of Canton and Kwangsi abruptly summoned Macao's chief officials. Perhaps remembering the fate of Tomé Pires sixty years earlier, the captain was afraid to go. Instead, the elderly judge and an Italian Jesuit accepted the call and set out for the capital at Shangking-fu with 4,000 cruzados worth of presents. The viceroy raged at the old judge and the Jesuit about the Portuguese gall in conducting a government not in accordance with the laws of China. He is even said to have threatened to break up the colony and expel the Portuguese from Macao. But the next day his attitude had changed radically and he intoned: "The foreigners, subject to the laws of the Empire, may continue to inhabit Macao."[30] In precedent-minded imperial China, this was tantamount to a binding contract. Official recognition had thus been granted, and thereafter there was little doubt about Portuguese status. As for the viceroy's about-face in the matter, it appears this represented another old mandarin tradition as well. For by then he had had time to inspect the velvets, crystals, mirrors, and mountains of other fine European goods which had been delivered to him.

Trade was, after all, the raison d'être for the whole colony in the first place, and it might have been reasoned by the Chinese that the Portuguese were of little use unless they brought benefit, individual and collective, to their hosts. No one knows the exact amount of income that accrued to the regional government via Macao, but the taxes from a market subsequently opened to foreign trade in Changchow brought in enough tax money to help support a provincial army.[31] In addition, Professor Boxer quotes the captain-major of the Japan voyage in 1582 — the very year of the visit to the Chinese viceroy — as saying that Goa-bound ships from Macao paid over 50,000 ducats customs duty in their transit through Malacca alone.[32]

Macao was founded — at least officially — in 1557. Yet within six years some 900 Portuguese lived there, excluding Malaccans and Malays, Indians, Japanese, and Africans, many of them slaves and servants.[33] Probably the city owed its rapid growth to the migration en masse of temporary

[30] Ljungstadt, *Historical Sketch of Macao*, p. 79.
[31] Chang, *Sino-Portuguese Trade*, p. 95.
[32] Boxer, *Fidalgos in the Far East*, p. 40.
[33] Chang, *Sino-Portuguese Trade*, p. 97.

residents from Lampacao and Changchun islands — in addition to which the tale of the new and more stable trading conditions in China must have attracted new settlers and business partners from Goa, Malacca, and even Ternate.

In many ways, burgeoning Macao was unique among all cities in the Portuguese world because there, more than anywhere else except possibly Brazil, business was the real king. Goa and the cities of India were under royal control: *fidalgos* dominated and the interests representing Lisbon prevailed (at least superficially); even on Ternate a resident captain-general made the decisions and set the pace, whether for good or evil. But the men who ruled Macao were *casados*, a relatively new breed of married retirees from state service, who had drifted into commerce and followed trading patterns that Asians had developed long before, but that the Portuguese crown had never integrated into its original guiding concept of profit by trade monopoly between India and Europe. By the time royal government became aware of what moneys were to be made in the Inter-Asian trade, it had run low both on its own shipping for the purpose and on ideas for organizing the extensive and impromptu Inter-Asian commercial activity which had sprung up among its subjects (see chapters 18 and 22). So it contented itself with merely a share in the trade from the annual concession voyages and the collection of whatever customs duties and licenses it could levy on the new commercial class.

Macao was founded and almost solely populated by these businessmen, and they dominated the *câmara*, or municipal government — which for nearly three-quarters of a century had no *fidalgo* command structure superimposed upon it in the form of a captain-general and his council. Hence the city represents the epitome of *casado* merchant power, whose business interests, and not those of a class of graft-and-advancement-hungry nobles, prevailed.

It is difficult today to establish all the varieties of business, legal and illegal, that the Portuguese residing in Macao pursued, but they were probably legion. Some, for example, took part in the financing and trade involved in the annual voyages to Japan and later in the clandestine trade with Manila. Others acted as business agents and fronts for Chinese traders in Malacca who had chosen to become exiles after the Ming prohibition took effect on foreign-trading activities.[34] Still others must have rep-

[34] Boxer, *South China*, p. 191.

resented the captains-general of Malacca and even more distant Portuguese officials who carried on illegal trade under another's name, and, finally, there were almost certainly a number of free-lance traders who supplied pepper, sandalwood, and cloves to the Chinese which they had bought in Java, Solor, or the Moluccas. Flexibility and ingenuity, if not loyalty, were properties which the *casado* class never found in short supply. Caught as they were between the strange and often horrible world of the Orient and the imperious world of their own upper classes, it would seem that nowhere more than here was the renowned Portuguese commoner's capacity to adjust to geography and circumstance shown to better advantage.

So far the role of the Portuguese in China has been examined without more than passing reference to what had developed in Japan between its first discovery by the Portuguese in 1543 and the foundation of the colony in Macao in the mid-1550s. In fact, the China trade became so integrated with the Portuguese activity in Japan that even Macao's chief officer bore as his title the captain-major (capitão-mór) of the Japan voyage. To complete the picture of Portuguese enterprise in the Far East, it is necessary to examine Lusitanian contracts with the islands of the Rising Sun.

Japan

Of all the Asian and African peoples whom the Portuguese visited during the sixteenth century, they were most impressed by the Japanese. And it almost goes without saying that the Japanese were the most taken with them. In fact, the Jesuit saint Francis Xavier, who arrived soon after Japan's discovery by Westerners, and the missionary fathers in general were so enthusiastic over the character of the Japanese and their receptivity to the Christian religion that they envisioned for a time an entirely Catholic island whose conversion might go far toward compensating Rome for England's apostasy. On the level of trade, Portuguese connections with Japan proved almost as satisfactory, for the European traders were not only well received by Japanese businessmen, but they were able to combine their connections between China and Japan in such a way that they made many of them rich beyond even their dreams.

Unlike most of the other Asian territories which the Portuguese made known to Europe, Japan was not located through the initiative of the king or one of his governors.[35] The reason for this does not seem to have been because Portuguese observers in the East failed to send home reports of its existence, but rather because these early reports made the Ryukyu (or Liukiu) Islands, which lie to the south, seem the more likely places of interest. Tomé Pires, in the *Suma Oriental*, mentioned above, which was written about 1514, provides perhaps the best clue to how Malacca-based Portuguese viewed the Far East before they actually visited Japan. From his testimony and the testimony of others, it is likely that after China the Ryukyus appeared to be the next logical objective for Portuguese penetration.[36]

Following his section on China, Pires speaks in turn of several islands, or groups of them, first of all the *Lequios* (Ryukyus) and the *Lucões* (Phillippines). By far the longest of these sections is on the Ryukyus, whose inhabitants Pires describes and whose extensive trading activities with Malacca, Fukien province, and Japan he dwells on in some detail. But to Japan he devotes only a vague paragraph, which sounds unpromising indeed, except for the statement that "all that comes from the Lequian traders comes from Japan."

Professor Boxer has observed that these traders as described by Pires sound far more like Japanese sailors than Ryukyu indigenes and that they were probably only based on the islands for more convenient trading access to Malacca and Fukien.[37] If so, the natural result would have been to mislead the Portuguese about the reconnaissance to be accorded first priority after the visit to Canton.

In his *regimento* for Fernão Peres de Andrade, King Manuel instructed him to find the Ryukyu Islands because he had heard "exciting news from Malacca" that "some junks of the peoples called *Lequios*" carried on a trade "which was for the most part in gold and other things of great value."[38] Andrade actually went so far as to dispatch one of his vessels to

[35] Father Georg Schurhammer has argued convincingly that Ptolemy and other ancient geographers had no idea whatsoever of Japan, and that Marco Polo was the first to transmit any information of it to Europe. But the trouble was, as he says, that from Polo's description, Europeans could form no idea of where his *Cipango* was located. See Georg Schurhammer, S.J., "O descobrimento do Japão pellos portuguêses (1593)" in *Anais da Academia da História Portuguesa*, 1, as conveniently reprinted in Georg Schurhammer, S.J., *Orientalia*, XXI, pp. 521–577.

[36] Pires, *Suma Oriental*, 1, pp. 128–134; see also the Schurhammer article "O descobrimento do Japão," *Orientalia*, pp. 510–520.

[37] C. R. Boxer, *The Christian Century in Japan*, pp. 10–14.

[38] Barros, *Da Ásia*, Dec. III, bk. 2, chap. 8.

discover these islands in 1518, but its captain instead wintered in Chüan-chu and then returned to Malacca.

With this episode, incidentally, ended the twenty-six-year period of Manueline discovery which had revealed territory to Portugal and the Western world from the Cape of Good Hope to China. Aside from the subsequent Coutinho mission, which Manuel sent out the year of his death and which arrived off China only in 1523 (in time for its celebrated shoot-out with the Cantonese navy), the skein of reconnaissance expeditions equipped and launched by the Portuguese crown had reached its farthest extension. King João III never initiated another, and Japan, the final great Portuguese discovery, remained to be found accidentally, most likely by three interloping common traders blown off course in 1543.

Whether or not the famous Portuguese tale-spinning adventurer Fernão Mendes Pinto, who claims credit for the discovery, actually preceded or followed the trio makes little practical difference. Circumstances would have been virtually the same: illegal traders plying along the coast of China in the period before Shang-ch'uan and Lampacao were safe for Portuguese merchants were driven far off course either by a violent typhoon or by flight from Chinese naval units. Most experts strongly favor the case for the three men, António da Mota, Francisco Zeimoto, and António Peixoto, whose merchandise-laden junk was driven off course by a terrible typhoon and made a landfall at Tanegashima Island, due south of Kyushu, in September 1543. Pinto almost certainly did visit the same island, but probably one to three years later than they, rather than one year earlier as he claimed.[39] Even if someone should verify his assertion one day, the news would cause more stir among the literati than among historians.

Diogo do Couto, who chronicles the storm-driven arrival of Mota, Zeimoto, and Peixoto, quickly adds that they were warmly welcomed by the scantily bearded and small-eyed Japanese, who took them home with them and entertained them royally. Moreover, the Portuguese disposed of their cargoes for silver before returning to Malacca.[40]

After such a reception, it was certain that the Portuguese would not wait long before returning to Japan. In fact, the word spread so fast that in

[39] See the discussion in Boxer, *Christian Century*, pp. 21–29. Also see Schurhammer, "O descobrimento do Japão," *Orientalia*, pp. 525–527.

[40] Couto, *Da Ásia*, Dec. V, bk. 8, chap. 12. Cf. Galvão, *Tratado dos descobrimentos*, p. 273.

the following year, 1544, Portuguese vessels turned up at Tanegashima again — this time in great numbers. More Portuguese ships visited Bungo, on the island of Kyushu. All of this was so unsettling to the illegal Chinese traders, who until this time had enjoyed exclusive intercourse with Japan, that they were provoked to attack the newcomers in hope of driving them away. But the Chinese "interlopers" were apparently ignorant of European cannonry: a battle ensued in which they were completely routed. Thereafter, the 100 or more Chinese junks that had been sighted in Japanese harbors were seen no more.[41]

It was either this open demonstration of pyrotechnics against the Chinese or some impromptu exhibitions given by the Portuguese at Tanegashima that enormously impressed the Japanese. Far from offending them, as Fernão Peres de Andrade's salute had offended the Chinese, the Portuguese armaments fascinated the islanders, even though the son of a chieftain seems to have been wounded in 1544 when a harquebus went off accidentally. Within a decade, the Tanegashimans had learned firearms manufacture from the Portuguese and were in business for themselves. The name "Tanegashima" was for many years a synonym for "musket" in Japan, although it was not long before that island incurred competition from Bungo and other manufacturers on Hokkaido and elsewhere.[42] Meanwhile, Portuguese traders continued to call in Tanegashima, Bungo, and, after 1550, Hokkaido. And in 1549, inspired by the tales of one Anjiro, a Japanese newly Christianized, Father Francis Xavier, two other European Jesuits, two servants, and three Japanese converts arrived at Kagoshima in southern Kyushu to introduce the Gospel. In one of his first letters written to his brothers in Goa, he reported (in sharp contrast to his feelings about the Spice Islanders) that "of all the newly discovered people among whom I have lived, those of this land are the best; none of the other heretical peoples can compare with the Japanese."[43]

Probably the main reason that the Portuguese and the Japanese struck it off so well was that they had many qualities in common. In China it was the mandarin bureaucrat and his writing brush who stood at the top of the social ladder and even symbolized the society; but it was the hereditary fighting class, the *samurai*, whose wearing of the sword symbolized Japan — and made the sword-wearing Portuguese feel at home.

---

[41] Probably from Malacca, the Ryukyus and Shang-ch'uan.

[42] Schurhammer, in *Orientalia*, pp. 76, 549.

[43] Xavier, letter of November 5, 1549, as reprinted in Boxer, *Christian Century*, p. 401.

Moreover, as Professor Boxer remarks, the *samurai* pride and rigid code of honor so admired by Xavier (himself of the Spanish *hidalgo*, or noble class) was similar to the chivalry and pride of the Iberian nobleman.[44] And, finally, as Sir George Sansom has observed, the very fact that the Japanese culture was itself a derivative culture, centered around foreign Chinese values, made the island people receptive to other kinds of overseas influence, in this instance European.[45] In the mid-sixteenth century, Japan was fighting an endemic civil war whose effects had even nullified the Ashikaga shogunate, the ruling clan whose chieftain, the *shōgun* directed the other clans in the name of the emperor. This struggle not only eliminated any chance that the shogun and Japanese emperor might wish to ban the Europeans from their country as the Chinese emperor had done, but, to the contrary — as with the Japanese eagerness to adopt firearms — it only made them more receptive to foreign influences. Both Portuguese merchants and Portuguese religionists took full advantage of their opportunities.

The Great Ships from Macao

In 1543, Portuguese trade with China was still very much sub rosa, and even the use of the Shang-ch'uan and Lampacao islands by Portuguese trading vessels was new and risky. Then Japan was discovered and merchants were pleasantly surprised in more ways than one. Not only did they find Japan to be a good market for Chinese silks, ceramics, and other trading items, European guns among them, but they discovered it possessed its own silver mines on Honshu and valued that metal in proportion to gold at about the same ratio the West did, about 12:1. China, on the other hand, possessed so little silver it would exchange it for gold at about 5½:1.[46] This meant that the Portuguese could buy or trade spice for Chinese silks and pieces of porcelain — prized in Japan above the native products — then sell them to the Japanese for silver, and, finally, exchange this silver in China for a large quantity of gold. It was fortunate for the Portuguese that in 1557 the Chinese had banned all further trading between their country and Japan, and that the raids of the *wako* on the China coast continued until 1588. For in practice the Portuguese were

[44] Boxer, *Christian Century*, pp. 37–38.
[45] Sansom, *Western World and Japan*, p. 107.
[46] See Boxer, *Christian Century*, pp. 426–427.

given a virtual monopoly, even though illicit trade between the two countries never stopped altogether.

The fundamentals of this trading scheme were apparently worked out by the private merchants in the 1540s, but it was not long before the Portuguese crown stepped in to limit and control the lucrative commerce. As indicated earlier, the device it used was to appoint a *capitão-mór*, or captain-major, of the Japan voyage. He was authorized to outfit a carrack or other ship at his own expense (or alternatively to borrow the money or supplies from the crown) and to make a round trip from Goa to Japan via China. While at Macao, as mentioned in the section on China, he was empowered to act as the governing officer of that city and, otherwise, as the royal representative vis-à-vis the Japanese and any Portuguese he happened to encounter in Japan or at sea.[47] In theory this meant that the China-to-Japan-to-China trading had become a royal monopoly; but in practice the crown never reaped an annual benefit representing more than about two-fifths to one-half of its value in the form of commissions and port duties paid at Malacca and Goa. Most usually, at least before 1580, the actual appointment of a *fidalgo* as captain-major of the China and Japan voyage was awarded in return for supposedly distinguished service, usually in the Indian wars, although sometimes it was sold for a fixed price far below its actual value. In contrast, unless his carrack was wrecked in a typhoon (which happened only once), the captain-major was able to salt away a tidy fortune, often amounting to some 50,000 cruzados.[48]

Since the captain-major had permission to operate only one ship per appointment (before 1580 Domingos Monteiro held the appointment three years in succession), he made it a big ship, in fact as big a nau or carrack as he could procure, usually one with three flush decks, a quarterdeck, and a forecastle. At Goa, he loaded it with Gujarati cottons and chintzes, woolen and scarlet cloths, wine, glassware, crystal, and Flemish clocks. After departure in April or May, the ship continued on to Malacca, where much of the original cargo was traded for Indonesian spices and sandalwoods and hides from Siam. Then, upon arrival in Macao, the cargo was again largely traded for silks of all types and grades,

[47] See C. R. Boxer, *The Great Ship from Amacon*, documental appendix, pp. 173–174; also see summary in Boxer's *Fidalgos in the Far East*, p. 17.
[48] Boxer, *Christian Century*, p. 106.

porcelains and Chinese objets d'art. The stay in Macao was of variable length — sometimes only weeks, but more often nearly a year if the ship missed either the China Sea southwest monsoons or the semiannual silk fairs at Canton, held in June and January. On the next monsoon, usually the following June to August, it set out for Kyushu in Japan, a sailing time of a fortnight to a month. There — before 1571 at Bungo, Hizen, and Omura, successively, and after 1571 at Nagasaki — it sold off its goods mostly for silver, some gold, and an assortment of Japanese lacquerware, painted screens, swords, and other curios. Then, in November, the ship caught the northeast monsoons for Macao, where its silver was converted to gold and copper (mostly for use in casting cannon in India), plus much ivory, many pearls, some new Chinese silks, and a few other items for Goa and perhaps, ultimately, Europe. Then it set sail again for India, when it hove to in the Mandovi roads after an absence of two or three years — depending on the length of the sojourn in China.[49]

Exactly what happened to the original independent entrepreneurs who flourished in the seven years between the discovery of Japan and the initiation of the captain-major's monopoly is not known positively. But it is most likely, as already suggested, that they found numerous ways of making their livings: through carrying on as if nothing had happened, through obtaining some cargo space on the official ship, or perhaps by joining the *wako*, or Japanese pirates, in their Chinese coastal raids. It is even likely that some of them, already wealthy, sat on the Macaonese *senado da câmara* or served as part of Macao's bureaucracy. But in 1571, after the Spanish settled in Manila, some absorbing new possibilities for illicit commerce opened for the Macaonese which were unlikely to be preempted by either Spain or Portugal, since both countries formally banned colonial trade with the other until 1580 — and even thereafter when under the same crown. The Macaonese interlopers then traded Chinese silks at Manila to Spaniards for South American silver. Macao, founded on smuggling, had no intention of turning its back on its heritage.

Finally in 1578, the commercial community of Macao found a more efficient way to market its goods when it joined with the Jesuit order then rapidly expanding in Japan. Under an arrangement made with the fathers there to help market the Chinese silk consigned to the annual *nau*, the

---

[49] See Boxer, *Fidalgos in the Far East*, pp. 15–16, also *The Great Ship from Amacon*, *passim*, but especially pp. 179–241.

merchants solved their chronic problem of what to do with unsold inventory after the great ship had sailed back to China en route home — and the Jesuits gained a badly needed source of additional income.

The Jesuits in Action

The conversions and the influence that the Society of Jesus achieved in Japan were noteworthy enough in their own right, but transcending that accomplishment is the thought of what the Jesuits might have achieved in the future had their work not been dramatically reversed in the late sixteenth and early seventeenth centuries. Uninterrupted, it might have made the most sensational impact on Christendom since the conversion of Ireland by St. Patrick, and Japan might never have turned its back on the West. Just thirty-one years after the first arrival of Father Francisco Xavier with only two clerical brethren, Anjiro, plus two Japanese servants to help him, the number of faithful had grown from one native believer in 1549 to an estimated community of 150,000, including generals, councillors, and high feudal lords. At the same time, the Jesuit numbers had increased from the original three to only fifty-four. Catholics had never seen a thing like it in modern times; for although there were by then many more Christian Indians in Mexico and Peru, they represented a more primitive society than the Japanese, the work was not undertaken by only a handful of missionaries, but by hundreds, and they possessed the advantage of having the Spanish soldiery first subdue the New World and almost destroy its culture before they moved in. In Japan, the lonely priests appeared to be better conquistadores without swords than ever Cortés or Pizarro had been with plenty of them. In all, it was a brilliant vindication of the new Jesuit order and its founding provincial, Francis Xavier, and indeed of the whole idea of papal donation in return for Christianization of the new areas opened by the oceanic sailing ship. It was pitiful indeed that within sixty years hardly a trace would remain of the Christian faith among the living, that some of the fathers would have renounced their beliefs to save their lives, and that the ground would have been bathed in the blood of crucified Japanese and European clergy and converts.

The visit by Xavier to Japan lasted only two years, from August 1549 until November 1551. During this time, he traveled from Kagoshima in Satsuma, Kyushu, all the way to the imperial court in Kyoto on Honshu and back to Funai in Bungo, on Kyushu. To Xavier and many of his overexpectant followers, the sojourn was something of a disappointment, but in retrospect it was clearly a reconnaissance mission that gave subsequent fathers a clear idea of how and where to concentrate their efforts. To read the detailed story of Xavier's travels and disputations in Japan is to have the feeling that one is viewing the opening episode in a drama which, beginning with the Jesuits, would ultimately lead Europeans to a study of foreign cultures on a scientific basis. For one can see in Xavier's movements and disputations a restless probing for a comprehension of Japanese religion and politics so that he and his brothers could better achieve their purposes.

Xavier's first move upon arrival in Japan was one he had planned in Goa. It reflected the military origins and pyramidal structure of his order and foreshadowed the standard Jesuit practice in years to come both in Europe and in Asia: immediately he sought out Japan's ruling elite and attempted to win it to his side. First he visited the *daimyō*, or feudal ruler, of Satsuma; after a polite reception by him, he asked where the king of Japan held court and whether he could obtain leave to see him. The ruler identified his overlord as the emperor at Kyoto and promised to take him there, but he explained that warfare had interrupted communications and would delay matters for a time. What he did not explain was that in Japan it had been many centuries since the emperor had been more than a figurehead. Xavier and his companions then spent ten months waiting patiently in Satsuma for transportation to the capital. Meanwhile, they made a few converts and drew up an elaborate statement of faith in Japanese. Xavier, incidentally, was never much of a linguist, but he fully realized and stressed the importance of language training for all future missionaries. During this interval, he also held some disputations with a Buddhist abbot and was somewhat amazed to learn that the man neither believed in an afterlife nor valued the sharp edge of reason.[50]

Xavier and his followers left Satsuma for Kyoto via Yamaguchi in southernmost Honshu, after realizing that the Satsuma *daimyō* never had serious intentions at all of taking them to the emperor. In Yamaguchi, Xavier and his companions received permission to preach, but narrowly avoided serious trouble when the interpreter reading their prepared text to the *daimyō* and his court struck a passage that strongly condemned homosex-

[50] See English extracts from Xavier's letter of November 5, 1549, in Boxer, *Christian Century*, pp. 401–405.

uality as a vile habit worthy of pigs. The *daimyō*, Ouchi Yoshitaka, it seems, happened to be a homosexual, along with many members of his retinue. On his way through Yamaguchi, however, Xavier continued to attack this sin, as well as those of idolatry and infanticide.

Ultimately in December 1550, Xavier set out on foot through the snow to Kyoto, over 200 miles away. When he reached the imperial city, he learned belatedly that the emperor was not a king in the European sense but that the shogun held this power. At this juncture in Japanese history, moreover, even the shogun was not up to his role.[51] When Xavier arrived at Kyoto, in fact, the emperor was living in seclusion and poverty in a badly maintained palace, but the shogun had left the city. After this on-the-scene demonstration of Japanese polity, or, rather, lack of it, Xavier decided that perhaps provincial Yamaguchi had not been such a bad starting point after all, for sodomy or no sodomy, at least its *daimyō*, Ouchi Yoshitaka, seemed to be among the more influential lords of Japan. As soon as Xavier returned from Kyoto, he sent a number of European-style gifts to mollify Ouchi, including a matchlock, a clock, some fine crystals, brocades, and spectacles. This list is interesting because it demonstrates that the Jesuits already recognized that the mechanical devices of the West were their best calling cards. Thirty-five years later, Xavier's coreligionist Matteo Ricci used the same tactics and demonstrated the same predilection of men in power when he penetrated the imperial court in China through the gift of a clock.

Xavier continued to teach and dispute with Japanese visitors in his quarters at Yamaguchi, and he and his followers learned much about Japanese concerns in matters of faith. Then in late 1551, he returned to Goa in a Portuguese ship which had called at Funai, in the province of Bungo.[52] Its ruler was reportedly so impressed by the awe in which the Portuguese sailors held Xavier that he sent an embassy of his own along with him to Goa, though probably, as Sir George Sansom suggested, rather to attract more trade than more Christians.[53] But the Jesuits

[51] For a succinct account of Japanese politics in relation to Portugal, the aging work by James Murdoch and Isoh Yamagata, *A History of Japan* is still the best, especially II, pp. 31–301.

[52] There was a foretaste of the martyrdom to come when, after Xavier's departure, his fellows returned to Yamaguchi just in time to be swept up in a revolution which overthrew Ouchi Yoshitaka; they lost their lives.

[53] See Sansom, *The Western World and Japan*, p. 123. Sansom's brief description of Xavier's mission is the best condensation in English, though more serious readers who can read German should consult Georg Schurhammer, S.J., *Franz Xavier, sein Leben und seine Zeit*, II, pt. 2.

needed no invitation. They sent new men as fast as they could be recruited, trained, and oriented.[54]

Despite Xavier's eagerness and the willingness of Loyola and King João III to follow up the initial Jesuit entrée, only six European fathers could be spared before 1561, and nine years later, in 1570, there were still only twelve in the Japanese mission field. In spite of this lag, the *daimyō* of Bungo in Kyushu, the Otomo Sorin, showed himself eager to cooperate with the fathers — and so did the other lords of Kyushu. As early as 1561, Otomo Sorin sent a finely decorated dagger to the child king Sebastião and a magnificent suit of armor to the viceroy of Goa.[55] A few years later, he even expressed the wish to conquer Yamaguchi, across the Suo Strait on Honshu, to help the fathers reestablish themselves there after Yoshitaka's overthrow in a civil war.[56]

The reasons for this, at least in the beginning, seem to have been closely tied to the economic plight of the lords of Kyushu and the benefits of Portuguese trade. As Father Valignano revealed in 1580, in a letter to his superiors, the Jesuits were not the only ones who needed some extra income: "After the grace and favor of Goa, the greatest help we have had hitherto in securing Christians is that of the Great Ship. . . . For as the lords of Japan are very poor . . . and the benefits they derive when the ships come to their ports are very great . . . they try hard to entice them to their fiefs."[57]

The feudal nobility of Kyushu gradually converted to Christianity, especially in Bungo, and about 1569, a Christian vassal of the *daimyō* Omura Sumitada (baptized as Bartholomeu) invited the Jesuit Father Gaspar Vilela to visit him in a fishing village on a deep inlet in southwestern Kyushu. The place was called Nagasaki, and Vilela had soon converted the townspeople and erected a Christian church on the site of its Buddhist temple. The Nagasaki harbor was splendid, and in 1571, the annual *nau* from Goa and Macao anchored there for the first time. Conditions were now propitious for a deal between the Japanese and the fathers, since the previous harbors in Kyushu (like Hirado and Kagoshima) frequented by

---

[54] Because of the long gestation period between novitiate and professed or working member of the Order, the great demand for Jesuit trainees in Germany and other parts of the world, and what seems an especially high mortality of brothers in transit, the increase of Jesuits was not great. Usually priests would arrive only three or four at a time.

[55] Boxer, *Christian Century*, p. 96.

[56] Sansom, *Western World and Japan*, p. 124.

[57] Quoted in Boxer, *Christian Century*, p. 93.

the captain-major's vessel either had been rendered dangerous by misunderstandings between the Portuguese and the Japanese or had been less than adequate as anchorages. In 1580, Bartholomeu and his vassal, eager to accommodate their "Bateren," or fathers, and to capture the rich trade permanently, actually completed the deeding over of Nagasaki and a nearby fortress called Mogi from Japanese into Jesuit hands. Thus it was that the Jesuits received their first — and only — sovereign territories in their history and the annual Portuguese ship its most famous harbor. No bargain resembled it before or since, although the actual Jesuit management lasted only seven years, or until Toyotomi Hideyoshi expropriated it.

By this same period of the 1570s, the Jesuits, always eager to convert those at the center of power, had again shifted their attention to Honshu, but this time they ignored the shogunate. The Ashikaga, who held this intermediate position between the emperorship and the rest of Japan, had now been definitely eclipsed by the upstart *daimyō* Oda Nobunaga, whose strategically located fief was modest enough in size but whose ambition and ability were first-rate. He had been introduced by a trusted lieutenant to the Jesuit Father Luis Frois (later author of a scholarly work on Japanese history), and he soon set Frois at liberty to move about and preach as he chose.[58] The emperor and the shogun seemed less enthusiastic, but Nobunaga was then running coastal Japan and scarcely heeded their wishes. Besides this, the Buddhists had consistently opposed Nobunaga, and he saw in the Jesuits a good antidote to their ambitions.

Nobunaga himself never converted to Christianity, but many of his subjects did, especially when they saw him entertaining the Jesuits and when he deeded them a plot of land for a seminary. The number of Christians in Japan was estimated at 30,000 by 1571, but in the same decade, another father, the Italian Organtino, estimated that his association had baptized 7000 Japanese within a six-month period. By 1582, the Jesuit Visitor-General Alessandro Valignano placed the number of Japanese Christians at 150,000 and their churches at 200.[59] At Nobunaga's

---

[58] For Frois's description of Nobunaga, as well as a scholarly evaluation of his work, see Schurhammer, *Orientalia*, pp. 581–609. His *Historia do Japão* was not published in his lifetime, or, for that matter, until 1926 when half of it appeared in a German translation by Georg Schurhammer, S.J. and E. A. Voretsch, S.J. as *Die Geschichte Japans, 1549–1578*. The second part was printed in the original version as: J. A. Abrantes Pinto and Y. Ohamoto (jt. eds.), *Segunda parte da História Japão, 1578–1582*.

[59] Sansom, *Western World and Japan*, p. 127.

death the same year, his successor, Toyotomi Hideyoshi, had among his trusted counselors half a dozen Christians, including his own son and a number of Christian generals who even went into battle with crosses on their banners. For a time Hideyoshi favored the Christians, and if he had continued to do so, they bode fair to have made their faith the country's dominant religion.[60]

But in August 1587, Hideyoshi suddenly issued an edict expelling the missionaries, a decision seemingly arrived at while drinking Portuguese wine at a feast the night before. It appears he had worked himself into a rage when his physician, who disliked the Portuguese, had criticized their methods and accused them of the forcible conversion of Hideyoshi's subjects to the Christian faith. The real reasons for the abrupt turnabout were as mysterious as those that prompted the French dowager and regent Catherine de Medicis to massacre Coligny and the Huguenots in France fifteen years before. But it would appear that in both instances the rulers felt suddenly that the new faiths and their protagonists were foreign to the traditions of the host countries and were about to entrench themselves beyond the rulers' control.[61] Both regents were insecure: Catherine was a woman and a foreigner; Hideyoshi was still new and relatively unsteady in his hegemony. Moreover, in Japan the Christians, a tiny minority, had the zealous, but undiplomatic habit of destroying Buddhist and Shinto shrines and temples; one Japanese writer assigns this as the chief reason for the public oratory that followed and Hideyoshi's action against them.[62] Even more fundamentally, perhaps, Hideyoshi and other Japanese of the ruling class must have feared that the consequence of the Christianization process would be the divided allegiance and ultimate disloyalty of their subjects.[63]

Having asserted himself, Hideyoshi did not prosecute the Christians actively for another ten years, but, meanwhile, a large number of apostasies followed in central Japan. Progress continued to be made in

[60]The Jesuits were not deceived about the manner in which conversions were made, at least initially. In his general report on the state of the Jesuit missions in 1580, Father Alessandro Valignano, S.J. observes, "Because the Japanese are so subject to their lords that they convert when those so command or make it understood it is their will, and this is the door through which those who are baptized enter in the beginning." See Silva Rego, *Documentação do padroado português na Índia*, 12, pp. 537–538.

[61]Boxer, *Christian Century*, pp. 145–149; Sansom, *Western World and Japan*, p. 128.

[62]Kiichi Matsuda, *The Relations between Portugal and Japan*, pp. 30–31.

[63]I regret that this subchapter had been all but sent to press when George Elison's *Deus Destroyed: the Image of Christianity in Early Modern Japan* came to my attention. His chapters 5, 6, 7 and 8 probe the matter in depth.

Kyushu, but in 1596 persecution began in earnest under Hideyoshi when, it is rumored, a Castilian captain whose galleon had run ashore and been confiscated, told the Japanese that the traders and priests were merely the vanguard of invading armies. Hideyoshi, by then in firm control of Japan, inaugurated the first of a series of crucifixions, executing twenty-six Christians at Nagasaki. The main victims in this instance were Japanese — and oddly enough, six Spanish Franciscans who had but recently arrived and whose presence had been regarded as a threat by the Jesuits. But Jesuit martyrdoms soon followed, and the bright hopes of the Society and Catholic Europe for the conversion of Japan tarnished. They were replaced by a Catholic martyrology unparalleled in the Protestant Europe of the Reformation and indeed in any period since the persecutions of Diocletian. Even the Romans had not had so much imagination as the Japanese, who in one series of executions crucified their Christian victims upside down in tidal flats, soon to be inundated by the incoming tide. It could have been but small consolation to the Company of Jesus and to the viceroy at Goa that all of this took place because the church had been on the verge of conquering Japan.

The persecutions were intermittent enough during the Hideyoshi years (1582–98) at least to allow Christianity to survive in Japan, if not to thrive, and the *naus* continued to come, though intermittently, until well into the seventeenth century. But long before the Portuguese were finally expelled nothing was left of Xavier's dream.

Xavier was a Navarrese, Valignano an Italian, and Frois a Portuguese, and so the Society's dream was not primarily a Portuguese one. But Portugal was the patron, the transporter, the financier, and the licensing agent of the Society in Asia, and it backed Jesuit projects with its money, its personnel, and its prestige. Xavier's mummy lies today in a silver tomb in Goa. The Apostle of the Indies and his men, if not all Portuguese, thoroughly represented the Portuguese cause and became its spiritual mercenaries. With better fortune, or greater tact, they might have changed the whole course of Japanese history.

CHAPTER 22

The Balance Sheet

The establishment of the Portuguese empire in Asia was anything but carefully contrived — it was the product of a strong national will and no more than a dash of planning. In fact, there was hardly any information available with which to plan in the beginning, and if the scout Pero de Covilhã's reports to King João II ever really did reach Lisbon, they seem to have been of little use to anybody.

For eighty years after Vasco da Gama's return to Europe in 1499, the Portuguese had sought the "alchemy" — the magic formula — which would make their discovery pay; indeed a vision of spices-turned-into-gold had been about their empire's only starting point. As information was fed back to Lisbon by dispatch and returning adventurer, the kings and their advisers strove to form assumptions and then translate them into policies that would bring money and power into Portuguese hands. As it turned out, none of these formulas worked for long, for a variety of reasons: the policies were not completely or properly executed, the ideas on which they were based were wrong or partly wrong, or circumstances beyond Portuguese control introduced entirely new elements. It is revealing to try to see what these assumptions and attempts were and what went amiss with them.

The Simple Profit

The first approach of the Portuguese to exploit their discovery of India was simple and direct, and, given the limited perspective brought home by da Gama, it seemed the logical place to begin. It was to barter for or buy spices, to haul them home, and to sell them in Europe for a big profit. If the Samorin of Calicut had been a Christian, if the Muslim traders had not interfered, and if the Portuguese had kept their tempers, this might have worked. Cabral's *regimento*, possibly prepared by da Gama himself, is a perfect blueprint for this stage of Portuguese planning. It says nothing about Portuguese shore installations beyond a simple *feitoria*, and it does not envision hostilities with Indian rulers. Naturally this blueprint did not remain in use very long. It took only the first hint of Arab intransigence to provoke a show of force by the Portuguese.

Chapter 13 has already dealt in some detail with Cabral and his actions against Calicut, and it is only useful to point out here that the crown was more a merchant than its men in command were good merchants' representatives. In fact, the pursuit of commerce was a peculiar characteristic of the Portuguese kings; in the Middle Ages other monarchs may have defended commerce out of selfish motives, but they never searched for money as directly as Portuguese rulers did. At the same time, the Portuguese nobles of the fifteenth century were much like the ordinary nobles of other European countries and not especially trade-oriented. Cabral was a better warrior than a businessman when he shot up Calicut's harbor.

Upon Cabral's return to Portugal, King Manuel's councillors set about to make a new plan; the old one had literally gone up in the smoke of Cabral's guns. It could not now be hoped that all the Portuguese had to do to turn a profit was to sail into Calicut with trade goods, or even specie, and sail home with spices which could be translated into many times the amount of the original investment.

The old idea of holy war against Muslims obviously came back into play at this juncture. The urge to cut throats of the infidel was never far removed from Iberian sentiments, and it is interesting how quickly a new concept that combined religion, war, and business replaced the original simple one, which had, in the main, hoped for a profitable trade with fellow Christians.

The Period of Geopolitics and Monopoly, 1520 to ca. 1550

Moderns can easily see that Cabral was a victim of instructions that did not take into account that the Samorin was not a coreligionist and that

Muslims in possession of a secure and successful living would surely fight for it when it was challenged, as by Cabral himself; the resistance he encountered seems only natural. But what one is not prepared to anticipate is that such apparent simpletons as the Portuguese appeared to be at this point would then leap from a patently naïve concept to behavior which took the academic world, at least, several hundred years to describe as "geopolitics." It has already been suggested in chapter 15 how the Portuguese probably came to identify the strategic nodal points around the perimeter of the Indian Ocean, and enough has already been said about how the Portuguese were prone to attempt a monopoly wherever they set foot outside Europe — witness Prince Henry's petitions to the pope to bar the Spaniards and others from travels along the African coast. Combining the correct identification of the geographical nexuses in Asia with the ideas of their capture and the subsequent enforcement of a Portuguese trading monopoly in the Indian Ocean was certainly a remarkable insight on the part of King Manuel and his advisers. But what made the scheme breathtaking was its gigantic scale; for as few as were the Portuguese, as numerous as were the Asians and Middle Easterners, and as vast as were the areas involved, it seems preposterous that King Manuel and his advisers would have had the nerve to entertain the idea, let alone try to put it into effect.

The military aspects have been considered in chapter 16 — namely, in the vital role Afonso de Albuquerque played in making into near-reality the instructions from his government. However, it will be recalled that he was not given the supporting forces by King Manuel, apparently because Manuel let himself be distracted by that fatal will-o'-the-wisp, the prospect of a Portuguese empire in Morocco. Even bad luck played its part when Albuquerque could not decide whether to slug it out with Aden or venture farther into the Red Sea and perhaps capture Jidda. His apparent plan to test Aden first and then try for Jidda was logical; but the monsoons did not cooperate, and the Portuguese failed to achieve the most vital objective of all — to close the Red Sea. (Albergaria, of course, had he seemingly not been born to fail, might in 1516 have remedied both the shortcomings of Manuel and of Albuquerque!)

Although the projected *mare clausum* was thus never achieved, other favorable events for the Portuguese offset their need for it during the years of their establishment in Asia. For one thing, in 1496, when the Mameluke ruler of Egypt died, an unusually severe succession struggle disrupted trade for the better part of a decade; often the routes from Suez were closed and the bazaars of Alexandria had no oriental merchandise to sell. Venice, meanwhile, was preoccupied by the Ottomans, and the rest of Italy was in the grip of invasions and battles; dozens of important financial houses were ruined. The Portuguese also helped their own cause by dealing blows to the established Muslim commerce centering on Calicut. Pepper prices shot sky-high in Egypt: in 1505, for example, a hundredweight cost 192 ducats, an all-time record.[1]

It took some years for the Portuguese to fill the void created by the collapse of the older trading system. All the networks of spice distribution radiated from Venice and, to a lesser extent, Antwerp (other emporia, like Lyons, were only of secondary importance). Lisbon, the Portuguese capital, was in no central geographical position to supplant these; at best it was an exchange point. Although Portugal did have its Italian commercial allies, the Genoese and the Florentines, and in 1500 had begun to attract German customers, these still were not sufficiently big or well connected to absorb great quantities of spices from India and then find customers quickly enough to keep their own purchases from Portugal brisk. Consequently, just as the Venetian prices were soaring, the prices at Lisbon were dropping, though not actually below the profit margin.[2] The problem as the Portuguese must have seen it was twofold: to stabilize prices and to reach a much larger market. King Manuel, however, was able to achieve price stability only through a certain amount of duplicity.

Until about 1505, the quantity of Asian spices King Manuel could market directly on his own account was limited. For at the time he had outfitted Cabral's great expedition in 1500, he had felt himself so pressed for funds that he had invited a number of bankers, mostly Florentine and Genoese, to invest directly in the expedition, much as had Prince Henry about a half century before. A number had accepted, and in return for equipping some ships at their own expense, they had been required merely to pay the *Casa da Índia* around 30 percent of their cargoes — whereupon they were free to market the rest wherever and at whatever amounts they saw fit. But then prices began to fall, and no doubt the crown blamed free selling on the merchants' part for the decline in its own profits, which, after all, followed the prevailing market.

For the next five years, King Manuel seems to have been torn between

[1] See table in Donald F. Lach, *Asia in the Making of Europe*, I, bk. 1, 145.
[2] João Lúcio de Azevedo, *Épocas de Portugal económico; esboços de história*, p. 102.

trying to please the merchants in case he needed them again and wanting to resume the monopoly and fix prices at a level he thought they should remain. As historian Donald Lach points out, the indecisive king had no sooner insisted on excluding foreigners by paying for his whole fleet (Albergaria's) in 1504, when he veered about and signed a contract with Lucas Rem on behalf of the German house of Welser and others now seeking the Portuguese market, and allowed them to outfit ships in his 1505 fleet (Almeida's) — under much the same conditions as he had given in 1500.[3] He soon repented of it. When the 1505 fleet, together with these private ships, returned to Europe in 1506, he blandly impounded the merchants' cargoes and forced the owners to obey retroactively a decree he had just made requiring private owners to sell their shares via the *Casa da Índia* at a fixed (and higher) price.[4]

The merchants, of course, objected furiously, and although they did not win this round, the crown relented in part by letting them market spices on a contract which imposed a minimum price but allowed the contractors more flexibility in marketing procedures and determining in what form and on what terms they should be paid. After their bitter disappointment of 1506, however, the merchants virtually ceased to press Manuel for direct participation in the annual fleets. Thereafter, it was the German Fugger who did most of the buying, and they and the other merchants contented themselves with making their acquisitions at the Ribeira do Paço warehouses of the *Casa da Índia*.[5]

The coming of the Germans to Lisbon in 1503–4 was the surest sign that the older trading system via the Middle East was breaking down and that Venice's luxury trade was in trouble. The south German banking families — such as the Fugger, the Welser, the Höchstetter, and the Imhof — were, after all, an integral link in the last lap of the marketing and distribution system which had begun at Calicut and Malacca; and the fact that these Germans switched in large part from Venice to Lisbon and the Portuguese for their oriental luxury goods affords decisive evidence about the trading revolution which had taken place. It was because the south German cities of Augsberg and Nuremberg lay between the Brenner Pass and northern Europe that the south German bankers had be-

---

[3] Lach, *Asia in the Making of Europe*, I, pt. 1, 108–111. Manuel, in the previous year (1503), had already signed a contract guaranteeing the Welsers preferential treatment.

[4] *Ibid.*

[5] The Fuggers were used to price-fixing arrangements from suppliers — the Venetians also imposed theirs when possible.

come important in the first place, and to see these houses shifting much of their business 1,000 miles to the west is far more dramatic than the fact that the Genoese and the Florentines had set up trading operations in Lisbon a century or two before. No doubt nothing would have surprised the same banking partners more in the fifteenth century, only a few years earlier, than to have been told they would all soon find themselves outside the Portuguese royal palace, hat in hand. In 1514, even the Venetians themselves purchased spices from Lisbon.[6]

King Manuel, meanwhile, did not rely on the world to beat a path to his new palace or, rather, to his *Casa da Índia*, both built on the very dockside where his ships from Asia were berthed. Just as the Venetians had carried a proportion of their spices to Antwerp for sale, he began experimenting with his own *feitoria* there as a means of spice distribution as early as 1501, only two years after this trading post's final move from Bruges. At that time he had introduced rather small amounts of pepper — no doubt because he had no more available for such speculation — but soon he came to recognize the advantages of doing business in Flanders: pepper brought there realized the crown up to a 13 percent increment above that sold in Lisbon.[7] The reason for this appears to have been that the Germans already did most of their actual buying in Flanders, were already in close contact with it both by land and by sea, and found it much more convenient to do business there than to trade in Lisbon.

Suddenly, in 1508, the whole marketing picture evolved still further when an Antwerp syndicate of Italo-Flemish merchants, headed by the Affaitati (in Portugal, "Lafetá") and the Gualterotti, reached an agreement with King Manuel to monopolize the entire Portuguese royal monopoly.

This idea of a merchants' monopoly in juxtaposition to the royal monopoly was bound to appeal to the king, if indeed it did not originate within the Portuguese camp. After all, the idea behind the impounding of the cargoes from the returning ships in 1506 had been to make sure that the merchants who owned the cargoes did not sell them below a price determined by the crown. By negotiating with a syndicate to buy all his pepper sent to Antwerp at a fixed price, Manuel must have felt he had solved his distribution problems at last and assured himself of a perma-

---

[6] See Heyd, *Commerce du Levant*, II, p. 550.
[7] J. Denucé "Privilèges commerciaux accordés par les rois de Portugal aux Flamands et aux Allemands," pp. 313–315.

nent profit. All he then had to do, according to his own concept, was to fix the buying rates at the Indian end of the system, agree on selling rates at the Lisbon end, and then sit back and watch the ducats pour in. They did, for a time; in 1510, for example, pepper bought in India for two cruzados per quintal sold at the *Casa da Índia* in Lisbon for thirty.[8] Soon, however, the instabilities of commercial life in the burgeoning new business capital of Antwerp turned what seemed like a secure proposition into a financial albatross.

The mercurial rise and fall of the city of Antwerp is roughly coincident with the presence of the Portuguese marketing of pepper there from its overseas discoveries, though to say that the city was dependent upon the sale of spices would be much like asserting that the city of Los Angeles was a creation of the motion-picture industry. At best, the pepper and other exotic goods for sale in Antwerp, like the movies in Hollywood, lent a certain glamour which distinguished the city and attracted other business. It may not have been sheer coincidence at all that the majority of the German bankers moved there from Bruges within a few years after the Portuguese *feitoria* had done so — but in any event, all the transfers were conditioned by the quickening pace of business in the Brabantian city. Among other things, it offered far better physical facilities than Bruges (whose Zwin River had silted too badly to accommodate large vessels) and a far less circumscribed business climate (a stone over Antwerp's principal gate proclaimed the city to be "for the merchants of all nations," whereas the Brugeois continually hampered foreign business transactions in order to favor themselves). By 1520, or even earlier, Antwerp had become the hub of capitalistic business transactions for all of Europe, and this not in spite of its newness as a great city but because of it. Some writers, most recently Herman van der Wee, have even postulated that it was the cradle of capitalism as it is known today because it was the first city to attract the complex of interdependent industry so characteristic of subsequent times: transport, distribution, finance, banking, commodities exchange, all forms of insurance, and publishing.[9] As a Venetian contemporary, Lodovico Guicciardini, has chronicled so unforgettably, one could buy anything there, from a piece of the king of Spain's indebtedness to a load of next year's Baltic wheat — and, he might have added, one could borrow the money to pay for it, contract for a ship to carry it, and then

[8] Azevedo, *Épocas de Portugal económico*, p. 110.
[9] Herman van der Wee, *The Growth of the Antwerp Market and the European Economy*.

find underwriters to insure it, including its arrival date.[10] Wool cloth, silks, majolica damask, grain, copper, and pewterware, iron, fish, armor, cannon, hats, and amber — as well as all the goods of the Portuguese and Spanish Indies — found their biggest markets there, and the convenience of doing all one's business in one place almost compelled merchants to make connections with the city. It was thronged with Italians, Spaniards, Portuguese, Frenchmen, Germans, Sephardic "New Christians," and even Russians and an occasional Armenian. Its population may have numbered 100,000 by 1568.[11]

All the complex machinery of modern capitalism may have been present in Antwerp, at least in rudiment, but what was totally lacking was any form of modern regulatory legislation. Businessmen of the era seem to have been born with a knowledge of the techniques of market cornering and rigging, so characteristic of the 1920s. Still other operators were more given to violence than stealth: they merely insured their partners' lives heavily, then hired assassins to murder them. Therefore it should not have been surprising that in negotiating to place its pepper in the hands of a syndicate of Antwerp merchants, the Portuguese crown made a serious mistake.

One problem seems to have originated with a Portuguese "New Christian," Diogo Mendes, who established himself in the city about 1512 and cast his lot with Giancarlo Affaitati and the existing pepper syndicate. Diogo Mendes, the Affaitati, and a group of *Marranos*, or Sephardic Jews, were thereafter the big buyers, contributing from 800,000 to 1,000,000 ducats each to a single shipment, and their lesser partners each put up amounts ranging from 10,000 to 20,000. By massing their purchases so that they bought not only all the spices destined for Antwerp, but almost everything for sale in Lisbon as well, they virtually succeeded in erasing the biggest German banking houses from competition. Then the Mendes-Affaitati group simply made the rest of Europe buy pepper from them at their inflated prices — even the mighty Fuggers were obliged to do so. It did not help Portugal that Diogo Mendes was arrested by the magistracy of Antwerp in 1532 for "Judaizing" and his goods sequestered, or that other *Marranos* were similarly arrested later. Although they may

[10] Lodovico Guicciardini, *Description de tous les Pays-Bas, autrement dict la Germanie Inferieure ou Basse Alemagne*, tr. F. de Belle Forest. Also in Italian original. See particularly the chapter "Discours sur les marchands d'Anvers et sur leur traffic."
[11] See E. E. Rich and C. H. Wilson, *The Economy of Expanding Europe in the Sixteenth and Seventeenth Centuries*, IV, 36.

have been the masterminds, their Christian associates were perfectly capable of carrying on the strategy without them.[12] So long as the double monopoly endured, there was not much that could be done to assure the Portuguese monarch a greater share of the total profit.

An obvious thing for the king to have done — or have tried to do — was to have renegotiated the basic price with the merchants of the syndicate. But in light of what was going on, it is unlikely that these merchants would have put up the huge sums necessary to take the year's fleetload from India off the hands of the Portuguese without first being assured of a very high profit margin. In the first place, the syndicate's own customers were notorious for their pepper speculation; hence, in the event of a price depression, there was always the risk that the merchants of the syndicate would not be able to resell what they had contracted to buy. Second, and even more basic than this, was the sad fact that by 1520, the Portuguese crown needed the syndicate's advance payment to finance the next year's India fleet. Even while King Manuel was still alive, Portugal had begun to slide into debt, undoubtedly as a result of his Moroccan policy. When King João III came to rule, the continuation of his father's policy in Morocco, plus his own dynastic extravagances and the Indian empire's mounting expenses, no doubt helped the slide gather dangerous momentum. As early as 1520, Portuguese officials had begun to ask the syndicate for advances on shipments which had not yet been received from fleets en route to Europe. This, of course, first put the syndicate in a position of "tiding over a friend"; then, as the "advances" persisted and the syndicate was faced with becoming a perpetual deficit banker to Portugal, it needed a high profit margin to recover what it had loaned.

By 1543, the royal debt to the Antwerp syndicate was estimated as 2,169,252 cruzados, and the financiers were becoming restless because João was not meeting the interest payments. Nor were things improved by the depredations of French corsairs and the renewed rivalry between the emperor and King François I, which after 1540 affected neutral shipping far more than it had in the past.[13] The increasingly unstable condi-

---

[12] Azevedo, *Épocas*, pp. 115–116. See also A. [Jan Albert] Goris, *Études sur les colonies marchandes méridionales à anvers de 1458 à 1567*, pp. 199–201. For a summary of Diogo Mendes's trials and that of an associate, together with their effect on the Antwerp merchant community, see Goris, *Colonies marchandes meridionales*, pp. 563–569.

[13] Sousa, *Anais de D. João III*, II, 265–266. Taco Hayo Milo, "Portuguese Trade and

tion dragged on until 1549, when, late in the year, King João was obliged to deliver a fatal blow to the Antwerp syndicate by stopping the royal transmission of spices to the Portuguese *feitoria* there. Buyers of pepper were invited to come directly to Lisbon, which was proclaimed open to all.[14] Then João announced that he was reducing the payments on his debts.

The Monopoly Fails (ca. 1550)

The period between 1549 and 1570 in Portugal was not marked by any imaginative new policies so far as Portugal's marketing problems were concerned. On the contrary, little was involved in the new European business strategy other than a reversion to the 1506 system of selling, i.e., at fixed prices through the *Casa da Índia*. It would have been wise for the crown to have raised these fixed prices to a point between the original price it received from the syndicate and the syndicate's selling price to its customers, for there could have been little sense in giving those customers who formerly bought from the Antwerp syndicate but now came to Lisbon the full wholesale price benefit that the syndicate had formerly enjoyed. The crown would have gained little better income than before and would only have missed the convenience of being able to borrow from a customer who was as dependent on the crown as the crown was upon it. But if it did work out that the crown was actually able to increase its income substantially while offering buyers a comparable saving at the *Casa da Índia*, then the elimination of the syndicate as middleman would have been logical, if desperate. Unfortunately, there are no known wholesale prices upon which to make any statements of fact.

The ruin of the syndicate and the unilateral scaling down of João III's debt might have been a successful maneuver if the Indian operation could therafter have been kept debt-free through an income from pepper which was sufficiently high to pay its costs. After all, the syndicate had been lending back to the king money he might have made in the first place, and since the Portuguese were not then involved in costly European wars, an impairment of Portugal's credit might not have hurt anything — provided

Shipping with the Netherlands after the Discoveries," p. 424. Netherlandish warships even had to convoy the Portuguese on several occasions.

[14] Francisco Paulo Mendes da Luz, *O concelho da Índia; esboço da sua história*, p. 57.

the king could remain solvent in the future.[15] Had not a new element entered the picture, the Portuguese might yet have shown a profit on their Asian enterprise. Until around the turn of the century, Portuguese assumptions had been predicated upon their enjoyment of a de facto spice monopoly. But it soon became apparent that they did not possess one any longer. This was because the old trade routes made a comeback around 1550, or just at the time King João had stopped marketing his pepper in Antwerp.

For decades on end in the sixteenth century, it did not matter much that the Portuguese had not closed the Red Sea, because the Muslim system was so adept at creating its own stumbling blocks. Among them were the overthrow of the Mamelukes by the Ottomans in 1516, the sharp Ottoman hostilities with Venice, and a subsequent period of instability probably to be explained by Venetian mistrust and an initial Ottoman greenness in mercantile affairs. Around 1550, however, a fundamental change occurred in the previously established trading system. First, the Ottomans were beginning to act more and more like the Mamelukes when it came to commerce, and the Venetians were beginning to do business with them much as they had with their earlier Turkish suppliers. Second, the Portuguese apparently gave up trying to stop the "leaks" in the spice trade to the Mediterranean world and instead attempted to license the Arab vessels by making them buy *cartazes* and pay duties as the Gujarati and the other purely Indian states did, as if to profit by what they could not prevent.[16] This need not have occurred had the Portuguese been in firm control of Aden or Jidda and thus could have blocked Arab trading entirely; but lacking this, they either had to intercept Arab competition while still in the Gulf of Aden which they were patently unable to do, or else to accept, as they seem to have done, their shortage of ships and manpower to patrol the area and try to realize what income they could from taxing to some degree whatever rival shipping they came across. This development must have paralleled the Ottoman revival of Red Sea commerce, for the impotence of the Portuguese naval patrols in the Indian Ocean would have become fully apparent to all parties only when the Ottomans sought to renew the commerce of the Red Sea. At any rate, in the last years of Suleiman I ("The Magnificent"), the stability of

[15] Probably nobody who had paid the Affaitati's high prices in Antwerp wasted much time feeling sorry for them when the Cremonese house went bankrupt in 1560.

[16] Godinho, *L'Économie de l'empire portugais*, pp. 774–780.

Red Sea traffic had been restored, and the Ottomans had begun to revive the heretofore moribund Basra-Aleppo desert route. Soon thereafter, spices had so obviously begun to flow back into the old channels — and at such competitive prices — that in 1558, for example, the Fuggers deserted Lisbon and turned to the Mediterranean for their procurement. There, despite the entry of new European commercial powers into the trade with Cairo and Alexandria, Venice quickly revived its leadership as a major distributor.[17] As remarked in chapter 15, Venetian shipping was sufficiently diversified in the years before the Portuguese discoveries that it had never really depended on the oriental luxury trade for its survival; it operated an important Mediterranean interport carrying trade, and it would appear that by 1510, its citizenry had turned from the spice trade and begun to invest heavily in agriculture on the mainland — with such success, incidentally, that the revenue from this source grew 400 percent in the course of the century.[18] When spices became available in large quantities once more via the Red Sea, Venice was therefore fit, and only too eager, to distribute them as in the old days. Thereafter, most customers of the Portuguese availed themselves of both sources of supply, Lisbon and Venice, and pepper prices entered a decade or two of wide fluctuation. This was good for the customers, no doubt; but for the Portuguese, the revival of the Middle Eastern routes and the reentry of Venice into the pepper competition meant that a new condition — and now one completely beyond their control — was preventing them from selling in Europe as dearly as they needed to if they wished to profit from their Asian operations. There was easily a market for all the spices both competitors could import into Europe during this period.[19] But any circumstance that tended to keep prices unstable could only have worked to

[17] The Fuggers, for example, even found a way to bypass Venice, via Dalmatia, as did the French, who traded directly with Egypt via Marseilles and did their marketing in Lyons. For Venice and the Fugger, see F. C. Lane, "The Mediterranean Spice Trade: Further Evidence of Its Revival in the Sixteenth Century," pp. 585–588. See also Hermann Kellenbenz "Autour de 1600: le commerce du poivre des Fugger et le marché international du poivre," pp. 1–28. For France, see René Gascon, "Un Siècle du commerce des épices à Lyon. Fin XVe-XVIe siècles," pp. 638–666.

[18] S. J. Woolf, "Venice and the Terraferma: Problems of the Change from Commercial to Landed Activities," as reprinted in Brian Pullan (ed.) *Crisis and Change in the Venetian Economy*, p. 182.

[19] F. C. Lane estimates that in 1500, annual pepper imports into Europe were about 1.5 to 2 million pounds, whereas by 1560, they had risen to 3 million. In Pullan, *Crisis and Change*, p. 54, no. 2. According to Lane, Venetian exports doubled in the course of the century, while Jaime Cortesão estimated that Portuguese exports between 1506 and 1598 increased almost ten times.

Portugal's further detriment. This was especially true when one considers that, besides the costs and dangers of the Cape route, Portuguese Asia itself was anything but efficiently or smoothly operated as an economic unit.

Asia: the Other Set of Books

The Portuguese kept two sets of ledgers concerning the finances of their Asian empire. One dealt with the long-distance Asia-to-Europe trade and balanced the European sales from the Asian monopoly goods against the specie transfers necessary to buy them, plus the transportation costs. The second set, as if the items it covered could really be divorced from the first, covered the empire's local sources of income in Asia — its rents, tributes, and customs revenues. Then it balanced against these the standing expenses of the Asian operation, consisting mostly of salaries to Portuguese Asian officials and soldiery. So far as is known, no document exists that rationalizes this dual system, but the implication is clear enough that the Portuguese Asian operation was supposed to pay its own way and the trade that flowed from it was intended to make a handsome profit for the crown. Actually, it never worked this way. Because the empire was limited in extent, the local sources of income were never more than barely enough to cover its minimum overhead, and moneys for anything beyond local salaries, i.e., those needed for armadas, campaigns, fortress remodeling, or repairs, had to come from Lisbon, either out of profits from the India-to-Europe commerce or out of general Portuguese revenues. No master books existed that balanced off the long-distance and Asian financial system, and, so far as the crown was concerned, money remitted to Asia for anything but spice procurement was a gift, grudgingly given. Both Manuel and João III, apparently, were reluctant to dilute European profits with Asian expenditures, no doubt because in their eyes the Asian empire was designed to create revenues, not absorb them. However, in light of the need for aggressive patroling of approaches to the Red Sea, or the various sieges of Diu or Malacca which had to be sustained, Asian sources of income were totally inadequate. It is well known that João de Castro even had to borrow the money in Goa to relieve Diu in 1545 and on his personal credit.

In addition to unrealistic bookkeeping, there were other aspects of the Asian operation that confused the crown, embarrassed it financially, or went completely unnoticed. One of these was that the government of Portuguese Asia was notorious for its corruption.

The reasons for this corruption among Portuguese public officials are not far to seek. All the European nobility of this era habitually believed their king owed them a living, and very few of them ever thought they should take the nominal and often minimal salary attached to their posts too seriously. Asian public officials, moreover, had raised peculation to a degree even more artistic than that of the Europeans, and the Westerners became their willing students. Finally, exile from their homeland and the enormous risks men incurred in sailing to the East seem to have attracted mainly the adventurous or the desperately penniless. The pattern is familiar in all the European overseas empires, and the old adage that men threw away their spoons when rounding the Cape of Good Hope proved true indeed. Surrounded by sickness, poverty, and death, by strange customs, incredible opulence, and easy companions eager to compromise the newcomer, many a Portuguese with basically good morals slipped them off on the eastward voyage, only to dress in them again if he ever returned home. While in Asia, the trick was to move from one office to a grander one every triennium and to invest the dishonest gains from one in the illicit opportunities peculiar to the next. The king paid double to his officials for the procurement of goods for the state, these officials paid their superiors for silence, and bystanders were forced to buy unwanted things or give up their property in state "emergencies" — receiving only a fraction of its value. Few of the abuses were unique to Portuguese Asia; many more were "modern" — or, rather, universal.

Ironically, it may not have been the peculators who helped ruin the empire so much as the honest or at least the not exactly dishonest. A more basic reason for Portuguese Asia's inability to produce revenue seems to have been that the crown inadvertently left the biggest source of potential profit to persons who either had dropped out of government service altogether or had invested their extra income and their best talents in work either unrelated to or in competition with their official jobs. As remarked in chapter 18, it was easy to leave royal employment, especially for the *soldado*, who could simply neglect to enlist at the annual muster. Then, also as remarked, the state, eager to preserve the native economy of the places Portugal had acquired or conquered — Ormuz, Goa, Malacca, Diu, and Daman chief among them — tended to keep the traditionally low customs rates charged by its predecessors, usually at from 4 to

6 percent on imports and exports, and merely to concentrate on making as many native vessels as possible stop and pay them via the *cartaz* and convoy system. (At the time, of course, the king and his councillors were only interested in and aware of the long-distance trade between Asia and Europe, and they absorbed themselves in trying to organize it successfully.) Apparently, Lisbon did not realize soon enough that it could make as much or more money if the crown were itself to enter into buying and selling commodities purely within Asia (the country trade), most of which did not concern the long-distance trade and hence were not under the royal monopoly. The royal employees, however, must have found out, almost as soon as they arrived, about the various trading opportunities from the same sources who told them about the Asian geography. Quickly, commanders of fortresses and exsoldiers, alone or in combination, went into business for themselves, and, as often as not, they fronted for viceroys, *vedores da fazenda*, and other administrators, or at least raised extra capital from those officials or paid them bribes. Essentially, they did the same things the Islamic traders had done, only with better capital and equipment, and they were not harassed by the armadas and patrols designed to suppress Muslim operations — in fact, as likely as not they were convoyed by royal ships, either officially as part of the *cáfilas* or unofficially (as when administrators owned a part of the cargo). It has been seen in the preceding chapter how they exploited the China trade — and even discovered Japan. In addition, they developed a flourishing commerce in the Bay of Bengal, settled permanently at Hugli, and kept the business with Pegu mostly to themselves throughout the sixteenth century. At a later date, they also founded an independent Portuguese community at Negapatam, near the Cape of Comorin. Obviously they were a formidable and innovative group whose success reveals that the royal grasp did not extend far enough to insure its own well-being.

The crown itself should have recognized and preempted this rich Asian interregional trade, as did the United East India Company of the Dutch in the seventeenth century (whose theoreticians, like Petrus Plancius, consciously learned from the Portuguese mistake). Had the crown become the entrepreneur, or even arranged for a bigger share of the take — for example by declaring certain inter-Asian commodities monopoly items and then collecting a royal Fifth on them, or had it provided some of the operating capital for the Inter-Asian trade itself, or both — the difference might have been one between profit and loss for the Asian set of books. The king did do something like this most notably with the concession voyages to Indonesia and China and Japan, and with the Ormuz trade; but his move came too late and, except for the Ormuz trade, gave the concessionaires as great a cut as the crown took. Perhaps the most one can say of this lost Inter-Asian trading opportunity is that, despite vast business experience in Europe, the Portuguese monarchy simply overlooked it while pursuing the trade between India and Lisbon. Private traders throughout most parts of the empire meanwhile paid their typically 3.5, 4 to 4.5, or even 6 percent custom duties to the *alfândega* — one trusts they paid even those — and waxed rich in spite of some private shakedowns by port officials, notably at Malacca. (And these, by the way, only go to show the crown was not taking in enough: otherwise the extortions would have ruined the trade). By the chronicler Couto's time in the 1580s, the consequences were plain to all but duty-minded Couto himself: a threadbare government existed in a wealthy state. Perhaps too few historians have pointed out in the past that Portuguese Asia was no failure before the Dutch arrived — only the treasury and the military apparatus were impoverished. In fact, instead of condemning Portugal for lack of business perspicacity, writers with capitalist inclinations should make the necessary distinctions and hold up the private merchants and even the officials leading double lives as models of successful enterprise.[20] The real trouble appears to have been that the

[20]The literature on Portuguese Asian corruption is vast but somewhat diffuse. Writers from Whiteway and Danvers to Justes Strandes, E. Denison Ross, and James Duffy have all dwelt upon it more or less at length, although the citations are too scattered to afford good concrete examples. My own book, *The Fatal History of Portuguese Ceylon; Transition to Dutch Rule*, though centered on the seventeenth century, supplies information. Chapter 6, "The Vicious Circle," provides a general description.

The classic evocation by a contemporary is that of the chronicler Diogo do Couto, whose *O soldado prático* is widely known, though there is no English translation. For those who wish more specific information on the period covered in this volume, it is desirable to read the version entitled *Observacões sobre as principães causas da decadência dos portuguêzes na Asia* because it contains two dialogues, the first written about 1580 and the second around 1612. The latter is more biting and more famous as literature, but the first is more specific and, of course, closer to the period encompassed by this text. There are also sections in the works of Jan Huighen van Linschoten and François Pyrard de Laval, both in convenient English translations published by the Hakluyt Society, which fully corroborate what Couto says. The text and bibliography of *The Fatal History* contain some additional sources.

Literature on the Inter-Asian trading of the Portuguese is much scantier. W. H. Moreland has called attention to it throughout his *India at the Death of Akbar*, as have M. A. P. Meilink-Roelofsz, in her *Asian Trade and European Influence*, and C. R. Boxer in a number of his writings, including *Francisco Vieira de Figueiredo, a Portuguese Merchant Adventurer in South-East Asia, 1624–1667*.

Portuguese writers frequently take the Inter-Asian trade into account. See for example,

royal corporation created — unwittingly, to be sure — too many profit-sharing opportunities and too many temptations for its employees and exemployees, kept unrealistic ledgers contrasting the wrong expenses, and then stood aside while the people who should have been enriching the corporation laid by their own fortunes out of its own natural substance.

An Era of Innovation (1570–77)

When Infante-apparent João predeceased his father, João III, in 1554, his own heir was still twenty days from birth. In those twenty days, Portugal waited anxiously to learn whether the baby would be male; otherwise, it was entirely possible that Don Carlos of Spain might eventually rule them. Portuguese joy therefore knew no limits when a boy, named Sebastião, was born posthumously to João by Joana of Austria. That Don Carlos was a Spaniard was enough for the Portuguese people, always less than lukewarm to their neighbor: little did they realize that they had escaped the shadow of the most incompetent crown price of the sixteenth century only to celebrate the nativity of the only person of the age who approximated him in unfitness to rule. Once Sebastião's majority had been declared in 1568, he ruined the country in slightly less than ten years.

João III died in 1557, and for the first six years of Sebastião's minority, his paternal grandmother, Catarina, a Spaniard, ruled in accordance with his grandfather's supposed deathbed wish. Although intelligent, she was very reluctant to rule, tried to resign immediately, and was only persuaded by her brother-in-law the Cardinal-Infante Henrique to stay on until 1562. It is interesting, and significant, that the occasion for her resignation was the popular outburst caused by her thoroughly sensible proposal to abandon the besieged fortress of Mazagão, in North Africa.

Henrique himself then replaced her. Ecclesiastical affairs and humanis-

---

Jaime Cortesão's appraisal in the (Barcelos) *História de Portugal*, IV, 76–77. There is primary evidence in the travel account written by Jean Baptiste Tavernier. See also Pyrard de Laval and Linschoten's descriptions of Goa, which when compared with the picture in Couto's *Soldado prático* are valuable. Couto himself condemns the fortress commanders and upbraids other public officials for trading privately under various guises. The religious orders, especially the Jesuits, were enterprising traders. There are frequent allusions in all the chronicles to *cáfilas* (groupings of merchant ships, whether convoyed or not) plying up and down in Asian waters, which from the context were plainly owned by Portuguese merchants. Finally, one gets the most vivid glimpse of the Inter-Asian traders in the accounts of the founding of trade with China and Japan.

tic learning had taken up his whole life until then; as inquisitor-general he was far too conscientious for modern tastes. Otherwise, he was uninformed and retiring by nature, rather than forceful. He did display occasional understanding for the subtleties of leadership, but it seems to have taken him nearly his whole regency to master his job. Regencies, in any event, are seldom distinguished or innovative, and Henrique had been too long in the provinces (first in Braga and then in Évora) and too much surrounded by fellow churchmen to have built much of a personal following among the former king's courtiers. The best thing he did was to bring some needed ecclesiastical revenues to the aid of the state.

When Sebastião's majority was declared in his fifteenth year, Portugal was delivered into the hands of a teen-ager whose unbalanced behavior and insolence were believed to have hastened the death of his grandmother Catarina and whose obnoxious companions so vexed the Cardinal-Infante that he pronounced them "such miserable favor-seekers and sycophants . . . that they deserve no less than roasting on the fires which burn Jews in the Holy Inquisition."[21] Sebastião showed no interest whatever in girls, either as dynastic vehicles or as playmates. Instead, he dreamed only of leading a holy Crusade against the Moors in North Africa. Though pale and unhealthy, he feverishly drilled himself and his favorites at arms, and worried his elders by long dashes on horseback through wintry terrain. The only sane men who had much influence over him were the Jesuits, and these only when they purported to go along with him.

Neither Catarina nor Henrique had had the training or the disposition to experiment with the home administration, and Sebastião was little more than a case of arrested development. Yet paradoxically, major experiments and innovations were undertaken in the overseas empire almost as soon as Sebastião came to power. More research is needed to establish cause and effect, but it could well be that Sebastião's need for money to finance his North African ambitions, plus his lack of any position concerning pressing Asian matters, actually permitted a variety of other approaches to surface — those fostered by foreign and domestic merchants, by members of the councils, and by the Jesuits. If one did not know better, one would almost suppose that an active and restless new captain had been guiding events. It only looked this way; in the absence of a

---

[21] Letter to Duke of Aveiro dated Alcobaça, 14 September 1573, in Joaquim Veríssimo Serrão (ed.) *Documentos Inéditos para a história do reinado de D. Sebastião*, p. 85.

captain, the crew members had twisted the ship's wheel this way and that.

The discontinuation of the Antwerp marketing system in 1549 may have given the crown a breather, but it cured neither the speculation in pepper among those who bought it from the *Casa da Índia* nor the need for royal credit.[22] At first, buyers who heretofore had been forced to deal with the syndicate must have hastened to Lisbon to avail themselves of a saving; but even increased revenues at the Casa da *Índia* could not have paid for the heavy drag of the Indian viceroyalty's expenses. Long before João III's death, the monarchy resumed its borrowing against future deliveries, this time amid the resentment of the banking fraternity and its universal suspicion that a king who had once repudiated his debts was no great credit risk for the future. Venice had begun to revive, and merchants shopped to find the best bargain between the two competitors, or else bought spices to see if the market would move upward; they were always dumping spices just as prices improved. The Portuguese could be expected to try a new approach.

On March 1, 1570, Sebastião signed a decree called "Regiment for the trade of pepper, drugs, and merchandise of India," which suddenly renounced the royal spice monopoly. Save only for the final pricing and marketing in Europe, reserved for the *Casa da Índia*, all phases of spice procurement in Asia and transport to Portugal were declared open to all comers at the Malabar cities of Cannanore, Chalé, Quilon and Cochin — plus others upon permission from the authorities in India. Malacca was declared a free port for all pepper destined for Goa and export to Portugal. Buyers could buy in whatever quality or quantity they wished and transport their purchases back to Europe in ships owned by the crown, or even in private ones if they thought they could effect savings over the official freight charges. The only restrictions (though some more were added in 1571) were that silver and copper could not be exported to the East by the private interests, and all ships transporting spices from the Orient had to call in Lisbon and pay the royal duties, upon pain of confiscation: 18 cruzados per quintal of pepper, 30 on cloves and most of the luxury spices, and 50 on nutmeg.[23] This was a stiff impost schedule,

[22] Some writers have stated mistakenly that the *feitoria* itself was closed. It existed in some form until the French Revolutionary period; only its identity with the *Casa da Índia* was broken.

[23] Azevedo, *Épocas*, pp. 136–137. See also Vincente M. M. C. Almeida d'Eça, *Normas*

indeed, and it amounted to considerably more than a royal Fifth, taken in kind, might have cost. Still, the profits must have been acceptable to the entrepreneurs; it has been estimated that during 1572 the crown cleared in the neighborhood of a half million cruzados on the new trading scheme.[24] Such estimates, of course, only measure the profits on European sales against the shipping costs and depreciation for a given year and neglected the Asian standing expenses entirely; the "surplus" would not have gone far in paying interest on past debts, rebuilding the cities shattered a year earlier in the allied assault on Portuguese India, and sending an adequate reinforcement to the beleagured São João de Ternate. Almost certainly, the "gains," if any, from the 1570 legislation never found their way back to India at all. Sebastião began to conceive his invasion of Morocco around 1574, and it is hardly to be imagined that money was spent on India which did not absolutely have to be.

Exactly what prompted the bold move of 1570 to free trade with India is not known for certain, but, undoubtedly, failing royal credit paved the way. Beyond this, the plan may have come from a proposal made by a councillor or even a merchant. It seems not to have been an entirely bad idea as far as it went, but its main trouble was that it did not go far enough. All such remedies that neglected the raising of adequate capital and the placing of merchants in control of the administration were superficial. What Portuguese Asia really needed was a fundamental reengineering to turn it into a more modern commercial operation — something which aristocratic Iberian councillors lacked the perspective to give it, but which the bourgeois Dutch displayed in their creation of an East India Company thirty years later.[25]

No really persistent desire to bring about a fundamental reform in Portuguese Asian trade could have prompted the 1570 *regimento*. Instead, Sebastião's sole motive seems to have been to lay his hands on

ecónomicas na colonização portuguesa até 1808; memória, pp. 62–66. He incorrectly gives the date as 1577.

[24] Lach, *Asia in the Making of Europe*, I, pt. 1, 132. I cannot find a contemporary statement for this particular year in order to examine what expenses it includes, but it seems virtually foregone that these followed the usual division.

[25] Once the Dutch company had demonstrated its success, numerous individuals and groups pressed the Philippine kings and even João IV and Pedro II to use its charter as a model for a Portuguese reorganization of the Indian empire. This actually came to pass in 1628 during the period of Spanish rule, but too much politicking had removed the important elements of the scheme and it was abandoned in 1633. See C. R. Boxer, "The Papers of Dom António de Ataíde."

money, the more the better, and he and his councillors probably thought that reducing the need to finance Indian fleets would free funds for activities in North Africa. For, certainly, his contract made five years later, in 1575, with Konrad Rott of Augsburg, suggests that a restless expediency, rather than any real vision, underlay all the changes his administration made in regard to Asia. The deal with Rott all but completely reversed the *regimento* of five years earlier. Rott was given a three-year monopoly on the procurement of pepper brought from India to Portugal. The heart of the arrangement was none other than Rott's promise to make a huge loan to Portugal at low interest rates.[26] Soon other commercial houses were given similar deeds for nutmeg and other spices, and with the one change of assigning each condiment to a different contractor, the Portuguese Asian trading pattern reverted most nearly to the practices of 1505, when German and Italian merchants had outfitted their own vessels.

Sebastião decreed yet another Asian innovation in the year 1569, the organization of Portuguese Asia into three separate entities, already mentioned in chapter 19. Exactly who and what prompted the move is as uncertain as who and what prompted all the other modifications; but a desire to effect fundamental administrative improvements is the least likely candidate among reasons. More probably, it was the by-product of other considerations: the desire to conquer the gold mines of Monomotapa in East Africa and the need to find the right man for the job. The right man seemed to be ex-Indian Governor Francisco Barreto, and he was no doubt an intelligent choice. But, as Sebastião's councillors must have reasoned, to have placed him in a position clearly subordinate to the governor at Goa would in effect have meant a demotion. So it must have seemed necessary to create a new captaincy-general just for him, and a second and similar new post for Malacca and the Far East was thrown in, as if for good measure, because the monarchy never got around to filling it after its initial appointee failed to take up his office. In Barreto's case, the new African title meant little, anyway. Sebastião's Jesuit friends imposed the opinionated Father Manclaros, S.J., upon him as an adviser, and conflict between cross and sword brought the whole expedition to naught (see chapter 19).

[26] See the article by K. Haebler, "Konrad Rott und die thüringische Gesellschaft."

The End of a Dynasty (1578–80)

The drama of Sebastião was soon played out. In 1574, the king had paid a visit to Ceuta and Tangier, and had tried, in vain, to provoke the Moors into doing battle with him. From that time on, all the visions of empire in Morocco which had inspired Sebastião's ancestors returned to delude him; he even spoke of sitting on the sultan's throne in Byzantium.[27] In 1576, he called for a meeting with his uncle King Philip II of Spain and proposed a joint expedition against the Moroccan port city of Larache. This place, he said, was about to become the base for vicious raids on the Iberian Peninsula, launched by the new Moroccan strongman Muley 'Abd-al-Malik, who recently usurped the throne of Sultan Muley Mohammed. King Philip, skeptical and afflicted with far more pressing worries, dutifully warned Sebastião of the grave dangers of taking on with unseasoned troops tough Berber fighting men; but he reluctantly promised some Spanish aid in two years' time if Sebastião persisted in his determination to go ahead.

Philip II's coolness keenly disappointed Sebastião, but it soon became evident to all that the young king was indeed going ahead and at a gallop. Cardinal-Infante Henrique resigned from his council. All relations with the disapproving Catarina were severed. Meanwhile, Sebastião's two executive advisers, Martim Gonçalves de Câmara and Martinho Pereira, helped him borrow every penny he could from every possible source and levy taxes on everything he could.

In spite of his kingdom's utmost efforts, Sebastião soon discovered he could not do without his uncle's offer of help and he could not have expected to field his own expedition much sooner than 1578. He pawned Portugal's future more deeply, contracted for auxiliaries, and tried to raise the money for them. When the spring of 1577 came, however, Sebastião's whole scheme went amiss. The governor of Larache, a friend of the overthrown Muley Mohammed, proposed delivering the city to Portugal, thus obviating the whole Portuguese plan for intervention. Muley 'Abd-al-Malik earnestly professed his desire for peace, not war. Philip II, whose finances, as always, were in bad condition, used all this as a legitimate reason for withdrawing his pledge of aid.

[27] A devastating description of Sebastião's fantasies and total incapacity to organize his expedition is in chapter IX, "Nas vesperas da catástrofe" by J. M. de Queiroz Velloso, *D. Sebastião, 1554–1578*, pp. 293–336.

In June 1578, Sebastião hoisted anchor in the Tagus and sailed for North Africa with some 800 ships of all varieties, loaded with some 17,000 men — 15,500 cavalry and 1500 infantry. When no Moor contested him, he marched in land from Arzila for a hundred miles, while the wiser of his nobles contemplated taking him into custody. Suddenly, the forces of 'Abd-al-Malik, 40,000 horsemen strong, swept down on the wandering European army and annihilated it. Sebastião and 7000 or Portugal's highest nobility and best fighting men lay dead in the wasteland near Al-Ksar-el-Kebir; in addition to this immeasurable cost, Sebastião had consumed a more measurable quantity to achieve what in effect became his annihilation: more than half of the whole state's annual budget.[28] The Moors carefully ransomed the survivors, according to rank, for nearly all the remaining cash in Portugal.[29] Many of the greatest families in the land spent nearly their last obtainable cruzado liberating their heads of household and sons and nephews.

Henrique, the Cardinal-Infante, was then crowned king; but he was tubercular and feeble at sixty-six. He had lost all interest in politics, and, indeed, in life. Only his sense of duty remained. Although the Portuguese chancery petitioned Rome for a marriage dispensation on Henrique's behalf, only the cautious Philip II, now bent on claiming Portugal, paid any attention to it. The real problem concerned who would follow the infirm man to the Portuguese throne.

João III had left no descendant besides Sebastião; all the claimants traced their lineage to Manuel. Manuel's fourth son, Luís, had a bastard, António, who became the prior of Crato, and two legitimate daughters, the deceased Maria, who married Alessandro Farnese and had a son, Ranuccio, by him, and Catarina, then married to the Duke of Bragança. Isabella, one of Manuel's own daughters, however, had married the emperor and mothered Philip II.

Modern historians are far less preoccupied with the tangle of such succession disputes than with the circumstances that decided the outcome. As Professor A. H. de Oliveira Marques points out, Ranuccio Farnese had by far the best claim, but his father worked for Philip II and this circumstance effectively stifled it.[30]

A certain amount of politicking took place on behalf of all the candi-

[28] António Henrique Rodrigo de Oliveira Marques, *History of Portugal*, I, 312.
[29] *Ibid.*
[30] *Ibid.*

dates, although the only two who actively represented their own causes were António and King Philip. Philip II's claim may have been debatable in terms of male versus female lineage, but it was by far and away the best claim in terms of practical considerations. For Philip, alone, through his Portuguese representative Cristóbal de Moura, was able to alleviate the poverty of those influential noblemen who could bring themselves to feel that he was the proper king for Portugal. And it has often been suggested, though perhaps without sufficient documentation, that many merchants and servants of the crown involved in the Indian trade believed that an affiliation with Spain would make Spanish bullion more easily available to them. It is indeed possible.

Cardinal-Infante Henrique was not enthusiastic over Philip's candidacy; but he did not favor the prior of Crato (whom he considered an ass), and he realized that Catarina totally lacked the pluck to stand up to Philip. With what little strength remained to him, he immersed himself in the ransom of the Moroccan prisoners and postponed the decision-making, almost until his dying breath. Finally, in 1579, he called the *Cortes* for advice. By that time Philip II's "silver bullets," as the Spanish king's bribes are sometimes called, had found their victims, and the division that confronted Henrique only made it more difficult for the fast-weakening monarch to make up his mind. Just before he died, at the end of January 1580, he reluctantly designated Philip as king-apparent of Portugal, as if only to avoid bloodshed. Philip's general, the Duke of Alva, thereupon moved across the border from Badajoz, captured Lisbon, and crushed an impromptu army thrown together by the prior of Crato. Philip himself then arrived for an extended visit, met the *Cortes* at Tomar in 1581, and promised that he would respect Portugal's integrity and not unite it with his other kingdoms.

The Tally

The Portuguese empire in Asia scarcely ended in 1580 — in fact the real challengers to its existence, the Dutch and the English, did not appear in force for another quarter century. Historians — Portuguese, Spanish, and English-speaking — have been of many minds over the question of Spanish intentions and influence for good or ill during the period of rule from Madrid, and there are so many questions regarding it which only future archival research can illumine — and so many imponderables —

that it is perhaps well for this volume not to attempt to answer them. Why, for instance, did Portugal's era of shipwrecks on the *Carreira da Índia* begin only after 1580? And might the Dutch and English have stayed out of Asia for decades longer had not Philip II seized Dutch shipping in the Tagus in 1592? It is obvious that the Spanish connection made dangerous enemies for Portugal of its old commercial allies and friends in Holland and England, and that these proved the scourge of Portuguese Asia beginning in the seventeenth century. If the forced marriage of Portugal to Spain had had no other effects for good or ill than turning those nations into enemies of the Portuguese, then it can hardly be maintained that the bride's lot proved in any way fortunate. The Spanish did not even bring to the union new ideas or compensatory naval or military protection which might have offset the inconvenience that the reversal of alliances caused Portugal.[31]

If one looks to the past from the year 1580 instead of to the future, it should become apparent immediately that the empire in Asia never enriched the crown for any considerable length of time. Failure to close the Red Sea may not have hurt its operation so much as people have supposed, for thanks to Turkish problems and mismanagement, the Portuguese enjoyed a de facto trade monopoly of Asian spices for half a century before the revival of the Middle Eastern routes and Mediterranean competition. Yet, after the first decades of profit, they would not, or could not, make their Asian operation successful. Probably this was a combined result of Kings Manuel and João III's careless financial practices on the European end of the *Carreira*, the growing expenses of personnel, fortresses, and maintenance on the Asian end, and the crown's rather too narrow approach to making the most of its trading opportunities. Following the Mediterranean revival, about 1550, pepper prices in Europe became even more unstable than they had been during the period before 1506 and the Portuguese hold on the market even less secure, in spite of increasing demands from the European consumer. Maneuvers like the shift from the Antwerp monopoly were at best palliatives; by 1564, the regent or one of his councillors complained in a *cédula* that "expenditures

---

[31] It is at least to Philip II's credit that he resisted proposals from his Spanish subjects to move in and take over the trading concessions. See the article by Paul E. Hoffman, "The Portuguese Crown's Cost and Profits in the India Trade, 1580. A Report with a Proposal for Increasing the Profits," pp. 22–32.

always run far ahead of receipts."[32] The abolition of the monopoly did not produce any better results, either.

The *regimentos* of Viceroy Antão de Noronha, already mentioned in chapter 18, make it clear that at best, the Asian empire's standing expenses, i.e., the salaries and perquisites of imperial officials and soldiers, as well as the expenses of hospitals and pensions, were barely offset by the customs tolls, tributes, and land rents from Asian possessions, and profits from concessionaires of the Japan and Moluccas voyages. All additional expenses — those for military campaigns, sieges, new fortifications, buildings, and naval construction and maintenance, plus all endowments of the religious orders — had to be paid out of Portuguese crown revenues, if not literally those acquired in Europe from the long-distance trade. These long-distance revenues themselves may have amounted to as much as 535,000 cruzados in 1587, but this hardly represented a great surplus; even if the money did not have to be directed into the next year's spice purchase after 1570, half of it must quickly have melted into interest payments on past borrowings, not to mention the cost of outfitting and replacing ships for the *Carreira*.[33] On the other hand, the crown's deficit in its Asian operation before 1571 probably ran to at least 25,000 cruzados per year in relatively quiet years, like those of Viceroy Antão de Noronha's tenure (1564–68).[34] One can be sure that in years of campaigning like 1560 (when Viceroy Constantino de Bragança invaded Jaffnapatam) or siege like 1570 (the Muslim grand assault), the deficit increased many fold. (Even then it was kept as low as it was by paring necessary expenses to the danger point.) It is no wonder that the Council of State in Lisbon would abolish the crown monopoly or even entertain such schemes as the conquest of Monomotapa in a wishful attempt to break out of the circle of limitations in Asia by acquiring a steady and plentiful supply of gold. Or that, more mundanely, it would try to "license" what competing trade to and from the Red Sea it did not have the power to stop — in an attempt to profit by its weakness and at least make ends meet. As it was, its Asian ledgers only approached the equilibrium point as closely as they did because of the revenue derived from the *cartaz*-custom-and-convoy

---

[32] Quoted by Pissurlencar in his introduction to *Regimentos das fortalezas*, p. x.

[33] Luís de Figueiredo Falcão, *Livro em que se contem toda a fazenda e real patrimonio dos reis de Portugal, Índia e Ilhas adjacentes, e outras particularidades, escripta no anno de MDCVII*, pp. 201–204.

[34] Pissurlencar, *Regimentos das fortalezas*, p. x.

scheme, which had long been imposed on Gujarat, Ahmadnagar, and other Indian maritime states.

The Dutch and English East India companies of the next century departed from the Portuguese imperial practice of depending on the long-distance trade on one hand and Asian tax revenues and tributes on the other, and made pursuit of the Inter-Asian trade a third feature of their corporate operations. Even when one concedes the efficiency of Dutch management, it is clear from studies like Kristof Glamann's that profits from the Batavia-to-Amsterdam trade never could have paid for United East India Company operations, even when these were supplemented by the same kind of land rents and tributes due the Dutch in Asia that the Portuguese collected.[35] The point, however, is that the Dutch never tried to make it do so, just as the Portuguese rulers never seriously tried to capture the trade between points in Asia for their own treasury, that is except for the relatively uneconomical (for the crown) concession voyages.

Hence one cannot escape the conclusion that what was such a brilliant success strategically and militarily in the sixteenth century became a white elephant economically because it was never properly conceived or organized to make ends meet. However, to have expected the kind of insight from the Portuguese pioneers that would have avoided from the outset the mistakes they actually did make, or would have remedied them before they became hopelessly institutionalized, is to expect more than it is reasonable for historians to demand of fallible human beings laboring under the hypotheses of their times. Until experience proved otherwise, the long-distance trade must have looked fabulously profitable not only to the empire's founders but to everyone in Europe, and obviously no one in authority realized soon enough that this trade alone could not be tapped without an extremely high investment and a permanently high overhead. Nor could men dazzled by the promise of wealth that the spice trade represented to them have possibly been aware that even greater wealth might lie in developing a systematic interport trade on the Indian Ocean and China Seas. No doubt kings and *fidalgos* could hardly have perceived these less glamorous operations as worthy undertakings for a king until a host of practical-minded traders had appeared from their own soldiery and demonstrated that many crumbs could be scraped together to make a mountain. In other words, isolated Europeans had to hit almost by

[35] Kristof Glamann, *Dutch Asiatic Trade, 1628–1740*, especially chapters IV, V, VII, VIII, and XII.

accident upon the possibilities inherent in Inter-Asian trade before the European world could grasp its significance and reap its profits in the seventeenth century.

Governments seldom are distinguished for innovating totally new structures; rather, they seek to reshape what they find to their own advantage. With the Inter-Asian trade, which grew almost unnoticed, the Portuguese crown had no institution readily at hand to tap any of its profits save the *alfândega*, or customs house; by the time of Albuquerque's death they had just finished the adaptation of this body to the preexisting native commercial patterns by retaining the percentages the natives were used to paying — which were low by European standards. At the same time, however, they sought to enlarge the scope of the collections made by compelling even the trade that was merely plying up and down the coast to other destinations to stop off and pay duties to the Portuguese crown. As remarked earlier, this only worked in a few places, notably India's west coast and in the Strait of Malacca. But probably, the innovation seemed so satisfactory at the outset in yielding up extra revenue that King Manuel and his advisers could imagine no more advantageous way to make money out of the royal presence in India. The Portuguese *casados*, however, did think of better ways, and they quickly waxed rich on them. Crown officials in Asia soon caught on, too, but they lined their own pockets rather than trying to convince Lisbon of opportunities overlooked.

It is difficult to see how, once the Portuguese crown had established its pattern of operation, it could have improved its basic condition without a fundamental job of administrative reengineering, one such as it never achieved. On the other hand, it must have been relatively easy for the Dutch — and to some extent the English — to see at a much later date that any organization trading in Asia would miss the best opportunities if it did not avail itself of the substantial revenues to be made by back and forth carrying and marketing there. (Of these two, the Dutch India company seems to have enjoyed better success than the English one in keeping its employees from private competition.) The Portuguese operation, however, belonged to an earlier epoch and its form had hardened like concrete before the opportunities had even been noticed.

While the Portuguese were operating their empire at such a great disadvantage to the royal treasury, what moneys did come into it as a result of their Asian imports appear to have been absorbed instantly into other state expenditures — so rapidly, in fact, that the crown normally even had to borrow the capital in Europe to finance its next year's cargoes of pepper in India. To a great extent, though in the almost total absence of data it is impossible to tell how much, the financial plight of the Asian empire must have been due even less to its confused bookkeeping, which kept Asian expenses separate from European spice revenues, than to an even more shortsighted practice of spending the Asian spice revenues, as they came in, on pressing needs of the crown, and then being caught short on that cash necessary to finance the next year's wholesale purchases. Morocco, dynastic marriages, the buying of Spanish claims to the Moluccas, and the outfitting of Tomé de Sousa's Brazil fleet in 1549 must all have become so intertwined financially with Indian and Asian affairs that if all the documents did exist today, they would probably make no sense at all, except in terms of how, figuratively speaking, Peter could be tapped to pay Paul, and then Paul to pay Peter, and Peter, James. Such a fiscal chaos existed in the Spain of Charles V and Philip II, and a parallel in Lisbon would hardly be surprising.

European monarchs have always been far more interested in what went on under their noses than in places thousands of miles away, and the only historic empires safe from periodic neglect were those built and operated by joint stock companies, which had no outside interests to distract them. The Spanish, the French, and the Portuguese kings all operated highly centralized empires in one sense; but the weakest point in them was precisely at the center. Once the rulers themselves became immersed in interests close at hand, their empires only came to notice whenever money was sent home which could be disbursed to keep the royal credit intact.

It is sad that this happened in Portugal, whose whole national history is inseparable from the expansion of Europe. But Portugal's was the pioneer empire in more ways than one, and it exhibited all the defects as well as all the glories of the age it inaugurated. No nation of the fifteenth or sixteenth century ever saw more, reported a greater variety of things, or left more of its imprint on the modern world, whose chief characteristic, after all, is mobility. People in northern European countries have never fully realized this because their own subsequent, and bigger, empires followed the same courses laid down by Portuguese pilots — and have received much greater attention from their schools and scholarship. And more recently, of course, the word "colonialism" has become an opprobrium among Westerners and Asians alike, who are fashionably blind to the fact that the world as we know it could never have evolved without the work of those who transferred the ways of the West to the East. Both of these considerations have tended to deprive Portugal of its due glory and credit.

There may be few formal monuments to Portugal in Asia today, but wherever one travels around its littoral, one finds a church, a fort, or a place name — or a family name — which is unmistakably Lusitanian. These are the true reminders that da Gama, Albuquerque, Almeida, their kings, their priests, and their soldiers were conquistadores not of the world, nor of the world's wealth, but of the world's isolation.

APPENDIXES

Discoveries and "Discoveries" in the Fifteenth and Sixteenth Centuries

Appendixes

Discoveries and "Discoveries" in the
Fifteenth and Sixteenth Centuries

The appendixes are intended to clarify some of the moot points and technical problems encountered by the historian of discoveries. If incorporated into the text, the materials that follow would slow up the essential narrative, which is concerned with the progress of Portuguese exploration. Some of the appendixes relate to alleged secret voyages for which there is little or no evidence. Other discussions treat the evidence deduced from early maps and the validity of some manuscripts and publications. A chronology of discoveries is included to help the reader see quickly the scope of Portuguese activities.

A considerable number of "discoveries" were supposedly made in the fifteenth century and kept secret by the Portuguese. Since none of these, even if they are accepted, as some historians have done, added anything whatever to Portugal's known, matchless explorations, they are mentioned only to facilitate further readings by those who wish to pursue the historiography as well as the history.[1]

---

[1] Charles Boland, *They All Discovered America*; Guiseppe Caraci, "The Reputed Inclusion of Florida in the Oldest Nautical Maps of the New World"; G. R. Crone, "The Alleged Pre-Columbian Discovery of America"; Gago Coutinho, "A intervenção portuguesa no descobrimento da América do Norte" in *A náutica dos descobrimentos*, I, 317–336; J. P. Oliveira Martins, *Les explorations portugais antérieurs à la découverte de l'Amerique*; Álvaro Júlio da Costa Pimpão, "A historiografia oficial e o sigilo sôbre os descobrimentos"; David B. Quinn, "The Argument for the English Discovery of America between 1480 and 1494"; E. Roukema, "The Coasts of North-East Brazil and the Guianas in the Egerton Ms. 2803"; Manuel Luciano da Silva, "The Meaning of Dighton Rock."

The Portuguese who have most strongly advanced a belief in "secret discoveries" are Jaime and Armando Cortesão, Admiral Gago Coutinho, and Costa Brochado. Among those historians who have belittled the "secret voyages" are Thomas Oscar Marcondes de Souza, Samuel Eliot Morison, and Duarte Leite. An excellent summary of the historiography is in Damião Peres's *Descobrimentos Portugueses*. He cast doubts on many of the voyages but tends to believe in some degree of secrecy.

I
The Map of 1424

The first of the alleged "voyages" came sometime before 1424, the date of a map showing a large number of islands in the Atlantic. None of these can definitely be identified with known islands. They were placed on the map of 1424 in the general region of the Azores and Madeira, as well as further north. The most interesting aspect of the 1424 map is the first appearance of a large rectangular figure called Antilia west of the false Azores. Armando Cortesão believes the Antilia of the map are the Antilles Islands and thus that the map provides evidence that a Portuguese voyage had discovered the Antilles (West Indies) before 1424.[2] The island with the name Antilia has the legend "this island is called Antilia" (*ista ixola dixemo Antilia*). Other islands pictured there are Satanazes, Saya, and Ymana. Cortesão says "the name Antilia corresponds to the Portuguese form Antilha and thus testifies to the arrival of Portuguese navigators in the area of the Gulf of Mexico at a date before the map." The word *Antilha*, he says, was "always Portuguese" and must have been used originally on the map that served the Venetian cartographers as a model. Satanazes, or Satanagio, and Saya are both Portuguese words, he says; Ymana may correspond to Iman or to Imam which appear on previous maps. He cites several etymological derivations to back his argument. These would seem to apply as well to any other language of Latin origin as to Portuguese.

The islands as they appear on the map are far to the north of the actual Antilles. The longitude cannot be estimated. Though Cortesão states his thesis well, there seems to be no reason to accept these islands as being different from the "islands" of Brazil or any other imaginary islands found

[2] Armando Cortesão, *The Nautical Chart of 1424*; A. Cortesão, *Cartografia portuguûesa antiga*; R. A. Skelton, "The English Knowledge of the Portuguese Discoveries in the Fifteenth Century.

on the fifteenth-century maps. Bartolomé de las Casas, writing more than a century after the map was made, cites the appearance in sea charts of islands, "especially the island called Antillia about 200 leagues west of the Canary Islands and the Azores."[3] The Antilles are about four to five times this distance.

Morison agrees with G. R. Crone, the English historian of navigation, who says that the name Antilla was probably derived from a "series of cartographer's blunders from Getulia, the classical name for the north-western part of Africa."[4] The Portuguese identified Antilia with "Ilha das Sete Cidades" — in 1474 Toscanelli wrote, "the island of Antilia which you [Portuguese] call the Seven Cities."[5]

The Las Casas version of the Seven Cities is that a Portuguese ship driven by storm landed at Antilia in the time of Prince Henry. The island was populated by people who spoke "Portuguese" and who invited the mariners to attend mass; but they in fear returned to Portugal, telling their stories to Henry at Sagres and expecting a reward for the gold found in the sand on the island. Henry, however, berated them as cowards and ordered them to return to Antilia, which they refused to do. No other reference to Henry mentions this incident. Nor is there any attempt to explain how descendants of people who left Portugal before the formation of the Portuguese language could speak Portuguese.[6] Morison notes that aside from Toscanelli, "it is curious that the full Seven Cities legend is first found in the Behaim Globe of 1492."[7] In addition to the Behaim reference and Las Casas, there are also the accounts of António Galvão and Ferdinand Columbus, which are later than Behaim.[8] Damião Peres thinks the story possibly reflects a true discovery and agrees with Galvão: "Some believe" says Galvão, "that these lands and islands where the Portuguese touched would be those which are now called the Antilles and New Spain." Peres believes "this supposition is borne out by a disputed legend on the André Bianco map of 1448."[9]

[3] Las Casas, *Historia*, bk. I, chap. 13.

[4] Morison, *Portuguese Voyages*, p. 16.

[5] Morison, *ibid.*, citing G. R. Crone, "The Origin of the Name Antillia."

[6] Morison, *ibid.*, p. 17, citing Las Casas, *Historia*, bk. I, chap. 13, translated in J. A. Williamson, *Voyages of the Cabots*, pp. 11–15.

[7] Morison, *Ibid.*, p. 17, note 25.

[8] Peres, *Descobrimentos*, pp. 173–176, and Morison, *Portuguese Voyages*, pp. 17–18, both cite F. Columbus, *Columbus*, chap. 9, and Las Casas, *Historia*, bk. I. chap. 13, as well as António Galvão, *Tratado dos descrobimentos*, fol. 19 of 1st ed.

[9] Peres, *Descobrimentos*, pp. 173–176.

These names and the names of lands that had actually been found continued to decorate the maps of fifteenth- and sixteenth-century cartographers who, except in rare cases, were not explorers but were merely trying to piece together the legends and reports coming to them. Occasionally, solid information reached them and they recorded true discoveries in the right place, i.e., the Azores and Madeira. But none of the other islands can be positively identified with any known land.

II
The Island of São Mateus

João de Barros, a sixteenth-century Portuguese historian of discoveries, records that in 1525 the Spanish fleet under the command of Loaysa en route to the Moluccas discovered an uninhabited island called São Mateus, 2°S, and that two trees on the island bore inscriptions saying that eighty-seven years before (hence 1438) the Portuguese had been in the island. Barros, says Damião Peres, was thinking of the Ilha de São Mateus, which cartographers of his time placed in the Gulf of Guinea. This nonexistent island remained on maps into the mid-nineteenth century. Since the island did not exist, a game sprang up among historians of identifying it with some other island. São Mateus, says Peres, was actually Fernando Noronha Island in the same latitude but "far to the west."[10] Indeed it is, some 22° or 25° West (1500 to 1800 miles). Peres says that the *Diario de navegação* of Hernando de la Torre describes an island similar to Fernando Noronha, hence São Mateus. Loaysa would have, so goes the theory, made the same navigational error as mariners who "discovered" the original nonexistent São Mateus.[11] Duarte Leite held the discovery of Fernando Noronha admissable if it was assumed the pilots did not return. This provokes the objections that the vessels would not likely have been carried there by accident if they had started from the area of Cape Blanco, then the outermost limit of Portuguese explorations and that there is no other historical proof, for none of the known accounts of the Loaysa voyage cite the discovery of such an island. Furthermore, as Peres points out, the carvings on the trees could hardly have remained legible in a tropic region for eighty-seven years. The identification with Fernando de Noronha is not proved in any way nor is the existence of São Mateus.

[10] *Ibid.*, citing Navarette, *Colección de viajes*, 1st ed., V, 241–313.
[11] Peres, *Descobrimentos*, citing Duarte Leite, *Coisas de vária história*, p. 149.

III
The André Bianco Map of 1448

A voluminous and fancy-filled historiography accompanies the André Bianco map of 1448. In London after completing a voyage from Venice, Bianco, known as a cartographer and mariner, drew a map; in the lower part is an inscription usually read "ixiola otinticha" (authentic island). Below this and partly cut away and indistinct is the inscription rendered "*xe longa a ponente 500* [or 1500?] *mia.*" In the photograph presented in the illustration section there is no apparent letter after X, and there is a break in what is usually read as "longa." Choosing 500 or 1500 is arbitrary. That the map was trimmed is evident from the photograph and more so from the personal examination made by this writer (Diffie). The meaning of the map has been debated for 100 years. The word *longa*, if indeed this is the proper reading has been interpreted as "long" or "distant from" 500 (or 1500) miles. Among those who have expressed views are Fernando Ongania, Theobald Fischer, Yule Oldham (who identified it with the land of Brazil), Jaime Batalha Reis (who accepted Oldham's reading), and others who opposed Oldham's interpretation, such as Ravenstein, Schlichter, Payne, Beazley, Carlo Errera, and more recently Duarte Leite.[12] Damião Peres argues that given the wind patterns of the Atlantic, a discovery of an island to the west of Cape Verde would be perfectly possible, that the Bianco map represents a real not an imaginary discovery, and that this would have been one of the Antilles. "Not all evidently, but one of the islands, was certainly the object of this . . . discovery; and this is what Bianco in 1448 gave . . . the denomination 'authentic' to distinguish [it] . . . from the Antilha of tradition."[13]

Others who have discussed the map are Taylor, Wieder, and Morison. Morison says "the ixola otinticha" legend is in the same ink and handwriting as the other legends on the map, and it is crowded in such a way that it proves no paring or clipping of the parchment was done after the map was drawn.[14] Thus Morison, who also saw the map, saw it differently from this writer (Diffie). There seems to be no reason why Bianco should have

---

[12] J. Cortesão, "The Pre-Columbian Discovery of America"; Leite, *Descobrimentos*, I, 339–349; J. Batalha Reis, "The Supposed Discovery of South America before 1448," who concludes: "The great probability is, therefore, in my opinion, in favor of the supposition that the north-east corner of South America had been seen on or before 1448 . . ."

[13] Peres, *Descobrimentos*, p. 184.

[14] Morison, *Portuguese Voyages*, p. 121; E. G. R. Taylor, "A Pre-Columbia Discovery of America."

written at the very margin of his map. Morison identifies the mysterious island with the Bissagos south of Cape Verde. Whether Morison is correct or not, his conclusion that it "is improbable to the point of fantasy" to connect Bianco's island with Brazil is the soundest conclusion from the viewpoint of strict critical history.[15] All guesses about what Bianco meant to convey are just that, guesses. No "discovery" or identification with any known land has been established.

IV
Diogo de Teive

Ferdinand Columbus and Las Casas both record that some forty years or more before Columbus discovered America a Diogo de Teive sailed from the island of Fayal in the Azores to the southwest "more than 150 leagues." Finding nothing he returned, sailing westward of the central Azores, and discovered Flores and Corvo, the westernmost Azores. After this he continued to sail "so far to the northeast (nordeste, sic) that he had Cape Clear in Ireland to the west," finding a calm sea with a strong wind from the west, from which he presumed land was close.[16] It was August; fearing winter, Diogo de Teive "resolved to return to the island from which he left." With Teive was Pedro de Velasco, a native of Palos. Morison translates this as: "afterwards it's said that they sailed to the N.E. so far that they had Cape Clear [which is in Ireland] towards the E, where they found winds to blow very briskly and the winds westerly and the sea to be very smooth, which they believed should be because of land that should be there, which sheltered them to the westward."[17]

Jaime Cortesão held this to be a discovery of Newfoundland, saying that the "northeast" in the account should be corrected to "northwest," as Antonio de Herrera had done in his *Décadas* in the seventeenth century. Furthermore, says Cortesão, because there was no land to be discovered to the east of Cape Clear in Ireland, the direction had to be to the west.[18] The Pedro de Velasco of Las Casas or the Pietro de Velasco of Ferdinand Columbus is identified by Cortesão with the Pedro Vasquez de la Fron-

---

[15] Morison, *Portuguese Voyages*, p. 125.
[16] Peres, *Descobrimentos*, pp. 184–185; F. Columbus, *Columbus*, chap. 9; Las Casas, *Historia*, bk. I, chap. 13; Marcondes de Souza, "Diogo de Teive e Pedro Velasco"; Carlos F. de Figueiredo Valente, *Os Teives e o Morgado*.
[17] Morison, *Portuguese Voyages*, pp. 21–22.
[18] J. Cortesão, "A viagem de Diogo de Teive e Pero Vasquez de la Frontera" and "The Pre-Columbia Discovery of America," cited in Peres, *Descobrimentos*, pp. 185–188.

tera who supposedly gave information on a westward discovery to Columbus. Cortesão holds that this shows that Teive and Velasco discovered
Newfoundland; but Ferdinand Columbus who, he says, was "one of the
most cynical falsifiers . . . of all time," refused to give them credit, and
Las Casas joined in the fraud. "Yet," says Morison, "all the evidence of
the Teive-Velasco voyage of 1452 comes from these two, and Valiente."
Valiente was a witness during the Columbus hearings in 1515 who testified that when in 1492 Columbus was recruiting a crew in Palos, a Perro
Vasquez de la Frontera, who had once gone on a discovery voyage, encouraged others to go with Columbus for "they would find a very rich
land."[19] Two who refuted Cortesão were Duarte Leite and Marcondes de
Souza. Damião Peres takes a position against Leite and Souza.[20]

The westerlies prevailing north of the Azores make a sailing to Newfoundland improbable, though not impossible. There have been many
"discoveries" of lands never found, even down to modern times. The
island "Brazil" has been "seen" by many sailors. The Italian Navy went
out in 1958 to seek an island supposedly unknown before but reported to
be in the Mediterranean. They did not find it.

Both Ferdinand Columbus and Las Casas were writing more than
three-quarters of a century after *this* alleged voyage of 1452 and long after
the discovery of America. Both were clearly recording gossip, not citing
from reliable records. In any event, neither of them states clearly that a
discovery was made. Until further proof can be found, this voyage must
be considered suspect. The lack of any corroborative evidence leads
Morison to conclude: "So much for the voyage of Diogo de Teive and
Pedro de Velasco. They probably discovered Corvo and Flores in the
Azores; they certainly discovered nothing else."[21]

V
Fernando, Vogado, Cassana, Teles, and Others

The search for the Atlantic islands shown on the various fifteenth-century
maps was encouraged by reported sightings of these nonexisting islands.[22]
By *carta régia* of February 19, 1462, João Vogado was granted two islands
called Lovo and Capraria, which can be identified with two of the mythi-

[19] Morison, *Portuguese Voyages*, p. 26.
[20] Marcondes de Souza, *O descobrimento do Brasil*, pp. 11–23; Leite, *Descobrimentos*, I,
354–357 and *passim*; Peres, *Descobrimentos*, pp. 185–188.
[21] Morison, *Portuguese Voyages*, p. 29.
[22] Peres, *Descobrimentos*, pp. 213–216; Morison, *Portuguese Voyages*, pp. 29–33.

cal St. Brendan Isles or the false Azores. On October 29, 1462, a *carta régia* granted to Fernando, brother of the king, island's allegedly seen by Gonçalo Fernandes when he was returning home from a voyage to Rio do Ouro. No island was found, for none existed in the region searched.

Luca de Cazana or Cassana, an Italian merchant of the Azores, financed three or four voyages to search for an island allegedly seen by Vincente Dias to the west of Madeira. The Vincente Dias-Cassana search was in vain.

On January 12, 1473, a *carta régia* referring to an island which Fernando had searched for "a few times" in the region of the Cape Verde Islands (hence before 1470 when Fernando died) granted to his widow, Beatriz, a concession to search again. There is no record that anything was found. Afonso V on June 21, 1473, granted to Rui Gonçalves da Camara "an island which he himself or his ships might find." No known discovery was made.

To Fernão Teles, on January 28, 1474, were granted islands which he himself or his agents might discover, provided the islands were not in the region of Guinea. There is no known result of this grant. On November 10, 1475, the king extended Teles's grant to include "the Seven Cities or other peopled islands, which up to the present have not been sailed to, found, or settled by my subjects."[23] The original grant to Teles was for unpeopled islands. Inasmuch as the Antilles or Sete Cidades were supposed to be inhabited, the extended grant covered the contingency that Teles might discover them. There is no record of any discovery whatever.[24]

VI

João Vaz Corte-Real and Álvaro Martins Homem

A "voyage" which has been taken far more seriously, and which some historians have considered the discovery of America twenty years before Columbus, is credited to João Vaz Corte-Real and Álvaro Martins Homem. João Vaz had been *porteiro mor* to Fernando, Duke of Vizeu, brother of Afonso V, and donatary of Terceira. The captaincy of Angra in Terceira in the Azores was granted to Corte-Real on April 2, 1474, by Beatriz, Fernando's widow. He had received another grant, São Jorge,

[23] Peres, *Descobrimentos*, p. 216, citing Jose Ramos Coelho, *Alguns documentos do Archivo Nacional da Torre do Tombo*, pp. 41–42.
[24] Morison, *Portuguese Voyages*, pp. 29–33; Peres, *Descobrimentos*, pp. 312–316.

between 1472 and 1474. Shortly before, on February 17, 1474, Álvaro Martins Homem was granted the captaincy of Praia — which he occupied for some years — for his services to Fernando, but not for any alleged discoveries.

The passage that supposedly relates a discovery of America, i.e., the area known as Codfish Land (*Terra do Bacalhau* or Newfoundland), in 1472 comes from Gaspar Frutuoso who wrote his *Saudades da terra* a century later, about 1570–1580. "The island of Terceira being without captain . . . João Vaz Corte-Real and Álvaro Martins Homem, who arrived from the Land of Codfish, which they went to discover by order of the king . . . petitioned Princess Dona Beatriz [for Terceira] . . . which they divided between them."[25]

In another passage Frutuoso names only João Vaz, saying he came from *Terra do Bacalhau*, that Jacome de Bruges released half of Terceira to him, and that after Jacome "went to his own land . . . and never returned," Beatriz gave the island to João Vaz and Álvaro Martins. This credits only João Vaz as discoverer and makes it seem that Álvaro Martins was in Terceira before Jacome left. The grant to João Vaz was in recognition of the expenses he had incurred and for services rendered; but nothing is said of discoveries.[26] It is clear he had received the first grant before 1473. Both Ernesto do Canto and Henry Harrisse rejected the "discovery" and compiled such a weight of evidence against it that the matter would seem to be utterly dead. Nevertheless, there are still historians who either do not reject or cautiously say it is possibly true — and it is now included in school history books in Portugal as a fact. It is also recorded in the beautiful mosaic sidewalk on the Avenida da Liberdade in Lisbon.[27]

The asserted discovery is not supported by any historian contemporary with Corte-Real and Homem nor is there any known document authorizing them to make discoveries. The eighteenth-century historian António Cordeiro repeats Frutuoso, adding only the error of 1464 for 1474.

Because of the lack of other evidence to support Frutuoso, the question of his reliability is essential. Morison enumerates many errors and confusions in his works. So does Duarte Leite, who sets most rigorous standards for documentation.[28] For example, Morison notes that Frutuoso

[25] Quoted in Leite, *Descobrimentos*, I, 364ff.
[26] *Ibid.*
[27] H. Braz, "A descoberta da Terra Nova" and "Descoberta pre-columbiana."
[28] Morison, *Portuguese Voyages*, pp. 33–41; Leite, *Descobrimentos*, I, 364ff.

credits João Vaz with discovery of Terceira, Cape Verde, and Fogo, though all were discovered before, and with the discovery of Brazil which occurred later. Furthermore, he supposedly won great battles from Castile, "as captain of great fleets," capturing from the Castilians "the best prizes that ever in this realm of Portugal were taken from them." But none of this appears in any known document, nor was it recorded by any historian before or contemporary with Frutuoso.

Frutuoso, says Duarte Leite, "fell into numerous confusions, gave wrong dates, and committed errors of fact. In spite of his diligence in recounting the discovery of Santa Maria, what he asserts is unacceptable *in totum*, and he also errs in what the says of the Island of São Miguel."[29] Leite describes Frutuoso's biography of João Vaz as "full of nonsensical legends and . . . various errors." Frutuoso does not mention, for example, Gaspar and Miguel, the two sons of João Vaz who were authentic discoverers. What definitely invalidates João Vaz as discoverer, says Duarte Leite, is that the *carta régia* of September 17, 1506 (which transferred to Vasco Eanes Corte-Real the lands discovered by his brothers Gaspar and Miguel and granted to them on May 12, 1500 and January 15, 1502), calls Gaspar "first discoverer" without reference to his father. The use of both words *descobrir* (to discover) and *achar* (to find) in the description of their discoveries rules out any interpretation that the Corte-Real brothers were merely exploring what had been discovered or found before.[30]

To the argument that João Vaz made the discoveries attributed to him because his name appears on maps such as those in the 1571 atlas of Fernão Vaz Dourado, the 1569 map of Gerard Mercator, and a Portuguese map of 1534, Duarte Leite offers the objection that if such discoveries had been made they would appear in earlier maps. The João Vaz notation does not appear in the maps of Cantino, Canerio, or Oliveriana of the early sixteenth century; and where it does appear on the maps of 1534 and later, it is placed on Greenland not Labrador. Furthermore, the name João Vaz appears alone on the maps and is not connected with the name Corte-Real; so even this "proof" is lacking.[31]

The efforts to connect the alleged discovery of Newfoundland by João

[29] Leite, *Descobrimentos*, I, 367.
[30] *Ibid.*, 369, and Peres, *Descobrimentos*, p. 221.
[31] Leite, *Descobrimentos*, I, 373; Morison, *Portuguese Voyages*, pp. 40–41.

Vaz Corte-Real with the known voyage of two Danish seamen, Pining and Pothorst, and with a trip by Johannes Skolp (Scolvus) in 1476, rest on no substantial information, though they have been widely discussed by numerous historians. Nor does anything indicate that the Pining-Pothorst or the Scolvus sailings went beyond Greenland, a well-known area in the fifteenth century.[32] The chief proponent of the João Vaz-Pining-Pothorst voyage was Sofus Larsen. Since neither Larsen nor any other historian has produced any evidence to show a common voyage by the three, there seems no reason to dwell on the overwhelming reason for rejecting the voyage. There is no known record of it in archives in Portugal or Denmark.[33]

Some sound historians, nevertheless, link João Vaz Corte-Real and Álvaro Martins Homem with exploration. Damião Peres, for example, without permitting himself to believe in a discovery, says: "In conclusion, everything leads to the belief that João Vaz Corte-Real . . . and his companion in adventures. Álvaro Martins Homem, belong to the numbers of Portuguese navigators who in the course of the fifteenth century arduously explored the Atlantic, searching to clarify the mysteries toward the west."[34] For Duarte Leite, however, there was no proof of the discovery: "I continue in the conviction that it is purely a fantasy to believe that Newfoundland was discovered by João Vaz Corte-Real."[35]

VII
Jean Cousin

The "discovery" of America by Jean Cousin of Dieppe, France, in 1487 or 1488 was recorded in the "Memoires chronologiques pur servir a l'histoire de Dieppe" in 1785. According to the story, Cousin, driven by a storm, discovered an immense river on an unknown coast. There is no other record of this alleged voyage. The people of Dieppe made no known efforts to follow this up nor did the French king record any interest nor make any claims based on this alleged discovery when a few years later the Spaniards and Portuguese were dividing the world.[36]

[32] Peres, *Descobrimentos*, pp. 224–226; Morison, *Portuguese Voyages*, pp. 36–41.
[33] Sofus Larsen, *The Discovery of North America*.
[34] Peres, *Descobrimentos*, p. 224.
[35] Leite, *Descobrimentos*, I, 370.
[36] Peres, *Descobrimentos*, pp. 483–484; Marcondes de Souza, *Descobrimento da América*, pp. 125–129.

VIII
Martim António Leme

Ferdinand Columbus and Las Casas[37] cite the case of Martim António Leme, resident of Madeira, who it was said sailed far west sometime before 1484 and saw three islands which, Peres says, "could not be any but some of the Antilles, [but] of this discovery nothing else whatever is known, though the history of António Leme shows him to be a person capable of such a sea voyage."[38] It is not clear on what basis Peres concludes Leme discovered the Antilles, a voyage that would have required several months and special preparations. No royal grant or other official or unofficial record of any sort mentions Leme as a discoverer. Martim António Leme was the son of Martim Lem, or Leme, a Fleming who had prospered in Portugal. In 1471 Martim António took part in the expedition to Arzila and the capture of Tangier, commanding military forces equipped by his father in Flanders. He was legitimized along with several brothers and sisters on September 6, 1464, and ennobled on November 12, 1471.

IX
The Anonymous Pilot

Las Casas, who recorded all the gossip he heard, tells a tale of a reported informant of Columbus, of unknown nationality but sometimes called Alfonso Sanches, who was said to have discovered land to the west before Columbus and to have told Columbus about it. Columbus does not refer to this anywhere. Ferdinand Columbus perhaps confuses this alleged voyage of the "Anonymous Pilot" with the real voyage of Vincente Dias to Cape Verde in 1444. Dias "saw" an "island" which he searched for in vain in three or four voyages financed by Luca de Cassano.[39]

X
Duarte Pacheco Pereira

A short passage in *Esmeraldo de situ orbis* by Duarte Pacheco Pereira, written ca. 1505–8, has stimulated the imagination and provoked speculation on its meaning. In chapter two, entitled "On the Quantity and Extent

---

[37] F. Columbus, *Columbus*, chap. 9; Las Casas, *Historia*, bk. I, chap. 13.
[38] Peres, *Descobrimentos*, p. 343.
[39] Las Casas, *Historia*, bk. I, chap. 14; Henri Vignaud, *Histoire critique de . . . Christophe Colomb*, I, 79, and II, 222–227.

of Land and Water and Which Is the Major Part," he upholds the thesis that land forms six-sevenths and water only one-seventh of the earth. For authority he cites several passages of the Bible and Pliny, and concludes that the ocean was placed "in between" two large bodies of land and consequently the water does not surround the land but "rather the land surrounds the sea" and that the "ocean sea is nothing more than a very large lake placed in the hollow of the land." A part of his argument is that since the land discovered toward the west — the American continent — had been found to run from 70°N to 28° 50S, with no ending either north or south, "it is certain that it runs entirely around the globe."[40]

In the middle of the chapter setting forth this argument he inserts the statement that some have taken to be a claim to discovery of some or all the lands he regarded as circling the earth. Writing as if addressing himself to King Manuel, he says: "Fortunate Prince . . . in the third year of your reign in the year of Our Lord 1498 . . . Your Highness sent us to discover towards the west, across the broad expansion of the ocean sea where there is found and sailed (*navegada*) a very large mainland with many and large adjacent islands, which extends to 70°N of the equator to . . . 28° 50S."[41]

The main questions arising from this statement are: what did he discover; did he claim to have discovered anything; did he even claim to have sailed? The debate on these issues includes such matters as whether the "us" in the expression "Your Highness ordered us to explore" is plural or singular. Some writers (among them Luciano Pereira da Silva) defend the thesis that he discovered Brazil; others (for example, Duarte Leite) that he discovered Florida. Still others (among them, Carlos Coimbra) contend that the discovery was made not by Duarte Pacheco himself but by another whose voyage he was recording. A recent opinion is, "that a Portuguese voyage to America, probably North America, took place in 1498 is indisputable; that Duarte Pacheco led it is disputed. However, it should not be forgotten that of these two conclusions, the fundamental one is the first" (i.e., that the Portuguese discovered the mainland of America in 1498).[42]

[40] Pereira, *Esmeraldo*, bk. I, chap. 2; Carlos Coimbra, "Duarte Pacheco e a viagem de 1498"; Luciano Pereira da Silva, "Duarte Pacheco Pereira, precursor de Cabral"; Lindolfo Gomes, "O 'Esmeraldo' de Duarte Pacheco."
[41] Pereira, *Esmeraldo*, bk. I, chap. 2; Morison, *Portuguese Voyages*, p. 134.
[42] Peres, *Descobrimentos*, pp. 421–425.

"What really is important," Duarte Leite says, is "to know whether Pacheco arrived in Brazil before Álvares Cabral" (April 22, 1500). In agreement with Luciano Pereira, such modern Portuguese historians as "Faustino da Fonseca, Brito Rebelo, Lopes de Mendonça, and Jaime Cortesão say he did, as does . . . Vignaud; and I believe he does not lack supporters in Brazil." However, says Leite, if Pacheco did discover areas east of the Line of Demarcation and did bring back news of this to Manuel, "the reason which induced Don Manuel to keep secret . . . such an important discovery escapes me."[43] As soon as Cabral returned in 1501, Manuel announced the discovery of Brazil to Ferdinand and Isabella of Spain. Why would he not in 1499, after the return of Vasco da Gama, make a similar announcement if Pacheco had already discovered Brazil? "No objection could come on the part of Spain," given the division made by the Treaty of Tordesillas, as "indeed none came in 1501" when Cabral's discovery was announced. "I am persuaded that Pacheco neither discovered Brazil in 1498 nor was present two years later at its discovery by Cabral."[44]

XI
Florida or Yucatan

The argument for a Portuguese discovery of Florida or Yucatan, or both, in 1498 rests on early sixteenth-century maps. Henry Harrisse held that clandestine Spanish voyages had been made to the region before Alberto Cantino's map of 1502, P. J. J. Valentini, in 1888, believed the map showed the discovery of Yucatan. George Nunn, in 1924, propounded the idea that the Cantino map merely duplicated a part of Cuba and bore names given by Columbus, most in Spanish but some in Portuguese. Gago Coutinho held that the map definitely established the Portuguese origin of the place names and connected the supposed voyage of Duarte Pacheco in 1498 with the voyage of Gaspar Corte-Real in 1499. The cautious judgment of Damião Peres is that "nothing can be said definitively, on the basis of known historical documentation."[45]

XII
Ojeda, Pinzón, de Lepe

Though Cabral made the effective discovery of Brazil (1500) which led to Portuguese colonization, some parts of the Brazilian coast had been vis-

[43] Leite, *Descobrimentos*, I, 501.
[44] *Ibid.*, 501–505.
[45] Peres, *Descobrimentos*, pp. 425–430.

ited briefly before Cabral's landing. Among the explorers who have been credited with Brazilian discovery are Alonso de Ojeda, Diego de Lepe, Vicente Yáñez Pinzón, and Amérigo Vespucci, all of whom sailed for Spain in 1499 or early 1500, touching or allegedly touching briefly on the northeast coast of Brazil from about the region of Cape St. Agostinho in Pernambuco and running northwestward to the Antilles.

A part of the Venezuelan coast had been discovered by Columbus on this third voyage in 1498; and thus knowledge of land to the south of where he touched could have reached Spain and Portugal before his return in 1500 and before any of the other discoverers sailed in 1499. The question to be answered is not whether any of these men sailed to the New World but whether they touched any part of Brazil.[46]

Ojeda sailed in 1499, having with him the mariner Juan de la Cosa as well as Amérigo Vespucci.[47] The coast along which Ojeda sailed reached some 200 leagues, about 600 miles, southeastward from Paria, i.e., approximately from the island of Trinidad. He would not have touched any part of Brazil on this voyage, if it can be assumed this distance is correct. He was in Hispaniola on September 5, 1499. It is difficult to believe that he had time to sail the Brazilian coast and still reach Hispaniola by that date. Vespucci's voyage is described as having taken place in July, August, and September. If they were indeed together at one time, they seemed to have separated at some point, Ojeda going to the Antilles earlier than Vespucci.[48]

Pinzón left Palos with four caravels in November 1499.[49] At a distance estimated at 540 leagues, about 1600 miles, from Cape Verde to the southwest, he found land at a point he named Santa María de la Consolación. From there, sailing northwest he passed a large river which he named Santa María de la Mar Dulce. After 600 leagues (ca. 1800 miles)

[46] The evidence for the 1499–1500 discoveries is found in the proceedings of the law suits between the family of Columbus, the Pinzón family, and the Crown of Castile, in *Documentos inéditos de Índias*, vol. VII. See also *HCPB*, I, 206ff.

[47] Duarte Leite discusses this and other voyages in his *Os falsos precursores de Cabral* and in *Descobrimentos*, I, 507–536; see also Gago Coutinho, "Teria Pinzón descoberto o Brasil?" in *A náutica dos descobrimentos*, II, 29–32.

[48] Among the historians accepting a separation of Ojeda from Vespucci in their 1499 voyage are T. O. Marcondes de Souza and Alberto Magnaghi. See A. Magnaghi, *Amérigo Vespucci*, and Marcondes de Souza, *Amérigo Vespucci e suas viagens*, São Paulo, 1949, and Carlos Seco, "Algunos datos definitivos sobre el viaje Hojeda-Vespucio," who rejects the Vespucci discovery; Peres, *Descobrimentos*, pp. 490–493.

[49] The voyage of Vicente Yañez Pinzón is described in Peter Martyr de Anghiera, *De orbe novo*, and three *diplomas régios* of 1500–1501, cited by Duarte Leite, *Descobrimentos*, I, 507–524.

along this coast he arrived in Paria, going then to Hispaniola in June and to Spain on September 30, 1500. Pinzón stated in 1513 that his Cape Santa María was the same as Cape St. Agostinho on the Brazilian coast. Spanish historians tend to accept this as a discovery of that part of Brazil, finding other evidence in the Juan de la Cosa map, dated 1500, though it was probably revised somewhat later.[50] In 1501 Pinzón received a royal grant as governor of the region from Cape Santa María de la Consolación "to the great river of the sweet sea," such territories lying presumably on the Spanish side of the Line of Demarcation. Since the Line of Demarcation had not been fixed, and could not have been fixed with the then existing knowledge of how to measure longitude, neither Pinzón nor the Catholic sovereigns who made the grant could be sure of what was donated.

Diego de Lepe, according to Las Casas, left Palos in December 1499, a month later than Pinzón. He sailed eastward along the coast he found until it turned toward the south, at which point he shifted northwest until he reached Paria, in April 1500. There he met for a time with Pinzón and returned to Spain sometime between August and November 1500.[51] Juan Rodrigues, brother of Diego and his companion on the voyage, testified that they explored 600 leagues to the southeast of Paria, which is approximately the distance claimed for Pinzón and would have placed them at some area long the northeast bulge of Brazil, perhaps in the state of Pernambuco. Neither the landfalls described nor the estimated sailing distances can be accepted with sufficient confidence to allow categorical answers to questions regarding those voyages. Portuguese historians have in general rejected these claims.[52] On the other hand, such Brazilian historians as Capistrano de Abreu, Marcondes de Souza, and Rodolfo Garcia have admitted the prior discovery claims of the Spaniards and Vespucci, while emphasizing the obvious fact that the only effective discovery was Cabral's.

The most thorough going challenge to the authenticity of these earlier discoveries was made in 1921 by Duarte Leite and repeated by him and others frequently since that time.[53] In addition to pointing out the rather

[50] G. E. Nunn, *The Geographical Conceptions of Columbus* and "The Mappamonde of Juan de la Cosa"; Marcondes de Souza, "A concepção geográfica dos portuguêses"; R. A. Skelton, *The European Image and the Mapping of America* A.D. *1000–1600*.

[51] Leite, *Descobrimentos*, I. 530–536.

[52] Peres, *Descobrimentos*, pp. 493–500.

[53] Peres, *Descobrimentos*, pp. 493–500. Much of the discussion about which explorers

equivocal evidence for pre-Cabral discovery, the opponents have asserted other reasons for rejecting it. They assert that a course southeast along the north coast of Brazil against contrary ocean currents and winds is all but impossible; that the disappearance from view of the Pole Star 300 leagues from Cape Verde Islands, as described by the historian Peter Martyr, was not possible inasmuch as the Pole Star would disappear only 445 leagues from the Cape Verde Islands; that the statement that Pinzón saw the Amazon River is disproved because he mentions only one such phenomenon, whereas the Orinoco also projects its waters far into the sea and therefore is the river Pinzón saw; that the Juan de la Cosa map is unreliable evidence since it lacks many place names given by Pinzón and Lepe, and the probable later alterations in the map render it still less reliable; and that the grant to Pinzón would have had to lie to the west of the Line of Demarcation, which passes through the mouth of the Amazon, to limit Pinzón's discoveries to Spanish territory. Damião Peres offers the argument that "it is necessary to observe furthermore the extreme difficulty of calculating latitude in regions south of the equator by those who then knew only the method of fixing on the Pole Star."[54] None of the men

---

crossed the equator is concerned with the position of the Pole Star. Today the so-called North Star (Polaris) is within 1° of the North Celestial Pole and can be used for simple estimates of latitude. The "Guards" in the Little Dipper can also be used, as can any other visible star. However, when any star other than Polaris is used, "time" must be taken into account, both the time of day (or night) and the time of the year. As an example, the Guards would be found directly below the Pole in early evening of mid-June and directly above in early evening of mid-January. Thus if the Guards were above the Pole and Polaris was no longer visible, it would indicate the equator had been passed. The south latitude could be approximately determined by the altitude of the Guards.

In 1500 A.D., Polaris was approximately 5° from the North Celestial Pole and was, consequently, less accurate than today as a rough guide to latitude. The height of the observer above sea level would also alter the estimate of the altitude as it would change the angle at which Polaris was seen. In 1500 a man who lost sight of Polaris would be at the equator or, supposing he could ideally see Polaris at exact horizon, approximately 5° south. When he lost sight of both Guards, he might be 20° south.

Polaris at 5° (or even near 6°) from the Pole would be at its highest at sunset in December 1499–January 1500 and at about the same altitude as the pole itself in April 1500. In other words, it would have been more visible to the navigator on the pole in December–January than in April when Polaris would rise and set with the sun. The navigator would probably have to be, for practical use of Polaris, about 5° north of the equator in April. It is a very large assumption to accept the belief that the navigators of 1500 knew this much about the position of Polaris. Their estimates of their latitude were precise only by chance. The efforts of modern historians to determine exactly where Vespucci, De Lepe, or Pinzón were with respect to the equator cannot be more exact. (Astronomical information supplied by the courtesy of Dr. Barbara Worcester, Professor of Astronomy, Texas Christian University.)

For the best discussion of De Lepe, Pinzón, and Vespucci see Duarte Leite, *Os falsos precursores de Cabral*, and *Descobrimentos*, as cited above.

[54] Peres, *Descobrimentos*, pp. 499ff.

mentioned, Ojeda, Lepe, Pinzón, or Vespucci, says Peres, could have known precisely where they were because they were incapable of taking solar observations. Whether Peres is correct in this view or not, or whether anybody at that time could fix latitude at sea precisely, is a matter for which no scientific base of judgement has been established. Peres's own conclusion is, "it may be thought extremely probable — in view of the lack of unquestionable documentary proof permitting a categorical affirmation — that only territories to the west of the Amazon were reconnoitered along the South American coast up to 1500 by Spanish navigators."[55] Duarte Leite had come to the same conclusion many years ago: "Neither Pinzón nor any other Spanish navigator antici- pated Cabral in the discovery of Brazilian territory."[56]

Without being dogmatic, we can agree with Leite that "it is astonishing how it is possible to extract from the same documentation, in good faith, conclusions that are diametrically opposed."[57] The most acceptable con- clusion to most historians is still, however strong the arguments of Duarte Leite, Damião Peres, and others, that De Lepe, Pinzón and Vespucci (but not Ojeda) saw some months before Cabral reached Brazil a part of what later became Brazil's northern coast.

XIII
Amérigo Vespucci

The "Vespucci question" has become one of the most debated issues among historians. What did Vespucci do that justified naming the New World for him? Did he make two, three, or four voyages to America? And whether two, three, or four, what did he discover? The evidence for what Vespucci did rests essentially on his own letters, or letters ascribed to him, with a few additional statements about him by his contemporaries.[58]

The letters may be divided into two groups: those published in his lifetime (two letters) and those found much later and attributed to him (three letters in manuscript plus a fragment). Strange as it may seem, the works published during his lifetime are generally considered to be less

---

[55] Ibid.
[56] Leite, Descobrimentos, I, p. 508.
[57] Ibid.
[58] Among the works on Vespucci are those of Roberto Levillier (who accepts four voyages by Vespucci), Alberto Magnaghi (who believes there were only two), Marcondes de Souza (two), Francisco A. Varnhagen, Ayres de Sá, Armand Marie Pascal d'Avezac, Frederick J. Pohl, and Gago Coutinho, all listed in the bibliography.

reliable and less certainly the direct work of Vespucci than those found long after his death.

In a letter sent to Lourenzo de Pier Francesco de Medici, published in Latin with the title *Mundus novus* while Vespucci lived, Vespucci described the voyage to Brazil in 1501–2 in the service of Portugal.[59] The second published in his lifetime was in Italian, the *Lettera di Amerigo Vespucci delle isole nuovamente trovate in quattro suoi viaggi*, commonly known as the *Lettera al Soderini*, dated from Lisbon, September 4, 1504.[60]

The manuscript group of Vespucci documents consists of three copies of letters written to Lourenzo de Pier Francesco de Medici, plus a part of a letter. The first is dated either the 18th or the 28th of July 1500 from Seville and describes a voyage in the service of Spain in 1499–1500.[61] It was first published in 1745 by Angelo Maria Bandini. The second letter, written from Cape Verde June 4, 1501, was first published in 1807 by Count Baldelli Boni, in his edition of *Il milloni di Marco Polo*. It contains the narrative of a voyage of 1501–2 from Lisbon to Cape Verde and gives detailed information about Cabral's voyage to India obtained while the ships of Vespucci and Cabral were anchored in Cape Verde (Bezeguiche) where they chanced to meet. The third letter was written from Lisbon in 1502, with neither day nor month but usually considered to be August, describing the voyage made in 1501–2 at the request of Manuel of Portugal. It is the continuation of the letter begun in Cape Verde and was first published in 1789 by Francesco Bartolozzi.

The "fragment" is a part of a Vespucci, or alleged Vespucci, letter published in 1937 by Roberto Ridolfi.[62] Made from an imperfect copy it was rejected by Alberto Magnaghi as unacceptable and hailed by Ricardo Levillier as further proof of the "first" voyage of Vespucci, 1497–98. The conflicting information and the sometimes quite indistinct descriptions have caused Vespucci's letters and alleged letters to be considered by some historians as falsifications. The many different analyses of the letters have led to completely contradictory interpretations by different histo-

[59] *Mundus novus*, 1st ed. 1504(?) or 1502: this and other letters in Magnaghi and Levillier; Arthur Davies, "The 1501–02 Voyage of Vespucci"; Marcondes de Souza, "A expedição de 1501–02 e Amérigo Vespucci."

[60] *Lettera*, Florence (1505? 1506?). This was translated from Italian into Latin and published by Martin Waldseemüller (Hylocamilus) in *Cosmographiae introductio*, St. Dié, 1507.

[61] Dated July 18 in the Codici Ricardiano 2112 bis and July 28 in number 1910.

[62] In Levillier, *El nuevo mundo*, pp. 154–169.

rians, among whom the Portuguese have treated Vespucci with the greatest disdain.

If we rely on the published works, that is the *Mundus novus* of 1504 and the *Lettera al Soderini* published in 1505 or 1506, there are descriptions of four voyages, 1497–98, 1499–1500, 1501–2, and 1503–4. Eliminating from consideration the *Lettera*, the three letters discovered later describe only two voyages, 1499–1500 and 1501–2. The "fragment" refers to three voyages, but it is not certain when it was written or if it is only a fragment of the *Lettera* in a more colloquial style. In the "fragment," Vespucci is answering the questions of some correspondent he considers stupid, which casts doubt on the attribution of the letters to Vespucci, for all his other writings show great respect for those addressed.

The chief proponent of the two-voyages theory after 1924 was Magnaghi. In an exhaustive review of the relevant writings and cartography, he concluded that Vespucci himself had not written the *Mundus novus* and the *Lettera al Soderini* but that they had been drawn from Vespucci's letters by someone who made a number of mistakes and interpolations because he was not acquainted with the areas discovered. Duplications had thus crept in which made two voyages seem to be four, causing many historians, especially the Portuguese, to accuse Vespucci of being an impostor. The chief modern proponent of the authenticity of all the letters, as well as the advocate of the most extensive exploration of Vespucci, has been Levellier of Argentina.

According to those who reject the *Mundus novus* as Vespucci's own work, it is composed of two of Vespucci's letters plus a third source that contains inaccurate information which did not come from Vespucci. It is perhaps the first composed or fabricated work about the new world of a type that became common later, including the *Four Voyages*. The *Mundus novus* contained principally the text of Vespucci's letter of 1502, his name having been used because he was known to have been a person who had traveled to the New World.[63] The letter of 1502, however, is free of many of the errors of the *Mundus novus*. The *Mundus novus* had a sensational reception. In the first year there were twelve editions and by 1550 there had been fifty editions. Immediately after the first edition in Latin it had been translated into Italian, French, German, Dutch, and other languages.

---

[63] Luis de Matos in Leite, *Descobrimentos*, I, 685; Marcondes de Souza, *Algumas achegas*, pp. 163–166; Henry Vignaud, *Améric Vespuce*, p. 16.

The *Lettera al Soderini*, also referred to as *Quattro viaggi*, was published in Florence in 1505 or 1506, though in Italian it never achieved the popularity of the *Mundus novus*. Only one early edition in Italian is known. The Library of Congress has recently acquired the Amoretti Codex, a sixteenth-century copy made from the original text of the *Lettera*. It is fuller in many passages than the published version and contains some variations which, though interesting, do not solve the essential problem of the Vespucci writings.

This brings us to a genuine mystery: why did the *Lettera* not receive more circulation in Italy? The interest of the Italians in exploration in the New World was intense. Columbus's letter to Rafael Sánchez on his discovery of the New World was published in Latin in April 1493. The secretary of the Venetian embassy in Spain, Ángelo Trevisan, sent to Admiral Domenico Malipiero in 1501 an account of the first three voyages of Columbus as well as of the voyages of Vicente Pinzón and Alonso Niño, which he had obtained from Peter Martyr and which Albertino Vercellese published in Venice in 1504 in a work entitled *Libretto de tutta la navigatione de rei de Spagna de le isole et terrini nuovamente trovati*. In 1507 Francanzano da Montalboddo published a famous collection of voyages under the title of *Paesi nuovamente retrovati et Novo Mundo da Alberico Vesputio, Florentino intitulato*, in which he included the *Libretto*, a translation of the *Mundus novus*, and the voyages of Cadamosto, Vasco da Gama, and Cabral, but not the *Lettera*. This work was immediately successful and was reedited in 1508, 1512, 1515, 1517, and 1521. It was published in Latin in Milan, 1508, in German in 1508, and in French in 1515.

Given this intense interest in the narrative of discovery, why was there only one edition of the *Lettera* in Italy? Florence was the city of Medici, Marchioni, Sernigi, and many other businessmen interested in Portugal. Could it be, as some think, that the answer is that it was known to be a falsification? The *Lettera* published in Florence bore no name of printer or date. The editor tried to stimulate its sale by annexing other works to it. According to the *Lettera*, which ascribes four voyages to Vespucci, three of them sailed May 10: that is May 10, 1497, May 10, 1501, and May 10, 1503, and the other May 16, 1501. It seems suspicious that four separate voyages from Cádiz and Lisbon should sail in May and three of them on May 10, all taking about the same period of time though greatly different in miles sailed. Whereas in Italy the *Lettera* achieved only that first edition, it was printed seven times in the Latin translation in Saint-Die in 1507 alone.[64]

Considering the *Mundus novus* and the *Lettera* as unacceptable evidence at the best and synthetic documents at worst, the only authentic writings of Vespucci are the three letters in which Vespucci claims to have made two voyages, not four, thus leaving out 1497–98 and 1503–04.[65]

According to the letter written from Seville either July 18 or 28, 1500, to Lourenzo de Pier Francesco de Medici, Vespucci sailed from Cádiz May 18, 1499, stopped in the Canaries for provisions and after about twenty-four days of sailing southwest sighted land 1300 leagues from Cádiz (roughly 4000 miles). The point reached was water-covered and dense jungle preventing landing. Sailing south they found two large rivers, one flowing east, four leagues across the mouth, and the other north, three leagues wide discharging sweet and potable water far out in the sea. They put out boats which rowed fifteen leagues up the river. When these had returned to the ship, they sailed further south finding an ocean current that ran west, so strong that it endangered the boat and prevented sailing southeast in spite of favorable winds. After reaching 6°S they turned northwest reaching an island 10°N, perhaps Trinidad. Entering the Gulf of Paria, they found another large river which discharged enough water to sweeten the sea. Along the coast of what is now Venezuela, they concluded they were in the region of Asia. Vespucci describes the progress further north and west, a two-month stay in Hispaniola, and a continuation still north when they took slaves and returned to Spain in June 1500. He reported a thirteen-month voyage, which covered almost 5000 leagues (15,000 miles).[66]

Vespucci's voyage resembles closely the voyage of Alonso de Ojeda and Juan de la Cosa made in 1499–1500, about which Ojeda testified he had with him "Morigo Vespucci and other pilots."[67] One explanation of why Ojeda did not make any reference in his testimony to sailing the Brazilian coast, which Vespucci did describe, is given in the documents among the papers of the family of the Duke of Alba. These documents describe two

[64] Marcondes de Souza, *Algumas achegas*, pp. 168–170; Magnaghi, *Vespucci*, I, 125, 210–248.

[65] Marcondes de Souza, *Algumas achegas*, pp. 170–172; Peres, *Descobrimentos*, pp. 484ff.

[66] Marcondes de Souza, *Algumas achegas*, pp. 173–174; Magnaghi, *Vespucci*, II, 145–146.

[67] Marcondes de Souza, *Algumas achegas*, pp. 177–178, and Navarette, *Colección de viajes*, in III, 528–531 (Buenos Aires, 1945 ed.).

expeditions that sailed together on May 18, 1499 from Cádiz. Two vessels were commanded by Ojeda and another two by Vespucci, some writers believe, though others object violently to this view. They sailed together to a coast 200 leagues southeast of Paria, some believe, from whence Ojeda sailed northwest and Vespucci southeast.[68]

Where then did Vespucci go? According to his own statement, in July, August, and September, he was sailing along the coast of the Guianas and Brazil, and finally arrived, in January 1500, in Hispaniola — that is, five months after Ojeda's arrival. Ojeda returned to Cádiz in April 1500 and Vespucci in June the same year. In Vespucci's letter written from Cape Verde, June 4, 1501, he referred to Cabral's discovery of the same land he, Vespucci, had found, but said his own discovery was farther toward the east.[69]

Pier Rondinelli wrote to Florence, October 3, 1502, saying that he expected Vespucci to arrive in Seville within a few days and added that "the king of Portugal gave a concession of the land he discovered to certain New Christians."[70] Giovanni da Impoli, who had accompanied Afonso de Albuquerque to India in 1503, wrote to his father on his return from India, September 16, 1504, referring to "the land . . . discovered by Amérigo Vespucci."[71] At a meeting of pilots and cosmographers in Seville in 1515 to determine a method to draw the Line of Demarcation, Vespucci's nephew Giovanni Vespucci stated that Amérigo Vespucci had made two voyages to Cape St. Agostinho 8°S and had there twice taken the "altitude of the sun."[72]

The evidence that Vespucci was along the coast of northeast Brazil in 1499 does not convince everyone, particularly not the Portuguese historians. Damião Peres, for example, writes at length to refute the pro-Vespucci position, calling Vespucci "more of a commercial agent than a notable explorer." Duarte Leite calls Vespucci "impostor, improvised astronomer and a fake discoverer," and a "mediocre merchant."[73] An

[68] Joaquim Caetano da Silva, *L'Oyapoc et la Amazone*, II, 382–387, and *Autógrafos de Colón*, cited in Marcondes de Souza, *Algumas achegas*, p. 180.

[69] Las Casas, *Historia* II, 394, cited in Marcondes de Souza, *Algumas achegas*, p. 181.

[70] Columbus: *Raccolta colombiana*, III, v. 2, pp. 120–121, cited in Marcondes de Souza, *Ibid.*, p. 181.

[71] *Ibid* cited in *Ibid*.

[72] Las Casas in Navarette, *Colección de viajes*, II, 525, and Navarette, III, 319–320 (Buenos Aires, 1945), cited in Marcondes de Souza, *Algumas achegas*, p. 181.

[73] Duarte Leite, *Os falsos precursores de Cabral*, p. 28, and Peres, *Descobrimentos*, pp. 490–500.

example of the sharp dialogue is a question posed by Marcondes de Souza, who asks, "merchant to sell to whom and to buy what . . . in a land of naked savages . . . monkeys and parrots?" Vespucci was, of course, among other things a representative of the Medicis' merchants; but all the missions of Vasco da Gama, Cabral, and their successors had commercial aims. The world was not discovered by men sailing aimlessly over a deep blue sea — they all had objectives, not the least of which was economic.

The best-known Vespucci voyage was 1501–2. As advised by Cabral and before Cabral's return from India, King Manuel sent an expedition to reconnoiter the newly discovered lands. Three ships were dispatched May 13, 1501, according to Vespucci, who was a member of this expedition, and returned to Portugal July 22, 1502. On the outward voyage after sailing sixty-four days in what Vespucci describes as a S-SW direction, they reached a coast which they ran for 800 leagues, reaching some 25°S or 32°S or 53°S, a matter of doubt and dispute. Although the precise details of this expedition have been the subject of a controversy as bitter as that surrounding the history of the first expedition, the most important result of the expedition — the opening of Brazil to European commerce and settlment — is not disputed. At the end of 1502 Manuel granted to Fernão de Noronha and others a three-year concession to trade in Brazil, with the stipulation that they explore 300 leagues of coast a year and establish forts. Portuguese colonization had begun.[74]

Any firm pronouncement that would be generally accepted as a solution of "the Vespucci question" awaits the discovery of new documentation of such authenticity that it will wipe away all doubts.[75]

[74] Marcondes de Souza, "A expedição de 1501–02," for a discussion of who commanded; see also Peres, *Descobrimentos*, pp. 503–517.

[75] In general, the Portuguese historians belittle Vespucci. The pro-Vespucci position is represented by Alberto Magnaghi and Roberto Levillier, though Magnaghi accepts only two voyages and rejects the authenticity of the *Mundus novus* and the *Lettera* but Levillier accepts all the writing and four voyages. Both praise Vespucci. Charles E. Nowell, reviewing Levillier's *América la bien llamada* (*HAHR*, 30:501–511, Nov. 1950), agrees with him in general. Relevant to this subject is the "fragmentary" letter attributed to Vespucci and published by Roberto Ridolfi in 1937. Written in a colloquial style that contrasts with the formality that characterizes the other letters attributed to Vespucci, and existing as a copy rather than in the hand of Vespucci, its authenticity is hard to check. Levillier accepts, Magnaghi rejects. See the review by C. E. Nowell in *HAHR*, 17:109–110, (Feb. 1938). In recent years the review *Imago Mundi* has published a running commentary on the "Vespucci question."

XIV
João Fernandes Lavrador and Pedro de Barcelos

King Manuel issued a license to João Fernandes Lavrador of Terceira on October 28, 1499, to "go in search of and discover some islands on [our side of the Line of Demarcation]" (*trabalhar de ir buscar e descobrir algumas ilhas de nossa conquista*).[76] João Fernandes was to pay the cost of the expedition and as a reward receive a captaincy and suitable honors on the model of grants made in Madeira and other areas. There is no record of a specific voyage made in accordance with this grant, but there are ample indications that Fernandes sailed and perhaps on more than one voyage.

Definitely connected with this is the career of Pedro de Barcelos, who was the owner of a large amount of land in Terceira. In 1506 he sued the sons of João Valadão who had seized some of his lands while he was away, because "I and João Fernandes Lavrador had an authorization from the King our Lord to go discovering, in which discoveries we spent a good three years." That they made discoveries is ample indicated from maps of the early sixteenth century, and it seems clear as well that Labrador was named for João Fernandes.

The answer to the question of whether these two explorers sailed over a three-year period from 1492 to 1495, or 1495 to 1498, or after 1500 rests on evidence so light and arguments so heavy that they need not be repeated here. The evidence set forth seems to suggest that it is highly unlikely that the discoveries were made before 1495, and they may have been as late as 1500–1501. The complicated arguments are set forth in Morison, *Portuguese Voyages*, and Damião Peres, *Descobrimentos Portugueses*.

Henry VII of England issued letters on March 19, 1501, for a João Fernandes, two other Portuguese, and three merchants of Bristol to make explorations. This is presumably, but not certainly, the same João Fernandes who received the license from Manuel in 1499. No record shows what, if anything, the English-Portuguese partnership discovered.

---

[76] The slender information about João Fernandes Lavrador and Pedro de Barcelos has been used by some historians to attribute to him the discovery of America in 1492 (before Columbus) or of Newfoundland in 1495 (before John Cabot and Miguel and Gaspar Corte-Real). Morison, *Portuguese Voyages*, pp. 51–72, rejects any discovery before 1500. Peres, *Descobrimentos*, pp. 407–421, believes 1495–98 are the right dates. Duarte Leite, *Descobrimentos*, I, 362–364, admits at most a "sighting" of Greenland between 1495 and 1498.

What happened to João Fernandes Lavrador after 1501 is unknown. The land that bears his nickname is his monument, though the land he touched was Greenland rather than present-day Labrador, the name having been transferred later. Duarte Leite remarks: "Nem em 1452 com Diogo de Teive, nem em 1472 ou 1473 com João Vaz e Álvaro Martins Homem, nem pouco antes de 1474 com João Vaz, nem entre 1492 e 1495 com Pedro de Barcelos e João Fernandes Lavrador descobriram os portuguêses terra algum da América. Entre 1495 e 1498 é possivel que João Fernandes Lavrador tivesse avistado a Groelandia numa expediçã portuguesa, que alias não desembracou na terra, conforme a legenda no mapa de Cantino; e nesse último ano veio a essa terra o nome de Lavrador."[77] Leite believes, however, that the Cantino map of 1502 shows that the Portuguese had discovered Florida before Ponce de León's voyage of 1512.

XV
Gaspar and Miguel Corte-Real

Between the years 1499 and 1502, the Corte-Real brothers, Gaspar and Miguel, discovered areas in North America that correspond to parts of Newfoundland and regions still farther north.[78] On May 12, 1500, King Manuel licensed Gaspar to continue to search for some islands and the mainland which Gaspar had already, at his own expense, "searched . . . to discover and find" and which he now desired to attempt again to discover. From this grant it seems clear that Gaspar had made a voyage or voyages before 1500. Whether or not he knew of the patent granted to João Fernandes Lavrador in October 1499 is not clear. Also he might have known of the two voyages made by John Cabot on behalf of Henry VII of England in 1497 and 1498. The best account of Gaspar's voyages comes from Damião de Góis (1502–74), chronicler of Kings João II and Manuel, who records that Gaspar with one ship sailed from Lisbon in the spring of

---

[77] Leite, *Descobrimentos*, I, 363–364.

[78] Morison, *Portuguese Voyages*, pp. 68–72; Peres, *Descobrimentos*, pp. 469–482; Leite, *Descobrimentos*, I, 364–373; Prestage, *The Portuguese Pioneers*, pp. 270–314 (who accepts the thesis of "secrecy"); Marcondes de Souza, *O descobrimento da América*, pp. 83–87, 215–217 (grant made to Gaspar Corte-Real by King Manuel), 218–220 (Cantino letter on Gaspar's voyage), 221–224 (Pasqualigo letters on Gaspar), 225–227 (brief notices from António Galvão and Damião de Góis). The chief work on the Corte-Real family is Henry Harrisse, *Les Côrte-Real et leurs voyages au Noveau Monde*.

1500, finding a cool land with large trees which he named *Terra Verde*. The people were described as "barbarous and wild," white when they were young but browning as they grew older. Also, if Góis gives a true account, Gaspar became well enough acquainted with them to discover that they were "very jealous of their wives." This area fits the description of Newfoundland north of Cape Breton somewhere in the region Cabot had reached.

In April or May 1501, Gaspar sailed again, this time with three ships. The best information concerning this voyage is contained in the letters of Pietro Pasqualigo and Alberto Cantino, two Italians writing from Lisbon. Gaspar reached Labrador, Newfoundland, and Nova Scotia, giving names to many of the features of the coast which they retain today in distorted English form. From this voyage he sent back fifty slaves, timber, and various other objects as well as silver earrings and a sword blade of Venetian origin, which presumably the Indians had obtained from the Cabot expedition. At some point Gaspar left his other ships and sailed south never to be heard of again.

King Manuel assigned half of Gaspar's discoveries to Miguel, elder brother of Gaspar, who sailed with two vessels sometime in 1502. He too was lost.[79] The importance of these expeditions for the Portuguese is clearly evident in the establishment of the codfishing industry off Newfoundland. As early as 1506, duties were paid on codfish being brought into Portugal, and the codfishing vessels of Portugal still sail annually.[80]

XVI
Chronology of Portuguese Expansion

Part I: 1415–1502

Date and Region*	Initiative
1415 Capture of Ceuta.	Initiative of the king, the princes, and João Afonso.
1415–1433 Fifteen(?) voyages along northwest African short of Cape Bojador.	Objectives, destinations, and results unknown. Source of information: Azurara.

---

[79] The disappearance of Miguel has led to the belief by some that he reached New England where the Dighton Rock allegedly records his arrival. See Edmond B. Delabarre, *Dighton Rock, a Story of the Written Rocks of New England.*

[80] Godinho, *Documentos*, II, 263–264, III, 318–322; Morison, *Portuguese Voyages*, pp. xiii–xiv; Peres, *Descobrimentos*, pp. 93–166, 213–226, and *passim*.

*Brackets indicate no sound evidence of voyage or discovery.

1419–1425(?) Rediscovery or discovery of Madeira and beginning of settlement.	Initiative of João Gonçalves Zarco and Tristão Teixeira. Porto Santo to Bartolomeu Perestrello.
1424 or 1425 Unsuccessful expedition of Fernando de Castro to the Canaries.	Initiative of the king and perhaps of Henry also.
1426 Gonçalo Velho to the "Terra Alta," somewhere short of Cape Bojador.	Initiative of Henry(?).
1427 Rediscovery or discovery of the Azores Islands by Diogo de Silves (or Sines?).	Individual initiative, by chance or on royal order(?).
1431 or 1432 Transplant of domestic animals to the Azores.	By action of Henry.
1434 First certain passage beyond Cape Bojador by Gil Eanes.	By order of Henry.
1435 Voyage beyond Cape Bojador by Gil Eanes and Afonso Baldaia.	Initiative of Henry.
1436 Afonso Baldaia to Rio do Ouro (an inlet, today Villa Cisneros, approximately 23°50'N latitude).	Initiative of Henry.
1437 Voyage to Rio do Ouro, unknown commander.	Initiative of Henry.
1437 Attack on Tangier, a bad failure: capture of Prince Fernando.	Initiative attributed to King Duarte and to Henry. Prince Pedro opposed to attack(?)
1440 Expedition to Canaries.	Initiative of the Regent Pedro and Henry(?).
1440 Two caravels along the Sahara coast.	Private initiative(?).
1441 or 1442(?) Antão Gonçalves takes first captives at Rio do Ouro.	His own initiative(?) or sent by Henry(?).
1441 Nuno Tristão to Cabo Branco (Cape Blanco) approximately 21°N latitude.	Initiative of Henry.

1443 Nuno Tristão to the islands of Gete and Garças in Arguim Bay, just south of Cape Blanco.	Initiative of Henry.
1444 Gonçalo de Sintra to Arguim.	Initiative of Henry.
1444 Antão Gonçalves, Diogo Afonso, and Gomes Pires on trade and raid to Rio do Ouro.	Initiative of Regent Pedro and Henry.
1444 Nuno Tristão to the Terra dos Negros (region of Senegal, approximately 14-15°S latitude).	Initiative of Henry.
1444 Lanzarote to islands of Naar and Tider, to raid for Negroes, just south of Arguim.	Individual initiative.
1444 Dinis Dias to Cape Verde and Ilha da Palma (Gorée) approximately 13-14°S latitude.	Inidividual initiative(?).
1445 Dinis Eanes, Álvaro Gil, Mafaldo (Gonçalo Coelho) to Terra dos Negros.	Individual initiative(?).
1445 Antão Gonçalves, Garçia Homem, Diogo Afonso to Cape Blanco and Arguim.	Initiative of Antão Gonçalves.
1445 Large expedition of Lanzarote and men of Lagos, plus others of Lisbon, etc., to region of Argium. Slave raids.	Initiative of Lanzarote and private individuals of Lagos and Lisbon.
1445 Lanzarote and Gomes Pires to Senegal region and Cape Verde.	Private initiative. Continuation of part of the large expedition.
1445 Álvaro Fernandes beyond Senegal and Cape Verde to Cabo dos Mastos (Red Cape?)	Private initiative.
1446 Gomes Pires to Rio do Ouro. Trade and raid.	Own initiative and perhaps collaboration of Regent Pedro.
1446 Estevão Afonso and six *caravelas* to Terra dos Negros.	Private initiative.

1446 Nuno Tristão to south of Cape Verde.	Private initiative.
1447 Diogo Gil to Messa, on Moroccon coast. Trade.	Private initiative or initiative of Henry.
1447 Antão Gonçalves to Rio do Ouro. Trade.	Private initiative.
1447(?) Vallarte, a prince from Scandinavia, to Terra dos Negros to south of the Cabo dos Mastos (identical with one of other voyages?).	Own initiative and help of Regent Pedro(?).
1448 Fishing voyage along coast beyond Cape Bojador and short of Cape Blanco.	Private initiative.
1448 Antão Conçalves sent to take possession of Lanzarote Island in Canaries, granted by Maciot to Henry.	Initiative of Henry.
1448 or before. Discovery of "Authentic Island" shown on Bianco map of 1448.	No other evidence of a discovery; many interpretations of the map.
1452 Diogo de Teive, discovery of islands of Flores and Corvo in Azores. Voyage to southwest of Azores, no discovery; to northeast or northwest, no known discovery.	Private initiative(?).
1452 or before. Three or more voyages on initiative of	Private initiative.
Luca de Cassano (or Cazana), one with Vincente Dias(?). No known discoveries.	
1450s and 1460s. Regular trade with islands and along African coast.	Private initiative under concession from Henry and and crown.
1455 First voyage of Cadamosto, in which he met Antoniotto Usodimare, who had sailed separately.	Private initiative with license and participation of Henry.

1455 or 1456 Voyage of António de Noli (and Diogo Gomes?) to Cape Verde Islands(?).

Extremely vague documentation.

1456 Voyage of Diogo Gomes to the region of the Geba River (same as above with Noli?).

Initiative of Henry.

1456 Second voyage of Cadamosto, with Usodimare, probably first to see Cape Verde Islands.

Private initiative with Henry's license.

1458 Capture of the Moroccan city of Alcácer-Seguer.

Royal initiative with the participation of Henry.

1460 or 1462(?) Diogo Gomes to realm of Barbacins (south of Cape Verde); discovery of Cape Verde Islands with Noli?

Royal initiative.

1460 or 1462(?) Gonçalo Ferreira to land of Barbacins.

Private initiative(?).

1460 First(?) voyage of Pedro de Sintra as far as Sierra Leone.

Henry's initiative, or the king's, or both.

[1462 Concession to João Vogado to search for two islands, Capraria and Lovo, shown on maps of the time. No islands found.]

Private or royal initiative(?).

1469 Concession to Fernão Gomes of Guinea coast beyond Sierra Leone.

Royal concession.

1471 João de Santarém and Pero Escobar to Guinea coast as far as Shama Bay (region of Cape Three Points).

Initiative of Fernão Gomes.

[1472–1474 João Vaz Corte-Real and Alvaro Martins Homem to America (Newfoundland). No sound basis for believing voyage made.]

Supposedly on concession of widow of Dom Fernando.

1472–1475(?) Fernando Pô,

Under the Gomes concession.

São Tomé, and Príncipe in Gulf
of Guinea. Various explorers
and merchants for Gomes:
Soeiro da Costa, Fernando
Pô, Lopo Gonçalves, and Rui
de Sequeira.

1474 or 1475 Rui de Sequeira to   Under Gomes concession.
to Cape St. Catharine, just
below the equator.

[1473–1481(?) Portuguese in   If a real voyage, it was under
the Pining, Pothorst, or   royal sponsorship.
Skolp voyage to Greenland(?).]

[1474–1476 Fernão Teles searched   Said to be under royal con-
for islands toward western   cession.
Atlantic(?). No evidence of
discovery.]

1479 Treaty of Alcáçovas
giving the Canary Islands to
Spain and the African coast
to Portugal.

1482 Construction of the   Royal initiative.
feitoria fort of São Jorge
da Mina on the Guinea Coast
about 1°W.

1482–1484 First voyage of   Royal initiative.
Diogo Cão beyond equator and
Congo River to Cape Santa
Maria, about 13°S.

[1484: António Leme's discovery
of Antilles. No proof of
voyage by Leme.]

[1484 Fernão Domingues do   Royal concession.
Arco. No known results — no
proof of voyage.]

1485–1486 Second voyage of   Royal initiative.
Diogo Cão to approximately
22°S (Walvis Bay).

1485–1486 João Afonso de   Royal initiative.
Aveiro to Benin (accompanied
Diogo Cão).

[1486 Projected voyage of Fernão Dulmo (Ulm or Olmos) and Afonso do Estreito west into Atlantic. No record of sailing or of discoveries.]	Royal initiative or private with royal concession.
1487–1488 Bartolomeu Dias sailed around Cape of Good Hope to east coast of Africa to about present-day Great Fish River.	Royal initiative.
1492–1493 First voyage of Columbus to America	For Spain, private initiative with royal support.
1494 Treaty of Tordesillas which demarcated Portuguese and Spanish spheres of activity.	
1497–1499 Vasco da Gama's voyage to east coast of Africa and to India.	Royal initiative.
[1498 Duarte Pacheco Pereira's alleged voyage to America. No proof of voyage or of any discovery.]	Alleged to be royal initiative.
1500–1501 Pedro Álvares Cabral's discovery of Brazil while en route to India.	Royal initiative with private participation.
1500 Most probable date of the João Fernandes Lavrador and Pedro de Barcelos voyage to Greenland (Terra de Bacalhau)	Private with royal grant.
1499–1502 Voyages of Gaspar and Miguel Corte-Real to America in the region of Labrador, Newfoundland, and perhaps New England.	Private with royal grants.

Part II: Conquest and Outreach, 1502–1580

Since most voyages after 1500 were the results of royal initiative, the formal category Initiative is eliminated below. Mention has been made in the text of the one instance in which a discovery was made privately.

1502 Vasco da Gama bombards Calicut and establishes a *feitoria* in Cochin.

1503 First trip of Afonso de Albuquerque to Asia.

1504 Duarte Pacheco Pereira repulses the Samorin of Calicut from Cochin; King Manuel grants concession to Lucas Rem and the Welsers to outfit ships in the 1505 fleet.

1505 Francisco de Almeida named first viceroy; he ravages Mombasa and conquers Quilon; his *regimento* contains beginnings of an imperial strategy; Pedro de Anaia takes Kilwa.

1506 Lourenço de Almeida visits Ceylon; King Manuel establishes spice trade as royal monopoly; Afonso de Albuquerque returns to Asia with Tristão da Cunha, and they capture Socotra; Albuquerque bears secret orders to succeed Almeida when term expires; Madagascar discovered.

1507 Albuquerque invests Ormuz, which agrees to accept Portuguese garrison, but reneges when Albuquerque's captains desert to Viceroy Almeida.

1508 Arzila besieged by Portuguese; Mameluke fleet descends from Suez into Indian Ocean, joins Malik Ayaz at Diu, and defeats small Portuguese fleet under Lourenço de Almeida.

1509 Quarrel between Afonso de Albuquerque and Viceroy Francisco de Almeida; Almeida defeats Mameluke fleet in Diu harbor, establishing Portuguese naval supremacy in Indian Ocean; Marshal of Portugal arrives and installs Albuquerque in power; Diogo Lopes Sequeira visits Malacca.

1510 Conquest of Goa by Albuquerque.

1511 Conquest of Malacca by Albuquerque; he sends Francisco Serrão to discover Moluccas.

1513 Albuquerque repulsed before Aden; he sails into Red Sea, becoming first Western commander to do so, but early reversal of monsoons forces him to lay over on barren Kamaran Island; Jorge Álvares arrives in China; Portuguese capture Azemmour.

1514 Probable date of António Fernandes's first trip into East African interior of Monomotapa.

1515 Albuquerque returns to Ormuz and captures it; is dismissed and dies on return to Goa; Portuguese overwhelmed at Mamora.

1516 *Book of Duarte Barbosa* published; Chaul fortified.

1517 Fernão Peres de Andrade arrives in Canton.

1518 Lopo Soares de Albergaria founds fortress in Ceylon.

1519 Ferdinand Magellan, in Spanish service since 1517, leaves Europe on voyage of circumnavigation.

1520 Diogo Lopes de Sequeira, on foray into Red Sea, drops off the embassy of Rodrigo de Lima at Massawa, whence it establishes contact with "Prester John," the Ethiopian emperor Lebna Dengal.

1521 Death of King Manuel; succession of King João III.

1522 Remnants of Magellan's expedition arrive in Moluccas, inaugurating hostilities there between Portugal and Spain over the next decades; Portuguese build fort of São João de Ternate.

1524 Luso-Spanish conference meets between Elvas and Badajoz to debate ownership of Moluccas on basis of Tordesillas agreement; Vasco da Gama sent back to India as first viceroy since Almeida; fort at Passumah (Sumatra) abandoned.

1525 Johore attacks Malacca, whose captain-general, Pero Mascarenhas, retaliates.

1526 Samorin of Calicut invests Portuguese fortress there.

1529 Treaty of Zaragoza over Moluccan question; double marriage between Emperor Charles V, King João III, and their sisters.

1532 Diogo Mendes arrested in Antwerp.

1533 Portuguese acquire Bassein.

1534 Portuguese occupy Bombay; Safi besieged by sheriff of Marrakech.

1535 Portuguese acquire fortress at Diu; concession system begun in Moluccas.

1538 First siege of Diu by Turks and Gujarati; Portuguese destroy Mombasa.

1541 Estevão da Gama expedition into Red Sea; leaves brother Cristóvão with small army to aid Ethopian Christians against Muslims.

1542 Safi and Azemmour abandoned; Francis Xavier arrives in Goa.

1543 Portuguese private traders reach Japan.

1546 Second siege of Diu by Gujarati.

1549 King João III ceases marketing operations for spices through *feitoria* in Antwerp; Alcácer-Seguer abandoned.

1550 Arzila abandoned; first contacts with Macau; Malacca attacked by coalition.

1551 Piri Reis captures Muscat from Portuguese, but abandons it.

1552 Turks besiege Ormuz unsuccessfully.

1557 Death of João III; Sebastião succeeds under regency of grandmother, Dona Catarina; Portuguese settle in Macau; captain-major of Japan Voyage first nominated.

1560 Portuguese capture Jaffnapatam in Ceylon and fortify Manar.

1562 Cardinal-infante Henrique succeeds Dona Catarina as regent; Mazagão besieged by Moors.

1567 Malacca besieged by Achinese.

1568 Sebastião's majority declared.

1569 Sebastião divides Portuguese Asia into three parts, appointing former governor Francisco Barreto as captain-general of East Africa (Monomotapa); Nagasaki open to Portuguese commerce.

1570 Sebastião decrees end to royal monopoly on Asian import and export; Asian coalition attacks Goa, Chaul, Bassein, Daman simultaneously.

1573 Death of Francisco Barreto on campaign.

1574 Sebastião makes first visit to North Africa.

1575 Contract with Konrad Rott of Augsburg.

1576 Fortress of São João de Ternate capitulates.

1577 Sebastião reoccupies Arzila.

1578 Battle of Alcácer-Kebir; death of Sebastião; Cardinal-infante Henrique succeeds him.

1580 Henrique names Philip of Spain as successor; he dies; Philip sends Duke of Alva to invade country and conquers it; at Cortes of Tomar he promises to preserve Portuguese separateness from his other realms.

XVII
Governors of Portuguese Asia to 1580

1. Francisco de Almeida, 1505–1509 (Viceroy)
2. Afonso de Albuquerque, 1509–1515
3. Lopo Soares de Albergaria, 1515–1518
4. Diogo Lopes de Sequeira, 1518–1522
5. Duarte de Menezes, 1522–1524
6. Vasco da Gama, First Count of Vidigueira, 1524 (Viceroy)
7. Henrique de Menezes, 1524–1526
8. Lopo Vaz de Sampaio, 1526–1529
9. Nuno da Cunha, 1529–1538
10. Garçia de Noronha, 1538–1540 (Viceroy)

11. Estevão da Gama, 1540–1542
12. Martim Afonso de Sousa, 1542–1545
13. João de Castro, 1545–1548 (Viceroy)
14. Garcia de Sá, 1548–1549
15. Jorge Cabral, 1549–1550
16. Afonso de Noronha, 1550–1554 (Viceroy)
17. Pero Mascarenhas, 1554–1555 (Viceroy)
18. Francisco Barreto, 1555–1558
19. Constantino de Bragança, 1558–1561 (Viceroy)
20. Francisco de Coutinho, Third Count of Redondo, 1561–1564 (Viceroy)
21. João de Mendonça, 1564
22. Antão de Noronha, 1564–1568 (Viceroy)
23. Luís de Ataíde, Third Count of Atougia, 1568–1571 (Viceroy) first term
24. António de Noronha, 1571–1573 (Viceroy)
25. António Moniz Barreto, 1573–1576
26. Diogo de Menezes, 1576–1578
27. Luís de Ataíde, Third Count of Atougia, 1578–1581 (Viceroy) second term

BIBLIOGRAPHY

Abbreviations

AAHP	*Anais da Academia de História*
ACL or ASL	Academia das Ciências (Sciências), Lisboa
AECA	Agrupamento de Estudos de Cartografia Antiga
AGC	Agência Geral das Colónias
AGU	Agência Geral do Ultramar
AHDE	*Anuario de Historia del Derecho Español*
AHML	*Arquivo Histórico da Marinha*
AHP	*Arquivo Histórico Português*
AHR	*American Historical Review*
AHU	Arquivo Histórico Ultramarino
APH	Academia Portuguêsa de História
BAGC	*Boletim da Agência Geral das Colónias*
BEP	*Bulletin des Études Portugaises et de l'Institut Français au Portugal*
BGSP	*Bulletin of the Geographical Society of Philadelphia*
BIH-IT	*Boletim do Instituto Histórico da Ilha Terceira*
BSGI	*Bollettino della Societá Geografica Italiana*
BSGL	*Boletim da Sociedade de Geografia de Lisboa*
BSGP	*Bulletin de la Societé de Geographia de Paris*
CEHU	Centro de Estudos Históricos Ultramarinos
III-CIEL-B	III Colóquio Internacional de Estudos Luso-Brasileiros
IV-CIEL-B	IV-Colóquio Internacional de Estudos Luso-Brasileiros
V-CIEL-B	V-Colóquio Internacional de Estudos Luso-Brasileiros
I-CHEPM	*Primeiro Congresso de História da Expansão Portuguêsa no Mundo*
CHR	*Canadian Historical Review*
CIHD	Congresso Internacional de História dos Descobrimentos (Lisbon, 1960)
CIHP	*Collecção de Livros Inéditos de História Portuguêza*
CMIH	Comemoração do V Centenário do Morte do Infante D. Henrique (1960)
CMP	*Congresso do Mundo Português*
DHP	*Dicionario de História de Portugal*
EHR	*English Historical Review*
EIP	*Estudos Italianos em Portugal*
GJE	*Geographical Journal, England*
GR	*Geographic Review* ·
HAHR	*Hispanic American Historical Review*
HCPB	*História da Colonização Portuguêsa do Brasil*

HEP	*História da Expansão Portuguêsa no Mundo*
IAC	Instituto de Alta Cultura
ICHS	*International Congress of Historical Sciences*
IM	*Imago Mundi*
JAH	*Journal of African History*
JEH	*Journal of Economic History*
JIU	Junta de Investigação do Ultramar
MM	*Mariner's Mirror*
RBPH	*Revue Belge de Philologie et d'Histoire*
RFCC	*Revista da Faculdade de Ciências de Coimbra*
RFLL	*Revista da Faculdade de Letras, Lisboa*
RH	*Revista de História*
RHES	*Revue d'Histoire Économique et Sociale*
RHSP	*Revista de História, São Paulo*
RIHGB	*Revista do Instituto Histórico Geográfico Brasileiro*
RIM	*Revista de Índias, Madrid*
RPH	*Revista Portuguêsa de História*
RSGM	*Real Sociedad Geográfica de Madrid*
RUC	*Revista da Universidade de Coimbra*
SGL	Sociedade de Geografia de Lisboa
SGM	*Scottish Geographical Magazine*
TAM	*The Americas*
TCHR	*The Catholic Historical Review*
TEHR	*The Economic History Review*
TGJ	*The Geographical Journal*
TGR	*The Geographical Review*
TI	*Terrae Incognitae*

Bibliography

BIBLIOGRAPHIES

Ameal, Conde de. *Catálogo da notável e preciosa livraria.* Ed. José dos Santos. Lisbon: José dos Santos, 1924.

Anselmo, António Joaquim. *Bibliografia das bibliografias portuguêsas.* Lisbon: Biblioteca Nacional, 1923.

————. *Bibliografia das obras impressas em Portugal no século XVI.* Lisbon: Biblioteca Nacional, 1926.

Arquivo Histórico Ultramarino. *Catálogo da exposição cartográfica e iconográfica comemorative do V [quinto] centenário do nascimento de Pedro Álvares Cabral, descobridor do Brasil.* Lisbon: AHU, 1968.

Arquivos de Angola. 7 vols. Luanda: Museu de Angola, 1943–.

Bibliografia geral protuguêsa, século XV. 2 vols. Lisbon: Imprensa Nacional, 1941–42. Incomplete.

Boletim da Filmoteca Ultramarina Portuguêsa, no. I. Lisbon: CEHU-AGU, 1954–. 37 vols. to date.

Brochado, José Idalino Ferreira da Costa. *Historiógrafos dos descobrimentos.* Lisbon: CMIH, Colecção Henriquina, 1960.

Carson, Patricia. *Materials for West African History in the Archives of Belgium and Holland.* London: Oxford University Press, 1962.

————. *Materials for West African History in French Archives.* London: Oxford University Press, 1968.

Carvalho, Joaquim Barradas de. "A Literatura portuguêsa de viagens (século XV, XVI, XVII)," *RHSP,* 40, 81:51–74 (January–March, 1970).

Catálogo bibliográfico da Agência-Geral das Colônias. Lisbon: AGC, name later changed to Agência Geral do Ultramar, 1943—.

Costa, Abel Fontoura da. *Bibliografia náutica portuguêsa até 1700.* Lisbon: AGC, 1940.

Costa, Mario. *Bibliografia geral de Moçambique.* Lisbon: AGC, 1946.

Coutinho, Xavier C. *Bibliografie franco-portugaise.* Oporto: Livraria Lopes da Silva, 1939.

Cox, Edward Godfrey. *A Reference Guide to the Literature of Travel, Including Voyages, Geographical Descriptions, Adventures, Shipwrecks and Expeditions.* 3 vols. Seattle: Greenwood, 1935–49.

Cunha, J. H. Rivara da. *Catálogo dos manuscritos da Bibliotheca Pública Eborense,* I, *América, África, e Ásia.* 4 vols. Lisbon, 1850–71.

Denucé, J. "Une visite aux archives de Lisbonne et de Seville," *Revue de l'Instruction Publique en Belgique,* 49:94–100 (1906).

Diffie, Bailey W. "Bibliography of the Principal Guides to Portuguese Archives and Libraries," *Actas do Colóquio Internacional d'Estudos Luso-Brasileiros de 1950* (Washington).
Nashville: Vanderbilt University Press, 1953, pp. 181–88.

Ferreira, Manuel. *Catálogo de uma excelente biblioteca de viagens, descobrimentos, história.* Lisbon, n.d.

Fontoura da Costa, Abel. See Costa, Abel Fontoura da.

Foulché-Delbosc, R. and L. Barrau Dihigo. *Manuel de l'hispanissant.* 2 vols. New York:
Hispanic Society, 1920–25.

Garraux, A. L. *Bibliographie brésilienne. Catalogue des ouvrages français et latin relatifs au
Brésil (1500–1898).* Rio de Janeiro, 1898; new edition, José Olympio, 1962.

Gonçalves, Júlio. *Bibliografia dos descobrimentos e navegações existente na Sociedade de
Geografia de Lisboa. Anexo BSGL,* 1954–56.

Gray, Richard and David Chambers. *Materials for West African History in Italian Archives.*
London: Oxford University Press, 1965.

Greenlee, William B. *A Catalogue of the William B. Greenlee Collection of Portuguese
History and Literature and the Portuguese Materials in the Newberry Library.* Compiled
by Doris Varner Welsh. Chicago, 1953.

Iria, Alberto. *Inventário geral dos códices do Arquivo Histórico Ultramarino.* Lisbon:
CEHU-AGU, 1966.

Laures, Johannes, S. J. *a Manual of Books and Documents on the Early Christians' Missions
in Japan and More Particularly to the Collection at Sophia University, Tokyo; with an
Appendix of Ancient Maps of the Far East, Espcially Japan.* 3rd ed. Tokyo: Sophia
University Press, 1957.

Magalhães Basto, A. de. *Catálogo dos manuscritos ultramarinos da Biblioteca Pública
Municipal do Porto.* Lisbon: Imprensa Nacional, 1938.

Manuel II, King of Portugal. *Early Portuguese Books (1489–1600) in the Library of His
Majesty the King of Portugal.* 3 vols. London: Cambridge University Press [and Maggs
Brothers], 1929.

Manuscritos da Ajuda (Guia). 2 vols. Lisbon: CEHU, 1966–73.

Mauny, R. "Contribution à la bibliographie de l'histoire de l'Afrique noire des origines à
1850," *Bulletin de l'Institut d'Afrique noire,* 28:927–965 (1966). (Excellent.)

Morel-Fatio, Alfred. *Catalogue des manuscrits espagnols et des manuscrits portugais [de la
Bibliothèque Nationale].* Paris, 1892.

Mostra dei navigatori veneti del quattrocento e del cinquecento. Venice: Biblioteca
Nazionale Marciana, 1957.

Palau y Dulcet, A. *Manual del librero hispanoamericano.* 2nd ed. 24 vols. Barcelona: Dulcet, 1948–.

Parker, John, compiler. *A List of Additions, 1951–54.* The James Ford Bell Collection.
Minneapolis: University of Minnesota Press, 1955.

———. *A List of Additions of 1955–59.* The James Ford Bell Collection. Minneapolis:
University of Minnesota Press, 1961.

Periódicos portuguêses de interesse ultramarino. 2nd ed. Lisbon: Centro de Documentção
Científica Ultramarina, 1967.

Pimpão, Álvaro Júlio da Costa. "A historiografia oficial e o sigilo sôbre os descobrimentos,"
I-CHEPM (Lisbon, 1938), 2:199–230 (1940).

Queiroz Velloso, José Maria de. *O arquivo geral de Simancas.* Coimbra: Imprensa da
Universidade, 1923.

Ráu, Virgínia. "Arquivos de Portugal," *Actas do Colóquio Internacional d'Estudos Luso-
Brasileiros de 1950* (Washington). Nashville: Vanderbilt University Press, 1953, pp. 189–
213.

Ráu, Virgínia and Maria Fernanda Gomes da Silva. *Os manuscritos do arquivo da casa de
Cadaval respeitantes ao Brasil.* 2 vols. Coimbra: Atlântida, 1956–58.

Ryder, A. F. C. *Materials for West African History in Portuguese Archives.* London: University of London, The Athlone Press, 1965.

Santos, Manuel dos. *Bibliografia geral ou descrição bibliográfica de livros tantos de autores portuguêses como brasileiros e muitos outrás nacionalidades, impressos desde o século XV até a actualidade.* 2 vols. Lisbon: Manuel dos Santos, 1914–25.

Schurhammer, Georg, S.J. *Die zeitgenössichen Quellen zur Geschichte Portugiesich-Asiens und seiner Nachbarländer zur zeit des hl. Franz Xavier (1538–1552).* Rome: Institutum Historicum Societatis Iesu, 1962.

Schutte, Josephus Franciscus, S.J. *Introductio ad historium Societatis Iesu in Japonia, 1549–1650; ac proemium ad catalogos japoniae propylaeum.* Rome: Institutum Historicum Societatis Iesu, 1968.

Serrão, Joaquim Veríssimo. *Historiografia portuguêsa.* Lisbon: Editorial Verbo, 1962.

———. *História e conhecimento histórico.* Lisbon: Editorial Verbo, 1968.

———. *Manuscritos portuguêses ou referentes a Portugal da Biblioteca Nacional de Paris.* Paris: Fundação Calouste Gulbenkian, Centro Cultural Português, 1969.

———. See *Documentos . . . D. Sebastião.*

Tovar, Conde de. *O Arquivo de Estado de Veneza.* Lisbon: Imprensa Nacional, 1933.

SOURCES

Adonias, Isa. "A cartografia vetustíssima do Brasil até 1500," *RIHGB*, 287:77–132 (1970).

Albuquerque, Bras de. *Comentários do grande Afonso de Albuquerque, capitão geral que foi das Índias Orientais em tempo do muito poderoso rey D. Manuel.* 2 vols. Ed. António Baião. Coimbra: Imprensa da Universidade, 1923.

Alfonso X, el Sabio. See: *Libros del saber de astronomía.*

Álvares, Padre Francisco. *Verdadeira informação das terras do Preste João das Índias.* Lisbon, 1540 and later. See the edition of AGU, Lisbon, 1943.

———. *The Prester John of the Indies.* Eds. C. F. Beckingham and G. W. B. Huntingford. 2 vols. London: The Hakluyt Society, vols. 114–115, 1961.

Álvares, Frei João. *Crónica do Infante Santo D. Fernando.* Ed. J. Mendes dos Remédios. Coimbra: Imprensa da Universidade, 1911.

Andrada, See Andrade.

Andrade, Francisco de. *Crónica do muyto alto e muyto poderoso rey destas reynos de Portugal Dom Joao III deste nome.* 4 vols. Lisbon, 1613.

Andrade e Silva, José Justino. Collecção cronólogica da legislação portuguêsa. 10 vols., plus 5 vols. of supplements. Lisbon, 1854–59.

Arquivo Português Oriental. Ed. A. B. Bragança Pereira. 11 vols. Bastora, Goa: Tipografia Rangel, 1936–40.

Azevedo, Pedro Agusto de, ed. *Documentos das chancelarias reaes anteriores a 1531 relativos à Marrocos.* 2 vols. Coimbra: Imprensa da Universidade, 1915–34.

Azurara (or Gomes Eanes de Zurara). *Crónica da tomada de septa por el Rey Dom Joham o Primeiro.* Ed. Maria Esteves Pereira. Coimbra: ACL, 1915.

———. *Crónica do Conde D. Pedro de Menezes.* Lisbon: in *Colecção de inéditos de história portuguêsa,* vol. 2, 1792. See later citation to this collection.

———. *Crónica do Conde D. Duarte de Menezes,* in CIHP, vol. 3, 1793.

———. *Crónica do descobrimento e conquista da Guiné.* Ed. Visconde de Santarém. Paris, 1841. See also edition edited by José de Braganza, 2 vols. Oporto: Livraria Civilização, 1937.

———. *The Chronicle of the Discovery and Conquest of Guinea.* English version by Charles Raymond Beazley and Edgar Prestage. 2 vols. London: The Hakluyt Society, Old Series, 95 (1896), 100 (1899).

———. Bourdon, Leon, ed. and trans. *Gomes Eanes de Zurara, Cronique de Guinée.* Ifan-Dakar, 1960.

Baião, António. *Documentos do Corpo Cronológico Relativos a Marrocos (1488–1514).* Coimbra: Imprensa Universitaria, 1925.

———. See Fernandes, Valentim.

Barros, João de, and Diogo Couto. *Da Ásia.* First complete edition Lisbon, 24 vols., 1777–88. This edition is used and compared with earlier publications of the first *decade*, Lisbon, 1552, and subsequent *decades* of both Barros and Couto. Modern editions have been edited by Hernani Cidade and Manuel Múrias, 4 vols., Lisbon: AGC, 1945, and António Baião, 1st *Decade*. Coimbra: Imprensa da Universidade, 1932.

Battuta, Ibn (also, Batuta). *The Travels of Ibn Battuta in Asia and Africa.* Ed. and tr. H. A. R. Gibb. London: Routledge and Kegan Paul, 1927, and reprinted Cambridge, 1958–62. Hakluyt, series II, 110, 117, 141.

Bensaúde, Joaquim. *Histoire de la science nautique portugaise a l'époque des grandes découvertes.* 7 vols. Munich and Lisbon: C. Kuhn, 1914–24. See later entries for other works issued by Bensaúde.

Berchet, Guglielmo. *Fonti italiani per la scoperta del Nuovo Mondo,* in *Raccolta Colombiana,* part 3, vols. 1 and 2. Rome, 1893. See: *Raccolta di documenti,* etc.

Berwick y Alba, Duquesa de. *Autógrafos de Cristóbal Colón y papeles de América.* Madrid, 1892.

Bontier, Pierre. *The Canarian, or Book of the Conquest and Conversion of the Canarians in the year 1402,* by Messire Jean de Bethencourt, tr. and ed. Richard Henry Major. London: The Hakluyt Society, 1st series, vol. 46, 1872. Based on an incomplete manuscript. See Margry, Pierre.

Boxer, Charles R., ed. *South China in the Sixteenth Century. Narratives of Galeote Pereira, Fr. Gaspar da Cruz, o.p.p. and Fr. Martin de Rada, o.e.s.a.* (1550–75). London: The Hakluyt Society, 2nd series, vol. 106, 1953.

———, ed. and tr. *The Tragic History of the Sea, 1589–1622. Narratives of the Shipwrecks of the Portuguese East Indiamen São Tomé (1589), Santo Alberto (1593) São João Baptista (1622), and the Journeys of the Survivors in South-East Africa.* London: The Hakluyt Society, 2nd series, vol. 112, 1957.

———, ed. and tr. *Further Selections from the Tragic History of the Sea, 1559–1565.* Cambridge: The Hakluyt Society, 2nd series, vol. 132, 1968.

Bragança Pereira, A. B. See *Arquivo português oriental.*

Brásio, António. *Monumenta missionária africana. Africa Ocidental.* Lisbon: AGU, 1952.

Brito, Bernardo Gomes de. *História trágico marítima.* New ed., 6 vols. Ed. Damião Peres. Oporto: Livraria Civilização, 1942–43. See translations by Charles R. Boxer and James Duffy.

Bulhão Pato, Raimundo de, ed. *Cartas de Affonso de Albuquerque seguidas de documentos que as elucidam.* 7 vols. Lisbon: ACL, 1884–1935.

———. *Documentos remitidos da Índia: livro das monções.* Lisbon: 1880–1975

Cabral: on Cabral see *Os sete únicos documentos de 1500, conservados em Lisboa, referentes a viagem de Pedro Álvares Cabral.* Eds. A. Fontoura de Costa and António Baião. Lisbon: AGC, 1940.

———. See also William B. Greenlee, ed. and tr. *The Voyage of Pedro Álvares Cabral to Brazil and India.* London: The Hakluyt Society, 2nd series, vol. 81, 1938.

Cadamosto: on Cadamosto see *Voyages of Cadamosto and Other Documentos on Western Africa in the Second Half of the Fifteenth Century,* ed. G. R. Crone, London: The Hakluyt Society, 2nd series, vol. 80, 1937.

———. See also *Viagens de Lúis de Cadamosto e Pedro de Sintra.* Eds. João Franco Machado and Damião Peres. Lisbon: APH, 1948.

———. See also Caddeo, Rinaldo. *Le navigazione atlantiche di Alvise da Cá da Mosto.* Milan: Edizioni "Alpes," 1928 and 1929.

Caminha, Pero Vaz de. *Carta a El-Rey D. Manuel.* Ed. Leonardo Arroyo. São Paulo: Domus Editora, 1963. See other editions by Jaime Cortesão, etc.

Canto, Eugenio do, ed. *Allegações feitas contra os portuguêses a favor do Rei de Castella no Concilio de Basilea por D. Affonso, Bispo de Burgos, sôbre a conquista das Canárias.* Lisbon, 1912.

————, ed. *Carta que El-Rey nosso senhor escreveo a el Rey e a Rainha de Castella seus padres da nova da Índia (1501)*. Lisbon, 1906.

"*Carta (uma) de quitação do Infante D. Henrique mencionando productos obtidos nos tractos de Guiné*," ed. Jorge Faro. *Boletim Cultural da Guine*, 12:255–58 (April, 1957).

Castanheda, Fernão Lopes de. *História do descobrimento e conquista da Índia pelos portuguêses*. 4 vols. Coimbra: Imprensa da Universidade, 1924–33. Earlier editions were 1551 and later.

Castanhoso, Miguel de. See Whiteway, Richard.

Castilho, António de. *Comentario do cerco de Goa e Chaul no anno de MDLXX, Viserey Dom Luis de Ataide*. Lisbon, 1573.

Castro, dom João de. *Roteiro em que se contem a viagem que fizeram os portuguêses no anno de 1541 partindo da nobre cidade de Goa atraues Suez que he no fim do Mar Roxo*. Lisbon: AGC, 1940.

Cha Masser. *Relazione di Lunardo de Cha Masser. Apéndice à carta de El-Rey D. Manuel ao rei cathólico*. Ed. Prospero Peragallo, in *Memorias da Commissão Portuguêsa no Centenário da Descoberta da America*. Lisbon, 1892.

Coelho, José Ramos. See Ramos Coelho, José.

Coleção (spelled Collecção and other variations).

Colección de documentos inéditos relativos al descubrimiento conquista y colonización de las posessiones espânolas en América e Oceania. 42 vols. Madrid: Real Archivo de Indias, 1842–95. 2nd series, 18 vols., Madrid, 1885–.

Collecção de documentos relativos ao descobrimento e povoamento dos Açores. ed. Manuel Velho Arruda. Ponta Delgada: Oficinas de Artes Gráficas, 1932.

Collecção de livros inéditos de história portugûeza dos reinados de D. João I, D. Duarte, D. Affonso, V, e D. João II. Ed. José Corrêa da Serra. 5 vols. Lisbon: Academia Real das Sciências, 1790–96.

Columbus, Christopher. The principal collection is *Raccolta di documenti e studi publicata dalla Real Commissione Colombiana pel quarto centenario della scoperta dell'America*. 15 vols. Rome, 1892–94.

————. See also: *De los Pleitos de Colón*. Ed. Cesareo Fernández Duro, in *Colección de documentos inéditos de Ultramar*. 2nd series. Vols. VII and VIII. Madrid, 1892; and a new edition by Escuela de Estudios Hispanoamericanos, Sevilla, 1964–.

Cordeiro, Padre António. *História insulana*. Lisbon, 1717.

Correia (Corrêa), Gaspar de. *Lendas da Índia*. Ed. Lima Felner. 8 vols. Lisbon, 1856–66.

Cortesão, Armando, ed and tr. *The Suma Oriental of Tomé Pires and the Book of Francisco Rodrigues*. 2 vols. London: The Hakluyt Society, vols 89 and 90, 1944.

————. *Descobrimento e cartografia das ilhas de S. Tomé e Príncipe*. Coimbra: AECA-JIU, LXIII secção de Lisboa, 1971.

————. *The Mystery of Vasco da Gama*. Coimbra: AECA-JIU, 1973.

————. *O descobrimento de Porto Santo e da Madeira e o Infante D. Henrique*. Coimbra: AECA-JIU, LXXXI secção de Coimbra, 1973.

————. *A história do descobrimento das ilhas da Madeira por Roberto Machim em fins do século XIV*. Coimbra: AECA-JIU, LXXXV secção de Coimbra, 1973.

———— and A. Teixeira da Mota. *Portugalia monumenta cartographica*. 6 vols. Coimbra: CMIH, 1958–63.

Costa, Abel Fontoura da. *Os sete únicos documentos*. See Cabral.

————. *Uma carta náutica portuguêsa, anónima, de "circa" 1471*. Lisbon: AGC, 1940.

Coutinho, Lopo de Sousa. *Livro primeiro do cerco de Diu, que os Turcos poseram a forteleza de Diu*. Coimbra, 1556.

Couto, Diogo do. *Da Ásia*. See Barros, João de.

————. *Observações sôbre as principães causas de decadência dos portuguêzes na Ásia*. Lisbon, 1790. (The M. Rodrigues Lapa edition is to be preferred for the second dialogue, ca. 1612, but only the edition cited here contains the first dialogue, ca. 1580.)

————. *O soldado práctico*. Ed. M. Rodrigues Lapa. 2nd ed. Lisbon: Sá da Costa, 1954.

Crónica dos cinco reis de Portugal. Ed. A. de Magalhães Basto. Oporto: Livraria Civilização, 1945.
Crónicas dos sete primeiros reis de Portugal. 3 vols. Ed. Carlos da Silva Tarouca, S. J. Lisbon: APH, 1952–53.
Diario da viagem de Vasco da Gama. See Gama, Vasco da.
Documentação para a história das missões do padroado português no Oriente. Ed. António da Silva Rego. 12 vols. Lisbon: AGU, 1947–58.
Documentaçao ultramarina portuguêsa. Lisbon: CEHU-AGU, 1960.
Documentos do Arquivo Histórico da Câmara de Lisboa: livros dos reis. Lisbon: Câmara Municipal, 1957–58.
Documentos (os sete únicos) de 1500 conservados em Lisboa referentes a viagem de Pedro Álvares Cabral. See Cabral.
Documentos inéditos para a história do reinado de D. Sebastião. Ed. Joaquin Veríssimo Serrão. Coimbra: Imprensa da Universidade, 1958.
Documentos referentes a las relaciones con Portugal durante el reinado de los Reyes Católicos. Eds. Antonio de la Torre and Luis Suárez Hernández. 3 vols. Valladolid: Consejo Superior de Investigaciones Científicas, 1958–63.
Documentos remitidos da Índia, livros das monções. 6 vols. Lisbon, 1880–1975. See Bulhão Pato, Raimundo de.
Documentos sobre os portuguêses em Moçambique e na África Central, 1497–1840; Documents on the Portuguese in Mozambique and Central Africa. 7 vols. Lisbon: National Archives of Rhodesia and Nyasaland and CEHU, 1962–.
Duarte Barbosa: *The Book of Duarte Barbosa*. 2 vols. London: The Hakluyt Society, 2nd series, nos. 44 (1918) and 49 (1921).
Duffy, James. *Shipwreck and Empire*. Cambridge: Harvard University Press, 1955.
Falcão, Luís de Figueiredo. *Livro em que se contem toda a fazenda e real patrimonio dos reis de Portugal, Índia, e ilhas adjacentes, e outras particularidades, escripta no anno de MDCVII*. Lisbon, 1859.
Fernandes, Valentim. *Reportório dos tempos, 1518*. Facsimile 1563 edition, by Joaquim Bensaúde, Geneva: A. Kundig, 1915.
———. *Manuscrito (0) de Valentim Fernandes*. Tr. Grabriel Pereira, *Boletim da Sociedade de Geografia de Lisboa*, 1898–99; also, edited by António Baião, Lisbon: APH, 1940.
Fernández de Navarette, Martín. *Colección de los viajes y descubrimientos que hicieron por mar los españoles desde los fines del siglo XV*. 5 vols. Madrid, 1825–37.
Fonseca, Henrique Quirino da. ed. *Diários de navegação da Carreira da Índia nos anos de 1595, 1596, 1597, 1600, e 1613*. Lisbon: ASL, 1938.
Foster, Sir William, ed. *The Red Sea and Adjacent Countries at the Close of the Seventeenth Century; as Described by Joseph Pitts, William Daniel, and Charles Jacques Poncet*. London: The Hakluyt Society, 2nd series, vol. 100, 1949.
Frois, Fr. Luis, S.J. *História do Japão*. 2 vols. Trs. and eds. G. Schurhammer, S.J. and E. A. Voretsch, S.J., as *Die Geschichte Japans, 1549–1578*; vol. II, J. A. Abranchos Pinto and Y. Ohamoto, eds. *Segunda parte da história do Japão, 1578–1582*. Tokyo: Sociedade Luso-Japonesa, 1938.
Galvão, António. *Tratado dos descobrimentos antigos e modernos feitos até a era de 1550*. Lisbon, 1563. 3rd ed. Eds. Visconde de Lagoa and Elaine Sanceau. Oporto: Livraria Civilização, 1944.
Gama, Vasco da. *Diário da viagem de Vasco da Gama*. Atributed to Alvaro Velho. 2 vols. Ed. A. de Magalhães Basto. Oporto: Livraria Civilização, 1945.
———. *A Journal of the First Voyage of Vasco da Gama, 1497–99*. Tr. and ed. E. G. Ravenstein. London: The Hakluyt Society, Old Series, no. 99, 1898.
Gavetas da Torre do Tombo. 11 vols. to date. Lisbon: CEHU-AGH, 1960–.
Godinho, Vitorino Magalhães. *Documentos sôbre a expansão portuguêsa*. 3 vols. Lisbon: Editorial Gleba, vol. 1 (1943?), vol. 3, 1956. (Best selection of documents.)
Góis, Damião de. *Crónica do Príncipe Dom Joam II, 1567*, and later editions. Coimbra: Imprensa da Universidade, 1905.

————. *Crónica do sereníssimo senhor Rei D. Emanuel*, 1st ed., Lisbon, 1566–67, and new ed., 4 vols. eds., Joaquim Martins Teixeira de Carvalho and David Lopes. Coimbra: Imprensa da Universidade, 1926. Republished, 7 vols., 1949–55.

Gomes, Diogo. *De prima inuentione Guinee, de insulis primo inuentis in Mar Océano Occidentis*. Códice de Valentim Fernandes, ed., António Baião. Lisbon, 1940. See Baião.

————. *As relacões do descobrimento da Guiné e das ilhas dos Açores, Madeira e Cabo Verde*. Tr. from text of Martin Behaim by Gabriel Pereira, in *BSGL*, 17th series, 1898–99.

Greenlee, William B., ed. *Voyage of Pedro Álvares Cabral*. See Cabral, Pedro Álvares.

Herrera, Antonio de. *Historia general de las Índias Occidentales y de los hechos de los castellanos en las islas y tierra firme del mar océano*. 4 vols., Madrid, 1601–15.

Ibn Battuta, see Battuta, Ibn.

Iria, Alberto. *Descobrimentos portuguêses: o Algarve e os descobrimentos*. Continuation of Silva Marques and numbered vol. 2 in two tomes. Lisbon: IAC, 1956.

Jacobs, Hubert M., S.J. *A Treatise on the Moluccas* (ca. 1544). Rome and St. Louis: Jesuit Historical Institute, 1970.

Jordão, Levy Maria. *Bullarium patronatus portugaliae regum in ecclesiis Africae, Asiae atque Oceaniae*. 3 vols. Lisbon, 1868–73; Appendix, vol. I, 1872; Appendix, vol. II, 1879.

Las Casas, Frei Bartolomé de. *Historia general de las Índias*. Ed. Marquès de la Fuensante del Valle. Vols. 62 to 67 of *Colección de documentos para la historia de España*. Madrid, 1875; new edition, ed., Augustín Millares Carlo, Mexico: Fondo de Cultura Económico, 1953.

Leitão, Humberto, ed. *Dois roteiros do século XVI, de Manuel Monteiro e Gaspar Ferreira Remão, atribuidos a João Baptista Lavanha*. Lisbon: CEHU, 1962.

Leo Africanus. *The History and Description of Africa Done into English by John Pory*. London: The Hakluyt Society, old series, vols. 92–94, 1896.

Libro del conoscimiento de todos los reynos y tierras y señoryos que son por el mundo y de las señales y armas que han cada tierra y señoryo. Ed. Marcos Jiménez Espada. Madrid, 1877.

Libros del saber de astronomia del Rey D. Alfonso X de Castilla. Ed. Manuel Rico y Sinobas. 5 vols. Madrid, 1863–67.

Linschoten, Jan Huighen van. *The Voyage of Jan Huyghen van Linschoten to the East Indies*. 2 vols. London: The Hakluyt Society, vols. 70–71, 1885.

Lisboa, João de. *Tratado da agulha de Marerar*. Lisbon, 1514.

————. *Livro de Marinharia*. Ed. Jacinto Ignacio de Brito Rebello. Lisbon, 1903.

Lopes, Fernão. *Crónica de D. Fernando*. 2 vols. Barcelos: Portugalense Editora, 1933 and 1935.

————. *Crónica de El-Rei D. João I*. 2 vols. Oporto: Livraria Civilização, 1945 and 1949.

Lopez, Duarte and Filippo Pigafetta. *Relação do Reino do Congo e das terras circunvizinhas*. 2 vols. Lisbon, AGC, 1949.

Lucena, Vasco Fernándes de. *Oração de obediência*, Rome, 1485, in Joaquim de Carvalho, *Excerpta bibliográphica ex Bibliotheca Colombina, Arquivo de História e Bibliografia*, Coimbra, 1925, pp. 563–71; also in A. Fontoura da Costa, *As portas da India em 1484*, Lisbon, 1936; and Francis Rogers, *The Obedience of a King*. Minneapolis: University of Minnesota Press, 1958.

Ma Huan. *Ying-Yai Sheng Lan: the Overall Survey of the Ocean's Shores (1433)*. Tr. and ed. J. V. G. Mills. Cambridge: Cambridge University Press [The Hakluyt Society Extra Series no. 42] 1970.

Mandeville's Travels. Text and tr. M. Letts. 2 vols. London: The Hakluyt Society, 2nd series, vols. 101–102, 1953.

Margry, Pierre. *La conquête et les conquérants des îles Canaries. Nouvelle recherches sur Jean IV de Béthencourt et Gadifer de la Salle. Le vrai manuscrit du Canarien*. Paris, 1896.

Mendes Pinto, Fernão. *Peregrinação*. New edition of work in 1616. Eds. A. J. da Costa Pimpão and César Pegado. 7 vols. Oporto: Portucalense Editora, 1944–45.

Mendonça, Jerónymo de. *Jornada de África*. 2 vols. Lisbon: Bibliotheca de Clássicos Portuguêzes, 1904.

Montalboddo, Fracanzano. *Paesi nouvamente ritrouate et nouo mondo da Alberico Vesputio florentino intitulato.* Vicenza, 1507.

Monumenta Henricina. Ed. António Joaquim Dias Dinis. 12 vols. Coimbra: CMIH, 1960–.

Mozambique: *Documentação avulsa mozambicana do Arquivo Histórico Ultramarino.* Ed. Francisco Santana. Lisbon: CEHU-AGU, 1966–67.

Nunes, Pedro. *Tratado em defensam da carta de marear.* 1st ed., 1537. Facsimile in *Tratado da sphera,* ed. Joaquim Bensaúde. Munich, 1915.

———. *Obras.* 2 vols. Lisbon: Imprensa Nacional, 1940–43.

Nunes de Leão, Duarte. *Crónicas del Rey Dom João de gloriosa memoria, o I deste nome e dos reys de Portugal o X e as dos reys D. Duarte e D. Affonso o V.* 2 vols. Lisbon, 1780.

Osório, D. Jeronimo. *Da vida e feitos de el-Rei D. Manuel.* 2 vols. Oporto: Livraria Civilização, 1944.

Pacifici, Sérjio J., tr. and ed. *Copy of a Letter of the King of Portugal sent to the King of Castile Concerning the Voyage and the Success of India.* Minneapolis: University of Minnesota Press, 1955.

Palencia, Alonso de. *Crónica de Enrique IV y Crónica de los Reyes Catolicos (Decadas).* 5 vols. Tr. Antonio Paz y Melia. Madrid: Tipografia de Archivos, 1904–9.

Pedro de Medina, a Navigator's Universe. The Libro de Cosmographia of 1538. Tr. Ursula Lamb. Chicago: published for the Newberry Library by the University of Chicago, 1972.

Pereira, A. B. de Bragança. See Bragança Pereira.

Pereira, Duarte Pacheco. *Esmeraldo de situ orbis.* Lisbon, 1892, 1905, and 3rd ed. Lisbon: APH, 1954.

———. *Esmeraldo de situ orbis.* Tr. George H. T. Kimble. London: The Hakluyt Society, vol. 79, 1937.

Pina, Rui de. *Crónica do muy excellente Rey Dom Joham de gloriosa memoria.* Lisbon, in *Colecção de livros inéditos de história portuguêza dos reinados de Dom João I, D. Duarte, D. Affonso V, e D. João II.* Lisbon, 1792–96.

———. *Crónica d'El-Rey D. Duarte,* in *Colecção* as above and Lisbon: Biblioteca de Clássicos Portuguêzes, 1901.

———. *Crónica d'El-Rey D. Affonso V,* in *Colecção* as above and in 3 vols. ed. Gabriel Pereira. Lisbon: Biblioteca de Clássicos Portuguêzes, 1901–2.

———. *Crónicas d'El-Rey D. Affonso II e d'El-Rey D. Sancho II.* Lisbon: Biblioteca de Clássicos Portuguêzes, 1906.

———. *Crónica d'El-Rey D. Affonso III.* Lisbon: Biblioteca de Clássicos Portuguêzes, 1908.

———. *Crónica d'El-Rey D. Diniz.* Lisbon: Biblioteca de Clássicos Portuguêzes, 1909. Also, Oporto: Livraria Civilização, 1945.

———. *Crónica d'El-Rey D. João II.* In *Colecção* as above and ed. Alberto Martins de Carvalho. Coimbra: Imprensa da Universidade, 1950.

Pisano, Mateu de. *De bello septense.* Lisbon: CIHP, 1790.

Polo, Marco. *The Book of Ser Marco Polo the Venetian Concerning the Kingdom and the Marvels of the East.* 2 vols. Ed. Sir Henry Yule; revised 3rd ed, H. Cordier. London: John Murray, 1903. There are many editions of *Marco Polo.*

(The) Portuguese Expedition to Abyssinia in 1543–1591, as Narrated by Castanhoso, with some Contemporary Letters, the Short Account of Bermudes' and Certain Extracts from Corrêa. London: The Hakluyt Society, 2nd series, vol. 10, 1902. See Whiteway.

Pulgar, Fernando del. *Crónica de los Reyes Católicos.* 2 vols. Madrid: Espasa Calpe, 1943.

Pyrard de Laval, François. *The Voyage of François Pyrard de Laval to the East Indies, the Maldives, the Moluccas and Brazil.* Tr. and ed. Albert Gray and H. C. P. Bell. 2 vols in 3. London: The Hakluyt Society, 1st series, vols. 76–77 and 80, 1887–90.

Queiroz, Frei Fernão de, S. J. *Conquest of Ceylon (Spiritual and Temporal).* 3 vols. Tr. S. J. Pereira. Colombo: A. C. Richards, Acting Government Printer, 1930.

Ramos Coelho, José, ed. *Alguns documentos do Archivo Nacional da Torre do Tombo acerca das navegações e conquistas portuguêzas.* Lisbon, 1892.

Ramusio, Giovanni Baptista. *Delle navigazione et viaggi.* 1st ed., 3 vols, 1550–56.

Ravenstein, E. G. ed. *A Journal of the First Voyage of Vasco da Gama*. London: The Hakluyt Society, old series, vol. 99, 1899. See also, Gama, Vasco da.

Regimento da declinação do sol (c. 1516 ou 1517), in *Histoire de la science nautique portugaise*, II, facsimile by Joaquim Bensaúde. Lisbon, 1916. See Bensaúde, Joaquim.

Regimento do estrolabio e do quadrante, in *Histoire de la science nautique portugaise* I, facsimile by Joaquim Bensaúde. Munich, 1914; 2nd ed., Lisbon, 1924. See, Bensaúde, Joaquim.

Remédios, Joaquim Mendes dos, ed. *Crónica do condestabre de Portugal, Dom Nuno Álvarez Pereira*. Coimbra: Imprensa da Universidade, 1911.

———. *Crónica do Infante Santo D. Fernando*. Coimbra: Imprensa da Universidade, 1911.

Resende, Garcia de. *Crónica d'El-Rey D. João II*. Lisbon, 1778.

Rico y Sinobas, Manuel. See *Libros del saber de astronomia*.

Rivara, Joaquim Heliodoro da Cunha, ed. *Arquivo Portuguêz Oriental*. 6 vols. Nova Goa, 1857–77.

Rodrigues, Bernardo. *Anais de Arzila, crónica inédita do século XVI*. Ed. David Lopes. 2 vols. Coimbra: Imprensa da Universidade, 1915–19.

Sá, Artur Basilio de, ed. *Documentação para a história das missões do padroado português do Oriente; Insulandia*. 5 vols. Lisbon: CEHU, 1954.

Santarem, Visconde de and Luis Augusto Rebello da Silva. *Quadro elementar das relações políticas e diplomáticas de Portugal com as diversas potencias do Mundo*. 18 vols. Paris, 1842 and Lisbon, 1864.

Sanuto, Marino. *I diarii di Marino Sanuto*. Eds. G. Berchet, R. Fulin, N. Barozzi, F. Stefani, and M. Allegri. 58 vols. Venice, 1879–1903.

Sanuto, Marino (called Torsello). *Secrets for True Crusaders to Help Them Recover the Holy Land*. Tr. Aubrey Stewart. London, 1896.

Seco, Carlos. "Alguns datos definitivos sobre el viaje Hojeda-Vespucio," *RIM*, 15:89–107 (1955).

Sergeant, R. B. *The Portuguese off the South Arabian Coast; Hadrami Chronicles with Nemini and European Accounts of Dutch Pirates off Mocha in the Seventeenth Century*. Oxford: The Clarendon Press, 1963.

Silva, L. A. Rebello da et al., eds. *Corpo diplomático Portuguez*. 15 vols. Lisbon: ASL, 1862–1910.

Silva Marques, João Martins da. *Descobrimentos portuguêses*. Vol. I and suplemento (2 vols. plus plates). Lisbon: IAC, 1944; vol. III, 1971. Documents covering 1147 to 1500 inclusive.

Silva Tarouca, Carlos da, ed. *Crónicas dos sete primeiros reis de Portugal*. 3 vols. Lisbon: APH, 1952.

Skelton, R. A., Thomas E. Marston, and George D. Painter, with foreword by Alexander O. Vietor. *The Vinland Map and the Tartar Relation*. New Haven: Yale University Press, 1965. Alleged first map to show Vinland. Now held by some to be a forgery.

Sousa, António Caetano de. *Provas de história genalógica da casa real portuguêsa*. Eds. of new edition, M. Lopes de Almeida and César Pegado. 6 vols in 12. Coimbra: Imprensa da Universidade, 1946—.

Sousa, Frei Francisco de, S. J. *Oriente conquistado a Jesu Christo*. 2 vols. Lisbon, 1710.

Sousa, Frei Luis de. *Anais de Dom João III*. Ed. M. Rodrigues Lapa. 2 vols. Lisbon: Sá da Costa Editora, 1938.

Tavernier, Jean Baptiste de. *Travels in India*. Tr. V. Ball. 2 vols. London, 1889.

Torre, Antonio de la. *Documentos sobre relaciones internacionales de los Reyes Católicos, 1479–1504*. 4 vols. Barcelona: Consejo Superior de Investigaciones Científicas, 1949–66.

———. *Documentos referentes a las relaciones con Portugal durante el reinado de los Reyes Católicos*. 3 vols. Valladolid: Consejo Superior de Investigaciones Científicas, 1958–63.

Trindade, Frei Paulo de. *Conquista espiritual do Oriente; em que da relação de algumas coisas mais notaveis que fizeram os Frades Menores da Santa Provincia de S. Tomé da Índia Oriental em a pregação da fé e conversão dos infiéis em mais de trinta reinos, do*

Cabo da Boa Esperança até as remotíssimas ilhas do Japão. Pref. e ed. Fr. Felix Lopes, O.F.M. 3 vols. Lisbon: CEHU, 1962–67.

Varthema, Lodovico di. *The Travels of Lodovico di Varthema in Egypt, Syria, Arabia Deserta and Arabia Felix, in Persia, India and Ethiopia, A.D. 1503–1508.* Tr. and pref. John Winter Jones. Ed. George Percy Badger. London: The Hakluyt Society, old series, vol. 32, 1863.

Velho, Álvaro. See Vasco da Gama.

Vercellese, Albertino. *Libretto di tutta la navigatione de Re de Spana de isole et terreni novamente trovati.* Venice, 1504.

Vespucci, Amérigo:

Bandini, Angelo Maria. *Vita e lettere di Amérigo Vespucci, gentiluomo fiorentino.* Florence, 1745. See also Henry Vignaud, *Améric Vespuce.* Paris: H. Welter, 1917.

Bartolozzi, Francisco. *Ricerche storico-critiche* with "a carta de Vespucio escrita de Lisboa a Lourenço de Medicis, 1502." Florence, 1789.

Lettera di Amérigo Vespuci delle isole nuovamente trovate in quatro suoi viaggi, Florence, 1505 or 1506. Reproduced in Vignaud, *Améric Vespuce.* Paris: H. Welter, 1917.

Quatuor Americi Vesputii navigationes. Latin translation of the Lettera in *Cosmographiae Introductio.* 1st ed., S. Die, 1507. Reproduced in Vignaud, *Améric Vespuce.* Paris: H. Welter, 1917.

Mundus Novus. Albericus Vespucius Laurentio Petri de Medicis salutem pluriman dicit. 1st ed., Florence, 1503; Italian translation Ramusio: 1 (1550); reproduced by Vignaud, *Améric Vespuce.* Paris: H. Welter, 1917.

Américo Vespucio, el Nuevo Mundo, cartas relativas a sus viajes e descubrimientos. Texts in Italian, Spanish, and English. Ed. Roberto Levellier. Buenos Aires: Editorial Nova, 1951; and *Américo Vespucio, cartas.* Madrid: Cultura Hispánica, 1966.

Viterbo, Francisco M. de Sousa. *Trabalhos náuticos dos portuguêses nos séculos XV e XVI.* 2 vols. Lisbon, 1898–1900.

Whiteway, Richard S., tr. and ed. *The Portuguese Expedition to Abyssinia in 1541–1543, as narrated by Castanhoso, with Some Contemporary Letters, the Short Account of Bermudez, and Certain Extracts from Corrêa.* London: The Hakluyt Society, 2nd series, vol. 10, 1902.

Zacuto, Abraham. *Almanach perpetuum, traduzido do hebráico em Latin por José Vizinho.* Leiria, 1496, in *Histoire de la science nautique,* vol. 3, facsimile by Joaquim Bensaúde. Munich, 1915.

BOOKS AND ARTICLES

Abeyasinghe, Tikiri B. H. *Portuguese Rule in Ceylon, 1594–1612.* Colombo: Lake House Investments, Ltd., 1966.

Abreu, João Capistrano de. *O descobrimento do Brasil pelos Portuguêses.* Rio de Janeiro, 1900, and later editions by the Sociedade Capistrano de Abreu, Rio de Janeiro, 1929—.

Abud, Katia Maria et al. "O descobrimento do Brasil através dos textos (edições críticas ou comentadas): a carta de Pero Vaz Caminha," *RHSP,* 36:185–228 (1968).

Aguado Bleye, Pedro. *Manual de historia de España.* 8th ed. 3 vols. Madrid: Espasa-Calpe, 1958–69.

Ailly, Pierre d'. *Imago mundo de Pierre d'Ailly (1410).* Ed. Edmond Buron. 3 vols. Paris: Maisonneuve, 1930–31.

Albuquerque, Luis de. "Sobre um manuscrito quatrocentista do tratado da esfera de Sacrobosco," *RFCC,* 28:82 (1959). (Excellent. Albuquerque is among the more erudite Portuguese historians.)

———. "O primeiro guia náutico português: o problema das lattudes na marinha dos séculos XV e XVI," *RUC,* 19:83 (1960).

————. "Sôbre a determinação de latitude no hemisfério sul na náutica portuguêsa no século XVI," *RPH*, 9:177–209 (1960).

————. *Introdução à história dos descrobrimentos*. Coimbra: Atlántida, 1962.

————. "Os almanaques portuguêses de Madrid," *RUC*, 21:1ff. (1962–63).

————. *O livro de marinharia de Andre Pires*. Lisbon: AECA-JIU, 1963.

————. "Sôbre a observação das estrelas na náutica dos descobrimentos," V CIEL-B (Coimbra, 1963), *Actas*, 2:103–147 (1965).

————. *A determinação da declinação solar na náutica dos descobrimentos*, Lisbon: AECA-JIU, XVI secção de Coimbra, 1966.

————. *O livro de marinharia de Manoel Álvares*. Lisbon: JIU, 1969.

————. *Os guias náuticos de Munique e Évora*. Lisbon: AECA, série memórias no. 4 (1970).

————. *Curso de história da Náutica*. Rio de Janeiro: Serviço de Documentação Geral da Marinha, 1971. (Best work on the subject of Portuguese navigation.)

————. "Quelques commentaires sur la navigation orientale a l'epoque de Vasco da Gama," *Arquivos do Centro Cultural Português*, 4:490–500 (1972).

Almagia, Roberto. "Planisferi, carte nautiche e affine dal sécolo XII al sécolo XVIII esitente nella Biblioteca Apostolica Vaticana," in *Monumenta Cartographica Vaticana*, vol. 1, Vatican City, 1944.

————. "Intorno alla antica cartografia nautica catalana," *BSGI*, ser. 7, vol. 10 (1945).

Almeida, Fortunato de. *O Infante de Sagres*. Oporto, 1894.

————. *História da igreja em Portugal*. 4 vols. Coimbra: Imprensa da Universidade, 1910–22; new edition, Oporto, 1967—. (Standard work. Conservative.)

————. *História de Portugal*. 6 vols. Coimbra: Imprensa da Universidade 1922–29. (Best for bibliography and institutions.)

Almeida, Justino Mendes de. "Princípio do Esmeraldo de situ orbis feito e composto por Duarte Pacheco Pereira," *BSGL*, series 82, 187–95 (1964).

Almeida Pessanha. See Pessanha.

Altamira, Rafael. *Historia de España y de la civilización española*. 4th ed., 4 vols. Barcelona: Juan Gili, 1929.

Andrada e Silva, Jacinto Freire de. *Vida de Dom João de Castro, quarto Vice-Rei da Índia*. Lisbon, 1759.

Aquarone, J. B. *D. João de Castro, gouverneur et vice-roi des Indes Orientales (1500–1548); contribution à l'histoire de la domination portugaise en Asie et à l'etude de l'astronomie nautique, de la géographie et de l'humanisme au XVI° siècle.* 2 vols. Paris: Presses Universitaires de France, 1968.

Arbman, Holger. *The Vikings*. New York: Praeger, 1961.

Arciniegas, Germán. *Amérigo and the New World; the Life and Times of Amérigo Vespucci*. Tr. Harriet de Onis. New York: Knopf, 1955. (Very pro-Vespucci. Best work on early life.)

Atiya, Aziz S. *History of Eastern Christianity*. South Bend: University of Notre Dame, 1968.

Avezac, Armand Marie Pascal d'. *Considerations geographiques sur l'histoire du Bresil: les voyages d'Améric Vespuce*. Paris, 1857.

Ávila, Arthur Lobo de. and Saul Santos Ferreira. *Cristóbal Colón: Salvador Gonsalves Zarco, Infante de Portugal*. Lisbon: Tipografia da Empressa Nacional de Publicidade, 1939.

Axelson, Eric. *South-east Africa, 1488–1530*. London, New York, and Toronto: Longmans, Green and Company, 1940.

————. "Prince Henry the Navigator and the Discovery of the Sea Route to India," *GJE*, 127, pt. 2:145–58 (June, 1961).

————. *Portuguese in South-East Africa, 1488–1699*. Cape Town: C. Struik, 1973.

————. *Congo to Cape: Early Portuguese Explorers*. New York: Harper and Row, 1974.

Azevedo, João Lúcio de. *História dos cristãos novos portuguêses*. Lisbon: Imprensa da Universidade, 1921.

————. *Épocas de Portugal económico; esboços de história*. Lisbon: Livraria Clássica Editora, 1929.

Babcock, William H. *Legendary Islands of the Atlantic.* New York: American Geographical Society, 1922. (A good study but uncritical.)

Baden-Powell, B. H. "The Villages of Goa in the Early Sixteenth Century," Extract from *The Journal of the Royal Asiatic Society*, London, April, 1900, 261–91.

Baião, António, Hernani Cidade, and Manuel Múrias, eds. *História da expansão portuguêsa no mundo.* 3 vols. Lisbon: Átiea, 1937–40.

Ballesteros y Berreta, Antonio, ed. *Historia de América y de los pueblos americanos.* 23 vols. Barcelona and Buenos Aires: Salvat, 1936—.

———. *Cristóbal Colón y el descubrimiento de América.* 2 vols. Barcelona and Buenos Aires: Salvat, 1945. Volumes 4 and 5 of above.

Barata, Jaime Martins. "O navio 'Sao Gabriel' e as naus manuelinas," separata, *RUC*, 24 (1970).

Barbosa António. *Novos subsídios para a história da ciência náutica portuguêsa da época dos descobrimentos.* Lisbon: Instituto de Alta Cultura, 1948.

Barreto, João. *História da Guiné, 1418–1918.* Lisbon: Imprensa Beleza, 1938.

Beaglehole, J. C. *The Exploration of the Pacific.* 3rd revised ed. Stanford: Stanford University Press, 1966.

Beaujouan, Guy. "Fernand Colomb et la traité d'astrologie d'Henri le Navigateur," *Romania*, 82:96–105 (1961).

Beazley, Charles Raymond. *Prince Henry the Navigator.* London: 1895; 2nd ed. New York: Barnes and Noble, 1923 and 1968. (Good but out of date.)

———. *The Dawn of Modern Geography.* 3 vols. London and Oxford, 1897–1906; New York: Peter Smith, 1949. (Standard work, best of its kind.)

Beckingham, C. F. "The Travels of Pero de Covilhã and Their Significance," CIHD (Lisbon, 1960), *Actas*, 2:1–14 (1961).

———. and G. W. B. Huntingford. *The Prester John of the Indies.* 2 vols. Cambridge, England: Cambridge University Press, 1961.

Bellio, V. *Notizie dele piu antiche carte geographiche che si trovano in Italia riguardante l'America.* In *Raccolta Colombiana*, part IV, vol. 2.

Bennet, Josephine Waters. *The Rediscovery of Sir John Mandeville.* New York: The Modern Language Association of America, Monograph series, no. 19, 1954.

Bensaúde, Joaquim. *L'astronomie nautique au Portugal a l'epoque des grandes découvertes.* Bern: Max Drechsel, 1912.

———. *Les legendes allemandes sur l'historie des découvertes maritimes portugaises.* Geneva: A. Kundig, 1917–22.

———. *Études sur l'histoires des découvertes maritimes.* Geneva: A. Kundig, 1917–31.

———. *As origins do plano das Índias.* (A reply to an article by Duarte Leite. Also published in French.) Paris: Aillaud, 1929 and 1930.

———. *Lacunes et surprises de l'histoire des découvertes maritimes.* Coimbra: Imprensa da Universidade, 1930.

———. "Estudos sôbre D. João II: o Roteiro de Flandres," AAHP, 2nd series 1:177–203 (1940).

———. *O cruzado do Infante D. Henrique.* Lisbon: AGC, 1943.

Note: Bensaúde published many other useful articles and books. Those cited above contain the essence of his work.

Betten, Francis S. "The Knowledge of the Sphericity of the Earth during the Earlier Middle Ages," *Catholic Historical Review*, 3:74–90 (1923).

Bettencourt, E. A. *Descobrimentos, guerras e conquistas dos portuguêses em Terras do Ultramar nos séculos XV e XVI.* Lisbon, 1881–82.

Birmingham, D. *Trade and Conflict in Angola. The Mbundu and Their Neighbors under the Influence of the Portuguese, 1483–1790.* New York and Oxford: Oxford University Press, 1966.

Blake, John W. *European Beginnings in West Africa, 1454–1578.* London: Longmans, Green and Co. 1937. (Based on sources published in next work, but not invariably reliable.)

────. *Europeans in West Africa, 1450–1560*. 2 vols. The Hakluyt Society, 2nd series, vols. 86–87, 1941–42. (Translation of extracts from sources.)

Blegen, Theodore C. *The Kensington Rune Stone*. Minnesota Historical Society, 1968.

Blitz, Rudolph C. "Mercantilist Policies and the Pattern of World Trade, 1500–1750," *JEH*, 27:39–55 (March 1967).

Bloch, M. R. "The Social Influence of Salt," *Scientific American*, 209:88–98 (July 1963).

Boehrer, George C. A. "The Franciscans and Portuguese Colonization in Africa and the Atlantic Islands, 1415–99," *TAM* 11:389–403 (January 1955).

Boland, Charles Michael. *They All Discovered America*. New York: Permabook by Pocket Books, 1963. An example of romantic "history" uncritical of sources.

Bonnet Reverón, B. "Las expediciones a las Canarias en el siglo XIV," *RIM*, 5:581–598 (1944) and running through several years.

Bovill, E. W. *The Golden Trade of the Moors*. 2nd ed. London: Oxford University Press, 1962.

Boxer, Charles R. *Fidalgos in the Far East — Fact and Fancy in the History of Macau*. Berkeley and Los Angeles: University of California Press, 1948.

────. *The Christian Century in Japan*. Berkeley and Los Angeles: The University of California Press, and London: Cambridge University Press, 1951.

────. "The Papers of Dom António de Ataide," *Harvard Library Bulletin*, V (Winter, 1951).

────. "S. R. Welch and His History of the Portuguese in Africa, 1495–1806," *JAH*, 1:55–63 (1960).

────. *Four Centuries of Portuguese Expansion, 1415–1825*. Johannesburg: Witwatersrand University Press, 1961.

────. "The Carreira da Índia (Ships, Men, Cargoes, Voyages)" in *O centro de estudos históricos ultramarinos e as comemorações Henriquinas*, pp. 33–82, Lisbon: CEHU, 1961.

────. *The Great Ship from Amacon; Annals of Macau and the Old Japan Trade, 1555–1640*. Lisbon: CEHU, 1963.

────. *Race Relations in the Portuguese Empire, 1415–1825*. New York: The Oxford University Press, 1963.

────. "Resposta a artigos de Armando Cortesão," *RHSP*, 28:405–408 (April-June, 1964).

────. *Portuguese Society in the Tropics; the Municipal Councils of Goa, Macao, Bahia and Luanda, 1510–1800*. Madison and Milwaukee: University of Wisconsin Press, 1965.

────. *Francisco Vieira de Figueiredo, a Portuguese Merchant Adventurer in South-East Asia, 1624–1667*. The Hague: Nijoff, 1967.

────. *The Portuguese Seaborne Empire: 1415–1825*. New York: Knopf, 1969.

──── and Carlos de Azevedo, eds. *Fort Jesus and the Portuguese in Mombasa*. London: Hollis and Carter, 1960.

Braga, José Maria. *The Western Pioneers and Their Discovery of Macao*. Instituto Português de Hong Kong. Macao: Imprensa Nacional, 1949.

Brásio, António. *A ação missionária no período henriquino*. Lisbon: CMIH-Colecção Henriquina, 1958.

────. "As relações da Cúria Romana com o Imperador da Etiópia na Época Henriquina: o seu porque e suas consequências," CIHD (Lisbon, 1960), *Actas*, vol. 5, part 1:85–92 (1961).

Braz, C. A. Moura. *O encontro da marinharia oriental e ocidental na era dos descobrimentos*. Lisbon: SGL, 1962.

Braz, Henrique. "Descoberta pre-colombiana de terras da América: João Vaz Corte-Real e Álvaro Martins Homem," separata no. 2 from *BIH-IT*, Angra do Heroismo, 1944.

────. "A descoberta da Terra Nova do Bacalhau," *BIH-IT*, 2:1–20 (1944).

Brazão, Eduardo. *Relações externas de Portugal, reinado de D. João V*. 2 vols. Oporto: Livraria Civilização, 1938.

────. *Les Côrte-Real et le nouveau monde*. Lisbon: AGU, 1967.

Bricker, Charles. *A History of Cartography: 2500 years of Maps and Mapmakers*; Maps chosen and displayed by R. V. Tooley. London: Thames and Hudson, 1969.

Brito, Domingos de Abreu e. *Um inquérito à vida administrativa e económica de Angola e do Brasil.* Coimbra: Imprensa da Universidade, 1931.

Brito, Mendes de. *O Infante D. Henrique, 1394–1460.* Lisbon: Livraria Portugália, 1942.

Brocahdo, José Idalino Ferreira da Costa. *Infante D. Henrique.* Lisbon: Editora Imperio [1942]. 2nd ed. Portugália Editora, 1958.

——. *Descobrimento do Atlántico,* translated as *The Discovery of the Atlantic,* both Lisbon: CMIH, Colecção Henriquina, 1958.

——. *O piloto Árabe de Vasco da Gama.* Lisbon: CMIH, 1959.

Brøndsted, Johannes. *The Vikings,* Baltimore, Md.: Penguin Books, 1967.

Brown, Lloyd A. *The Story of Maps.* Boston: Little, Brown and Company, 1950.

Bruyssel, Ernest van. *Histoire du commerce et de la marine en Belgique.* 3 vols. Brussels, 1861–64.

Burke, Fred. *Africa.* New York: Houghton Mifflin, 1969.

Burstyn, Harold L. "Theories of Winds and Ocean Currents from the Discoveries to the End of the Seventeenth Century," *TI,* 3:7–32 (1971).

Cabreira, Antonio. *Calendários solar e lunar perpétuos.* Coimbra: Imprensa da Universidade, 1918.

Caetano, Marcello. *O Conselho Ultramarino, esboço da sua história.* Lisbon: AGU, 1967.

Camargo, Ana Maria de A. "O descobrimento do Brasil através dos textos (edições críticas e comentadas)," *RHSP,* 32, no. 66:495–530 (April–June, 1966).

Campos, José Moreira de. *O Infante D. Henrique e os descobrimentos dos portuguêses (Da fantasia a realidade).* Lisbon: Edição do Autor, 1957.

Campos, Viriato de Sousa. *Viajens de Diogo Cão e de Bartolomeu Dias.* Lisbon: Parceria A. M. Perreira, 1966.

——. "O descobrimento do Brasil na historiografia e no ensino em Portugal," *Studia* (Lisbon), 103–121 no. 23, 1967.

Canale, F. *Storia del comercio, dei viaggi, delle scoperta e carte nautiche degli italiani.* Genoa, 1866.

Canale, Micheli Giuseppi. *Degli Antichi navigatori genovesi.* Genoa, 1846.

——. *Nuova istoria della republica di Genova.* 4 vols. Florence, 1858–64.

Canto, Ernesto do. "Diogo Gomes de Cintra, descobrimentos das ilhas dos Açores," *Arquivo dos Açores,* 1878–90, vol. 1.

Carci, Giuseppe. "The Reputed Inclusion of Florida in the Oldest Nautical Maps of the New World," *IM,* 15:32–39 (1960).

——. "The Vespucian Problems — What Point Have They Reached?" *IM,* 28:12–23 (1964).

Cardozo, Manoel. "The Idea of History in the Portuguese Chroniclers of the Age of Discovery," *TCHR,* 49:1–19 (April, 1963).

Cardozo, Mario. "A tradição náutica na mais antiga história da Península Hispânica," *CIHD* (Lisbon, 1960, *Actas,* 3:15–42 (1961).

Carrère, Claude. *Barcelone, centre économique a l'époque des difficultes, 1380–1462.* 2 vols. Paris: [Mouton] 1967.

Carvalho, Joaquim Barradas de. "A decifração de um enigma: o título Esmeraldo de Situ Orbis," *RHSP,* 58:339–48 (April–June, 1964). First of a series of studies on the sources of the history of Portuguese exploration and the discovery of Brazil, running through successive issues to 1973. Excellent and critical.

Cary, Max and E. H. Warmington. *The Ancient Explorers.* Baltimore: Pelican, 1963.

Cassidy, Vincent H. *The Sea around Them; the Atlantic Ocean, 1250.* Baton Rouge, La.: Lousiana State University Press, 1968.

Casson, Lionel. *The Ancient Mariners, Seafarers and Sea Fighters of the Mediterranean in Ancient Times,* New York: Minerva Press, 1959.

Castro, Armando. *A evolução económica de Portugal do século XII a XV.* 12 vols. to date. Lisbon: Colecção Portugália, 1965—.

Castro, D. João de. *Roteiro de Lisboa a Goa.* Lisbon, 1882.

Chang, Kuei-Sheng. "Re-examination of the Earliest Chinese Map of Africa," *Papers of the Michigan Academy of Science, Arts, and Letters*, 42:151–160 (1957).

———. "Africa and the Indian Ocean in Chinese Maps of the fourteenth and fifteenth Centuries," *IM*, 24:21–30 (1970).

———. "The Ming Maritime Enterprise and China's Knowledge of Africa Prior to the Age of Great Discoveries," *TI*, 3:33–44 (1971).

Chang, Tien'tse. *Sino-Portuguese Trade from 1514 to 1644*. London: E. J. Brill, 1933.

Chapman, Charles E. *A History of Spain*. New York: Macmillan, 1st edition, 1918 and later reprints.

Chaunu, Pierre. *Conqête et exploitation des nouveaux mondes*. Paris: Presses Universitaires, Nouvelle Clio, 1969.

———. *L'Expansion européenne du XIII° au XV° siècle*. Paris: Presses Universitaires, Nouvelle Clio, 1969. (Highly complicated and not clear.)

Cheyney, Edward P. *The Dawn of a New Era, 1250–1453*. New York: Harper and Row, Harper Torchbooks, 1962.

———. *European Background of American History*. New York: Collier Books, 3rd paperback ed., 1966. (Out of date.)

Chumovski [Shumovski], T. A. "Uma enciclopédia marítima árabe do século XV," CIHD (Lisbon, 1960). *Actas*, 3:43–56 (1961).

———. *Três roteiros desconhecidos de Ahmed Ibn Madjid o piloto árabe de Vasco da Gama*. Lisbon: Comissão das Comemorações do V Centenário da Morte do Infante D. Henrique, 1960.

Cidade, Hernani. *A literatura portuguêsa e a expansão ultramarina*. 2 vols. Lisbon: AGC, 1943.

Cipolla, Carlo M. *Guns, Sails and Empires*. New York: Minerva Press, 1965. (Significant work.)

Coelho, António Borges. *A revolução de 1383*. Lisbon: Portugália Editora, 1965.

Coimbra, Álbaro da Veiga. "Ordens militares de Cavalaria de Portugal," *RHSP*, 26 no. 53:21–34 (1963).

Coimbra, Carlos. "Duarte Pacheco e a viagem de 1498." *CMP*, 3:357–72 (1940).

———. "O Infante e o objectivo geográfico dos descobrimentos," CIHD (Lisbon, 1960), *Actas*, 4:77–98 (1961).

———. "Os objectivos portuguêses do Tratado de Tordesilhas," V CIEL-B (Coimbra, 1963), *Actas*, 2:199–208 (1965).

Coles, Paul. *The Ottoman Impact on Europe*. New York: Harcourt, Brace and World, 1968.

Colloquium: Proceedings of the International Colloquium on Luzo-Brazilian Studies, Washington, 1950. Nashville: Vanderbilt University Press, 1953.

Colloquium: III CIEL-B, Lisbon, 1957; *Actas*, Lisbon, 1959.

Colloquium: V CIEL-B, Coimbra, 1963; *Actas*, Coimbra, 1965.

Columbus, Ferdinand. *The Life of the Admiral Christopher Columbus by His Son Ferndinand*. Ed. and tr. Benjamim Keen. New Brunswick, N.J.: Rutgers University Press, 1959, (Good translation and notes.)

Congreso Internacional de História dos Descobrimentos. (Lisbon, 1960). *Actas*, 6 vols. Lisbon: Comissão das Comemorações do V Centenario, 1961.

Congreso do Mundo Português, Publicações. 19 vols. Lisbon: Imprensa Nacional, 1940. Cited as *CMP*.

Cordeiro, Luciano. *Descobertas e descobridores — Diogo Cão*. Lisbon, 1892.

———. *Diogo D'Azambuja*, Lisbon, 1892.

———. *Portuguêses fora de Portugal: uma sobrinha do Infante, Imperatriz da Allemanha e Rainha da Hungría*. Lisbon, 1894.

Corrêa, Marqês de Jacome. *História das descobertas das Ilhas*. Coimbra: Imprensa da Universidade, 1926.

Correia, Fernando da Silva. "Um Notável Médico conselheiro do Infante D. Henrique," CIHD (Lisbon, 1960), *Actas* 3:57–78 (1961).

Correia, Virgílio. *Livro dos Regimētos dos officiaes mecanicos da mui nobre e sēpre leal cidade de Lixboa* (1572). Coimbra: Imprensa da Universidade, 1926.

Côrte-Real, João Afonso. *"Problemática das navegações para noroeste."* CIHD (Lisbon, 1960), *Actas*, 3:79–92 (1961).

Côrte-Real, Maria Alice M. "As Índias Orientais no plano henriquino," CIHD (Lisbon, 1960), *Actas*, 3:93–96 (1961).

Cortesão Armando. "Subsídios para a história do descobrimento da Guiné e Cabo Verde," *BAGC* no. 70 (1931). (Excellent historian of cartography who accepts unwarranted conclusions about pre-Colombian discoveries.)

———. *Cartografia e cartógrafos portuguêses dos séculos XV e XVI.* 2 vols. Lisbon: Seara Nova, 1935.

———. *The Nautical Chart of 1424 and the Early Discovery and Cartographical Representation of America.* University Coimbra and Minneapolis: University of Minnesota, 1954.

———. *Cartografia portuguêsa antiga.* Lisbon: CMIH, Colecção Henriquina, 1960.

———. *History of Portuguese Cartography.* Vol. 1, Lisbon: JIU, 1969.

———. "Pizzigano's Chart of 1424," separata, *RUC*, 24 (1970).

———. *The Mystery of Vasco da Gama.* Coimbra: AECA-JIU, 1972.

———. "O descobrimento da Australasia e a 'Questao das Moluccas," *HEP* II, p. 147 and n. 6.

———, and A. C. Texeira da Mota. *Portugaliae monumenta Cartographica.* 6 vols. Coimbra: CMIH, 1958–63.

Cortesão, Jaime. *A Expedição de Pedro Álvares Cabral e o descobrimento do Brasil.* Lisbon: Aillaud e Bertrand, 1922. (First of a long list of publications which insisted that there were secret Portuguese discoveries and led to distortion of Portuguese exploration history.)

———. "Do sigilo nacional sôbre os descobrimentos," *Lusitânia* I, 1924.

———. *L'expansion des portugais dans l'histoire de la civilization.* Brussels: Exposition Internationale de la Civilization, 1930.

———. "The Pre-Columbian Discovery of America," *GJE*, 89:29–42 (January–June, 1937).

———. *A carta de Pero Vaz de Caminha.* Rio de Janeiro: Edições Livros de Portugal, 1943.

———. *A política de sigilo nos descobrimentos.* Lisbon: CMIH 1960.

———. *Descobrimentos portuguêses.* 2 vols. Lisbon: Editorial Arcádia, 1960–62. (See remarks above.)

Costa, Abel Fontoura da. "A vila do Infante, antes Terça Nabal e Sagres," *Arquivo Histórico da Marinha*, Vol. I, no. 1 (1933–36).

———. *Ás portas da Índia em 1484.* Lisbon: Imprensa da Armada, 1936.

———. *A marinharia dos descobrimentos.* 2nd ed. Lisbon: AGC, 1939.

———. *Cartas de achaménto das ilhas do Cabo Verde de Valentim Fernandes (1506–1508).* Lisbon: AGC, 1939.

———, ed. *Roteiro da primeira viagem de Vasco da Gama, 1497–1499, por Álvaro Velho.* Lisbon: AGC, 1940.

———. *Uma carta náutica portuguêsa anónima de "circa" 1471.* Lisbon: AGC, 1940.

———. "Descobrimentos portuguêses no Atlântico e na costa ocidental africana do Bojador ao Cabo de Catarina," CMP, III:243–86 (1940).

———. "Ciência náutica portuguêsa: cartografia e cartógrafos," CMP, III:537–78 (1940).

———. *A ciência náutica dos portuguêses na época dos descobrimentos.* Lisbon: CMIH-Colecção Henriquina, 1958.

Costa, António Dominguez de Sousa. "O Infante D. Henrique na expansão portuguêsa," *Itinerarium* (Braga) 5:419–568 (1959).

Costa, Didio J. da. *O Brasil e o ciclo das grandes navegações.* Rio de Janeiro: Imprensa Nacional, 1940.

Costa Brochado. See José Idalino Ferreira da Costa Brochado.

Coutinho, Carlos Viegas Gago. *A náutica dos descobrimentos.* 2 vols., 1951–52. 2nd ed. Lisbon: AGU, 1969.

Couto, Diogo do. *Da Ásia.* See Barros, João de and Diogo do Couto.

Crone, G. R. "The Alleged Pre-Columbia Discovery of America," *GJE*, 89:455–60 (1937).
———. "The Mythical Islands of the Atlantic Ocean: a Suggestion as to Their Origin." International Geographical Congress, Amsterdam, 1938. *Comptes Rendus*, vol. II, section iv, pp. 164–71.
———. "The Origin of the Name Antilia," *GJE*, 91:260–62 (1938).
Cunha Matos, R. J. da. *Compêndio histórico das possessões de Portugal na África*. Rio de Janeiro: Arquivo Nacional, vol. 52, 1963.
Curtin, Philip D. *Africa Remembered*. Madison: University of Wisconsin Press, 1968.
———. *The Atlantic Slave Trade*. Madison: University of Wisconsin Press, 1969.
Cuvelier, J. and L. Jadin. *L'ancien Congo d'après les archives romaines, 1518–1640*. Brussels: Académie Royale des Sciences Coloniales, 1954.
Dantas, Hélio. "Pedr'Alvares Cabral, êsse desconhecido," *RHSP*, 36 no. 74:289–300 (April–June, 1968).
Danvers, Frederick Charles. *The Portuguese in India*. 2 vols. London, 1894, and second impression, Frank Cass and Co., 1966.
Danvila, Alfonso. *Felipe II y la sucesión de Portugal*. Madrid: Espasa-Calpe, 1956. (Good for Spanish view.)
Davenport, Francis Gardiner, ed. *European Treaties Bearing on the History of the United States and Its Dependencies to 1648*. 4 vols. Washington, D.C.; Smithsonian Institution, 1917–37. (Standard, excellent work.)
David, Charles Wendell, ed. and tr. *De expugnatione Lyxbonensi (The Conquest of Lisbon)*. New York, 1936, reprint New York: Octagon Books, 1969.
Davidson, Basil. *The African Slave Trade*. Boston: Little, Brown and Company, 1961.
Davies, Arthur. "A navegação de Fernão Magalhães," *RHSP*, 22 no. 45:173–90 (January–March, 1961).
———. "The 1501–02 Voyage of Amérigo Vespucci," *CIHD* (Lisbon, 1960), *Actas* 3:111.122 (1961).
———." João Fernandes and the Cabot Voyages," *CIHD* (Lisbon, 1960), *Actas* 2:135ff. (1961).
Davies, Oliver. "Native Culture in the Gold Coast at the Time of the Portuguese Discoveries," *CIHD* (Lisbon, 1960), *Actas*, 3:97–110 (1961).
———. *West Africa before the Europeans*. London and New York: Methuen and Barnes and Noble, 1967.
Davis, D. B. *The Problem of Slavery in Western Culture*. Ithaca: Cornell University Press 1966 and 1969. (Excellent, common-sense treatment).
Dawson, C., ed and tr. *The Mongol Mission*. New York: Barnes and Noble, 1955.
Deacon, R. *Madoc and the Discovery of America*. New York: Barnes and Noble, 1967. (Romance, weak history.)
Delabarre, Edmond B. *Dighton Rock, a Story of the Written Rocks of New England*, New York: W. Neale, 1928. See, Silva, M. D. Manuel.
Delgado, Ralph. *História de Angola*. 4 vols. Benguela: Edição da Tipografia do Jornal de Benguela, 1948–55.
Denucé, Jean. *Les origines de la cartographie portugaise et les cartes des Reinel*. Ghent: E. van Goethem, 1908.
———. "Privileges commerciaux accordés par les rois de Portugal aux Flamands et aux Allemands." *AHP*, 7:313–15 (1909).
———. "The Discovery of the South America, according to an Anonymous Map in the British Museum," *GJE*, 2 (1910).
Dias, Carlos Malheiro, ed. *História da colonização portuguêsa do Brazil*. 3 vols. Oporto: Litografia Nacional, 1921–26. (Standard. Needs to be replaced.)
Dias, Gastão Sousa (compiler). *Relações de Angola*. Coimbra: Imprensa da Universidade, 1934.
Dias, Manuel Nunes. "A organização da rota atlântica do ouro da mina e os mecanismos dos resgates," *RHSP*, 21, no. 44:369–98 (1960).

————. *O capitalismo monárquico português (1415–1549)*. 2 vols. São Paulo: Editorial Comercial Safady, 1957 and Coimbra, 1963. (Excellent compilation, not always easy to follow.)

————. *O descobrimento do Brasil*. São Paulo: Universidade de São Paulo, 1967.

————. "Descobrimento do Brasil — tratados bilaterais e partilha do Mar Oceano," *Studia* (Lisbon), 25:7–30 (December 1968).

Diffie, Bailey W. *Prelude to Empire: Portugal Overseas before Henry the Navigator*. Lincoln: University of Nebraska Press, 1960. (Some points are corrected in the present volume.)

————. "Foreigners in Portugal," *TI*, 1:23–34 (1969).

Dinis, António J. Dias. "O testamento do Infante D. Henrique num livro de uso de Fr. Antão Gonçalves, de 1461." Coimbra: separata de Biblos, 21 (1946).

————. *O V [quinto] Centenário do descobrimento da Guiné Portuguêsa a luz da critica histórica, 1446–1946*. Braga: Tipografia das Missões Franciscanas, 1946. (Good documentation; his views differ from previous views.)

————. *Vida e obras de Gomes Eanes de Zurara. Introdução a "Crónica dos feitos de Guiné."* 2 vols. Lisbon, AGC, 1949.

————. "As crónicas medievais portuguêsas: adulteração de Rui de Pina?" *Colectanea de Estudos* (Braga), 2nd series, 1:299–345 (1950).

————. "Regimento do Infanto Dom Henrique sôbre os direitos da pesca em Castro Mirim," *Colectanea de Estudos*, 2nd series, 3 (1952).

————. *Estudos Henriquinos*. Coimbra: Atlantida, 1960. (Very useful.)

————. "Qual o cabo dobrado em 1434 por Gil Eanes?" separata, *AAPH*, 2nd ser. 13:139 (1963).

————. "Em torno dos testamentos do Infante Santo," *Ultramar*, no. 40, 1970.

Do tempo e da história. 5 vols. Ed. Virginia Rau. Lisbon: IAC, 1965–.

Doehaerd, Renée. *L'expansion économique belge au Moyen Âge*. Brussels: La Renaissance du Livre, 1946. (Highly useful.)

————. *Études anversoises (Documentos sur le commerce international à Anvers — 1488–1514)*. 3 vols. Paris: S.E.V.P.E.N.. 1963–64.

Doran, Edwin. "The Origin of Leeboards," *MM*, 53:39–55 (February, 1967).

Dória, António Álvaro. "O problema do descobrimento da Madeira," in *Estudos de História dos Descobrimentos*, Guimarães: Minerva Press, 1945.

Dozy, Reinhart P. A. *Histoire des Musulmans d'Espagne*. Ed. E. Levi-Provençal. 3 vols. Leyden: E. J. Brill, 1932.

————. *Spanish Islam: A History of the Moslems in Spain*. Tr. Francis Griffin Stokes. London: Frank Cass, 1972.

Duffy, James. *Shipwreck and Empire*. Cambridge: Harvard University Press, 1955.

————. *Portugal in Africa*. Cambridge: Harvard University Press, 1962, Penguin, 1963. (Critical of Portugal.)

Eça, Vicente M. M. C. Almeida d'. *Normas económicas na colonização portuguesa até 1808; memoria*. Coimbra: Imprensa da Universidade, 1931.

Elison, George. *Deus Destroyed: the Image of Christianity in Early Modern Japan*. Cambridge, Harvard University Press, 1973.

Elliot, J. H. *Imperial Spain 1469–1716*. New York: Mentor Books, 1966. Extremely useful.

————. *The Old World and the New 1492–1650*. London: Cambridge University Press, 1970.

Errera, Carlo. *L'epoca delle grandi scoperte geografiche*. Milan: Hoepli, 1902; 3rd ed., 1926.

————. "Noli, Antonio da (Antoniotto Usodimare)" in *Enciclopedia Italiana*, vol. 24. (This article shows former confusion of Noli with Usodimare.)

Eventail de l'histoire vivante, hommage a Lucien Fevre. 2 vols. Paris: Armand Colin, 1953.

Faria, Francisco Leite de. "Uma relação de Rui de Pina sôbre o Congo escrita em 1492," *Studia (Lisbon), no. 19*:223–304 (1967).

Faro, Jorge. "Duas expediçoes enviadas a Guiné anteriormente a 1474 e custiadas pela fazenda de D. Afonso V," *Boletim Cultural da Guiné Portuguêsa*, 12:47–104 (January, 1957).

Federzoni, Luigi, ed. *Relazione storiche fra l'Italia e il Portogallo*. Rome: Academia Real d'Italia: Memorie e Documenti, 1940. (Very useful work.)

Ferrand, Gabriel. "Le pilote arabe de Vasco da Gama," *Annales de Geographie*, no. 172:289–308 (1922).

Ferraz, Maria de Lourdes Esteves dos Santos de Freitas. "A Ilha da Madeira na época quatrocentista," *Studia* (Lisbon), no. 9:143–98 (January, 1960).

———. "Povamento e economia da ilha da Madeira," *Arquivos do Centro Cultural Português*, 3:13–53 (1971).

Ferreira, Maria Emilia Cordeiro. "India, Casa da," *DHP* II, 505–13.

Ficalho, Conde de. *Viagens de Pedro de Covilhã*. Lisbon, 1898.

———. *Memória sôbre a Malagueta*. Lisbon: AGC, 1945.

Figueiredo, Fidelino de. "Les idées nouvelles sur les découvertes geographiques des portugais," *RH*, 14:135–51 (1925).

Figueiredo, João M. P. "Goa pre-portuguesa." *Studia* (Lisbon), no. 12:141–259 (1963).

Filgueiras, Octavio Lixa and Alfredo Barroco. "O caíque do Algarve e a caravela portuguêsa," separata, *RUC*, 24 (1970).

Finot, Jules. *Étude historique sur les relations commerciales entre la France et la Flandre au Moyen Âge*. Paris, 1894.

———. *Étude historique sur les relations commerciales entre la Flandre et l'Espagne*. Paris: Annales du Comité Flamand de France, 1899.

———. *Étude historique sur les relations commerciales entre le Flandre et la Republique de Gênes au Moyen Âge*. Annales du Comité Flamand de France, 28 (1906).

Fitzler, M.A. Hedwig. "Der anteil der Deutschen an der kolonialpolitik Philip II, von Spanien in Asien." *Vierteljahrschrift für Sozial- und Wirtschaftgeschichte*, 28 (1935).

Fonseca, Henrique Quirino da. *Os portuguêses no mar; memórias históricas e arqueológicos das naus de Portugal*. Lisbon: Tipografia do Comercio, 1926(?).

———. *A caravela portuguêsa e a prioridade técnica das navegações henriquinas*. Coimbra: Imprensa da Universidade, 1934. (Fine work.)

Fontoura da Costa, A. See Costa.

Fontvieille, Jean. "A lenda de Machim," CIHD (Lisbon, 1960) *Actas*, 3:197–238 (1961).

Foote, Peter G. and David M. Wilson. *The Viking Achievement*. New York: Praeger, 1970.

Francisque-Michel, R. *Histoire du commerce et de la navigation à Bordeaux*. 2 vols. Bordeaux, 2:154–55, 1867–70.

———. *Les Portugais en France, les Français en Portugal*. Paris, 1882.

Freire de Andrade, Jacinto. See Andrade.

Freire, Anselmo Braamcamp. "Maria Brandoa, a do Crisfal," *AHP*, 6:293–442 (1908); 7:53–79, 123–33, 196–208, 320–26; 8:21–23 (1910). (On the Feitoria in Flanders, very fine documentation.)

———. *Expedições e armadas nos anos de 1488–89*. Lisbon: Livraria Ferin 1915.

Freire de Oliveira, Eduardo. See Oliveira.

Freitas, Jordão de. *A vila e a fortaleza de Sagres nos séculos XV à XVII*. Coimbra: IAC, 1938.

Friederici, Georg. *Carácter da descoberta e conquista da América pelos europeus*. Rio de Janeiro: Instituto Nacional do Livro, 1967.

Frutuoso, Gaspar. *Saudades da terra* (1580–91). Ed. Álvaro Rodrigues de Azevedo. Funchal, 1873; new edition Instituto Cultural de Ponta Delgada, Azores, 1963—. (Gossipy and unreliable.)

Gad, Finn. *The History of Greenland*. Vol. 1. McGill-Queen's University Press, 1971—. To be four volumes.

Gago Coutinho. See Coutinho.

Gama Barros, Henrique da. *História da administração pública em Portugal nos séculos XII–XV*. 2nd ed., 11 vols. Lisbon: Sá da Costa, 1945–54. (Excellent, useful, and erudite. A mine of documentation.)

Gandi, Attílio. "Os caminhos do Sahara," *Universo* (Florence, Italy) March–April, 1968.
García, Carlos Alberto. *Paulo Dias de Novais e a sua época*. Lisbon: AGU, 1964.
———. "A Ilha de São Tomé como centro experimental do compartamento do luso nos trópicos," *Studia* (Lisbon), no. 19:209–21, (1966).
García Gallo, Alfonso. "Las Bulas de Alejandro VI y el ordenamiento jurídico de la expansión portuguesa y castellana en África e Índias," *AHDE*, 1958.
Gascon, René. "Un siècle du commerce des épices à Lyon. Fin XV°–XVI° siécles." *Annales: Economies, Societes, Civilizations*, 15:638–66 (1960).
Gathorne-Hardy, G. M. (tr. and discussion). *The Norse discovery of America: The Wineland Sagas*. Reprint. With new preface by the author and new introduction by Gwyn Jones. New York: Oxford University Press, 1970.
Genofre, Edmundo. "Os mestres da colonização," *RHSP*, 23 no. 47:145–48 (July–September, 1961).
———. "Cristóvão Colombo e a acção papal," *RHSP*, 26 no. 53:129–44 (1963).
Glamann, Kristof. *Dutch Asiatic Trade, 1628–1740*. The Hague: Martinus Nijhoff and The Danish Science Press, 1958.
Glezer, Raquel. "O descobrimento do Brasil através dos textos," *RHSP*, 33 no. 68:481–88 (October–December, 1966).
Godin, O. I. *Princes et princesses de la familie royale de Portugal, ayant par leurs alliances regné sur la Flandre. Rapports entre la Flandre et le Portugal de 1094 a 1682*. Lisbon: Imprensa Nacional, 1892.
Godinho, Vitorino Magalhães. *Historiografia contemporânea*. Lisbon: Officina Fernandes, 1942. Separata da Revista da Faculdade de Letras, 8:1 and 2. (The works of Godinho are sound and thorough, with an emphasis on economics. To be preferred to Cortesão, Gago Coutinho, Brochado, and other romantic writers.)
———. *Dúvidas e problemas acêrca de algumas teses da história da expansão*. Lisbon, 1943.
———. *A expansão quatrocentista portuguêsa*. Lisbon: Emp. Contemporanea, 1944.
———. *História econômica e social da expansão portuguêsa*. Lisbon: Terra-Editora, 1947.
———. *Comemorações e história: a descoberta da Guiné*. Lisbon: Cadernos de "Seara Nova," Secção de Estudos Históricos, 1947.
———. "Les grandes découvertes," *BEP*, new series 16:3–53 (1952).
———. "Le repli venetien et egyptien et la route du Cap 1496–1533." *Eventail de l'histoire vivante: hommage à Lucien Febvre*, 2:283–300. Paris, 1953.
———. *A economia dos descobrimentos henriquinos*. Lisbon: Sá da Costa, 1962.
———. *Os descobrimentos e a economia mundial*. 2 vols. Lisbon: Portugália, 1965–71.
———. *L'economie de l'empire portugais aux XV° et XVI° siècles*. Paris: École Practique des Hautes Études, S.E.V.P.E.N., 1969.
Goldstein, Thomas. "Florentine Humanism and the Vision of the New World," CIHD (Lisbon 1960), *Actas* 4:195–208 (1961).
———. *Fifteenth Century Geography against the Background of Medieval Science*. Salem, Mass.: Society for the History of Discoveries (November, 1964).
Gomes, A. Sousa. *Descobrimentos geográficos dos portuguêses no século XV*. Lisbon: Sociedade Tiopgráfica Primarose, 1968.
Gomes, Lindolfo. "O'Esmeraldo' de Duarte Pacheco." *CMP*, 11:357–60.
Gonçalves, Júlio. "Marco Polo e os portuguêses — duas fases da geografia do Oriente," *BSGL*, series 73:315–24 (1955). (Excellent scholar.)
———. *O Infante D. Pedro, as "sete partidas" e a génese dos descobrimentos*. Lisbon: AGU, 1955.
———. "Also Sprach: . . . assim falou Sardar K. M. Panikkar," separata, *BSGL*, series 74 (October–December, 1956).
———. "Alvise de Ca da Mosto e o V centenário caboverdeano," separata, *BSGL* series 75 (October–December, 1957).
Goode, Kenneth C. *A Concise Afro-American History*. Berkeley: University of California, 1969.

Goris, A. [Jan Albert]. *Études sur les colonies marchandes méridionales, portugais, espag-noles, italiens, à Anvers de 1488–1567.* Louvain: Libraire Universitaire, 1925.
Gracias, J. B. Amâncio. *Alemães na Índia nos séculos XV à XVIII.* Lisbon, 1941.
Greenlee, William B. Also see Cabral.
Greenlee, William B. "The Captaincy of the Second Portuguese Voyage to Brasil, 1501–02," *Tam*, 2:3–12 (July, 1945).
———. *Catalogue of the Greenlee Collection,* 2 vols., compiled by the Newberry Library, Chicago. Boston: G. K. Hall, 1970.
Guedes, Armando Marques. *A aliança inglêsa (notas de história diplomática).* Lisbon: Editorial Enciclopedia, new ed., 1943.
Guedes, Max Justo. *Descobrimento do Brasil.* Rio de Janeiro: Directoria de Hidrografia e Navegaçao, 1966.
———. See *História Naval Brasileira.*
Guerreiro, Amaro D. *Panorama econômico dos descobrimentos henriquinos.* Lisbon: CMIH, 1961.
Guicciardini, Lodovico. *Description de tous les Pays-Bas, autrement dict la Germanie Inferieure ou Basse Alemagne.* Tr. F. de Belle Forest. Antwerp, 1567.
Guimarães, Vieira. *A Ordem de Cristo.* Lisbon: Imprensa Nacional, 1936.
Gunther, R. T. "The Astrolabe: Its Uses and Derivatives," *SGM,* 43:135–77 (1927).
Haebler, K. "Konrad Rott und die thüringische Gesellschaft," in *Neues Archiv für Sachsis-chegeschichte und Altertumskunde,* 16, 177–218 (1895).
Halecki, Oscar. "Diplomatie pontificale et activité missionaire en Asie aux XIIᵉ–XVᵉ siècles," *XII ICHS,* II:5–32 (Vienna, 1965).
Harden, Donald. *The Phoenicians.* New York: Praeger, 1962.
Harrisse, Henry. *The Discovery of North America: A Critical Documentary and Historic Investigation, with an Essay on the Early Cartography of the New World.* Paris, 1892. (Still a fine work. See next item.)
———. *Les Côrte-Real et leurs voyages au Nouveau Monde.* Paris, 1883.
Haskins, Charles Homer. *The Normans in European History.* Boston-New York, 1915, reprint New York: Norton, 1966.
Heaton, Herbert. *Economic History of Europe.* Cambridge-New York: Harper-Row, 1948, 1952.
———. *The Economics of Empire.* Minneapolis: James Ford Bell Lectures, no. 3, 1966.
Heers, Jacques. "L'expansion maritime portugaise à la fin du Moyen Âge: la Mediterranée," *RFLL,* 2nd series, 22:84–112 (1956).
———. 'Portugais et génois au XVᵒ siècle; la rivalité atlantique-mediterranie," III CIEL-B (Lisbon, 1957) *Actas,* 2:138–47 (1960).
——— et al. "Concurrences des voies maritimes et des voies terrestres dan le commerce international depuis la fin du Moyen Âge jusqu'au XIXᵉ siècle," *XII ICHS,* III:159–67 (Vienna, 1965).
Heissig, Walther. *A Lost Civilization: The Mongols Rediscovered.* New York: Basic Books, 1966.
Heleno, Manuel. *Os escravos em Portugal.* Lisbon: Tipografia da Empresa do Anuário Comercial, 1933.
Henry the Navigator. *Commemoração do quinto centenário do Infante Dom Henrique.* Lisbon: Imprensa Nacional, 1894.
Herculano, Alexandre. *História de Portugal* [to 1279]. Lisbon, 1854–56. Many editions. (Finest work on Portugal to 1279.)
Hernández Sánchez-Borba, Mario. *Las tendencias expansivas portuguesas en la época del Infante Don Enrique.* Madrid: Consejo Superior de Investigaciones Científicas, 1960.
Hess, Andrew C. "The Evolution of the Ottoman Seaborne Empire in the Age of Oceanic Discoveries, 1453–1525," *AHR,* 75:1892–1919 (December, 1970).
Heyd, Wilhem von. *Histoire du commerce du Levant au Moyen Âge.* 2 vols. Leipzig, 1885–86.

História da colonização portuguêsa do Brasil. See Dias, Carlos Malheiro.

História da expansão portuguêsa no Mundo (HEP). See Baião, António.

História Naval Brasileira, coordinated by Max Justo Guedes. 2 vols. to date. Rio de Janeiro: Ministerio da Marinha, Serviço de Documentação Geral da Marinha, 1975. (With excellent contributions by Luis de Albuquerque on the maritime development of Portugal and by Max Justo Guedes on the discovery of Brazil.)

Hoffman, Paul E. "The Portuguese Crown's Cost and Profits in the India Trade, 1580. A Report with a Proposal for Increasing the Profits." *Journal of the American Portuguese Cultural Society,* V, nos. 1 and 2, 22–32 (winter–spring, 1971).

Hooykaas, R. "The Impact of the Voyages of Discovery on Portuguese Humanist Literature," separata, *RUC,* 24 (1970).

Hourani, George F. *Arab Seafaring in the Indian Ocean in Ancient and Early Medieval Times.* Princeton: Princeton University Press, 1951.

Humboldt, Alexander von. *Examen critique de l'histoire de la geographie du Nouveau Continent et des progrès de l'astronomie nautique dans le XV° et XVI° siècles.* 5 vols. Paris, 1831–39.

————. *Cristóbal Colón y el descubrimiento de América, historia de la geografia del Nuevo Continente y de los progreses de la astronomia náutica en los siglos XV y XVI.* 2 vols. Madrid, 1892.

(XII) International Congress of Historical Sciences, Vienna: Verlag Ferdinand Berger and Sohne, cited as *XII ICHS.*

Iria, Alberto. *Porque foi o Algarve, e não outro sítio do país, a região eleita do Infante D. Henrique?* Lisbon: Instituto de Alta Cultura, Separata do Mensario das Casas do Povo, 1953. (Iria's works show fine, critical scholarship.)

————. "Da fundação e govêrno do castelo ou fortaleza de São Jorge da Mina pelos portuguêses e da sua acção missionária após o descobrimento desta costa," *Studia* (Lisbon), no. 1: 25–69 (January, 1958).

————. *Itinerário do Infante Dom Henrique no Algarve.* Faro, 1960.

————. "Novas cartas régias Afonsinas acêrca dos descobrimentos e privilégios do Infante D. Henrique — documentos inéditos," *Studia* (Lisbon), no. 25:51–116 (December, 1968).

Jackson, Gabriel. *The Making of Medieval Spain.* New York: Harcourt Brace Jovanovich, 1972.

Jackson, Melvin. "The Labrador Landfall of John Cabot: The 1497 Voyage Reconsidered," *CHR,* 44 no. 2 (June 1963).

Jacob, Ernst Gerhard. "Quelques points controversés dans l'histoire des dècouvertes faites par Colomb, Magalhães et Behaim," CIHD (Lisbon 1960) *Actas,* 3:239–248 (1961).

————. "A descoberta da África Sudoeste pelos portuguêses," *RHSP,* 29 no. 59:39–52 (July–September 1964).

Jadin, Louis. "L'Afrique et Rome depuis l'époque des découvertes jusqu'au XVIIIᵉ siècle," *XII ICHS,* II:63–69 Vienna (1965). Cites Verlinden to support his position based on documents in Almeida, *História de Portugal,* III, 759–789.

Jayne, C. K. *Vasco da Gama and His Successors: 1460–1580.* London: Methuen, 1910; reprint, New York: Barnes and Noble, 1970. (Still good.)

Jervis, W. W. *The World in Maps — A Study in Map Evolution.* London: George Phillip, 1937.

Jones, Gwyn. *The Norse Atlantic Saga: Being the Norse Voyages of Discovery and Settlement to Iceland, Greenland, and America.* London and New York: Oxford University Press, 1964.

————. *A History of the Vikings.* London and New York: Oxford University Press, 1968.

Keith, Henry H. and S. F. Edwards, eds. *Conflict and Continuity in Brazilian Society.* Columbia, S.C.: University of South Carolina Press, 1969.

Kellenbenz, Hermann. "Autour de 1600: le commerce du poivre des Fugger et le marché internationale du poivre," Paris: *Annales: Économies, Societés, Civilizations,* 11 (1956).

————. "Le front hispano-portugais contre l'Inde." *Océan Indien et Medterranie (travaux du*

Sixième Colloque International d'Histoire Maritime et du Deuxième Congrès de l'Associa-tion Historique Internationale de l'Océan Indien-Section de Lourenço Marques, 13–18 Aout, 1962, pp. 263–90. Paris: S.E.V.P.E.N., 1964.

Kimble, George H. T. "Some Notes on Mediaeval Cartography, with Special Reference to M. Behaim's Globe," *SGM*, 49:91–98 (1933).

———. "Portuguese Policy and Its Influence on Fifteenth Century Cartography," *TGR*, 23:653–59 (1933).

———. "The Laurentian World Map with Special Reference to Its Portrayal of Africa," *IM*, 1:29–33 (1935).

———. *Geography in the Middle Ages*. London: Methuen and Co., 1938. (Accepts romantic Portuguese view of secrecy.)

Konetzke, Richard. "Entrepreneurial Activities of Spanish and Portuguese Noblemen in Medieval Times." *Explorations in Entrepreneurial History*, 6:115–20 (1953).

Kroll, Heinz. "Algumas designações portuguêsas para um sítio muito remoto e descon-hecido," V-CIEL-B (Coimbra 1963) *Actas*, 5:335–42 (1966).

Krueger, Hilmar C. "Genoese Trade with Northwest Africa," *Speculum*, 8:377–95 (1933).

Kup, A. P. *History of Sierra Leone, 1400–1787*. Cambridge, England: University Press, 1961.

Lach, Donald F. *Asia in the Making of Europe; The Century of Discovery*. Vol. 1, parts 1 and 2, and vol. 2. Chicago: University of Chicago Press, 1965—. (Extremely useful and erudite scholarship.)

——— and Carol Flaumenhaft. *Asia on the Eve of Europe's Expansion*. Englewood Cliffs, N.J.: Prentice-Hall, 1965.

Lagôa, Visconde de. *Fernão de Magalhães (a sua vida e a sua viagem)*. 2 vols. Lisbon: Seara Nova, 1938.

Laguarda Trias, Rolando A. *La aportación científica de mallorquines y portugueses a la cartografía náutica en los siglos XIV al XVI*. Madrid: Instituto Histórico de Marina, 1963.

———. "Elucidario das latitudes colombianas," *Boletín de la Real Sociedad Geogrfica*. Madrid: 99:181–245 (1963).

———. "Importancia de las mas antiguas latitudes de la costa Brasileña," *RIHGB*, 287:314–94 (1972).

Lane, Frederic C. *Venetian Ships and Shipbuilders of the Renaissance*. Baltimore: Johns Hopkins University Press, 1934.

———. "The Mediterranean Spice Trade; Further Evidence of Its Revival in the Sixteenth Century," *AHR*, 45:581–90 (1939–40).

———. "Tonnages, Medieval and Modern," *TEHR*, 2nd series, 17 no. 2:214–33 (1964).

———. "Pepper Prices before Da Gama." *JEH*, 28:590–7 (December, 1968).

———. "Venetian Shipping during the Commercial Revolution." In Brian Pullen, ed., *Crisis and Change in the Venetian Economy in the Sixteenth and Seventeenth Centuries*. London: Methuen, 1968.

La Roncière, Charles de. *La découverte de l'Afrique au Moyen Âge*. 3 vols. Cairo: Societé Royale de Geographie d'Egypte, 1924–37. (Standard, useful work, well organized, but less thorough than reputed.)

———. "Reflêts de la cartographie portugaise sur la cartographie dieppoise de la renais-sance," *CMP*, 3:479–84 (1938).

———. *Histoire de la découverte de la Terre*. Paris: Hachette, 1939.

Larsen, Sofus. *The Discovery of North America Twenty Years before Columbus*. Copenha-gen: Levin and Munksgaard, 1925. (Doubtful value — stretches interpretation of mate-rials.)

Latrie, M. L. de Mas. *Traités de paix et de commerce et documents divers concernentes les relations chrétiens avec les Arabs de l'Afrique septentrionale au Moyen Âge*. Paris, 1866–72.

Leitão, Humberto. *Os portugueses em Solor e Timor de 1515 à 1702*. Lisbon: Tipografiia da Liga dos Combatentes da Grande Guerra, 1948.

Leite, Duarte. *Os falsos precursores de Álvares Cabral.* 2nd ed. Lisbon: Portugália, 1950. (One of the sounder and more critical Portuguese historians.)

————. *Descobrimentos portuguêses.* 2 vols. Lisbon: Cosmos, 1958–60. (Principal writings of Leite, collected by Vitorino Magalhães Godinho, with excellent comments and notes.)

Leite, José Gervásio. *Comentários do grande capitão Rui Freire de Andrade.* Lisbon: AGC, 1940.

Leonard, Irving A. *The Books of the Brave.* Ann Arbor: University of Michigan Press, 1953.

Levellier, Roberto. *Américo Vespucio: el Nuevo Mundo.* Buenos Aires: Editorial Nova, 1951. (Enthusiastic pro-Vespucci view.)

————. *América: la bien llamada.* 2 vols. Buenos Aires: Kraft, 1948, and Madrid: Cultura Hispanica, 1966.

————. *Américo Vespucio: Cartas.* Madrid: Ediciones Cultura Hispánica, 1966.

————. "Novamente contra Vespucio na Iberia," *RHSP,* 37, no. 76:485–98 (October–December, 1968).

Levenson, Joseph R., ed. *European Expansion and the Counter-Example of Asia: 1300–1600.* Englewood Cliffs, N.J.: Prentice-Hall, 1967.

Ley, C. D. *Portuguese Voyages, 1498–1663.* London: Everyman, 1917, and many later printings. (Good anthology.)

Lima, José Joaquim Lopes de. *Ensaios sobre statística das posessões portuguêzas na África occidental e oriental, na Ásia occidental, na China, e na Oceânia.* 5 vols. Lisbon: Imprensa Nacional, 1844–62.

Lima, M. C. Baptista de. "Deux voyages portugais de découverte dans l'Atlantique Occidental," *BEP,* 10:42–108 (1945).

Lisboa, João de. *Livro de marinharia.* Lisbon, 1903.

Livermore, H. V. *A History of Portugal.* Cambridge, England: University Press, 1947. (Sound, narrative history.)

————. *Portugal and Brasil.* Oxford: Clarendon Press, 1963.

————. *A New History of Portugal.* Cambridge, England: University Press, 1969.

Ljungstadt, A. *An Historical Sketch of the Portuguese Settlements in China. A Supplementary Chapter Entitled Description of the City of Canton.* Boston, 1836.

Lobato, Alexandre Marques. *A expansão portuguêsa em Moçambique, de 1498–1530.* 4 vols. Lisbon: CEHU-AGU, 1959.

————. "Dois novos fragmentos do regimento de Cabral para a viagem da India em 1500," *Studia* (Lisbon) no. 25:31–50 (December, 1968).

Lopes, David. *Cousas arábico-portuguêsas: algumas etimologias.* Coimbra: Imprensa da Universidade, 1917.

————. *História de Arzila durante o domínio português (1471–1550), e (1577–1589).* Coimbra: Imprensa da Universidade, 1925. (Good historian, now being superseded in some views.)

————. "Os portuguêses em Marrocos." In *História de Portugal,* ed. Damião Peres. Barcellos, 1928–54, 3:385–544; 4:78–129.

Lopes, Fernão. *Crónica de D. Pedro I.* Barcelos and Porto: Livraria Civilização, 1932 and 1972.

Lopes, Francisco Fernandes. *Os Irmãos Côrte-Real.* Lisbon: CEHU-AGU, 1955.

————. *A figura e a obra do Infante D. Henrique.* Lisbon: Portugália, 1960.

————. "The Brothers Côrte-Real," *Studia* (Lisbon) no. 16:153–65 (1965).

Lopez, Roberto S. *Genova marinara nel duecento.* Milan: G. Principate, 1933. (Excellent information on Italian activity in this and other works by Lopez.)

————. *Studi sull'economia genovese nel medio evo.* Turin: S. Lattes, 1936.

————. *Storia delle colonie genovese nel Mediterraneo.* Bologna; N. Zanichelli, 1938.

————. "European Merchants in the Medieval Indies," *JEH,* 3:164–84 (1943).

————. "Majorcan and Genoese on the North Sea Route in the Thirteenth century," *RBPH,* 29 (1951).

————. *Nascimento da Europa.* Tr. A. H. de Oliveira Marques. Rio de Janeiro: Cosmos, 1965.

———— and I. W. Raymond, eds. *Medieval Trade in the Mediterranean World*. New York: Columbia University Press, 1955.

Luca de Tena, T. "The Influence of Literature on Cartography and the Vinland Map," *TGH*, part 4, 132:515–18 (1966).

Lusitano, Cândido. *Vida do Infante D. Henrique*. Lisbon, 1758.

Luz, Francisco Paulo Mendes da. *O conselho da India*. Lisbon: AGU, 1952.

Lybyer, A. H. *The Influence of the Rise of the Ottoman Turks upon the Routes of the Oriental Trade*. 2 vols. Washington: AHA Annual Report, 1914.

————. "The Ottoman Turks and the Routes of Oriental Trade," *TEHR*, 30, no. 120 (October 1915). (A still ignored viewpoint.)

Macedo Soares, J. C. *Fronteiras do Brasil no regime colonial*. Rio de Janeiro: Colecção de Documentos Brasileiros, no. 19, 1939.

McEwan, P. J. M. ed. *Africa from Early Times to 1800*. London: Oxford University Press, 1968.

MacGregor, I. A. "Notes on the Portuguese in Malaya," *Journal of the Royal Asiatic Society, Malacca Branch*, 28. no. 2 (1955).

Machado, João Franco. "O conhecimento dos Arquipélagos Atlánticos no século XIV," in *HEP*, I; 269–74 (1937).

Machado, José Pedro and Viriato Campos. *Vasco da Gama e a sua viagem de descobrimento*. Lisbon: Camara Municipal, 1969.

Machado, L. Saavedra. See Saavedra.

MacKenna, James B., ed. *A Spaniard in the Portuguese Indies: the Narrative of Martin Fernández de Figueroa*. Cambridge: Harvard University Press, 1967.

MacKinder, Sir Halford John. *Democratic Ideals and Reality, a Study in the Politics of Reconstruction*. New York: Holt, 1942, and other editions.

Madison, Francis. "Medieval Scientific Instruments and the Development of Navigational Instruments in the XVth and XVIth Centuries," separata, *RUC*, 24 (1970).

Magalhães Basto, António de, ed. *Fernão Lopes, suas crónicas perdidas e a crónica geral do reino*. Oporto: Progredior, 1943.

————. *A antiga, mui nobre e leal cidade*. Oporto: Progredior, 1954.

Magnaghi, Alberto. *Amérigo Vespucci, studio crítico*. 2 vols. Rome: Treves, 1924 and 1926.

Magnino, Leo. "António de Noli e a colaboração entre portuguêses e genoveses nos descobrimentos marítimos," *Studia* (Lisbon) 10:99–115 (July, 1962). (Confuses Noli and Uso di Mare.)

Magnusson, Magnus and Herman Palsson. *The Vinland Sagas*. Baltimore: Penguin Books, 1959.

Major, Richard Henry. *The Life of Prince Henry of Portugal, Surnamed the Navigator*. London, 1868. (Now outdated.)

Makino, Myoko. "O descobrimento do Brasil através dos textos," *RHSP*, 34 no. 69:179–186 (January–March, 1967).

Manzano Manzano, Juan. *Cristóbal Colón. Siete años decisivos de su vida (1485–1492)*. Madrid: Ediciones Cultura Hispánica, 1964.

Marcel, Gabriel. *Reproduction de cartes et de globes, relatifs a la découverte de l'Amerique, du XVIᵉ au XVIIᵉ siècles*. Paris, 1893.

Marchant, Alexander. "Colonial Brazil as a Way Station for the Portuguese India Fleets," *GR*, 31:454–65 (1941).

Marcondes de Souza, T. O. *O descobrimento da América*. A revision of 1912 work. São Paulo: Editora Brasiliense, 1944. (Highly critical of alleged "secrecy" in discoveries advocated by Cortesão brothers. Excellent.)

————. *O descobrimento do Brasil de acôrdo com a documentação histórico-cartográfica e a náutica*. 1st ed., 1946. 2nd. ed., São Paulo: Gráfica-Editora Michalany, 1956.

————. "A expedição de 1501–02 e Amérigo Vespucci. (Réplica ao Prof. Damião Peres)," *RHSP*, 1 no. 3:391–411 (July–September, 1950).

————. *Amérigo Vespucci e suas viagens*. 2nd ed., São Paulo: Instituto Cultural Italo-Brasileiro, 1954.

————. *Algumas achegas à história dos descobrimentos (críticas e controvérsias)*. São Paulo: Editora Herder, 1958.

————. "O descobrimento do Brasil (questões correlatas)," *RHSP*, 20 no. 43:185–98 (July–September, 1960).

————. "O 'Infante D. Henrique e a Escola Naval de Sagres (um reparo a 'História do Brasil' do Acadêmico Pedro Calmon)," *RHSP*, 21 no. 44:451–64 (October–December, 1960).

————. "Diogo de Teive e Pedro Velasco supostos descobridores do Banco da Terra Nova," *RHSP*, 22 no. 45:161–72 (January–March, 1961).

————. "Agricultores portuguêses no Brasil antes da arribada de Álvares Cabral," *RHSP*, 22 no. 46:441–44 (April–June, 1961).

————. "O conhecimento pre-colombiano do Brasil pelos portuguêses," *RHSP*, 23 no. 47:149–56 (July–September, 1961).

————. "Um suposto descobrimento do Brasil antes de 1448," *RHSP*, 25 no. 52:439–48 (October–December, 1962).

————. "A concepção geográfica dos portuguêses após o descobrimento da América," *RHSP*, 26 no. 53:145–54 (1963).

————. "A divulgação pela imprensa da notícia do descobrimento do Brasil por Álvares Cabral," *RHSP*, 28 no. 58:389–404 (April–June, 1964).

————. "A viagem de Pedro Álvares Cabral sob o ponto de vista náutico," *RHSP*, 29 no. 59:53–66 (July–September, 1964).

————. "A carta de Pero Vaz de Caminha e o descobrimento casual do Brasil," *RHSP*, 30 no. 61:177–80 (January–March, 1965).

Margry, Pierre. *La conquete et les conquerants des iles Canaries*. Paris, 1896.

Mariejol, Jean H. *The Spain of Ferdinand and Isabella*. Ed. Benjamin Keen. New Brunswick, N.J.: Rutgers University Press, 1961.

Marquard, Leo. *A Short History of South Africa*. New York: Praeger, 1968.

Marques, A. H. Oliveira. See Oliveira Marques.

Martins, José Ferreira. "Casa de Índia," *CMP*, 4:365–84.

Masson, P. *Histoire du commerce francais dans le Levant au XVII° siècle*. Paris, 1896.

Mateos, Francisco. "Bulas portuguesas e españolas sobre descubrimientos geográficos," CIHD (Lisbon, 1960) *Actas*, 3:327–415 (1961).

Matos, José Dalmo Fairbanks Belfort de. "O recuo do meridiano de Tordesilhas, em face do direito internacional (Resumo)," III-CIEL-B (Lisbon, 1957) *Actas*, 2:311–29 (1960).

Matos, L. de. *Les portugais à l'Université de Paris entre 1500 et 1550*. Coimbra: Imprensa da Universidade, 1930.

————. *Les portugais en France au XVI° siècle*. Coimbra: Imprensa da Universidade, 1952.

Matsuda, Kiichi. *The Relations between Portugal and Japan*. Lisbon: JIU-CEHU, 1965.

Mauny, Raymond. "Les navigations medievales sur les côtes sahariennes anterieures a la dècouverte portugaise (1434)," CIHD (Lisbon, 1960) *Actas*, 3:421–22 (1961).

Mees, Jules. *Henri le Navigateur et l'Academie Portugaise de Sagres*. Brussels, 1901. (Outdated.)

Meilink-Roelofsz, Maria Antoinette Petronella. *Asian Trade and Eruopean Influence in the Malay Archipelago between 1500 and about 1630*. The Hague: Martinus Nijhoff, 1962.

Menander, J. "Phantom Islands of the Atlantic," *BGSP*, 26 (1928).

Mendes dos Remédios, Joaquim. *Os Judeus em Portugal*. 2 vols. Coimbra: França Amado, 1895–1928.

————. *Os Judeus portuguêses em Amsterdam*. Coimbra: França Amado, 1911.

Mendonça, Henrique Lopes de. *Estudos sôbre navios portuguêses nos séculos XV e XVI*. Lisbon: ASL, 1892.

Milo, Taco Hayo. "Portuguese Trade and Shipping with the Netherlands after the Discoveries." *Actas*, 3:424. Lisbon: CMIH, 1961.

Moita, Grisalva de Nóbrega. "Os portuguêses no Congo. (1482'–1520)," *Studia* (Lisbon) 3:7–35 (January, 1959).

Mollat, Michel. *Le commerce maritime normand à la fin du Moyen Âge*. Paris: Plon, 1952.

Mollat, Michel and Paul Adam, eds. *Les aspects internationaux de la découverte Océanique aux XVᵉ et XVIIᵉ siècles.* Paris: Plon, 1966.

Morais, José Custódio de. *O conhecimento dos ventos do Atlántico e do Índico, nos séculos XV e XVI.* Coimbra: University of Coimbra Memórias e Notícias no. 10, 1941.

——. "As tempestades no percurso de Pedro Álvares Cabral em 1500 entre as ilhas do Cabo Verde e o Brasil," separata, *RUC,* 19 (1960).

Morales Padrón, F. "Las relaciones entre Colón y Martín Alonzo Pinzón," CIHD (Lisbon, 1960) *Actas,* 3:433–42 (1961).

Moreland, William H. *India at the Death of Akbar: an Economic Study.* Delhi: Atma Ram and Sons, 1962, reissue.

Morison, Samuel Eliot. *Portuguese Voyages to America in the Fifteenth Century.* Cambridge: Harvard University Press, 1940; New York: Octagon, 1965. (Devastating attack on "secrecy.")

——. *The European Discovery of America: the Northern Voyages.* New York: Oxford University Press, 1971.

Mota, Avelino Teixeira da. "A viagem de Bartolomeu Dias e as concepções geopolíticas de D. João II," separata, *BSGL* (October–December, 1958).

——. *Méthodes de navigation et cartographie nautique dans l'Ocean Indien avant le XVIe siécle.* Lisbon: AECA-JIU, 1963.

——. *A cartografia antiga da África Central e a travessa entre Angola e Moçambique, 1500–1860.* Lourenzo Marques, 1964.

——. "As rotas marítimas portuguesas no Atlántico de meados do século XV ao penúltimo quartel do século XVI," *Do Tempo e da História* (Lisbon) no. 3 (1970).

——. *A vigaem de António de Saldanha em 1503 e a rota de Vasco da Gama no Atlántico Sul.* Lisbon: AECA-JIU, LXIV, secção de Lisboa, 1971.

——. *Mar, Alem Mar: estudos e ensaios de história e Geografia.* Lisbon: AECA-JIU, vol. I, 1972.

——. *O Comandante Abel Fontoura da Costa, historiador da Marinharia dos descobrimentos.* Lisbon: AECA-JIU, LXXXIV, secção de Lisboa, 1973.

——. *Reflexos do Tratado de Tordesilhas na cartografia náutica do século XVI.* Coimbra: AECA-JIU, LXXX, secção de Lisboa, 1973.

——. *A contribuição dos irmãos Rui e Francisco Faleiro no campo da* náutica em Espanha. Separata from *A viagem de Fernão de Magalhães e a questão das Molucas.* Lisbon: Centro de Estudos de Cartografia Antiga, no. 16, 1975.

—— and Jaime Cortesao. *El viaje de Diogo de Teive: Colón e los portugueses.* Valladolid: Cuadernos Colombinos no. 5, Casa-Museo de Colón, 1975.

Murdoch, James and Isoh, Yamagata. *A History of Japan.* 3 vols. London: Routledge and Kegan Paul. 3rd Impression, 1949.

Múrias, Manuel. *História breve da colonização portuguêsa.* Lisbon: Ática, 1940.

——. "Legitimidade do direito de Portugal ás terras descobertas: Tratado de Tordesilhas," *CMP,* 3:687–709.

——. *O descobrimento do Brasil.* Lisbon: AGC, 1942.

Naia, Alexandre Gaspar de. "Não é um mito a escola náutica criada e mantida pelo Infante D. Henrique em terra Algarvia," *RHSP,* 26:83–128 (January–March, 1963). (Romantic school.)

——. "Quem foi o primeiro descobridor do Rio da Prata e da Argentina? Em prol da verdade histórica," *RHSP,* 39 no. 79:51–68 (July–September, 1969).

Nambiar, O. K. *Portuguese Pirates and Indian Seamen.* Bangalore: M. Bhakta-Vatsalam, 1955.

Neiva, Rubens Viana. "Ensaio de críítica náutica sôbre a viagem transatlántica de Pedro Álvares Cabral (1500–01)," *RIHG-B,* 287:36–76 (April–June, 1970).

Nemeiso, Vitorino. *Vida e obra do Infante D. Henrique.* 3rd ed. Lisbon: Edições Panorama, 1967.

Newton, A. P., ed. *Travel and Travellers of the Middle Ages.* New York, 1925; reprinted, Barnes and Noble, 1968.

Nordenskjold, A. E. *Facsimile Atlas of the Early History of Cartography*. Stockholm, 1889.
———. *Periplus, an Essay on the Early History of Charts and Sailing Directions*. Stockholm, 1897.
Nougarède, M. P. "Qualités nautique des navires arabes." *Océan Indien et Mediterranée*. Paris: S.E.V.P.E.N., 1964: and in *Studia* (Lisbon) 11:95–122 (1963).
Nowell, Charles E. "The Discovery of Brasil — Accidental or Intentional?" *HAHR*, 16:311–38 (August, 1936). (Careful, erudite studies with some conclusions different from those in this volume.)
———. "The Rejection of Columbus by John of Portugal." *University of Michigan Historical Essays*. Ann Arbor, 1937.
———. "Reservations Regarding the Historicity of the 1494 Discovery of South America," *HAHR*, 22:205–10 (February, 1942).
———. "The Treaty of Tordesillas and the Diplomatic Background of American History," in *Greater America, Essays in Honor of H. E. Bolton* pp. 1–18. Berkeley: University of California Press, 1945.
———. "Prince Henry the Navigator and His Brother Dom Pedro," *HAHR*, 28:62–67 (1948).
———. *History of Portugal*. New York: Van Nostrand, 1952.
———. *The Great Discoveries and the First Colonial Empires*. Ithaca, New York: Cornell University Press, 1954.
———, tr. *A letter to Ferdinand and Isabella — 1503*. Minneapolis: University of Minnesota Press, 1964.
Nunn, George E. *The Geographical Conceptions of Columbus*. New York: American Geographical Society, 1924.
———. *The Mappemonde of Juan de la Cosa: a Critical Investigation of Its Date*. Jenkintown, Pennsylvania, 1934.
———. *The Diplomacy Concerning the Discovery of America*. Jenkintown, Pennsylvania, 1948.
Oleson, Tryggvi J. *Early Voyages and Northern Approaches, 1000–1632*. Toronto: McClelland and Stewart Ltd., 1963.
Oliveira, Eduardo Freire de. *Elementos para a história do município de Lisboa*. 19 vols. Lisbon: Typografia Universal, 1882–1911, 1942–43.
Oliveira Marques, A. H. de. *Hansa e Portugal na idade média*. Lisbon: Tipografia Albano Tomas dos Anjos, 1959.
———. "Navegação prussiana para Portugal nos princípios do século XV," *RUC*, 10:1–24 (March, 1960).
———. "Notas para a história da feitoria portuguêsa na Flandres no século XV." *Studi in onore di Amintore Fanfani*. 3 vols. Milan: Dott. A. Giuffrè, 1962, II, 439–76, and in author's *Ensaios da história medieval*. Lisbon: Sá da Costa, 1965, pp. 217–67.
———. *History of Portugal*. 2 vols. New York: Columbia University Press, 1971–72.
Oliveira Martins, J. P. de. *Portugal nos Mares*. Lisbon: A. M. Pereira, 1889 and later.
———. *Les explorations des portugais antérieurs à la découverte de l'Amerique*. Paris, 1893. (Many conclusions now considered outdated and romantic.)
———. *Os filhos de Dom João I*. 5th ed. Lisbon: A. M. Pereira, 1926.
———. *A vida de Nun'Álvares. História do estabelecimento da dynastia de Avis*. 5th ed. Lisbon: A. M. Pereira, 1928.
———. *O príncipe perfeito*. 4th ed. Lisbon: A. M. Pereira, 1933.
Oliver, Roland, ed. *The Dawn of African History*. 2nd ed. Oxford: The University Press, 1968.
——— and J. D. Fage. *A Short History of Africa*. New York: New York University Press, rev. ed., 1963.
——— and Caroline Oliver. *Africa in the Days of Exploration*. Englewoods Cliff, N.J.: Prentice-Hall, 1965. Global History Series, Spectrum, 1968.
Olschki, Leonardo. *L'Asia di Marco Polo, introduzione alla lettura e allo studio del milione*. Venice, 1957. English version, Berkeley: University of California Press, 1962.

Owen, W. F. W. *Narrative of Voyages to Explore the Shores of Africa*. 2 vols. London, 1833.
Özbaran, Salih. "The Ottoman Turks and the Portuguese in the Persian Gulf, 1534–1581," *Journal of Asian History*, 6 no, 1:45–87 (1972).
Panikkar, K. M. *Asia and Western Dominance*. London: George Allen and Unwin, 1959, and other editions. (See for the Indian view of Portugal in India.)
———. *India and the Indian Ocean*. 3rd ed. London: George Allen and Unwin, 1962.
Parry, J. H. *The Age of Reconnaissance*. New York: Mentor Books, 1963.
Paula, E. Simões de. "O Infante D. Henrique e as responsabalidades do desastre de Tanger," *RHSP*, 23 no. 47:141–44 (July–September, 1961).
Payne, Stanley G. *A History of Spain and Portugal*. Madison: University of Wisconsin Press, 1973.
Pearson, M. N. *Merchants and Rulers in Gujarat*. Los Angeles and Berkeley: University of California Press, 1977.
Penrose, Boies. *Travel and Discovery in the Renaissance, 1420–1620*. 1st ed. Cambridge, Mass: Harvard University Press, 1952.
Peragallo, Próspero. *Cenni intorno alla colonia italiana in Portogallo*. Genoa, 1904; revised ed., 1907.
Pereira, Carlos Renato Gonçalves. *História da administração da justiça no estado da Índia, século XVI*. 2 vols. Lisbon: AGU, 1965.
Pereira da Silva, Luciano. *A astronomia dos Lusíadas*. Coimbra: Imprensa da Universidade, 1915.
———. "A arte de navegar dos portuguêses desde o Infante á D. João de Castro," *HCPB*, I, chap. 2.
———. "Duarte Pacheco Pereira, precursor de Cabral," *HCPB*, I, chap. 4.
———. *Obras completas*. 3 vols. Lisbon: AGC, 1943–45.
Peres, Damião, ed. *História de Portugal*. 8 vols. Barcelos: Portucalense Editoria, 1928–38. (Collective work — some parts excellent. Little bibliography. Needs complete rewriting. Peres has made numerous and excellent studies — among sounder of Portuguese historians; takes moderate position on "secrecy." Compare with Marcondes de Sousa.)
———. *Como nasceu Portugal*. 2nd ed. Oporto: Portucalense Editora, 1942.
———. *História dos descobrimentos portuguêses*. Oporto: Portucalense Editora, 1943; 2nd ed., privately printed, 1960. (Best one-volume study — especially good on historiography.) The 1960 edition is used in the citations in the footnotes.
———. *Regimento das cazas das Índias e Mina*. Coimbra: Imprensa da Universidade, 1947.
———. *Diogo Cão*. Lisbon: CEHU-AGU, 1957.
———. *Viagens de Luis de Cadamosto e de Pedro de Cintra*. Lisbon, 1958.
———. *Uma prioridade portuguêsa contestada mas incontestável: a circumnavegação da África Austral por Bartolomeu Dias*. Lisbon: APH, 1960.
———. *O descobrimento do Brasil por Pedro Álvares Cabral: antecedentes e intencionalidade*. Oporto and Rio de Janeiro: Portucalense Editora, 1949; 2nd ed., 1968.
Pereyra, Carlos. *La conquista de las rutas oceánicas*. Madrid: M. Aguilar, 1940.
Pérez Embid, Florentino. *Los descubrimientos en el Atlántico y la rivalidad castellano-portuguesa hasta el tratado de Tordesillas*. Seville: Escuela de Estudios Hispano-Americanos, 1948. (Excellent for comparison with Portuguese views.)
———. "La política del Infante y la marina de Andalucía, según la nueva edición crítica de los Pleitos Colombinos," *CIHD* (Lisbon 1960) *Actas* 3:153–62 (1961).
Pessanha, José Benedito de Almeida. *Os almirantes Pessanhas e a sua descendência*. Oporto: Imprensa Portuguesa, 1923.
Phillips, Eustace D. *The Mongols*. London: Thames and Hudson, 1969.
Pike, Ruth. *Enterprise and Adventure: the Genoese in Seville and the Opening of the New World*. Ithaca: Cornell University Press, 1966.
Pimpão, Álvaro Júlio da Costa. "A historiografia oficial e o sigilo sôbre os descobrimentos," *I-CHEPM*, Lisbon (1938).
Pinto, Sérgio da Silva. "O problema da época do achamento das Canárias pelos portuguêses (reinado de D. Afonso IV ou de D. Dinis?)" *CIHD* (Lisbon, 1960) *Actas*, 3:443–48 (1961).

Pissurlencar, Panddaronga S. S. *Regimentos das fortalezas da Índia*. Bastorá, Goa: Tipografia Rangel, 1951.
Po, Guido. "Navigatori italiani nel Medio Evo al servizio del Portogallo," *CMP*, III, 579–620.
————. "Le Scoperte marittime de portoghesi — Cartografia nautica," *CMP*, III, 621–44.
————. "La Marina Italiana in Portogallo," *CMP*, III, 653–84.
Pohl, Frederick J. *Amérigo Vespucci: Pilot Major*. New York, 1944; Octagon Press, 1967.
————. *Atlantic Crossings before Columbus*. New York: Norton, 1961.
Postan, M. and E. E. Rich, eds. *The Cambridge Economic History of Europe*. Cambridge, England: The University Press, 1952. See vol. 2, chap. 4, and pp. 531–36.
Poujade, Jean. *La Route des Indes et ses navires*. Paris: Payot, 1946.
Prestage, Edgar. *The Portuguese Pioneers*. London, 1933, and New York: Barnes and Noble, 1967. (Romantic and outdated.)
————. *Descobrimentos portuguêses*. Oporto: Imprensa Portuguêsa, 1934.
Pullan, Brian, ed. *Crisis and Change in the Venetian Economy*. London: Methuen, 1968.
Queiroz Velloso, José Maria de. *D. Sebastião, 1554–78*. 3rd ed. Lisbon: Empresa Nacional de Publicidade, 1945.
Quinn, David B. "The Argument for the English Discovery of America between 1480 and 1494," *GJE*, 127:3 and in CIHD (Lisbon, 1960), vol. 2.
————. "Exploration and the Expansion of Europe," *XII ICHS*, 1:45–59 (Vienna, 1965).
Ramalho, Américo da Costa. "Sôbre a data da morte de Diogo Cão," *RPH*, 2:319–21 (1947).
Ramusio, Giovanni Battista. *Delle navigationi e viaggi*. 3 vols. 1st ed., Venice, 1550.
Randles, W. G. L. "South-East Africa and the Empire of Monomotapa as Shown on Selected Printed Maps of the 16th Century," *Studia* (Lisbon) 2:103–64 (July, 1958).
————. "La signification cosmographique du passage du Cap Bojador," *Studia* (Lisbon), 8:221–56 (July, 1961).
Ráu, Virginia. *Os holandeses e a exportação do sal de Setúbal nos fins do século XVII*. Coimbra University Press, 1950. (Excellent, erudite studies.)
————. *A exploração e o comércio do sal de Setúbal*. Lisbon: Bertrand, 1951.
————. "Uma família de mercadores italianos em Portugal no século XV- os Lomellini," *RFLL*, 2nd series, 2:56–69 (1956); and *Estudos de História*. Lisbon: Verbo, 1968, pp. 13–58.
————. "Rumos e vicissitudes do comércio do sal português nos séculos XIV–XVIII," *RFLL*, 3rd series, 7 (1963).
————. "Feitores e feitorias — instrumentos do comércio internacional português no século XVI," *Brotéria* (Lisbon), 81:458–78 (July–December, 1965).
————. "Um grande mercador-banqueiro italiano em Portugal: Lucas Giraldi," separata, *EIP*, no. 24 (1965), and Ráu, *Estudos de História*, Lisbon: Verbo, 1968, pp. 75–130.
————. "Para a história da população portuguêsa dos séculos XV e XVI," *Do Tempo e da História*, Lisbon, 1 (1965).
————. "A grande exploração agrária em Portugal a partir dos fins da Idade Média," *RHSP*, 30, 61:65–74 (January–March, 1965).
————. *Estudos de História*. Vol. I. *Mercadores, mercadorias, pensamento económico*. Lisbon: Editorial Vestão, 1968.
————. "Bartolomeo di iacopo di ser Vanni Mercador-Banqueiro Florentino 'Estante' em Lisboa nos meados do século XV," *Do Tempo e da História*, Lisbon, 4 (1971).
————. "Alguns estudantes e eruditos portugueses em Itália no século XV," *Do Tempo e da História*, 5 (1972).
————. *Portugal e o Mediterrâneo no século XV*. Lisbon: Centro de Estudos de Marinha, 1973.
———— and Bailey W. Diffie. "Alleged Fifteenth-Century Portuguese Joint Stock Companies and the Articles of Dr. Fitzler." *The Bulletin of the Institute of Historical Research*, 26:181–99 (1953).
———— and Jorge de Macedo. "O açucar na ilha de Madeira — análise de um cálculo de produção dos fins do século XV," CIHD (Lisbon, 1960) *Actas*, 5:189–210 (1961).

————. *O açucar da Madeira nos fins do século XV*. Funchal: Junta-Geral do Distrito Autónomo do Funchal, 1962.

Ravenstein, E. G. *Martin Behaim, His Life and His Globe*. London: G. Phillip and Sons, 1908. (Excellent, critical study.)

Rawlinson, H. G. "The Flanders Galleys: Some Notes on the Seaborne Trade between Venice and England, 1327–1532 A.D.," *MM*, 12:145–68 (April, 1926).

Reboredo, Armando de. "Os descobrimentos, a expansão ultramarina — as linhas de comunicação marítima," separata, *BSGL* (April–June, 1960).

Rêgo, António da Silva. *História das missões do padroado português do Oriente; Índia (1500–1542)* 1 vol. to date. Lisbon: AGC, 1949.

————. *Portuguese Colonization in the Sixteenth Century: a Study of Royal Ordinances*. Johannesburg: Witwatersrand University Press, 1957. (Compare with Charles Boxer's views.)

————. *Reflexões sôbre o primeiro século da história Cabo Verdiana (1460–1580)*. In *Cabo Verde, Guiné, São Tomé e Príncipe*. Lisbon: Instituto Superior de Ciências Sociais e Política Ultramarina, 1966, pp. 67–84.

Reindorf, Carl C. *The History of the Gold Coast and Asante, 1500–1860*. Accra: Ghana Universities Press, 1966.

Reis, J. Batalha. "The Supposed Discovery of South America before 1448 and the Critical Methods of the Historians of Geographical Discovery," *GJE*, 9:185–210 (February, 1897).

Renouard, Yves. *L'hommes d'affaires italiens du Moyen Âge*. Paris: Armand Colin, 1968.

————. "Pour les recherches sur les relations entre pays de la Mediterranée et pays de l'Atlantique au Moyen Âge," *RPH*, 4:253–61 (1949).

Reparaz, Gonçalo de. "Mestre Jacome de Malhorca, cartógrafo do Infante," separata, *Biblos*, vol. 4 (1930).

Ribeiro, João Pedro. *Dissertações cronológicas e críticas sôbre a história e jurisprudência ecclesiástica e civil de Portugal*. 5 vols. Lisbon, 1857–96.

Ribeiro, Orlando. *Portugal, o Mediterráneo e o Atlántico*. Coimbra: Coimbra Editora, 1945.

————. "Originalidade da expansão portuguêsa," separata, *BSGL* (April–June, 1956).

————. *Aspectos e problemas da expansão portuguêsa*. Lisbon: JIU, 1962.

Ribeiro, Patrocínio. *A nacionalidade portuguêsa de Cristóvam Colombo*. Lisbon: Livraria Renascença J. Cardoso, [1927].

Ricard, Robert. *Les sources inédite de l'histoire du Maroc*. Paris: P. Gouthner, 1934–53.

————. *Études sur l'histoire des portugais au Maroc*. Coimbra: Imprensa da Universidade, 1955.

Rich, E. E. and C. H. Wilson. *The Economy of Expanding Europe in the Sixteenth and Seventeenth Centuries*. Vol. 4. *The Cambridge Economic History of Europe from the Decline of the Roman Empire*. Cambridge, England: The University Press, 1941–67.

Riley, Carrol L. and others, eds. *Man across the Sea: Problems of Pre-Columbian Contacts*. Austin: University of Texas Press, 1970.

Rita, J. G. de Santa. "Os conhecimentos geográficos no princípio do século XV," *HEP* 1:213–22 (1937).

Robinson, Arthur H. *Marine Cartography in Britain; a History of the Sea Chart to 1855*. London: Leicester University Press, and MacEachern, 1962.

Rodrigues, José Maria. "O Infante D. Henrique e a universidade," *O Instituto* (Coimbra) 1:485–508 (1894).

Rodrigues, M. M. Sarmento. "Prioridade portuguêsa das invenções científicas no Ultramar," separata, *BSGL* (April–June, 1958).

Rodrigues, Vicente and Diogo Afonso. *Roteiro da navegação e carreira da Índia*. Lisbon: AGC, 1940.

Rogers, Francis M. "Valentim Fernandes, Rodrigo de Santaella, and the Recognition of the Antilles as 'Opposite-India'," *BSGL*, series 75, 279–309 (July–September, 1957).

————. *The Obedience of a King of Portugal*. Minneapolis: University of Minnesota Press, 1958.

————. "Union between Latin and Eastern Christians and the Overseas Expansion of the Portuguese, a Thematic Study of the 'Libro del Infante Don Pedro de Portugal,'" III CIEL-B (Lisbon, 1957) *Actas* 2:148–63 (1960).

————. *The Travels of the Infante Dom Pedro of Portugal*. Cambridge: Harvard University Press, 1961.

————. *The Vivaldi Expedition*. Offprint, 73rd Annual Report of the Dante Society.

————. *The Quest for Eastern Christians: Travels and Rumor in the Age of Discovery*. Minneapolis: University of Minnesota Press, 1962.

————. "The Attraction of the East and Early Portuguese Discoveries," *Luso-Brazilian Review*, 1, no. 1 (1964).

Roncière, Charles de. See La Roncière.

Roukema, E. "A Discovery of Yucatan prior to 1503," *IM*, 8:30–38 (1956).

————. "The Coasts of North-East Brazil and the Guianas in the Egerton MS. 2803," *IM*, 16:27–31 (1960).

————. "Brazil in the Cantino Map," *IM*, 17:7–26 (1963).

Ruddock, Alwyn A. "Italian Trading Fleets in Medieval England," *History*, 106:192–202 (September, 1944).

————. *Italian Merchants and Shipping in Southampton, 1270–1700*. Southampton, England: University College, 1951.

————. "Columbus and Iceland: New Light on an Old Problem," *GJE*, 2:178–189 (June, 1970).

Russell, P. E. "Prince Henry the Navigator." Offprint, *Diamante* (London), vol. 11 (1960).

————. "Fontes documentais castelhanas para a história da expansão portuguêsa na guiné nos últimos anos de d. Afonso V," *Do Tempo e da História*, Lisbon, 4 (1971).

Sá, Aires de. *Recherches sur Améric Vespuce et sur ses prétendues découvertes*. Paris: BSGP, 1837 and 1842; *reproduced in Opúsculos e esparos*. Lisbon, 1910.

————. *Essai sur l'histoire de la cosmographie et de la cartographie au Moyen Âge*. 3 vols. Paris, 1849–52.

————. *Frei Gonçalo Velho*. Lisbon: Imprensa Nacional, 1899–1900.

Sá, A. Moreira de. *O Infante D. Henrique e a universidade*. Lisbon: CMIH, 1960.

Saavedra Machado, L. "Os ingleses em Portugal," *Biblos*, vols. 8–13, *passim* (1937—).

Sanceau, Elaine. *Portugal in Quest of Prester John*. London–New York: Hutchinson, 1943. (The works of this author are well written and the best introduction in English, but not sufficiently critical of sources.)

————. *The Land of Prester John*. New York: Knopf, 1944.

————. *Henry the Navigator*. New York: Norton, 1947.

————. *The Perfect Prince: Dom João II*. Oporto, 1959.

————. "Uma narrativa da expedição portuguêsa de 1541 ao Mar Roxo," *Studia* (Lisbon) 9:199–234, CEHU (1962).

————. *Good Hope, the Voyage of Vasco da Gama*. Lisbon: Academia Internacional de Cultura Portuguêsa, 1967.

————. *The Reign of the Fortunate King, 1495–1521*. Hamden, Connecticut: Archon Books, 1969.

————. *Knight of the Renaissance, a Biography of Dom João de Castro, Soldier, Sailor, Scientist and Viceroy, 1500–1548*. London: Hutchinson, n.d.

Sanches, António Nunes. "Origim da denominação de Cristão Velho a Cristão Novo em Portugal," *Arquivo de Bibliografia Portuguêsa*, 8:247–79 (October–December, 1956).

Sansom, Sir George B. *The Western World and Japan*. 5th printing. New York: Knopf, 1965.

Santa Rita, José Gonçalo de. "O govêrno central e o govêrno local," *HEP*, 2:73–83.

Santarém, Visconde de. *Recherches sur la priorité de la découverte des pays situés sur la côte occidentale d'Afrique*. Paris, 1842.

Santos, Domingos Maurício Gomes dos, S.J. *D. Duarte e as responsabilidades de Tânger (1433–38)*. Lisbon: Editora Gráfica Portuguêsa, 1960.

Santos, Eduardo dos. *O antigo reino do Congo*. Lisbon: AGU, 1964.

Santos, Maria Emília Madeira H. "O carácter experimental da carreira da India. Um plano de João Pereira Dantas, com fortificação da África do Sul (1556)," separata, *RUC*, 24 (1970).

Sanz, Carlos, ed. *Biblioteca americana vetustíssima*. Madrid: Carlos Sanz 1960. (Sanz has published numerous, excellent studies of cartography and history.)

————. *La carta de Colón anunciando el descubrimiento del Nuevo Mundo, 15 febrero–14 marzo 1499*. Madrid: Carlos Sanz, 1962.

————. *Mapas antiguos del mundo, siglos XV–XVI*. Madrid: Carlos Sanz, 1962.

————. *Mapa (un) del mundo verdaderamente importante en la famosa Universidad de Yale*. Madrid: Carlos Sanz, 1966.

————. "El primer mapa del mundo con la representación de los dos hemisferios." *RSGM*, series B, no. 455 (1966).

Sapori, A. *Le marchand italien au Moyen Âge*. Paris, Armand Colin, 1952.

Sar Desai, D. R. "The Portuguese Administration in Malacca, 1511–1641." *Journal of Southeast Asian History*. 10, 3 (December, 1969).

Saraiva, António José. *Para a história da cultura em Portugal*. 3rd ed. 3 vols. Lisbon: Publicações Europa América, 1969.

————. Inquisição e cristãos-novos. 3rd ed. Oporto: Editorial Inova, 1969.

Saraiva, Cardeal (D. Francisco de S. Luiz). *Obras Completas*. 10 vols. Lisbon: Imprensa Nacional, 1872–83.

Sardella, P. "Nouvelles et speculations a Venise au debut du XVI⁰ siécle." Paris: Armand Colin, Cahiers des Annales, I, [1948].

Saunders, John J., ed. *The Muslim World on the Eve of Europe's Expansion*. Englewood Cliffs, N.J.: Prentice Hall, Spectrum, 1967.

Schaefer, Henrique. *História de Portugal*. 7 vols. Lisbon: 1893–1926.

Schurhammer, Georg. S.J. "O descobrimento do Japão pellos portuguêses no ano 1543." Tr: P. Francisco Rodrigues. *Anais*. Lisbon: APH, 1946.

————. *Franz Xavier, sein Leben und seine Zeit*. 2 vols, in 3 parts. Freiburg im Breisgau: Herder, 1955–56.

————. *Orientalia. Biblioteca Instituti Historici, S.I*. Rome and Lisbon: Institutum Historicum Societatis Jesu, and CEHU, 1963.

———— and E. A. Voretsch. *Die Geschichte Japans, 1549–78*. Leipzig: Verlag der Asia Major, 1926.

————. *Francis Xavier; His Life and Times*. Tr. M. Joseph Costelloe. Rome: Jesuit Historical Institute, 1973.

Sérgio, António. "A conquista de Ceuta (ensaio de interpretação não romântica do texto de Azurara)." *Ensaios*, 5 vols. Rio de Janeiro: Anuario do Brasil, 1920–46, 1:279–305. (Realistic, economic interpretation.)

————. *Obras completas*. 8(?) vols. Lisbon: Sá da Costa, 1971–.

Serpa, António Ferreira de. *O descobrimento do arquipélago dos Açores*. Oporto: Livraria Civilização, 1925.

Serra Rafols, Elías. "Lançarotto Malocello en Canarias," CIHD (Lisbon, 1960) *Actas*, 3:467–78 (1960). (Compare with views of Verlinden.)

————. "Portugal en las islas Canarias," *CMP*, III, 209–42.

Serrão, Joaquim Veríssimo. "A conquista de Ceuta no diário veneziano de António Moroseni," CIHD (Lisbon, 1960) *Actas*, 3:543–50 (1960–61).

Serrão, Joel. *O carácter social da revolução de 1383*. Lisbon: Seára Nova, 1946.

————. ed. *Dicionário de história de Portugal*. 4 vols. Lisbon: Iniciativas Editoriais, 1963–71.

Shillington, V. M. and A. V. Wallis. *The Commercial Relations of England and Portugal*. London: G. Routledge, and New York: Dutton, 1907.

Silva, L. Gentil da. *Alguns elementos para a história do comércio da Índia de Portugal existentes na Biblioteca Nacional de Madrid*. Lisbon, 1951.

Silva, Luciano Pereira de. See Pereira da Silva.

Silva, M. D. Manuel Luciano da. "The Meaning of Dighton Rock," *Medical Opinion and Riview*, pp. 82ff. (February 1966). (Compare with S. E. Morison's views).
——. "Words from the Portuguese." *Medical Opinion and Review*, pp. 108–113 (June, 1966).
——. *Portuguese Pilgrims and Dighton Rock*. Bristol, R.I.: Privately printed, 1972.
Silva, Padre Fernando Augusto da, and Carlos Azevedo de Meneses. *Elucidário madeirense*. 2nd ed. Funchal, 1940–1946.
Silva, L. A. Rebello da. *Memória sôbre a população e a agricultura de Portugal*. Lisbon: Imprensa Nacional, 1868.
Silva Correia, Alberto C. Germano da. "Os franceses na colonização portuguêsa da Índia," *Studia* (Lisbon) 4:7–105, (July, 1959).
Simões, A. de Veiga. *La Flandre, le Portugal et les débuts du capitalisme moderne*. Brussels: offprint from *Revue Économique Internationale*, 1932.
Skelton, R. A. *Explorers' Maps*. London: Routledge and Kegan Paul, 1958.
——. "The Cartographic Record of the Discovery of North America," CIHD (Lisbon, 1960) *Actas*, 2:343–63 (1961).
——. "The English Knowledge of the Portuguese Discoveries in the Fifteenth Century: a New Document," CIHD (Lisbon, 1960) *Actas*, 2:365–74 (1961).
——. *The European Image and Mapping of America, A.D. 1000–1600*. Minneapolis: University of Minnesota, James Ford Bell Collection, 1964.
——. *The Vinland Map and the Tartar Relation*. New Haven, Connecticut: Yale University Press, 1965.
Slessarev, Vsevolod. *Prester John, the Letter and the Legend*. Minneapolis: University of Minnesota Press, 1959.
——. "Raphael Maffei's Contribution to the History of Portuguese Discoveries," CIHD (Lisbon, 1960) *Actas*, 3:551–76 (1961).
Smith, Vincent Arthur. *The Oxford History of India*. 3rd ed. Ed. Percival Spear. Oxford: Clarendon Press, 1967 [1968].
Soranzo, Giovanni. *Il Papato, l'Europa Cristiana e i Tartare*. Milan: Societá Editrice "Vita e Pensiero," 1930.
Sousa, J. M. Cordeiro de. "O Infante D. Henrique e os primeiros descobrimentos marítimos," *CMP*, 3:99–104.
Sousa, Luiz de. Robert Ricard, ed. tr. *Les portugais et l'Africa du Nord de 1521–57*. Lisbon: Livraria Portugália Editora, 1940.
Sousa Costa, O. F. M., António Domingues de. "O Infante D. Henrique na expansão portuguêsa," *Itinerarium* (Braga), 5:419–568 (1959).
Sousa Holstein, Marquês de. *A escola de Sagres e as tradições do Infante D. Henrique*. Lisbon: Academia das Sciências, 1877.
Souto, A. Meyrelles do. *Portugal e Marrocos*. Lisbon: AGU, 1967.
Spear, Thomas George Percival. *History of British India under the Company and the Crown*. 3rd ed. London: Oxford University Press, 1952. See also under Thapar, Romila.
——. *India, A Modern History*. Ann Arbor: University of Michigan Press, 1961 and 1972.
Stephens, Henry Morse. *The Story of Portugal*. New York, 1891; reprint, New York: AMS Press, 1971.
Stevens, Henry N., and George F. Barwick. *New Light on the Discovery of Australia*. London: The Hakluyt Society, Series II, 64, 1930. (Attributes discovery to Diego de Prado y Tovar, 1605–6, of Fernandez de Quiros expedition. Discounts alleged earlier Portuguese discovery.)
Strandes, Justus. *The Portuguese Period in East Africa*. Tr. Jean F. Wallwork. Nairobi: The East-African Literature Bureau, 1968.
Stripling, George W. F. *The Ottoman Turks and the Arabs, 1511–1572*. Urbana: University of Illinois Press, 1942.
Suárez Fernández, Luis. "El Atlántico y el Mediterráneo en los objetivos políticos de la casa de Trastámara," *RPH*, 5:287–307 (1951).

514   FOUNDATIONS OF THE PORTUGUESE EMPIRE

Sykes, Percy. *A History of Exploration from the Earliest Times to the Present Day.* New York: Harper Torchbooks, 1961. (Excellent general survey.)

Tavares, Luiz C. Nozes. *O Infante D. Henrique e os descobrimentos.* Braga: Edições Nozes Tavares, 1960.

Taylor, E. G. R. "A Pre-Columbian Discovery of America," *GJE*, 67:282–83 (January–June, 1926).

———. "Ideas of the Shape and Habitability of the Earth Prior to the Great Age of Discovery," *History*, pp. 54–58 (June, 1937).

———. *The Haven-Finding Art: a History of Navigation from Odysseus to Captain Cook.* London, 1956, and New York: Elsevir Publishing Co., 1971.

Teixeira, Luiz. *Lisboa e os seus cronistas.* Lisbon: Câmara Municipal, 1943.

Teixeira, Fr. Manuel. *Portuguese Missions in Malacca and Singapore, 1511–1958.* Vol. 1 of 3 vols. Lisbon: AGU, 1961–63.

Teixeira de Aragão, Augusto C. *Vasco da Gama e a vidigueira.* Lisbon: Imprensa Nacional, 1898.

Teixeira da Mota. See Mota.

Thapar, Romila. *A History of India.* 2 vols. Baltimore: Penguin Books, 1965–66. Volume 2 by Thomas George Percival Spear.

Thieury, Jules. *Le Portugal et la Normandie jusqu'à la fin du XVIe siècle.* Paris, 1860.

Tibbets, G. R. "The Navigational Theory of the Arabs in the Fifteenth and Sixteenth Centuries," separata, *RUC*, 24 (1969).

Tindall, P. E. N. *A History of Central Africa.* New York: Praeger, 1968.

Tonneaux, Albert. "La découverte de la route martime des Indes," *BSGL*, series 66, pp. 19–72 (1948).

Tooley, Ronald Vere. *The Printed Map of the Continent of Africa, 1500–1900.* Map Collector Series no. 29. London: Map Collector Circle, 1966.

———. *Maps and Map-Makers.* 2nd ed., New York: Crown, 1971.

Ure, John. *Prince Henry the Navigator.* London: Constable, 1977.

Usher, Abbot Paysan. *The Early History of Deposit Banking in Mediterranean Europe.* Cambridge: Harvard University Press, 1943.

Valente, Carlos F. de Figueiredo. *Os Teives e o morgado instituido por Diogo de Teive á seus filhos.* Lisbon, 1934.

Vandenbussche, Émile. *Flandre et Portugal.* Bruges, 1874.

Varnhagen, Francisco Adolfo de. *História geral do Brazil.* 1st ed. 2 vols. Madrid, 1854–57, and many other revised and annotated editions. 4th ed. Rio de Janeiro-São Paulo: Companhia Melhoramentos. 1948. Standard nineteenth-century work. Basic research.

———. *Les voyages d'Améric Vespuce.* Paris, 1858.

Vasconcelos, Basílio de. *Itinerário de Dr. Jerónimo Münzer.* Coimbra: Imprensa da Universidade, 1932.

Vasconcelos, José Augusto Amaral Frazão de. *Pilotos das navegações portuguêsas dos séculos XV e XVII.* Lisbon: Instituto de Alta Cultura, 1942.

———. "Pero Escobar." Lisbon: CEHU-AGU, 1957.

Vausse, Petit de. "Croisades bourguignonnes," *Revue Historique*, 30:269ff. (1886).

Verlinden, Charles. "Deux aspects de l'expansion commerciale du Portugal: Harfleur au xive siécle, Middlebourg au xive et au xve siécle. *RPH*, Coimbra, 1951.

———. "Italian Influence in Iberian Colonization," *HAHR*, 33:199–211 (1953).

———. *Precédents medievaux de la colonie en Amerique.* Mexico: Pan American Institute of Geography and History, 1954.

———. *L'esclavage dans L'Europe medieval.* Brussels: De Tempel, 1955.

———. "La colonie italienne de Lisbonne et le développement de l'économie metropolitaine et coloniale portugaise," in *Studi in onore di Armando Sapori.* Milan, 1957, pp. 617–28.

———. "Navigateurs, marchands et colons italiens au service de la découverte et de la colonisation portugaise sous Henri le Navigateur," *Le Moyen Âge*, 64:467–97 (1958).

———. "Lanzarotto Malocello et la découverte portugaise des Canaries," *RBPH*, 36:1173–1209 (1958). (Based on documents believed to have been fabricated, perhaps in the nineteenth century, and first published by Fortunato de Almeida, *História de Portugal*, III, 759–89.)

———. "Formes féodales et domaniales de la colonisation portugaise," *RPH*, 9:1–44 (1960).

———. "Les découvertes portugaises et la collaboration italienne d'Alphonse IV à Alphonse V," CIHD (Lisbon, 1960) *Actas*, I:593–610 (1961). (Also uses the Almeida "documents.")

———. "António de Noli e a colonização das Ilhas de Cabo Verde," *RFLL*. 3rd series, 7:28–45 (1963).

———. "Un précuseur de Colomb: le flamand Ferdinand van Olmen (1487)," *RPH*, 5:453–465 (1963). (Overstates case on the basis of documentation.)

———. "La signification de l'année 1487 dans l'histoire de la découverte et de l'expansion portugaise," *RHES*, 42:485–498 (1964).

———. "Les Ganois dans la marine portugaise avant 1385," *Actas do Congresso de Portugal Medievo* (Braga) 3:388–407 (1966).

———. *The Beginnings of Modern Colonization*. Ithaca, New York: Cornell University Press, 1970.

——— and Florentino Pérez Embid. *Cristóbal Colón y el descubrimiento de América*. Madrid: Ediciones Rialp, 1967.

Vidago, João. "Os Côrte-Real e os seus objetivos geográficos (1500–1502)," *Studia* (Lisbon) 15:123–40 (1965).

———. "Conceito da Palavra descobrimento no século XV," *Vertice* (Coimbra) 153–56.

Vignaud, Henry. *Histoire critique de la grande entreprise de Christophe Colomb*. 2 vols. Paris: H. Welter, 1911.

———. *Améric Vespuce, 1451–1512*. Paris: H. Welter, 1917.

Vigneras, Louis-André. "Etat present des études sur Jean Cabot," CIHD (Lisbon 1960) *Actas*, 3:657–70 (1961).

———. *The Discovery of South America and the Andalusian Voyages*. Chicago and London: University of Chicago Press, 1976. (An excellent study of the methods of financing exploration.)

Vilhena, Thomaz d'Almeida Namoel de. *História da instituição da Santa Ordem da Cavalaria e das ordens militares em Portugal*. Coimbra: Imprensa da Universidade, 1925.

Viterbo, Francisco M. de Sousa. "O monopólio da cortiça no sécula XV," *AHP*, 2:41–52 (1904).

Vlekke, Bernard H. M. *Nusantara, a History of Indonesia*. Revised (2nd) edition. The Hague: W. van Hoeve, 1965.

Walter, James. "O Infante D. Henrique e a medicina," *Studia* (Lisbon) 13–14:31–39 (1964).

Washburn, Wilcomb E. "The Meaning of Discovery in the Fifteenth and Sixteenth Centuries," *AHR*, 68:1–21 (October, 1962).

———, ed. *Proceedings of the Vinland Map Conference*. Chicago: University of Chicago Press, 1971.

Waters, David. "The Iberian Bases of the English Art of Navigation in the Sixteenth Century," separata, *RUC*, 24 (1970).

Weckman, Luis. *Las bulas alejandrinas de 1493 y la teoría política del papado medieval*. México: Instituto de Historia, 1949.

Wee, Herman van der. *The Growth of the Antwerp Market and the European Economy, Fourteenth-Sixteenth Centuries*. 3 vols. The Hague: Nijoff, 1963.

Weinstein, Donald. *Ambassador from Venice: Pietro Pasqualigo in Lisbon, 1501*. Minneapolis: University of Minnesota Press, 1960.

Welch, Sidney R. *Europe's Discovery of South Africa*. Cape Town and Johannesburg: Juta and Company, 1937. (See critique of Welsh by Boxer.)

———. "Portugal's Discovery of South Africa and Its First Effects upon the Culture of Europe," *CMP*, 3:287–310, 1940.

———. *South Africa under Manuel I, 1495–1521*. Capetown: Juta and Company, 1946.

Whiteway, Richard S. *The Rise of Portuguese Power in India, 1497–1550*. London, 1899. (Good though now partly outdated.) 2nd ed. London and Santiago do Compostelo: Susil Gupta, 1967.

Wilson, W. J. "The Historicity of the 1494 Discovery of South America," *HAHR*, 22:192–205 (February, 1942). (See Nowell's caveat.)

Winius, George Davison. *The Fatal History of Portuguese Ceylon; Transition to Dutch Rule*. Cambridge, Mass.: Harvard University Press, 1971.

Winter, Heinrich. "Who Invented the Compass?" *MM*, 23:95–102 (1937).

———. "Catalan Portolan Maps and Their Place in the Total View of Cartographic Development," *IM*, 11:1–12 (1954).

———. "The Origin of the Sea Chart," *IM*, 13:39–52 (1956).

Witte, D. Charles-Martial de. "Une lettre inèdite du Roi Jean II au Pape Innocente VII sur l'affaire de Graciosa," *Studia* (Lisbon), 1:90–100 (January, 1958).

———. "Les bulles pontificales et l'expansion portugaise au XVe siècle," *Revue d'Histoire Ecclesiastique*, 48 (1953), 49 (1954), 51 (1956), 53 (1958), and in book form, Louvain, 1958. (The fundamental study on the subject.)

Woolf, S. J. "Venice and the Terrafirma; Problems of the Change from Commercial to Landed Activities." In Pullen, *Crisis and Change*, cited, 182ff.

Wright, J. K. "Notes on the Knowledge of Latitudes and Longitudes in the Middle Ages," *Isis*, 5:75–98 (1923).

INDEX

Index

519